D1064286

1998

Harry Partch

Yale University Press   New Haven & London

Bob Gilmore

H
a
r
r
y

P
a
r
t
c
h

a

b
i
o
g
r
a
p
h
y

B
PARTCH

The publishers gratefully acknowledge the support of the American
Musicological Society and the Harry Partch Foundation.

Frontispiece: Partch playing the Cloud-Chamber Bowls, c. 1953.
Photo by Fred Lyon.

Printed in the United States of America.

Library of Congress Cataloging-in-Publication Data

Gilmore, Bob, 1961–
Harry Partch : a biography / Bob Gilmore.
p.   cm.
"Chronology of compositions" : p. 395
"Chronology of writings" : p. 405
Includes bibliographical references and index.
ISBN 0-300-06521-3 (cloth)
1. Partch, Harry, 1901–1974. 2. Composers—United States—
Biography. I. Title.
ML410.P176G55 1998
780'.92—dc21
[B]   97-39140
MN

A catalogue record for this book is available from the British Library.

The paper in this book meets the guidelines for permanence and
durability of the Committee on Production Guidelines for Book
Longevity of the Council on Library Resources.

10 9 8 7 6 5 4 3 2 1

To Maria

Contents

Preface, ix

Prologue, 1

1 Oakland and the Old West, 9

2 Los Angeles and San Francisco, 35

3 New Orleans and California, 71

4 New York and Europe, 96

5 Western States, 113

6 Chicago, Ithaca, and New York, 136

7 Madison, 156

8 Gualala and Oakland, 180

9 Sausalito and Urbana, 215

10 Yellow Springs, Chicago, Evanston, and Champaign, 253

11 Petaluma, 296

12   Del Mar, Van Nuys, Venice, and San Diego, 319

13   Encinitas and San Diego, 353

     Epilogue, 388

     Chronology of Compositions, 395

     Chronology of Writings, 405

     Notes, 411

     Acknowledgments, 453

     Index, 457

Preface

This book is a biography of Harry Partch, not an analytical study of his work. Although I discuss all of Partch's compositions and a great many of his writings in the pages that follow, my primary intention is to offer a narrative account of his life. In so doing I have flown unashamedly in the face of Partch's own belief that the individual's path "cannot be retraced, because each of us is an original being."[1]

This biography attempts to illuminate the purposeful self behind Partch's work—his music, his instruments, his written texts. In the spirit of an investigative journalist I have gathered information about all aspects of his life, many of them hitherto undocumented. In the spirit of a cultural historian I have sketched the broader musical and artistic contexts within which that life unfolded. And in the spirit of a musicologist I have approached his compositions with the view that works of art, as the biographer Richard Ellmann argued, are not objects of autotelic purity: they may also be seen as the result of a momentary convergence of energies, in which past works and deeds, present circumstances and pressures, play a determining role.[2] Although not in any sense "explaining" the music, biography can shed light on how and why the total oeuvre developed as it did. In this view, biography is falsifiable hypothesis, situated somewhere between portraiture and chronology.

Like many creative artists, Partch's own attitude to biography was paradoxical. Among his papers is a scribbled memo which reads: "Biography—it is so trivial. The larger world is trivial beyond belief. So let us be less trivial than that larger world." Yet this was a man who, finally, was inclined to explain all his work in terms of his own experience, and thus on one level to view it as deeply autobiographical. "One is what his experiences, his genesis, and his milieu make him," he wrote to a friend in 1950, "and if he pretends that his experiences are lies, then he's a liar."[3]

Partch has long had the reputation of being a difficult biographical subject, and this book has been beset with a number of obstacles and potential pitfalls. Before I traveled to California in 1987 to embark on my research, several friends warned me that my time there would be wasted. Partch's instruments, his scores, and his papers were in San Diego in the possession of his long-time assistant and now his heir, Danlee Mitchell, who, I was told, would not let me near them: the instruments were kept in storage, under lock and key; the scores, virtually all of which were unpublished, were inaccessible; and Mitchell himself was much too busy to spend time with an unknown researcher, much less allow him access to Partch's papers.

None of this proved to be accurate. Danlee Mitchell agreed to talk with me, at first reluctantly, but in the months that followed we met often and spent hours conversing together. He proved courteous and cooperative beyond my wildest dreams, eventually allowing me access to all the materials in his possession. The greatest initial excitement was in playing Partch's instruments, but I also spent hours studying scores and worked late into the evenings listening to tapes and going through unpublished papers and rare documents—letters, articles, sketches for dramatic works, lecture texts, drawings, photographs. I traveled to look at archival collections elsewhere in the United States. And I talked to a great many of Partch's friends, gradually sketching out a chronology of his life.

Rather than dispelling all the mysteries, my research revealed that Partch was a complex individual, an inexplicable, almost unknowable figure. This impression can be attributed partly to the sparsity of documentary sources for large stretches of his life, creating obscure, shadowy areas in the resulting portrait. But it is due also to the disconcerting imbalance in the pattern of Partch's life, where prolonged spells of vibrant, thrilling creativity alternate with years of aimlessness, of time-wasting, of lack of achievement. In 1980 the composer Kenneth Gaburo wrote, with apparent seriousness, that "what we know about Harry Partch is mostly a matter of hearsay";[4] and more recently Thomas McGeary, in his introduction to a collection of Partch's writings, declared that "little will ever be known of the first forty years of Partch's life."[5]

There are reasons for this pessimism. The problem posed by the very real lack of first-hand documentation of Partch's early life cannot satisfactorily be solved. Most of what we know about his childhood and teenage years has to be extrapolated from later accounts, such as the passage recalling his youth in Arizona and New Mexico in the preface to the second edition of his book *Genesis of a Music,* written in 1969, or reflections recorded three years later during the making of the documentary film *The Dreamer That Remains.* Most of the autobiographical sketches Partch provided record only the development of his musical work, and take as their starting point the year 1923. Recollections of his childhood and youth, whether in form of asides in his letters, or anecdotes remembered by others, are fragmentary, often tantalizingly so, and sometimes inaccurate.

If the conventional first stage of the biographical process, the assembling of materials, was difficult enough in Partch's case, embarking on the second stage was harder still. This second stage I understand to be the creation and maintenance of a steady though imaginary relationship between biographer and subject; not just a fixed "interpretation" but an ongoing dialogue and exchange, a ceaseless discussion and reviewing of motives, actions, and circumstances, a kind of voyeuristic friendship across time.

The elusiveness of this second stage was brought home to me vividly when I was in Santa Fe visiting composer and author David Dunn, one of Partch's last assistants. We had driven to nearby Albuquerque where we succeeded in finding the house on South High where Partch had composed his first music, where his father had died, and from where he cycled on his way to play piano in the local movie house. That night I had the first of many dreams about Harry Partch as a teenager. The backdrop in my dream was a flickering sequence of images of the central New Mexico landscape at twilight: a mound of dark earth with a curious reflection on it, the orange-pink and blue-black of the sky, the brilliant stars, the last light slanting across the terrain. A misfocused, black and white photographic image of Harry, in the half-dark by a mound, was beckoning me over, as though he wanted to tell me something, to confide some secret. He seemed desperately unhappy, shy and rather removed. In the dream, because he appeared as a photographic image, he only moved in the way one tilts a photo, from side to side or up and down, the image staying fixed. It was as though something was possessing him, tearing at him, as a photograph tears and frays at the edges. Each time I tried to move toward him the image blew further away, always beyond reach. All the contained, complex emotions of the photograph were trapped within the still vibrant background. By then the biographical quest had begun, and there could be no turning back.

Prologue

My first encounter with the work of Harry Partch was on a January day in 1979, when I was seventeen. I came across a library copy of his book *Genesis of a Music* and sat gazing at the photographs of the intricate forms of Partch's handcrafted instruments as though they were a set of curiously fashioned mandalas. In the course of that single winter afternoon the coordinates of my musical world changed. The image that grabbed my attention most powerfully was a detail of the staging for the dance-drama *Delusion of the Fury*, which showed the array of instruments on the stage floor in clusters, void of players and dancers, looking like a strange external landscape from a lost time. The very materials from which they were built were enticing and beautiful in themselves: bamboo from the Philippines, Japan, San Diego; American redwood, Brazilian rosewood, African padouk, eucalyptus, sitka spruce; light bulbs, bottles, guitar strings, Pyrex bowls, brass cartridge shells, hubcaps. The collected ensemble looked like the artifacts of some imaginary ethnic group, a compost of allusions to flower stems, tendons, human sexual organs, claws, stamens, dismembered limbs, petals.

These associations, although personal, were not merely adolescent psycho-biological ramblings. In his descriptions of the instruments Partch's most frequent types of metaphor were biological, drawing from the natural world of plants and living creatures, and corporeal, deriving from the forms of the human body. He wrote of the Gourd Tree, a tall eucalyptus bough from which are suspended twelve Chinese temple bells bolted to gourd resonators, that the rods which attach the bells to the bough "are rather flexible and can be bent in order to position the bells for easy playing, as well as to give the impression of ripe fruit growing at various angles on stems, somewhat like a papaya tree, with the smallest fruit at the top."[1] Again, in a letter explaining how to assemble a sound sculpture he had built as a birthday present for a friend, he described the fourth of the sculpture's five parts, a row of tuned pieces of bamboo, as "eleven stiff pricks of varying sizes."[2] And, describing a bamboo marimba he called the Eucal Blossom: "This is the third instrument in which I used the contorted boughs of eucalyptus as part of the base structure. A branch with an appropriate crotch extends from a redwood base; one arm above the crotch is cut at the top at the angle desired for the disk holding the bamboo, and is there bolted to the disk; the other extends upward through a slot in the disk and holds the music rack."[3] In this instrument the "blossom" of bamboo appears to grow from a eucalyptus stem. The whole ensemble seemed full of this sort of life, as though it were a living species in need of a newly invented morphology to explain its forms and structures.

Much of the excitement of getting to know *Genesis of a Music* lay in discovering the organic nature of Partch's work, any given detail of which is always part of an equally compelling larger interweaving of diverse strands. Not only is all his music written for instruments of his own design and construction, but those instruments are tuned to a microtonally extended just intonation scale that is wholly different from the equal temperament of the piano keyboard. A few of his instruments have been duplicated, but there remains only one complete set, the original. Almost none of Partch's music has been—and, arguably, could be—satisfactorily performed using only conventional Western instruments.

Partch's work is thus inseparable from his own handmade ensemble, the visual aspect of which, moreover, is important to the impact of his work in performance and was central to its evolution. The layout of blocks or strings or found objects on the instruments was determined in part by an abstract visual aesthetic, by the patterns created by different projections of the relationships within Partch's microtonal tuning system—projections of interval and scale patterns that demanded new geometric forms of their own. The often large

Detail of staging from *Delusion of the Fury,* UCLA, 1969. Photo by
Ted Tourtelot.

physical spaces occupied by the playing areas of the instruments calls for a
bodily awareness and grace from the player that is almost choreographic, an
antidote to the usual comportment of performers on the concert platform.
Partch insisted, for example, that the players bend at the knees, not at the waist
"like an amateur California prune picker."[4] The correct bodily attitude on the
part of the player would transform the act of instrumental performance into an
integral part of the dramatic focus of Partch's theater works, in which players
and instruments were always to be on stage, "in the act." In 1967 he commented:

> The direction in which I have been going the last forty-four years has much in
> common with the activities and actions of primitive man as I imagine him. Primitive
> man found magical sounds in the materials around him—in a reed, a piece of
> bamboo, a particular piece of wood held in a certain way, or a skin stretched over a
> gourd or a tortoise shell: some resonating body. He then proceeded to make the
> object, the vehicle, the instrument, as visually beautiful as he could. His last step was
> almost automatic: the metamorphosis of the magical sounds and visual beauty into
> something spiritual. They became fused with his everyday words and experiences—
> his ritual, drama, religion—thus lending greater meaning to his life. These acts of

primitive man become the trinity of this work: magical sounds, visual form and beauty, experience-ritual. . . . One has to go back four hundred years to the Italian Renaissance to find anything like it, and even then the situation is not very similar.[5]

The sum total of these demands—together with related, behind-the-scenes aspects such as instrument maintenance, adequate rehearsal space and time, and so on—is a life's work that presents an enormous problem of access. Rarely has a body of music been so closely bound, in a purely practical sense, to its creator.

Many aspects of Partch's work continue to arouse the same controversy more than twenty years after the composer's death in 1974 as they did in his lifetime. Before I read the theoretical chapters in *Genesis of a Music,* the idea of microtones—to the limited extent that I had considered it at all—seemed a rather lateral solution to the problems of contemporary music and the exhaustion of tonality, which at the age of seventeen I took very seriously. It was as though a crisis of language was being addressed by adding new vocabulary. It came as a surprise to find Partch discussing actual microtones and the exhaustion of tonality comparatively little, while saying a lot about subjects such as tuning, consonance and dissonance, and the reanimation of ancient traditions of knowledge stemming from Pythagoras and Ptolemy about the relationship of number and vibration. The microtones were a by-product of these more ancient concepts. My fascination with the psychobiological forms of the instruments became bound up with an interest in their tuning, and in the mathematics of tuning systems in general.

Although Partch readily accepted the "sad compromise" of recordings and films, he insisted nonetheless that the only investigation of his work which had "genuine integrity" was the "seen and heard performance."[6] He attached great importance to the multifaceted nature of his oeuvre, to its status as music integrally bound up with text, drama, or dance, to the sculptural beauty of his instruments and to the *corporeality* of the performing musicians. Kenneth Gaburo argued that to focus on any one aspect of Partch's work in isolation

becomes reductionist; the parts are regarded as-if they are the whole; as-if *ends*, and not *means*. But: one needs constantly to ask such questions as: *just intonation* in the light of what?; *music* in the light of what?; *acting* in the light of what?; *anti-intellectualism* in the light of what? By not so doing, it is easy to see how Partch's work can be rendered "simple," and crucially, how certain kinds of violence can be done to it, even when one speaks eloquently in his behalf. Contrarily, with Partch, musical thought *cannot* be separated from corporeal-theatrical thought . . . what is demanded is that *parts* must give up their *partness* in favor of a *wholeness* which includes them.[7]

Partch himself wrote: "I must decline to limit the dimensions of my rather intense beliefs by the modernly specialized word *music*."[8] He insisted that all his work was theater, and was flattered when a critic once described him as a dramatist. "I do not aim toward *interesting* music—structurally, thematically, formalistically. If it is, this is incidental, because I aim at convincing drama, dynamism, spontaneous emotional reactions."[9]

For all its genuine integrity, even the "seen and heard performance" is not without problems as a way of approaching Partch's work. There can be a peculiar aura around live presentations of his work, which since his death have come to assume the guise of spectacles, of rare opportunities. Too often, the whole phenomenon of the Partch instrumentarium tends to deflect critical attention away from the work itself. Any criticism at all—of composition, performance, theatrical presentation—seems so mean-spirited that one holds silent.

Yet perhaps the most controversial aspect of the entire enterprise is the sheer unavailability of much of Partch's work. Its practical inaccessibility continues to be the largest single cause of the neglect it has suffered. While the music spoke directly and powerfully to sympathetic listeners—the writer Anaïs Nin, for example, commented that "it was as if one had drunk the music instead of accepting it through the ears. . . . The affinity of his music with water, with the poetry of space, with fusion appealed to me"[10]—live performances are an enormous undertaking in terms of time, money, and effort, and have always been few and far between. No recordings of Partch's music were commercially available outside the United States in his lifetime, and few have been since. Only three scores have been published, two of them in small magazines and the third in a hard-to-come-by book: the rest are unpublished and, effectively, unavailable. Even with a score, the music cannot be played unless one has the use of his instruments or is prepared to build duplicates.

To complicate matters still further, Partch's use of greatly expanded pitch resources meant that conventional musical notation was useless for his purposes. His scores were written in a newly invented, elaborate set of tablature notations—graphic codes, different for each instrument, based on the peculiarity of the layout of blocks or strings or found objects on that instrument. These tablatures cannot be "read" as one would read a conventional score: a given symbol indicates which string to pluck, or which block to hit, but not what sound will result, and has to be "translated" to its pitch value. "To promote a youthful vitality in music," he wrote in 1947, "we must have students who will question every idea and related physical object that they encounter . . . they must question, constantly and eternally, what might be called the philosophies behind device, the philosophies that are really responsible for these things."[11]

I have sketched my own initial problems of access to Partch's work because, on a larger scale, the same problems stand in the way of the apprehension and assimilation of that work by the wider musical community. He is a composer whose importance in American music has long been recognized, but the nature of whose achievement is anything but accurately established.

Harry Partch is today viewed as one of the central figures in the nascent evolution of contemporary American music. He has been described by the composer Ben Johnston as an exemplar "of an artistic and philosophic independence and individualism that has few peers," and by Kyle Gann in the *Village Voice* as "the most American composer of all, the center and progenitor of our indigenous music culture."[12]

Partch's name is invariably, if often indiscriminately, linked with that group of musical iconoclasts known collectively as the "American experimental tradition." With an occasional co-opted precursor, this "tradition"—the ironic quotation marks are unavoidable—begins at the turn of the century with Charles Ives, and emerges full-blown in the 1920s in the work of Carl Ruggles, Dane Rudhyar, Henry Cowell, and Ruth Crawford and in the 1930s and beyond with John Cage, Conlon Nancarrow, Henry Brant, and others—composers at odds with that more pervasive and politically more powerful strain in American composition that modeled itself on European tradition. In 1930 Henry Cowell wrote, in the best polemical manner:

> The real division among the modern American composers now, a sharp one, is between those who regard music as something for the purpose of amusement, and those who regard it as a medium for expressing greater depths of feeling. The former group, that work together closely, is composed of men who have studied for the most part in Paris, and have become distinctly influenced by certain modern French philosophical trends. The latter group are for the most part made up of men who have studied in America, and who, although often cruder in technique than the others, are building up a style distinctly rooted in the feelings and traditions of this country.[13]

What this "latter group" of composers had in common was not a shared musical language but an aesthetic imperative: the carving out of an indigenously American musical identity, as distinct from simply writing European symphonic music with an American accent. The music of Ives epitomizes this sensibility, with a rich vein of musical and philosophical allusion underlying its multilayered textures. Like Ives, Ruggles and Crawford forged complex, dissonant idioms, distinct in technique from those of their European counterparts. The Californian strand of this individualism is personified by Cowell, a musical inventor and thus as authentically American as his more famous student John Cage, who introduced the prepared piano. In the late 1930s and early 1940s Cage and Lou Harrison opened a Pandora's box of new percussion resources, using brake drums, flowerpots, and other ready-mades. Nancarrow's radical innovations have been in the domain of rhythm, in particular polymeter and polytempi; Brant's in the exploration of spatial music and ensemble dispersion. In the 1950s Cage and his younger colleagues brought about more far-reaching upsets of musical language and aesthetic with the use of chance and indeterminacy. Harry Partch's place in this schema is clear, qualifying as an inventor of new plectra and percussion instruments, and as a composer who exerted a revolutionary impact by his use of a microtonal tuning system.

Yet to speak of an "experimental tradition" and to assess Partch's place within it is already to offer a reductionist view of twentieth-century American musical life. Like all such simplifications, this one, while containing a germ of truth, masks a more complex and interesting reality. Partch's reasons for building new instruments were quite different than those of other twentieth-century innovators. Edgard Varèse, for example, spoke of the parabolic and hyperbolic effects of the sirens he used in *Amériques* (1918–21) and *Ionisation* (1931), and envisioned new means, mostly electronic, of expanding the registral, timbral, and spatial dimensions of music. The intent behind Partch's instruments was less to provide for new timbres, though that, too, than to realize accurately the pure intervals in his microtonal scale and, in particular, to enhance the corporeality of musical performance—a motivation that dominated all others as time went on. His use of microtonal intervals, moreover, was not the result of an identification with the avant-garde, but rather stemmed from his desire to recapture the vital connection between speech intonation and music that he believed characterized ancient cultures such as the Greek. In this sense, no matter where music historians locate him, Partch remains a true American original.

It would perhaps have pleased Harry Partch that his influence on the American arts has extended beyond his considerable achievements as a composer. The imposing and beautiful forms of his instruments have long commanded the attention of critics and photographers, often at the expense of other, equally important aspects of his work; and, posthumously, the influence of his theoretical work in just intonation on a number of significant composer-theorists of the next generation seems ever more fruitful.

During his lifetime, moreover, Partch was known to friends not only for his professional work but also as a man with a profusion of less public talents: as a writer who left a body of satirical, aesthetic, and autobiographical pieces (among others), an artist who left a cache of modest but characterful pen-and-ink drawings, a raconteur, and a carpenter of considerable gifts and originality, one of whose more routine creations, a driftwood couch, was admired by Henry Moore.[14] His role as producer and distributor of recordings of his own work impressed fellow artists such as Anaïs Nin, and served as a model for several younger composers in the 1960s and 1970s.

Some of these activities were mere adjuncts to Partch's central work as a composer. Others, in particular his writings, served more directly as a kind of pressure valve, as a medium in which aesthetic or conceptual aspects of a work in progress could be argued out and clarified. Yet however integral all the diverse sides of his creative self may have been to Partch the man, it is his activity as a composer that formed the point at which they all met and for which he shall, in the long run, be remembered.

To a younger generation of composers and new-music enthusiasts in America, and increasingly in Europe as well, Harry Partch, the man and the artist, has acquired the trappings of legend. In *The Dreamer That Remains* the composer himself declared, with a dramatic flourish, that he would prefer his work to be anonymous, like that of the cave painters of Altamira—to be remembered for its own virtues, independently of the struggles and frustrations of its creator. This apparently self-effacing remark has occasionally been cited as evidence of a self-defeating or even self-destructive element in his work; as though its sheer inaccessibility, and its remoteness from stable forms of cultural appreciation and dissemination, was a sign of an anarchic or nihilistic insularity, a sign even of a disdain for the attentions of posterity. Ben Johnston, however, has argued that to take the statement at face value "is to elevate a neurotic self-defense mechanism into a philosophy of art. He defended himself ahead of time against the obscurity he almost guaranteed. [It is] futile to attempt to reconcile keeping his music alive for all of us with trying to imitate his own penchant for self-defeat, which masqueraded as anarchism."[15] The work of any artist that is so fragile, that seems so threatened by obsolescence, exerts a powerful, if morbid, fascination, a fascination perhaps with darker aspects of personality and artistic vision. Inevitably, attention and interest is drawn to the man behind this phenomenon, whose ghostly presence draws on and compels.

Oakland and the Old West

The backdrop for Harry Partch's boyhood and adolescence is
the American Southwest. Although he was born in California, his earliest memories concerned the handful of scattered
locations in southern Arizona and in New Mexico where he
grew up. The territory of Arizona at the beginning of the
twentieth century was experiencing "the declining years of
the Old West," the "dying gasps" of the old frontier life.[1] The
images of that life familiar from its celluloid double—of
cowboys brandishing lassos; of outlaws pursued by a posse on
horseback; of low adobe buildings encircled by rambling
verandas; of the spiky desert landscape itself, with its subtle
hourly changes of light and shadow—these images were
among Partch's earliest recollections.

In pinning down the exact chronology of these early years
we are dependent to a large degree on a single, time-worn
sheet of paper: Partch's father's employment record as maintained by the U.S. Immigration Service. Other documents
that have come to light—land deeds, voter registration rec-

ords, entries in city directories and the like—support in a general way the trajectory mapped out by that document, though seem occasionally to be at odds with it on specifics. Partch himself explained that his father "was transferred rather frequently in the Arizona-New Mexico area, always to some railroad junction near the Mexican border."[2] Curiously enough, the details of his father's postings make the family life seem relatively stable, at least in comparison to the chronology of Partch's own adult life. Perhaps part of the confusion was that he retained vivid memories of towns that the family evidently visited but in which they did not live (Yuma, for example, and El Paso), while speaking rarely or not at all about towns in which they did live (Tucson). Yet none of this is truly surprising: it was hardly a place, nor a time, for permanence.

This chapter is not so much about Harry Partch's childhood as his memories of that childhood. What the lived experience of those years felt like we have little hope of knowing. The scarcity of documentary materials is such that there are stories to be told, but no narrative structure from which to fashion an account. Given the arbitrary nature of the historical record, Partch's own recollections as presented here form a necessarily incomplete selection. He himself imposed certain constraints on those memories he wrote down and made public, as would any artist: other memories that came to the surface in interviews, letters, or conversations with friends add further detail to the picture he had sketched out, but they do not present an unbroken chronology.

The value of any autobiographical materials is not that they record things as they were, but that they present an interpretative gloss on the past dictated by the needs of the present. Experiences, and in particular the emotional impact of those experiences, expand and enrich themselves later, often when the lived events to which they refer are long in the past: and that "expansion" process is accomplished principally through language. It is this living, growing, transforming nature of memory that resolves the past into the present.

The importance of the memories collated in this chapter is not so much what they tell us about Harry Partch's past, but that they formed a continuing part of his mental and emotional present. They became, in their telling or writing, part of his *repertory*, and thus determining of aspects of his mature behavior and sensibility, of his self-projection as a man and as a creative artist. The context of their utterance is inseparable from the "content" of the memory. If read as biography, or at least as the subtext of one, their effect is to keep us dependent on unverifiable materials from the end of Partch's life in the attempt to reconstruct and imagine his beginnings, trapping us within his later mind and memory.

The present chapter is thus an exigetic study, a reading of this collation of memories. In making sense of them we are trying less to understand what the years 1901–19 felt like for Partch—the biographical aim—than to map out what Freud called the "psychic economy" of the artistic self, in which the incidents and impressions that the composer himself recorded claim, if only by default, center focus.

Harry Partch was not especially interested in his lineage, though it would probably be wrong to read into this any conscious urge to detach himself from the family stem. Tracing the family history through the generations before the composer's birth we uncover a very American chronicle of rootless generations of solid but unremarkable men. The recorded history of his father's side of the family begins in England in the early eighteenth century, with Quinton Patch (as the name was spelled then) and his twin sister, Mary, who were brought to the U.S. from Tiverton, in Devon, by their foster parents. Quinton and Mary were not the first Patches in the New World: a branch of the family whose relation to them has never been properly established appears in the annals of American history in the mid-seventeenth century.

Harry himself probably learned of old Quinton from a mention in a letter from his brother, Paul, who reported having read, in the summer of 1951, a revised copy of the family "stud book" *Quinton Patch and his Descendants,* compiled by their uncle George Enos Partch and Mary Dunlava Tellefson. Paul even suggested that parts of the book read like "the sort of thing you might set to music." Quinton's last will and testament, he reports, "makes it thoroughly understood that he was on the side of the angels, and that he was going to expect reciprocity, and the personal property inventory showed that the Salvation Army couldn't have gotten many discarded possessions from the Patch family . . . one of Q's boys really blew things wide open by getting the hell out of Connecticut and going to Alabama and buying some slaves."[3]

With Quinton's eldest son we find the origin of the name Partch. Sometime between 1810 and 1820 Thompson Patch, the composer's great-great-grand-father, born in Connecticut in 1750, changed his name and that of his seven sons to Partch. The first record of this appears on the census of 1820, although there the name is given as Parch: a decade later it is spelled as it was to remain. The reason for the change is not known. One family legend has it that Thompson and his three brothers quarreled and two of them had their names changed by an act of legislature, but there is nothing in the files of the state legislature of Vermont, where they lived, that would confirm or dispel this.

Another legend is that a will sent from England had the name spelled incorrectly, and as a would-be beneficiary Thompson thought it wise to change his name accordingly. Thompson built the beginnings of the Vermont nest that housed three generations, including the composer's grandfather.

None of Partch's grandparents receive more than a passing mention in the surviving documentation. His paternal grandfather, Homer Warren Partch, born in Vermont in 1834, is the first scholarly man that can be recorded in the family annals. He maintained a farm most of his life but moved frequently, first to Iowa and thence to Kansas, from where glowing reports were emanating about the fertility of the soil and the quality of the crop yield. Later we find him in Nebraska, where he superintended a missionary school for Native American boys and girls. He outlived his three wives, the second of whom, Laura Ann Young, bore his first son, the composer's father.

Virgil Franklin Partch was born in Oakdale Township, Howard County, Iowa, in 1860. He was twelve when the family moved to the farm in Kansas, where the remainder of his education took place. Virgil attended Highland University, receiving a bachelor's degree in 1881.[4] Following his graduation he went to sea for almost two years. Upon his return he worked briefly as a schoolteacher before deciding to train for a career in the church. The Christian seed was planted deeply in the family, and Virgil's half-brother, George Enos Partch, recorded that "missionary interest was being promoted" at Highland University.[5] Virgil graduated from McCormick Theological Seminary of the Presbyterian Church in Chicago in 1888 and was ordained, back in Kansas, by Highland Presbytery in the same year.

Harry's maternal grandparents were from the South. John Childers was from Virginia, and his wife, America Lee, from Tennessee. Partch claimed that their forebears, like Virgil's, were descended from English, Scottish, and Irish settlers. From his maternal grandmother the young Harry picked up a store of "pure Appalachia," colloquial wisdom and old sayings—one of which, "he was not born in the woods to get scared by an owl," even found its way fifty years later into the second edition of his book *Genesis of a Music*.[6] Partch's mother, Jennie Childers, was born in Lucas, Iowa, in 1863. Her son liked to stress her hillbilly origins, describing her as being from the "mountains of western Virginia, eastern Kentucky and Tennessee."[7]

Jennie's education was less extensive than that of her husband-to-be. However, at the age of twenty she entered the preparatory department of Simpson Centenary College in Indianola, Iowa, which provided a foundation course for students wishing to do undergraduate study. She began a course called "Latin

Virgil Franklin Partch and Jennie
Childers Partch in the year of their
marriage, 1888. Photo by Uhlman, Harry
Partch Estate Archive.

and Scientific," but is listed in the college records for only the first year of what was normally a two-year course. The drop-out rate after the first year was quite high, and it is possible that she may not have passed the examinations (a hurdle that forced out the majority of the students). The college also offered music, among other subjects. Although we have no record of Jennie's participating in musical activities, she seems to have learned to read music as a girl and had possibly taken piano lessons. In the 1886–87 academic year she re-enrolled at the college as a Selected Studies student, but pursued this only for a year, after which the college has no further record of her. It seems, though, that in vocational terms her mind was already made up. She had received the "call" of the Lord, and had decided to undertake missionary work.

In 1888 the Board of Foreign Missions of the Presbyterian Church in the United States appointed Virgil Partch and Jennie Childers to be missionaries. They were married on August 24 that year. A photograph, taken in the year of their marriage, shows the couple as they prepared for passage to the Orient: it is easy to read into their features signs of those character traits later ascribed to them by their youngest son. Virgil, in a dark frock coat, is seated, his face registering both solemnity and, thanks to the shy, slightly turned left eye, a kind of introspection. Jennie, in white, stands at his left; her full lips suggest kindness, even sensuousness, yet in the curious way she looks toward but not quite at the camera there is a hint of self-involvement, even—by a stretch of the imagination—obstinacy. Five weeks after their marriage they left the U.S. to serve as Presbyterian missionaries and teachers in China.

By December 1888 Virgil and Jennie Partch had arrived at the Ningpo station of the Central China mission. Ningpo (now usually written Ningbo) is a port on the Yung River in eastern China, in the Zhejiang province. Their first task was to learn the Ningpo dialect, as fluency in spoken language was crucial to their forthcoming missionary work. In Ningpo their first child, Paul Chester Partch, was born in 1891.

Living conditions were difficult, and by early 1893 Jennie had contracted malaria. The family then returned to the United States. Virgil spent two years doing missionary work in Nebraska and Oregon, and Jennie slowly regained her health. Early in 1895 they returned to China, this time to Chinanfu. They now had to learn the Mandarin dialect of the Shantung Province, forgetting in the process the dialect they had learned in Ningpo. Here in 1899 they had a second child, Irene.

It is difficult to avoid seeing Partch's parents' missionary experience in symbolic terms: so much of their youngest son's artistic stance is prefigured in their shifting attitudes, which encompassed evangelism, a sympathy to Oriental culture, and finally an apostasy and flight. During the last decades of the nineteenth century, missionaries went deep into the villages of the impoverished Shantung in large numbers, converting people, tearing down the traditional temples, and building churches. The self-righteousness with which most American missionaries approached China is well known, and Virgil and Jennie initially were probably no different. The missionary felt China needed God and Christianity, the "one true religion," to bring about a moral rebirth. The Chinese in their turn felt indignant at these Westerners, many of whom they regarded as their cultural inferiors, acting as schoolmasters to their children. As the years passed, and possibly to their own surprise, Virgil and Jennie began to develop a respect and even an admiration for the culture of the people they were supposed to be converting. Partly as a consequence of this, and partly as the concatenation of various repressed doubts and questions within himself, Virgil began in 1898 to study "the Higher Criticism" and to entertain heterodox ideas.

The widespread missionary activity soon led to a series of violent reprisals. Young Chinese men banded together and began to study the ancient arts of self-defense—"Chinese boxing"—eventually forming a kind of anti-dynastic secret society that became known as the Boxers. By the end of 1899 they were openly attacking Western missionaries as well as Chinese Christians, most numerously in the villages of Shantung, where Virgil and Jennie were stationed. With two small children, they must have begun to fear for their lives. "They had a hell of a time just staying alive," Partch later explained. "And yet they were very sympathetic with the Chinese: it made their situation very precarious."[8]

As well as the troubling social conditions in China, Virgil was engaged in another, and ultimately more transforming, crisis, of which he makes no mention in this later account: his growing doubts about Christian belief. Some of this was due to his increasing sympathy for Chinese culture, which he retained to the end of his life. As Harry put it, he "simply couldn't go along with the 'heathen' epithet that was thrown at the Chinese." These doubts culminated in a resolve to write to the Missionary Board, expressing the full measure of his heterodoxy. In a letter dated April 28, 1900, he recorded his doubts about the evangelical work in which he had been engaged and asked to be recalled from service. The request was granted, and resignations from both he and Jennie were recorded on June 18, in the middle of the Boxer Rebellion—the peasant uprising that formed the culmination of the Boxers' activity.

Attempting to flee from the country under those conditions was both difficult and dangerous. Virgil's own account, in a letter written near the end of his life, downplays the danger of their situation, but we get a glimpse of the harrowing events of that year. "In 1900, at the time of the Boxer trouble, I was in charge of an academy at Chinanfu, and teaching in the Mandarin dialect algebra, geometry, trigonometry and natural philosophy. This rebellion destroyed the school and caused the immediate return to the United States of myself, wife, and two children born in China."[9] Virgil and Jennie and the two children were ordered to the coast for protection. The Chinanfu station was looted only days after they fled. Recounting the story, Partch did not refrain from embellishing details, but his outline is accurate enough: "The exodus was long and gruesome. Bribes, murders, the ship they were on was rammed and sank in the harbor of . . . Tsinan-fu."[10] The Partch family departed in June on a steamer chartered by the American consul. The passage lasted a grim seven weeks.

They arrived in San Francisco in August. Even though the social and political situation in China was beginning to return to normal by the end of the year, the family seems to have made no attempt to return. This was no doubt chiefly because of their severing of ties to the missionary service, though there was a contributing factor that became clear that autumn: Jennie was pregnant again. Years later Virgil explained matter-of-factly that "for the sake of the family I remained here and entered the Civil Service . . . three children were to be educated and the United States was the best place for the purpose."[11] In November 1900 he took the civil service examinations for the job of postal clerk.

The timing of the family's return to the United States is important in that Harry Partch often stated, and apparently believed, that he had been conceived in China—"either a Boxer prison camp in Shantung Province . . . or the broad Pacific."[12] He even recounted that his mother, pregnant with him, had fallen off the gangplank getting onto the boat leaving China and into the water.[13] And, with reference to the terrifying conditions of their exodus, he remarked that "I've always had a weak stomach, and my mother says that this was true when I was a baby. I'm sure that some of her fears were bequeathed to me."[14] Sadly, the facts dispel these possibilities, however apt their mythic significance. Given the date of his birth he must have been conceived in California, a few weeks after the family's return. He was born in Oakland on June 24, 1901, in their home at 5861 Occidental Street.

Our only substantial knowledge of the Partch family in the San Francisco area at this time is of Virgil's employment. From information in a personal questionnaire that he compiled at the request of the Department of Commerce and Labor in July 1904, we know that he began working as a postal clerk some seven weeks before Harry's birth, on a salary of $50 per month. In October 1901 he started as a gauger for the Internal Revenue Service at a rate of $5 per diem, but the job lasted only until December. The job of postal clerk, however, continued until the following July, implying that for some weeks he held the two jobs concurrently: presumably the family had financial problems. In August 1902 he started working as a customs inspector on the waterfront in San Francisco, on a salary of three dollars per diem; this job he held for some eighteen months. In October 1903 he sat for the civil service examination for the job of Chinese Inspector, and obtained the highest exam grade of anyone in the country. Accordingly, the following January he was appointed to a new post in the Immigration Service. This was a step up in salary, but his being stationed in Arizona is the first visible manifestation we have of a family drama that was played out away from the historical record: Jennie's tuberculosis. It is sadly ironic that Virgil and Jennie and their three children came to Arizona not as an oasis on the way west, following the pioneer trail, but as a refuge from the Pacific Coast necessitated by Jennie's health.

Of his mother's tuberculosis we know only what Partch himself recalled in his later years. It seems that when he was about two and a half years old Jennie's condition was critical enough to require a move to a desert climate in search of better air. Southeastern Arizona provided such a climate and, although lower in elevation than parts of New Mexico, had a thin atmosphere that relieved the pressure on her weakened lungs. In February 1904 Virgil began working as Chinese Inspector for the U.S. Immigration Service on a salary of $4 per diem, and was stationed at Tucson.

In the early years of the century, a diagnosis of tuberculosis was tantamount to a death sentence. It was not incurable, but the fatality rate was so high that it was even normal to withhold the identity of the illness from friends and family. The mythology surrounding tuberculosis linked it to poverty, deprivation, malnourishment; it was believed to be a disease of damp cities, of unhealthy urban environments. In 1882 it was discovered to be a bacterial infection and was treated as a disease of the lungs. In those cases that were not yet advanced beyond the hope of a cure, the medical advice was always to find better air. Jennie herself probably received treatment in a sanatorium. In any event these first years in Arizona must have been difficult ones for the family, and indeed for the young Harry. It was the second time Jennie found herself seriously ill with an infant son dependent on her.

In August 1904 Virgil began a new posting some fifty miles east of Tucson, in the desert whistle-stop railroad town of Benson. Benson is described in period accounts as a forbidding, sleepy village. It was initially a stage station where the stagecoaches crossed the San Pedro River, to the east of town, but by the turn of the century had become a railroad town. The landscape surrounding it was, and remains, spectacular: dry, half-covered yellow earth scattered with yuccas, cacti, and century plants that sent up tall flower stalks in the rainy season and then perished. Ranches were often located near a spring, which were invaluable sources of water in the midst of the broad areas of barren sand. Little vegetation grew in the arid, half-desert land, and the Partch family was dependent on mail-order deliveries of canned food.

Located in a slight depression, out on the mesa, Benson was often wind-swept, and the most solid buildings in the town were the saloons. Partch recalled the town as having "about three hundred population and with eleven saloons for transient railroaders along its board walks": a feature in the *Tucson Citizen* in 1906, however, describes Benson as having "eight saloons . . . the population figures as high as 1500."[15] Yet whatever the truth of statistics, the down-at-heel image is clear. The same newspaper reported that the suggestion of building a Presbyterian church in the town foundered for lack of expertise, for while "there is an oasis of men in Benson who will tell you how to construct a saloon building, it is a barren desert when it comes to suggestions for church buildings."

It was a time of relative prosperity. In keeping with the pattern common in the Southwest, many of the general stores, saloons, hotels, and restaurants were run by Chinese immigrants. Only recently had a company secured franchises for water works and for lighting the town electrically, though Partch as an old man recalled the Arizona night sky of his boyhood, as seen from his parents' ranch, with "no street lights, millions of stars."[16] Horse-drawn carriages with lanterns were still common. Some thirty years later the *Arizona State Guide* noted of Benson: "Cowboys, miners, and Mexicans still frequent this town that for many years was filled with saloons, tinhorns, rustlers, cribs, and crap games."[17]

In the "declining years of the Old West" aspects of frontier days would spasmodically spring to life. Partch recalled "watching through a telescope 'bad men' holed up in some nearby rocks. . . . I was always for the bad men. I didn't have any real reason except that the idea of retribution was a ghastly idea to me. Whatever they had done, here they were being *trapped,* hunted and trapped! I had seen my father and sister hunt animals, and I had this terrible feeling about anyone who was hunted."[18]

The first home that Partch recalled was his parents' ranch, which he remembered as being a mile and a half from Benson. No property deed for this ranch has come to light, but we have details of the land the family bought in June 1907. The grant deed records it as: "Lot number fourteen in block number six in the plot of ground known as 'Bryans Addition' to the Town of Benson, Cochise County Arizona, said lot being fifty feet wide and one hundred and fifty feet long." Three weeks later, on July 19, they bought for the sum of $160 three additional lots from the Pacific Improvement Company.

The family's home was full of Chinese objects, books, paintings, and furniture. Early in 1950, in northern California, Partch saw some black bamboo which, as he wrote to friends, was "quite the most beautiful plant I've seen in a long time. It brought back very small childhood—black bamboo furniture my parents brought from China—the first time I've ever recalled it."[19] Chinese was occasionally spoken in their home, always when there were Mandarin-speaking visitors. "My father read and even wrote Mandarin, and corresponded for a number of years with Chinese friends. I remember seeing him write."[20] Although both Virgil and Jennie retained some measure of fluency in the spoken language, they made no attempt to teach it to Harry; but the sound of the language imprinted itself on him. They also had a library in which "there were more books in Chinese, accordion folded, with ivory thongs, illustrated by gory colored lithographs of the beheading of missionaries, than there were books in English."[21]

His earliest conscious musical impressions were associated with his mother. Unlike her husband, who turned to atheism, Jennie remained a Christian. She sang her son hymns, including "Rock of Ages," accompanying them on a reed organ, and also Chinese songs and lullabies—"the only lullaby she ever sang was Chinese." Harry remembered a few of these songs and could still sing them, in Chinese, into his twenties. Jennie was probably not an especially accomplished musician; in her son's description her performances sound redolent of her missionary days. "My mother—who could play chords on the organ—taught me to read music when I asked her to."[22] Harry showed an interest in playing the organ, and both parents seem to have encouraged musical activity in their children. Before long musical instruments joined the range of mail-order items on which the family, because of the comparative isolation of their ranch, were dependent. Virgil and Paul, the eldest son, "loved to look through Sears, or Monkey-Ward catalogues, and order some new instrument." "I recall a cello, a violin, a mandolin, a guitar, a cornet, and numerous harmonicas," Partch noted. "These were not just passing fancies. My older sister learned to play the violin very well, and my older brother the mandolin."[23] Harry himself, at "age 5–6," began playing, "in order—the old pump reed organ, a mandolin, and a cornet. I mean seriously. Whatever plucked-string technique I later developed started with that mandolin. . . . There was also a violin and a cello, but I did not play them seriously."[24] One can indeed hear the influence of the mandolin on his later guitar technique. "But I do not think that any of my family devoured as avidly as I did the *idea* of music."[25]

There were also musical impressions from other sources. An enclave of Yaqui Indians, native to Sonora, Mexico, had settled around Benson. In 1906–07 the Mexican government began a series of initiatives aimed at breaking the Yaqui resistance to encroachment upon their territory near the Yaqui River. Large numbers were forcibly deported and sold to plantation owners in Yucatan and Tehuantepec, and others were enrolled in the army. There followed a wide-spread scattering of the Yaqui, the majority throughout Mexico, though a smaller number headed north and crossed the border into southern Arizona. The young Harry could hardly have encountered the Yaqui at close range—he remembered them as "very timid and aloof"—although years later, "when I heard the Yaqui Indian Spring Ritual on a record, the sounds seemed amazingly familiar to me."[26] Growing up in proximity to Native Americans he was able to develop a sympathy for their plight, which matured into a lifelong respect.

Virgil maintained a small woodshop on the ranch, so Harry grew up "familiar with common tools."[27] Many years later he explained to a correspondent, with disarming simplicity, the importance of this small fact to his life's endeavors. "I grew up using tools. The combination of instruments of many varieties all around, and a woodshop, made my decision to build my own instruments very easy, when that time came."[28]

Partch's memories of Benson included the sounds of the whistles of steam engines reverberating around the mountains. "My first awareness of being alive came to me on the southern Arizona desert, where the mountainous horizons were some sixty miles distant in any direction. And my first and most poignant aural memories are the whistles of the trains which ran across that valley, from one mountain range to the opposite range."[29] The haunting loneliness of the sound, in the vast darkness of the desert night, came to symbolize the immensity of the terrain. Fifty years later, the sound itself found its way into Partch's *U.S. Highball,* where it evokes a blast of uncertain exhilaration, the isolation and danger of long journeys on autumn nights. Asked near the end of his life by filmmaker Stephen Pouliot why he had not been afraid to spend so much of that life alone, Partch replied: "I suppose I got used to it when I was young. I had to play alone, I had to create my own worlds. There was no-one to help me create a world. Out in the Arizona desert I had very few playmates."[30] And one of his last writings contains the following: "The small child feels that he is the center of the world, in both his joys and his disasters. It is redundant to say *the world he knows.* There is no other. And every lonely child builds worlds of his own, both with objects and in fantasy, a dozen a year, or even a dozen a day."[31]

In the summer of 1909, when Harry had just turned eight, his brother, Paul, left home to join the navy. Paul joined ship in San Diego, and far at the back of his younger brother's mind was a memory of southern California that summer—a first taste of the area that, half a century later, would become his home.

Beyond isolated glimpses of family life, we have little idea of the individuals or the important friendships that shaped the young boy's personality. Partch stressed, in contrast, the loneliness of his childhood. In 1969, on the wall of a projection room of a company in Los Angeles specializing in children's films, he came across an inscription, "painted, illuminated, by the child-author": "Once upon a time/ There was a little boy/ And he went outside."[32] It was an image that haunted his last years. Going "outside" meant many things: as a boy, going outside into the "big ranch country of Arizona"—the pioneer spirit; in his teens, going "outside" his family, by not going "the way a happy pair of parents would have liked";[33] later, going "outside" in music; and later still, going "outside" society as a hobo, with almost devastating consequences. In a 1969 draft of the preface to the second edition of *Genesis of a Music,* he wrote: "The only way to build a conceivable optimism (with pollution of resources and constant intimations of annihilation) is somehow to find a way *outside.*" The finished preface says it best: "When I feel optimistic, it holds brilliant promise, like an Arizona morning before dawn, with its cardboard stage set and dark eastern silhouette in honor of the sun's holy rising." Optimism is the paper-thin patina on the "outside," loneliness its necessary corollary.

Yet for all that, he was far from unhappy. Danlee Mitchell has the impression that both parents regarded Harry as something of a favorite child. In *The Dreamer That Remains* Partch as an old man speaks of the "little anodynes for peace, content, comfort" that symbolized the Benson of his youth. He recalled "many benches along the plank and roofed-over sidewalks, . . . and in front of the post office. And where else would you want a bench to read your mail and love your mail and in front of the bank to contemplate your circumstances and in front of the saloon to contemplate your soul?"

Virgil's job turned out to have involved a misunderstanding on the part of the Immigration Service. He understood and spoke Mandarin, which the immigration officials thought would be useful in dealing with the Chinese laborers who were coming illegally from Mexico to work on the railroad. The majority of the immigrants, however, spoke Cantonese, which, as Harry put it, was as incomprehensible to Virgil "as Manx-speaking Gaels would be to Melanesian Islanders."[34] He recalled also that "my dad seemed to scoff at the lack of understanding."[35] Virgil's job was to help enforce the restrictive new Chinese Exclusion Act of 1902. By the turn of the century Chinese inspectors and immigration officials had made it almost impossible for Chinese to enter the United States through busy ports in densely populated areas, and as a result most shifted to the sparsely inhabited border areas of the Southwest. Virgil probably alternated, at least initially, between work in an office and scouting assignments, maintaining surveillance, perhaps on horseback, of backcountry areas, and inspecting passenger trains and freight cars. His knowledge of Chinese manners, habits, and reactions and his familiarity with local topography and transportation facilities would have been assets in the job—which must have been arduous and probably dispiriting—of ferreting out illegal aliens in the range of Arizona weathers, sometimes extremely hot or bitterly cold.

Virgil's employment record shows that for a period of nine months in 1910 he was stationed at Tucson. That the transfer was not in the nature of a promotion is indicated by the fact that his salary at first remained as it had been in Benson for the previous three years, $1,600 per annum. We have no way of knowing if the family moved to Tucson with him. There is one counterindication, which is that in November that year Virgil received a land grant patent to 160 acres of land in Benson, for the "east half of the southeast quarter, of Section eight, and the south half of the southwest quarter of Section nine in Township seventeen, south of Range twenty east of the Gila and Salt River Meridian, Arizona." This made for a considerable holding—it was in addition to the land they had bought in the summer of 1907, which was not sold until twenty years later—and indicates the strength of the family's ties to Benson.

Tucson, with thirteen thousand inhabitants, was the largest city in Arizona Territory. The look of the place was dominated by flat-topped one-story adobe buildings, plastered mud brown or dirty white, and narrow, rutted streets. Like most of the larger towns in the Southwest it had a Chinatown, as well as a Mexican section of one-room earthen-floored shacks. Downtown there was an affluent business district. Most of the town's commercial and professional establishments were run by Anglos; restaurants and laundries were run almost entirely by Chinese. Horse-drawn wagons were plentiful, but there were also several automobiles, regarded as expensive curios for the wealthy rather than as a means of transportation. Harry doubtless visited Tucson to see his father, as the distance would have been too great for Virgil to commute from the ranch in Benson every day. Virgil's pay increase in July, four months into the posting, of an extra $20 per annum, was to be the last increase he would ever receive.

It may have been during the time Virgil was stationed at Tucson that the most traumatic event of Harry's childhood took place. We are not sure exactly when it happened—Partch believed he was about eight at the time—but there is general agreement among the friends to whom he confided it that it happened when his father was out of town. The incident was his mother's decision to have the young Harry circumcised. We do not know what prompted Jennie's action—whether she was following medical advice or observing some pseudo-religious practice—but the effect on the boy was traumatic. What is worse, Partch claimed that his mother took him to the doctor to have the circumcision performed without having warned him of the reason for their visit.

Partch's recounting of this incident is captured in an outtake from the film *The Dreamer That Remains,* when he describes the act to Stephen Pouliot as "a conspiracy . . . a woman obsessed with controlling her son, and taking that little skin off gives her control":

> My father was not circumcised, my brother was not, and they were naked in front of me constantly. But my mother decided I was going to be different. I was going to be a modern child who was going to be cleansed, as it were, by having a little piece of skin cut off. It wasn't that—I didn't object to this humiliation so much as that I was then different from everybody else, except for the Jews. . . . And I resented that. I resented my mother, yes, and she didn't have it done until my father was away because I'm sure he would have objected . . . this is a cabal, a conspiracy between doctors and mothers—mothers who want their sons symbolically castrated. Of course, all mothers want to castrate their sons. If they can castrate them then they can keep them close.

In the telling of this, Partch was aware he was on camera, on the record, but it is impossible to believe that his passion and anger are anything but genuine. Perhaps Jennie was determined to exercise control over a young son who, in his father's absence, was becoming difficult. On the other hand, she may simply have been following medical fashion; circumcision was becoming widespread in the U.S. at the time, following the increasing belief by the medical profession in its hygienic necessity, although the operation was usually performed at birth. Perhaps, as her son suggested, she regarded the act symbolically as a form of cleansing or purification. Or perhaps there was a genuine medical reason which the young Harry did not understand and later, as an adult, chose to ignore. But why his mother didn't *tell* him that she wanted to have the operation per- formed—which only added to its traumatic impact—can only be conjectured, dependent as it was on the total fabric of their relationship. The episode and the anger it generated led to an intense and sometimes stifling love-hate relation- ship between the two until Jennie's death in 1920.

The incident left an indelible mark. Partch's friend Francis Crawford, talking to him about it fifty years later, had the impression that the composer regarded it as a rite of passage that abruptly terminated his childhood, and at an earlier age than normal. Crawford feels too that the boy never recovered from the sense of emotional betrayal, and in consequence never regained a full measure of trust in his mother.[36] Danlee Mitchell was told the story in the early 1960s, when it was recounted without undue rancor or distress; only years later, Mitchell contends, did it begin to "play on his mind."[37] The writing of the autobiographical passages of the new preface to *Genesis of a Music*, perhaps, and certainly the making of *The Dreamer That Remains,* dredged up many repressed emotions.

Somewhat connected to this, at least in terms of its effect on the adult Partch, is a second traumatic experience. Among the normal childhood illnesses he contracted as a boy was mumps. In keeping with the Christian Science beliefs she then held, Jennie did not seek any form of medical treatment for him, believing bodily illness to be a delusion that could be dispelled by a closer knowledge of God, and medical science therefore to be irrelevant. Accordingly she took her son to a Christian Science practitioner, a professional healer of a type that was not uncommon by then, who read to Harry from the Bible and prayed for his recovery. As a result, because the mumps had not been treated, Partch all his life believed himself to be sterile.[38]

Whether or not he really was sterile probably matters less than his own belief on the matter. The attribution of this to the mumps is certainly possible. If he developed orchitis, an inflammation of the testicles and the most common of the complications from mumps among males, this could have led to atrophy of the testicles and hence to sterility. With this complication he would have been all the more in need of medical treatment.

However, there is another explanation for Partch's supposed sterility. There is a claim from one apparently reliable source—a former lover—that Partch had "no balls at all." If so, this would not have been a consequence of orchitis: although the testicles would atrophy and no longer function, they would not simply disappear. Rather, one (wholly conjectural) possibility is that he was born with the condition known as undescended testicles. In this case he would almost certainly have been genuinely sterile, and his having contracted mumps as a boy would have played no part at all.

In combination, these two incidents played a part in shaping an important aspect of Partch's mature sensibility. At least one of his friends, to whom he confided much of this, saw a connection between his belief that he was sterile and his sexuality. Lou Harrison comments: "The circumcision that his mother caused, in addition to the atrophy, must have given him a whale of a castration complex, and must certainly have inhibited him immensely in seeking sexual partnership, especially with other men . . . these must have contributed strongly to what I somehow felt were Harry's reluctances or tentative qualities with regard to approaching other men."[39]

In November 1910 Partch's father was transferred to Phoenix. The Phoenix Elementary School District has a record of Harry in fifth grade in the school year 1910–11. Driving through Arizona more than half a century later, he was "surprised and delighted" to find his old school building in Phoenix still standing, and recalled his schooldays there to a newspaper reporter, who wrote that "the building was two-story with stairs on each side and he used to sit beneath the stairs and play the piano while the kids marched to their class-rooms."[40]

In Phoenix a new avenue of musical exploration opened up thanks to a music store owner in the town. "I began to hear music on Edison cylinder records when I was ten, but I can't recall exactly what. Later, when I knew, I reacted to certain small shafts of intense life—Hebrew chants, Chinese theater, and Congo ritual—with a kind of intimate passion."[41] He recalled his mother taking him to Jewish burial ceremonies, and the chants remained in his memory.[42]

By the age of twelve Harry had his own corner of the garden where he planted and grew things. "My mother insisted that I learn the 'meaning of money,' so I had to take a small cart and sell my produce from door to door. I hated it. Luckily, she went off to northern Mexico as a correspondent for the Villa-Carranza revolutionary expedition and by the time she returned the growing season was over."[43] Jennie's activity as a newspaper reporter took her occasionally away from home which, far from providing a relief from her attention, seems to have been hard for her son.

In the 1912 Phoenix city directory the Partch family is listed as living at 511 East Willetta. The Maricopa County recorder has a warranty deed, made in December 1913, recording a purchase of land by Jennie in Phoenix, of "All of Lot Thirteen in Block Thirteen in East Evergreen, an addition to the City of Phoenix . . . together with all water rights and ditch rights belonging to said land." Yet a few weeks before the purchase took place, according to his employment record, Virgil was transferred to Albuquerque, New Mexico; it may be that on this occasion the family did not move at once. The land in Phoenix was sold nine months later.

Virgil began his job in Albuquerque in November 1913; his office was on the third floor of the federal building in the center of town. In the 1915 Albuquerque city directory the Partch family is listed as living at 208 South High, where they remained for some five years. The writer Paul Horgan, two years Partch's junior, who arrived with his own parents in Albuquerque around the same time, remembered his fascination as a youth with the Rio Grande, which bounded the western edge of town, and noted that "at that impressionable age, the physical splendors of the New Mexico landscape entered into me—piercing light from on high; sovereign thunderheads ten miles above; pink gold in fine sandy bottoms edged by cottonwood groves; great lazy heat of summer after-noons; grinding spring dust storms; veiled blue of distant mountains; mer-cifully undeveloped solitudes."[44]

Harry started at Albuquerque High School in August 1915, and he seems to have been a promising student. During his four years at the school his grades steadily improved from good to excellent. In his first year he took English, algebra, Spanish, American history, mechanical drawing, and music; algebra was replaced by plane geometry in his second year. He enjoyed history, English, geography, and geometry, but seems not to have distinguished himself in music. "I was asking too many questions that couldn't be answered by the people around."[45] After his second year music no longer appears on his transcript, and in the first two years of his studies it is unique among his subjects in that no grade was conferred for it.

Yet music was on his mind now more than ever before. During early 1916, at the age of fourteen, he made his first serious attempts to compose music. The first piece to stay in his memory was *Death on the Desert,* composed, as he recalled nearly fifty years later on the original score of *And on the Seventh Day Petals Fell in Petaluma,* in March–April 1916. Prophetically enough, from the standpoint of his later work, this was a story to be read with piano accompaniment. He composed more of these "whimsical, melancholy 'stories'" and set them to music.[46]

If Partch had any kind of instruction in composition outside his music classes at Albuquerque High, we know nothing of it. From the outset, such formal study of music as he undertook seems not to have been greatly successful. There is a curious remark in a letter of 1954 to a reviewer of his records where he notes: "Until late in my teens I couldn't 'carry' a tune. I know now that this was not because I couldn't hear, but because I heard too much."[47] By "too much" Partch seems to imply that his sensitivity to the nuances of intonation impaired his ability to abstract and remember melodic contour, of its essence a more approximate way of hearing. He would occasionally muster this rather curious argument in defense of people generally considered "unmusical," notably the Irish poet W. B. Yeats, citing Yeats's line "I hear with older ears than the musician" in support of his claim that music with discrete scale steps—particularly tempered ones—had led to an impoverishment in our sensitivity to the inherent music of spoken words. The result of this inability to carry a tune was that his teachers probably concluded he had a poor ear. From the standpoint of his musical development this was the most helpful mistake they could have made.

A significant change in the family's life during Harry's first year of high school was his mother's enrollment at the University of New Mexico, beginning in January 1916. The university acknowledged one hundred credit hours from her last year of study at Simpson College in Iowa in 1886–87 toward her degree in social science, so she was officially regarded as a transfer student. Her degree work included a course in the department of education, which complied with the requirements of the state board of education for a professional certificate. Jennie officially received her B.A. in social science from the university in May 1917, at the age of fifty-three. Her graduation photograph and a brief notice appeared in *The Mirage,* the University of New Mexico yearbook. "If you, gentle reader, do not believe in 'votes for women,' just challenge Mrs. Partch to a debate on the subject and then prepare to have your pet theories and arguments shattered and your views completely changed. Yes indeed, Mrs. Partch won glory to the cause when she defended Women's Suffrage in a debate in Social Science class one morning. . . . Now our suffrage friend has designs on a Master's degree and we know she will take it, for Mrs. Partch succeeds where she attempts."

By this time, and no doubt due in part to Jennie's enrollment at the university, the family had economic problems. Paul, who was still in the navy, had by this time married Anna Pavloff, daughter of the last Russian governor of Alaska, and had a family of his own to support.[48] Harry explained that "we simply didn't make enough money: I had to start working."[49] The U.S. had entered World War I in April 1917, but he was still too young to be drafted into military service. As it turned out, the family's economic situation led Partch into work that proved to be among the most satisfying of all his early musical activities.

It came, appropriately enough, from outside the classroom. "My last two years of formal education in high school I supported myself partially, sometimes wholly, by bell-hopping (Kansas City [where the family sometimes visited relatives for holidays] and Albuquerque), and playing in bands for silent movies and mechanical organs for silent movies (Albuquerque). This helped [financially] also, and I liked doing it. It strengthened my belief in dramatic or theatrical music."[50] Near the end of his life he recalled: "I played in movie theaters and I played in church. I much preferred movie theaters. They paid better, too."[51] As a bellhop Harry worked in an Albuquerque Harvey House, a restaurant that provided speedy service for passengers on stopovers during train journeys. He also found gainful employment delivering prescriptions all over town on his bicycle, "including the wide-open red-light district," probably for the maladies of the prostitutes. He recalled one woman there offering him his first cigar, which he smoked all the way through without getting sick.

The adolescent Harry had several opportunities to befriend the women of Albuquerque's red-light district. "Interspersed at this time are recollections of my mother visiting jails, complaining loudly about their condition, and occasionally bringing a prostitute home to spend the night. (My father would bring hobos home also, but he insisted that they work. I do not recall that my mother ever demanded that the prostitutes work.)"[52] It is easy at first reading to miss the wry humor of this reminiscence. But it does point up the complex image of the female sex that surrounded Harry in Albuquerque: a very strong and domineering mother, the occasional prostitute brought home from jail, and his beautiful sister, Irene, two years older than he, who seems to have shared some of their mother's colorful, outgoing personality. A couplet from the Albuquerque High 1919 yearbook's "High School A.B.C.'s" reveals that "I stands for Irene/ Loved by the boys"; while "The Writing in the Sand," a humorous piece predicting the possible futures of the 1919 senior class, quips that Irene now "travels with the Redpath Chautauqua. She is an ideal teller of fairy tales."

Set against this was Harry's deteriorating relationship with his father. Toward the end of his life he attributed this situation, philosophically, to the inevitable conflict in the biological world between old males and young males.[53] Virgil had become a quiet, reserved, and possibly rather embittered man. "My dad . . . was a Sphinx, [and] I remember the few times he ever spoke," Partch recalled; "a very scholarly guy, but not one to mix with people at all."[54]

His parents' apostasy had taken different forms. Virgil turned to agnosticism and "aggressive atheism": "he had many of the writings of Robert Ingersoll about."[55] Partch took pains to point out that the aggressiveness of Virgil's atheist position was doctrinal rather than evangelical: he did not want to make it sound "as though my father went around ramming atheism down the throat of everyone he met . . . he was so silent that only his own family even knew that he was an atheist."[56] Jennie, however, "remained a Christian," and took up at various times Christian Science, Unity, New Thought—"anything that flew through the wind. That became pretty annoying."[57] Virgil, as a convinced atheist, would surely have found much of this hard to tolerate.

Indeed, religion was the primary cause of tension between Harry's parents. He himself "got so sick" of their religious arguments.[58] It is possible that this doctrinal division had repercussions in other aspects of their relationship. Partch told an interviewer pointedly that his parents "slept in different beds through all their life that I remember," and another interviewer that "my own home was certainly not a happy home as far as marriage was concerned. It was never over the subject of love or fidelity . . . the whole basis was economic and religious."[59] But there is no real reason to suppose that his parents' marriage was disintegrating.

The question of religious and philosophical doctrine, even given the committed and passionate interest it aroused in his parents, was of lesser interest to Harry. It "simply did not stack up, in excitement, beside the wild immoralities of Greek mythology or, in adventure, with the *Anabasis* of Xenophon."[60] His parents' library, besides its large collection of Chinese books, contained many volumes on religion and philosophy, and much Greek mythology. Virgil instilled a love of Greek writers in both his sons. It is rather easy to imagine Harry as a young boy eavesdropping on Paul—who was ten years older—reading, picking up on the enthusiasm and excitement of his father and older brother, before he was able to read them for himself.

Partch acknowledged that the basis of his absorption in Greek mythology was that it "ignored nothing that was basic to the human psyche."[61] It can scarcely be coincidental that both the Oedipus drama and the Bacchae, the two myths that most obsessed him over many years and both of which became the subjects of major theater works, treat with the dark side of the mother-son relationship: his fascination with them had without doubt an element of personal catharsis. Significantly, though, in his setting of W. B. Yeats's translation of *King Oedipus* the emphasis is less on the fact of incest than on the gradual revealing of the true network of relationships through which Oedipus is destroyed. In *Revelation in the Courthouse Park* it is again the sons who are destroyed—"actually, in the ancient Greek myth, but psychologically, in the American scene"—by their inability to face the schizoid incompatibility of stifling family relationships with their ambivalent fascination with, and rejection of, their mothers' abandonment to orgiastic hedonism.[62]

Some of the material Partch uses in Chorus Four of *Revelation,* the fragmented, dreamlike passages sung by Mom witnessing an attack on her son, turns out to have a complex personal symbolism. His Depression-era journal *Bitter Music* contains this beautiful passage, bringing to life memories of the Arizona landscape of his boyhood:

> Down in the country where I was reared, cottonwood trees line the dry stream beds, the rivers and canals. For several weeks each spring they snow their tiny bolls of cotton down on the desert fields.
>
> My friends and loved ones burst upon my consciousness like the cottonwoods' whitenesses. The gentlest breeze loosens them from their pods. A few of them brush against my cheeks, and fewer still touch my lips, ever so softly, as they fall. They hardly stop at all, and in the briefest moment they are away.[63]

This image had a mesmeric hold on the composer. Twenty-five years later, and a decade after destroying the journal, fragments of this passage and the music he sketched for it in 1935 came to him in composing Chorus Four of *Revelation,* where, in a moment of transference, he puts these last words into the mouth of the sleepwalking Mom. Partch, wistfully acknowledging the fragility of his own personal relationships, gives these same words to a mother who in some respects resembles his own, reflecting on the drifting away of her children, and her loss of control over them.

During his teenage years a further, crucial aspect of Partch's mature identity began to emerge: his homosexuality. Throughout his life Partch was reticent about making his sexual orientation a matter of public knowledge. He left virtually no written material that discusses explicitly his sexual awakening nor his early experiences, although he would talk about these matters to close friends. The only creative work in which his homosexuality features prominently is *Bitter Music;* in it he recounts two stories of his schooldays that seem to be connected, in his own mind, with his emerging sexuality and the anxieties associated with it. The first is of his early schooldays in Benson.

> One time when I was six and in the first grade I sat at my desk drawing a stallion on my tablet. I took great pains with it, and drew his symbol of fertility as I had often seen it, long and portentous.
>
> It didn't occur to me to be ashamed of it. I didn't reason, of course, but it meant something elementally right.
>
> I then showed the drawing to the little girl sitting in the double desk beside me. She banged me on the head, cried "Shame!" and with her eraser vigorously rubbed the sex out of my horse.
>
> "This is the way to do it," she said, redrawing a simple belly line, and leaving my once virile stallion presumably female or ambiguous.
>
> I took my humiliation quietly. But my inward ferocity burned for days—in fact, never stopped.
>
> Thus in early years did this Christian abstract female age cow me.
>
> Wherever you are, young woman, long-deferred nuts to you![64]

The story illustrates what Partch called the "conspiracy of false modesty" about sexual matters that surrounded him as a young man. The display of male virility is seen as shameful, and the small boy is humiliated and made to feel anguish for his violation of a taboo. In this little parable, the values of "this Christian abstract female age"—three adjectives that, in Partch's lexicon, have almost wholly pejorative associations—threaten not simply virility or masculinity, but the whole sense of the body: what many years later he was calling the *corporeal.*

In 1972, in the pages of a notebook in which he was sketching ideas for the film *The Dreamer That Remains,* Partch retold the same story in note form, this time giving it quite a different significance.

> We had a black stallion named Prince in Benson. One had only to observe him when he loitered to know that he was a stallion.
>   I was six
>   She cried, "Shame! Shame!"
>   If I had fucked her right then and there my life might have been somewhat different.
>   That little girl destroyed a potential in me—lost—lost[65]

In this later retelling the emphasis has changed from the humiliation suffered by the six-year-old to the bitterness and frustration of the old man, who sees his "potential" for sexual fulfillment as having been "destroyed." At the end of his life he is still able to relive his outrage at the girl's attempts to shame him, and decries a lost opportunity.

In a later passage in *Bitter Music* he describes being taunted by a group of drunken hobos. They shout insults at him as he walks past with a hobo pal, calling Partch a "Fruit." He laughs it off and walks away; unlike his pal, who wants to start a fight, he feels no compulsion to take issue with the men, acknowledging: "I am a coward because theirs are physical standards." The episode reminds him of being bullied by school friends for being a sissy: "Time flashes back twenty years or more. I am standing grimly with my back against a wall—unmoving from terror—while a group of my schoolmates—always groups—pummels me and taunts me with 'Sister!' "[66] His response—both as a terrified schoolboy and as a mature adult—is not to strike out in self-defense, but rather to cultivate "an insistent attitude that denies the right of others to disrespect" and "an intense fervour in the justness of my life." This fervor would always remain for Partch more a matter of inner conviction than of outward behavior. To the end of his life he would retain a decorum in sexual matters, which was as much the result of his natural reticence as it was a sign of the times. Yet he never lost the ability to shock polite society or uncomprehending friends with an occasional pointed remark or reference to the subject.

"Harry's homosexuality was, I think, perfectly natural," his friend Lou Harrison has remarked;[67] nonetheless, his emerging sexual identity seems to have cast a shadow over Partch's adolescence, contributing to what he described in later years as an unhappy time. It was part of an ongoing search for self-identity, in which several other factors—including his troubled relationship with his parents and his growing commitment to creative work in music—also played a part. It would be many years before that identity could manifest itself with any confidence.

After a hiatus from which no correspondence survives, we encounter Partch's mother and father again in their letters within a few weeks of each other in the summer of 1918. The only surviving letter from Jennie Partch to her youngest son was mailed on June 27, 1918, from Kansas City, Missouri. At least Jennie and Irene, and perhaps Virgil too, were with their relatives in Kansas City in the early part of that summer, while Harry stayed at home in Albuquerque. The letter bears out our image of Jennie as a smothering parent; yet there is no mistaking the genuine affection that comes across as well. It reads, in part:

> Dearest Harold;
>
> How I would love to see you. It will soon be two months, the longest time I have ever been away from you. I hope you are not feeling so blue as your last letter seemed to indicate. Don't worry about not finding work. I am sure you will have some very soon and we may all get to go to the [mountains] later. While you didn't have work it would have been well for you to have been in the hills but of course you have hoped all the time to find something.
>
> I will be so glad when I can get home. It truly is hot here night and day. We hope to have breakfast with you 3 weeks from this Thursday morning. Hurrah and suppose Paul and Anna come then too Whoop la.
>
> We sent the money for you to do just as you pleased with.
>
> I hope the Bible suited you in size. It was the best I could do to get a real good one with a clear type. That will last you many years with care and the button keeps it from getting hurt in pocket. I got the things downtown and had them done up in the store and forgot to put my name inside. I was so tired and hot and afraid you would not get them in time for your birthday. The money was to get what you needed for your birthday too. A cake etc or not as you liked.
>
> Love, Mother

His mother's buying him a Bible for his seventeenth birthday is revealing: it implies that Jennie was concerned to give him a Christian education, which Virgil was not, and is another biographical component in the negative equation of "female" and "Christian."

On August 22, 1918, Virgil wrote to the Commissioner-General of Immigration in Washington, D.C., applying for "any pending or future vacancy" in the post of vice-consul in China. "When I first learned of the appointment of inspectors for service in Chinese ports," he writes, "I was naturally interested, but felt my duty to my family was paramount at the time; three children were to be educated and the United States was the best place for the purpose. Now, however, that education is so near complete, that the presence is not necessary." Returning to China in his late fifties—he cannot have known at this time that he had only eight months to live—would possibly have meant saying goodbye to his children for the last time. We may wonder if Harry knew of his father's plan; or, indeed, if Jennie was prepared to return to China with her husband.

Harry's extracurricular activities seem to have had only good effects on his last two years of high school. In his third year at Albuquerque High he took English III and IV (grade—excellent), algebra II and solid geometry (good), and economics (commendable); and in his final year journalism and public speaking, civics, and U.S. history (all excellent) and physics (good). He was a member of the chorus for three of his four years, but otherwise distinguished himself in theater more than in music. In his final year he took the part of André, Count DeGrival, in Arthur W. Pinero's *The Amazons;* the 1919 school yearbook *La Reata* notes that "Harold Partch as the passionate Frenchman was a scream throughout the play." He also took part in a comedy called *The Man Who Married a Dumb Wife,* presented by the journalism and public speaking class, about which the yearbook noted that "Harold Partch as the judge played his part enthusiastically to say the least," adding that one of the other characters in the play "was very dignified in comparison." His senior year credits included the school oratorical contest. His interest in oratory is reflected in the Senior Quotations section of the 1919 school yearbook, where he states: "A good orator must be Cicero and Roscius in one man."

The school had an orchestra, in which his sister Irene played violin and which she seems to have led at one time. The yearbooks, however, record no involvement by Harry in any musical activities at the school; these took place elsewhere. The Albuquerque city directory for 1919 lists one "Harold W. Partch" whose occupation is given as "pianist, Pastime Theatre." As the directory would probably have been compiled late in 1918, it seems clear that Harry was holding down this job while still at school. The Pastime Theatre, on West Central Avenue, was Albuquerque's main movie house. Harry's silent movie repertoire included "Hearts and Flowers" and other familiar tunes—"one did not have to be very good in the small town that Albuquerque then was."[68] He experimented with playing comic music for tragic scenes and vice versa. "I can't remember the story, but I remember getting pretty annoyed with something

Graduation photograph, Albuquerque High School, 1919.
Photograph reproduced courtesy of Albuquerque High School.

that was obviously crap, and when somebody got shot and was being buried I put in some very happy bird calls. Nobody noticed it."[69] His job had some unexpected benefits. One was that the gangs of Mexican boys who hung out in Albuquerque at night and beat up passing Anglo boys left Harry alone when they saw him, knowing that if they hurt his hands they would have no music at the movie theater the following day.[70]

Virgil was ill in the early part of 1919. By March his condition had become critical and he was obliged to stop work. Once he took to his bed he declined rapidly and died on March 21. Two days later the *Albuquerque Morning Journal* announced that his funeral service "will be private and the body will be taken to San Francisco by his son, Paul, for cremation in accordance with a request made by him." Three months later, on June 20, Harry Partch graduated from Albuquerque High School. From this point, the trajectory of his life was firmly in his own hands.

Los Angeles and San Francisco

Partch's mature creative work springs from the clash between
his view of an implanted culture for which he had little use—
the concert tradition of eighteenth- and nineteenth-century
European music—and what he liked to call ancient values, a
"deep and abiding tie with peoples and animals and things
removed in time and space."[1] From this tension much in his
artistic personality took root. His move to Los Angeles at the
age of eighteen provided his first encounter in full force with
the American concert world of the time, and any discussion
of this period of his life is drawn inevitably into anticipating
the future. From the tension between his urge for approval by
that institutional world and his caustic rejection of many of
its pretensions his own musical character began uneasily to
develop.

Partch often speaks of beginnings in terms of such dualisms. In the program notes for *The Bewitched* he describes
the beginning of time as "that ancient time when the first
single cell moved itself in such autoerotic agitation that it

chapter

2

split in two": in the notes for *Even Wild Horses* he speaks of human life emerging "through the double heartbeat of mother and enwombed child." And in the summer of 1957, preparing a small booklet with photographs and descriptions of his instruments, he states, most pointedly: "Affirmation of parentage provides the primary substance of rebellion." Throughout the 1920s what he was rebelling against, and thus affirming as his cultural parentage, were the attributes and the essence of eighteenth- and nineteenth-century European music, its intonational system and its concert forms. The rebellious art that was slowly taking shape in his mind was little concerned with effecting a reconciliation with that parentage. Rather, such was the force of his convictions in this decade that the two would be maintained in sharp opposition all his life.

The summer of 1919 marks a watershed in Partch's life. Following his father's death, and his own and his sister's graduation from Albuquerque High, the family home broke up, even though "it had broken up before that, because I 43wasn't getting along with my father. . . . I had left home several times and made my way."[2] Yet for our purposes, his way leads not into the light but even deeper and apparently more irretrievably into the shadows. The dearth of documents of his life throughout this crucial decade—his twenties—is in large part responsible for, and indeed justifies, his reputation as a mythical, unknowable figure. For large stretches of the 1920s all we have are fragments of information. What we are able to trace is not his journey from the end of adolescence to artistic maturity, a passage of spirit that lasted over ten years, but the emergence of a cultural critique: a system of values, aesthetic and musical.

Partch's arrival in southern California is marked by three photographs of him with friends, in the Flintridge Hills and elsewhere in the Los Angeles area, inscribed "fall 1919." The photographs are copies, not originals, and were made for him in 1969 by a friend known only as Gertrude, who appears in the photographs as a young woman. These faded images offer a poignant glimpse of the young Partch: even in the midst of friends he seems apart, as though torn away from the prevailing air of relaxed camaraderie by a quiet sadness. In one photograph, his left hand holds gently onto a branch of an overhanging tree, as though for support; in another, perched on a rock, he alone among the six friends looks away from the camera into the distance.

To judge from the fragmentary evidence available, he seems to have gone to California initially on his own. His sister, Irene, drops out of the picture at this point until her marriage the following year: we encounter her again a few years later living in Hawaii. Partch's mother had certainly joined him in Los Angeles

Partch with friends in California, 1919. The caption, in Partch's hand, was written fifty years later. "Top: H. Partch, Gene Oakley (and this silly fool is putting his hat over your face). Carrick Oldham is looking under the sign—Half-Way Bridge. Carl Busch is to the right of the sign. On ground—Gertrude and Helen Oakley (whoever the hell she is). Fall 1919." Unsigned photograph, Harry Partch Estate Archive.

by January 1920. With her husband dead, her elder son, Paul, with a family of his own, and Irene about to be married, Jennie was probably determined to keep a close watch on her younger son's development.

Los Angeles in 1919 was just entering a boom period. California was witnessing a large-scale shift of population and economic initiative from north to south, and in Partch's first years there some 100,000 people poured into the city each year. In the early 1920s Los Angeles

> was still relatively provincial. It acknowledged, perhaps mistakenly, the cultural hegemony of longer-established San Francisco. . . . The various cities of the basin, such as Glendale, Hollywood, and Pasadena, were still separated from one another by orange groves and connected by a system of electrified interurban rail lines. Souvenir photos from the period tend to show modest frame farmhouses set amid groves of orange trees that extend for miles to snowcapped mountains in the background, a reminder of the great physical beauty as well as the semirural quality of the Los Angeles basin.[3]

The city felt more like a network of small communities, and not yet the cosmopolitan cultural center it soon became. Musically, however, it was anything but a desert, providing an environment that was much more active and diverse than that of Partch's boyhood and adolescence in the Southwest. Soon after his arrival he began to attend concerts in the first season of the Los Angeles Philharmonic Orchestra, then a new organization with an English-born principal conductor, Walter Henry Rothwell. Partch also took such opportunities as arose to see other events. "Both in San Francisco and Los Angeles in the twenties there were travelling opera companies. There's no such thing anymore. They were small companies: you got to know the music very well that way . . . it was all Italian and some French."[4]

He eagerly embraced these opportunities, steeping himself—at first—in concert life. He later remarked to an interviewer, somewhat tongue-in-cheek, that in this period "I went [to concerts] so much that I never wanted to go again."[5] The Los Angeles Philharmonic provided Partch with his real introduction to the symphonic repertoire. The orchestra's programs emphasized music of the nineteenth century. There was little of what was then called the "ultra-modern" music of Stravinsky or Schoenberg: Rothwell's conservative tastes precluded much adventurous programming. When in 1922 the young composer Dane Rudhyar's *Soul of Fire* won a competition sponsored by the orchestra for a new symphonic work, a small scandal was created by Rothwell's refusal to play the piece on the grounds that it was too modern.[6] Yet there is some irony in the fact that the Los Angeles Philharmonic's repertory at that time was, broadly speaking, the period of Western music for which Partch had a certain fondness, though a fondness that never went publicly unqualified. He could be sympathetic to the color and drama of the musical language of the Romantics and he responded to the compelling emotional content of Beethoven's music, although he remained unmoved by Mozart and Haydn.

While this type of cultural environment was precisely what the young Partch doubtless thought he was looking for, his contact with it gave rise to a host of ambivalent and contradictory impressions. He seems to have found, almost immediately, much that repelled him as well as much to which, insecurely, he wished to aspire. His later inveighing against the Los Angeles concert world of the early twenties had little to do with the cautiousness of repertory—indeed, little to do with the actual music at all—and was directed instead against the pretentiousness of concert personalities, the self-importance of the audiences who applauded them, and the prevailing aura of "pure black-and-white tails, pure orchids on a pure bosom," the "inhibitory incubus" of formal concert garb.[7] His most lasting impression of the Los Angeles Philharmonic concerts, in that very first season, was the "sea of blue-haired ladies" that he observed flooding the audience.[8] These "blue-haired ladies" became for him a symbol of the identification of a particular social class—wealthy, generally aged, and often not particularly musical—with the symphonic repertoire, and it planted the seed of his distaste for the pernicious social snobbery that could flourish at concerts of this type. In 1967, lamenting to students how little that concert world had changed in fifty years, he remarked: "Any backward community, culturally or musically, makes up for its backwardness by indulging in symphony concert chit-chat, concert personality gossip, the latest interpretations of Rodzinsky—back in the twenties." This concert chit-chat, he added sardonically, is "the last refuge of sterility."[9]

The young Partch determined to maintain a distance from the economics and social behavior of that world. He took some delight in telling an interviewer that at these concerts "generally I ushered. I never paid my way, never."[10] Ben Johnston comments that, to a boy from the desert towns of the Southwest, "the urban culture of America was as exotic . . . as a foreign country. When he encountered it he did not identify with it, but rejected it passionately, stubbornly maintaining against it an art and a life-style drawn directly from his early influences . . . he continued to draw almost all his artistic and cultural sustenance from non-European sources rich in the California environment."[11]

While this is true in the broadest sense, it overstates the immediacy of this rejection. In affirming this music as his cultural parentage, his relationship with it became as fraught with feelings of guilt and confusion as any intense parent-child relationship. Grafted onto the encounter was an uncomfortable measure of personal identification. Partch's mother was hell-bent on seeing him succeed in that world, and so, uneasily, she and he came to assume rather clearly defined symbolic roles: Jennie, the essentially uninvolved proponent of the values of high culture and its milieu, and of what could be reaped from it in terms of social status and economic stability; Harry, his head already filled with "doubts and ideas," engaging in a quiet struggle with the first small shoots of rebellion against the cultural environment into which he had just arrived. This role-playing can only have brought the clash of cultural worlds closer to home.

Whether formal music study was the immediate purpose of his move to Los Angeles we do not know, although it seems likely. Before those studies were properly under way, however, a tragedy befell him, the importance of which to his development can scarcely be exaggerated. On November 28, 1920, "I had a date to meet my mother at a certain street intersection in Los Angeles. She did not appear, and when I phoned the school where she was teaching I was informed that she was dead."[12] Jennie died of a skull fracture after being hit by a streetcar on her way to meet her son. The *Los Angeles Evening Herald* the following day reported six persons killed in traffic accidents that weekend, among them "Mrs. Jennie Partsch [*sic*], instructor at Westlake Military School," and described her death in what must have been, for her son, unbearably graphic detail: "Mrs. Partsch was caught by the fender of a Los Angeles railway car and met death beneath the wheels when she attempted to pass in front of the car after alighting from another car at Avenue Forty-three and Marmion way." Partch was obliged to see to her funeral arrangements himself. Jennie's death certificate was filed on December 1: it records that she had been resident in California for only ten months.

Jennie's body was cremated, as Virgil's had been the previous year. Partch kept her ashes for some time on his mantelpiece, unable to bear parting with them. Stephen Pouliot recounts the story of her son's final resolve to scatter the ashes: "It was illegal to empty ashes, so he got a little hootched up one night and . . . went down to the Santa Monica pier. It was about three o'clock in the morning. I guess he had his own little ritual."[13] This story was related by Partch to various of his friends, some of whom seem to have seen it as rather morbid—a clinging to his mother even in death, an apt symbol of his stifling attachment to her. But the mixed emotions caused by the presence of his mother's ashes are hardly unusual: similar reactions are experienced by the bereaved partner of even the happiest of relationships, and the decision to release the last physical traces is not usually an easy one. Even if he needed the emboldening power of alcohol to help him pluck up courage to scatter the ashes, the act of release seems more a sign of psychic health—an acceptance of death and a perfectly normal act of bidding farewell. He loved his mother and admired her strength and independence of spirit, for all the pain it inflicted on the obliquities of their life together, but without her he was free of her high hopes for him. Recalling this decade at the end of his life, he told an interviewer: "If I had had a mother who was demanding that I get someplace, which she would have been if she had been alive, because that was her purpose in life, that I had to amount to something. . . ."[14] And his voice trails off.

The details of Partch's clash with formal music education must be pieced together, although the overall image seems clear enough. There is, first, his repeated insistence that after leaving high school he began searching the music shelves of the Los Angeles Public Library and other places for books on music theory, "pursuing ideas to their sources." Set against this, however, are several periods of formal study. The extent to which he continued with conventional musical studies at this time and even as late as 1922, however unsuccessfully, is surprising in view of the determined search he was starting to make on his own.

In an autobiographical sketch written in 1945 he noted: "I had run the usual gauntlet of music subjects and teachers in my education. Work in composition for piano through my adolescent years led me, at eighteen, to begin an independent search for satisfactory explanations of musical phenomena I knew as facts of experience, but which both the teachers and the books I had encountered either ignored or left to a dark world of groping."[15] Years later he elaborated: "In 1919, as I recall, I had virtually given up on both music schools and private teachers, and had begun to ransack public libraries, doing suggested exercises and writing music free from the infantilisms and inanities of professors as I had experienced them."[16] This date—1919—may seem somewhat exaggerated in the light of what we know about Partch's studies in Los Angeles in the years up to 1922, and is probably expressive of his disillusionment at the end of his schooldays. He goes on: "Before I was twenty, I had tentatively rejected both the intonational system of modern Europe and its concert system, although I did not realize either the ultimate scope or the consequences of that rejection."

In a grant application submitted in October 1932, the earliest of his surviving accounts of these years, he continues the story.

> My academic education was carried through high school. Until 1921, when 20 years of age, I studied piano and harmony with private teachers in various parts of the southwest, including Los Angeles and Kansas City. Two of these years were spent in piano work with Olga Steeb in Los Angeles. In 1920 I entered the College of Music at the University of Southern California but after a few months I left. Since that year, when I began as copyholder in the proofroom of the Los Angeles Times, I have made my living in newspaper offices. In 1921, entirely alone, I completed the acquirement of the academic musical knowledge.[17]

Of his studies at the Kansas City Conservatory we know nothing, other than that they seem linked to the presence of relatives in the city.[18] His studies in Los Angeles, about which we know only a little, were almost certainly a highly formative experience.[19] By 1920 the University of Southern California had a large and flourishing music school. It was the obvious place in the city for Partch to enroll; UCLA was only becoming established and was not yet empowered to grant degrees.

The question of when precisely Partch enrolled at USC is significant in that it sheds some light on the effect on his studies of his mother's death. By his own account, he enrolled first in the autumn of 1920, when his mother was still alive; if so, his dropping out "after a few months" may conceivably have had as much or more to do with his distress at her death at the end of November than with any dissatisfaction with his studies. Partch's name is indeed inscribed in the USC School of Music ledgers for the academic years 1920–21 and 1921–22. In these documents, however, the first record of him is not until February 15, 1921, when he is listed as having matriculated for the second semester of that year, with a major in piano. The next mention of him is not for some time, but we find his name twice in the following academic year: he enrolled on June 5, 1922, near the end of the second semester (which seems odd); and again on June 22, for the summer session. Whether or not he actually did begin his studies during his mother's lifetime, Partch's enrollment—or reenrollment—in February 1921, some three months after her death, is a strong testament to his willingness to live up to her expectations in a way she would doubtless have approved. Whether this was the principal motivation for his enrollment, in the face of his ambivalence about pursuing formal study, must remain speculation. In any case, the testament did not stand for long.

Partch states that he studied "piano and harmony" in these earliest years in southern California. In his later writings he offers a vigorous polemic against the shortcomings of these two fields of musical study in particular: numerous satirical pieces that mock the exhausted rituals and the corrupt values of the concert world, and theoretical writings that offer a precise analysis of the malpractice in Western music—the adoption of equal temperament—that, in his view, had undermined the relationship of harmony with its basis in acoustics. Yet nowhere in these writings does he offer any details of his own studies. This perhaps signifies an intentional avoidance of the autobiographical voice, lest the recourse to personal psychology color his argument unnecessarily; but there is a sense, too, of Partch rewriting his own history, of his casting a shadow over figures who had played a part in his development so that he might seem all the more self-made. It is worth itemizing whatever small details we can in exploring the autobiographical aspects of his dissatisfaction.

His piano teacher, Olga Steeb, was then the newly appointed head of the department of piano at USC. She charged the highest fees of the instrumental teachers at the school—five dollars for a thirty-minute lesson. Born in Los Angeles in 1892 of German parents, Steeb was at that time one of the most brilliant young pianists in southern California. While still in her teens she had performed in Berlin, to great adulation in the German press; and she was known from her recital and concerto performances in Los Angeles as a pianist of extraordinary memory, technical command, and a broad, eclectic repertory, which encompassed even the "ultra-moderns" of the time.[20]

The myth of Partch as an uneducated primitive, a cultural desert plant, receives a fatal blow by the fact of his being accepted into Olga Steeb's piano class. To the contrary, he must have been a gifted performer. It seems he even entertained the idea of training to be a concert pianist, though whether this idea was implanted by his teacher or by his mother, or arose from ambitions of his own we cannot say. A tape recording survives from 1966 in which Partch, in the course of a drunken conversation with Danlee and Georgie Mitchell, sits down at the piano and plays fragments from a Brahms intermezzo, the Chopin B minor Sonata and the F minor Concerto, all of which were presumably in his repertory as a young man. In the same conversation he displays a familiarity with the nocturnes of John Field, and his remark that "the John Field Concerto for piano is the best Concerto for piano that has *ever* been written" leaves us in no doubt about the high regard in which he held the Irish composer-pianist.[21] The composer Henry Brant, who knew Partch in New York in 1944, recalls: "He said that he had studied piano and that he had certain ideas from his teacher. For instance, how Chopin should be played. He demonstrated a Chopin nocturne and displayed a considerable familiarity with keyboard styles."[22]

Regrettably, we have no knowledge of how the nineteen-year-old Partch responded to Olga Steeb's teaching. On the basis of his later writings one would be inclined to believe that this whole period of serious piano study was anathema to him, and that he felt his creative spirit being submerged under the discipline of regular practice. Passages like the following certainly have auto-biographical resonances: "The current musical values, symbolized by the average good music student's prayer to be able to play or sing a scale more skillfully, smoother, and faster than anybody else, are exactly as ennobling as a competitive armaments race."[23] Or, speaking of his dissatisfaction in his twenties with "the body of knowledge and usages as ordinarily imparted in the teaching of music," Partch recalls his annoyance with "the widespread emphasis on skills at an instrument, emphasis on the 'technique' of playing and composing music, both by authors of books and by teachers. All too rarely did I find consideration of intrinsic content by either author or teacher. Various degrees of intrinsic content were simply accepted, having long ago been determined for us."[24]

Partch's objections to the emphasis placed on technique are easy enough to dismiss. Indeed, the distinction he draws between "technique" and "intrinsic content" seems a slightly empty one, overlooking as it does the subtle interaction between the two. Yet to carp at these arguments is surely to miss the central tactic of these and the majority of his writings about music: that of rendering the possibility of growth by evoking—in however overstated, black-and-white terms—the context of decay. His words are perhaps better taken as part of the struggle to give vent to his inchoate critique of the musical values of the time than as part of the substance of the critique itself.

In fact, Partch may well have been an earnest and diligent pianist—he later claimed to have damaged his health by long hours of piano practice—and, in that sense, a good student. Signs of his later rebellion against the instrument and the musical values it symbolized may not yet have been in evidence. His studies of harmony, on the other hand, seem to have fueled his latent dissatisfaction with the formal study of music. He told a newspaper reviewer on one occasion that after spending "three long months on the resolutions of the dominant seventh chord" he could see no reason to continue his studies.[25] Years later he told another interviewer:

> I certainly don't care whether I'm writing perfect counterpoint, or whether voices are moving in the way that I was taught to move them. . . . I spent I think about three months on the dominant seventh chord, and I thought: Well, this is the end, I'll never touch this sort of nonsense again. . . . I decided one time to observe every damned rule, every one, and write something totally outrageous, which I did; and it was put up on the blackboard and ridiculed, because it wasn't musical. . . . Of course, I knew it wasn't! Oh, it was an absurd experience. I didn't want to learn; I think I knew more about the resolutions of the dominant seventh chords than he [the teacher] did.[26]

Partch's jeremiads about the inadequacies of his formal music studies scarcely mark him as unique. Few young creative spirits show much patience with such exercises in pedantry. Yet what is curious about Partch's complaints is that there is not the slightest grudging admission that such studies inculcate anything finally worthwhile, almost as though such an admission would amount to cutting his own throat. His attacks on the blinkered, reactionary ethos of twenties pedagogy, while having a ring of truth, seem willfully one-sided and hence damagingly superficial. We can perhaps begin to understand why— however passionate his convictions and however exciting the rebelliousness to which they attest—his objections and arguments impressed few people at the time, and why their sheer lack of reasonableness turned away several otherwise sympathetic ears in the decades ahead. The point seems to lie more in the *vehemence* of his rejection of official education, as though nothing less extreme could unleash the explosive energy needed to propel him toward the new worlds of his creative imagination.

His refuge lay in moving "from the classroom where I had to *listen* to teachers who were telling me nothing, to the public library where I could *discard* a book that was telling me nothing. I was less than twenty when I separated myself in mid-semester from the USC Music School, in the unshakeable conclusion that my teachers were not older and wiser. They were just older. . . . On the day that I left that school, if I could have taken my disgust into the public library and assuaged it in a book like *Genesis of a Music,* I would have felt that the future was not all black, after all. The person I was at twenty is the person I really wrote my book for."[27]

In one of his favorite metaphors, Partch views the potentates of music education as members of a secular priesthood: "Ritual of classroom double-talk and creed of safety-deposit-box dogma have vested the high priests of the musical academy with a calcification the envy of every other bone of human endeavour."[28]

Even though we have no record of him studying composition formally at this time in Los Angeles—nor indeed at any other time—his creative work underwent at least a temporary transformation during the early 1920s. "When I had formal music classes and formal teachers I did rebel, because my philosophy was already established, though it was certainly not articulated. I actually became somewhat ashamed of my first creative efforts" (the "whimsical, melancholy stories" with piano accompaniment that he had written in his teens in Albuquerque).[29] "I got to feeling that this wasn't the highest expression in music, and that I must be abstract; so then I began to write pieces for the piano. Finally I did a piano concerto which I still think [1974] was pretty damn good, except that I never finished it. I did the first two movements."[30] This period was the only one in which "I visualised any presentation of my music on the concert stage. I thought of the music that I wrote both immediately before and immediately after this period as intimate."[31] He contended that throughout these early years "I didn't change my basic feeling that I had a direction of my own, which was toward dramatic ideas . . . coincidentally with this, however, was a desire to understand the mechanics or the intricacies of concert music, so called, of absolute music; and that was when I began to train myself in the disciplines of concert music."[32]

Of his becoming "somewhat ashamed" of his earliest music and pursuing instead the "disciplines of concert music," Partch commented that it wasn't until a few years later "that I began to realize my mistake. . . . The reason is very simple. This was the artificial (to me) world of reality. I finally knew that I could not reconcile it with my real child-world. And I had to find my real child world again."[33] This reconciliation process involved an acceptance of his own essentially childlike perception of the interconnectedness of music and other art forms and, more profoundly, of the fusion of art-making activity with everyday life. What was "artificial" about music education, he contended, was its insistence on the need to unlearn this perception and to undergo a training in which extramusical impurities must be extracted, one by one, leaving only a central body of abstract musical relationships.

The stimulus provided by the urban culture of Los Angeles in the twenties did not consist exclusively of concert music. A great deal of music-making, and hence employment, existed in the vaudeville theaters or on the movie lots in Hollywood, where live mood music was played as the silent films were being shot. Yet despite his involvement with movie houses in Albuquerque, we have no record of Partch doing the same in Los Angeles. Nor was he drawn to the musical activities, many of them public, of the Theosophists and the other pseudo-religious orders that flourished in the city; his later devotion to W. B. Yeats, who for a time was deeply immersed in Theosophy, did not extend to the poet's fascination with esoteric doctrine. Los Angeles became a blatant symbol of the pressures and demands of the moneyed minority who supported high culture, and of the hollow values of the symphonic world.

Partch's dissatisfaction with his studies and his "dismissal" of his teachers caused him considerable anguish. In an article written a quarter-century later on the values of the American concert world as he experienced it, he expresses the matter thus: "Perhaps no element of modern life is so stifling—so destroys a human being—as this idol of digital and laryngeal proficiency. I know; I experienced it, and had to die and find still another womb to emerge from."[34] This metaphor of life and death reads at first as an instance of his typical overstatement, but his own period of intense piano practice had a critical effect on his health. In a letter of January 1932 he offers an alarming account in explanation of his withdrawal, for the first time, from USC: "At nineteen came the first of a succession of physical breakdowns—as the result of a heady ambition, overstudy, overpractice, and many long hours in a newspaper of-fice—that turned a love of the piano and tradition into a devastatingly intense aversion to the piano and to music as it now exists."[35]

This "succession of physical breakdowns," for which we have no surviving medical evidence, seems in keeping with the "devastatingly intense" nature of

Partch's impassioned convictions as an artist, convictions that, however untenable or idiosyncratic, never cooled off or abated throughout his life. But there were contributing factors. With both parents dead, and with no one to support him financially, he was probably working full-time at the *Los Angeles Times*.[36] In addition to this was the crushing ambivalence of his desire for approval by the concert music world, which involved a commitment to honoring his mother's wishes for him, and the intensity of his search for musical ideals true to his vision and his experience—yet with no certainty that the search would lead him anywhere. And this considerable strain was operating on a sensitive adolescent recently bereft of both his parents.

Danlee Mitchell has suggested that a romantic disappointment may have played a part in one of these breakdowns. Partch's circle of acquaintances included those he met through drama workshops, which he attended in hopes of learning "something about stage mechanics."[37] He befriended a struggling young actor, two years older, who like Partch himself occasionally worked as an usher at concerts of the Los Angeles Philharmonic: Ramon Novarro. Novarro became famous as a silent movie actor around 1921, by which time Partch and he had become close. Their relationship was dissolved by the demands of Novarro's sudden fame.[38] Although he was homosexual Novarro became known on screen as a ladies' man; having a young male friend in the wings would make for gossip that could damage his career. The breakup of the relationship and the subsequent feelings of rejection must have weighed heavily on Partch.

A period of recovery was made possible through the intervention of his sister. Partch spent the months January to April 1922 in Hawaii, visiting Irene and her husband, Leslie Dustin. "My beautiful sister . . . went to a School of Music, now part of the University [of Hawaii]. And she was then teaching school at Kaneohe, and we lived on Kaneohe Bay. I was a daredevil 20-year-old and I went swimming in that savage surf on the Windward side, all the way from Haleiva to Wananalo, walking mostly."[39]

His intention seems to have been not to abandon his musical studies altogether but to gain a clearer perspective on them, away from Los Angeles and the pressures it represented, to which the Hawaiian sun and surf must have seemed the perfect antidote. "Everyone told me: 'You won't do a thing in Hawaii.' Well, I never wrote so many fugues in my life."[40] In a lecture he gave in 1971 at the University of Hawaii he reminisced: "I wrote counterpoint, fugues, in between getting tossed about on the north shore waves, trying to body-surf in waves that I am sure a merciful god never intended bodies to be in." It was a very happy time. "I threw my gardenia lei into the harbor when I left, meaning that I *would* come back."[41]

In June, back in Los Angeles, he enrolled again at the USC School of Music, a decision that may have been encouraged by the more conventionally minded Irene, who still kept up her violin playing. After the exhilarating freedom of his sojourn in Hawaii, it is all too easy to imagine a combative Partch approaching the school with the attitude of giving it one last chance. Los Angeles that summer offered a new attraction in the form of open-air concerts at the Hollywood Bowl, an imposing amphitheatre that was to be the new summer home of the Los Angeles Philharmonic; a wide range of symphonic music was presented there in ten-week seasons of "Symphonies Under the Stars." Partch recalled nostalgically that in those days, "long before Hollywood Bowl became a cemented, be-shelled, be-uniform-ushered stadium, a few of us would take sandwiches and bottles of pop high up on the hillside there, and consume them quite without regard to whether we liked or did not like the music being played. That is a singular memory. Never since has the idea of the symphony orchestra seemed so painless in contemplation."[42]

The second chapter of his studies at USC proved to be the last in his formal musical education: again the studies led nowhere. As a result he essentially abandoned serious study of the piano, and renounced any lingering hope of a career on the concert platform. In a grant application he submitted to the Guggenheim Foundation in 1932 he declared, with a hint of defiance, "I am without institutional musical training." Although this was true more in spirit than in fact, it was to become a crucial part of his self-projection as a musician.

Partch's solution to the impasse and confinement of Los Angeles was physical escape, which remained necessary to his psychic health all his life. By April 1923, the twenty-one-year-old Partch was working as a proofreader for the California State Legislature in Sacramento, in northern California. That month he found in the Sacramento Public Library Hermann Helmholtz's *On the Sensations of Tone*, the classic exposition of the foundations of music theory in the scientific study of sound.[43] Helmholtz's book, in the 1885 translation and edition by Alexander J. Ellis, provided Partch with what was, at the time, the most cogent and persuasive answer available to the question that most obsessed him: "whether there was any logical reason for 12 tones in an octave. . . . I was always dissatisfied with the explanation of musical phenomena given in school and by music teachers."[44] Helmholtz was "the key for which I had been searching," the key that was to unlock the door to his creative future. That spring Partch's lifework began to take shape.

Although many experts in acoustics and music psychology today find fault with Helmholtz, those disciplines still remain in important ways under his long shadow. Musical revolutionaries in the twentieth century have often found the needed catalyst for their radical departures in disciplines other than music itself, and it is perhaps not surprising that some composers, including Varèse, should have turned to a scientist for inspiration. Helmholtz, with his exploration of the "natural affinities . . . of *physical and physiological acoustics . . .* and *musical science and esthetics,*" provided a solid foundation for radical musical ideas.[45] In exploring these "natural affinities" Helmholtz was effectively reestablishing a connection between music theory and the natural sciences, the roots of which stretch back to antiquity—in the Western world to Pythagoras, to whom is generally accredited an important discovery: that proportional lengths of a vibrating string, in small-number ratio relationships, produce basic musical intervals. "If, as is probable, [Pythagoras's] knowledge was partly derived from the Egyptian priests," Helmholtz wrote, "it is impossible to conjecture in what remote antiquity this law was first known."[46] This "law"—the relationship of musical intervals to the rational proportions of a vibrating string—is the starting point for all of Partch's innovations in music theory. Under the impetus of Helmholtz's work, "doubts and ideas achieved some small resolution, and I began to take wing."[47]

The conception of musical intervals as describable in mathematically precise terms marks the first revolutionary step, the real breakthrough in Partch's thinking. Although sanctioned in ancient Greek thought, the concept remains controversial. Music theory, in the 1920s as today, describes the pitch resources of Western music not in numerical terms but by an arbitrary but consistent system of letter names, from A to G. The fact that there are exactly seven such letters, on the other hand, is far from arbitrary: the seven letters have a structural correlate in the seven degrees of the diatonic scale. As the seven pitches are not equally spaced, a sub-system of sharps and flats are affixed to the letter names to indicate other pitches that fall in the gaps between those described by adjacent letters. Filling the gaps yields five new tones which, added to the original seven, combine to form twelve equally spaced pitches in the octave, an array that is duplicated in all other octaves throughout the audible spectrum.

This explanation of the "logical reason for 12 tones in an octave" is in fact a deeply unsatisfactory one, and it is precisely the evasions and question-begging of such explanations that must have vexed the young Partch. Helmholtz showed that the true nature of the diatonic scale was quite independent of the system of letter names, and its constituent intervals revealed themselves—as the ancient Greeks had known—as small-number vibrational relationships, analogic to the vibration patterns produced by a sounding body. In Part III of his book, Helmholtz explored ancient Greek modes and the divisions of the tetrachord found in ancient texts, as well as the scales, keys, and harmonic relations of Western tonal music, from the standpoint of ratio relationships. His description of musical intervals in ratio terms was consistent with his scientific objective of formulating quantitative rules according to which perceived pitches of sounds can be related to physically specifiable properties.

Far from proving the inevitability of the system of twelve-tone equal temperament, Helmholtz showed it as one of numerous solutions that had been proposed, historically, to the problem of how to tune instruments, principally keyboards, with a small number of fixed tones. In equal temperament all the degrees of the scale are falsified, or tempered: exact tuning is sacrificed in order to achieve a viable, practical system. Reading Helmholtz, Partch saw that the compromise of equal temperament could be abandoned, and a return made to *just intonation,* the tuning system of the later Greek modes, and the aesthetic ideal of the Renaissance theorists. This involved abandoning the conventional Western nomenclature for pitch, which would be replaced by "the language of ratios." In adopting ratio terminology in his own musical investigations, Partch was less concerned with its relevance to the formal and acoustical underpinnings of the existing system of equal temperament than he was with opening the door to a "new" tuning system—just intonation—for which ratios provided a language. Much of his early theoretical work derives its energy from the exciting sense of exploring a new system of thought incommensurate with that of conventional music-theoretic knowledge.

Although almost every music theorist of the time alluded to ratio terminology and to the phenomenon of overtones, Helmholtz presents the concept so precisely, and applies it at such length, that it became the most important of the lessons Partch learned from him.[48] The "language of ratios" is the language in which all of Partch's own theoretical concepts are described, and his introduction of this terminology into twentieth-century composition has been one of his most enduring legacies.

In describing Partch's early explorations in music theory it is tempting to draw parallels with his father's heterodoxy in matters of religious faith. Both father and son were caught up in a difficult and painful process of questioning widely accepted ideas, and of examining, from admittedly different standpoints, the foundations of culture and human experience. Just as Virgil's years of doubt eventually gave way to a firm commitment to atheism, so too his son's immersion in Helmholtz marks the point at which the free-thinking openness of his early musical investigations began to close. With the finding came an intolerance toward those who had not found, or who demurred in the face of his own discovery. And yet, part of the "fire of youth" that illuminated his search continued to smolder, even to the end of his life.

Partch's embracing of these new ideas happened gradually. *On the Sensations of Tone* "was still too feeble a ray to alter greatly fifteen years of musical thought habit. I had spent four years on a piano concerto, and now I devoted more years in studying orchestration, entirely alone, and in writing a symphonic poem and a string quartet."[49] The fact that it was five years from the initial encounter to the first of his achievements that the book helped to spawn suggests that the time was not the logical aftermath of a religious conversion but a period of slow assimilation and growth, in which his new ideas were caught up in a carousel of motives and possible directions, pulling and disorienting them.

His life during these years was likewise unsettled. The symphonic poem and string quartet mentioned above were preceded by a brief period in the winter of 1923–24 teaching piano privately in La Jolla, in southern California. This involvement with the piano—and he was to teach piano again, in Santa Rosa, at the end of the decade—shows that his "aversion" to the instrument was perhaps not quite as total as he sometimes implied. Although his motivation was doubtless primarily financial, his creative imagination was brought into play, and his somewhat lateral thinking on matters of piano technique suggested compositional applications: "I attempted to expound in composition a revolutionary manner of piano technique based upon a five-finger utilization of the hand . . . in passage work at all possible times."[50] In this brief description there is the faint suggestion of a demented ex-piano student exacting his revenge upon the digital proficiency and muscular co-ordination of the unsuspecting aspiring virtuoso. We have no knowledge of the practical results of Partch's new method of piano pedagogy. These experiments lay dormant for nearly a decade: in 1932 they influenced his design of the Ratio Keyboard.

Although he had moved away from Los Angeles "and all that it implied," Partch was obviously keeping at least one eye on the musical activities in the city. In 1924–25 he composed a symphonic poem and submitted it for a competition sponsored by the Los Angeles Philharmonic, "without result." We know nothing about this piece: the orchestra's archives contain no documentation on Partch's submission, nor on the competition itself. His study of orchestration was probably connected to its composition. Given his already highly selective attitude toward the orchestral repertory—Partch's taste in symphonic music seems not to have extended past Brahms and Mussorgsky—we may wonder about the musical language of this symphonic poem. In *Genesis of a Music* he casts a rueful eye over what he calls the "series of revolving Ixion-wheels, of major fashions in music" that were predominant in America during the first half of the twentieth century, all of them with roots in Europe: "the influence of Sibelius in my teens and twenties, of Paris-trained composers in my twenties and thirties, of the twelve-tone row in my thirties and forties." It seems unlikely that Partch's composition was as "modern" as the prize-winning work Dane Rudhyar had submitted to the orchestra a few years earlier.

Sometime in the mid-1920s Partch moved north to San Francisco, and from this point onward came to regard the Bay Area as his home. He continued to earn his living in newspaper proofrooms, as he had done in southern California. Musically, San Francisco proved to be a quite different environment. Like Los Angeles it had a flourishing symphony and opera world, but was no more attuned to contemporary music. The main difference was the greater access it provided to Oriental cultures, in particular to Chinese theater, which was then undergoing a renaissance in the city. San Francisco's Chinatown had been devastated in the earthquake of 1906 and, twenty years later, was once more a thriving, growing community. Partch regularly attended performances at the Mandarin Theater, an attractive new venue on Grant Avenue that opened its doors in June 1924. "And there was nothing strange about it."[51]

At the Mandarin Theater Partch was witnessing a new concept of Chinese drama. One critic wrote in 1925 that "the Chinese theater now uses scenery that is identical with that used in our own modern drama—drops and sets portraying interiors and landscapes. It is, however, combined with the imaginative scenery of the ancient Chinese drama."[52] The performances introduced Partch to a theater tradition unfamiliar in the West. They were based on traditional plots, melodies, and dance forms, and the lead performers combined the skills of actor, dancer, singer, mime, and acrobat.

Audience etiquette at these events, to his delight, proved to be a far cry from that at Los Angeles Philharmonic concerts. Performances began at 6:30 and continued until midnight, but the audience members could come and go as they pleased. The Chinese in the audience maintained, as one critic put it, "their undemonstrative mien and their habits of talking during performances, reading newspapers, and snacking on various edibles that were hawked by peddlers in the aisles."[53] Partch remarked of these events, in connection with what became one of the central concerns of his own work a few years later, that "present-day Cantonese music-theater . . . is certainly a far cry from the classic Chinese type, yet even here there is frequent and illuminating evidence that the audience understands the words, despite the percussion and the tiresome cracking of peanut shells."[54]

Immersion in Chinese culture, even to the limited extent possible for one not able to speak the language, was the needed corrective to the symphonic world of Los Angeles. Thanks to the legacy of his parents, Chinese culture was something for which Partch felt a ready affinity, and he felt free to respond to and absorb any aspects he pleased as a sympathetic outsider. Chinese instruments, with their nontempered intonation, had a lasting appeal; and he observed with great interest the conventions of Oriental dance.[55] This dynamic form of theater, with the greater interweaving of the constituent arts than is conventionally found in Western opera, was to have a clear impact on Partch's own dramatic works twenty-five years later.

Partch's fascination with Oriental culture did not supplant his study of acoustics. In San Francisco he "bought a violin and a viola (my previous practical experience had been with keyboard instruments only) and began experimenting with string proportions," putting into practice some of what he had read in Helmholtz.[56] His musical work entered a vital period of experimentation during which the largely negative ethos of the Los Angeles years turned, in a slow dissolve, into something positive. "The years from 1925 to 1928 were spent in experiment with systems of just intonation and notation, and in the composition of music to demonstrate them. In 1926, with the intention of experimenting with instruments of unfixed tones I began study of the violin and later of the viola, which instrument I played in the University of California Symphony Orchestra."[57]

In view of Partch's later assertions that the piano keyboard—"twelve black and white bars in front of musical freedom"[58]—hemmed in all attempts at the exploration of expanded pitch resources, his beginning the study of bowed strings was a decisive liberation. Partch remarked modestly that he played the violin only "a little bit: and later I played viola—better, but I really had to work hard at it, because I hadn't gained the expertise when I was very young."[59]

Stimulated by these experiments he composed a string quartet in just intonation, for violin, two violas, and cello, the first substantial compositional result of his new theoretical ideas. The work seems to have provided his first taste of some of the practical problems involved in music that moves beyond equal temperament and its associated complex of performance habits. Partch tells us that the quartet was "written in an experimental notation which because of its novelty made reading difficult."[60] If the piece used a microtonally extended just intonation, with fine divisions of intervals resulting in a large number of discrete tones in the octave, a new notation would clearly be necessary. Partch continued his experiments in notation, at times independently of his compositional activity or of new developments in his theoretical thinking, for a further decade before they achieved a relative stability. However, in 1933 he wrote that during the later 1920s "at different times I invented types of notation for twelve just tones to the 2/1 [octave], and wrote music for each to be played on unfretted string instruments."[61] The relation of this music to the string quartet is not clear, unless the quartet used a variety of notations within its span; and if the earliest notations were for scales of twelve just tones in the octave, the need for a new notation system is less obvious—it would be possible to retain the conventional notation system and simply redefine its symbols to correspond to the scale employed by the music.

The quartet posed a further problem: how the string players, trained to match their intonation to the equal temperament of the piano and the instruments of the orchestra, could learn the experimental tuning scheme Partch had devised for the work. To this he had an amusing solution: "paper coverings" for the fingerboards of the instruments, on which were computed and precisely marked the exact places where the string should be stopped to achieve the desired intonation. Quite what these paper coverings looked like, and how they were attached to the fingerboards, we shall probably never know. If they were designed to wrap around the fingerboard under the strings, they must have altered the tone quality of the instruments; if they attached somehow at the side of the fingerboard so as not to touch the strings, it is hard to imagine how they would not have interfered with the movements of the left hand, and indeed how the ratios indicated on these "paper coverings" could be read while the instruments were being played.

In all probability the quartet was never performed in public.[62] It was an important step from theoretical speculation to compositional application, but most of the solutions the work offered must have seemed less than compelling. Partch was clearly not content with the composition itself and destroyed it a few years later. Soon after completing the quartet he compiled a "set of just intonation resources."[63]

All of these experiments were carried out in isolation. "I had not tried to interest anyone in my unset ideas nor even spoken of them."[64] The loneliness of his endeavor was a fact that Partch stressed all his life. It is important to remember how atypical his development, during this formative decade, actually was.

Partch was of the same age as that generation of East Coast American composers who, after World War I, began to flock to Paris, where they found a mentor in Nadia Boulanger: chief among them were Aaron Copland, Virgil Thomson, Roy Harris, and Walter Piston. The mid-1920s, when the first wave of exiles began to return home and establish themselves, represents in many ways a flowering of American musical life. During their studies in Paris most of these young Americans had fallen unashamedly under the influence of Stravinsky, whose music they studied, besides much else, in Mlle. Boulanger's classes; and although their own compositions transcended mere pastiche, all the hallmarks of Stravinsky's musical language are to be found there. The music of Copland, Thomson, Harris, and Piston shares Stravinsky's firm commitment to tonality—a tonality given a Modernist, dissonant edge or subjected to Cubist-like distortion; and the rhythmic vitality of Copland's early scores owes much to the energy and, sometimes, the aggressiveness of Stravinsky's rhythmic language. This music was intimately bound up with the very concert tradition from which Partch was beginning to distance himself.

At the time, the emphasis of the critics who reviewed this music was less on the French influence on the new generation than on the fact that American composers were writing music of substance and originality. In 1926, for example, the critic Pitts Sanborn, writing for the newly founded quarterly review *Modern Music,* enthused about the new works that had impressed him that season: among them were Varèse's *Amériques,* Copland's *Music for the Theater,* and Carl Ruggles's *Portals.*[65] Thus, works by a European-born and European-trained composer working in America (Varèse), an American-born and European-trained composer (Copland), and an American-born and American-trained composer (Ruggles) could command equal respect.

Partch himself felt quite removed from what little he encountered of this Francophile American music in the 1920s. He felt no sympathy with the musical language nor with the aesthetic position of Copland and the others, and he reacted strongly against the snobbishness of those who felt that European training was essential for an American composer. We must remember, too, that the great majority of this activity was centered on the East Coast and, more specifically, in New York, where by the mid-1920s the International Composers' Guild and the League of Composers kept up a respectable profile for contemporary music. In California the situation was very different, and it took the entrepreneurial skills of one man, Henry Cowell, to effect a change.

It was thanks in large part to the ferment of activity generated by Cowell's efforts as composer, performer, concert promoter, publisher (of the quarterly *New Music,* beginning in 1927), teacher, and propagandist, that a vein of radical new music opened up in California. Gradually, San Francisco began to foster a viable alternative to the concentration of new music activity on the East Coast. In 1925, while not yet thirty, Cowell founded the New Music Society of California, which was based initially in Los Angeles and, from October 1927, in San Francisco.[66] A crucial aspect of Cowell's music, and as time went on an increasingly important part of the collective self-image projected by those composers most closely associated with him, was its experimental nature, its determination to strike a distance from the techniques and aesthetics of European music.

The fact that Partch was living in San Francisco at the time of Cowell's first New Music Society concerts there might suggest a degree of involvement in Cowell's circle that, upon closer examination, turns out not to be the case. We have no record of Partch's having attended any of the New Music Society concerts at this time—indeed, no certainty at all that he knew any of Cowell's work until he read Cowell's book *New Musical Resources* shortly after its publication in 1930.

It is perhaps surprising that the first composer we know Partch to have turned to for advice was the rather more conservative Howard Hanson, with whom he corresponded in the winter of 1927–28. Hanson was a year older than Cowell and five years older than Partch. A symphonist whose early output is audibly influenced by Sibelius, Hanson had, by the late twenties, established himself as one of the most promising young voices of his generation. He was already known as a champion of the work of younger composers. Partch sent him the score of his string quartet, and "a short theoretical exposition," which was probably the "set of just intonation resources" that he compiled soon after the composition of the quartet.[67] "He showed a great deal of interest," Partch recalled. "I even sent him the paper fingerboard coverings, but he never tried to get it played."[68] This professional contact was maintained over a period of two decades, although it never quite became a friendship.

Partch's personal life in these earliest years in San Francisco is a mystery. He evidently had few musical contacts: the little that can be established of his activities suggests a painfully solitary path. He was working full-time and pursuing his investigations by night, but such basic questions as the company he kept, what he was thinking, what he was reading, remain unanswered. On

April 2, 1927, he presented himself before a notary in San Francisco, to sign away his claim to his mother's land in Benson. On February 5, 1927, Paul and Irene had appeared before a notary in Los Angeles to initiate the sale. Paul had been released from active duty in the Fleet Naval Reserve some five months earlier, but the timing of the event suggests that the sale may have been some form of financial expedient for Irene, whose husband had died in January.[69]

Partch is listed in the San Francisco city directories for 1928 and 1929, where his occupation is given as proofreader: an article on him published in February 1931 records that he "was copyholder on the *San Francisco News* three years ago."[70] The balance of Partch's daytime occupation with his nocturnal forays as an artist seems to have been critically different than that struck by Charles Ives, who had two mutually supportive careers, or so he claimed, in life insurance and in composition. Ives found in life insurance a profession that could contain the effusive outpourings of his ideas for the philosophical and political betterment of mankind, and that at the same time provided an ample livelihood. Partch valued proofreading for the opposite reason: it did not dissipate his creative energies. The work "was easy for me because I was always a good speller. I knew sentence structure . . . I even tried working on the copy desk, but I didn't like it because it took too much out of me. Proofreading took nothing out of me. I could be almost as fresh after eight hours as I was at the beginning."[71] He seems to have regarded proofreading simply as a way of making a living, and was quite content to keep it separate from music.

The 1931 article just cited also sheds light on one of the more surprising of Partch's musical activities. At the time he was working for the *San Francisco News* he played the viola in the symphony orchestra of the University of California. This apparently recursive act of involvement in a milieu long since abandoned—and it was not the last such act—shows that he was keen to profit from the mainstream cultural life available in the city and testifies to the diversity of his musical endeavors. The orchestra in which Partch played was known officially as the California Music League Symphony Orchestra; it became known formally as the University of California Symphony Orchestra only in 1930. It presented concerts under the auspices of the university at Berkeley, but membership was not limited to students. Partch found in it an opportunity to measure his proficiency as a string player. Moreover, despite all his railings against the orchestra and against the "persons with shattered English and long noses" engaged to conduct them, his later ensemble writing shows signs of having learned much from first-hand experience of the inner dynamics of a group of musicians playing under a conductor.[72]

In the spring of 1928 he worked at putting his theoretical ideas on paper in an extended form. On May 20, while living at 1166 Clay Street in San Francisco, he completed the first draft of a treatise entitled *Exposition of Monophony*. It was the first real consolidation—although in embryonic form—of his "initial divergent gropings";[73] as he remarked five years later, it felt like his first significant accomplishment. Perhaps as a mark of recognition of this fact he had the manuscript notarized. The completion of the treatise created few waves in the musical world at large, and did not earn him any critical attention. Nor does he seem to have made any significant attempt to disseminate it widely; he showed the manuscript to only a few professional musicians, among them Julius Gold, violinist in the San Francisco Symphony and a theorist.[74] The *Exposition* nonetheless represents a high-water mark in his achievements to that time.

By June he was in Santa Rosa, where he lived in one of the rental units owned by a woman named Martha Zoller. She and her three children lived in an old house on Second Street, with five acres of ground encompassing a prune orchard. At first, like any normal tenant, Partch paid rent: as the family grew fond of him, and gradually realized the impermanence and precariousness of his finances, Martha suggested that he could live rent-free in exchange for music lessons for the children. Partch taught piano to the daughter, Wanda, known as Sissy; and violin to the younger son, Nicholas, known as Buddy. The lessons took place in their living room, where Partch was made to feel at home. He even took meals with the family. He began to develop a paternal attachment to the children, insisting on good table manners and on the use of napkins, and took great pride when Nicholas played solo violin upon his graduation from junior high school. The Zollers became as close to a family of his own as he had at this time.[75]

As an outlet for his musical ambitions, the role of pedagogue was far from ideal. Nonetheless, he was now more confident about mentioning his work to professional musicians, however hesitantly. He made the acquaintance of Josef Walter, a young music teacher at Santa Rosa High School. "He introduced himself to me," Walter recalls, "and proceeded to show me some changes he would like to make on the viola and possibly other string instruments. Since I did not play viola at the time, I was not much impressed. . . . I was not very comfortable with his modern ideas."[76] Walter's response was probably typical, and faintly disheartening. And although Partch's first achievement was now behind him, "My own direction, as it finally evolved, had more to do with lonely daydreaming than with revolt."[77]

Despite the significant start he had now made in his theoretical work, the events of the later part of 1928 took Partch away from any sustained work in music. This may have been the unexpected consequence of a decision taken for precisely the opposite reason: to jolt himself into a way of life that better suited the restless promptings of his creative spirit. In a letter in 1960 he recalled, "After years at various jobs in Los Angeles and San Francisco, I rebelled. . . . I'd lived outdoors so much of my early life, and I resented this adventureless existence, punching time clocks, even soft beds and regular meals. So in 1928 I quit the job I was on in Sacramento and started out on the fruit harvest. This was my first real hoboing, and it came at a time when jobs were fairly easy to find. I followed the harvest most of the rest of that season."[78]

Although this first taste of "real hoboing" was not perhaps particularly arduous, it was a crucial preparation for the events of the next decade. A song written in 1929 describes the experience, and although the words—Partch's own—seem neither heartfelt nor particularly well-crafted, they are not without interest:

I've gone away—
Away forever—
Away from tries and tears,
Away from loves, hates, thrills, fears—
The stars above—
The winds beneath me—
In spreading sails,
In hobo trails where I'm
Bound away for Sacramento Jungle,
For the joy o'living I'm—
Strumming, a-strumming on my vocal chords a-tingle
While my heart keeps beating time.

The hobo "jungle" to which the lyric refers was a gathering place established by the hobos, usually in a dry, shady spot on the outskirts of a city and in close proximity to a railroad division point. The hobos governed the jungles with their own self-imposed rules. In such locations Partch learned the ethics as well as the ethos of hobo life.

When he returned to composition it was in yet another direction, and one influenced by his recent experiences. By now he had turned his back almost completely on concert music, and struck out on a new tangent, composing popular songs for voice and piano. "In a period of about two weeks I wrote one a day, words and music." The words were "obscene by the stringencies of the twenties, with my Greek mythology background, but very mild today."[79] Many years later he recalled: "I had the nerve to send [one of the obscene ones] to a publisher. He didn't turn me over to federal authorities, but he did write me a blistering letter. I replied to it very calmly, and then I had a second letter from him saying that he thought I had talent, and I ought to channel it properly. Mostly, they were hobo songs."[80] One of them, *My Heart Keeps Beating Time,* quoted above, was published, by Lloyd Campbell Publications in San Francisco, "but it was certainly never popular. . . . My hobo words were deleted— that appalled me, but I went along. Ted Lewis wrote new lyrics for it—they were so silly I don't even remember them." Partch published the song under the pseudonym Paul Pirate; the lyricist credited on the printed version of the song is Larry Yoell.

He quickly became dissatisfied with these songs. Writing in 1933 he attributed this to the limitations of the piano scale for vocal settings, but we might wonder if he was somehow uncomfortable with the medium of the popular song as a whole. For many years his work had been aimed at something quite different. The lucrative but ultimately conservative medium of the popular song was scarcely a promising vehicle for his far-reaching experiments in tuning theory and performance practice. The publication of one of them under a pseudonym implies the creation of a temporary persona through which he could maintain distance from an involvement that lacked the full measure of his artistic sincerity. Following this experience, he wrote, "came the determination to allow the spoken words of lyrics to govern the melody and rhythm of the music. There was no conscious influence in the conclusion except, possibly, the knowledge that the ancient Greeks had used some such manner of song."[81]

If Partch's outer life remains concealed during the 1920s, at least one of the streams of his inner life was flowing toward the treatise *Exposition of Monophony,* the one substantial source of our knowledge of his early theoretical investigations. It comes as a sobering corrective to the anarchic, irreverent aspects of Partch's creativity to realize how many hours he must have spent poring over Helmholtz's book and leafing through innumerable lesser works, drier than dust, on music theory and acoustics. Yet this search was undertaken in a spirit of evangelical seriousness. W. B. Yeats offers the comforting thought that "truth flourishes where the student's lamp has shone," and Partch's lamp guided his way into what remains for most musicians an arcane, tangential area, far removed from the central concerns of composers and theorists of the time.

It seems paradoxical, in the light of the difficulties the subject continues to hold for many musicians, that Partch's theoretical work in just intonation should remain far more widely studied than any of his individual compositions. This is largely due to the wide circulation and influence of *Genesis of a Music,* into which the *Exposition of Monophony* was gradually transformed, in comparison with the relative inaccessibility of his scores.

The prevalent assumption has been that *Genesis* presents the "pure" form and the definitive statement of Partch's theoretical thinking. This overlooks the fact that, not surprisingly, his theoretical work had a long and fascinating history of evolution and crystallization. Some of its most apparently central concepts and terminology do not seem to have been formulated until a rather later stage than we might suppose; and, conversely, some important early aspects of his work are passed over without mention in the book. A further misconception, prevalent among those who have studied only the book and not the music itself, is that his music functions in accordance with the ideas and theories expounded in the book. While the assumption is not unreasonable, closer examination shows that it is only partly true, and is a misleading starting point for an exploration of his music.

Although the main principles and postulates of Partch's theoretical system were developed between 1923 and the completion of the first draft of the *Exposition of Monophony* in 1928, they were still in an embryonic state at the end of that decade. The treatise went through five drafts in the years up to 1933: only the fifth draft, completed in Los Angeles in June 1933, is extant. At least some of the earlier drafts may have been destroyed by Partch, or dismantled, as he extracted pages containing diagrams and tables from one manuscript for use in a new one. Happily, the fifth draft includes a brief review of his work to that point, and tells us something of the contents of earlier drafts.

In his foreword to the 1933 draft Partch announces: "Throughout the history of music there has been a slow and only half-recognized revelation of the universe of tone created by the overtone series. This work is an attempt to found the theory of music definitely on the origin of intervals. It is an exposition of the so-far-accepted in the light of that origin and a disclosure of a further small part of its universe. Understanding of musical structure does certainly devolve upon an understanding of this one source of tonal relationships. Without this, a true knowledge has only chance existence in the arbitrary, traditional, or intuitive." The overtone series, or harmonic series, is a natural phenomenon well known to physicists and is discussed at length by Helmholtz. When an elastic medium of any sort is set in periodic motion, it will produce sound waves corresponding to twice, three times, four times, and so on in infinite series, the lowest (fundamental) frequency of vibration. These overtones, also known as harmonics or partials, are constituents of any compound tone: the lower overtones are often audible, and even partials as high as the eleventh can sometimes be emphasized on acoustic instruments. The relationships between adjacent overtones can best be described by mathematical ratios, in an analogous way to the intervals produced by proportional lengths of a vibrating string.

Helmholtz's work moved far beyond the specific question of string lengths and dealt with all sound-producing bodies—the voice, orchestral instruments, even sirens. He wrote that, in the eighteenth century,

> the law governing the motions of strings became known, and it was thus found that the simple ratios of the lengths of the strings existed also for the pitch numbers of the tones they produced, and that they consequently belonged to the musical intervals of the tones of all instruments. . . . This relation of whole numbers to musical consonances was from all time looked upon as a wonderful mystery of deep significance. The Pythagoreans themselves made use of it in their speculations on the harmony of the spheres. From that time it remained partly the goal and partly the starting point of the strangest and most venturesome, fantastic or philosophic combinations, till in modern times the majority of investigators adopted the notion accepted by Euler, that the human mind had a peculiar pleasure in simple ratios, because it could better understand them and comprehend their bearings. But it remained uninvestigated how the mind of a listener not versed in physics, who perhaps was not even aware that musical tones depended on periodical vibrations, contrived to recognise and compare these ratios of the pitch numbers.[82]

The study of the vibrational patterns produced by two musical tones whose fundamentals are related by small-number frequency ratios led Helmholtz to a new solution to the problem left "uninvestigated" in Euler's time. His influential contention was that the recognition and comparison of these ratios depended upon the coincidence, or lack of coincidence, of the upper partials of two or more musical tones. These processes, taking place in the ear, "render sensible the difference between consonance and dissonance."

Partch's wish to disclose "a further small part of . . . the universe of tone" meant extending the musical palette of consonance and dissonance, as these terms are defined by Helmholtz, by admitting higher prime-number relationships of the harmonic series—analogous to the higher partials—as potential consonances. He acknowledged that a great deal of familiarity was needed with the more complex ratios before they could be heard and reproduced accurately, and that this complexity was hierarchical: Partch held the intervals derived from the remote eleventh partial to be more complex relationships both physiologically and in terms of historical usage than the intervals derived from the seventh partial, and these seventh-partial intervals in turn as more complex than those from the fifth partial, which are the familiar basis of Western tuning practice.

In the first chapter of the *Exposition of Monophony* Partch appends a small caveat to the tangled question of interval derivation. "It is not important whether one chooses to say that musical intervals have their source in the ratios of simple numbers, as did Pythagoras of Samos in the sixth century B.C., or that their source is in the overtone series, the phenomenon discovered by Marin Mersenne, French monk of the seventeenth century. The result is the same. . . . Just intonation is any system of tuning with intervals exactly the same as the intervals of the overtone series."

By the time of the first draft of the *Exposition,* in 1928, Partch had adopted just intonation as the basis of his theory, and had already fixed the eleventh partial as "the limit of the source of . . . intervals."[83] This meant that he accepted as valid musical material all of those pitch relationships analogous to the intervals between any two of the first eleven elements of the harmonic series, and the inversions of those intervals. Not only does this scheme encompass the familiar intervals from the lower reaches of the harmonic series—the octave (in ratio terms 2/1), perfect fifth (3/2), perfect fourth (4/3), just major third (5/4), and just minor third (6/5)—but also unfamiliar kinds of every interval class, derived from the seventh partial and the eleventh partial. If all the intervals generated by this process, and the inversions of those intervals, are measured from a given fundamental, a set of twenty-nine different pitches within the octave is obtained. In his 1933 terminology, Partch described this set as "the 29 tones within 11": later he termed it, more clearly, the twenty-nine primary ratios within the 11-limit. His term *limit,* as applied to a just intonation system, refers to the highest prime number found in the ratios of the pitches in that system—an 11-limit system is therefore one that includes ratios of 2, 3, 5, 7 and 11, but no higher.[84]

These twenty-nine tones gave him an already very complex microtonal scale. However, this twenty-nine-degree sequence contains some very wide gaps between some of its adjacent degrees (particularly at the two "ends") and some very narrow ones, so he decided to divide the wider gaps and produce a more even contour by allowing himself the practice of deriving further pitches by tuning simple intervals above some of the degrees of the scale. These additional pitches he later termed secondary ratios. The number of them that he included in the scale varied during the period 1928–35: reviews of his work from the early

1930s report the number of tones in his scale as being, at different times, twenty-nine, fifty-five, and thirty-seven tones, and his early theoretical writings contain descriptions of these and scales of thirty-nine and forty-one tones, among others, before he settled on the forty-three-tone scale he analyzes in *Genesis of a Music.* The frequent change in the constitution of his scale, although an interesting aspect of this period of Partch's work, is secondary in importance to the fact that the body of principles underlying the generation of the scales remained consistent.[85]

The term that Partch frequently uses to describe the pitch resources of his system of extended just intonation is *fabric.* The word appears in his earliest extant theoretical writings, and it was a usage he retained throughout his life. The metaphor is not merely poetic. The word *fabric,* with its connotations of texture, places emphasis on the system's internal *coherence*—and on the fact that it can grow if woven further—rather than viewing it as a closed structure. The scale is seen as an expanding fabric of relationships capable of informing, shaping, and ordering the pitch domain: a *laying down* of the total pitch space.

Although from the later 1920s Partch had abandoned the idea of twelve pitches in the octave, he never abandoned—at least in theory—the idea of a scale with a fixed number of degrees: it was simply the number of tones in the octave that he set as limits that changed. Yet although incipient in his theory, the idea of an expandable source scale—a fabric of tones—is in fact a more accurate description of his music than that of a fixed structure of forty-three tones, of which any given work might use only a subset. His music offers a fully fledged example of the principle: scattered throughout his output we find numerous works that seem, as it were, to lay down their pitch terrain as they unfold, sometimes using only a small piece of the fabric, and occasionally extending that fabric to many more than forty-three tones.[86] As with any real composer, we find that Partch's theory, at least in this respect, lags behind his compositional practice.

⅄ The difference between Partch's method of scale generation and the concept of twelve-tone equal temperament—the tuning system that is the norm throughout the Western world—may perhaps be clarified by a visual analogy. Twelve-note equal temperament, Pythagorean in its origins, is a closed system analogous to a circle on which are marked twelve equally spaced points.[87] The generative process of Partch's scale, in contrast, resembles the division of a whole into proportionally smaller parts—two halves, three thirds, and so on, with the thirds in turn being divided in half. This process is by definition theoretically infinite, bounded only by the limits of what is perceptible.

Table 1. Chronology of the development of Partch's scale, 1928–1935

June 1928	Partch marks a discarded cello fingerboard with twenty-nine indications in the octave: this later becomes the fingerboard of his Adapted Viola. The indicated ratios correspond to "my 1928 theory of the more essential tones."
November 1930	Mayfield's review in the New Orleans *Times-Picayune* reports Partch as having devised a twenty-nine-tone scale: its exact relation to the ratios marked on the Viola fingerboard is not known.
February 1932	The previews and reviews for Partch's concerts with Rudolphine Radil in the San Francisco area describe his music as using fifty-five tones to the octave.
September 1932	The chart showing Partch's Ratio Keyboard design depicts a layout with thirty-nine tones to the octave.
October 1932	In his Guggenheim application submitted this month, Partch is still describing his work as involving a fifty-five-tone scale.
February 1933	The reviews for Partch's concerts with Calista Rogers in and around Los Angeles still describe his music as using fifty-five tones to the octave.
June 1933	The (fifth) draft of the *Exposition of Monophony* describes a thirty-seven-tone scale and makes no mention of the fifty-five-tone scale.
October 1933	In his Guggenheim application submitted this month, Partch describes his work as involving a scale of thirty-seven tones in the octave.
Winter 1934–1935	Partch's new keyboard instrument, the Ptolemy, is built in London; its keyboard seems (from the surviving photograph) to have forty-three tones to the octave. The layout of keys, in concentric arcs, is the same as the Ratio Keyboard designs of 1932 but with four extra keys apparently added forming the bottom row (39+4=43).
June 1935	Partch's article "A New Instrument" is published in *Musical Opinion*; it describes his "system of intonation" as involving forty-three tones in the octave.

The resulting microtonal scale, then, contains all the interval relationships found in the twelve-tone chromatic scale, as well as many others derived from the unfamiliar seventh and eleventh partials. (Many of these unfamiliar intervals occur, as Helmholtz recorded, in ancient Greek theory and in the music of non-Western cultures.) Indeed, one of the premises of Partch's theory is that the ear can distinguish several different kinds of (say) "major third"—independent and distinct pitch materials that are confounded in conventional theory. Partch compares the situation to an artist's scale of colors: "In his mind he approaches the reds. For his brush's immediate use he sees a carmine, a vermilion, a scarlet, a crimson, a cerise, a garnet, a ruby, and verging off into other color values are an orchid and a magenta, a nasturtium and an orange, and a sienna, a rust and an ochre . . . Consider the writer of music. Before him is also a scale. It holds seven white keys and five black ones. In his mind he approaches C sharp, one of the five blacks. He approaches it, and he lands on it. His action is direct, simple, predetermined. There are no shades of C sharp, no shades of red, for him."[88]

In Western musical performance we hear many such "shades of red" without always realizing it, especially on unfretted string instruments and in voices. Performers instinctively introduce tiny shadings or inflections into the size of intervals for expressive purposes almost constantly. In this sense, "microtones" are a familiar part of our musical experience. Partch wanted to make conscious and rational use of these inflections, and thus to refine our vocabulary of intervals so that new compositional materials could be described and would become practicable.

Beyond the direct use of microtones in scales and melodic passages, an important consequence of his use of extended just intonation was in the domain of harmony. A postulate about chord formation, the necessary corollary of his theory of consonance and dissonance, seems to have been present in Partch's theoretical work from as early as can be documented. He considered as legitimate harmonic entities those just intonation intervals analogous to the relationships of the first six *odd-number* elements of the harmonic series to their fundamental. Hexadic chords of this type are equivalent in Partch's music to major triads in conventional "classical" harmony in being the normative elements of his harmonic language.

Partch did not attempt to set down, either in the *Exposition of Monophony* or in the later *Genesis of a Music,* any fully worked-out theory of chord movement—a theory of harmony, in fact, as that idea is usually construed. Two theoretical concepts that might be regarded as steps toward such a theory were apparently already present in the 1928 draft of *Exposition of Monophony:* a theory of resolution and a classification of intervals. The theory of resolution was devised in the attempt to account for "departure" and "attraction" in his type of hexadic chordal movement. These terms are somewhat analogous to the idea of tension and release in tonal analysis, and form part of his attempt to reconceive that idea in quantitative terms—based on the "pull" of different strengths exerted by the different pitches ("identities") of the chord.

The "classification of intervals" in his early writings is essentially the same as that embodied in the later "graph of comparative consonance" in chapter 9 of his book.[89] He divided the intervals in his scale into four "arbitrary" categories—Intervals of Power (the "perfect" intervals), Intervals of Emotion (corresponding to major and minor thirds and sixths), Intervals of Suspense (which at one time he called Psychic Intervals, and which correspond to the augmented fourth and diminished fifth), and Intervals of Approach (corresponding to major and minor sevenths and seconds). It is tempting to see in this scheme a link with Partch's idol W. B. Yeats, whose involvement in esoteric doctrine predisposed him toward mystic quarternaries; with, perhaps, the Four Faculties that form one of the cornerstones of Yeats's *A Vision* (1925), with their echoes of the four elements of magic, the four humors of medieval medicine and psychology, and much else. Partch never explained the symbolism of his scheme. In purely musical terms, the classification was an acknowledgment that in his system not only was the idea of enharmonic equivalence—the sense in which C sharp is the same as D flat—redundant, whereas it is crucial to an equal-tempered system, but also that the whole idea of interval classes had to be reexamined. As arbitrary as he acknowledged this fourfold classification to be, it, like his theory of resolution, has some bearing on his compositional practice. The scheme operates in conjunction with a different hierarchical disposition of intervals based on the complexities of their prime-number limits.

The ideas outlined above, all of which and more are included in the 1933 draft of the *Exposition of Monophony*, remained present in Partch's thinking with only slight modifications, if any, in the years to come. However, quite a few concepts that are important to his later work do not seem to have been formulated by this point, and his terminology, in particular, was in greater flux than is at first apparent. This latter point is suggested by the first ever review of his work, from November 1930, which describes his ideas and quotes Partch on his theoretical work.[90] In the article, Partch is quoted as stating that for practical purposes he chose to "close the field" at the eleventh harmonic, because

"the 13th enters into territory as yet unfathomed by our ears, though years from now it may be familiar. Most theorists of today stop at the seventh harmonic. The third, fifth, seventh, ninth and 11th harmonics, each of which sets up a new [overtone] series within this field, are called magnets in [M]onophony, as they seem to attract the illegitimate transposed notes, called satellites."

By exact calculations, which, like all researches into the science of sound, lead through what their maker admits is "a night of numerology," the magnets and satellites form the scale of 29 notes within the octave (though "octave" is a word meaningless in such a scale and Mr. Partch calls it "aura").

This passage contains examples of terms that Partch coined and then dropped (aura); terms that he coined, apparently dropped, and then resurrected (magnets and satellites, which do not appear in the 1933 *Exposition* but are used later in the published *Genesis of a Music*).[91] Yet a term as central (and, in retrospect, obvious) as Otonality—to describe a 1:3:5:7:9:11 chord, as discussed above—appears neither in this review nor in the 1933 draft of the *Exposition,* although by the time of the latter Partch was already using the word *tonality* to mean a chord of this type and referring to its constituent degrees as "identities" of the chord, both usages that he retained.

One possible reason why the term *Otonality* had not yet occurred to him is that by 1930 it seems he had not formulated its complementary concept, Utonality. A Utonality is a hexadic chord that is the inversion of an Otonality: it is formed by building the same interval sequence as that of an Otonality *downward* from the root of the chord, rather than upward. The analogy, in this case, is not to the harmonic series but to the subharmonic, or undertone, series. Partch included the concept when he revised his theoretical exposition the following year, 1931, stimulated—or, by his own admission, "hastened"—by reading Henry Cowell's discussion of undertones in his book *New Musical Resources,* which had just been published.[92] In retrospect, it is easy to see that Utonalities are implicitly present in the system Partch had already developed— indeed, they are his "minor" hexads, the complement of the "major" Otonalities. In forming the concept and giving it a name he was merely identifying a pattern that was already there.

Viewed as a whole, Partch's theoretical work was not undertaken in the spirit of wishing to replace one exhausted paradigm by another, by a "different set of rigid stipulations."[93] It was the result of what was, for him, a searching, creative investigation, and needs to be seen in that light, not as a dogmatic prescription (or proscription), every detail of which is set in amber. In a letter in 1952 he wrote: "I do not always *achieve* the just intonation which I hold as desirable— the clear choice of consonance or dissonance. Someone has said that ideals are like stars. We can't touch them but we look to them for guidance. I believe in a rational—that is, acoustical—approach to the problems of musical materials, as the *only* one leading to genuine insight."[94]

Several composers and theorists have seen in Partch's theoretical investigations implications that extend well beyond his own work. Partch was, in the

1920s, largely unfamiliar with the crisis of contemporary European music—the so-called "breakdown of tonality" and the exploration of atonality and serialism in the works of the Second Viennese School, of Schoenberg, Berg, and Webern. Yet Ben Johnston has argued that Partch in fact formulated, from quite different motivations, a music-theoretic standpoint that implies a striking diagnosis of the immense strain underlying this phase of European music. In Partch's view, twelve-note equal temperament is not merely a tuning system, but a conceptual vehicle that sets limits on the nature of the musical thought possible within it. The "crisis of tonality" in turn-of-the-century European music may thus be a manifestation of the strain resulting from the attempt to forge new nontriadic harmonic units and distant reaches of tonal space out of a conceptually exhausted *intonational* framework that was incapable of realizing them. Partch's own music sidesteps this crisis and creates an idiom that refuses to push the harmonic language of European music further beyond the breaking point.

Partch's revolutionary work in intonation creates a new conceptual milieu and a language in which problems of harmony and subtleties of musical pitch relations can be addressed. What he might have called the "wide-consciousness intuition" underpinning these investigations offered a bridge not only to past and present eras of Western music, but to the great civilizations of the ancient world and the East. His friend (from later years) Erv Wilson, one of the few people in his lifetime who Partch felt understood his theoretical work, has suggested the radical idea that Partch intuitively perceived the rightness of using the unfamiliar ratios from higher in the overtone series because those relationships had existed in the music of ancient Greece and non-Western cultures; as Wilson puts it, a kind of "ancestral memory" had awoken in him. He believes that Partch "may have perceived in archetypal melodic patterns, archetypal scales, on an unconscious level. . . . I think that embedded in the substrata of our own European music is its own memory of its own past, and that [Partch] as a purely intuitive genius was able to bring forth these ancient memories and give expression to them again in an utterly valid form. It may have been glances against other cultures that caused some of these to trigger, to awaken, but I think that he was remembering."[95]

The 1920s ended for Partch with a memorable experience. He registered in Philadelphia on December 31, 1929; after a little over three weeks of service as an ordinary seaman he was discharged on January 22, 1930. His certificate of discharge states that his ship was an oil tanker on an intercoastal voyage. It rates Partch's "character, ability, and seamanship" all as "very good." Evidently still under the sway of his songwriting persona, he registered under the name of Paul Pirate.[96] He dismissed this experience, at the end of his life, as having occupied "just a little time."[97] (There were compensations: during his time in service he learned how to do macramé.)[98] Yet, however short lived, the episode can hardly have failed to make a mark. From our point of view, it heralds his step from the shadows toward the light.

New Orleans and California

Upon his discharge from service as an apprentice seaman Partch hitchhiked down the East Coast and over to New Orleans, arriving in February 1930 toward the end of a winter that proved to be "among the most miserable in my life, mostly because the houses aren't equipped for cold. I can also recall practically burning up in heat on the first of April."[1] He explored the city on foot, taking in the heady mixture of old and new world cultures of what Edmund Wilson a few years earlier had described as the "dull chocolate and slate-lilac city with its high roofs and narrow windows," with "that perfume of Southern trees and plants in the air . . . the delicacy of vines against the exquisite laces of wrought-iron balconies . . . the trains, the steamboat sounds, the whistling and songs from the street . . . the chattering sound of Creole French."[2] Partch's earliest points of orientation included the cheapest places to eat. At first he lived on green bananas for three days on the docks, fruit discarded from the large shipments arriving from Central America; and later "for about a dime you could go to the French Market . . . and get a bowl of soup that was really good."[3] Before long he found a job as a proofreader for the *Times-Picayune*.

His gravitation to New Orleans is unlikely to have been prompted primarily by musical considerations. Jazz was the thriving musical attraction and was all over the city, from the night clubs on Bourbon Street to the inimitable funeral processions with jazz band in attendance. Despite his flirtation with popular songwriting the previous year, jazz itself appealed to him less than the air of relaxed spontaneity that characterized much of the city's music-making. Twenty years later he recalled "the little Negro boys of New Orleans street corners (their 'instruments' might be frowned on by our serious musicians), who play washboards, tubs, tin cans, anything that intrigues their aural imaginations, and who dance and make sounds from their mouths and grimacing wrinkles on their faces."[4] Another, perhaps not irrelevant attraction was that New Orleans was, of all the larger American cities of that time, probably the one where a homosexual man could feel the least need for decorum, and could lead an active life with relatively little fear of discrimination on the grounds of his sexuality.

Among the belongings Partch brought to Louisiana was the fingerboard from a discarded cello that he had begun to mark with ratio indications two summers earlier in Santa Rosa. In New Orleans in April a local violin maker, Edwin Benton, attached the fingerboard to a lengthened neck which was then joined to a viola body, creating a new hybrid instrument that Partch called the Monophone, after the name he had given to his scale fabric. By 1933 it had become known as the Adapted Viola, the name it was to retain. The instrument is held between the knees in playing, like a viol. Open strings, because of their unconventional length, are tuned a fourth below the usual viola tuning (or an octave below the open strings of a violin); he used cello strings, which gave the best sound. The lengthened fingerboard has twenty-nine indications for ratios within the octave, corresponding to his "1928 theory of the more essential tones":[5] tiny bradheads have been hammered into the fingerboard at these points *beside* the strings, so that they act as guides for the fingers of the left hand, not as frets. Pitches other than the twenty-nine indicated are found with reference to those marked.

The idea of a *new* instrument was motivated ostensibly by the desire for a medium that could readily project the full pitch resources of his tuning system, and the two principal adaptations Partch made to the conventional viola—the elongated neck and fingerboard, and the bradheads in the fingerboard—have the same purpose: to permit greater accuracy in the precise stopping of the strings for the microtonal degrees of his scale. (In the light of Partch's previous experiments, the bradheads can be seen as a refinement of the paper fingerboard coverings he had devised for the string quartet composed around 1925.) However, a new instrument conferred an additional advantage. In view of the frustration and annoyance with the "widespread emphasis" on technique that he felt as a piano student, a new instrument of his own devising represented terra incognita; in playing it he could have, by definition, no competition, and so he was placing himself outside the discussion of the vicissitudes of technique. More than this, he was free to develop his own technique, one that could grow together with his compositional needs.

Partch's own playing of the Adapted Viola was intended from the outset as a partner or complement to his voice. It clearly invokes the ancient bardic tradition of a singer or chanter of stories accompanying himself on a stringed instrument. His intent was that voice and Viola together form a sinuous couple, with a liquid and sensuous gliding movement, close to human speech, in place of the technique of organlike "precise discrete steps" into which he felt Western bowed string players were indoctrinated. The "*one-finger* technique" which he devised is dependent on the careful control of the speed and timing of the finger glides, and on the nuances of bowing. In terms both of musical resources and of performance manner the instrument became the arbiter between theory and compositional practice.

The completion of the Adapted Viola marks the true point of no return in Partch's early musical development. It seems to have determined him to make a more drastic break with his musical past. Soon thereafter he burned all of his compositions to that time in a pot-bellied iron stove, an act that he later described as "a kind of adolescent auto-da-fé."[6] The stack of fourteen years' worth of manuscripts—including the unfinished piano concerto, the symphonic poem, the string quartet, and numerous short piano pieces and songs— had been "accruing to the point where I couldn't stand to have it around . . . there was a lot of unhappiness involved, too, both economic and romantic."[7]

The "auto-da-fé" involved more than simply the destruction of a particular body of work that no longer held any value for him. Rather, especially given the symbolic portent of destruction by fire, it is not too fanciful to regard the act as one of purification: the renunciation of a whole world of past aspirations and values, not only musical ones, and the "reaching for a supernal freedom." It was "a confession, to myself, that in pursuing the respectable, the widely accepted, I had not been faithful." Yet he was "at the same time enduring a kind of anguish in abandoning all that I had struggled to learn of the old ways (*and not so old!*)." "I wanted to be free," Partch wrote toward the end of his life, and—in the wake of the auto-da-fé—"in the tiny vortex of my being I found freedom."[8]

The apparently direct, unambiguous symbolism of this act is offset to some extent by his wholly uncharacteristic vagueness about its date. All his life he claimed to be able to relive the great surge of freedom that swept through him then, and the precisely remembered detail of the appearance of the big, pot-bellied iron stove in which the manuscripts were burned lends the memory a touch of authenticating vividness. Yet among his writings we find datings as much as four years apart—the earliest being 1926, which would place the event years before his arrival in New Orleans[9]—discrepancies so great as to suggest that behind the apparently blatant intent of the act lurks a telling, and still mysterious, inability or unwillingness to remember precisely its timing and location. Erv Wilson recalls Partch's saying that the act was prompted by a vivid dream he had one night in New Orleans, in which "he was given to understand all that was wrong with the music that he [had been] making [until then], how hideously unsuited it was to his needs, and was shown . . . the kind and quality of music that he should be doing . . . [as] I understand it, some part of his inner psyche was revealing to him a much deeper level of his musical abilities."[10] The nature of this dream, of which Wilson's recollections are the only available testimony, cannot be verified; but in any case it would have only been the trigger for the act itself, intimations of which may have been on the composer's mind for some time. Whatever its cause, the effect of Partch's auto-da-fé was to clear the way for the compositions to follow.

By the autumn of 1930 his theoretical ideas were firmly on his mind again. His solitary walks around the romantic new city in which he found himself, with its hazy southern light, acted as a spur to his more cerebral flights of the imagination. He recalled "walking along the levees of the Mississippi River," his mind awhirl with the proliferations of the tonal relationships within his scale fabric.[11] On October 21, in his lodgings at 828 Camp Street, a few blocks away from the offices of the *Times-Picayune,* he completed a revision of the *Exposition of Monophony,* "giving a more thoro explanation of the ideas." He showed the new draft to Selby Noel Mayfield, music critic and colleague at the *Times-Picayune,* who published the first review of Partch's work in the paper on Sunday, November 16. The article, entitled "Student Devises 29-Degree Octave Theory of Music," gives a serious and intelligent discussion of Partch's ideas and an accurate account of his theoretical work. Mayfield introduces Partch as a "musician by interest and proofreader by profession," and explains that although "music is his major interest, he wanted to keep it apart from his daily work, as he believes his own theories would color too deeply a musical profession, and turned to proofreading." Mayfield likened Partch's scale fabric "to the Persian and Arabian scales which also largely subdivide the octave," an association probably prompted by a remark by Partch, who in turn may have picked it up from his readings of Helmholtz (who discusses the "Arabic and Persian musical system" in *On the Sensations of Tone*). Mayfield also presents Partch's aesthetic position, and his disdain for the whole debate about "modern music," which "has been on the wrong track from the beginning centuries ago . . . and should return to the musical method of the ancient world: voice accompanied by one instrument. . . . The high civilization of Greece and Rome used unerring taste in choosing voice with accompaniment for its music, says Mr. Partch."

By November, with the Adapted Viola as his stimulus, Partch had begun work on settings of verses by the eighth-century Chinese poet Li Po, for intoning voice and Adapted Viola in his system of microtonally extended just intonation. He completed the first, "The Long-Departed Lover," in December. The following month he set "On Seeing Off Meng Hao-jan" and "With a Man of Leisure"; a fourth, "On the Ship of Spice-wood," followed in April.

The idea of writing music that would be first and foremost an exemplification of his new theoretical ideas was totally foreign to Partch, a motivation that he considered too abstract. These first mature compositions start from his devotion to the expressive power of human speech: from the intimacy of the speaking voice, and the implied situation of person-to-person communication and confession that it connotes. They are not so much "about" particular ways of combining musical tones as they are "about" a particular kind of performance projection or bearing.

The vocal manner in these settings, which in December he described in a short article entitled "The Art of Song," represents on one level a reaction against the last compositions he had written prior to the auto-da-fé, the popular songs for voice and piano. Following his dissatisfaction with these "came the determination to allow the spoken words of lyrics to govern the melody and rhythm of the music." *In Genesis of a Music* he elaborates, that around 1930 "I came to the realization that the spoken word was the distinctive expression my constitutional makeup was best fitted for, and that I needed other scales and other instruments. This was the positive result of self-examination—call it intuitive, for it was not the result of any intellectual desire to pick up lost or obscure historical threads. For better or worse, it was an emotional decision."[12]

His intention in these settings was not to reduce melody to the less distinctive contours of speech, but rather to maximize understanding of the words by showing that speech contained within it the *condition* of music. In this art, he wrote, "the vitality of spoken inflections is retained in the music, every syllable and inflection of the spoken expression being harmonized by the accompanying instrument," which provides in addition "an enhancement of the text-mood and . . . a musical elaboration of ideas expressed."[13]

On the most immediate level, "the intrinsic music of spoken words" meant a sensitivity to those musical elements that poetic speech can be heard to contain—repeated notes, cadence figures, hierarchies of pitches, even harmonic relations between pitches, and so on. Yet in the Li Po settings he was not trying merely to compose vocal lines with a speechlike contour. He experimented with transcribing actual speech patterns as heard—first his own, and later, perhaps realizing the limitations of this approach, those of other people. On some occasions he would first reproduce the pitches on his Adapted Viola and then notate the result: the exact nuances of the spoken inflections could be captured with great precision by the resources of the microtonal scale he had devised. The notations then became a kind of "given," the first step of the compositional process. Not all of the Li Po settings were done strictly in this way, but Partch's use of the technique is extensive enough to lend the songs a coherence of musical language and manner. In those settings where he traverses the spectrum between transcribed speech and melody he evokes a haunting sense of speech metamorphosing into song: in essence, the bardic ideal. Because of the close adherence to "the vitality of spoken inflections" and the intended style of vocal delivery the settings were described, both in his early manuscripts and in the notices for the first public performances, as "tone declamations."

Partch's attraction to Li Po was more deeply rooted than simply that of a Californian (which, by now, he regarded himself) looking naturally to the Pacific Rim cultures for inspiration. There was the Chinese legacy from his parents' missionary activities, the second period of which they had spent in Shantung Province (where Li Po was born in the time of the T'ang Dynasty); and his attending performances at the Mandarin Theater in San Francisco. In New Orleans he was reading widely in the works of Chinese antiquity: his copy of Lao-tzu's *The Canon of Reason and Virtue* bears the inscription "March 28 1931."[14] The composer Peter Garland has even suggested that Partch's attraction to the poetry of Li Po contained a measure of identification with the poet: "Partch, I bet, had the Chinese hermit-poet's appreciation of nature: a bottle of wine, drunkenness, the brief instant of total being, awareness, a flock of geese overhead, petals falling, the wind; in the train yards, even; beyond the wounds of our personal selves."[15] To a limited extent, the identification of poet and composer holds. In the biographical sketch of Li Po that Partch includes in the manuscript of one of his later settings, the poet is depicted as an impulsive, headstrong, sensuous romantic, prepared to endure penury and exile rather than bear the duplicity of imperial patronage. Partch's own life, by this time, had begun to take on the aspect of the vagabond poet; having little hope of earning a living from his music, he careened from East Coast to West and back again in the years ahead, torn by the problem of patronage and support in an America darkened by economic recession. More important, in Li Po Partch found a point of view that set itself in opposition to accepted beliefs and social decorum, warring with them enthusiastically and eloquently; and his example conferred the benediction of antiquity on those individuals who sought to do likewise.

He did not, of course, attempt to set Li Po in the original language: the versions he used were from the book *The Works of Li Po, the Chinese Poet*, translated by Shigeyoshi Obata.[16] Partch was attracted to Li Po's intimate observations of detail and the universality of feeling thus expressed, an aspect of the verse that is captured elegantly in the uncluttered surfaces of Obata's translations.[17] During the filming of *The Dreamer That Remains* in 1972 Partch quoted Li Po's "On the City Street"—which he had set to music some forty years earlier—as an instance of "one little specific . . . that says the universal in a more beautiful way":

> They meet in the pink dust of the city street.
> He raises his gold crop high in salute.
> "Lady," says he, "Where do you live?
> "There are ten thousand houses among the drooping willow trees."

Capturing the detail and poise of these verses gave Partch the impetus to explore the new manner of vocal writing that, it seems, had already begun independently to suggest itself to him: one in which, in the words of W. B. Yeats which Partch would later quote with enthusiastic approval, "no word shall have an intonation or accentuation it could not have in passionate speech."[18]

Nowhere is Partch's spoken-word principle more clearly evident than in the first of the settings, "The Long-Departed Lover." In the score the syllables of the text are assigned pitch values but the rhythm is left free: the words are to be intoned on pitch following the natural rhythms of spoken delivery. The vocal line could plausibly be a straight notation of the rise and fall of the text as spoken, with its sense of quiet yet intense yearning for a former love. Nowhere does the line seem to have been composed into melody in anything like the conventional sense. Indeed, it seems almost prosaic in its avoidance of "expressive" gestures and literal repetition. It conveys, rather, an austere faithfulness to the particular spoken rendition with which Partch has imbued the text: yet that very austerity is itself filled with expressive significance. The voice moves within a constricted range (approximately a major sixth) and within that space there is a high degree of microtonal saturation: a total of nineteen different, unequally spaced, pitches. The vocal line as a whole is evocative of a sigh—the very smallness of the microtonal intervals is itself an expressive device—and as such poignantly renders the sense of the verse. This demonstrates, of course, how a carefully intoned recitation of the verse is itself an act of composition.

Harmonically, the terrain within which this setting lies is highly unfamiliar. In Partch's own terminology, the reiteration of the single pitch of the opening acts as a temporary "magnet" around which the other "satellite" pitches cluster. Voice and Viola, when they play together, are strictly in unison much of the time; when the line divides into two parts—which feels more like a step from monophony into polyphony than from melody into harmony—the only vertical intervals used (with one exception) are different sorts of "thirds," Partch's Intervals of Emotion. The one exception comes at the setting of the poet's question "where are you, Beloved?": here the voice rises to the highest pitch in the song's range, and Partch introduces a single 3/2 interval (a perfect fifth) between voice and Viola. This, the only occurrence in the setting (vertically or horizontally) of an Interval of Power, seems to embody—and more than just metaphorically—the assertiveness in the question. The Viola's carefully controlled flowing in and out of unison with the voice manages at once to render, by the choice of vertical intervals, the expressive significance of the words and, more practically, to support the voice in pitching the often difficult intervals of the vocal line. This earliest exemplification of Partch's "intoned speech" manner feels fully purified of unwanted residues of past compositional techniques, of what he had "struggled to learn" in the music he had burned in the auto-da-fé. In an interview near the end of his life Partch remarked that the Li Po settings were "what really started me. Until I got hold of that music, I thought that I was going nowhere. But then I knew, after I wrote 'The Long-Departed Lover' . . . that I wasn't going to destroy that, probably."[19]

Considering the musical thinking manifested in "The Long-Departed Lover" and in subsequent Li Po settings in the light of Partch's theoretical work in the early 1930s—which can only tentatively be reconstructed, given the few source documents of value that have survived from these years—we find a complex and interesting correspondence. Sometimes the theory provides for an accurate and complete description of what is happening in the music, at least at the level of pitch; at other times the music uses ideas that are present only by implication or not at all in the theory, while the theory draws some distinctions that seem only peripherally important when considering the music. At still other times the appearance of a new theoretical concept leads to significant departures in compositional practice, while a practice that is present in the music finds articulation in the theory only much later.

Partch's working method in the earliest Li Po settings must be deduced from close examination of the sketches that have survived from some of the later settings, although the principle seems clear and consistent. He began by setting out the text, in full, on a sheet of manuscript paper. In the surviving sketches the texts are written out neatly at the top of the staves, with no sign of the uneven spacing that would result if the notes had been written first and the text spaced accordingly: rather, it is the notes that are spaced unevenly. With the entire text before him on the page, his—or, later, someone else's—intoning of the text could be notated quickly without the interruption of filling in the text as he went along.

One aspect of these sketches comes at first as a shock. The notation system employed in them is the conventional one, with ad hoc additions of quarter tones and sixth tones to represent the microtonal contours of speech more accurately. It seems almost sacrilegious to see Partch resort in these manuscripts to the irrational divisions of the tempered scale he opposed so vitriolically. This apparently recursive use of an equal-tempered framework for purposes of speech transcription, rather than a notation system that could record the intervals of his just intonation system more directly, is perhaps not as anomalous as it first appears. The primary criterion was that the notation in the sketches be first and foremost a form of shorthand: complete accuracy would be less important than that the system be sufficiently familiar to allow him to record the inflections fairly accurately with reflexlike speed, before the creative spontaneity of the recitation was lost in a momentary hesitation over the precise notational symbol. Partch had been experimenting with new notation systems for several years and continued to devise new ones during the years he was setting Li Po, but the majority of them were abandoned before they had become sufficiently ingrained to become a habit. The "language of ratios" was the common denominator in all the systems, but few actually used ratios per se. He was therefore probably still not sufficiently comfortable with ratio notation to think of using it in this particular situation.

In working the sketches into first drafts of the settings, Partch was not simply translating the makeshift system of quarter and sixth tones into their closest ratio equivalents within his scale fabric, but was doing what might be termed *fine-tuning:* reconceiving the "raw" transcriptions in terms of precise interval relationships, and integrating those intervals, as part of tetrachords or modes, within a harmonic, and even structural, context—in essence, a compositional act. This part of the compositional process, like accuracy of intonation in performance, is important precisely because it clarifies (in many of the settings) structural relationships. The point of the transcriptions was not to be faithfully accurate: Partch felt no compunction about introducing slight modifications in notating what he heard, at which point his compositional imagination was already at work. The transcribed speech patterns are thus already shot through with compositional decisions.[20]

If the microtonal possibilities of Partch's system of Monophony gave him the means to capture the inflections of speech, exploring its harmonic and modal resources suggested ways of relaxing the severity of this initial compositional approach. "On Seeing Off Meng Hao-jan" shows a straightforward form of the fusion of the intoned speech principle with harmonic techniques derived from Partch's theories of chord formation: the speechlike vocal line is set in a new and distinctive harmonic context made possible by the microtonal intervals of his scale. The song is played using the option of lowering the third string of the Adapted Viola at the bridge, so that three strings can be bowed at once; with the addition of the voice it is therefore possible to sustain a four-part chord. The harmonic movement in this setting was to become characteristic of his music— densely chordal, in which the constituent degrees of one chord travel by narrow resolving distances to the next chord.[21] Later he termed it "tonality flux," preferring the neutral sense of the word *flux* to the usual implications of terms like *progression* or *modulation*.

The four Li Po settings written in August 1931, after his return to California, make *structural* use of this type of tonality flux, using two modes (or sometimes chordal formations from a mode), the constituent degrees of which are microtonal distances apart. In "On the City Street" and the beautiful "The Intruder," the two modes are used to symbolize opposing tensions in the verse. The text of "The Intruder" reads:

The grass of Yen is growing green and long
While in Chin the leafy mulberry branches hang low,
Even now while my longing heart is breaking,
Are you thinking, my dear, of coming back to me?
—O wind of spring, you are a stranger,
Why do you enter through the silken curtains of my bower?

The opening mode, a straightforward Dorian without microtonal embel-
lishments of any kind,[22] provides a sense of stability which is associated
throughout with the poet's mood of contemplation—the grass of Yen, the
mulberry branches in Chin, even the sense of heartbreak. This is gradually
disrupted by intrusive elements of an alien mode—an identical sequence of
intervals a microtonal interval apart, thus sharing no common degrees with the
opening mode—which is used consistently for the disquieting images of the
poem: the addressing of a question to the loved one, the intrusive and deceptive
spring wind, and finally the bower which, we may assume, brings back disquieting memories. The two modes are used together, in flux, in setting the line
of the poem in which the poet confronts the intruder ruffling his silken
curtains; but the intruder proves to be the spring wind and not the returning
lover. The careful consistency with which Partch applies this haunting and
audible relationship invests this tiny song with a depth of expressive significance and provides a striking example of the compositional craft found in these
early works.

In later settings these techniques are expanded still further. We begin to see
some degree of convergence of Partch's radical technical means with more
familiar compositional principles, amounting to a reinterpretation of those
principles in his own terms. "The Night of Sorrow" makes use not of two
contrasting modes, as did "The Intruder," but of what in Partch's terminology
would be described as two "magnets" to articulate the structure. Here the music
seems to suggest an expansion of the theoretical concept. The magnets are two-
note chords, rather than single pitches, although only the second is sounded
harmonically (and then in passing); and new distinctions can be seen to apply
among the pitches classed as "satellites." For the first half of the poem, in which
a woman is pictured sitting "deep within" her house, the magnet is a just major
third. In the second half of the poem this narrows to a just minor third, the
space of which is subject to a greater degree of microtonal saturation: the fifth
and sixth lines of the text are set to an ascending sequence of eight divisions of
the interval. This more microtonal contour coincides with that moment in the

text when the poet begins to describe the woman's suffering. Throughout, the satellite tones, although (by definition) close to the magnet tones, derive sufficient melodic identity of their own from the pull of the magnets to be heard as "expressive" inflections. The closing Viola phrase, which repeats the opening one and thus frames the setting, is wholly ambiguous with regard to the two magnets and leaves any feeling of tonality or tonal progression open and inconclusive. Several of the settings have a similarly inconclusive feel in their final moments, giving the sense that the poem and the scene encapsulated in it have faded from view rather than ended.

The Viola phrase that frames "The Night of Sorrow" is one of the rare instances in the early settings where the Viola presents independent melodic material of its own. During the period of composition of the Li Po settings the Viola attains an increasing degree of independence, and begins to be cast in roles different from its former one as "complement" to the voice. In "On Hearing the Flute at Lo-cheng One Spring Night" the voice begins with quiet pentatonic strains evoking the distant, muted sound of a bamboo flute; the Viola part, played tremolo and pianissimo throughout, is used to symbolize one of the elements of the poem—the spring wind, which carries the sound of the bamboo flute "hovering over the city of Lo." The increasing command of the compositional techniques Partch had been developing forms the ground for "A Dream," the thirteenth to be written and the longest of the Li Po settings, a real tour de force for both composer and performer, manifesting a virtuoso range of styles of articulation.

By the spring of 1931 a return to California was in prospect. The tentative steps Partch had taken to interest persons of influence in the New Orleans musical world in his work had come to nothing,[23] and he probably felt that California offered more potential outlets for his work than did the culturally isolated world of the South. He left New Orleans with "a firm intention to return some day": the intention was never to be realized.[24]

By August he was back in northern California, staying with his friends the Zollers in Santa Rosa, composing, and playing viola in the Santa Rosa Symphony—"it wasn't a very good orchestra, but it was a small town then."[25] This was only a temporary measure, and in September he relocated to San Francisco, now with a new determination to make inroads into the musical circles in the city. His work had acquired a much greater definition since his previous period of residence there: not only had his ideas in music theory and aesthetics developed further, but he now had an instrument and a handful of composi-

The first manuscript of "A Dream" from the *Seventeen Lyrics by Li Po,* 1932, showing ratio notation.
Reproduced by permission of the Harry Partch Estate Archive.

tions that afforded him an immediate, practicable way of gaining himself a hearing. He was correspondingly more confident in his self-projection as an artist; and he had turned thirty.

It is hardly surprising that his path led almost straightaway to Henry Cowell, whom he met shortly before Cowell's departure for Europe in September. The two men were in many ways unalike, both temperamentally and artistically. Cowell personified the untamed spirit of Californian new music, his own work brilliant and hopelessly unselfcritical by turns. A man of simple candor, whose appearance of naivete belied a blustering Irish capacity for self-promotion, Cowell was then active in championing and publishing the music of Charles Ives, Carl Ruggles, Adolph Weiss, Wallingford Reigger, Dane Rudhyar, Ruth

Crawford, and many others. His tastes were nothing if not wide-ranging, but he had a temperamental aversion to the currently fashionable Francophile musical language of the East Coast—of Copland and his Paris-trained colleagues—and much of his work as propagandist centered on homegrown composers. In contrast, Partch in person was more reserved and hesitant, his work more careful, and his spirit less gregarious and generous to the work of others. His artistic stance was squarely in line with Cowell's interests, however; and although the two men "got along well at first,"[26] and although courteous and prepared to a limited extent to be supportive, Cowell showed no serious interest in the work of his young colleague.

Cowell's longer-term lack of support for Partch's music is not easy to explain. If it was based primarily on musical grounds, it may be that Cowell found Partch's techniques and artistic outlook too insular, at too great a distance from the concerns of the more "experimental" musical languages of the composers he was promoting. Although Partch's voice and Viola works are technically unprecedented, they lack several characteristics of musical modernism which to Cowell himself were as natural as breathing. When he did eventually hear the Li Po settings, Cowell was unmoved—"he didn't like any of my early work," Partch remarked.[27] It seems just as likely that Cowell's attitude was determined by some quirk or incompatibility of personality about which we have no substantial knowledge.

One of the things the two men discussed was Cowell's book *New Musical Resources,* a short theoretical treatise substantially completed a decade earlier but which had been published only the previous year, 1930. Of most immediate interest to Partch, as we have seen, was Cowell's discussion of undertones, which seemed to legitimize his own idea (not yet included in his *Exposition of Monophony*) that interval sequences that formed the inversion of those in the overtone series could be built downward from the root of a chord, rather than upward. The result would be what Partch later termed a Utonality: a hexadic chord analogous to the first six odd-number elements of the undertone (or subharmonic) series. From this autumn onward we begin to encounter unequivocal uses of Utonalities in his compositions. Shortly after meeting Cowell, Partch set to work revising the *Exposition of Monophony* to include the idea of undertones (as well as overtones) "as the source of intervals." A new third draft was completed on October 2, 1931, while he was living at 175 Sixth Street in San Francisco.

Cowell's most immediate act of practical help was in introducing Partch to the singer Rudolphine Radil, with a view to their presenting a concert of

Partch's work for the New Music Society. Radil had considerable experience performing the "ultra-modern" music of the time. She had performed Schoenberg's *Pierrot Lunaire* for the New Music Society a year earlier, and must have discussed with Partch the similarities and differences between Schoenberg's Sprechgesang and Partch's own concept of the intoning voice.[28] The experience and attitudes of a performer like Radil brought Partch in touch with musical modernism, allowing him the better to clarify his own position with regard to it. Their rehearsals of Partch's own songs proved to be "a revelation; I learned that the voice is extraordinarily susceptible to alteration provided that the ear hears."[29] He taught her by rote, playing the voice part on the Adapted Viola. This method may well have been a consequence of her inability to read his notation, but was also necessitated by his insistence on accuracy in realizing the very difficult voice parts of the settings.

The notation that Partch seems to have been using during this period in San Francisco was still rather experimental. The manuscripts were written on blank paper, using the ratios themselves to denote the pitches, with no staff or graphic component of any sort other than the occasional use of upward or downward inflection marks above syllables in the text that were intoned to a glide of two or more pitches.[30] The immediate visual impression it makes is not inelegant, but is somehow curiously unmusical. As Partch himself later pointed out, this seems due largely to the absence of graphic signification of pitch movement, which facilitates reading, and which seems so intimately connected with our whole perception of pitch and so intractably embodied in the language with which we describe it. A further disadvantage of this ratio notation is that it does not allow for much sophistication in notating subtleties of rhythmic articulation, nor indeed of even moderately complex rhythmic configurations.

By the middle of November 1931 Partch and Radil were ready to give private hearings of the songs, in preparation for the New Music Society concert which had been arranged for February. They performed on several occasions in private homes and studios of musician friends of Radil's in Oakland and San Francisco, inviting critics to attend. These gatherings provided Partch's entrée to the musical circles in the city, and the scattering of reviews that appeared were greatly encouraging. A reviewer from the *Oakland Tribune* noted of the songs—much to Partch's amusement—that "the effect when heard is eerie, exotic and unmodern";[31] while Redfern Mason, influential critic of the *San Francisco Examiner,* was quite swept away by the attempt of this "young San Franciscan . . . to rationalize, so to speak, the musicality of speech."[32] These reactions, and the stimulus of working directly with a singer, acted as a spur to further composition, and through the turn of the year Partch worked on additional Li Po settings. The thread binding together the rather diffuse group of new settings was the impulse not so much to develop new compositional techniques as to explore the range of mood and expression possible within the voice and Viola medium, probably with an eye to building repertory for a diverse and interesting concert program. With this in mind he began transcribing the spoken inflections of voices other than his own. Those of Radil herself became the basis for a setting of a quite different literary source, "The Potion Scene" from Shakespeare's *Romeo and Juliet;* and Cantor Reuben Rinder of the Congregation Emanu-El in San Francisco, whom Partch approached in hopes of getting a "truly Hebraic interpretation," recited for him Psalm 23, "The Lord Is My Shepherd." This last formed a pair with his setting of Psalm 137, "By the Rivers of Babylon," written in August in Santa Rosa.

Throughout these months he was leading a hand-to-mouth existence. When he arrived in San Francisco with no job, the city was already in the grip of economic recession: he was unable to find even a proofreading job. In consequence he had almost no money, and was dependent much of the time on charity. He took the only available recourse and "shuffled forward along some sidewalk near Howard Street in San Francisco with other derelicts—four abreast and sometimes several blocks long—in the 'bread line.'"[33] He resolved to devote his energies fully to his creative work, and to scrape by as best he could. By the new year his financial problems had become critical, and somewhat in desperation he wrote on January 13 to Elizabeth Sprague Coolidge, well known in California as an active and influential patron of the arts, asking for support: "In less than a week I will be homeless and a burden to organized charity unless someone sees and appreciates. I have been homeless before, and have not complained—but then I was not burned with a consuming purpose." She refused his request for money, but, as would remain the case throughout his life, close friends and associates helped him. Rudolphine Radil "hocked her gold jewelry so that I could pay my rent."[34] He remained determined nonetheless to pursue his music and to get "into the breadline when I couldn't make ten dollars giving a demonstration of my philosophies before a women's club."[35]

On the evening of Tuesday, February 9, 1932, the first public performance of Partch's work was given for Cowell's New Music Society at the Rudolph Schaeffer Studio at 136 Anne Street in San Francisco. It began with a demonstration by Partch of the Adapted Viola—still called the Monophone—and of his system of intonation, which was reported to "produce accurately 55 tones to the octave." The works performed, billed as "Tone Declamations," were two passages from Shakespeare—"Dialogue from *The Merchant of Venice*" (a setting of the dialogue of Lorenzo and Jessica, which he subsequently destroyed), and "Potion Scene from *Romeo and Juliet*"; seven of the then ten Li Po settings; and the *Two Psalms*. The responses of both the audience and the critics were favorable; the *Chronicle* and the *San Francisco News* carried reviews the following day. The reviewers were keen to record Partch's premise that, as Alexander Fried in the *Chronicle* put it, "insofar as music departs from the intonations and rhythms of speech it becomes artificial."[36] Marjory M. Fisher, in the *San Francisco News,* demurred that "Partch's ideas are more interesting than his exposition was convincing," adding—a point that had not gone unnoticed by others—that "many of the declamations which he and Miss Radil originated to expound his theories presented a distortion of words so great as to deny his thesis."[37] Whatever their reservations, Partch was encouraged by the critical response and was not shy about approaching critics to help further his activities. Marjory Fisher read the manuscript of the *Exposition of Monophony,* and Partch was beginning to use the names of critics who had heard earlier performances, among them Marie Hicks Davidson and Redfern Mason.

Partch and Radil presented two further public concerts. The next, in Oakland on February 29, drew puzzled critical response, one reviewer noting that although the music "is interesting always, hypnotic in its power and capable of expressing great subtlety," still "at present the idiom seems strange and unnatural."[38] The reviewer from the *Oakland Tribune* "blandly (and perhaps smugly)" confessed that for him "Monophony . . . offers little of musical value."[39] Their last public concert together was in San Francisco on April 14.

Although these concerts mark the inception of Partch's public career as a composer, and although the critical response was nonpartisan and encouraging, far from feeling the exultation of professional arrival he maintained a kind of sullen detachment. He complained mournfully to a reviewer a few years later that even in the "city of his adoption," and even though invitations had been sent out to members of the New Music Society for the February 9 concert, "in the audience was to be found not one of the club's invited members."[40] It seems a portent of what was to come.[41]

Toward the end of April, with no further recitals in prospect nor any solution to his economic survival, Partch, clutching at straws, resolved to try his luck in southern California. San Francisco, he noted a few years later, was where "I . . . began my apostasy and my zealousy"; now he was being "driven out of this great city by two hungers: hunger for bodily sustenance and hunger for understanding."[42]

Migrating down the coast, he broke his flight first in Santa Barbara to look up Mildred Couper, a composer then in her mid-forties, who had written some quarter-tone music for two pianos: her *Xanadu,* written as incidental music for Eugene O'Neill's *Marco Millions,* was to be performed at a New Music Society concert in San Francisco the following month.[43] They discussed the problem of a keyboard suitable for microtonal pitch systems. Couper's solution in *Xanadu* had been to tune the two pianos a quarter tone apart. Although her advocacy of quarter tones was anathema to Partch—quarter tones, as divisions of equal-tempered semitones, uphold the very intonational paradigm that his just intonation system was attempting to contravene—she showed no corresponding aversion to his ideas. Encouraged by the meeting he began to design a keyboard layout, rather like a typewriter keyboard, that could accommodate his just intonation scale.

By early May he was in Los Angeles, where his initial contact seems to have been the pianist Richard Buhlig;[44] at the beginning of the month Partch was sending and receiving mail from Buhlig's studio at 102 S. Carondelet. Buhlig set about to introduce him to his circle, and to arrange for him to give small-scale demonstrations for interested parties. The earliest of these, for a group of Buhlig's Los Angeles musician friends, took place in Eagle Rock at the home of the music critic Bertha McCord Knisely. She published an extended and appreciative review in the Los Angeles weekly *Saturday Night* on May 14.

Partch's encounter with Bertha Knisely this spring was to prove crucial to his immediate future. In fact their relationship, in some respects, would set the pattern for similar attachments throughout his life. She was a few years older and was recently widowed, but was nonetheless comfortably off, with a secure position as music reviewer and editor for *Saturday Night.*[45] Moreover, she had a formal music education, which he lacked, and a degree in music: she had studied piano in Berlin, New York, and, with Richard Buhlig, in Los Angeles.[46] Yet she was genuinely and vocally enthusiastic about his revolutionary ideas. She took him under her wing, inasmuch as he would allow it, encouraging him to accompany her on her interview assignments with concert personalities visiting the city,[47] and introducing him to those of her professional friends likely to be sympathetic to his work.

The hospitality readily offered by musicians like Buhlig and Knisely eased Partch's way to a considerable extent, but Los Angeles provided no obvious solution to the immediate problem of earning a living. He took occasional jobs "hoeing weeds and mowing lawns for suburbanites," and was prepared—when nothing better presented itself—"to shovel gravel to earn a few dollars."[48] He recalled poignantly a few years later "the five days in 1932 I lay on Imperial Beach [near the Mexican border in San Diego] without food—because I was determined to have surcease from continual begging for my music."[49] His lack of a stable position in Los Angeles puzzled some people and worried a few others. One interviewer concluded almost apologetically that "because he doesn't want to accept the judgement of one or two cities and because of a restless disposition, he is journeying around the country looking for opportunities to present his music."[50] The spring and summer were very unsettled as he stayed with anyone who was prepared to take him in. His correspondence of these months gives quite a range of addresses: in mid-June that of a friend in Covina, northeast of the city; in mid-July that of his sister, now Mrs. Irene Clabaugh, at 4924 Hub Street. He remained fond of her, and of his brother, even though their conservative lifestyles became increasingly hard to reconcile with his more bohemian, rootless existence.

Despite all his wandering he was still able to work. In August he drifted north to the San Joaquin Valley, bringing the Adapted Viola with him, and on August 24 in Visalia he completed the fourth draft of the *Exposition of Monophony*, which contained a new "history of intervals," and incorporated, in slightly revised form, his short exposition on "The Art of Song." A few days later he completed the charts of the new keyboard design that had been on his mind since April. Despite the productivity of these months, he described the time three years later as one of "undirected wandering," which, from a professional standpoint, was true; but clearly he had already acquired the ability of the vagabond poet not to let circumstance affect the quality of his work—indeed, to use his unease with his surroundings as a way of enclosing himself in his work with added intensity and determination. "September 21, the date of my escorted exit from the San Luis Obispo jail, where I was an overnight guest"—he had probably been arrested for vagrancy—"marked my entrance into respectability after a spring and summer of roaming."[51]

The respectable society he now entered was that of Pasadena, an affluent city in the foothills of the Sierra Madre mountains, about nine miles from central Los Angeles. He was drawn to the city to be close to the singer Calista Rogers, to whom Bertha Knisely had introduced him, and who had agreed to perform his songs in the new season. Rogers was one of the best-known figures in the Pasadena musical world. She owned a beautiful brown-shingle Swiss-chalet-style home at 511 South Marengo Avenue, where she held an informal recital

series, musical soirees that presented performances by Rogers and local musicians of a wide range of songs, chamber and piano music. She was sympathetic
to contemporary music, and her distinctive voice—described by one of her
accompanists as "round and clear but not naturally 'expressive' or 'warm,'
almost without vibrato and with accurate pitch control"[52]—must have struck
Partch as a promising vehicle for his songs.

᛭ By the end of October 1932 Partch was preparing materials for a grant
application to the Guggenheim Foundation in New York, one of the few such
organizations at the time which supported the creative arts. The application, in
the first instance, was for funds to help him continue his work "in a multiple-
tone music system based on the one natural source of tone relationships, the
overtone series, the writing of a review of the historical uses of those relationships, and the adaptation of a keyboard to the theories." He confessed to the
foundation that he had no present occupation "aside from the projects listed
within, which are not remunerative." He proposed, if awarded the fellowship,
to travel, first to study "over a period of six months, at the Tokyo Academy of
Music and at one or all of the following three Chinese institutions: Yenching
and Peking Universities, Peiping: Shanghai University, Shanghai"; then on to
Europe, to study at the "Bibliotheque Nationale and at the Library of the
Conservatory of Music in Paris (I am capable of doing research in French), and
at the British Museum, London." He submitted with his application a copy of
the Ratio Keyboard charts completed a month earlier, explaining that he was
then "attempting to interest the California Institute of Technology at Pasadena
and others in constructing the Ratio Keyboard," adding rather optimistically
that "it is quite possible the keyboard may be completed before the beginning
of a fellowship incumbency." Although the application was unsuccessful, the
prospect of travel sustained him through the turn of the year.[53]

Between November and January, prompted by his rehearsals with Calista
Rogers, he revised some of his earlier compositions. First he reworked the
ending of "The Potion Scene," then—in a new notation system he had devised—three of the settings written in New Orleans. The new notation system
involved a new staff consisting not of the conventional five lines but of five pairs
of lines with spaces separating them, amounting to "an eighteen-line staff—
five pairs of lines visible, the other [four pairs] assumed," with "a line or space
for each of thirty-nine ratios."[54] The advantage of this new notation was that it
restored the graphic component that had been absent from the earlier ratio
manuscripts, and had made them impossible to read without considerable
familiarity with ratios. Even if Calista Rogers, like Rudolphine Radil, had

learned the voice parts by rote and used notation simply as a memory aid, this very graphic quality—an up-and-down visual representation of pitch movement—would have been of considerable help. By mid-November she and Partch were ready to give a private hearing of the songs in her home.[55]

At the same time, probably in the attempt to trigger the interest expressed by the Institute of Technology, Partch busied himself constructing a model of his keyboard design, which he completed on December 28. The model, "constructed of enameled thread spools, the ends filled with plastic wood and corrugated board varnished,"[56] was guaranteed to make some of the musicians in Rogers's circle blush: but it already indicated the fastidious attention to detail Partch was prepared to pay in order to make his wilder visions a reality.

Partch and Rogers gave their first public concert in the recital series at her home on February 17, 1933, to an audience of some sixty people. As he had done in his concerts in the San Francisco area the previous year, Partch began the presentation with a talk on Monophony and a demonstration of the Adapted Viola. Photographs of the charts he used in this and subsequent presentations are still extant. They display the overtone series through the sixteenth partial and the relation of the diatonic scale to the intervals of the series; "The Progress of Consonance"; Partch's new notation system (the wide staff with five pairs of lines); and a Keyboard Analysis chart showing his Otonalities and Utonalities and a "color analogy" system. He also demonstrated scales on the Viola, including an East Indian scale and two ancient Greek kithara scales according to Ptolemy. The works performed were the *Two Psalms,* a group of seven Li Po settings, "The Potion Scene," and a second group of six Li Po settings. In her review in *Saturday Night,* Bertha Knisely was effusive in her praise and called Partch "a young genius."[57] The concert attracted several other notices and previews. While Partch's presentations in San Francisco had met with a sober critical response, the Pasadena performance stretched the credulity of some reviewers to the limits. One of the preview notices began: "Hollywood has consulted numerologists for successful names and other pieces of luck, but it has remained for a serious student of music to consult the science of numbers for inspiration in music."[58] Partch admitted years later that at this period he actively sought out such "news hounds": "Very indirectly, they helped. That is to say, some people decided that I ought to be given the job of cutting the lawn around the Campfire Girls' Clubhouse for four dollars a week."[59]

Throughout the spring months Partch and Calista Rogers performed repeatedly in and around Los Angeles, including, by demand, a repeat performance at her home in Pasadena on April 28. In the notices for their concerts the descrip-

Partch in 1933 with the Monophone (soon to be renamed the Adapted Viola) and the Ratio Keyboard model. The score of the Li Po songs is on his lap. Behind him is one of the charts he used in his presentations with Calista Rogers in southern California. Danlee Mitchell recalls that, on seeing this photograph later in life, Partch remarked of his younger self: "Typical L.A. fag." Unsigned photograph, Harry Partch Estate Archive.

tion of the settings as "tone declamations," as was the case for Partch's San Francisco concerts, disappears, and they are described simply as "songs"; the whole performance was billed as a presentation of "The Spoken Word in Song." Although there was only one new composition in the repertory since the previous year—a setting of Li Po's "A Midnight Farewell"—these labelings were not arbitrary. The distinction is reflective of a reassessment, whether fully conscious or not, of the developments in Partch's compositional activity throughout the period in which he had continued to set Li Po's verse.

Through one of Rogers's friends, an opportunity to earn some money presented itself in February, when the folklorist and performer Eleanor Hague hired Partch to transcribe a number of old Edison cylinder recordings of American Indian songs at the Southwest Museum in Los Angeles.[60] These were mostly field recordings, made by the ethnologist Charles F. Lummis on reservations in the early years of the century. Hague considered Partch well suited for the task, as the museum's bulletin the *Masterkey* noted, "on account of the research which he has carried on in musical intervals smaller . . . than the ordinary diatonic intervals. Indian tunes are replete with such intervals." Straining to catch the precise intervals on the cylinder recordings, with their tiny signal and considerable background noise, must have been demanding work, but "after many repetitions of a part of a record I duplicated its tones on my Viola and notated the result."[61]

His analyses in fact refuted the original premise on which he had been hired. "In analysing the five California Indian melodies," he reported, "I have the feeling that there is a constant striving for very simple intervals. . . . Those places where the voice wavers, slides up or down to a tone, or rises under excitation do not alter that feeling since at no time, I believe, is there a deliberate use and repetition of a more complex interval."[62] His conclusion was that the singers were "aiming at a five-tone scale and sometimes they don't hit the right note."[63]

As interesting to Partch as the melodic aspect of the songs were the rhythms. One of the songs, the "Stick Game Song" of the Hupa Indians of northern California, he analyzed as a thirteen-beat pattern, and eleven-beat patterns occur in his transcription of the Cahuilla "Bird Dance Song." The music, and the "distressingly mournful," haunting qualities of the voices on the old cylinder recordings, moved him deeply. He retained his rough copies of the transcriptions, and his love for the music remained with him for the rest of his life. The "Cancion de los Muchachos" of the Isleta of New Mexico was used in "Cloud-Chamber Music" in 1950; a Cahuilla chant in *The Bewitched;* and he had planned to use the Hupa "Stick Game Song" in his music for the film *The Dreamer That Remains* nearly forty years later (he ultimately did not because the producer and the director "decided I'd written enough music").[64] *The Masterkey* published, in 1934, transcriptions of Spanish California songs made by Eleanor Hague concurrently with Partch's work on the Indian songs, but none of his own transcriptions made it into print.

Despite the affection he retained for Calista Rogers, leaving Pasadena proved to be no hardship. With their concerts and his transcription work coming to an end, he moved into Los Angeles. Two years later, ravaged by guilt about the parasitism of the hobo life he was then living, Partch noted in his journal: "And to what end is this body sustained when it is thwarted in its reason? Women hold a keen sympathy for the physical needs of men, but it is blind instinct. It was this blindness that maddened me in Pasadena. They recognized and guaranteed my body for a time, but, having done so, dropped it into a pit. Its purpose in being was not within their ken."[65]

By the beginning of May 1933 he was living at the Sawyer Apartments at 327 South Hope Street in Los Angeles. By now Bertha Knisely had become his lifeline. Over the course of the year their friendship had deepened and they had become very close, settling into a crepuscular state between affection and love that stopped short of full commitment. The extent of their closeness is apparent from a special delivery letter she sent him on the morning of Tuesday, May 9:

> Thoughts on awaking—5:30 A.M.
> Precious *Music!*
> *Precious* Music!
> *Precious Music!*
> Endlessly, Bertha

"Music" was the nickname she had coined for him. Partch kept her letter for the rest of his life.

Throughout these weeks he was working on a fifth draft of *Exposition of Monophony*, which he completed in his room on South Hope Street on June 8. This draft, which is still extant, was prompted by Knisely's comments on the previous draft, of which the new one was "principally a condensation."[66] The work contains seven chapters, on "The 11 Diatonic Intervals" from both overtones and undertones, with a section on "The Phenomenon of Resolution"; "The 37 Monophonic Intervals" and the "12 tonalities within the one," six Otonalities and six Utonalities; "History of the 37"; a "Classification of Intervals" into four "arbitrary" categories (as already discussed)—"intervals of power," "emotional intervals," "psychic intervals" (which is scored out in the manuscript and "intervals of suspense" inserted), and "intervals of approach"; "Notation and Instruments," illustrated with pictures of the Adapted Viola and the Ratio Keyboard and music examples on his staff of five pairs of lines; "The Spoken Word in Song"; and a brief "Review" of the history of his work to that point.

Whatever the truth of his feelings for Bertha Knisely, during these months a plan was hatched, with her active support and encouragement, for Partch to go to New York. The most likely motivation for this plan would be to make a second attempt to secure Guggenheim Foundation support. In the application he had submitted the previous October six of his eight referees had been Californians, and Partch may well have felt that his application would carry more weight if some well-known East Coast names could be persuaded to speak on his behalf. Knisely set about to establish a fund to help get him to New York, soliciting contributions from friends in the Los Angeles area. On July 3 Partch received an initial check of twenty dollars, probably for a train ticket, and the contributors each pledged five dollars per month for the period July to January.[67] Early in July he headed east.

New York and Europe

Partch's initial impression of New York in the summer of 1933 was not favorable. In *Bitter Music* he recalls "one of my first days in New York. I am walking down Thirty-Fourth Street depressed by many things—the noise, the long dark faces, the commercial cackle, the gluttonous light of the eyes."[1] This may be simply the reaction of a Californian used to a slower pace of life than that of New York's teeming streets, or it may be Partch showing us one of his characteristic sides: the attainment of his goal—in this case, finally reaching the energy and excitement of the great metropolis with its promise of cultural fulfillment and economic reward— provokes a morose resistance, an unwillingness to accept the full measure of his achievement. This ambivalence perhaps explains why he seems merely to have touched base briefly in New York before quitting it for the remaining weeks of the summer.

He did, however, manage to make contact with the first on what would grow to be a long roster of persons of position in the New York musical world. A letter to Partch dated July 12, 1933, records a meeting with someone—the signature on the letter is illegible—at the music publishers G. Schirmer Inc. Thanking Partch for the "remarkable demonstration that you were kind enough to give," the writer of the letter continues: "I trust that you have forgiven me my outburst aroused by your 'Juliet' music. It is not my custom to express dislike so positively, but I should not have done so in that particular case, if the other things you had previously played for me had not so keenly interested and charmed me."[2]

This schizoid response to Partch's performance served as a warning of the unpredictable reaction he was likely to find in the city, and of the cost to his ever-excitable nerves of these encounters. Having tested the waters, he withdrew almost immediately to the comparative calm of New England, and spent the next few weeks visiting contacts in the northeastern states and pursuing his lifelong habit of working on the run.

By early August he had arrived in Gloucester, Massachusetts, where he composed what were to be the final three Li Po settings, "Before the Cask of Wine," "By the Great Wall," and "I Am a Peach Tree." Of these, the first and the last stand out by virtue of their considerable difference in mood from the preceding settings. It is tempting to ascribe the exhilarating high spirits of these two songs to the optimism of Partch's cross-country journey a month earlier— as though this hopefulness, rather than the depression of his arrival, had found its way into his art. "I Am a Peach Tree" is the brashest song of the whole set: in it, the poet reels through a sequence of outrageous, self-assertive images which Partch intersperses with breathless outbursts of rhythmic abandon, the Viola adding mandolin-like pizzicato chords throughout. Although the songs introduce no new technical procedures they are expertly crafted, and the balance of the speech-rhythm delivery of the texts and the metric passages of wordless vocalize seem to prefigure the next period of Partch's work.

With the composition of these three settings Partch seems to have regarded his voice and Viola output as complete, and there is the sense that he felt this whole chapter of his work drawing to a close and new projects beginning to take shape. He inscribed a collective title, *Seventeen Lyrics by Li Po*, into the typescript copy of the new revision of the *Exposition of Monophony* which he mailed to himself care of Bertha Knisely in Los Angeles on August 10. This act seems, too, one of summation, of preserving a record of his work in the face of the new adventures that were to open up for him on the East Coast. Included with the manuscript were "a few pages from the 1928 draft, notarized, pictures of instruments and charts, programs and newspaper clippings, and the only three designs of the Ratio Keyboard." Back in California the envelope containing this little archival collection was to remain unopened for fifty years.

The principal new project on his mind, and the one for which at the end of October he applied for Guggenheim Foundation support, was a setting of W. B. Yeats's translation of Sophocles' *King Oedipus* "on the principle of intrinsic melody and rhythm in spoken words."[3] Many years later he wrote: "I had been drawn to Yeats because of that marvelous experience of seeing eye to eye with him through his writings over a period of years—writings in which he expounded, and hoped for, a union of words and music in which no word shall have an accentuation it could not have in passionate speech."[4] In the Guggenheim application he had submitted the previous year Partch wrote that he had "anticipated for several years the production of a musical spoken drama," but that "the drama that is to be the inspiration for the musical conception I have only tentatively selected."[5] By this autumn, however, his decision was resolute, and he had given the matter a great deal of thought.

> Approximately half the lines will be spoken in improvisation without accompaniment. Choruses, climaxes, and lines that directly concern the fate of Oedipus will be heightened by music and the words spoken to set tones. From the final entrance of Oedipus the music will continue to the end, intensifying the sense of fatality and alleviating the horror of the conclusion. Orchestration is to be light, and probably muted, for viola, cello, bass, and possibly other instruments or duplicates of the three. If the Ratio Keyboard, having all the Monophonic tones within the ordinary piano octave span, is completed in time it might also be used in the orchestration.

His main problem a year earlier had been that the work "must await the adaptation of several other instruments and the training of persons for execution of instrumental and vocal parts."[6] As a modest beginning he had managed to find one further musician who had taken enough of an interest in his work and his theories that he was prepared to adapt his own instrument to Partch's Monophonic system: Yves Chardon, a cellist in the Boston Symphony Orchestra. From Gloucester, Partch traveled north to stay for much of the rest of August with Chardon in Middlebury, Vermont. Partch's attempts to play his Adapted Viola with Chardon playing the cello seem to have sown the seed of composing for a consort of the lower-pitched strings. In his October 1933 Guggenheim application Partch wrote that he was "adapting another cello and a string bass during this present winter": and at the end of the year, in Los Angeles, Bertha Knisely reported in *Saturday Night* that, among other projects, "Partch . . . has worked on the adaptation of a cello and is already engaged in writing [M]onophonic music for three string instruments."[7] This music was presumably intended for Chardon, among others, and was conceived as a way of working up toward the ensemble for *King Oedipus*. The music for three strings remained unfinished, and no manuscript of it has survived.

With autumn approaching, and the November 1 deadline for his Guggenheim application pending, Partch returned to New York, determined to drum up support for the application. In a letter of September 20 he wrote that he was "now in New York to remain indefinitely though I am not located."[8] He stayed at first in the YMCA on 34th Street, and received mail at the West 11th Street apartment of Clara Shanafelt, a friend of Bertha Knisely's. Shanafelt was to remain an important friend and contact for him in New York. She was a painter, a cultured and intellectual woman with radical views on politics and the arts. She also wrote poetry, and the diversity of her talents and the keenness of her intellect contributed to Partch's fondness for her. In her early forties, unmarried, she supplemented the meager income she made from her paintings by teaching art privately.[9]

Partch worked in September on a new set of scores of all the works for voice and Adapted Viola, in yet another new notation system that he had devised the previous month in Gloucester while working on the final group of Li Po settings. He had decided that his existing notation system, the one using the staff of five pairs of lines, was unsatisfactory: its disadvantage was that "the area the eye was obliged to cover defeated the object—easy reading through a completely graphic notation."[10] The new notation was devised in an attempt to correct this deficiency, and used "the ordinary five-line staff, involving the same paper distance as in ordinary notation, . . . with altered note-heads."

At the same time, he was beginning to expend much energy in the attempt to establish himself professionally. The extent to which Partch pursued the attentions of fellow composers, critics, and other persons of influence during the autumn and winter in New York shows that, far from maintaining a splendid isolation, he evidently cared desperately at this time that his work receive the attention of the professional music world.

A good opportunity to immerse himself in that world came thanks to Bertha Knisely, who visited New York in the middle of September, and who persuaded Partch to accompany her to the new music festival at Yaddo, near Saratoga Springs. The Yaddo festival was a showcase for young composers and, like all such festivals, a convenient springboard for fledgling talent. The work at the festival for which Partch felt the greatest sympathy was the First Sonata for solo cello of 1924 by Otto Luening, a young composer with whom Knisely had already put him in touch. On his return to New York, Partch wrote to Luening that he was much in sympathy with the sonata's tendency "toward an individual, unhazardous, linear expression, and away from the complex, and to me more artificial symphony and choral forms." He apologized for the inadequacy of this description, adding that "this feeling of mine always brings a storm on my head when it is expressed."[11] Yet even this early in his career, what we see Partch value in the work of another composer is an implied aesthetic standpoint that he perceived as similar to his own, rather than an objective consideration of the composition's individual merits. In fact, Luening had by 1933 written quite a lot of symphonic and choral music, and whatever he (and Aaron Copland, who submitted the work for the festival) valued in the sonata would have been unlikely to rest on its supposed aesthetic standpoint.

Partch's admiring reference to the sonata's "linear expression" can be seen, in retrospect, to mark the start of a web of confusion between him and Luening, centering on Luening's misunderstanding of Partch's use of the term "Monophony," a confusion that would be shared by others. Luening's sonata is not Monophonic in Partch's sense, not being conceived in just intonation; and yet it is certainly as monophonic—lower case—as some of Partch's voice and Viola songs, and is broadly in sympathy with the aesthetic concept that Partch would later formulate of the One Voice. Although Partch's admiration for the work feels a little overstated, it was probably genuine.

Luening willingly agreed to write a letter of reference in support of Partch's Guggenheim application. Other composers that Partch sought out included Walter Piston and Aaron Copland, who "understood little about my theories and I gathered were not especially interested. But they liked my music."[12] Piston even "said he would try to arrange a demonstration at Harvard." Other referees were Henry Cowell, George Antheil, and Adolph Weiss. Weiss agreed to recommend the application on the basis of Partch's music, feeling, Partch wrote, "that perhaps none of us had really divined the nature of tonal relationships. Perhaps not, I only interpreted them according to my lights."[13]

At Weiss's suggestion Partch took the crucial step of establishing direct contact with Henry Allen Moe, secretary of the Guggenheim Foundation. Following their first meeting at the end of October Partch maintained contact with Moe, whose evident interest in his work must have been highly gratifying. Partch's actual application, when it arrived in November, presented Moe with an unusual problem: how could one evaluate the merits and the feasibility of so unconventional a project? While most of the composers who wrote in support were enthusiastic about the music, the fact that several of them felt unable to comment on Partch's theories—together with the stress on his theoretical work placed by Partch himself in his application materials—left a question mark about that aspect of his proposal. Accordingly, to set Moe's mind at rest, Partch furnished letters of recommendation from acousticians whom Moe judged able to attest to the validity of the acoustical basis of his theories, among them Dayton C. Miller and Frederick A. Saunders. Even this did not settle the matter, as the projected setting of Yeats's *King Oedipus* rested on "the principle of intrinsic melody and rhythm in spoken words." At the end of December Partch wrote to Moe with the names of two persons from the School of Speech at the University of Southern California, who had heard his recitals with Calista Rogers and who would speak in his favor.

The coup de grace, however, came toward the end of January, when a letter arrived from none other than W. B. Yeats himself. In October Partch had written to Yeats in Dublin, detailing his approach to word-setting and asking for permission to set Yeats's translation of *King Oedipus*. Yeats's letter, dated January 6, 1934, granted him "permission with pleasure" to proceed with the projected setting "subject, in case of performance or publication, to the usual business arrangements." At the end of the letter Yeats added: "What you say in your letter is exceedingly interesting and has, so far as I can understand your methods, my complete sympathy."[14] Partch forwarded the letter to Moe on January 27, writing of his plans to visit Yeats in Ireland, should he be awarded the fellowship, and to record "on phonograph records" the interpretations of the Abbey Theatre actors reading "certain of the lines" of the play; these recordings, "notated, would become the basis for a setting," following the procedure he had used the previous spring at the Southwest Museum in transcribing the Native American recordings. Two days later he wrote again to Moe, quoting a long passage from Yeats's appendix to his *Dramatical Poems* of 1907 which, Partch said, "explains the two generative ideas of my musical settings: first, the intrinsic music of spoken words; second, meaningless syllables in pure vocalization."

The energy and determination of Partch's pursuit of Guggenheim support, and his constant efforts at selling himself and his work, seem only to have contributed to the unhappiness and loneliness of this winter in New York. The problem of his livelihood still loomed large, and was exacerbated by situations such as the one he describes in a letter to a friend in California: "In New York I spent some three weeks being psycho-analyzed, interviewed and examined, medically and musically, by Adjustment Service. At the end I was solemnly informed that my life had been wasted because I should have been a book-keeper."[15] A further complicating factor was the winter weather itself, to which he found it hard to adapt. The poet Wallace Stevens remarks that only with "a mind of winter" can one regard the frost and the snow properly,[16] and this kind of mind was not natural to Partch. Yet a measure of his desire to come to terms with his surroundings can be seen in his gesture of sending his friends the Zollers in California some photographs he had taken of New York in wintertime.

Creatively, he was not short of ideas, but the impermanence of his situation, the difficulty of establishing a foothold for himself in the city, and his desire to travel to Europe meant that nothing could be brought to fruition. Added to this were his frustrated attempts to find a vocalist to perform his voice and Viola works. He explained to Moe that the "greatest difficulty is that my vocalist must give an unusual amount of time for rehearsal. After we begin practice it would still be a month or six weeks before we could give a satisfactory demonstration."[17] As a stopgap he gave a few solo performances, both privately and in public. The only prestigious concert appearance was on February 11 for the Town Hall Club on West 43rd Street, to which he invited Moe, among others, explaining that "the exposition will not be technical since only a few in the audience will be musicians, but I will play Greek and Hindu scales not possible in our present musical system and give settings of seven Li Po lyrics and one of a scene from Shakespeare."[18] Three further small-scale lecture-demonstrations followed in May.

In presenting himself to the cognoscenti of New York, the issue of Partch's lack of academic pedigree naturally arose. Insofar as the matter had become a conscious one, Partch seems to have resolved to exploit it as a positive token of self-identity. This is suggested in a satirical story he wrote in the spring, which he called "A Modern Parable I" (a second parable followed four years later). In it, he juxtaposes two nonmomentous encounters: a newsboy "engaged in half-friendly wrangling" with his boss about the lack of business on his corner; and, a stone's throw away, the president of a university addressing a degree ceremony. Partch contrasts the unfettered curiosity of the streetwise boy with the pompous intellects of the professors arraigned on the platform. At the denouement, the newsboy's boss asks him in mock desperation what he should do with that corner if the boy intends to desert it. At the same instant the president grandly asks the assembled gathering of scholars the rhetorical question: "What shall we do with this magnificent learning?" The newsboy's answer—which, by implication, Partch offers also to the president's question—is that he can stick it up his ass. "There was something great and epic and timeless in the marching footfall words . . . It seemed as though the sky had opened, and that a transcendent flood of light enveloped a moving earth."

Early in June he was staying for a few weeks on a farm in East Chatham, New York, belonging to his New York friends the Flanders, to whom he had been introduced by Clara Shanafelt. Donald Flanders was a mathematician and an amateur violinist. He took an interest in Partch's theoretical work, which, as his son Peter remarks, "appealed to the latent Pythagoreanism that most musical mathematicians seem to harbor; and, of course, to the interest in intonation that any violinist must have."[19] The family invited Partch to spend time with them on their farm and to work for his board and room. During that June he earned a reputation among the family as the only person capable of picking a quart of sweet wild strawberries—tiny, and very hard to find—in the course of an afternoon.

The abandoned farm adjoining the Flanders' was owned by Donald Flanders' sister-in-law Roberta Fansler, an art historian and an arts adviser to the Carnegie Corporation of New York. One day early in June she broke the news to Partch that his grant application for his projected studies in Europe had been successful—but not through the expected source, the Guggenheim Foundation, but through the Carnegie Corporation, which had awarded him $1,500 for the purpose. She added: "You have only Moe to thank. He was dismayed because he could do nothing for you."[20]

Official notification was slow to arrive, leaving Partch somewhat paralyzed. Not knowing the conditions of the grant nor when it would be available, he felt unable to make clear plans. He wrote immediately to Bertha Knisely to tell her of the news. She replied exultantly that "it means a great boost to . . . my faith in the ability of a flame like yours to lap up the cold waters of indifference and sweep all before it. I believe in you that much. . . . I do wish you a year of deep joy in your cherished work—and certainly all the other good things that can be interpolated. Do be good to your health—but I must not lapse into a maternal attitude, to bring down ridicule on my head! Anyhow I'm fond of you."[21] He stayed at East Chatham for the next few weeks, and on June 22 wrote to Henry Allen Moe, expressing "a deep and simple gratitude." A letter finally arrived from the Institute of International Education (which was to administer his grant) dated June 26, confirming the award.

He spent the summer months in the city making preparations for departure, and checking out shipping lines. Meanwhile, his musical work continued apace. Toward the end of June *Exposition of Monophony*, which he had been circulating around various contacts, received a "gracious" rejection from the musicologist A. H. Fox-Strangways, who was unconvinced by Partch's arguments in favor of just intonation. Undaunted, Partch bought a guitar and during July and August began work adapting it, trying to "evolve effective frets in Just Intonation."[22] In August another letter arrived from W. B. Yeats, who agreed to see Partch "with pleasure" in Dublin, but doubted that his "unmusical mind would be of much help to you. Your work interests me very much but I have no knowledge of music."[23] With the *King Oedipus* project now seeming destined to become reality, Partch approached several organ builders in the New York area about building a working instrument from a new Ratio Keyboard model that he had built in New York to replace the one he had brought from Pasadena.[24] His inquiries caused "reactions of indifference or downright antagonism." Stoically, he concluded: "Well, my tight little imaginationless businessmen, you have lost your opportunity."[25] He applied for a passport and an English visa, and on September 22 set sail on the British freighter S.S. *Gourko,* bound for London.

After a whole year of marking time in New York, Partch's period of study in Europe was one of fulfillment. He had actively sought out, and had now found, a tradition of English-language poets—of whom Yeats was the most eminent—who shared aspects of his vision of what a music rooted in the spoken word might be, and whose own work suggested ways of enriching that vision. In England, moreover, he was in the midst of an eccentric collection of musicologists and theorists researching intonation and ancient tuning practice, scholars of a breed that barely existed in the United States at that time. During his six months in England, Italy, and Malta, he explored potentially fruitful ways of extending the scope and the technical range of his voice and Viola works, charting the terrain for an art that, starved and buffeted by the events of the remaining years of the decade, would never quite emerge in the way he envisaged it in the dark London autumn of 1934.

He arrived in London around October 8, and immediately headed in the direction of the British Museum, where he had determined to locate himself. Wandering around the side streets near the museum he chanced upon a royal procession. "King George and Queen Mary pass before me. All the men on the street remove their hats. I wear none, which is well, since I am too astonished to remove it."[26] Once the initial charm of disorientation had worn off he fell prey to his habitual feelings of maladjustment. London seemed to him at first not only alien but hostile, and stiffly formal. A few days after his arrival he wrote mournfully to the IIE in New York that "I cannot say that I am happy in London or that I like it. Of course, it is unimportant."[27] He felt insignificant and out of place, and was snubbed by officials at the American University

Union, with whom he was obliged to register, on account of his lack of degrees. However, almost immediately he realized that, for purposes of his work, the city would become the temporary center of his universe.

The biggest initial excitement came from the long hours he spent researching the history of intonation in the British Museum, which provided access to a much more extensive library of works on intonational theory and practice than had been available to him in California. "Day after day, from the reading room's opening hour to its closing hour, I go through ancient and modern volumes on music." As his notebooks piled up he had the sense, as he wrote a year later in mock-heroic tones, of his theoretical treatise becoming a book, finally "emerging into the grandeur of its conception."

He settled down to a routine of work every day at the museum, discovering there a wealth of resources on arcane, tangential aspects of music theory. One of the books he came across was Wilfrid Perrett's *Some Questions of Musical Theory*, of 1926. Perrett's theorizing on just intonation, resulting "from disparate conjectures regarding the famous auloi player Olympos in ancient Greece, the phenomenon of difference tones, and the Greek notation,"[28] was broadly in accord with his own ideas. Moreover, Perrett had actually applied his theories on an "evolved-keyboard harmonium" that he called the Olympion. Partch succeeded in tracing Perrett, finding him to be a "plain-spoken retriever of basic values," and had a chance to play the instrument and to discuss the technicalities of its construction. He also visited the South Kensington Museum and examined the quite different just intonation organ of General Perronet Thompson. He met Ernest Clements, authority on Indian music and theory, and, perhaps best of all, Kathleen Schlesinger, musicologist, theorist, and ancient Greek scholar, who had built several models of ancient Greek instruments. Partch would have encountered only her articles, specifically one in the *Encyclopedia Britannica;* her celebrated book *The Greek Aulos* was still some four years away from publication. All of this was fuel for the parallel activity to his research: investigating organ builders in and around London who might transform his Ratio Keyboard model into a functioning instrument.

After a month in London he was ready for his trip to Ireland to meet Yeats. On November 12 he traveled by bus to Liverpool to take an overnight ferry to Dublin.[29] The boat, scheduled to leave at 10 P.M., was grounded by fog—"a dark blind form crawling up the Mersey"—and the sailing was postponed for twenty-four hours. Partch finally arrived in Ireland on the morning of the fourteenth, feeling wretched from the boredom and anti-climax of the journey,

but telephoned Yeats on arrival and was invited to the poet's home in Rath-
farnham on the outskirts of Dublin.

The meeting had an inauspicious beginning. Nearing seventy, and his health
prone to fluctuation, Yeats welcomed the young composer in a way that seemed
"perfunctory," and Partch sensed "worry and uninterest in his voice."[30] Partch
insisted nonetheless in singing and playing for the poet his setting of "By the
Rivers of Babylon"; and "the flood of comment" that Yeats offered at the end
epitomized "the total comprehension" for which Partch had been searching for
so long. Yeats was overwhelmed, and although admitting that he didn't much
care for Partch's voice, told him that "a play done entirely in this way, with this
wonderful instrument, and with this type of music, might really be sensational."

Partch had brought with him "a musical outline of my proposed setting of
his version of the ancient drama [Oedipus]. There was not yet a single musical
note written down, but the outline presented a rather clear idea of what I
proposed to do."[31] Yeats offered no objections, and gave Partch a copy of his
book of Irish legend plays, talking about what might be done with them. Yeats
"invited some persons to his house to hear me,"[32] and "spoke of a theater and
chanters for an eventual performance."[33] Both Yeats and an Abbey Theatre
actor read parts of *King Oedipus* while Partch "made a rough graph of their
spoken inflections . . . on a blank page."[34]

If Partch showed Yeats some of his manuscripts they must have brought to
Yeats's mind his own essay of more than thirty years earlier, "Speaking to the
Psaltery," in which he describes his practice of intoning his verse to the tones of
a chromatic psaltery built for him by his friend Arnold Dolmetsch.[35] Yeats gave
Partch a letter of introduction to Dolmetsch, and one to the artist Edmund
Dulac, encouraging him to look them up on his return to London. Further, as
Partch reported some weeks later to Henry Allen Moe: "Yeats and T. S. Eliot are
writing experimental plays to be produced at the Mercury Theatre, London,
next spring. There was talk of my writing music for one of them, nothing
definite. . . . I seem to have my work planned for me for a good long time."[36]
Yeats's high regard for Partch's art was quite genuine, and of the seven days
Partch spent in Dublin he was with the poet on four. In a letter to his young
friend Margot Ruddock a few days after Partch's initial visit, Yeats wrote:

> A Californian musician called a few days ago and is coming again tomorrow. He is
> working on the relation between words and music. He has made and is making other
> musical instruments which do not go beyond the range of the speaking voice but
> within that range make a music possible which employs very minute intervals. He

speaks (does not sing or chant) to this instrument. He only introduces melody when he sings vowels without any relation to words. . . . We cannot however use him in our work at present, he is on his way to Spain to perfect his discovery; it is still, I think, immature. He is very young, and very simple.[37]

Yeats offered Partch his blessing, telling him: "You are one of those young men with ideas, the development of which it is impossible to foretell, just as I was thirty years ago." He told Partch he would be in London in April, and hoped to see him and to introduce him to persons in the city.

Yeats was as good as his word, and a few days after his return to London Partch received a note from Edmund Dulac, inviting him to his home in Holland Park "quite informally next Saturday after dinner," and requesting that he bring the Adapted Viola.[38] Partch found Dulac charming, and was impressed by his multifarious talents. They discussed Dulac's settings of Yeats's plays on Irish legends using zither, harp, flute, drum, and gong and with the syllables of the text allotted exact pitches, which Dulac told him had been unsuccessful in performance.

These meetings were an enormous spur to Partch's compositional aspirations, and he resolved to waste no more time in making his plans for a Ratio Keyboard a reality. "I procured some brilliantly colored celluloid and spent three weeks in November and December constructing the new keyboard, using the keys from my NY model."[39] He brought the newly completed model with him on the occasion of another auspicious meeting, this time in Surrey with the musicologist, performer, and instrument builder Arnold Dolmetsch. Of this meeting the two men give quite contradictory accounts. In Partch's version of the meeting, Dolmetsch, talking effusively about ancient writings on music, refers to Marin Mersenne's *Harmonie universelle* and is astonished when Partch asks him which edition of the book he is referring to, stammering out: "For *twenty years* I have been talking about Mersenne, and nobody even knows who I am talking about. And now you—you ask me which edition!"[40] In a letter of December 17 to Yeats, Dolmetsch gives a different impression of the erudition of the young Californian.

Harry Partch came a few days ago—He talked volubly about ratios and true intonation and he showed me a cardboard model of a most complicated keyboard to which someone might make a musical instrument—I cross-examined him—I don't think he had ever met anyone who could do that—He did not come off very well— However, I told him that both music and poetry being *for the ear,* first, I wanted to hear what he could do—He did not bring the kind of viola he uses—He could not (why?) use one of my instruments. He departed rather suddenly saying he would come again—I have heard no more from him—I am willing to give him every chance—I shall listen to his "new art"—(no *new* art is conceivable) and then I shall tell him what I think.[41]

Partch's bringing the Ratio Keyboard model rather than the Adapted Viola—his performance with which may well have impressed Dolmetsch more—was a miscalculation, and probably discouraged him from attempting further contact (although in his account Partch notes that "I leave very happy").

His enquiries to organ builders in London met with "courteous and interested answers," but none considered his offer of a "paltry hundred pounds" sufficient.[42] He made further enquiries to builders in Germany and Italy before settling, in December, on Edwin Malkin of Wimbledon, in London, who gave him an estimate of £70. Malkin had an idea to simplify the mechanical difficulties, and hence to produce a three-octave instrument during the winter months. Although his decision to gamble on Malkin had been taken, Partch exchanged letters with Wilfrid Perrett in the next few weeks about details of organ construction, for although trusting Malkin's professionalism Partch was keen to oversee and to understand the whole process himself.

The keyboard problem now in hand, he put his mind to his book. He felt that "my work at the British Museum can't go on until my notebooks, which have piled up phenomenally, undergo consolidation and organization. Loneliness—darkness at 3 P.M.—I decide I must have sunshine to effect this organization, and I buy a third class ticket to Rapallo—$25—on the longer and cheaper Channel Crossing, Folkstone-Boulogne."[43]

On the way south he passed through Paris, but decided not to stay: "The language barrier was too much, and Paris, in December 1934, was just as dismal as London."[44] He went on to Italy, and arrived in Rapallo on December 22 to "lots of cold sunshine and cold tile floors." Rapallo, for more than a decade, had been a favorite retreat for writers and artists: the steep rise of the hills behind the town kept it from spreading out into an overpopulous tourist resort. Yeats had been there several times during the 1920s, and had described the place in an essay: "Mountains that shelter the bay from all but the south wind, bare brown branches of low vines and of tall trees blurring their outline as though with a soft mist; houses mirrored in an almost motionless sea; a verandahed gable a couple of miles away bringing to mind some Chinese painting. . . . Rapallo's thin line of broken mother-of-pearl along the water's edge."[45] Partch himself described how from the high mountainside he would gaze down upon the harbor of Rapallo and upon Portofino in the distance. "Tall, slim cypresses march upward toward the heights. They are young gods—wistful, melancholy."[46]

Yet the beauty of the place—and its Mediterranean climate—were not its only attractions for him. Living there was the poet Ezra Pound, about whom Yeats must have spoken, even though by this time the two were keeping their distance. Pound, early in his career, had read extensively in the troubadour poets of medieval Provence, and much of his early poetry shows their influence. Pound had developed a manner of half-singing the old texts, and had impressed Yeats as having gotten close "to the right sort of music for poetry . . . it is more definitely music with strongly marked time and yet it is effective speech."[47] The problem was, as Pound himself admitted, he had the vocal "organ of a tree toad,"[48] and although in 1921 he had even written an opera on the fifteenth-century poetry of François Villon, his musical activities as a whole were rather eccentric and were taken with a pinch of salt by many of his friends. Partch met with Pound in January 1935, and found him "a most difficult man."[49] Pound's "difficult" nature, however, lay less in his musical or poetic attitudes than in the fact that by 1935 he was rarely willing to discuss any subject at length except economics or politics, which Partch must have found hard to endure.

From Rapallo on December 24 Partch wrote to Henry Allen Moe in New York that "I have come to the Riviera to organize my research material and to compose." His work at the British Museum, he wrote, "has given me a great deal of assurance . . . my ideas have changed in no way: their presentation has changed." He reported also that "the Riviera is much less expensive than London. I pay about $10.50 per week for full pension and I expect to do even better later."[50] He kept the IIE in New York informed of his travels, above all because of the continual worries he entertained about his monthly grant installments not arriving on time. At the beginning of December he had even wired the office in New York—an expensive operation—to inquire about a small delay in the arrival of his funds. The officials of the American University Union in London, who seemed to regard him as slightly odd, found his wanderings highly amusing. He struck the director of the AUU as "not of the common run of students. He seems highly talented, but as is often the case with those of an artistic bent, his fancy may sometimes lead him to eccentricity, to hypersensitiveness, to put the worst interpretation on things, and even to a regrettable tendency to be a bit exorbitant when he quotes either himself or others."[51]

Partch was still in Rapallo on January 21. "I work on my book, in my room—a front room, in a Dutch woman's *pensione*. I work on my book despite lurking *carabinieri*, my exasperating *biglietto di sojorno*, cold tile floors, cracked houses, cold fires, short change, but at last it becomes unbearable. I buy a third-class ticket for Malta, blood oranges, and the Union Jack—$20."[52] He travelled south via Naples, arriving in Malta after a "thoroughly miserable" crossing on a small Italian passenger ship, its only compensation being an Italian sailor named Mario who let him share his bunk and his blanket during the night. Partch recalled with evident contentment that "[we] snuggle together . . . and sleep warmly and soundly."

He established himself in Valletta and continued work on his book. From there on February 5 he sent the IIE a "Six Months' Report on Projects to be Executed Under Carnegie Grant for the Year 1934–35." In it he described his compositional plans, confidently including the new organ in the projected drama: "*King Oedipus* is scored for four voices (the remainder of the cast speaks, as usual) and four instruments; ptolemy [the name he had chosen for the organ], viola, guitar and double bass. Generally, only one instrument is used at a time, and qualities are allotted to characters. . . . In addition to *King Oedipus* I expect to set to music four chapters from the *Song of Solomon* and a Sapphic trilogy (fragments of poems translated by Arthur Weigall) on the same principles, and for ptolemy and guitar accompaniment." By this time he had changed the title of his book to *Monophony Is Expounded*.

How long Partch had planned to stay in Malta is not clear. A letter arrived from Bertha Knisely, who unexpectedly—or, he felt, nonchalantly—had "crossed the broad Atlantic" with a new husband, "and is now in a tiny fishing village near Gibraltar. It is too late now, being utterly unwarned, to see her on my meager funds."[53]

Bertha Knisely's marriage to Harold Driscoll marked the turning point in what had become an uneasy relationship with Partch, and her apparent disinclination to let him know of her travel plans until it was too late may perhaps be taken as a sign of this. Her visit to him in New York sixteen months before seems to have brought about some sort of crisis; Partch admitted to a mutual friend when she left that he missed her "dreadfully."[54] There is even some evidence that the question of marriage had arisen between them, and if so it was almost certainly Partch, and not Bertha, who felt unable to make the commitment. Asked about this by a friend near the end of his life, Partch replied calmly that he had simply never been "tempted . . . by any emotional relationship that is going to hamper me in what I believe I must do."[55] Toward the end of February he returned via Southampton to London. "I see the grandeur of the Sierra Nevada, on the southern Spanish coast, and the nearness of my friends— on the Mediterranean shore so few miles away!"

His return to London this time was rather pleasant, and he found lodgings in one of the streets near the British Museum. Throughout March he did some final research for his book, though by now it was clear to him that there was "no prospect of getting it into presentable typewritten form" before his year was up. The organ, the Ptolemy, was now completed, and he worked for two weeks tuning the reeds. It had "forty-three tones to the octave over a three-octave extent, and 268 rainbow-colored keys in a practical analogy with tones."[56] In terms of intonation, the results were everything he had hoped for, "but its mechanical workings—the ideas that made its construction cheap—are faulty. The action is extremely uneven. . . . I cling to the hope that adjustments can later be made, and I find that it will cost only $40 to ship it direct to Los Angeles." He invited a few people around to hear it, including Edmund Dulac, who graciously declined due to pressure of work;[57] and he wrote a short article on it, "A New Instrument," which was published in *Musical Opinion* in June. The Ptolemy was shipped to Los Angeles via the Panama Canal.

Partch's greatest hope had been to meet Yeats again in London in the spring, but owing to Yeats's ill health and convalescence his trip to England was postponed. Yeats wrote that he regretted not seeing him again, adding: "I return your biographical essay which I found exceedingly interesting. You have a narrative gift and a remarkable power of explaining yourself."[58] It is frustrating to record that we have no idea what this "biographical essay" was; perhaps an (autobiographical?) product of his sojourn in Italy or Malta, it was subsequently destroyed. Nonetheless, Yeats's praise for Partch's skills as a writer can be seen to have influenced the direction of Partch's work in the next few years.

With his money almost gone he made preparations to return to the United States. The person he was most determined to see again before his departure was the "gracious and sympathetic" Kathleen Schlesinger. On "one of those much-fictioned London days, gray fog in the shadows, silver in the light," he telephoned her, explaining he had very little time left in London, and inviting himself to tea that same afternoon.[59] What he most wanted to see was her kithara, an instrument inspired by a depiction of a Greek instrument on a vase in the British Museum, which Schlesinger had had built by a local handyman during World War I, using the wood from an orange box. Partch, characteristically, was impressed that her investigation of the ancient Greek harmoniai had been practical as well as theoretical. Her speculations regarding ratio tunings encompassed intervals analogous to the thirteenth partial for some of the Greek modes, and these tunings were embodied in her collection of flutes and auloi. Partch was unable to inspect the wind instruments fully in his brief visit, but she left him alone to examine the kithara and was delighted by the sketches he made of a design for one of his own. A few days after the meeting she sent him a touching note telling him: "You are a worker after my own heart, and I wish you every possible success."[60]

Partch's farewell to polite London society came on the evening of March 26. At a party he met George Russell, better known as the poet A.E. and a friend of Yeats, who read some of his own poetry. When Partch told him he had been working with Yeats on *King Oedipus,* Russell told him dismissively that Yeats was unmusical and could not tell one tone from another. Partch, "distraught by so many things—my leaving, my mental confusion, my momentary frustration in my work, and . . . tongue-tied by the smart sayings of the salon people around me,"[61] was unable to muster a coherent objection. The riposte that failed to come to his lips is one he would always use to counter this often-voiced accusation: that "the inability to carry a tune is more like hypersensitivity to tone. Such a person hears all the tones in the gamut, instead of the seven or eight or twelve our musical fathers have insisted must be our limit. In answer to such critics I like to quote Yeats's own words: 'I hear with older ears than the musician.'"[62]

The following day he departed for Cornwall and set sail for the United States, "the only passenger on a freighter loaded with china clay, bound for Portland, Maine. . . . I say goodbye to ginger beer, yellow primroses, general civility, unfailing courtesy from the powers that be. I do not want to go."[63]

Western States

"My return was to a jobless America, and I took my blankets out under the stars beside the American River (the river of gold!), carried my notebook, kept a journal, and made sketches."[1] The late spring of 1935 marked the beginning of the first of several periods of hobo travels, of "living in jungles and skidrow rooming houses, working on the ranches of the three Pacific coast states."[2] This existence would come to an end only in 1943, although "there were periods when I had jobs; and so it wasn't a continuous thing."[3]

Shored against the personal chaos of this way of life—the "more or less constant hunger, loss of sleep, filth, and a good deal of petty apprehension and danger"[4]—are two substantial creative works, which come at either end of the eight-year period: an "occasional diary" of "eight months spent in transient shelters and camps, hobo jungles, basement rooms, and on the open road," which became the journal *Bitter Music* (1935–36); and a "musical account of a transcontinental hobo trip," *U.S. Highball* (1943). Both works draw directly on

Partch's own experiences as a vagrant: yet this very directness should not blind us to the fact that both attained their final form years after the lived episodes from which they spring. It is hard to disentangle the emotional actuality of Partch's hobo existence from his artistic recreations of it, as indeed from his much later defiant and yet sentimental recollections of this period: for at no other time do his life and his art seem to attain a more authentic interfusion.

On his return to the United States early in April 1935 Partch made his way first to New York, and presented himself at the offices of the Institute of International Education. He was shunted from one desk to another in the search for someone who could locate the six months' report he had sent from Malta. The officials proved true to his image of them, meekly admitting they hadn't understood his report nor had they made any effort to show it to someone who might—an admission that, while leaving him feeling "hollow," gave him the ammunition that he would later use to pre-empt their demand in October that he submit a further report.[5] Behind his back they were dismissive and cynical about his work, one official at the Carnegie Corporation writing that, in the photograph Partch had sent them, "not only does 'The Ptolemy' resemble an adding machine, but it seems to be a combination of a typewriter, checkerboard, Mah Jong and chocolate fudge."[6]

The Ptolemy prompted his immediate plans to return to southern California, as he wanted to be there himself to clear it through customs in Los Angeles and to arrange for storage. After "seven humorless days" hitchhiking from New York he reached Indianapolis, where he bought a bus ticket for the remainder of the journey. He arrived in Los Angeles with only $15 remaining from his Carnegie grant but, by dint of perseverance, managed to persuade the customs officials to waive the duty charges on the Ptolemy. Mildred Couper, whom Partch nominated the instrument's "godmother," agreed to pay for its transportation from the docks to Santa Barbara, and to store it there indefinitely.

Los Angeles, "the one city that really encouraged me,"[7] was different now in one crucial respect: Bertha Knisely, the principal source of that encouragement, was still out of the country, and remained so for some time. Partch somewhat cautiously sounded out his former supporters, finding the response "various" but on the whole "not cordial." In truth, he himself probably felt little desire to re-enter the artistic circles in southern California in which he had moved during 1932–33; but an alternative source of support seemed further away than ever. He headed north and spent most of May with his friends the Zollers in Santa Rosa. He found that his "beloved Santa Rosa prune orchard, of bygone dreams, is all but uprooted." Nonetheless, the Zollers' home offered him the stability to get on with writing letters in an attempt to further his work. On May 23, on "a small fruit ranch near Santa Rosa: ten acres of prunes with a beautiful creek running through it and teeming with polywogs," he wrote to Roberta Fansler of the Carnegie Corporation in connection with the rather optimistic request he had submitted to the IIE that his grant be renewed for a further year so he could continue his work, especially in composition. He assured her: "I am now expecting to remain in California—I expect very little more expense with my instruments, so that I could live comfortably on the amount I am asking."

The Zollers were, as ever, "very kind," yet Partch was wary of imposing. His temper, exacerbated by the strain of living from week to week without definite plans, flared up one day in a row with Buddy Zoller and he made a sudden exit. The rupture was not permanent—Partch's "terribly retentive memory" for any slight or insult notwithstanding—and in December Zoller wrote to apologize "for a lot of the things that I did and said to you."[8] However, it provides a glimpse of Partch's lifelong tendency in times of stress to push even his staunchest ally beyond the breaking point. What sparked the quarrel is not known; but Partch's covert intention, having heaped on his young friend what Zoller called "all that palaver about your being of no importance," was surely the calculated one of decrying his own worth to provoke a conciliatory reaffirmation of friendship and loyalty. At times the technique worked: at others, as now, it failed.

Partch now felt that he had to make a choice. It would be conceivable to return to Los Angeles "and resume begging under the apology of my music," but—as he recalled at the end of his life, with a gritty defiance that was perhaps less evident at the time—"I just was not going to be a sycophant for those wealthy people. I could have been; I had enough youth and perhaps enough integrity and charm . . . to have done it, and gotten away with it: but it sickened me."[9] The alternative was, "with a whoop and a holler," to take to the road. The previous month, passing through Indianapolis on his way west, he had spoken with some youths in a transient bureau who had told him of their existence riding freight trains and living in a transient shelter, a new institution for homeless men that had been established under the New Deal while he was in Europe. Vagrancy now seemed to have the ghost of government approval, a necessary evil while the Depression lasted. That way of life was, after all, not new to him; and although still mindful of the hunger and jail experience of his wanderings three summers earlier, his mind was made up. Eighteen months later he explained candidly to Henry Allen Moe that, upon his return from Europe, "the one person who had the desire and power to assist me in California [Bertha Knisely] had left the country. I was tired of begging for myself and sought the relief and surcease of wandering about as a bum."[10]

We must beware of imparting too teleological a reading to the beginnings of what Partch euphemistically called his "gypsy existence"—of retracing the steps that led to his "sudden descent into hobo jungles" only to show how much of the path he had paved himself. He had, he always claimed, no other recourse. And yet, the "glow of attractiveness" that the experience would come to hold for him in retrospect he may have glimpsed in advance, beckoning and compelling.[11]

On June 11, just prior to his departure from Santa Rosa, he began to keep a journal. *Bitter Music* directly confronts the alienation of his hobo existence, the anguish of living always at the rim of his nerves. The act of diary-keeping, through the first eight months of his wanderings in California, Oregon, and Washington, thus partly served a therapeutic function; it provided a retreat from, and a means of transcending, the depressing sense of redundancy that he (and many American artists, in painful isolation from one another) felt increasingly at this time. "Certain extremes of feeling were peculiarly characteristic of those times of economic depression, due in part to the continuing endeavours of many of us to cling to hope, to be something virtually impossible."[12] The resulting journal, with drawings and notations of fragments of speech from the voices of his fellow itinerants, was intended not merely as a document but as aspiring to the status of a work of art—and not a musical composition but a literary work of a hybrid nature, "an excursion into an art form as old as history."[13]

Any assessment of *Bitter Music*—in relation to Partch's work as a whole, or in terms of the picture it draws of the lives of vagrants in the Depression and Partch's relationship to them—must take into account the fact that he destroyed the manuscript of the journal sometime around 1950, thereby registering his dissatisfaction with it. We owe its continued existence to his friend Lauriston Marshall, who had borrowed a collection of Partch's manuscripts, including *Bitter Music,* to have them put on microfilm for archival purposes. Partch's correspondence of the time shows that *Bitter Music* was not a casualty of one of his occasional black moods of self-criticism, but that its destruction was quite premeditated; in February 1950 he wrote to Marshall asking him to return the manuscript so he could have the satisfaction of destroying it himself. It is not clear if he knew at the time that the journal had been put on microfilm—as distinct from his music manuscripts, the copying of which was the ostensible purpose of Marshall's efforts.[14]

Partch never offered a satisfactory explanation of his decision, saying only that the journal had outlived its usefulness. It had given him, he wrote, a "faintly delineated canvas" for the compositions of 1941–43;[15] yet this seems unconvincing, as of these works only *The Letter* bears any direct relationship to *Bitter Music*. Partch included the journal in his list of works until 1950, in which context it seems somewhat anomalous: the speech transcriptions are given for voices and piano in conventional notation with no trace of the microtonal pitch usages that had characterized his music of 1930–33. But this fact in itself scarcely seems sufficient reason for him to have destroyed it. It may, perhaps, have outlived its usefulness not so much as art but as autobiography: fifteen years on he no longer felt close to the self described in its pages.

Bitter Music treats explicitly and unashamedly all of the facets of Partch's hobo existence. Nowhere does he shy away from the sordid or degrading aspects of that life. The main subjects that weave in and out of the text are those basic to human survival, food and shelter; to these must be added a third, sex. For, as Partch announces unequivocally: "There is a strange alliteration in the three principal desires of bums. Food and flops are the most important, but they get the least attention in conversations."[16] Humor, in fact, is the saving grace of the journal and, one suspects, the means by which Partch himself managed to avoid the morbid inwardness and pessimism that are characteristic of the vagrant condition. It turns on their head what threaten to become maudlin or acrid lines of thought—when, for example, with just a shade of self-mockery, he quotes this description of an artist friend: "He is an artist of unusual ideas, he gets financial backing from many patronesses, and he is best hung of any man I ever saw. Considering the constitution of our society I feel that an artist might as well give up who isn't blessed either with a substantial dependable income or a substantial dependable ring dang doo."[17]

The sex talk among the hobos, and their constant urges for sexual gratification, is juxtaposed with the Christian symbolism that is laced through the journal. In *Bitter Music* the evangelical ministry of lay preachers and the refuge provided by Salvation Army hostels represent the world outside, the ordered Christian society from which the hobos have escaped, and the encounter with that world provokes in them a range of emotions from outright hostility to shame and guilt. In one passage Partch provides this autoerotic description of his own naked body in the darkness under an oak tree in Ojai, where he is resting for the night, and juxtaposes it with his recollections of the words of a

Filipino preacher who had given him a lift out of Santa Barbara the previous day, extolling the primacy of the spirit over the flesh. This snatch of Christian rhetoric is seen as an annoying intrusion in a context of onanistic contentment.

> Last night I laid my bag on the dry leaves under a pepper tree in Ojai Valley. The berries are red and dry now, and sweet to taste. Tonight I am camping under a live oak tree with a heavy roof of leaves.
>
> I take off all my clothes, as I always do before crawling in, and gaze down at a body pale in the blackness. It is beautiful.
>
> My hands stroke its belly, and I am very happy this November night looking up into the inky O-high oak.
>
> *. . . I don't want your body. Jesus doesn't want it . . .*
>
> But I do, and I think it is beautiful.[18]

The affairs and relationships among the hobos, and the convenient round of casual homosexual encounters, figure prominently in his descriptions of them. In June, in the San Joaquin Delta, he writes of a new friend he had met in a transients' shelter in Stockton: "What chance has a refined and sensitive bum like Pablo really to possess a woman worthy of him? About as much chance as that such a woman will move in his orbit. If the homosexuality in prisons, navies, and in any other circumstances which segregate men is similar to such tendencies as I have seen in this camp it is mostly pure lust. Few of these men desire tender affection. A female sheep would often prove satisfactory."[19] Partch's descriptions of his own encounters, on the other hand, make it clear that "tender affection" was exactly what he himself was starved of. In December he writes:

> Night.
>
> Four black walls—I don't like them after all the lacy heavens that I have slept under so much before this.
>
> Four black walls surround a month that is marked by turmoil.
>
> When a friend who has lived with me has suddenly gone he is still present in my mind—he is in the feeling of the rug under foot and between the leaves of my manuscripts and I cannot shake him out overnight.
>
> And so with this December.

Despite its fixation upon the omnipresence of sex in the lives and conversations of the vagrants, *Bitter Music* as a whole seems to contradict the impression gathered by some friends of the composer that the casual sex and, in Lou Harrison's phrase, the "male bonding" of the vagabond lifestyle was one of its chief attractions for the homosexual Partch.[20] Of all the passages in the journal, he seems to speak most directly from the heart in a conversation he records with his young friend Pablo, who tells him ashamedly of a homosexual affair with a hobo pal, assuring Partch that it was an indiscretion and that "it is women who fill my thoughts." Partch replies: "Any real love is a beautiful experience . . . and real love is apt to fluctuate over the whole idea of sex, and beyond, too. I wouldn't give it another thought."[21]

The "food and flops" at the shelters provide the hobos with a secondary level of conversation, giving them a yardstick by which to measure the quality of their existence. Partch's hobo letters are replete with discussions of food and of the bodily functions and evacuations that precede and permeate sleep. A letter dated July 28 from Camp Milan, Washington, to his hobo pal Jimmy (hobo Kain-tuck of *Bitter Music*) begins:

> They give you real butter here, and, believe it or not, a big pitcher of real cream on each table. And the pie isn't filled with cornstarch. When I saw bread pudding I thought: O, O—the old stand-by, but it proved to be hoky-doke, the best I ever ate.
>
> Also, they pay every Friday, one buck. There are things I don't like. We are on the grounds of the Seattle water system and you can't take a piss except in the can without being liable to 30 days' imprisonment. And there are only two places they will let you even walk. Besides, these gorillas are not very friendly.
>
> They haven't taught the dogs to use the can. They seem to think that the good people of Seattle are not too good for dog piss.[22]

The company he encountered in the shelters, and the lack of privacy—in *Bitter Music* one hobo, hustled back hurriedly from a trip to the "can," complains "they sure don't give you time to shake off no drops"—provoked in him at first a desolate loneliness. He masks this in the early pages of the journal by an uncharacteristic tone of aloofness—"my company is barely tolerable," he writes in disgust on June 14, and a week later "the ignorance hereabouts is of two kinds—hopeless and irremediable." But he settles into a mode of detached observation and finally, toward the end of the journal, into a sustained interior monologue punctuated by snatches of remembered conversation, most of which is given in musical notation. Throughout, the "music in the voices all about me" rarely lets up, and ranges from "such little things as a quarrel in a potato patch" to the "sequential snorgles from forty human exhausts" that assail his ears as he tries to get to sleep. The journal also contains abundant quotations of hymns, folk songs, and popular songs (*Hand Me Down My Walking Cane, Rock of Ages, Oh, Susanna, He Walked Up to the Queen of Spain*), as he heard them sung or as he sang them himself.

Partch's attention to the hobo voices sustained him, at least intermittently, in

A drawing by Partch from *Bitter Music,*
1935. Harry Partch Estate Archive.

the conviction that there was an aesthetic dimension to his existence, that he was tapping an uncounterfeit source of inspiration that could feed directly into his work. *Bitter Music* leaves us in no doubt that the interest was genuine, and not merely an affectation. Nonetheless, there was ever on his mind the painful realization that, however potentially fruitful, his existence was distracting him from the work he had been doing in Europe. On September 3, from Camp Ingot, California, we find him writing to the IIE in New York, applying for a further $1,000 to enable him to continue his work. "All of my work has been in abeyance since June 1st when I started on a gypsy existence, seemingly my only recourse. I am with hobos, log men, ex-convicts and all tail-enders of relief, in camps, shelters and on the road. It is not time entirely wasted since I am collecting really American folklore and songs. Still, I am unhappy contemplating my unfinished projects." The more or less constant physical hardship he was obliged to endure, however, was itself taking its toll, sapping his energies for creative work. Throughout the autumn he cleaned ditches, hoed weeds, and worked on the grape harvest. By the middle of October, even in southern California, the nights were getting colder, but he often had to sleep in the open if he missed the transient shelters' 10 P.M. curfew. In the mountains near Gilroy, sleeping in oat straw, "tiny ice crystals cover the top of my [sleeping] bag, when I awake." Sometimes these nights under the stars are recorded in the journal with a sweep of bravado, as when he writes: "I am weary, so I lay my bag in a vineyard and am in it. (Tomorrow morning more sweet grapes than I can eat are within the lazy reach of an arm.)"[23] Near the end of October he discovered the spectacular natural beauty of Big Sur, where he slept "under the bay and redwood trees" in the landscape "where the ichor of Robinson Jeffers courses."

The coastline seemed "like paradise," and the spell it cast on him was enhanced by his falling prey unexpectedly to heartbreak: he was smitten with a man, one of a group of convicts, working on the unfinished mountain road at Anderson Creek. His feelings came "out of the void": when the two parted, "out of the cold reaching blackness an endless anguish descends."[24]

His health, too, was suffering. He writes poignantly one October morning of struggling to his feet "in spite of trench mouth, poison oak, and an aching back" to look for work. And his self-esteem was diminished by the need to resort to begging: in November, "at fourteen homes in San Luis—at fourteen sets of steps I mortified myself—"Please lady I'd gladly work for something to eat"—and when I was through I held a can of milk and a can of pea soup. Not even these would I have gotten had I not insisted on my need like a homeless please-eyes dog." Much of his feeling of humiliation was channeled into anger and resentment of the powers that be. Mildred Couper, whom he visited in Santa Barbara in mid-November, noticed the change in him, advising him: "I know you are bitter and I can see why you are, but you simply antagonize people because of it. . . . And you must get off the road. It has done something frightful to you."

By January 1936 Partch had come to regard his diary jottings as aspiring to the condition of a literary work, and accordingly he set about putting them into shape. This very impulse seems to have led him to take refuge from the road, and in the new year he stayed for brief spells with friends in the Los Angeles area—Glendale, La Crescenta, and Covina—using their "homes and pianos"

A drawing by Partch from *Bitter Music*,
1935. Harry Partch Estate Archive.

to notate the music for his journal. The text itself comes to an end in December, but for a lengthy final entry dated February 1, 1936, chronicling an evening in San Bernardino, trying to escape the pouring rain, still unable to get a lift, but with the prospect of imminent employment as a proofreader.

On one page of *Bitter Music,* choked by the futility of his "aimless wandering," Partch quotes Lao-tzu: "I am drifted about as on the sea. I am carried by the wind—As if I had nowhere to rest."[25] It is one of those recurrent images that seize the unconscious with inexplicable power and authority, giving support during times of confused action and ill-defined aims. This clinging to a fragment of literature, a remnant of the artistic world he used to inhabit, was a means of "clinging to hope," and the writing of *Bitter Music* as a whole can likewise be seen an affirmation of his art in the midst of the chaos of his life. How, then, should we read the journal—as a personal or artistic document? Or is the problem not precisely that the work is a hybrid which sits on the border, exposing the delicacy, the artificiality, of the boundary between the two?

Partch's proofreading job in San Bernardino in February 1936—his first steady employment in nearly five years—put an end to his diary-keeping, and we have no more trace of him until early August in Arizona. He was probably drawn there at the invitation of his brother, Paul, and his family, who had been living for some years in Tucson, where they owned an acre of land on which Paul and his eldest son, Virgil, had built "a regular hacienda" from adobe mud. Partch's first inclination was to look for a newspaper job, but immediately he came up against the problem of Arizona residence requirements. (Ironically he was unable to claim California residence, either: the previous winter his Los Angeles friend Louis Curtis had tried to recommend him for a position as a lecturer in an adult education project, but the plan had been scotched, and Partch discouraged from pressing his application, because of his failure to comply with residence requirements.)[26]

As luck would have it he was referred, in looking for proofreading work, to Ross Santee, director of the Federal Writers' Project in Arizona, an offshoot of the Works Progress Administration established by President Franklin D. Roosevelt to combat the Depression. The Writers' Project was engaged in a number of projects on overtly American themes. Partch wrote to Santee in Phoenix, making no secret of the fact that his primary aspirations lay in his musical work, but detailing his achievements and experience as a writer and offering a not unimpressive résumé: "During the years of my experimenting, 1923–31, I read proof in various offices—Los Angeles Times, Sacramento State Printing Office,

Spokane Spokesman-Review, New Orleans Times-Picayune."[27] He offered to let Santee read the manuscript of his journal, then still with its original title, *Cause All Our Sins Are Taken Away*, recently returned from hopeful outings during the summer to the publishers Viking Press and Covici-Friede, both of whom had rejected it. Santee forwarded the manuscript to George W. Cronyn, associate director of the Writers' Project in Washington, D.C., who was duly impressed, and recommended that Partch be employed on the Arizona project. On September 21, the residence problem somehow overcome, Partch began work on a salary of $85 per month rewriting parts of the tours section of what would become the WPA *Arizona: A State Guide* (New York, 1940). In December he wrote to Henry Allen Moe, in evident contentment: "To be doing work for somebody which pleases him and for which there is immediate recognition is a beautiful and a long lost experience."[28] Years later, even though his recollections of the job had been soured, he admitted how glad he was to have work that at least took him "out of the tomato and apricot fields and their 10 to 15 cents an hour."[29]

If Partch was pursuing any musical work during the relative stability of these nine months' employment in Phoenix we know nothing of it, although it is possible that the "sixth writing" of *Monophony Is Expounded*, embodying the research he had done in Europe, was completed there. In May he had written to W. B. Yeats asking him to write a preface. Yeats, who had been ill, was slow to reply, and when a letter arrived toward the end of August it was a disappointment: "I wish I could do that preface for you, but even if I had enough knowledge of the subject I could not do it now. Great arrears of work are crowded into my convalescence. I wish you good luck."[30] Partch enclosed the manuscript with a letter to Henry Allen Moe in December, calling it the result of his "thirteen years of experiment and research": "I find, in completing it, that those thirteen years were spent on a subject that apparently interests no-one. This is a discovery that does not amaze me and against which I do not complain." Yet, admitting to "a childish desire" to display his "zealous folly before someone," he asked Moe to forward the manuscript to Otto Luening, who was then teaching at Bennington College in Vermont. He also sent Moe, with "no anticipations whatever," the manuscript of his journal, now back with a rejection letter from Story Press.

By May 1937 Partch was restless in his job, largely because of temperamental differences with Santee. In the middle of the month he wrote to George Cronyn in Washington, hinting that all was not well and that he was intending to quit the job and go back on the bum around the Southwest. Cronyn urged him not to leave and to wait for the arrival of a Dr. Ed Kennard, their "Indian consultant and in spite of the 'Dr.' a good fellow," who was coming to Phoenix in a few weeks and who, he hoped, would rekindle Partch's commitment to the job. "I believe," Cronyn wrote, "you may have some ideas in common that can be worked on":

> I and other editors have read some of your recent city copy and agree that it is among the most finished we have received. There may be criticisms of details but the stuff is *good*. . . . Your essay style, combining color with detachment, is a rarity. You can write well about anything you turn your hand to. But if I were your classroom instructor (God forbid!) I would advise you to avoid the autobiographical form for a year or two. It's the métier of the present school but has pitfalls. There are few enough people in America with a shrewd observing eye, but that eye, turned inward, may see too many snarls. An outsider might consider you maladjusted; that's the penalty of looking clearly at a maladjusted world. And "adjustment" is generally the sign of insensitivity or conformity.[31]

By the time the letter reached him, Partch had had a blow-up in the office with Santee and had no option but to leave. He reported this to Cronyn, who advised him: "You might go commercial by setting out on a long cross country jaunt and turning up with a sheaf of material but you would have to delete the passages that no run of the mill editor wants to read. Or you might do it uncensored, leaving out some autobiography, and interest a publisher. With your shrewd eye for detail and fewer scruples, you no doubt could be highly successful."[32] Cronyn's enthusiasm for his talents as a writer was highly gratifying, but if Partch's cross-country travels following his departure from Phoenix in July sparked off any writings, autobiographical or otherwise, they have not survived. He was writing more prose in these years than we have knowledge of: in the letter just quoted Cronyn agrees to read a "fantasy" Partch had written, and we have record of Yeats's praise two years earlier for a "biographical essay." It may even be that Partch was, at this time, seriously considering writing as a possible direction, a way out of the apparent stalemate he had reached in his musical work—in *Bitter Music* he had written in exasperation, "Oh, if music were as simple to use as words, requiring but pencil and paper for a nickel or a dime!"[33]

In taking to the road again Partch virtually disappears from the historical record for the next two years. This period, far more than his early hoboing—which is salvaged for us by the existence of *Bitter Music*—is a mysterious one; his activities, his aims and motives, become more and more unfathomable. Leaving Phoenix he seems to have headed north, and in September we find him briefly in Boise, Idaho, then at the end of October back in California, where his address is care of his friend F. G. Oldham in Glendale. Thereafter we have only the most fleeting glimpses: a handful of stray letters, some from hobo pals, one or two of his own small attempts to promote his work or, more painfully, to ensure that his manuscripts are returned to his painter friend Clara Shanafelt in New York for storage. The fact that he leaves so little trace personally, professionally, or musically for quite some time may simply be dismissed as attributable to the swallowing-up, anonymizing effect of the hobo existence he continued to lead; but that itself seems to beg the question of why he chose to resume, and to maintain, that lifestyle when, as his experience in Phoenix demonstrated, he could find a job if he was willing to stay in one place for long enough.

Between October 1937 and December 1940 there are no letters to Henry Allen Moe, Partch's main professional contact and someone to whom he was in the habit of writing simply to keep him appraised of his progress. There was clearly no significant progress on which he could update Moe. When Partch finally broke his silence toward the end of 1940 he mentioned a "series of illnesses" that had been responsible for the long delay in his work reaching fruition. The most devastating of the illnesses he contracted as a hobo, which may be the explanation of so much in these years, was syphilis.[34] Always a threat among vagrants, syphilis was an ever-present specter in the hobo camps. In *Bitter Music* Partch writes chillingly of one of his companions: "He now has no home, no realizable wishes, no work, and so he plants the meadows of Hell with Charm and Syphilis."[35] We do not know when Partch contracted the disease, but in April 1941 he wrote to a friend about his treatment at a clinic in Monterey; and, as his body was not autopsied and his medical records destroyed, the course and effects of his infection are impossible now to determine precisely. It seems an ineluctable part of the Partch legend that this most central medical catastrophe remains a mystery.

The one piece of writing from this period that does survive—in a later typescript copy, not in manuscript—is the short, satirical "A Modern Parable II," dated "April 26, 1938, Camp Devore, Cajon Pass, San Bernardino County." This piece, in the manner of its predecessor four years earlier, juxtaposes the dialectical techniques of bums sitting around a pepper tree in California with those of a group of musicologists around a walnut table in New York City. The piece is humorous but wholly inconsequential, and its only point appears to be that of extolling the virtues of the bums' manner of deflating each others' pretensions—"for deflation is something which happens when bums tire of bums, but which *never* happens in this world of abundant revelation where musicologists *never* tire of musicologists."

The bums' courage in remaining stoically humorous in the face of even the gravest misfortune was a value Partch treasured, and it comforted him in the realization that, however depressing his own existence, things could always be worse. A letter dated June 17, 1938, from his hobo pal Don (addressed to Partch in San Bernardino, which suggests that his stay there lasted for most of the spring) recounts Don's attempt to get from San Fernando back to Camp Devore, where he had worked. Don explains in the letter that the reason he hadn't yet returned was that on the way he had been overtaken by discomfort with a swollen testicle. This understandably curtailed his mobility, and much else. "As I told you in my last letter, I went too work, well one of my nut's started to swoll up on me. I went to a private doctor, and he told me to keep working, well by Monday, I was so sick, and my nut was as big as [my] head. Anyway I couldn't go to work Monday, so I stay in bed all day. Tuesday I started out for Devore, hitchhiking, got as far as Pomona, and couldn't go any further, because I was so sick."

The letters from hobo pals that Partch retained are as diverse as the personalities that speak through them. Some are vulgar and comic, others are heartbreaking tales of loneliness and deprivation. A letter the following summer from his friend Jack Brooks attempts to soothe Partch's "highly sensitive feelings" after Jack's "unconscious but nevertheless cruel attitude" in declining without explanation to accompany Partch on a planned expedition to Colorado, which hurt Partch deeply. "There is one *confession* I will make. And that is this—in some strange manner you have affected me as no-one has ever done. It is true that I desired ever so much to make the Colorado trip with you. And it is also true that I was afraid to do so *with you*. . . . You say I slipped a strait jacket over you—I also slipped one over me. Since receiving your last letter, I have fought with myself over the desire to make with you your Lower California trip and the half-hearted desire to finish college. For once, I must be ruled by the intellect and not by emotion."[36]

By the time of this last exchange Partch was back in southern California. In the autumn of 1938 he had followed the fruit harvest again, which led him up near Spokane, Washington; thereafter he seems to have made a determined attempt to base himself in Los Angeles.

Despite the comforts of human contact, Partch's years of transient existence had by now become "very onerous."[37] The attractiveness that the hobo lifestyle had at first held for him, notwithstanding its abundant hardships and dangers, had been superceded by feelings of aimlessness and underachievement, and by 1939 he was desperate somehow to find his way back into civilized society. During his wanderings he had several times been picked up by the police for vagrancy, and spent occasional nights in jail if it was too cold to sleep outside— "in total maybe two dozen [times]."[38] When he first took to the road following his return from Europe in 1935 he had gotten by relatively easily: "I always looked younger than I was; and they thought I was a kid, a lost kid from California."[39] But as the Depression worsened even the life of a migrant worker became increasingly difficult. "At Marysville there were at least a hundred peach pickers for every job, and the banks of the American River were so thick with hobos that—at night—you'd have thought it was the site of an Army bivouac."[40]

By March 1939 he was attempting to settle in Los Angeles.[41] He stayed for a time at the YMCA on South Hope Street—the rooming house on "that futile Hope Street" (as he later described it to Peter Yates), near where he had lived in 1933—but as each of the few surviving pieces of mail to him that spring bears a different address (and often more than one, as mail was readdressed) he was clearly as unsettled as ever.

In Los Angeles he reestablished contact with the young musician Noel Heath Taylor, who had published an article on him in the magazine *Pacific Coast Musician* the previous year.[42] Partch and Taylor shared a trenchantly anti-establishment outlook, and an equally unorthodox, although different, approach to composition. Taylor played Partch a piece using common sounds,

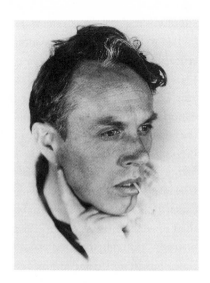

Harry Partch, c. 1938. Unsigned portrait,
Harry Partch Estate Archive.

"L.A. street cars and dripping faucets among many others."[43] Many years later it was Taylor whom Partch had in mind when he wrote, in his article "A Somewhat Spoof": "The young man in Los Angeles who makes music out of common sounds during the late 'thirties is ignored to extinction, but some young Europeans doing the same thing under the fancy title *Musique Concrète*—ten years later—are celebrated from New York to California." Although there was little new to report since the previous year, Taylor produced two articles, one in *California Arts and Architecture* magazine in July and the other in *Pacific Coast Musician* in August, discussing Partch's ideas, and describing the Adapted Viola and the Ptolemy, the latter still not fully functional. Taylor pointed out—a compliment that Partch would later repay in "A Somewhat Spoof"—that "for years American critics have decried the seeming inability of this country's artists to strike off on their own, to create music that does more than merely follow in the footsteps of European tradition. And here is Harry Partch, who has found a new necessity, developed new tools, created a new and vital art. If his music were beyond the comprehension of the average man, too abstract, too mystical, there would be reason to ignore him. But nothing in music was ever so simple as that which he has composed. It has the immediate appeal of lyric Irish speech, the charm of spontaneous Negro music, the power and emotion of the Hebrew chant."[44] One project that Taylor did not mention, and which remained incomplete, was the building of a new instrument, a kithara. Partch had taken the sketches he had made at Kathleen Schlesinger's home in London to his sculptor friend Gordon Newell, who improved them, and Partch began to work on the body of the instrument, using large pieces of redwood, in the adult education night classes in the woodshop of a Los Angeles high school.

Taylor's publications in the summer of 1939 are, sadly, not indicative of any renewal of compositional activity on Partch's part, and it was almost two more years before any new work would come to fruition. During the latter half of the year he was engaged on another WPA project, and is credited among the editorial staff for *California: A Guide to the Golden State* (New York, 1939). As the book was in print by August, and Partch's employment (according to WPA files) only began in mid-July, he may have submitted some written material before officially beginning the job—perhaps the product of something like the freelance travel writing that George Cronyn had suggested to him two years earlier.[45] He felt more comfortable working for the Federal Writers' Project than for one of the several WPA projects in music. Many years later he explained: "through the Depression and the WPA days . . . I saw the most ridiculous things happening in the arts because of a particular bureaucrat in music . . . Musicians weren't supposed to be [creative]."[46] He worked for the Federal Writers' Project in Los Angeles throughout the summer and autumn, quitting the job on January 13, 1940, and moving on.

What he moved on to was a project that had been on his mind for some time: a photo trip in the southwestern desert. The beginning of the trip is marked by a photograph showing Partch at the wheel of his car, with his later inscription on the back: "On beginning of search for my soul into desert." Despite this caustic self-mockery, the intense, haunted look on his face tells its own story. Since his childhood, the desert had represented a constant value—the confrontation with "the terrible fact of every person's aloneness" and the hope of self-renewal.[47] It would always hold for him a sense of suspended eternity, with the guarantee that each day will be the same, will hold the same "brilliant promise."[48]

The photo trip that he undertook in January and February 1940 had the aspect of a pilgrimage. The photographs from the trip, labeled and dated, he preserved in a small, handmade wooden box; and besides their documentary value as a beautiful evocation of the journey, they show a fine eye for the medium. Partch proceeded out of southern California heading for Arizona, and the images along the way are conjured up in his incantatory inscriptions on the back of the photographs: Smoke Tree on Salton Sea, Yuma Street, Fort Yuma barracks, Fort Yuma hoboes, Colorado River jungle camp near Yuma, the Colorado River and the Needles, Cantu Station near Pilot Knob, Topok Highway bridge from California side, Picacho Ghost Doorway with Desert Holly in front, Painted Canyon, Laguna Salada Shadows, Campplace at Picacho.

In February, making his way by hitchhiking, he was walking along the highway just north of the Mojave Desert junction of Barstow, California, when, sitting down on the highway railing to rest and wait for a ride, he began to read the hitchhiker inscriptions scribbled on the railing. The first inscription that caught his eye was "both weak and strong, like unedited human expressions always are," and "eloquent in what it fails to express in words."[49]

It's January 26. I'm freezing.
Ed Fitzgerald. Age 19. Five feet, ten inches.
Black hair, brown eyes.
Going home to Boston, Massachusetts.
It's 4:00, and I'm hungry and broke.
I wish I was dead.
But today I am a man.

The graffiti along the railing immediately suggested to him musical possibilities and, "thoroughly aroused by this sudden fountainhead of Americana," he

A group of hobos, photographed by Partch in 1940
during his trip in the southwestern desert. This
image was used on the cover of the 1962 record of
The Wayward, Gate 5 Records, Issue B. Harry Partch
Estate Archive.

copied down all eight legible inscriptions into a little notebook. Their appeal
lay in qualities they shared with the hobo lore he had recorded in *Bitter Music*—
an uncensored stream of consciousness, sprinkled with expletives, recording
the small frustrations and the unpretentious sensibility of his fellow travelers.
But there was the difference that, unlike the inscriptions in *Bitter Music,* they
came without voices attached, without the inflections of the speaker, thus
opening the way to new musical possibilities. However, it was to be more than a
year before he was able to realize them.

In the autumn of 1940 Partch returned to the coast south of Big Sur, the area he
had fallen in love with some five years earlier. "The little house on the ledge—
beside the lilac trees at the edge of the cliff—now has other occupants, but I am

invited to lunch, and lunch conceives days, and days months."[50] Lillian Bos Ross, who lived in the little house at Lime Creek, recalled the encounter many years later in an article in the *Monterey Herald*: "One autumn day of 1940 I was in the kitchen. So was my typewriter with my almost finished first novel beside it. . . . I heard voices. My husband said, 'This is Harry Partch. He's been in the Big Sur before and wanted to see it again, so he's hitch-hiked and walked.' . . . Lunch over, my husband was starting up to his shop. Mr. Partch stood up ready to leave. I said, 'I wish you'd stay here and rest a little while. Then you could go over to the Hot Springs, the hot water is wonderful—so healing. Have dinner with us and spend the night. We can put you up.'" Her husband added: "Nothing like that hot sulphur water for trail kinks." In the course of conversation it emerged that Partch had in the past worked as a proofreader and could type. She asked him if he would be willing to stay and type her novel in exchange for food and a bed. He agreed, and settled in "the little south room where the jasmine and heliotrope tapped at the window," and began cleaning and oiling her old typewriter.[51] The Rosses induced him to stay in the area, and by November they and their friends had helped him move into one of the abandoned offices—formerly the camp superintendent's office—of the old Convict Camp on the coast at Anderson Creek.

Partch was, in fact, never far from a typewriter that autumn. On November 22 he completed a new preface to his journal of 1935–36, which he now entitled *Bitter Music*. The experience the journal chronicles had, in retrospect, "a glow of attractiveness, but five years later there is still something underneath that is not so attractive. I remember each new fragment of music as an essence slightly bitter."[52] He had finally secured a contract for its publication, with Caxton Printers of Caldwell, Ohio, "but with war in Europe," and the high cost of paper, "the contract was cancelled."[53]

In addition to *Bitter Music* he had also been at work at a new draft, the seventh, of his theoretical treatise, now called *Patterns of Music*. He completed the preface, the last part to be written, in Big Sur on December 10. The table of contents of the book, still extant—unlike the remainder of the typescript—shows seven main parts: an introduction to experimental instruments and to measurement of scales and intervals in cents; a history of intonation systems from the ancient world through meantone and equal temperament to "modern proposals" including 19-, 24-, 36-, and 53-tone equal temperaments, the systems of Ellis, Perrett, and Yasser and the ideas of Schoenberg, Scriabin, and Cowell; a study of "Diatonic Intervals" derived from both the overtone and undertone series and the "14 tonalities" and "tonality relationships"; "Monophonic Intervals," discussing his 11-limit system, the twenty-four "tonalities" primary and secondary, modulation and resolution, and a classification of intervals; "Contributors to Just Intonation," beginning with Pythagoras and Archytas and ending with Helmholtz and Riemann; "Notations and Instruments," the latter including his own Adapted Viola and Ptolemy, plus a "survey of keyboards" for other than the tempered scale; and finally a section on "Spoken Words in Song," including a section called "Along the Road to Abstraction" and a section on his own settings, with subsections entitled Li Po, Psalms, Shakespeare, Song of Solomon, Sappho, and Sophocles (of which only the first three sources had yielded finished results, though a setting of part of the Song of Solomon is found in *Bitter Music*). On December 13 he sent the preface and the table of contents to both the Carnegie Corporation as "a final report of my activities under grant" (although the "report" was five years late) "looking toward publication of the exposition," and to Henry Allen Moe at the Guggenheim Foundation in "undiminishing gratitude for very real aid." Exactly four years earlier he had sent Moe the previous drafts of these two manuscripts, the journal and the treatise, and the fact that history should repeat itself so closely is at once a tribute to Partch's tenacity and a reflection of the lack of any significant new work in the interim.

Meanwhile, the abandoned office he had taken over was turning into a functioning and quite beautiful studio, and he began to turn his attention to work on his instruments. Rummaging around the bottom of the canyon at Anderson Creek, Partch had found a huge piece of redwood, a remnant of the old bridge supports, and used it to fashion a base for the Kithara he had begun to build in Los Angeles. He also worked at developing stainless-steel frets for the guitar he had bought in New York seven years earlier, and in December wrote to Moe that he was completing an "entirely new keyboard instrument"—probably the new model of the Ptolemy keyboard that he had begun to build in night classes in the woodshop of a high school in Los Angeles. This further attempt to turn the Ptolemy into a working instrument was unsuccessful, and the project was abandoned "a year later."

The Big Sur coast was an inspiring place to work. The anthropologist Jaime de Angulo, whom Partch befriended in the area, wrote of it: "Imagine: only a trail, for a hundred miles, bordering the ocean, but suspended above it a thousand feet, clinging half-way up the side of the sea-wall, and that wall at an incredible angle of forty-five degrees, a green wall of grass (. . . in winter— throughout the summer the green is brown-yellow) and canyons with oaks, redwoods, pines, madronyos, bluejays, quail, deer, and to one side the blue

Partch's photograph of his studio at Anderson Creek,
California, 1941: the instruments shown are the Kithara,
Adapted Viola, Adapted Guitar, and the model of a new organ
console. Harry Partch Estate Archive.

ocean stretching away to China."[54] The beauty and remoteness of the area
attracted a number of artists. In March Partch attended a poetry reading by Ella
Young, who gave him a copy of her book *Marzilian,* texts from which he was to
set in 1942 and again in 1949. Ella Young was an Irish-born poet, described by
the philosopher Alan Watts in his autobiography as "a Celtic white witch and
nature mystic" who believed that "flowers and vegetables, trees and mountains,
animals and birds, are *people* . . . this frail, transparent, bewitching old lady
talked . . . like a true shaman, about the personalities of mountains, and about
talking to the weather and to wild animals."[55] Another Big Sur friend was the
painter Jean Varda, known as Yanko, whom Partch met while hitchhiking in
the area, and who persuaded him to take care of his ranch in December and
through the New Year of 1941. Varda was a collage artist of Greek origin, a
charismatic and colorful individual, and always penniless. Partch recalled that
"Varda was living in . . . Anderson Creek—$15 a month—and when the wood
ran out, he used to tear down a shack."[56]

Despite friends like these, Partch later claimed that he had felt very lonely and abandoned during these months in Big Sur. He recalled that the locals would boast that "not everyone can TAKE Big Sur!" and was not ashamed to admit, many years later, "No, I couldn't, by God."[57] He recalled with a shudder "a typical Big Sur party," where he was greeted with the words, "Who the hell are you? WE are from BIG SUR!" His friend Preston Tuttle remembers Partch in Anderson Creek as "an acutely paranoid sensibility. I can remember Harry staying in bed for one or two days, then growling around for a week because of some alleged insult vented by a party guest. It was all so trivial but his feelings were so aggravated that we could not take the matter seriously—except to be pleasant, cheerful, and try to coax him back to normal."[58] Partch's sentiments were shared, at first, by the writer Henry Miller, who would a few years later become the area's most famous resident; but passing through Carmel early in June 1941, Miller wrote to Anaïs Nin that he "didn't like the looks of the place— so arty."[59]

Partch's unhappiness in Big Sur was compounded by his health problems. A letter of April 8, 1941, to Bertha Knisely and her husband, Harold Driscoll, gives some impression of his confused, vacant state of mind:

> The delay has been caused by my waiting to know exactly what I might do. I was somewhat demoralized, not entirely by your letter, and didn't know whether I could stay in the south much longer. I am due to return to my clinic at Monterey Co. Hospital very soon, but perhaps I can put it off another week or two. If I leave here Saturday [April 12] for La Mesa, I may have a ride, and I may decide to bring all my encumbrances. Morton Grant, the scenario writer who has been interested in keyboard, has a friend in La Jolla, and may see him to provide excuse for delivering me in La Mesa. Also, parties here wish me to see one Ned Guymon, in San Diego. I am a class Z dope, and don't seem to be able to emerge from my daze long enough to write intelligent letter. Now with Herbert Childs in La Crescenta.[60]

One way or another the trip south did take place, and in La Mesa on April 14 he began work on a new composition: *Barstow: Eight Hitchhikers' Inscriptions,* settings of the graffiti he had copied from the highway railing a year earlier. He completed the work back at Anderson Creek on May 18. Breaking five long years of compositional silence, *Barstow* ushers in a new phase of his creative life.

In its original form, the piece was written for voice and Partch's Adapted Guitar, with the intention that he could perform it as a solo work. The manuscript is in ratio notation on blank pages, with the voice part given additionally in approximate staff notation. Partch set the eight inscriptions with only slight editing of the texts as he had found them. The musical language is closer to the songs of American folk singers than to the art-song tradition, and the piece as a whole is more diatonic and metrical than the voice and Viola works of 1930–33. In a letter many years later he acknowledged that the vernacular tradition of such singers as Woody Guthrie and Leadbelly were important sources for his work of this period; in *Barstow* the voices of old folk singers are more apparent than anywhere else in Partch's output.[61]

The text of *Barstow* is very different from the exquisite verse of Li Po, or the texts of Sappho, Shakespeare, the psalms, or the Song of Solomon, which had occupied Partch's musical imagination to that time, and the contrast was a liberating one. Even the most prosaic scribblings from the highway railing— such addresses as "530 East Lemon Avenue," "118 East Ventura Street," "915 South Westlake Avenue," or curses, "To hell with it," "Damn it anyhow," "Why in hell did you come anyway?"—are given distinctive and often funny musical treatments. Sometimes this takes the form of unexpected microtonal inflections in the voice part against diatonic harmonies from the Guitar. The resources of Partch's scale here add new qualities of sourness or quasi-drunkenness to familiar harmonic and melodic patterns. Despite the new departures in this piece—some of them foreshadowed by *Bitter Music*—Partch himself tended to emphasize the similarities in intent between *Barstow* and his earlier works, rather than their differences. Writing about the work the following year (1942), he declared that it was "spiritually allied" to "the songs of the medieval troubadors. . . . *Barstow* is simply 'speech-music,' or a music based on speech, in which every syllable and inflection of the voice is harmonized by the accompanying musical instruments . . . [it] thus combines a harmonic music with the pristine concept of melodic word forms."[62]

Although *Barstow* is the only composition to come from Partch's Big Sur period, he wrote four newspaper articles toward the end of his stay there. His residence in the old convict camp had come to the notice of a local reporter, Mary P. Drake, who published an article on him in the *Carmel Pine Cone* in February 1941. Thanks to this contact he wrote and offered the paper four articles later in the year. The first, "Bach and Temperament," published in the July 18 issue, was prompted by the local Carmel Bach Festival. The other three—"The Kithara," "Barstow," and "W. B. Yeats"—dealt with aspects of his own work. By the time these appeared in print in the *Carmel Pine Cone,* in September and October, he was no longer in California.

Chicago, Ithaca, and New York

Partch's loneliness in Anderson Creek, and his sense of
desperation and of being trapped, perhaps explains his
willingness to gamble on a chance encounter during the
summer of 1941. "Quite casually, I met a man, a divinity
student, who became interested in my work and described
it to a friend in Chicago. The friend wrote to me almost
immediately, invited me to Chicago if I could get there on
my own, and ended his letter: 'May God's richest blessings
be upon you.' Having been through more than six years of
California depression, I jumped at the chance to see some
midwest depression."[1] He made hasty preparations for
departure, put the Kithara and the Ptolemy console in
storage in Carmel, and "got galvanized." On the evening
of September 17, "I left San Francisco with $3.50 or
thereabouts in my pocket—$3.29 after paying the 21 cents
ferry and train fare across the bay to Berkeley. Getting
around the country during the Great Depression was
generally no large problem. . . . One had his thumb,

and when that failed there was always the last resort—the drag, the slow freight."[2]

On the second day out of San Francisco he began to keep a notebook, jotting down "fragments of conversations, remarks, writings on the sides of boxcars, signs in havens for derelicts, hitchhiker's inscriptions, names of stations, thoughts." The notebook and his subsequent memories of the trip, a year and a half later, became the basis for *U.S. Highball*. He made his way across the country mostly by freight train. The first excitement came in leaving California on top of a boxcar, riding through the Sierras, and coming to "a non-exhilarating end at the division yards of Sparks, Nevada." From there he moved on, with "days and nights of hobo confabulation atop or in boxcars, 'gon-*do*-las,' tank cars, and around fires in the yards," ending up at Green River, Wyoming.[3] He found a dishwashing job in Little America, Wyoming, which provided him with a week of "rest, food, and economic refurbishing." Thanks to a cleaner appearance he was able to get a lift on the highway. The high point of the trip came in the Illinois plains, with the approach to Chicago in sight, the exhilaration of the journey more important than the prospect of arrival: he knew the city would bring "a gulf of new problems, a new set of dismal difficulties."[4] He had been feeling hopeful throughout that the trip "would be the last ordeal of my personal Great Depression"; but "another year and a half of dirty dishes, in Chicago hash houses, in a Michigan lumber camp, and in a New York evacuation center," were still ahead.[5]

Partch arrived in Chicago "in the dull, dirty light of early dawn, on October 1, with one dime in my pocket."[6] The ending of *U.S. Highball*, the protagonist's depressing anticlimax in confronting the "dingy, pre-dawn smogginess of industrial Chicago," must surely mirror his own experience.

He stayed first with the divinity student's friend, who had invited him, and managed to establish contact almost immediately with the new music activities in the city. His new surroundings, and the new set of faces in the Chicago music world, gave him at first the energy to promote his work as energetically as he had done in New York eight years before. On November 18, some seven weeks after his arrival, he performed *Barstow* (billed as "Hitch-hikers Ballad") and some of the Li Po settings at an evening held at Chicago's School of Design. Also on the program was an "Improvisation by the Class in Sound Experiments" directed by a composer, not yet thirty years old, whom Partch found "rather charming, albeit shallow."[7] The young man was John Cage.

This Chicago concert was probably the first time the two composers had met. Their not dissimilar paths had persistently failed to cross in California, where Cage had grown up, and later in New York. Although he was more than ten years younger, Cage was the better established of the two, his name well known in avant-garde circles and beyond: the previous year *Time* magazine had even published an illustrated feature on his work.[8] His output by this time consisted largely of pieces for percussion ensemble and for the prepared piano, which he had recently introduced. Recordings of percussion works by Cage and Lou Harrison were played at the School of Design concert following the "Improvisation." Partch found Cage's actual music "precious and vapid," though he declared himself "all for common sounds as valid materials."[9] Partch's own primary interest in new instruments at this time—as a way of expanding possibilities in the domain of pitch, and of making provision for subtleties of tuning—Cage "dismissed . . . as of no consequence."

Partch's encounter with Cage—and his growing resentment of Cage and his work throughout the 1940s and beyond—has many similarities with his first meeting a decade earlier with Cage's former teacher, Henry Cowell. In both cases Partch's manner was aloof and somewhat unfriendly, his attitude that they, being the more established, should acknowledge and support his work, while he felt under no obligation to extend any generosity toward theirs. And Cage, like Cowell before him, complied, publishing a report on Partch's Chicago activities in the magazine *Modern Music* the following spring.[10]

Chief among those activities was establishing a functioning keyboard instrument that would fulfill the purpose for which the Ptolemy, lying moribund in California, had been intended. Partch first adapted and retuned an old melodeon, loaned to him for the purpose by two harpsichordists he had met in Chicago, Philip Manuel and Gavin Williamson. This proved only partly satisfactory, and in January 1942 he adapted "one of the more unusual five-2/1 [five-octave] harmoniums," which he was to use for the next three years.[11] He used the reeds from the Ptolemy, and set them in an instrument that, in Cage's words, looked "like an old-fashioned harmonium." The name Partch gave it, the Chromolodian (the spelling was soon changed to Chromelodeon), arose from the fact that each key was banded with colors, following the plan of the keyboard designs he had been developing over the previous decade. He regarded the result as "an instrument of expediency," and still had the intention of completing what he was then calling his Chromatic Organ, planning to use the keyboard console he had built the previous winter in Big Sur.[12]

The Chromolodian proved more useful than he imagined. Around the turn of the year he transcribed his setting of "The Lord Is My Shepherd" for voice and Chromolodian, and added parts for the instrument to *Barstow* and "By the

Rivers of Babylon." He found a musician to play it: Gilman Chase, director of music in Chicago's First Unitarian Church. The two of them, together with a young tenor named George Bishop, began at the end of February to present concerts of Partch's compositions.[13] In March they made a set of acetate recordings of the *Two Psalms, Six Lyrics by Li Po,* and *Barstow.* Although Partch felt the recordings had technical problems because he "was not able to experiment to any appreciable extent with placings of the microphones and instruments," they provide an invaluable record of how his compositions sounded with the three instruments he was then using.[14]

A further project on his mind was the publication of his theoretical treatise. Following a solo performance he had given in January for the Poetry Group of the Friends of the Library of the University of Chicago, he met an editor from the University of Chicago Press who gave him "some encouragement in the form of an assurance that if [the book] is put in the scholastic form required of any ms. submitted to them" it would be given "serious and sympathetic consideration."[15] To this end he put together an application for a residency at the artists' colony at Yaddo, near Saratoga Springs, New York, where he proposed to work at a final revision of the text. Henry Allen Moe, Otto Luening, and others were prepared to write in support of his application, but he felt his chances of success would be improved if he went to see Elizabeth Ames, the executive director of Yaddo, in person. He telephoned her, and she agreed to see him "rather reluctantly, since she said they generally didn't count on interviews in making decisions." His quite staggering incompetence in managing the meeting is recounted in a letter to Luening.

> It was only after I called her I began to realize the difficulties in reaching her. She gave no directions, but I made enquiries, and started walking out there a little before two. A taxi was quite out of the question for me—I didn't see how I was going to eat on the trip as it was. I was actually on the grounds of Yaddo before 2:30 but I couldn't find a soul to direct me except a gardener who spoke no intelligible English. I spent nearly two hours wandering around the section before finding anyone who knew where she lived, and then when I called her by phone she was unavailable. The effort to see her had already depleted my funds woefully, and so I hastened back to Albany to try to get a through ride west. . . . Of course, I wrote to Mrs. Ames as soon as possible. I couldn't send a telegram, except collect, which was naturally absurd.[16]

It took him four days and nights of bad luck on the highway to make it back to Chicago. Not surprisingly, the Yaddo application was unsuccessful.

Just prior to his ill-fated trip to Yaddo in April he was briefly in New York, where he met Otto Luening for the first time. In his autobiography, Luening recalled that after "corresponding with me for ten years, he appeared at our New York studio door, saying, 'I'm Harry Partch. It's been so nice this way; let's never become friends.'"[17] That same evening Partch had planned to attend a concert featuring music by Luening, but a few hours after his visit in the afternoon he had a minor hemorrhage. It was not serious, but by the time the bleeding had stopped he had missed the beginning of the concert, including a Luening piano work. Fortunately he arrived in time to hear Luening's wife, Ethel, sing, and, struck by her voice and by her powerful stage presence, he wrote to Otto a few days later, dropping the hint that he might like to write something for her. Attending a recital of this sort made Partch realize how "very ignorant about modern music" he was;[18] and, although aware of Partch's naiveté, Luening was very impressed by him and proposed that Partch give a lecture and a concert at Bennington College in Vermont in the autumn.

The spring and early summer in Chicago were difficult, and Partch was plagued by bouts of ill health and extreme poverty. He directed what energies he had toward promoting his work. He and a friend compiled a ten-page booklet, intended as publicity material which they would distribute around interested parties, giving a brief biography, an introduction to his theoretical work, and a list of all his compositions. He managed somehow to scrape together enough money to pay for the pressing of several sets of the acetate recordings he had made earlier in the year, and distributed sets to Luening, Henry Allen Moe, and the Mexican composer Carlos Chavez. He also sent one, with an explanatory letter, to Columbia Records. This latter gesture did not receive even an acknowledgment, and in the autumn he went to the record company's New York office in person to retrieve the set, which had not been opened. (Partch would take great delight in telling this story on the occasion of Columbia's recording *Barstow* in 1968.)

These efforts at self-promotion were difficult to sustain, not least because of the lack of significant new work to promote. As ever, there were ideas in his mind for new compositions, but he held little hope of realizing them.[19] His inability to concentrate on composition was not helped by the fact that since his arrival in Chicago he had been lodging with one friend after another, being unable to afford a room large enough to accommodate his instruments permanently. The Chromolodian had been stored in a friend's basement since the time of the recordings in March, and although another friend had offered to pay transportation expenses for the instruments still in storage in Carmel, they were not sent until later in the year.

In June, plucking up courage, Partch wrote to Henry Allen Moe of his intention to apply again for a Guggenheim Fellowship. He explained that he had intended to re-apply every year since his return from England in 1935 but had "put off this application from year to year with the intention, when application was made, of having overwhelming evidence (1) that both music and I had profited from the assistance given me by Carnegie, and (2) that I knew my direction, and would pursue it regardless of circumstances and eventualities." Now, he confessed, he was still not certain that he had such "overwhelming" evidence; "but in the last few months two persons have urged me to re-apply, and have assured me support."[20] The application had to be submitted formally, which could not happen until the autumn, so for the moment he had to bide his time. On July 11 he wrote to Luening: "My musical work has been in complete abeyance since my trip east in April. And for just one reason: a precarious means of existence. I have had two dishwashing jobs in Chicago restaurants in the past two months and I have occasionally been aided by friends who can ill afford the luxury of a penniless composer. . . . Day after tomorrow I am taking a blanket and going north to try to participate in the fruit and grain harvests." His wanderings took him up to northern Michigan, where he had a job as a "flunky" in a lumber camp dining room. While working there he received a reply from Moe that encouraged him to apply for Guggenheim support.

By early September 1942 he had moved to Chappaqua, New York, staying first with Donald Flanders and his family, to whom Clara Shanafelt had introduced him several years before. Their home was about thirty miles north of the city on the New York Central rail line. The Flanders family's fondness for Partch had not been tainted by the fact that by now they had broken off their friendship with Clara herself over the Stalin-Hitler pact—she had aligned her sympathies with Stalin, or rather with the very distorted idea of Stalinism prevalent in the West at that time. When the Flanders learned that Partch needed a place to stay, they offered him the use of their attic and agreed to let him set up his instruments there. The Kithara and the Chromatic Organ console were crated and sent from Carmel, and the Chromolodian from Chicago. Partch planned to stay with them until he received word of his status with respect to military service, which was to be decided within a few weeks. (In June in Chicago the U.S. Department of Commerce had issued a certificate of service classifying him as an "ordinary seaman" and stating that he was endorsed for the "Engine Dept. and qualified to serve in the rating of Coal Passer and Wiper.")[21]

Partch fitted harmoniously into the Flanders' household. He was content for the most part to keep his own counsel, but participated from time to time in the social round. The Flanders' sixteen-year-old son, Peter, who was learning the cello, took an interest in their houseguest, and following some mild coercion from Partch marked the fingerboard of his instrument with the degrees of Partch's scale. "I also spent quite a bit of time in the attic," Peter Flanders recalls, "listening to Harry talk about his theories and to his playing his instruments. My mother was a little uneasy about my spending all that time with Harry alone, but there was no sexual overtone, and she had sufficient confidence in his integrity not to interfere."[22]

Working conditions in the Flanders' attic proved ideal. Partch began a setting of the last two paragraphs of Thomas Wolfe's essay "God's Lonely Man," a text in which Wolfe extols the joys of loneliness and isolation, declaring that loneliness is a more common shared experience for modern man than the experience of love as advocated by Christ. Partch's setting would emerge the following year as *Dark Brother*, for voice, Adapted Viola, Chromolodian, and Kithara, a somber and angst-ridden work, the emotional world of which could scarcely be further from that of *Barstow. Dark Brother* was the first composition to be conceived originally for the Chromolodian. The music is a prolonged passage of what Partch termed "tonality flux": a nondirectional sequence of chords, each of which resolves onto the next by narrow, microtonal intervals. This principle often characterizes his writing for the instrument, the keyboard layout of which, with its wide physical spans producing relatively narrow intervals, seems to have influenced him toward the narrow resolving distances in this type of harmonic movement. (The span of an octave on the keyboard, moving up twelve of the degrees of Partch's forty-three-tone scale, produces an interval of approximately a minor third.) Thomas Wolfe may have been on Partch's mind at this time because among the friends of the Flanders family was Edward Aswell, Wolfe's last editor.

Dark Brother was planned as one item in a seven-part "Monophonic Cycle," the composition of which was the basis of the Guggenheim application Partch took to Henry Allen Moe in person in New York on September 17. The Cycle was also to include *Barstow* and the projected works *San Francisco, U.S. Highball, Variations on a Theme* (based on "Yankee Doodle"), settings from James Joyce's *Finnegans Wake* (intended for Ethel Luening and the idea for which may have come from Otto, who had met Joyce in Zurich during World War I), and a vocal work called *God, She*, described as "a musical satirization of women as the arbiters of the nature and color of American expression." Partch drafted a text for this last work, but it alone among the works of the Cycle would never materialize in quite that form. The "Plans for Work" section of his application did not include his projected setting of *King Oedipus*, which had "progressed no farther than the 'interpretation' I sketched with Yeats [in 1934]. The lack of instruments—capable of my musical system—suitable to the drama's scope and grandeur has held this work in abeyance. I fully intend to complete the setting, but . . . I see no prospect of getting the instruments during the war, with the attendant scarcity of materials."[23]

The only two names he had given the Guggenheim Foundation as referees were Otto Luening and Howard Hanson, and so during the autumn he continued to approach prominent persons in the musical world of the East Coast for support, much as he had done nine years earlier. On October 5 he wrote to composer Virgil Thomson, at Luening's suggestion: "I would like to talk to you for two extremely selfish reasons: first, I am applying for a Guggenheim fellowship and I need references, and second, forthright proponents of liberal musical thought are rare in this world: it is always gratifying to meet one." The letter, which is a fairly typical one of his of this time, goes on briefly to describe his work, to propose a meeting so he can play his records for Thomson, and to offer a copy of the "Plans for Work" section of his Guggenheim application. Like other letters to his professional contacts, this short exchange with Thomson makes for dispiriting reading. There seems something anomalous about Partch's avowed claim to be looking for "proponents of liberal musical thought" in the light of the utterly gray, humorless tone of these letters. He seems to be cloaking himself so completely in this garb of respectful formality that the possibility of any real ferment or exchange of "liberal" ideas seems in danger of being smothered before it can draw breath; it is as though he felt the mere profession of doctrinal allegiance was itself somehow enough. The trials of his hobo years, understandably, had further complicated his always uneasy stance toward musicians who for him represented the establishment. In attempting to gain a foothold in the professional musical world he seems to have felt, initially, a need to downplay the facts of his hobo existence in the belief that if it became any kind of central issue or identifying tag it would disqualify him from the serious attention of the figures he was approaching. Luening wrote to Thomson, recommending Partch's work highly but warning him that Partch "has few friends (because he is a left handed customer who doesn't know how to talk to people anyhow) and his project is special."[24]

Early in October Partch was interviewed by the army, a prospect that he had known for some time was awaiting him. The war was on everyone's mind. During the summer he had been sitting one day in a park in Escanaba,

Michigan, writing in a notebook. Some passerby found this suspicious and alerted the police who, a short time later, arrested Partch on suspicion of being a Nazi spy. When they examined his notebook and discovered he had been only making notes about his musical work, he was released.[25] Following his interview in October, as he recounts in a letter to Luening, the army turned him down.

> Reason, among others: "emotional instability." This conclusion was reached after the following conversations:
>
> 1st Psychiatrist: Do you think you would fit into the army?
>
> A. I think I am adaptable. But I can't see myself toting a gun. I have a horror of violence.
>
> 2nd Psychiatrist: Did you ever have any nervous trouble?
>
> A. I have had nervous collapses as the result of too strenuous work with my music and insecurity shock.
>
> 2nd Psychiatrist: I don't think you belong in the army. Do you?
>
> If these answers indicate emotional instability I'm a monkey's grandmother. But I'm not inclined to argue.[26]

In fact, the rejection renewed his determination to make a go of things professionally, and he began once more to solicit and to give guest lectures and presentations on his work. On October 22 and 23 he gave a pair of lecture-demonstrations at Bennington College in Vermont at the invitation of Otto Luening, one a discussion of his theoretical work and the other a performance. The Luenings were still slightly unsure what to make of him socially, and Otto found it odd that the ten dollars that Partch received for personal expenses—in addition to a modest lecture fee—was divided half on sleeping accommodation and half on Irish whiskey, which he shared with anyone around. Ethel threw a party for him after the lectures, at which she introduced him to the theater director Arch Lauterer, whose stage sets for dance productions at the college the Luenings had admired, and who became, nine years later, Partch's first theatrical collaborator.

From Vermont he went on to the Eastman School of Music in Rochester, New York, where Howard Hanson had invited him. The two lectures he gave there on November 3 were recorded in their entirety on six twelve-inch glass-base acetate discs, which have not survived, but which he forwarded by railway express to the Guggenheim Foundation some weeks later in support of his application. Hanson was impressed by his abilities as a lecturer, and upon his return to New York Partch pursued the prospect of further engagements, writing to Paul Hindemith (at Virgil Thomson's suggestion) "and offering to visit Yale . . . to see him."[27] On November 21 he reported to Henry Allen Moe that Douglas Moore, at Columbia University, had "asked me to make a presentation of my music for one of his classes this coming winter."

Whether stimulated or not by these modest professional successes, Partch returned to composition at the end of 1942, and the months ahead were among the most productive of his life. In December he composed three songs for voice and Adapted Guitar, with the collective title *December, 1942*. The first, a setting of Shakespeare's "Come Away Death" from *Twelfth Night* (which he dedicated to Clara Shanafelt), is an exquisite song quite in keeping with the finest of the Li Po settings. The other two—"The Heron," setting a poem by Tsurayuki as translated by Arthur Waley, and "The Rose," setting a poem by Ella Young—he seems not to have been satisfied with, and he destroyed the manuscript of all three songs some years later. Fortunately, as is the case with *Bitter Music,* a microfilm copy made a few years after composition for archival purposes has survived. Looking at the songs now, we may perhaps agree with Partch's assessment that the last two settings are in need of revision: he himself was to take up both texts again seven years later in the *Eleven Intrusions*. In all probability he was simply out of practice at working something up to finished form. The Thomas Wolfe setting, *Dark Brother,* remained a sketch, and a similar handicap at first befell the composition he began a few weeks later: *U.S. Highball.*

At the end of January 1943 he visited friends in Ithaca, New York, supposedly for a few days, and ended up staying for almost nine months. He was able to afford a warm room for the first time that winter, thanks to a part-time bookkeeping job he had taken with a small scrap-iron company. In his room at 329 West Seneca, on February 14, he began to write *U.S. Highball,* originally for voice and Adapted Guitar, which, like the original score of *Barstow,* was notated in ratios on blank paper. The text of the work was elaborated from the phrases he had noted in the pocket notebook he had carried with him on the trip from San Francisco to Chicago eighteen months before. He completed the score a little over five weeks later, in the early hours of the morning of March 24. He wrote to Luening that the creative fever in which he had been working on the piece was the most intense he had experienced in years.[28] Although the composition was originally conceived as a solo work for voice and Adapted Guitar, as work progressed he seemed to realize the need for other instruments; Kithara and Chromelodeon—Partch had by now changed its spelling—are indicated in the score at various points. These instruments had been left in storage in Chappaqua, which made work on the piece "a little difficult"; the manuscript has, for this reason, an unfinished feel.

The completion of this first version of *U.S. Highball* coincided with a piece of momentous news: the award of his first Guggenheim Fellowship, as of April 1. Partch quipped many years later that the award marked the end of his personal Great Depression, and for the first time in eight years he had the financial security needed to devote himself fully to his musical work. On March 26 he wrote to Moe to thank him, and in the next few days dispatched other letters to the various people who had supported his application. He decided to remain in Ithaca indefinitely to concentrate on the projects his fellowship had made possible. "I am in congenial surroundings," he told Moe, in "almost complete isolation . . . and I find that I work very well here."[29]

Immediately he arranged for all his instruments to be transported to Ithaca, at a cost of forty dollars: their physical presence was necessary to his pragmatic way of composing. With the instruments around him he began, on May 1, a "second draft" of *U.S. Highball,* now scored for voice, Adapted Guitar, Chromelodeon, and Kithara. Concurrently with work on the score he produced other pieces, all intended for the projected "Monophonic Cycle." On June 21 he completed the Wolfe setting, *Dark Brother,* and at the end of the month he added Kithara parts to the *Two Psalms* and *Barstow.* On July 1 he finished *San Francisco,* a setting of his recollection of the cries of two newsboys on a foggy night in the 1920s; and a few days later *Letter from Hobo Pablo,* a setting for voice, Adapted Guitar, and Kithara of the letter he had received in the autumn of 1935 from his old hobo friend, telling him of his wedding (the text of which he had included in *Bitter Music*). July and August were spent mostly repairing his instruments, chiefly the Kithara; and during September and October he worked at copying and revising his new scores. The new version of *U.S. Highball,* with three instruments, was completed on October 1.

With "the creative part of my project . . . pretty well in hand,"[30] he made plans to leave Ithaca permanently at the end of October. He wanted his new compositions to be heard in concert, to prove to the Guggenheim Foundation—and to himself—that this was work that could hold the attention of the New York musical world. His idea, until he could establish and rehearse an ensemble, was to make the rounds of his professional contacts giving demonstration performances on his own, in the hope that this would lead to an opportunity to present the works in a more prestigious context. He confessed to Virgil Thomson that he had some anxieties about how well his recent work would "come off the paper," especially in the "skeletal way" he was proposing to present it, "without the ensemble for which it was conceived, but only with voice and guitar or viola."[31]

For the next few weeks he was essentially homeless. He traveled first to Vermont, visiting Otto and Ethel Luening at Bennington College. There, Luening introduced him to the composer Douglas Moore, who was tremendously impressed by Partch's run-through of parts of *U.S. Highball* and enthusiastic about helping. It was the beginning of a long friendship. In his autobiography Luening describes Moore as "distinguished-looking and solidly built, with a fine head of hair and friendly, alert, twinkly, expressive, keen brown eyes. He was a chain smoker and walked with just a hint of a nautical roll."[32] Although his compositional language was far removed from Partch's own—Moore had studied with Horatio Parker at Yale and Vincent d'Indy and Nadia Boulanger in Paris—they had a common interest in Americana themes and in popular musics.

From Vermont, early in November, Partch went to Boston where he met and befriended the composer Quincy Porter. He played *Barstow* and *U.S. Highball* at a lecture-demonstration Porter had arranged at the New England Conservatory of Music on November 4. In the audience was the redoubtable Nicolas Slonimsky, whom Partch had first met in Henry Cowell's company in San Francisco in 1931. Slonimsky was captivated by the bawdy text of *Barstow* and talked about publishing the score. Although flattered by his interest, Partch confessed in a letter to Luening, "after three cocktails and a big dinner, [these] and Slonimsky were too much for me."[33] Quincy Porter proved to be highly supportive, even encouraging Partch to settle in Boston. Partch decided to stick to his plan to make a trip to New York, and perhaps return thereafter to Boston and try to find a room.

He was in New York for about a fortnight. There, he renewed his acquaintance with Henry Cowell, who seemed "much more sympathetic than ever before."[34] Cowell had settled on the East Coast after his humiliating, and much-publicized, four-year imprisonment in San Quentin following his conviction on charges of homosexual assaults on underage boys at his home in Menlo Park, California. Both he and his work had changed. His sympathy to American folklore and traditional musics perhaps made him well-disposed toward the subject matter of Partch's recent work. Partch played *U.S. Highball* for him, and Cowell was enthusiastic. Partch also played the work for Martha Graham, who talked of choreographing it the following summer.

While these meetings had been encouraging, no offer of any major concert opportunity had yet resulted. It was thus gratifying to discover, on his return to Boston on November 23, a telegram from Douglas Moore inviting him to audition the following week for the League of Composers, the principal forum for new music concerts in New York. Partch traveled back to the city for the audition on November 29, which was successful, and he was offered a performance under sponsorship of the League at Carnegie Chamber Music Hall the following April.

Moore was keen to help in other ways. Making no secret of the fact that he didn't understand Partch's theories, he held a gathering at his apartment on Riverside Drive at which he introduced Partch to someone who would: the composer Henry Brant. Brant, then thirty years old, had written some wonderful experimental works in his teens which had been championed by Henry Cowell, and his mature compositions were no less unconventional. Among them were *Angels and Devils* (1931), a concerto for flute and flute choir; *Music for a Five and Dime Store* (1932) for violin, piano, and kitchen hardware; and *The Marx Brothers* (1938), a "tone poem" for tin whistle and ensemble. Brant was then earning his living as a commercial orchestrator in New York. In Moore's expansive living room overlooking the Hudson, he listened to Partch talk animatedly about his work. Brant immediately understood Partch's explanation of his Otonal and Utonal chords and their relationship to the intervals of the harmonic series. "I immediately had the impression," Brant recalls, "of an important and substantial musical mind. The thing that impressed me most was a point of view of considerable breadth comparable to Ives. He . . . was writing directly from his own experience . . . it wasn't a little funny avant-garde noise or a quick novelty entertainment. What he was after was a new kind of musical expression of the principal issues in the world, as he understood them, and he was prepared not just to *talk* about a musical revolution but to make it in practical terms. And I saw there that that was something bigger than anything I'd heard of since Ives."[35] Brant was also a gifted multi-instrumentalist, and was prepared to do what he could to help Partch recruit an ensemble of musicians for the forthcoming League of Composers concert. Nonetheless, staying in New York was a daunting and expensive prospect, so Partch returned to Boston, intending to settle for a time and to continue his preparations from there.

In Boston on December 3 he gave another solo performance of *U.S. Highball,* this time for Howard Hanson, in town to conduct his Fourth Symphony, who "seemed quite pleased." And yet, finding a satisfactory studio in Boston proved no less difficult than in New York. He told Henry Allen Moe that he was "running up against the problem of a vastly overcrowded city. I have moments of feeling that the two weeks, and wasted time, of unsuccessful searching aren't worth the advantages. In this time I have found just one room where there is no objection to my instruments, and I have taken it for one week. But from other standpoints it is highly undesirable, and I don't know whether I can make a go of it."[36] Finally, on December 21, he wrote to Moe that he had installed his instruments, which had been sent from storage in Ithaca, in a "large, old-fashioned room" at 23 Hancock Street on Beacon Hill. He received some "expert advice" on his Chromelodeon from "the organ repair man at the Conservatory," and spent Christmas working at improvements.[37]

He had hoped to have an ensemble in rehearsal by early January 1944, and to be ready to make a recording of *U.S. Highball* around the middle of the month. However, being "unable to find the type and amount of assistance" he needed from musicians in Boston, he recorded the work himself in mid-January, at Quincy Porter's home, by overdubbing parts one at a time—first voice and Adapted Guitar, then Chromelodeon, then Kithara. The result, he told Moe on January 27, was not totally satisfactory because of the resulting loss of clarity of the voice and because of a buzz from the Kithara. Porter hand-delivered the records and the manuscripts of the completed works of the *Monophonic Cycle* to the Guggenheim Foundation—to which Partch dedicated the rewritten version of *U.S. Highball*—in New York on January 28.

In February Partch rethought the decision he had made some weeks before and packed up and moved to New York. He established himself and his instruments in a couple of rooms at 38 West 92nd Street. Rehearsals began for the April concert. Henry Brant recruited a third member of the ensemble, to play the Kithara: Alix Young Maruchess, a viola da gambist who had been a friend of Calista Rogers in Pasadena. In the last week of March, inspired by Brant's virtuosity on the tin whistle, Partch composed his long-projected composition on "Yankee Doodle," which he called *Y.D. Fantasy.* It is scored for soprano voice (a part he offered to Ethel Luening), two tin whistles (whose pitches he measured carefully against the Chromelodeon and notated accordingly), tin oboe (a tin whistle played by an oboe mouthpiece and reed, one of Brant's inventions and, as he recalled in 1985, "an instrument on which at that time I had few rivals in Manhattan"), Chromelodeon, and Flex-a-tone. The energy and commitment given by Alix Maruchess and Henry Brant, Partch felt, were "little less than heroic," especially as neither expected any remuneration for their efforts.[38] The rehearsals were high-spirited affairs, and Brant recalls that Partch was not above making an occasional pointed remark about his homosexuality, knowing it would shock Ethel Luening.[39] Just as he was completing the score of *Y.D. Fantasy,* news came that his Guggenheim Fellowship had been renewed for a second year.

The League of Composers concert took place on April 22, at 5 P.M., in the

Partch seated at the Chromelodeon with Alix Maruchess and
Ethel Luening, rehearsing for the League of Composers
concert, New York, 1944. Photo by Larry Gordon.

Carnegie Chamber Music Hall at Seventh Avenue and 57th Street. The works
performed were *Barstow*, *U.S. Highball* (before which, the *Herald Tribune*
reported, Partch gave "a brief oral glossary" of the unfamiliar hobo expressions
in the text), *San Francisco*, and *Y.D. Fantasy*, which was encored. The response
was positive, although there were a few dissenting voices. The League of
Composers audience consisted largely, in Brant's words, of "a lot of people who
I would call stuffy, self-satisfied hacks as composers; [yet] I believe that everyone
felt themselves in the presence of a formidable new contender. They reacted in
various ways. Some were annoyed, irritated, perhaps envious, a little hostile . . .
many of them took [Partch to be] an eccentric amateur. But in 1944 things were
so Stone Age that many of those same people would have said the same thing of
Ives."[40] The concert was reviewed in several New York papers. Paul Bowles in
the *Herald Tribune* commented that Partch had "found an excellent medium

for expressing a kind of all-embracing unhappiness; when the music was moving, it was so only in so far as it cursed, groaned, released sounds of pain." Most reviewers found *U.S. Highball,* though striking, too long and amorphous (at their estimate of forty-five minutes). Henry Simon in the magazine *P.M.* felt it was too exclusively dependent on an "emotional tone of disillusioned misery throughout, even in the flashes of humor." (A week later the magazine published a letter of mild protest against Simon's review from Clara Shanafelt.) All the critics recognized the importance of the texts as the focus of the works, though the *New York Times* concluded that the value of the works was "almost exclusively literary," the instruments merely adding secondary—though "admirable"—atmosphere. Bowles noted that Partch "not only lacked sufficient voice to make himself heard above the accompanying strains, but was also busy playing the guitar, which he constantly bent his head to watch." These reservations notwithstanding, the reviewers were impressed by the virtuosity of the playing, especially Partch's, and by Brant's impression in *Y.D. Fantasy* of what Bowles called "a phonograph whose governor is broken and whose turntable is doing three hundred revolutions a minute." The May–June issue of *Modern Music,* however, carried a disparaging review by Lou Harrison, who complained that Partch's forty-three tones "seem never to do much but decorate a comparatively simple basis. . . . The actual music was on the whole negligible, but the special sounds were often interesting. I wondered what a composition really involving an integral use of the forty-three tones would sound like." Harrison was obliged to admit that *San Francisco* had moved him deeply: around its newsboys' cries "Mr. Partch has woven a spell of about the foggiest and dampest music I have ever heard. I got homesick."

At the beginning of May Partch composed *Two Settings from Joyce's Finnegans Wake* for soprano, Kithara, and double flageolet (another instrument in Brant's collection), his long-promised showpiece for Ethel Luening. The first of the settings, "Isobel," was included in a repeat of the concert given on the evening of May 22 at Brander Matthews Theater, Columbia University, which had been arranged by Douglas Moore.[41] Following the performance, the *New Yorker* magazine published an article on Partch. Despite the frivolous tone of its introduction, it is a serious and accurate piece, which concludes by stating the composer's conviction that the tempered scale "is a form of regimentation, and he has long been opposed to regimentation. This is evidenced by the fact that he has drifted restlessly from one occupation to another: schoolteacher, fruit picker, apprentice seaman, writer, and proofreader, as well as indigent transient and composer. 'My father was a Presbyterian minister who turned agnostic,' he told us. 'Maybe that had something to do with it.' "[42]

In its visionary sense of the lonely, unmoving emptiness of urban America in the early 1940s, *U.S. Highball* is unique in twentieth-century music. It combines heady evocation of the isolation of long journeys on autumn nights with snatches of drunken hobo ribaldry in an America peopled by police and by vagrants who appear and disappear like ghosts. The mistiness and iridescence of sound; the exhilaration of early morning distances; the feeling of urban dissolution, of the city as a condenser of anxiety—these images spring from the work as the result of a deep identification with a specific locale and specific people, not from a momentary desire to add touches of Americana color. The hobos that rollick and swagger their way through *U.S. Highball* emerge from firsthand experience of "hobo confabulation." Partch's bawdy "account" is a matter of detail, observation, and empathy.

The work begins with Slim, the protagonist (whose name was changed in the 1955 rewrite to Mac), intoning the opening line: "Leaving Carmel, Californiel." Thus begins an identification of place with motion, which is maintained throughout the work. Partch's hobos are rarely *in* a place, they are either arriving or leaving. The brief moments of physical stasis in the work exist in supernormal emotional states, from the frustrated to the metaphysical. As the work, and the journey, progress, we encounter these states sequentially: yet in the persistent jumping backward and forward in language and states of mind, Partch evokes an ever-changing emotional landscape by means of montage—the juxtaposition of two pieces of material, the combination of which forms a third quality unlike either of the other two in isolation.

Despite the West-East trajectory of its journey, *U.S. Highball* contains little more than the skeleton of a linear narrative. Such linearity as does emerge is evoked by many nonlinear techniques: fragmentary images, snatches of speech, the play of contrasting tempi; phrases and episodes that falter and peter out with the text's frequent degeneration into childish rhyming; the restless shifting of gears and tempi; the juxtaposition of meters, in the text and in the melodic lines; the sudden lurch of hopeful accelerandi that grind down into stasis; the range of different tones of voice, from the crapulous and farcical—"You exclamation mark bum! Get your semicolon asterisk out of these yards!"—to the expectant, tense—"Sssstuck. In Green River." The contrasting rhythms and tempi over the work's twenty-five-minute span manage not merely to express the despairs, hopes, and exhilarations of the hobos' transient existence but, by their quick succession and shifts, to embody them.

Partch uses the notated hobo language in several ways in *U.S. Highball,* crossing over various levels between direct representation and symbolism. The ludicrous wordplay of the rhymings of station names and their states—"Winnemucca, Nevaducca," "North Platte, Nebras-ass-katte"—are the protagonist's attempt to while away the boredom of the journey. In extremes of boredom, such wordplay—however purposeless—serves a kind of lulling instinct: the mind simultaneously spurts word associations and, in so doing, squanders its attention still further. The *music* of the language, Partch himself suggested, gives "a peculiar introspective intensity, a peculiar humor, a peculiar drama, and a peculiar urgency—an illusion or hallucination that the things of the story situation are being said and are happening here and now—which only this music can convey. It integrates and intensifies the fragments of word thoughts, remarks, and signs, into an account."[43]

Partch is careful to call the work a "musical account," as distinct from a narrative account. *U.S. Highball* is not a distant experience viewed through the panes of later wisdom or disillusion: it is too close to the real thing. Partch doesn't artfully step back from the lived journey to give us a crafted vantage point on the protagonist's moods, his exhilarations and depressions—the progression of the emotional meaning of the trip. It is more like a musicalized diary, like Partch's little notebook itself brought to musical life. His method— which stems from the directness of his dealing with the jotted-down material— is *not* to build up any composed, narrative shape, in order to make more vivid the aimlessness and haphazardness of the existence he is recreating.

Yet we should not overlook the obvious selectivity involved in what phrases he chose to record, or to remember and then later write down, in the notebook itself. This process of selection was the first compositional act, and was done right then and there, on the road. His next compositional act, the placing of the phrases into a sequence, was only partly determined by the West-East trajectory, as he allows himself a certain measure of poetic license in departing from the sequence in which the phrases occur in the notebook. This notebook, moreover, unlike *Bitter Music,* contains no musical notations: these were all remembered, and in the interim period before their actual working into the score can only have become more infused, however subconsciously, with Partch's own characteristic intonations. This is not at all inappropriate aesthetically, because Partch is identifying himself—as an "unseen supernal commentator"—with the hobos: the characters become imaginary selves. "The action and words have no integration but geography and the implied fortunes of the protagonist, the composition as a whole no integration but music."

Only rarely does the text seem to have overtly symbolic significance. One such moment is a quiet, nocturnal interlude in Nevada, which beautifully captures a stillness that disappears as soon as the image has been evoked. "Look at them Northern Lights! See them long streaks up in the sky? You can't ride outside in weather like this. We'll build a fire so when the next drag stops all the 'bos'll come running over to get warm." The image of the Northern Lights—one of reflected, not true, light—is evoked as a symbol of the hopefulness and the dreams of the transients. Behind the symbol is the suggestion that the colored play of the Northern Lights betrays, by its ephemerality, the illusory nature of the hobos' aspirations. The true light of the sun does not figure in *U.S. Highball*.

The lengthy final section of the work depicts the fury and excitement in the protagonist's approach to Chicago. The buildup of tension is repeatedly dissipated by slower passages, still more station names, and irrelevant episodes. After the exhilaration of the approaching end—"a-ga o-go a-ga Chicago!"—the work dissolves into anticlimax in the "dingy, pre-dawn smogginess of industrial Chicago, and with just one pocketed dime."

The technique of montage, which is the structural heart of *U.S. Highball* as well as of the later film score *Windsong* (rewritten as *Daphne of the Dunes*), provides a foretaste of what would become Partch's most characteristic compositional method in later extended works: the multiple exposure. This related technique creates the larger structures of both *Castor and Pollux* (1952) and *And on the Seventh Day Petals Fell in Petaluma* (1963–64), where a sequence of short sections—respectively, dances and "verses"—is played once, then played through again with the sections combined into simultaneous groupings. The technique, like that of montage, has the effect of refocusing aural perspective and of creating a playful distortion of chronological progression.

Whereas Partch judged *Bitter Music* a failure, *U.S. Highball* would remain one of the compositions for which he felt the greatest affection. Conceptually they spring from the same impulse, being (as Partch wrote of *U.S. Highball*) "art that surges up and out of the strictly literal, the experienced narrative, even out of the abysmal. And because it is art, the strictly literal time and place of its concept form merely the flight deck for what follows. . . . The intensity of the experiences preceding it and the intensity of my feelings at the time forced me into a different welter of thought—one that I had to mold in a new way."[44]

Collectively, *The Wayward*—the title he appended in 1956 to *Barstow, San Francisco, The Letter,* and *U.S. Highball,* "musical compositions based on the spoken and written words of hobos and other characters . . . the result of my wanderings in the Western part of the United States from 1935 to 1941"[45]—is perhaps the first underground masterpiece in American music. A piece like *Barstow* was quite clearly thumbing its nose at the myth of the cultivated, refined masterpiece tradition, as was *Y.D. Fantasy,* whereas *U.S. Highball*'s peculiar anti-epic grandeur seems distilled from the shards and dregs of society. Yet despite the vein of mordant satire that laces through them, these compositions do not depend for their effect on subverting the norms of Western concert tradition. With the benefit of hindsight Partch appears neither a heretic within that tradition nor an infidel outside it. The compositions of *The Wayward* are the work of a passionate and deeply committed humanist who remakes cultural symbols where he cannot sustain belief in existing ones.

Madison

There is a sad irony in the fact that Partch's principal achievements in the eight years or so following his New York concerts in the spring of 1944 concerned projects associated with the previous decade: the putting of "the final word to the final draft" of his book in Madison, Wisconsin, in the spring of 1947,[1] and the production of his long-projected setting of *King Oedipus* in California in March 1952. Although these achievements stand as testimony to his artistic fortitude, we grow painfully aware, tracing the paths he followed after leaving New York, of the other avenues of growth that were bypassed or thwarted in bringing them to fruition. For all its fleeting moments of fulfillment, this period of Partch's life is characterized by a growing sense of painful isolation, by frustration, struggle, by lack of achievement.

Partch's New York concerts branded him with a small but permanent reputation as a cultural outlaw who had wandered off well-worn tracks in order to contemplate and develop a sort of lateral extension of his art. In this light his next substantial undertaking, the rewriting of the book that would be published as *Genesis of a Music*, can be seen as a bid for academic legitimacy. The book had essentially lain dormant since his unsuccessful application to the Yaddo artists' colony two years earlier, and his settling to the task of completing it was due as much to circumstance as to any inner necessity: it was only one item on the carousel of unfulfilled projects that he, like most artists, kept in spin.

Partch's compositional work under his Guggenheim Fellowship in 1943–44 brought about a change in his attitude toward his theoretical treatise, then still entitled *Patterns of Music*. A note of dissatisfaction with it creeps into his exchange of letters with Virgil Thomson.

On the occasion of their first meeting, in the autumn of 1942, Thomson had expressed interest in reading the manuscript, and keen though Partch was to receive Thomson's criticism, it proved impossible to find a time when "my exposition and your leisure" could coincide.[2] Partch needed to hold on to it for use in the lectures he was then trying to obtain, explaining that as it "is full of tables and various data that I use more or less continually, and since it is my only copy and I can't make another at this time it is difficult to part with it for a long period."[3] A year later, after intense work on the compositions of the *Monophonic Cycle*, we find him writing to Thomson: "As for the theoretical work, I would prefer to let it ride for the present. Although it still represents my theories, it has ceased to represent my attitude, and must be revised. When that is done I shall be much interested in your appraisal."[4]

A quite unexpected proposal of an opportunity to revise the book came from the pianist Gunnar Johansen, then artist-in-residence at the University of Wisconsin, Madison, who attended a rehearsal for Partch's Columbia concert in the company of Douglas Moore.[5] Johansen enthusiastically suggested the possibility of Partch's working in Madison to prepare the book for submission to the University of Wisconsin Press. Almost immediately after their meeting, Partch set out on an exploratory visit to the university.

Contrary to the anti-institutional image he liked to project, and which history has perpetuated, Partch was flattered by the offer of an academic affiliation and would at this time readily have accepted a lecturing post. A few years later he complained in a letter: "My friends Howard Hanson and Douglas Moore are directors of music schools and could have removed me from the edge of dish-washing jobs, destitution and frustration that I am constantly teetering on. They didn't. Why? Ambivalence, their own faculties, who were definitely hostile."[6] Moreover, despite the moderate amount of attention the New York concerts attracted, no offers of anything more permanent were forthcoming from the New York musical world, which was a considerable disappointment. "I really did have something vigorous and new; that was the time of my life I should have gotten some notice, and it didn't come."[7]

The ambivalence with which those in musical academia viewed his work was by now a familiar response, and in all probability Partch came to Madison expecting something similar. The understanding of his work that musicians like Hanson and Moore showed was, he realized, limited. "Even Douglas Moore, who arranged demonstrations and applauded vigorously, still waved ratios aside and contended stubbornly, 'Music has nothing to do with acoustics.'"[8] The book was to be his attempt to set matters right. He discussed the proposal with Carl Bricken, director of the School of Music at the University of Wisconsin, who was encouraging; many of Bricken's colleagues on the music faculty were less supportive of Partch's appointment, not least because of his lack of academic credentials.[9] He submitted a document describing his proposed "Research in a Non-Tempered Musical Scale, and Instruments to Implement and Exemplify the Results" to the University Research Committee, and at their meeting on June 5 they decided in favor of awarding him a grant for the forthcoming academic year.

With no further prospects in New York he headed back to California, and spent the summer staying with friends and beginning work on the new draft, the eighth, of his book. By the middle of August he was staying on Gunnar Johansen's ranch in Gualala, on the Pacific coast north of San Francisco, from where on August 14 he wrote to Henry Allen Moe: "I am pursuing my work in this seacoast mountain retreat, and finding it a great comfort and source of spiritual rehabilitation after three years in the populous East."

Partch's affiliation with the University of Wisconsin, his first with an academic institution, gave him a status that was effectively a limbo position between research student and faculty member, without the full benefits of either. One of his Madison friends recalled that Partch "lived on the scale of a University student,"[10] an impression that may have been prompted by the nature of his living accommodation, which Partch described as a "very warm room—frightfully small, and in a house with one bathroom to seven boys—who aren't too considerate about where they do their reading of mystery stories."[11] The house was at 824 W. Johnson, about a block away from Gunnar Johansen's studio.

Johansen, who was some five years younger than Partch, was a virtuoso pianist and a composer with a largely unknown but impressive output, mostly of piano and chamber music. It may have been Johansen's interest in the Italian composer and pianist Ferrucco Busoni that provided the background to his enthusiastic support for Partch. In his *Sketch of a New Esthetic of Music,* published in English in 1911, Busoni had outlined his interest in sixth tones, a division of the major second into six equal parts resulting in thirty-six-tone equal temperament. Johansen recalled, on encountering Partch's work, that "I was convinced that what he had to contribute was really significant. Of course, having been brought up somewhat within the realm of Busoni's philosophy . . . I was already aware of the potential and begging for these innovations. So I felt that Harry was on a very vital track."[12]

Following Partch's arrival in Madison in October, Johansen set about to introduce him to a circle of friends outside the music department, whose faculty—with the exception of Carl Bricken, who was leaving at the end of the year—were not especially sympathetic. One such friend was the painter Marshall Glasier. Glasier was nearly the same age as Partch, and turned out in many ways to be a kindred spirit. He too had spent his twenties drifting, getting by on routine jobs, and had begun serious work in painting only when he reached thirty, studying in New York with George Grosz; like Partch, he had worked on WPA projects during the Depression. Glasier projected himself essentially as an outsider. He had no connection with the university and lived at home with his parents, painting in the attic—rather to the disdain of some of the middle-class residents of that part of Madison, who regarded him as somewhat eccentric. Partch found him sympathetic company and he became a close friend and ally, as did his composer brother John.[13]

Marshall Glasier, in turn, introduced Partch to his psychiatrist friend Dr. James Jacobs and his wife, Marian. Jacobs was an intelligent, dapper man with a keen interest in the arts and who was also something of a painter. He took an immediate interest in Partch personally as well as professionally, advising him in his occasional periods of ill health, much of which stemmed from his hypertension and the side effects of the medication he had to take for it. Jacobs was one of the relatively small number of people with whom Partch was truly able to relax, perhaps sensing that Jacobs understood his complex nature more than most and yet accepted him. Jacobs was to be one of the mainstays of Partch's years in Madison and an important part of his circle of friends; Partch maintained the friendship to the end of his life.

In finding musicians to form an ensemble Partch was once again helped substantially by Johansen, who suggested to some of his more talented piano students that they meet Partch and try his instruments. Two students who took up the offer were Christine Charnstrom and Lee Hoiby, who learned to play the

Chromelodeon and the Kithara, respectively. Soon they were joined by the young singer William Wendlandt, whose voice Partch admired: "He had a kind of a cry in his voice, which I thought was just beautiful."[14] These three, with Partch himself, formed the nucleus of the ensemble throughout his stay in Madison. They began to rehearse together in November, usually during the afternoon, in the large, cluttered basement room Partch had been assigned in the physics department in Sterling Hall. The sessions were long and intense, their tone set by Partch's patient but insistent perfectionism.

In the staid atmosphere of Madison Partch struck many of those who came in contact with him as highly eccentric. This was due not to his appearance, which was quite elegant—he looked younger than his forty-three years although he was graying at the temples, and a thin moustache gave him a distinguished if slightly affected air—but to his behavior. Sometimes only the effects of his current fixations were visible and not their causes, as in the case of the strange diets necessitated by his health problems, real or imaginary—at one time only orange juice, at another only pablum.[15] He would worry over the notion that the malnutrition he had endured during his hobo days had done permanent damage to his already delicate health. His occasional allusions to his hobo travels must have seemed an odd counterpart to his apparently esoteric musical endeavors. And although capable of great kindness and warmth, he could also by turns be morose and self-pitying, a side of him that Lee Hoiby recalls as being sometimes hard to bear: "In a way, he was really very much like those bums that he hung out with as a hobo: excessive whiners, blaming the world for their self-imposed misfortunes. When things were going well musically, he would never show artistic delight; he would just stop complaining. It was as though for him art didn't elevate, it merely pulled us up out of the mire briefly to a tolerable level." Hoiby also recalls that Partch was quite open about his homosexuality, which was "taken quite for granted among us, his co-performers. And considering the repressive atmosphere of the period we were all pretty nonchalant about it. . . . I can remember only a couple of specific references to the subject. Once in my presence he produced an unforgettable drawing that he had done [in 1937] of a man masturbating on a beach. The other instance was a remark he made about someone he had met as a hobo, who was 'the best-hung man I ever knew.' At the time I didn't know what that meant, but have since learned. He never made the slightest advance to either me or Bill Wendlandt."[16]

With all the various settling-in activities and his supervising rehearsals, Partch at first made little progress with his work in composition. Among his projects was a musical setting of a transcription of a BBC broadcast of glider pilot Warren Ward describing the Normandy invasion. On December 27 he wrote to Otto Luening: "The record of the glider-pilot account is being put on a graph for me; the idea was to put a musical accompaniment under the actual record, using this voice as a solo, and I still think it a fine idea, since spontaneity is predetermined." This idea was to materialize early the following year as *"I'm very happy to be able to tell you about this . . ."* and is clearly a response—unique in Partch's output—to contemporary political and social events in Europe. It may have been prompted to some extent by pangs of conscience: Christine Charnstrom recalls "one music professor's jibe that while other men were fighting and dying in the war, Harry sat warm and comfortable over in Sterling Hall, a parasite on taxpayers."[17] Yet there is no reason to dismiss the project as an act of opportunism. It is ironic that Partch should finally have found a relatively stable base and funding for his work with War still very much in progress, and after so many years of homelessness—years in which he had suffered more than many Americans from the economic and social turbulence that preceded the United States's entry into the war.

To all external appearances Partch's situation in Madison was satisfactory. He had been allocated sufficient space for his instruments and had been given keys to a wood and metal shop on the same floor in Sterling Hall. His letters to friends at the end of the year, however, bristle with his customary complaints. He was bothered by the coldness of the Wisconsin winter, which in 1944–45 proved to be exceptionally severe: Gunnar Johansen responded by giving him a huge sheep-lined overcoat as a Christmas present. Even though it was the fourth winter in a row he had endured away from California he still missed his native state, especially at this time of year. On Christmas Eve he wrote to Bertha and Harold Driscoll: "Dammit I'm just not indigenous to this country—a fact I can forget if living conditions and circumstances surrounding my work are happy, which they are not, and so I can't." In an article the following February the *Milwaukee Journal* quoted Partch as saying that Carmel was "still home."[18]

The first opportunity for those in Madison to hear any of Partch's music was in the context of two Wednesday afternoon lecture-demonstrations that he gave in the University's Music Hall on February 28 and March 7, 1945. They were presented under the auspices of the Graduate School Research Committee, and formed a nearly complete retrospective of his work to that time. At the first Partch gave a "talk on theory, including a demonstration of scales, triads and hexads, Pythagorean, tempered, and just," and he and his ensemble performed

By the Rivers of Babylon, The Potion Scene (performed by Partch solo), *San Francisco,* and *Barstow.* The second concert featured *Two Settings from Joyce's Finnegans Wake, U.S. Highball,* and *Y.D. Fantasy.* The concerts provoked considerable controversy. One of the members of the music faculty "admitted with some chagrin that it was the largest crowd for a music event in several years," and the responses of those who attended ran the gamut from enthusiasm to disgust. "The band leader declared that my talents should be spent in the local ammunition works and that my instruments should be scrapped for the war effort. One of the French profs opened his class with—'Shi-shi-shi-shi-shi-*cah*-go!' in a voice of great derision. One of the philosophy profs got very excited over *U.S. Highball* and the music was made the subject of a seminar for the sociology dept."[19]

The music department on the whole remained "cool"—in Partch's later accounts this becomes "hostile"—and Partch claimed to have overheard remarks to the effect that "both Lee Hoiby and Christine Charnstrom . . . give up their work with me."[20] Those partisan to his cause were quite vocal in their support. Following the first recital Gunnar Johansen joined forces with Scudder Mekeel, associate professor of social anthropology, and the philologist Freeman Twaddell, and, aware that Partch's Guggenheim was about to expire, they authored a joint letter to the Rockefeller Foundation in New York attempting to secure the financial support needed to keep him at Madison for a longer period. Mekeel described the three of them as an "officious and enthusiastic Triumvirate of Cervical Extrusion" (meaning that they were prepared to stick their necks out on Partch's behalf).[21] The Rockefeller Foundation's decision, however, was a sympathetic refusal, on the grounds that music as a discipline did not feature in their program. The following month the "triumvirate" tried the Carnegie Corporation, also without success.

On May 3 Partch and his ensemble gave a full evening concert as part of the university's May Music Festival. It included works given in the lecture-demonstrations together with the premières of *Dark Brother* and *"I'm very happy to be able to tell you about this. . . ,"* the work based on the recording of the glider-pilot's account of the Normandy invasion, scored for soprano and baritone voices, Kithara, and Indian Drum. The concert was highly successful and was one of the notable events of that year's festival. Partch wrote to Henry Allen Moe that he was pleased to have succeeded in his aim "to instil a little ferment";[22] privately, however, he did not rejoice in the fact that other events at the festival had attracted as much interest and attention as his own. The members of his ensemble were all active in other events, Hoiby and Charnstrom playing solo piano works by Busoni and Prokofiev, respectively. Hoiby recalls he and his fellow students attending a concert by the resident Pro Arte Quartet, which included some of the string quartet pieces by Webern, music little known at that time and which had Hoiby, himself a composer, "on the edge of my seat."[23] Indeed, the amount of purely *musical* influence that Partch's work was exerting was disproportionately small in comparison with the aesthetic controversy it provoked. Hoiby remarks in retrospect that "in spite of all the rationales that he generated, there's something in his music which deliberately defies being made into anything seminal."[24]

Partch had arrived in Madison with the manuscript of the new draft of his book, which he had worked at the previous summer and part of the autumn in California "in preparation for submission to the University of Wisconsin Press," substantially complete. In March 1945 he sent the finished typescript to Otto Luening, who had agreed to write a foreword, and two months later submitted it to the press. It now had the title *Monophony*, and the typescript came to 440 pages with some fifty photographs and diagrams.[25] The text had been read by some of his Madison friends—in its entirety by Freeman Twaddell, and in part by Scudder Mekeel and Gunnar Johansen. They offered a few criticisms, "particularly regarding the occasional use of colloquialisms," feeling that Partch's lively but uneven prose style would detract from the scholarly import of the book.[26] They also criticized "the lack of topical headings and topical paragraphs," which made it difficult to follow the interdisciplinary and sometimes elliptical paths of Partch's argument. He decided to submit the text as it was and "to abide by competent editorial advice," knowing that the text would be carefully scrutinized by the press's readers as well as by his editor, Livia Appel.[27]

Partch himself suggested three requirements for a competent judge of his work: "That he be an American"; "That he be either a composer of music or a creative theorist"; and "That he have an open mind to arguments for Just Intonation."[28] In a letter of May 9 which accompanied his delivery of the manuscript, he explained: "The subject matter of *Monophony* is unusual in that it cuts across several fields presently constituted as scholastic entities, in any one of which there are a few or numerous authorities. Taken as an integrated subject, as a synthesis of ancient and contemporary musical theory, the physical basis of tone, and the psychological attitudes toward music of the past two thousand years, there are very few authorities." The only two authorities he recommended were Otto Luening and Howard Hanson, both of whom wrote to the press in Partch's favor. Another supporter was the influential musicologist Jacques Barzun at Columbia University, who had attended Partch's concert there the previous year, and to whom Partch sent the then final chapter, "Some Trends in Music." Barzun expressed his approval and suggested the inclusion of one of his own main enthusiasms, Berlioz, into Partch's panorama of music history.[29]

Although the typescript was now in the hands of the press there was still a long way to go, and Partch was keen to remain in Madison to see the book through publication. With the term of his Guggenheim at an end the problem of funding remained unsolved. At the end of the academic year in May, "the Graduate College wanted the music school to take me on its staff. The vote, as I recall, was 40 to 1—only Gunnar Johansen supported me."[30] Partch instead submitted a grant application to the University Research Committee. Leon Iltis, who had replaced Carl Bricken as chairman of the music school, advised the committee that "we are in sympathy with carrying on experiments in music theory but we do not wish this attitude to imply that there is or will be in the near future a place for Mr. Partch on the School of Music faculty."[31] Following more positive recommendations from others, including an eloquent letter of testimony on behalf of Partch from Johansen, the Research Committee in June appointed him as a research associate, providing $1,500 "for supplies" and a salary of $2,000 per annum from university funds.[32] In their official letter of confirmation the University Regents added the curious stipulation that his appointment was "subject to any action of the Board of Regents in relation to patents" on his instruments.[33] Partch reassured them that he had no serious intention of patenting his instrument designs: "My ultimate purpose is cultural and esthetic—that is, the creation of new music which might act as a stimulus to a more widespread investigation into aural sensations. . . . I have never considered my instruments as having commercial possibilities."[34]

Partch's continuing lack of official connection with the School of Music had its disadvantages. It meant, first, that it was not possible for students to obtain credits for their work with him and, as Partch told the Research Committee, "to expect devotion to a musical ideal to compete with a system of credits, when the student's time is already pressed to the limit in the obligation to acquire credits, imposes an almost insuperable handicap."[35] Second, it meant that his wish to give "a lecture-laboratory course in comparative and historic intonations"—an idea perhaps encouraged by the belief shown in him by Mekeel, who had told the Rockefeller Foundation that the exposition Partch had given at his February recital was presented "with a skill and ease which to us argues teaching ability of a high order"—came to nothing.[36] Indeed, perhaps partly in self-defense, he grew increasingly uncomfortable around an academic music program. Christine Charnstrom recalls that "although he was pleasant with those of us who worked with him at Sterling Hall, Harry was not known for his amiableness while at Wisconsin. . . . [He] went about freely speaking his mind on the evils of academia and the 'system.'"[37]

His artistic distance from the activities and concerns of the School of Music is evident in a composition written in July: a satirical, unaccompanied soprano-alto-tenor-bass setting of the Tsurayuki/Waley text he had previously set as the second song of *December, 1942,* which he called *Polyphonic Recidivism on a Japanese Theme.* The piece was conceived as a parody of bel canto singing, transplanted to the context of a madrigal group with ludicrous results. It was probably never performed publicly, and he seems to have considered it as a private act of letting off steam, too insubstantial to include in his list of compositions.

Partch's other main activity during his first two years in Madison centered on repairing, adapting, and building instruments. For the first time he had access to the necessary facilities and personnel to work on electronic amplification. The quiet voices of the Adapted Guitar and the Kithara were always in danger of being drowned in ensemble passages by the louder Chromelodeon. With the help of a physics professor he met in Sterling Hall, H. B. Wahlin, and two physics majors, Partch worked first at the amplification of the Kithara, which entailed a certain amount of rebuilding, then at adapting a new Guitar. The Guitar had the same tuning he had devised for his original Guitar in Carmel, but the new instrument had a fretless fingerboard with small brass rivets embedded in it, making amplification essential in compensating for the quieter tone that resulted from stopping with fingers. Encouraged by these experiments with electronics he began to plan an electronic organ which he hoped, rather optimistically, to build (with help from the physics department) in the 1945–46 year. He also built a new string instrument, the Double Canon, a precursor of his later Surrogate Kithara. It was intended for Margaret H'Doubler in the dance department and the students in her dance group Orchesis, and was used for the first time by them at a dance recital in Langdon Hall toward the end of April 1945. He also added a part for the instrument, as well as an extra voice part (singing, rather than intoning) to *U.S. Highball* in preparation for the forthcoming performance in the May Festival.

During the latter part of 1945 he adapted another Guitar, which would become Guitar II, with ten strings and played bottleneck-style with a brass rod (later he used a weighted plastic rod).[38] When it became clear that the electronic organ project was unlikely to materialize, he adapted and tuned an old reed organ, producing the instrument that would become known as Chromelodeon I, replacing his existing instrument. The following year he designed and built a new keyboard, with the usual black-and-white layout of keys in a five-octave span and additional rows of red keys (above the black) and yellow keys (below the white), which he attempted to attach to an old chapel organ, although at the time he could "only guess at the skills needed." Although the instrument worked for a few years "it did not have the facile rebound of keys or levers that is necessary in a keyboard instrument intended for an intense compositional purpose," a problem similar to the one that had beset the Ptolemy.[39]

Even more significant for the future direction of his instrument building was a new instrument from the latter part of 1945 which he named the Harmonic Canon. It was an extension of the ancient Greek monochord principle, the name Canon in this case meaning "law." Originally it had one set of forty-four strings with a movable bridge under each string: the oak-ply body was built with the assistance of his friend John McKinney, Jr., and the redwood base designed by Norman Harms. The concept was significant both musically and aesthetically. Open strings were all tuned in unison, and the use of the movable bridges provided for an infinite number of possible scale settings—either Partch's own forty-three-tone gamut or any other conceivable sequence, historic or speculative. The placing of the bridges resulted in a geometric array of lines and arcs across the body of the instrument, and one that could be changed for each new composition. Partch later offered the analogy that the open strings without bridges were like a white canvas to a painter; devising the bridge settings was in itself an imaginative, creative challenge. His aesthetic concern extended to building the music rack and the performer's stool, the latter mostly from scraps from the redwood base, retaining—another portent of one of the characteristic concerns of his later work—the shapes of the scraps as he found them.[40]

Some of the new instruments were used in a set of acetate recordings of his music made in Madison in the autumn of 1945. Through James Jacobs, Partch met Dr. Warren Gilson, a research associate in medical electronics at Madison's General Hospital. Gilson had a consuming interest in sound recording and had assembled a complete studio in his home, much of the equipment for which he had built himself. He was, moreover, as Partch described him, something of a

Partch with Harmonic Canon I, University of Wisconsin, 1946. Photo by John
Newhouse, *Wisconsin State Journal.*

"poet and philosopher," and quickly became a good friend. Gilson grew interested in making recordings of Partch's work, "for fun and for aesthetic satisfaction," as he later put it,[41] realizing from the start that there was no real
commercial potential in the idea. Their first project was to record most of the
works presented in the concerts earlier in the year— *Barstow, Two Settings from
Joyce's Finnegans Wake, By the Rivers of Babylon, Yankee Doodle Fantasy, Dark
Brother, San Francisco,* and *U.S. Highball:* some fifty-five minutes of music,
which filled sixteen sides on the 78 rpm acetate discs. Although the recordings
are not faultless, their interest is much more than historic: they contain some of
the most breathtaking moments ever captured of Partch as a performer.

Partch spent the latter half of 1945, when not working on his instruments,
"extensively" rewriting his book "under guidance of" the University of Wisconsin Press, finishing a further draft by early December.[42] His editor, Livia
Appel—who, as chance would have it, was an old high school friend of Henry
Allen Moe—had developed an almost maternal interest in him and his un-
kempt manuscript, exercising an unusually severe editorial hand and asking for
two complete rewrites before he put "the final word to the final draft" in the

spring of 1947.[43] By most accounts her affection for him was not altogether returned, but he realized the value of her assistance with his book and remained grateful for it.

It seems surprising from what we know of Partch's considerable ability as a writer that Appel should have felt his manuscript was so badly in need of censoring. It had provoked a scathing outburst from one of the press's readers, an American history professor, who berated Partch for his "bad writing";[44] and even Howard Hanson, in his otherwise positive response, had quipped that in places the exposition needed to be "translated into English."[45] Although these reactions were probably triggered by the theoretical sections of the manuscript rather than the historical passages, it is not impossible that the numerous rewrites since the time of his researches in Europe, rather than making the exposition more detailed and cogent, had led to a diffuseness of impression and an inconsistency of style. In any case, other than the "meticulous editing" of the details of his prose for which Partch credited her, the only generalization we can make about Appel's editorial hand, on limited evidence, is her tendency to curb the excesses of his humor.[46]

In the middle of February 1946 he received the good news that the book had been formally accepted for publication, although Appel insisted that a final rewrite would be necessary. The news was heartening for many reasons, and acted as a buffer against the continued indifference of the music department, with whom he still had no official connection, and increasingly little connection of any sort. Even the theater department, to whom he suggested his idea of a version of *King Oedipus,* reacted "as though I were insane."[47] Partch might in fact have been somewhat less willing to spend yet more months at the typewriter had events in the early part of 1946 not conspired against him: the good news of his book's acceptance in fact came in the midst of the most sustained difficulties in the history of his interdepartmental affiliation.

In January he had been obliged to vacate his studio in the physics building, and the university assigned him space in the storage basement of Blackhawk Garage "in the middle of a huge machine shop, where experiments were being carried on by the Navy. It was not only the noise that bothered me—I had no privacy, and various sailors were constantly puttering around, taking my tools."[48] His complaints to the president and his assistant in the university provoked no change, and after six difficult weeks there Livia Appel put him substantially in her debt by offering him the basement of her home, which he promptly took, notifying the university only after he had moved. Her basement provided adequate storage for his instruments but could not function as a rehearsal space, which effectively scotched any plans he might have had for further concerts; and, given his pragmatic approach to composition, it made any concentration on creative work difficult.

He managed nonetheless to fulfill two projects in these months. One was a series of three lectures, given fortnightly beginning on March 21 at the Play Circle in the university's Memorial Union under the auspices of the departments of anthropology and music and the University Lecture Committee, with the collective title "Expanding the Musical Consciousness." "At the first two I discussed, compared, and demonstrated tempered and just intonation, in intervals, chords, and modulations, using the Chromelodeon and Harmonic Canon. I also played 'Studies' on the Harmonic Canon, using historic scales: Terpander's hexatonic, Archytas's Enharmonic, Olympos's pentatonic, and the ancient Mixolydian harmonia as deduced by Schlesinger. At the third lecture I discussed current trends in composition, demonstrated my Kithara, and played settings of Chinese poems on my Adapted Viola."[49] This would seem to imply that there were originally four studies, of which he retained two, which became the *Two Studies on Ancient Greek Scales,* originally for Harmonic Canon solo (a Bass Marimba part was added four years later): the two scales are Olympos's pentatonic and Archytas's enharmonic.

The second project was a new recording of *U.S. Highball,* for two voices and four instruments—the Harmonic Canon appears briefly at the end—which was recorded in Warren Gilson's home and released on three twelve-inch Vinylite 78 rpm records on his GME label (which Partch liked to refer to as "God alMighty Enterprises").[50] The performers were Partch, Lee Hoiby, Christine Charnstrom, William Wendlandt, and Hulda Gieschen, and the recording was made with technical assistance from James Jacobs and Edgerton Paul. Gilson did not do any serious advertising for the records, and they sold purely by word of mouth: yet all one hundred sets (which retailed at $6.75 each, plus tax) were sold in the next few years.

Many years later Partch remarked that on studying the *U.S. Highball* recording he felt an "urgent need" for percussion instruments in his ensemble. This was not because the performance seemed rhythmically lifeless: rather, he perhaps felt that the musical language of *U.S. Highball* and of his other recent compositions could not evolve further without them. In Gilson's shop, and with his advice and assistance—the extent of which Gilson would later take pains to downplay—he began work building a Diamond Marimba. The instrument's name derives from the layout of its blocks, which are arranged in tiered rows, forming a diamond shape of thirty-six blocks with a total pitch range of nearly three octaves. The six lines of blocks from lower left to upper right give Partch's hexadic Otonality chords, the six lines from upper left to lower right the hexadic Utonalities. The consequent dual identity of each block and the overall correspondence of the layout to his geometric "tonality diamond" model—which will be discussed below—reflect his initial intention that the instrument be mostly a vehicle for the demonstration of his tuning system. However, it proved to be more genuinely musical than he had hoped. The blocks originally were of tulipwood, cocobolo, and Brazilian rosewood, but this proved unsatisfactory, and Partch replaced most of the blocks three years later with Pernambuco wood. The resonators for the blocks were lengths of Brazilian bamboo, "bought in a Los Angeles bamboo furniture factory" that year. Before building the Diamond Marimba he visited the instrument builders J. C. Deagan and Company in Chicago, where many of his observations on marimba-making were corroborated and developed. He also inspected a Bass Marimba that the company had built, which he thought was unsatisfactory. Progress on the Diamond Marimba had sufficiently advanced by June for Partch to include the instrument in that year's Report to the University Research Committee, but the final stages of construction and tuning caused him a lot of effort. The instrument can be seen retrospectively to mark a turning point in his activity as an instrument builder, and to herald the beginning of a new phase in composition.

In July 1946 he was reappointed as research associate for a further year, his salary now $2,400 plus $600 for expenses. He wrote to Otto Luening that the decision was "very generous": "I am still not under a department—the music dept. and I are farther apart than ever—and that is the source of the only trouble, a place to work."[51] In fact it was to prove a difficult and rather unhappy year, and rather than branch out into further projects Partch seems to have regarded it as a chance to wind up the activities that were not yet complete. From July until the following April he concentrated on preparing a final draft of his book. The title he had settled on was *Genesis of a Music,* a name that had been mentioned as early as October 1945 in a letter from Livia Appel to Howard Hanson. The only musical accomplishment during the year was the recording of *Ten Settings of Lyrics by Li Po,* in performances by Partch and William Wendlandt, which Warren Gilson released on his GME label in 1947.

Indeed, Partch was to spend far more time as a writer this year than ever. As an offshoot of the vein of satire unleashed in part one of his book, he produced two essays lampooning the values of the American concert system of the time, "Show Horses in the Concert Ring" and "On G-string Formality." The latter, ostensibly an attack on the cultural snobbery of musical education, is the most cynical of his many pronouncements on the subject. Beneath the sarcasm and vitriol there is a strong undercurrent of bitterness, perhaps provoked by his own frustration at the lack of recognition accorded him at the University of Wisconsin.

> Our schools are doing a bang-up job of preventing any absurd anarchy—creativity is what the wretched radicals call it—in music. No investigation—it's not in the rules. No curiosity—it's not in the rules. No more than a superficial interest in exotic musics (confidentially, there will never be One World until *everyone* loves Bach as much as we do!) . . . they could offer two initial degrees—B.B. and M.F. (the second degree available only to female candidates), that is, Bachelor of Bach, and Mistress of the Fugue (need I remind you? there was only one Master of the Fugue). . . . The penultimate degree—which would really get tough—would be D.B.D., Doctor of Bachic (not to be confused with *bacchic*—no, never!) Divinity. . . . And—finally, the *ultimate* degree, B.V.D.—Bach verus Dominus, requiring that the candidate possess the ability to rewrite the entire *B minor Mass* from memory under massive injections of pentathol.[52]

Another essay, "Musicians as 'Artists,' " is a more dignified reflection on some of the same themes. He had been reading Oswald Spengler's *Decline of the West,* whose focus on the "basic philosophic attitudes, or values, or approaches" of cultural forces in society impressed him enormously, although he was dismissive about Spengler's musical views and not much in sympathy with his attitude to Eastern thought, particularly Buddhism.

Despite the passion of his convictions and the humor with which he could express them on the page, these writings harbor an intensely personal irritation which Partch in company was finding increasingly hard to repress. The provincialism of some of the midwestern attitudes he encountered was becoming a frustration, and added to his growing conviction that he was out of place. A lecture entitled "Hopes for a Creative Age in Serious Music" that he gave in November 1946 in Decatur, Illinois, met with antipathy from a largely uninterested student body. Then, early in 1947, Livia Appel sold her house, and he was obliged to move his instruments yet again. "I again went to the presidential assistant, but he insisted there was no space."[53] His only recourse was to scatter "instruments, manuscripts, tools, materials, etc. . . . wherever storage was offered," "in basements, attics, garages, of various friends," particularly Marshall Glasier. The situation was clearly becoming intolerable, and his patience with the university bureaucracy had reached its limit.

By early in 1947 Partch had made a positive resolve to get out of Madison once his book was finally laid to rest. He had no feeling that his music had engendered a following of any real permanence at the university. He wrote on February 21 to Otto Luening: "I'm planning to build a trailer just as soon as the snow is gone and then pack my instruments in it and take off for California, and try to make a new start." After Partch had made the decision to leave, Gunnar Johansen again came to his aid by offering him the use of the abandoned smithy on his ranch at Gualala for an indefinite period, or just for the summer as an immediate port of call in California. Even more impressively, Johansen managed to get "a fund together for reconstructing the [smithy], and for living expenses for a year."[54]

Despite his frustrations in Madison, Partch was not inclined to resort to alcohol as a relief from tension, as he would later in life under similar difficulties. Hulda Gieschen, who performed in the *U.S. Highball* recording, recalls him occasionally lacing a root beer with scotch largely, she feels, for humorous effect.[55] James Jacobs remembered him as a mild social drinker, drinking mostly wine, but never (or almost never) to excess,[56] and Warren Gilson did not recall his drinking at all.

Some of his friends came to the conclusion that Partch would prefer to complain about his ill-treatment than take, or have someone else take, diplomatic steps to improve his situation. After completing the trailer, a two-wheel affair that he built from the floor up, intending to store it in the Glasiers' driveway in Madison, he ran into Lee Hoiby, who asked to see it. "Rather than describe the accomplishment (which indeed it was) with pride, he bemoaned it and complained about all the work it took, about how many screws he had to put in the plywood, etc. 'I had to build this whole thing; do you know how much work that was? I had to have a special screwdriver.'"[57] The incident of his searching out the special screwdriver was witnessed by Kenneth Lindsay, then Christine Charnstrom's fiancé, who was given a lift by Marshall Glasier, driving Partch to the hardware store. Partch complained all the way about Glasier not having adequate tools, behaving (as Hoiby puts it) like a "spoiled child."[58]

Quizzed many years later by Peter Yates about the label "difficult" that had become attached to him in Madison, and which he would never shake off, Partch recalled an incident that happened in the summer of 1947, a week before he left Madison, defending it as the one time during his years at the university that justified the label. "I was called to the administration building and conducted to several large rooms, completely vacant, and asked whether any of them were suitable for a studio. When I learned that these rooms had been vacant throughout my three-year stay at Wisconsin—well, that was when I became difficult. One day spoiled a three-year record that was otherwise perfect."[59] He paints a rather blacker picture of his leaving in a letter two years after the event, carping that ending his association with Warren Gilson "was virtually the only thing that hurt when I walked out of that foul situation."[60]

Partch remarked near the end of his life that he should have been writing his book then and composing in the 1940s.[61] Although the thought is striking, it does not reflect the reality of his situation in Madison: there is no sign of his having begrudged, nor even shown more than mild impatience with, the time spent on *Genesis of a Music,* regarding it philosophically as the fulfilling of an obligation both to himself and to the professional musical community.

Genesis of a Music is not a summation of Partch's work but a spirited polemic written in midstream, at a time when his music and his artistic vision were in the midst of a period of change. The prevalent assumption—that the book presents the definitive statement of his theoretical and aesthetic standpoint—is a mistaken one. The book as it finally appeared in print in 1949 is more like a temporary resting-point, a progress report on the searching, creative investigation that had prompted it rather than the encapsulation of its every last detail. To some extent, the book can be seen as intellectual autobiography, an account of the "wayward trail" Partch had traveled for two decades and would continue to follow. Although its inner core of ideas had remained largely unchanged since the 1920s, that core had become embedded in layers of progressive revision, and the manner of its presentation had bowed somewhat to the pressures of the professional music world.

The subtitle of the first edition of the book gave a clear statement of its subject matter: "MONOPHONY: the relation of its music to historic and contemporary trends; its philosophy, concepts, and principles; its relation to historic and proposed intonations; and its application to musical instruments." As if to emphasize the subjectivity of his approach, Partch stresses the fact that *Genesis of a Music* purports to explain and to justify his own "musical system," Monophony. The book is thus not an historical treatise nor a work of music theory in the conventional sense, but rather a detailed exposition by a composer of his own work and the theoretical and aesthetic issues pertinent to it.

In part one of the book, "Corporeal versus Abstract Music," Partch presents his ideas of Monophony and the One Voice in the guise of an extended historical analysis, based around the distinction he draws between "abstract" and "corporeal" music. This distinction is woven into the central thesis of the first part of the book: that the prevalence of "abstract" musical thought, especially in Western music of the past three hundred years, has been to the detriment of the ancient and venerable tradition of "corporeal" music, which he defines as "the essentially vocal and verbal music of the individual," a tradition stemming from epic chant and continued in the ancient cultures of China, Greece, Arabia, and India, "in all of which music was physically allied with poetry or the dance."[62]

In tracing the history of "corporeal" music, Partch examines the treatment of words in music as set down in writings spanning the centuries from ancient China through Plato, the Florentine Camerata, Cantonese opera, Gluck, Berlioz, Wagner, Mussorgsky, Schoenberg, to his own contemporaries. The point was to not so much to offer a new reading of music history for its own sake but to formulate the intuitions that had found expression in his own work—itself the embodiment of the corporeal ideal—and to contextualize them by relating them to (and occasionally confounding them with) various wide-ranging cultural expressions through history: actual works of music, or aesthetic positions, that have points of contact with his own.

In searching for expressions of corporeality, Partch traces a path through highly diverse eras of musical activity. At times the points along the way are drawn together at the expense of important distinctions among the works in question, the immediate connection of which to his own endeavors sometimes seems more hypothetical than real. In the case of Schoenberg's *Pierrot Lunaire*, although he acknowledges its somewhat anomalous place in Schoenberg's output, the implied kinship with his own compositions for intoning voice is persuasive enough. But in viewing Mahler's *Das Lied von der Erde* as the realization of "a Corporeal perception" late in its composer's life, and thereby implying its qualitative difference from the rest of Mahler's output, the cracks in the cement become all too noticeable. In passages like this one, and several times in the chapter that follows on "American Musical Tendencies," the ignorance "about modern music" that Partch had confessed some years before to Otto Luening makes itself plain.

The historical thesis in part one of *Genesis* is boldly conceived and executed with humor and literary flair. Today, however, we can see these chapters as an instance of an artist giving himself just enough rope to hang himself. Read as a theory of history, Partch's central thesis—regarding the subordination of the corporeal to the abstract—is easy enough to pull apart; but if taken as an unashamedly personal stab at artistic self-justification the chapters make enjoyable and stimulating reading. Jacques Barzun was one of the few musicologists at the time who was enlightened enough to regard them in this way; after reading a draft of the text he wrote to thank Partch for the profit he had gained in "jotting down notes and ideas suggested by your essay" and the pleasure he had felt in his sense of "sympathy, interlarded with delight in your wit, with much that you had to say . . . in this superb review."[63]

The concept of Monophony is used to link part one of *Genesis* to the discussion of music theory and intonation that constitutes the larger part of the book. "Monophony," in Partch's special use of the term, is "an organization of musical materials based upon the faculty of the human ear to perceive all intervals and to deduce all principles of musical relationship as an expansion from unity, . . . 1/1."[64] This definition, which accords with his use of the term since the 1920s, alludes to the idea of one tone both as a generator and as a symbol of the system of pitch relationships that proliferates from it, and aptly represents the hierarchical nature of those relationships. However, he also uses the term "the Monophonic concept" to signify a particular type of vocal expression, by one voice, as "manifested through . . . the individual's spoken words." "Monophonic" in this latter sense has a meaning close (though not identical) to its conventional one, that of one voice as the focus of a musical texture. He explains the connection between the term Monophonic as it pertains to his tuning system and the Monophonic as a specific vocal aesthetic by the stunning non sequitur that the two had formed a union in ancient Greece—by "the long and coexistent presence . . . of ratio-idea and music-enhanced word-vitality in the same culture, the Greek."[65] But if the linchpin connecting the historical and the theoretical parts of the book is placed under too great a strain, and if the lapses in argument in part one of the book are now all too apparent, we are on much more solid ground in the sections devoted to the theory and history of intonation, which have had a permanent influence on composition in the late twentieth century.

The theoretical ideas that Partch presents in his book had been undergoing a process of refinement for nearly twenty years. The theory itself, as he points out, is not an ex post facto extrapolation from an existing body of music—for example, a theory of harmony applicable to eighteenth- or nineteenth-century music. Rather, he offers a discussion from several perspectives of the subject of tuning. Starting from first principles, and assuming no prior knowledge of the subject on the reader's part, he introduces a body of terminology and "definitions pertaining to intonation," some standard and some of his own invention; then he offers an introduction to the "language of ratios" and presents some "basic Monophonic concepts," including the principles of scale formation using just intonation and his theory of extended consonance and dissonance. Then follows a detailed analysis of his own forty-three-tone scale and its melodic and harmonic resources, and an account of his instruments and notation. The last part of the book gives a "thumbnail sketch of the history of intonation" through the centuries, biased (as he acknowledges) toward just tunings, but scrupulously researched and accurately and engagingly written.

Although a very different kind of music theory than that offered by most writers of the time, Partch's theories are by no means as idiosyncratic as they may at first seem. The ideas expressed in *Genesis of a Music* draw on a number of traditions from different historical eras, ancient and modern (including some, like just intonation itself, supposedly abandoned in the name of "progress"), and from diverse disciplines—music theory, natural philosophy, and acoustics. His theory of consonance and dissonance, for example, relates not to the work of music theorists like Rameau and others—who held that these terms describe the function of chords in a given musical context, a "dissonance" being that which requires resolution to a "consonance"—but to the definition proposed by Helmholtz, according to which "consonance" and "dissonance" refer to the perceptual character of individual chords quite independent of musical context. Retained from his early *Exposition of Monophony* is a related concept, that of "The Progress of Consonance," which phenomenon is equated with the progressive acceptance through music history of intervals derived from the higher prime-number partials as musical materials. (This appears in *Genesis* in diagrammatic form as a "Chronology of the Recognition of Intervals.") In this evolutionary view, consonance is a comparative matter—a view essentially the same as that held by Schoenberg, who wrote in his *Harmonielehre* (1911): "the expressions 'consonance' and 'dissonance,' which signify an antithesis, are false. It all simply depends on the growing ability of the analyzing ear to familiarize itself with the remote overtones, thereby expanding the conception of what is euphonious, suitable for art, so that it embraces the whole natural phenomenon."[66] Elsewhere Schoenberg states his position that "what distinguishes dissonances from consonances is not a greater or lesser degree of beauty, but a greater or lesser degree of comprehensibility"[67]; Partch would say exactly the same.

One of the central new concepts of the book is the Tonality Diamond, which was to prove the most fruitful of his several geometric projections of his pitch resources (table 2). The Diamond does not figure as an image in the 1933 *Exposition of Monophony,* though all the relationships that it embodies are made explicit in that early text.[68] The model arranges all twenty-nine "primary" ratios of the 11-limit (with a few ratios appearing more than once) into a diamond pattern, with the tones that form Partch's hexadic Otonalities running diagonally from bottom left to top right, and the Utonalities diagonally from bottom right to top left.[69] The resulting configuration is precisely symmetrical around its vertical axis: the complement (or in musical terms, the inversion) of a given ratio (i.e., interval) can be found at the corresponding point in the other half of the Diamond. The model embodies the complementary nature of major and minor—of Otonalities and Utonalities—in that if one tunes Utonality hexads *downward* from all six tones of the 1/1-Otonality, all the remaining *Otonality* hexads appear in the process, without needing any independent generative mechanism.[70]

The relationships symbolized in the Tonality Diamond are embedded deep within the substratum of much of Partch's music, both before and after the time of *Genesis of a Music,* as the result of two main modes of thought. First, its form is projected directly in the layouts of several of his instruments, most obviously the Diamond Marimba,[71] and that in working pragmatically with the instruments and composing idiomatically for them he was working directly with the Diamond configuration itself. Second, the nature of the configuration suggested a particular kind of harmonic language, with which he was then able to work directly, even on an instrument that had no structural connection with

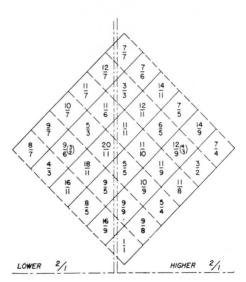

Table 2: Partch's eleven-limit Tonality Diamond.

the Diamond layout (for example the Chromelodeon)—a language that stems straight from the interlocking nature of the Diamond's constituent hexads.

On this latter subject—the relationship of his theoretical models to his compositional practice—*Genesis of a Music* has next to nothing to say. It is clear that Partch felt disinclined, perhaps out of modesty, to offer any musical analyses of passages from his compositions, even in those cases when the music manifests his theoretical precepts fairly directly, or when an example of this sort might have helped illuminate a complex theoretical point. Subsequent generations of readers seem to have taken Partch's silence on these matters as a sign that there is really nothing to be said, drawing in the process the unwarranted conclusion that his music adheres directly and straightforwardly to his theories. In fact, nothing could be farther from the truth. If the aesthetic standpoint set out in part one of *Genesis* describes Partch's work of the 1930s and 1940s best, and if much of it seems rather beside the point when considering the later theater and dance works, the theoretical exposition that forms the major part of the book should likewise be taken as representative of the state of his thinking when he wrote it: it cannot be applied indiscriminately to all periods of his work.

The overall image of Partch's creativity that emerges from his book is as disconcerting as it is invigorating. Given the subjectivity of his approach, the views the book expounds are necessarily colored by its author's anti-establishment sentiments, feelings exacerbated by his situation at the University of Wisconsin, where the book underwent its final revision. One of the themes that runs through *Genesis* and through Partch's other Madison writings and lectures, and one of the bases of his dislike of "abstract" values, is the misplaced emphasis on the interpretative rather than the creative. Christine Charnstrom recalls that he "held the unpopular opinion that it was only composers who could lay claim to being creative musicians, that performers were mere drones."[72] In "Show Horses in the Concert Ring" Partch satirizes the "average good music student's prayer" for greater technique as being "exactly as ennobling as a competitive armaments race," remarking that "the noncompetitive spirit of an Aztec village, in which virtually everyone is an artist, begins to show what the human race is capable of." By now he would unashamedly argue that the heritage of European classics, products in general of the abstraction he claimed to detest, was a stifling, paralyzing heritage, and that its prestige in the minds of the moneyed minority of Americans who patronized the arts was a form of necrophilia that only innumerable individual acts of creative anarchism would dissipate. Partch's is an art that, in William Blake's striking phrase, drives a cart and plow over the bones of the dead. It exudes an earthy, revitalizing spirit that must first subvert before it can create. The truly and fully creative society that Partch envisages in the writings of this period would be an anarchic society: *Genesis of a Music* is likewise a book for the young in spirit, and its erudition and daring have never failed to inflame and to inspire.

Gualala and Oakland

Partch wished to return to northern California in the summer of 1947 in no small part because he considered it his only
real home. On leaving Madison in June he first made a rather
hectic trip east, its most noteworthy features "some strange
old houses in Canada" and a brief stop at Niagara Falls.[1]
Early in August he arrived at Gunnar Johansen's ranch in
Gualala, spending the first weeks nervously waiting for mail
to be forwarded (from Carmel) and for a response from Livia
Appel concerning the proofs of his book.

Gualala was then a small lumbering town in an isolated
area 140 miles north of San Francisco. The Johansens' ranch
was on a steep hill on the Pacific coast. The two main buildings—the Johansens' house and an old abandoned smithy,
not used since the last century—were on either side of a dirt
road leading up the hill: a little way further up was an old
herdsman's cottage. The ranch was sheltered from the winds
blowing in from the ocean by a stretch of evergreens. Almost
immediately Partch busied himself with tasks around the

place, beginning to put the herdsman's cottage, which he liked to refer to as the Cherry house, in order. Gunnar and Lorraine Johansen arrived a few weeks later to find that he had built a picnic table under their grapevines, and planted bamboo in an area out back. Partch wrote to Livia Appel that he spent most of the day sunbathing and occasionally joining Lorraine in "picking apples and blackberries, making apple and pear cider . . . last week I cut a huge arena out of a patch of eucalypts, and called it Barena, the area where you go bare."[2] They would also go swimming, Partch impressing them with his fearlessness in diving into the sometimes chilly waters of the Gualala River; then they came home and had supper outdoors, around a fire built from manzanita nuggets.

Partch was at first content to enjoy the freedom and the sunshine that Gualala offered him, not thinking of his work or his instruments, which were still stored in the trailer parked in Marshall Glasier's driveway in Madison. Friends in Wisconsin wrote to warn him of the dangers of stultifying, but things were not at a complete halt. The Johansens brought with them the news of a possible job prospect: they had spoken to Clarence Dykstra, the provost of UCLA, who was prepared to talk with Partch about an appointment on the fine arts faculty. Partch wrote to suggest a meeting in October, for he was determined before anything else happened to carry out an idea he had had for years at the back of his mind: to explore the desolate section of the northern California coast from Rockport to the mouth of the Eel River, which was among the most uncivilized coastline left in the continental United States. He told Livia Appel: "I'm determined to take my hiking trip up the north coast wilderness before I do anything else. . . . Charis Weston (now in Eureka, the northern end of my projected trip) wrote to me ridiculing my plan, saying many had never found their way out again, but I'm going, anyway. I've been assured that I can live on seaweed, limpets, sea snails, madrone tips, and leached acorns, which abound in this country, virtually forever. Then for dessert there are huckle and salal berries, and abalones. I ain't afraid."[3]

He gathered supplies in Santa Rosa for the trip, and in September, armed with two woolen sleeping bags with rubberized covers, a knapsack, a canteen, a mess kit, a marine jungle knife, an air pillow, and about twenty pounds of dehydrated food, he spent two weeks clambering over coastal paths and attempting to hitchhike around the most inaccessible points of the coastline. Fresh water was available in most of the springs in the cliffs, and when fresh food could not be found or caught he survived on his supplies—for breakfast, dried lemon juice dissolved in water, dried prunes, coffee; for supper, salt pork or smoked herring, dry Pablum, bitter chocolate, and a shot of dark rum.

However, the travels were plagued by fog, the inaccessibility of some of the most beautiful beaches, problems with his sinus infection, and sore feet after "man-killing hours [climbing] strange ridges."[4]

In Rockport on September 9 he began documenting his travels and making sketches of the coastline in a journal he called *End Littoral*, which he typed up on his return.

The trip over, he decided not to return to Gualala but instead managed to get rides all the way south, ending up early in October at his brother Paul's in San Diego. He stayed for some weeks, busying himself at work on the tables and illustrations for *Genesis of a Music*. He traveled to Los Angeles for his long-awaited meeting on October 24 with Clarence Dykstra at UCLA. They discussed a joint appointment with the music and physics departments, oddly similar to his unsatisfactory situation in Madison. Indeed, Partch's pursuit of the idea seems a strange twist of fate in view of the atmosphere of his leaving Madison: the past three years had clearly not altogether soured his interest in an affiliation with a university. While visiting UCLA he followed up on a suggestion that he write incidental music for a production of Stephen Vincent Benét's play *John Brown's Body*, to be produced at the university the following March; but following discussions with Kenneth Macgowan in the theater arts department, he concluded that the time was too short—given that his instruments would first have to be retrieved from Wisconsin—and in any case he felt uninspired by the play. A few days later he reported to Livia Appel that he had

Drawing by Partch from *End Littoral*, 1947. Harry Partch Estate Archive.

received a note from Dykstra "saying that he was stymied (in regard to a position for me) for the academic year. I am quite light-hearted about it. I am living in a climate and a circle of mountains that I revel in."[5]

Partch's feeling of contentedness in California was fortunate, for he had no real career prospects. Rather than return north to Gualala he spent the winter in Borrego Valley, a desert region about eighty miles northeast of San Diego, and found a job in the new desert resort town of Borrego Springs, working for the planning commission. Although the financial relief was welcome, he was lonely and found himself "aching for something to fill" the long hours on his hands.[6] He was laid off at the end of February 1948 but took the news calmly, staying in the area for several weeks, camping in nearby Coyote Creek "amid the wild flowers and cactus skeletons," and enjoying the beauty of the desert landscape.[7] He began to collect cactus skeletons, which he saved and dispatched in the summer to Marshall Glasier. He passed the time reading Colin McPhee's *A House in Bali,* which Glasier had sent him. The book elicited mixed feelings: a perpetual annoyance, tinged with envy, at the fact that McPhee did not explain in any detail how his research was funded; an impatience with McPhee's reliance on the piano in assimilating and explaining the music of Bali; and disappointment at the fact that the use of voices, which interested Partch "tremendously . . . he seems not to understand at all."[8]

Although the problems of an income and a place to work remained unsolved, he was determined to base himself in California. With the coming of spring he drove across country in an old 1933 Studebaker to Madison to retrieve his trailer of instruments. He stayed for three weeks, checking on the progress of the publication of his book. In May he drove back to southern California with instruments in tow. Marshall Glasier's brother John and his family in El Centro had offered to let him stay, and Partch had planned to get a part-time job so that he would have money and time to pursue his work.

The plan is a clear indication of the lack of direction that had once again overcome him, and any hopes he might have had of pursuing his musical work were to be frustrated. The instruments remained in the trailer in John Glasier's driveway just as they had in his brother's driveway in Madison. "I have all my things," Partch told Marshall Glasier, "but they're stored, or packed away, or in sheer chaos. It seems impossible to find a place to work in. I'm quite discouraged. In the last ten years I've had my things *right with me* only about two and a half. Some record. . . . John talks about getting a bank loan to fix up his garage. But that's a long process, to say nothing of the work."[9]

To keep body and soul together he took a job as a proofreader for the *Brawley*

News, and drove from El Centro to Brawley every day to work. This thirty-mile daily round-trip entailed the upkeep of his Studebaker, and in the course of the summer he had to spend $100 on car materials and repairs from a weekly salary of $21.82. His life became quite uneventful—"work mornings, stay in the office afternoons to work on index [for his book], go to lunch counters (another activity I can't afford), and back to the El Centro garage to sleep. The trailer is crammed into a tiny space at the back of the garage. They have a beautiful backyard but it is surrounded by a concrete block wall—no place to park at all. I can only get into the trailer with difficulty. O, I could get a room in Brawley anytime, eat at greasy spoons, and stare into space during leisure hours. But the whole point of my part-time job is thus defeated."[10]

The index of his book, the final large task, was completed and sent to Livia Appel on June 21, but whatever relief it may have brought him was over-shadowed by his constant irritation with the slowness of the publication process. He grumbled about Livia Appel, rather ungratefully, in his letters to Marshall Glasier. "She says her doctor won't let her work nights, which means, I suppose, that more months will pass. . . . It is a completely dispirited, even uninterested, preparation of a book. What th' hell! I have to impose self-discipline in the face of it to maintain any interest myself."[11]

John Glasier was himself a composer, of a rather conventional kind, but one for whose lyrical gifts Partch was to develop a genuine liking. One Sunday he attended a performance of a Glasier choral work in a local church, an occasion he described in a letter to Marshall. Glasier's piece, Partch complained, didn't make much impact: "I never heard such uninspired singing in my life, and I've heard a lot." Rubinstein's "Kamenei Ostrow," which followed, "was apocalyptic in its stink"; and overall the experience was greatly depressing. "John baffles me. Here I thought I had drunk the very dregs of human degredation. But anyone who would deliberately make himself an integral part of such a business for an entire year has out-plumbed me, and endured more self-flagellation. I sat and gazed at a stained glass window, there in front of me, of Jesus Christ kneeling by a rock, with the sun streaming down on him. And all I could think of was how hot he must feel, there in the Palestine desert, with all those clothes on."[12]

Although the Glasiers proved a source of moral and practical support during these months, by the middle of August Partch had come to feel that his existence was "one long exhaustion . . . between my diurnal exhaustion and my nocturnal exhaustion there is little to choose." He had started to hitchhike to Brawley and back every day, partly to save money, and partly because of the unreliability of his car. "The daily walk to the edge of El Centro to get a ride up—and the daily walk to the edge of Brawley to get a ride back. There's no adventure in it—sheer monotony."[13]

His only recourse—with the book finally laid to rest—was to move north and take up Gunnar Johansen's standing offer of setting up a studio on his ranch in Gualala. San Diego, which had never seemed a particularly promising base for his activities, was in any case "getting hotter, and the rents higher. It would be insane to stay."[14] In the middle of August, after a few days of "enjoying the calm and silence of John's ghostly house" when the Glasiers were away, he started north up the coast.

The abandoned smithy on the Johansens' property was Partch's home for the next two and a half years, although throughout he was simply living from month to month with little feeling of permanence or stability. He and Johansen had never formalized any agreement regarding Partch's occupancy of the ranch. Johansen's invitation was an open-ended one; Partch could stay as long as he liked, until something more permanent came along. On his return from Madison the previous summer Partch had made no real attempt to settle in Gualala—perhaps the amount of work needed to make the smithy habitable had seemed daunting, or perhaps the prospect of a position at UCLA had deterred him from starting it. In either case, the increasing sense of alienation he soon began to feel in this secluded paradise shows that his acceptance of Johansen's offer was not a sign of his wishing to root himself in a remote corner of the California landscape and to draw artistic nurture from the wilderness; rather, it was a desperate denial of the urbanite he essentially was, a temporary admission of defeat.

Partch drove up the coast from San Diego with his trailer of instruments, his Studebaker miraculously making it all the way upstate and getting stuck only on the almost impossible turns near the foot of the hill that led up to the Johansens' ranch. The car refused to pull the trailer up the hill, and all but failed to make it up itself, so Partch had to unload the instruments and carry, push, or pull them up individually on his own. He set about immediately renovating the smithy, which was in considerable disrepair.[15] The proprietors of the general store at the foot of the hill, Jamie and Ruth MacNamee, distressed at finding he had been sleeping in his car while the studio was not ready, offered him a job in their store. Partch declined, but the MacNamees' store was to become one of his lifelines; it had a telephone, and it served as his postal address.

The smithy itself, as Partch wrote to Marshall Glasier, was in a "beautiful spot . . . with a field of azaleas in a little glen sweeping down from my balcony, lined by firs and redwoods above the creek";[16] this small, dark rainforest, about one hundred yards from the smithy, would become the major source of his building materials during his time in Gualala. At first, life there was not easy: "To indulge in any intellectual activity one just has to have a little freedom from personal problems. Ever since May in Madison they have plagued me: health, finances, car, trailer. Sometimes singly, sometimes simultaneously. I am over-whelmed by them. There are thousands of things demanding doing, a wood supply, a weather tight house, apples and huckleberries to put away for the winter, endless treatment for my sinus infection. O Lord! And a good part of this must be done before the heavy rains start."[17] The building and rebuilding work occupied him all through the autumn and winter months, his efforts hampered by a broken rib. He moved into the studio in January 1949, although the process of repairing it had "still not ended, nor are the leaks of California rain and the cracks that let in the current Arctic air of California corrected."[18] He told Thompson Webb, now his contact at the University of Wisconsin Press, not to be "too impatient over the slowness of communication"; "because of the condition of the road, in the rains, I sometimes go down the hill only once a week. Consequently even a telegram is not necessarily a quick means."[19]

As the year wore on the isolation became oppressive. The Johansens spent the academic year in Madison, coming to Gualala only on vacations. There were people around, but for the most part not the kind of people with whom Partch, in his gregarious moods, would choose to keep company—"puritans, winos, fat tycoons wading in rivers, and slot machine addicts. Is it any wonder I'm lonely?"[20] Consequently, such rare new friendships as came along were pursued with considerable intensity.

The most important of these was with Lauriston (Larry) Marshall, then professor of electrical engineering and director of the Microwave Laboratory at the University of California at Berkeley, and his wife, Lucie, friends of the Johansens. Although they were not musicians, the Marshalls were to become staunch professional allies and, for a time, Partch's closest friends. Their visits over the next two years, as well as proving an invaluable source of moral support, aided his material existence considerably. They brought things he needed from Berkeley, everything from supplies of food and coffee (which could only be purchased sixty miles north in Fort Bragg) to parts for his instruments or his car.

More important, the Marshalls were necessary to his psychic well-being. In July he had warned them: "I'm getting touchy like a hermit, and I'm sure if I stay here another year—alone—I'll be a confirmed recluse, rejecting everything. I find myself hoping someone will come weekends, and then being sorry they did come. Incipient psychosis."[21] He wrote frequent and lengthy letters to them, often over a glass of rum after supper, and the anticipation of their visits (and the occasional visits of others, such as his brother, Paul, and his wife) made the isolation more bearable and gave him the impetus to carry on with renovation work around the ranch. He built steps up the hill "to make it easier to carry water," and finished a small cabin guesthouse, annexed to his studio in the smithy, where the Marshalls could stay, avoiding what Partch called "the too-close intimacy and egregiously phallic symbolisms of my house."[22] His letters to them show clearly how much he treasured their visits, even at times adopting a mock pleading tone. Early in October he wrote: "Please come soon—the little cabin is cold and damp and forlorn—no fire in it yet. I redesigned the fireplace so it wouldn't smoke, hung Japanese prints on the walls, tarred the front porch so water wouldn't seep onto the floor. Please bring, send, exile anyone up here you feel inclined to."[23]

There were continual chores to keep him busy. With no refrigeration he had to salt, smoke, or pickle meat and fish; he also canned huckleberries and tomatoes (those not eaten by gophers) and made his own cider. In the dry season he spent much time chopping wood and taking care of occasional emergencies—such as trying to chase off rats who had made a nest in the Chromelodeon.

One of the things he discussed with the Marshalls, chiefly Larry, was *Genesis of a Music*. The book had finally been published in the spring by the University of Wisconsin Press in an edition of one thousand copies, at a selling price of ten dollars, high by 1949 standards. Reviews had already begun to appear in journals and magazines, and although on the whole they were favorable—with the occasional exception, such as Henry Cowell's cold and dismissive one in *Saturday Review* in November, which Partch heard about but did not see until much later—he was highly sensitive about his friends' reactions to the book. He never truly forgave Gunnar Johansen for, as he thought, never having read it properly, and was guardedly receptive to Lauriston Marshall's criticisms of his prose, telling him: "I am of course sorry that you don't like my manner of exposition. I shall quit defending it, but I think that it will be a year or two before anyone comes along who can reduce the philosophy behind seven thousand years of musical usage and misusage to an MV-over-ZX-divided-by-Gamma formula, and who can then explain his formula in the simple narrative style of the *Cleveland Torso Murders!*"[24] It was, of course, highly gratifying to receive occasional letters from sympathetic readers, especially from strangers. In November an enthusiastic letter arrived from a young master's student at Cincinnati Conservatory of Music, Ben Johnston, who proposed to come out to California to study composition with him. Even though in his correspondence with Johnston he took pains not to paint very brightly the kind of existence he led, Partch was thrilled at the prospect, sensing relief from his isolation.

In the summer of 1949, with the new studio finally ready, Partch gradually began writing music again, pulling himself out of the almost complete standstill his compositional work had reached. It had been fully five years since his last prolonged creative spell, years that had seen only occasional minor forays into composition amid work on his instruments and his book. The Madison years, and especially the fruitless year following his return to California, show a mind too distracted, and finally too despondent, too clouded with troubles and melancholy, to sustain for long the intense energies needed for creative work. The years from 1944 to 1949—foreshadowed by the even longer period from 1935 to 1941—make a dispiriting record of compositional underachievement.

Although the nature of this underachievement has more to do with the endlessly recurring, never-to-be-solved problems in the external *conditions* for his work than with internal problems with the work itself, such as a shortage of inspiration or an incapacity for hard work, these external problems are themselves partly attributable to an inner psychological conflict. The conflict was between, on one hand, Partch's temperamental aversion to permanence, to the feeling of being rooted or trapped, and, on the other, his persistent pushing of any individual who showed constancy and belief in him to the limits of their loyalty, which the Gualala years would bear out in his growing disillusionment with Gunnar Johansen.[25] He confessed to Lauriston Marshall that "perhaps the one thing I've done more efficiently than any other in my musical life is the burning of my bridges behind me," and the same could be said of his life as a whole.[26]

In one sense, his creative underachievement seems partly willful. Partch's pragmatic way of composing tied his creative activity to an unusual extent to the maintenance of a reasonably permanent studio for his instruments. He placed considerable demands on those individuals, like Johansen, who helped make such studios possible, and thus became caught in a downward spiral of constant struggle and mounting anxieties, gradually destroying the conditions that made for that stability.

In Gualala he worked at two compositional projects. One was the exquisite *Eleven Intrusions,* a set of songs which, compositionally, are squarely in line with the voice and Adapted Viola works of 1930–33, a seasonal change rather than a new departure. The other project, unique in his output to that time, was an instrumental work initially called *Tonality Flux* and subsequently renamed *Sonata Dementia,* an experiment in writing absolute music quite independent of text or extramusical reference. This latter work was felt by Partch himself to be at best a qualified success, although the music was never intended as anything more than an experiment: an attempt at a purely instrumental musical language as a complement to the nearly exclusive dependency on text in his earlier work.

An initial set of *Three Intrusions* was written in August: "The Rose," "The Crane," and "The Waterfall," for voice, Adapted Guitar II, and Diamond Marimba.[27] The first two were new settings of texts he had set unsuccessfully in *December, 1942,* and the third set another poem by Ella Young. On New Year's Eve he wrote to enlist the Marshalls' help in recording these and other pieces, asking them to bring a tape recorder on their next visit. As well as the *Intrusions* there were

> two brief sketches on ancient Greek scales that I've been practicing; I used them in lectures in Madison; for Harmonic Canon. A comparatively short composition I wrote in Ithaca seven years ago [*Letter from Hobo Pablo*], for voice, Guitar I, Kithara. It's never been performed, or even rehearsed. It's on a hobo theme, and I began to get touchy over so much criticism of my hobo music. The kithara supplies tonality and rhythm, so voice and Kithara would have to be done first, which might be difficult, and guitar added. . . . Anyway, I began to wonder what this composition sounds like—I never have known really—so I've been working it up. Also, we could do four parts of *Tonality Flux,* the composition I started last summer but didn't have time to finish, Chrom., Guitar II, Kithara, Har. Canon. A marimba part will have to wait till the instrument is rebuilt. . . . Now that I am working on my music, after 15 months of feverish preparation, I find myself in a blue funk. . . . This dreadful loneliness bothers me more now than when I was knocking myself out every day with hard work.[28]

No manuscript or sketches for *Tonality Flux* have survived. The music seems to have been derived in part from a chordal exercise for Chromelodeon called "Progressions Within One Octave," written, to guess from the handwriting and type of manuscript paper, in New York in 1943 or 1944. The title *Tonality Flux*—an accurate description of the densely textured voice-leading of the opening music—was abandoned when he resumed work on the piece in favor of the less didactic *Sonata Dementia,* with three movements entitled "Abstraction and Delusion," "Scherzo Schizophrenia," and "Allegro Paranoia." The work was essentially complete in that form by February 1950, although Partch was probably never truly satisfied with it.[29] The three movements were later reworked into *Ring Around the Moon.*

In addition to composition, he was able to concentrate for the first time since Madison on his instruments. Lauriston Marshall had had the idea of submitting a joint application to the Guggenheim Foundation for funds to build an electronic organ for Partch's work. This had Partch's enthusiastic support, not least because the damp northern California climate was wreaking havoc on the Chromelodeon, which was not staying in tune. At the end of February he wrote to Marshall in exasperation: "I shall use the Chromelodeon very little from now on; its musicality doesn't satisfy me, though it is indispensible from the standpoint of theory." All of these problems reinforced "the need either for an electronic tone or a reed made out of some alloy less susceptible to temperature changes than brass."[30]

Besides the organ project, his main concentration was on percussion instruments. He had begun repair work on the Diamond Marimba, replacing the blocks with new ones of Pernambuco wood. Concurrently with this he began building a Bass Marimba, using large Sitka spruce blocks over redwood resonators, the whole mounted on a redwood frame. Because of the size of the materials involved—the resonator for the lowest-pitched block was so large that Partch decided that the player would have to stand on a riser to play the instrument comfortably—the building process entailed an enormous amount of physical labor, most of which he carried out entirely on his own, with one or two friends who happened to be around, such as the MacNamees' son, Vernon, lending a hand. Even though he studied closely textbooks like Sir James Jeans's *Science and Music* (1937), which confirmed a few technical points on matters such as damping, much of the time he was shooting in the dark: any work with resonators and couplings for such low tones was frankly experimental. The early months of 1950 were spent at the seemingly endless work of determining resonator lengths, couplings, and block mountings; Partch exchanged weekly letters with Marshall, who provided useful advice and acted as a willing resource, obtaining tools and supplies of Pernambuco wood.

By the beginning of March Partch had started work tentatively on an instrument he named the Cloud-Chamber Bowls. It used the tops and bottoms of large Pyrex carboys (obtained, thanks to Marshall, at the glass shop of the Radiation Laboratory at Berkeley), which were hung on ropes from a redwood frame. Struck with a hard mallet they produced a beautiful, inharmonic, bell-like tone. Without the tools to grind the bowls, Partch could not tune them, so the instrument-building process became one of selecting those bowls whose fundamental pitch most closely matched one of the tones on the Chromelodeon. He also began putting together an instrument of miscellaneous percussion sounds that he called the Spoils of War.

These activities were briefly interrupted on March 5, when, by the raspberry and blueberry bushes outside his studio, he was bitten on the leg by a wood tick and had an allergic reaction. Two days later he wrote to the Marshalls: "There is still a big swelling there, about 4 inches across. Last night I dreamed that a marimba block emerged from the swelling. How appropriate! (I thought, in my dream). Get raped by a woodtick and you give birth to a marimba block!" When he had recovered sufficiently to resume work, completing the Bass Marimba became the priority.

Later that month, spurred by the urge to put the Bass Marimba to compositional use, he wrote another set of *Three Intrusions:* "The Wind," setting a poem by Ella Young with lines from Lao-tzu appended; "The Street," setting the closing paragraphs of Willard Motley's novel *Knock on Any Door,* both for voice, Harmonic Canon, and Bass Marimba; and a revision of *Letter from Hobo Pablo* as *The Letter,* with expanded ensemble. (This latter would ultimately not be included in the *Eleven Intrusions.*) He also rewrote *Two Studies on Ancient Greek Scales* to include a Bass Marimba part.

On April 6 the good news came that the Guggenheim Foundation in New York had awarded a joint grant to Partch and Marshall for "studies toward the development of an electronic instrument with electronic tone and manual keyboard." The idea of building an electronic organ was not a new one—a similar proposal had foundered at Madison some five years before—and even now, with the necessary funds, Partch harbored a certain amount of understandable pessimism about the likely success of the venture. Marshall enlisted the help of a master's student at Berkeley, William Max Mueller, to work on the project, while he put much of his own share of the grant into purchasing lumber and other materials for Partch's instruments. Since his arrival in Gualala Partch had been scraping by on thirty dollars a month: his monthly allowance now worked out at eighty-five dollars.

The tick bite proved to be only the beginning of Partch's health problems that spring. At the end of April he suffered an attack of hyperadrenalism. "I . . . stumbled down this hill in the middle of the night," he told Lauriston Marshall, who had teased him for being a hypochondriac, "in a state of mental panic because of irritation and discomfort."[31] On May 1 he was admitted to the hospital at the University of California, where surgeons removed a suspected tumor of the adrenal gland, which turned out to be a cyst. He stayed in the hospital for three weeks. Back in Gualala on June 1 he wrote to Marshall Glasier: "Now I've been out two weeks and here at the homestead a week, alone, and I feel not a bit different than before they cut me open. . . . I can't even concentrate enough to read a book." And there was more bad news to come. On June 10 he reported to Lauriston Marshall: "Two of the worst attacks I've had yet came on the last two successive days. I managed to get some of your medicine down me, although it was all I could do to hold the bottle for a minute in two hands. I pray for nothing more than dissolution into nothingness, when these attacks come. . . . I also have two swollen legs, because I seem to be allergic to the aqueous testosterone solution. . . . The three shots of Perandren I had left when you brought me up I took on alternate days, because it seemed to help get me over the condition of panic. Then I started on this aqueous solution."

The illness had a more profound impact on his general health, both physical and mental, than was perhaps apparent to those close to him at the time. A few years later he wrote to a friend that after going through the illness and the weeks of hospitalization "in rather fundamental ways I am a different person, and the change was anguishing both to me and others."[32] With these problems he was naturally worried about being on his own so much of the time, although he acknowledged that he was "no magnet of attraction right now." In this state it was all the more distressing to receive a letter from the one person he had interested in coming, Ben Johnston, who, although now quite determined to work with him, wrote in early June to announce that he would not be arriving for another couple of months. Partch told the Marshalls that he read the letter "with something close to despair. Two more months of this."[33] To Henry Allen Moe he was more circumspect, writing that, despite the advantages of life in Gualala, "For one of my temperament there are also many serious disadvantages. I am alone, off the highway on a rugged road, . . . without a phone, and without a dependable doctor, a drugstore, or a close friend within sixty miles. By close friend I mean someone who is an outlet for intellectual and musical intercourse, which is almost as necessary to me as food."[34] In need of escape, he traveled to San Diego in July to see his brother, Paul. While down south he briefly looked up Noel Heath Taylor, then music editor of a new, broadminded magazine, *Frontier:* "He suggested something that has been on his mind a good deal—a short film about my music, which he offered to write a script for."[35] The idea remained in the air for some months, but never came to anything.

In August 1950 Ben Johnston arrived in Gualala with his new wife, Betty, and found Partch "a lot more gruff and overtly unfriendly" than he had imagined.[36] At first Partch was cool toward Betty and tried openly to embarrass her by maintaining his Gualala custom of gardening in the nude; only after some weeks did he become more cordial.[37] Subsequently Johnston realized that some of Partch's curtness might have had to do with the fact that his arriving in California with a wife had put an end to Partch's "pipedream that I might become his lover": Partch's letters to Johnston prior to their arrival had expressed dire warnings about the wisdom of his decision to get married, which Partch considered a "biological trap."[38] The Johnstons also found him obsessed with his health problems. Knowing little of what he had just been through, they read most of his concern as hypochondria and found it hard to take seriously, as he seemed, on the face of things, not altogether frail. Yet the problems were real; and with increasing age—he was only some months away from his fiftieth birthday—little money, and the weight of his aloneness very much upon him, his anxieties were well founded.

The Johnstons found conditions on the ranch rather primitive, quite unlike anything they had experienced. They were at first surprised and ultimately charmed by the eccentric features that Partch had added around the place, notably an outdoor privy he called the "Throne," incorporating an ornate driver's seat from an antique horse-drawn sled, which had a commanding view of a mountain meadow with the Pacific Ocean visible in the distance through the redwoods.[39] The view had been achieved by Partch isolating the exact trees that were originally blocking the way and chopping them down.[40] Betty Johnston took over most of the cooking for the three of them. Partch would occasionally cook, his speciality being Mexican dishes, in particular very hot enchiladas, but in general he cared little for cooking and was glad to have help.

Ben Johnston had been attracted to Partch's work by *Genesis of a Music,* rather than by any of his compositions, none of which he had heard before his arrival in Gualala. Although he had successfully completed his master's degree he had felt out of place in the traditional atmosphere of a conservatory of music, and was keen to explore the radical ideas in Partch's book. Even before he had reached his teens, Johnston had become curious about tuning and about musical acoustics after he attended a lecture on Debussy, in which the speaker discussed the relevance of Helmholtz's theory of consonance and dissonance to the harmonic language of Debussy's music. "The lecturer used a monochord to demonstrate the basic premises of just-tuned intervals and the phenomenon of overtones," Johnston recalls. "I never lost the feeling of mystery and unfolding new possibilities that world of simple mathematical ratios opened to me. . . . Later, when I studied music theory, it was a disappointment and finally a disillusionment how cavalierly it sidestepped the principles of acoustics."[41]

If Johnston had hoped to spend long hours in Gualala discussing such matters with Partch, he was to be disappointed: only after some persuasion would Partch talk about theoretical matters at all. Johnston was first pressed into service helping Partch renovate the herdsman's cottage, where he and Betty were to live, Partch disregarding his protestations of lack of competence with tools. The Johnstons soon settled into the spirit of things and even managed, with Partch's help, to install a bottle wall in their cottage, forming a structure whose pieces of broken colored glass (courtesy of the MacNamees' store), cemented into the wall, would glow when the sun hit them. Partch had built a similar structure in the guest room annexed to his studio. Thereafter Ben Johnston became a kind of apprentice, helping Partch by tuning the instruments every morning in preparation for the day's work, and he and Betty learned to play them. Partch encouraged him to practice the percussion instruments, dismissing Betty's objection that Ben was not a percussionist with the retort "Hell, I'm not either." The "apprenticeship" worked as intended from the start, and in September, for the newly expanded ensemble forces available to him, Partch composed a setting of his Berkeley friend George Leite's poem "Lover," using speaking voice, soprano, Adapted Guitars II and III, Bass Marimba, and four Cloud-Chamber Bowls.

Although Partch was making little headway on the electronic organ project, one of the most satisfying offshoots of the Guggenheim funding was Lauriston Marshall's decision to hire professional help to make recordings. At the beginning of October Harry Lindgren, a sound technician from Paramount Studios, brought an MGM sound truck up into the forest at Gualala. With the help of Johnston's friend Bill Snead, who had come for the purpose, Partch and the Johnstons started to record the *Intrusions*. Partch described the session to the Marshalls as a "once-in-a-lifetime experience," praising both Lindgren and Johnston for their work.

Johnston was impatient to begin composing for Partch's instruments himself. An opportunity arose when he was asked to provide incidental music for a play entitled *The Wooden Bird* by his friend Wilford Leach, which was to be performed in January of the following year at the University of Virginia. He suggested to Partch that they make the project a collaborative effort, and together they produced some twenty minutes' worth of incidental music, most of it short fragments of songs, music for scene changes, and sound effects. The music was recorded and the tape used in the production in January. *The Wooden Bird*, with its casual mishmash of styles, stands as an interesting curiosity in this phase of Partch's work, but nothing more: as Johnston describes it, "it probably wasn't very typical of any of us—Leach included."[42]

By December Bill Snead had had enough of the difficult living conditions, and went home. Johnston brought another friend, Donald Pippin, who, although somewhat too "prim" for Partch's taste, managed to stay on cordial terms with him. Partch was encouraged by Pippin's presence to persevere with composition, and to press ahead with his plans for further recordings. The previous month he had set Giuseppe Ungaretti's poems "Soldiers," "War," and "Another War," using intoning voice, Harmonic Canon, Diamond Marimba doubling Cloud-Chamber Bowls, Guitar III, and Bass Marimba, and on December 19 he completed a setting of Ungaretti's "Vanity" for voice and Guitars I, II, and III. Together with "Lover" these formed a new set of *Five Intrusions* ("Soldiers," "War," and "Another War" he only later regarded as one). He found the Ungaretti poems in the summer 1948 issue of George Leite's *Circle* magazine, in which his article "Show Horses in the Concert Ring" had appeared, and had told Marshall Glasier at the time that he found the whole issue, especially the poetry, "exceptional." Ungaretti's work, in translations by William Fense Weaver, shared something of the same kind of delicate, specific, haiku-like imagery that Partch had admired in Li Po. "Soldiers," for example, reads: "We remain like leaves on the trees in autumn"; and "Another War": "In this darkness with my frozen hands / I can make out my face / I feel myself abandoned."

On December 30 he completed "Cloud-Chamber Music," for Adapted Viola, Guitar III, Kithara doubling an Indian Deer Hooves Rattle, Diamond Marimba doubling Cloud-Chamber Bowls, Bass Marimba, and, at the end, voices; it became the last of the *Intrusions*. The piece incorporates the melody of the "Cancion de los Muchachos" of the Isleta tribe, a recording of which he had transcribed at the Southwest Museum in Los Angeles in 1933. While rehearsing the piece he had the first of many accidents with the Cloud-Chamber Bowls, then identified by Greek letters, which he reported to Lauriston Marshall: "We had an accident with Psi yesterday. I broke it myself, I whacked it—it was a cold morning, and . . . changes of temperature will weaken glass."

Early in the new year, 1951, another recording session took place, and all the remaining *Intrusions, Dark Brother* (with a new Bass Marimba part), and *Sonata Dementia* were recorded, although the overdubs necessary for the *Sonata* were never completed. As with the previous session, not everything was recorded to Partch's satisfaction. He told Marshall that the performance of "Soldiers, War, Another War" in particular was poor, hampered by bad placement of microphones, just as in the earlier session he had not been completely satisfied with the recordings of the "Study in an Ancient Phrygian Scale" or "The Crane." Yet in retrospect the technical deficiencies of these Gualala recordings seem minor in comparison with Partch's marvelous performances: his voice sounds rather abandoned, giving these melancholy little compositions the pallor of night settling over the sky.

In their quiet, forlorn way, the *Eleven Intrusions* are among the most compelling and beautiful of Partch's compositions. They seem a product of the loneliness and introversion that haunted the months in which he wrote them. Although put together simply as a collection, they function successfully as a cycle, with their central nucleus of eight songs framed by two instrumental preludes and an essentially instrumental postlude. The work calls for a total of ten instruments, but was conceived for only five musicians: as a whole the music projects a new ensemble sound from the compositions of 1943–44, distinguished by the pairing of strings and percussion, and by the absence of the Chromelodeon.

The *Two Studies on Ancient Greek Scales,* for Harmonic Canon and Bass Marimba, which opens the work, were written in Madison fully three years before he began the other pieces. Stylistically they are less adventurous than the ensuing songs, their texture dividing rather conventionally into melody, simple strummed accompaniment, and bass line, but the quasi-vocal nature of the melodic line provides a bridge to the songs that follow.

The first group of songs uses Adapted Guitar II and Diamond Marimba, and the music grows from chordal configurations on the two instruments. "The Waterfall" offers an extended example of tonality flux, with a sequence of mostly Otonal hexads flowing nondirectionally one into the next: these are articulated by strummed chords on the Guitar and arpeggiated chords on the Diamond Marimba.

By contrast, the dark, haunting settings that follow, "The Wind" and "The Street," are more linear. The Harmonic Canon is set for a continuous microtonal sequence of Partch's forty-three-tone scale in baritone register, and its glissandi, shadowing the wailing contour of the voice, work texturally in suggesting the hollow moaning of wind rifling a deserted landscape. In "The

Street," the low-pitched sweeping movement on Harmonic Canon, coupled with delicate, fast pianissimo repeating figures on Bass Marimba played by gloved hands, brings to life the cinematic sequence of moving images thrown up by the text: the expensively clad mannequins in shop windows, the gloom of doorways, boys under lampposts, old houses, the corner prostitute.

The next group, "Lover," "Soldiers—War—Another War," and "Vanity," offers a presentiment of the future direction of Partch's use of his ensemble forces. The songs depend on timbral contrasts and gestural patterns on the instruments in articulating their form, and avoid the more usual structural relationships in harmonic terms. The songs mark the first use of the Cloud-Chamber Bowls, which in "Soldiers—War—Another War" provide a hesitant chiming that is effectively juxtaposed with low tremolos on Diamond Marimba. In "Vanity" Partch creates an appealing and original texture from tremolos and slides on his three Guitars.

"Cloud-Chamber Music" opens with a sonorous carillon on four Cloud-Chamber Bowls, their distinctive bell-like tones with complex, inharmonic spectra yielding to a mournful microtonal lament on Adapted Viola and Adapted Guitar. Following this, in a faster tempo, the Viola introduces the melody of "Cancion de los Muchachos," which is then sung by all the musicians, accompanying themselves on their instruments, except the Kithara player, who takes up a Native American deer-hoof rattle. This ritual provokes another outburst on the Cloud-Chamber Bowls. Ben Johnston has suggested a scenario implicit in this sequence of musical events: "Bearing in mind the origin of the bowls in the atomic energy program and the role of the Southwest in that development, Partch's exhortation to the downtrodden is not hard to read. . . . 'Cloud-Chamber Music' begins as a depressed reaction to a false clarion, but then seizes American Indian incentives as a reinvigorating antidote."[43] Johnston also sees the piece in part as autobiographical, an allegory of their situation in Gualala. Partch had cast himself, an aging man, in the role of inciter, with his Viola, by far the most "traditional" of his instruments, undergoing the change first, and exhorting the youthful ensemble to follow him in the transformation.

In February 1951 Partch received another tick bite, which set off a much more serious allergic reaction than the one a year earlier. The swelling became very alarming, and as night fell the Johnstons and Donald Pippin decided that they had better rush him to the hospital in Fort Bragg. His treatment proved straightforward, but the doctors advised him to get out of the woods at once and not run the risk of another bite. The advice threw the inhabitants of the ranch into confusion, because not only was there the problem of Partch's relocation, but that of the Johnstons as well.

Partch's own immediate plan was to head south and follow up on Harry Lindgren's suggestion that he meet with some of Lindgren's contacts at Paramount Studios with the idea of doing music for a Hollywood film. He visited the studios and had lunch with a couple of directors and a composer. "It seems they have a completed picture, *Worlds in Collision,* that they would like some 'weird' effects for. [The composer] wanted to know if I'd written any music for movies. No. Would I care if he used my instruments to write music for *Worlds in Collision?* No, not at all, if he were capable—if he had the background, but the background means a good deal of thought and study. . . . When he continued to assume that all he had to have was my instruments, and that they would automatically produce 'weird' effects, I'm afraid I got a little annoyed."[44] The meeting was all the more frustrating because of the appeal that writing music for films held for Partch, and he was appalled by the crassness of the approach he encountered.

From there he went on to San Diego, to be with his brother, Paul. Early in December he had received upsetting news that Paul's health was deteriorating. Paul had been suffering for two years with what was thought to be rheumatoid arthritis, but now he had been diagnosed as having an incurable bone disease. "It's a terrible blow," Partch wrote. "He spent 20 years with a bedridden wife [his first wife, Anna], raising two kids—now for some three years he has really been happy, and in just that time began to paint, and this winter was voted into the San Diego Guild because of his fine work."[45] Paul was in low spirits, knowing his case was critical and that little could be done.

Partch spent about a month in San Diego, wanting to avoid Gualala and its ticks while trying to solidify plans for his next move. There he began work on his long-projected setting of W. B. Yeats's version of Sophocles' *King Oedipus.* His resolve was to have the work produced at Mills College in Oakland, in collaboration with the director Arch Lauterer, whom he had met at Bennington College some years before, and who was then professor of speech and drama at Mills. On March 21 he wrote to the Marshalls: "I have sketched the entire *King Oedipus* roughly, dynamically, and I have composed in some detail the introduction, first scene, and first chorus; I'm just starting on the second scene. I hope to have about half of the drama finished in this manner before I return. Of course, there will be much filling in of parts and polishing to do later. I am writing Arch Lauterer today to inform him. . . . I expect to take a slow trip north, arriving Oakland about April 9th, and my present idea is to go on north, to pack up, about a week later."[46] He also hoped that Mills College would take on Ben Johnston as a student.

Partch arrived at Mills in April 1951 with the score of *King Oedipus* in progress. Oakland, even then, had become saddled with the reputation as the ugliest city on San Francisco Bay—because, as the writer John Krich remarks, "Oakland . . . was a natural warehouse, a storage depot, the end of the line . . . [having] always done the dirty work that keeps San Francisco young and beautiful."[47] Mills College itself was a pleasant enough environment, and after years in the comparative wilderness of Gualala, Partch suddenly found himself with numerous avenues of escape: to the Marshalls' apartment in nearby Berkeley, and to the allure of San Francisco itself across the Bay Bridge.

The éminence grise at Mills was the composer Darius Milhaud, who had been offered a teaching post there when he fled from Europe in 1940. Partch and Johnston were introduced to him at a dinner party given by a mutual friend, Agnes Albert, who was on the board of the college, and thanks to her intercession Milhaud was able to accept Johnston as one of his students, even midway through the academic year. Partch himself kept his distance from the Frenchman. He was uncomfortable with Milhaud's old-world sophistication and his identification with the symphony and opera world of San Francisco and its high society, complaining later that he had sensed that Milhaud and his wife, Madeleine, "resented my presence at Mills to the point of being calculatingly rude."[48] Some money from his Guggenheim Fellowship still remained, so he was free from the need to angle for a position or a salary from the college: and none seemed likely, as long as new appointments on the composition faculty came under the purview of Milhaud.[49]

The composition of *King Oedipus* proceeded swiftly during the early summer months, and he completed the 157-page score on July 31, the whole compositional period—sandwiched around his relocation to Oakland—having lasted only some twenty weeks. The work was conceived for four "intoner-actors," who take the parts of Oedipus, Jocasta, Tiresias (who doubles as the Herdsman, as "[t]ogether they personify Oedipus's fate"),[50] and the Spokesman of the Chorus; actors for the other principal roles—the Priest, Creon, the Messenger; dancers, chorus, and an ensemble of twelve instruments, his own instruments augmented by clarinet, cello, and double bass. He cut some passages of Yeats's dialogue, in particular "all of the self-analysing and oracular expatiations," wanting instead to let the music become more prominent as the drama neared its end. What we do not know is to what extent, if at all, the transcriptions he made in Dublin in 1934 of Yeats reading passages from the drama were incorporated into the score, as the transcriptions themselves have not survived. It is perhaps more likely that, at a distance of seventeen years, Partch was working quite freely with his impressions of Yeats's voice. As he had written a few years after their meeting, "I made diagrams of his inflections, but my memory of his vibrant tones is more accurate than my marks."[51]

In October, soon after the beginning of the fall semester, rehearsals got under way in the "beautiful studio in the theater building [Lisser Hall], bigger and better than anything I had at Wisconsin," that Arch Lauterer had earmarked for him.[52] "I began training Mills students to play the instruments and to read my musical notation. Others, outside the college, volunteered to play their own instruments in unusual ways, and professional singers undertook to adapt their talents to a new manner of word delivery."[53] The lead performers included Allan Louw, who played Oedipus, and the part of Jocasta was taken over by Partch's very first professional collaborator, Rudolphine Radil, after his original Jocasta, who had worked with him for months, "found the strain too great— not vocally, but psychologically."[54] The majority of student performers were female, as was the conductor, Marjorie Sweazey. Even given his latent misogyny Partch found the interest in his work displayed by the young women at the college gratifying: several of them found him personally rather attractive and his lack of flirtatiousness appealing. He even seems not to have minded the embarrassment of having one of the performers try unsuccessfully, at the post-production party, to lure him into her bed.

After weeks of individual practice a short preview performance of excerpts from the work was given in Lisser Hall on November 28. It was combined with an informal talk by Partch, illustrated with some of the recordings from Gualala, which Lauriston Marshall had brought out as a five-record 78-rpm set called *Partch Compositions*. The following day he wrote to Marshall that the occasion allowed him to become "acquainted with the hall. Its coefficient of sound absorption is simply terrific." It may be that a concern to put the acoustics of the hall to compositional use was one of the motivations behind the new instrument he was building by the end of the year: a huge marimba, the majestic size and acoustical profundity of which was conceived purposely for the Oedipus drama. He called it at first the Hypo-bass Marimba, but had changed its name to the Marimba Eroica by the time of the production in March. Originally the instrument had three enormous vertical redwood blocks giving very low frequencies around the bottom of the piano register. He also worked at improvements to the Bass Marimba and the Cloud-Chamber Bowls in preparation for the performances.

Over the Christmas period he went south to visit friends. In San Diego he saw Harold and Bertha Driscoll, who entertained him to an "excellent dinner and liquid refreshments."[55] He also paid a brief visit to his old Los Angeles friend Richard Buhlig, who was dying; and, saddest of all, a farewell visit with his brother, Paul, whose condition had become critical. When news of Paul's death reached him in February, in the midst of the rehearsal activity at Mills College, it came as no surprise. He wrote a moving letter of sympathy to Paul's wife, Adeline, known as Doll, although he decided not to attend the funeral. Paul was buried beside Anna, his first wife, "and space is reserved for me," wrote Doll. She told him to "think of Paul as he was before he was so ill," begging him to come and see her after the production: "It will seem like a little of Paul around."[56]

The collaboration with Arch Lauterer was a very satisfying experience. In the preface to *Genesis of a Music* Partch had written that the aspects of his art that drew attention—his misunderstood theories, his cryptic notation, his strange instruments—had only been his creative tools, the paints and brushes that enabled him to work; toward the end of his life he added that he had been "explaining paints, brushes—until I met Arch Lauterer."[57] "Here was a man who understood what I wanted almost without talking about it. He wanted it too. He was used to being in authority, and he was a strong over-all director. I did not intrude in his particular domain at all—that is, lights and set. But I did have in mind a particular kind of dignity, in regard to costumes, acting, dancing, and generally—I got that dignity."[58] Above all, Lauterer rose to the challenge of basing his ideas about stage direction and design for the drama around Partch's music and, more important, his instruments. In Lauterer's words,

> It is the music that determines the *manner* of showing every aspect of the dramatic action. The music is not only the expression of the emotional climate of the tragedy, but is the style and measure that orders every movement and line of the drama. It is so significantly related to the dramatic action that it must be seen with it on the stage. The instruments, massive in their arrangement in the stage space and archaic in their separate appearance, set the visual style for the production. Even the single color note derives from the tawny red of the instruments. This reddish glow develops and intensifies through other stage shapes, reaching its ultimate in the blood-drenched face and beard of Oedipus at the close of the tragedy.[59]

A scene from the first production of *King Oedipus* at Mills College, 1952. Photo by Carl Mydans, *Life* Magazine, ©Time Inc.

Working with Lauterer planted the seed of one of the recurring ideas in all Partch's subsequent theater work: that his instruments be an integral part of the stage set. In *King Oedipus* their statuesque presence enhanced the monumental nature of Lauterer's production: Lauterer's bold use of lighting, with its shifts from sudden enveloping shadow to penetrating, sharp sunlight, worked creatively to denote the passage of time, "as movement rather than static."

Partch learned a lot about stagecraft and about the concurrence of music and drama from the rehearsal process. He later confessed to Douglas Moore: "Once we put the thing on stage, I was immediately aware . . . that I had made some dreadful mistakes—mistakes which had the effect of impeding drama rather than intensifying it. I hurriedly made a few changes, but the needs were too many, and it was too late, to do a thorough job."[60] He resolved to make the necessary revisions in full after, and with the benefit of, the production.

Partch's conception of the theater was essentially a traditional one—indeed, an ancient one, its roots lying much deeper than the "specialised theatre of dialogue," as he called it, of contemporary western Europe. This theater of dialogue, under which rubric he included most of the work of his own American contemporaries, he rejected as artificially cerebral and as one which, in piling device upon device in an attempt to heighten psychological undercurrents and formal sophistication, had lost the redemptive value possessed by the older forms of ritual theater. Partch's theater world—attempting a reintegration of music, dialogue, action, mime, and dance—was intended to *hit lower* than more conventional forms of contemporary theater. In his treatment of *King Oedipus* the music was conceived "as emotional saturation, or transcendence, that it is the particular province of dramatic music to achieve."[61]

Throughout the score the acoustical terra incognita of the Marimba Eroica provides a blatant and yet majestic medium for this particular form of visceral assault and emotive saturation. Conceptually, the enormous redwood instrument and the dance-drama belong together: both have a stylized grandeur that was a new quality in Partch's work to that time, and one consistent with the epic nature of the subject. From the heavy opening Eroica strokes through the sustained low notes on the Chromelodeon, the mournful cello glissandi, and the wordless, wailing chorus lamenting the desperation that has befallen the city of Thebes, the drama unfolds amid stark, unsettling, dark-hued sonorities.

In the score of *King Oedipus* Partch takes the intoned speech principle to its extreme. In the twenty years since the early Li Po settings he had found ways of expanding the range of the intoning voice medium—by his sensitivity to the differences in musical feel suggested by the prose styles and types of meter of the writers whose texts he set—but in this work it is stretched to the limit. His earlier practice of surrendering considerations of form to the unadorned unfolding of the texts mattered less or not at all in short works, but the seventy-five minute drama showed the intoning voice medium, paradoxically, as a limited mode of expression. Indeed, the work stretched the attention span too far for some of its original listeners, and made demands that were not helped by Partch's sometimes overdone, histrionic sense of drama.

The intoned passages and the passages of freely spoken dialogue are offset by quite beautiful stretches of harmonically derived music, specifically the First Chorus, the Antiphony, and the Coda. Harmonically Partch ranges from extended consonance, however tragic in feeling—the most poignant example is perhaps found in the Antiphony, at the words "O coppice and narrow way where three roads meet"—to the extended dissonance of the Coda, extended by the integral use in the harmony of the higher "identities" of the chords, the (just) seventh, ninth, and eleventh. By the time of *King Oedipus* both this sustained, nondirectional harmonic movement (the tonality flux principle) and the spoken word manner had become natural to him: less natural was the percussive-based dance music toward the end.

King Oedipus was performed on March 14, 15, and 16, 1952, to sold-out houses. It was a considerable success, and Partch was deluged by admirers after the performances. The production received extensive Bay Area news coverage and several national reviews, although Partch cannily took note of the fact that only the *Herald-Tribune,* of the New York papers, bothered to cover the event. The reviewers were by no means unanimous in their view of the work. Most found it rather avant-garde, quite missing the fact that its starting point in Partch's youthful enthusiasm for Yeats's Abbey Theatre productions—which had acquired a historical dimension by virtue of the fact of Yeats's death thirteen years earlier—marked the work, at least in theatrical terms, as comparatively mainstream.

Most of the reviews praised Lauterer's production, but reactions to the music varied. *Time* commented that "the Partch orchestra produced cacophonous sounds sometimes reminiscent of a Hollywood sound track for a Chinese street scene, sometimes like a symphony orchestra tuning up";[62] while one reviewer in the *Oakland Tribune* wrote that "the results were rather horrendous, and Sophocles came out low man on the totem pole with his tragic story completely lost while actors 'intoned' to a strange sort of Oriental musical background . . . every time an actor had a key speech there was either a zither effect or a tom-tom dissonance to distroy its values."[63] The reviewer of the *San Francisco Chronicle,* however, felt that "his score—fragmentary, subdued, elusive—vastly enhanced the menace, torment, and bewildered, ominous tension of the tragedy";[64] and some months later Wilford Leach in *Theatre Arts* wrote that "with the production of Harry Partch's *King Oedipus* the western theater has been given one of the most challenging and revolutionary potentials in its history."[65]

The excitement of the *King Oedipus* production wound quickly down into the inevitable anticlimax, and in the middle of April he decided to escape to southern California for a few weeks. The primary reason was to visit his sister-in-law in San Diego, but the idea of further performances of *Oedipus* was very much on his mind, as well as the larger question of where to go next. Mills College had made "not the slightest gesture"[66] concerning a permanent appointment, which was discouraging; and there was a need to find a new source of income, as the funds remaining from his Guggenheim were enough to sustain him only through the summer.

The most serious interest in a new production of *King Oedipus* was shown, albeit briefly, by the music school and cinema department of the University of

Southern California. During the previous autumn a proposal by Otto Luening to produce the work at Columbia University had been considered, but fell through because there seemed no likelihood of finding sufficient funding. The episode had made Partch painfully aware of the large sums of money needed to mount the work and had brought home to him the increasing likelihood of such schemes running aground in the future. His playwright friend Wilford Leach, meanwhile, was sounding out contacts in New York and elsewhere, including Martha Graham; and the musicologist Peter Yates suggested a performance of *King Oedipus* for his "Evenings on the Roof" concert series in Los Angeles. Partch also visited Paramount Studios again. "They played my tapes, but didn't have the nerve to invite in even the alley cat. Exactly one man, a sound man, heard them all the way through. I was too disgusted to do more than say thank you and walk out."[67]

Back in Oakland he felt like a "lost soul." Arch Lauterer was going to Maine for the summer and Partch felt that it was time for him, too, to bow out. He considered moving to Marin County, where he had made a couple of acquaintances, telling the Marshalls: "There are so many artists, writers, designers over there, and they aren't stuffy. So—I've been thinking of hiring a truck and moving my instruments over to one of those substandard houses over in Mill Valley."[68] Once it became clear to him that there was no real need to vacate his studio until the end of the summer he decided to sit tight and to distract himself from the anxieties of waiting with some creative work.

During the summer of 1952 in Oakland he composed what he would later collectively entitle *Plectra and Percussion Dances,* three short and essentially independent dance works that "have no obvious integrating tie," although he felt that "in the matter of inherent quality they belong together." He wrote to Peter Yates on June 17 that he was writing them "for no one in particular, trying some new techniques both on instruments and in form." The first, *Castor and Pollux,* "A Dance for the Twin Rhythms of Gemini," was completed on July 1.[69] The second, *Ring Around the Moon,* "A Dance Fantasm for Here and Now," was largely a reworking of *Sonata Dementia* but with a new vocal part of "nonsense phrases": it was the last of the three to reach its final form. The third, *Even Wild Horses,* "Dance Music for an Absent Drama," setting (in French) fragments of Rimbaud's *A Season in Hell,* was completed on August 31.[70]

Although foreshadowed by the dance sequences of *King Oedipus,* the *Plectra and Percussion Dances* are the first of his major works to be wholly instrumental in conception. They stand in relation to *Oedipus* as a satyr play in relation to a Greek tragedy—hence the work's subtitle, "Satyr-Play Music for Dance Theater." He felt that after the prolonged period of composition and production of *Oedipus* it was "almost a necessity to give vent to feelings and ideas, whims and caprices, even nonsense, that seems to have no place in tragedy."[71] Musically, much of the impetus came from the rhythms of Latin American and Afro-American dance and popular music, which are used quite freely and wholly without prophylactic irony. In an article on the work written that summer Partch explains rather apologetically that after sitting through a session with a good jazz band in a nightclub—by no means a frequent occurrence, and something he would generally only undertake with his Berkeley friends under mild protest—his musical imagination was both fascinated and annoyed by the rhythmic practices of the music: fascinated by its immediacy and physicality, and annoyed with its steady pulse. He supplemented these responses by analyzing and transcribing recordings of Latin American dance bands. The very ambivalence of his response, and the urge to do better himself, had a revitalizing effect on his musical language.

Like *Oedipus* itself, *Castor and Pollux* draws on an ancient Greek source, but this time one with an optimistic tone: Castor and Pollux are the twin stars of good luck. "Far from treating with the story of a man [Oedipus] who is destroyed simply because he is who he is, it treats of a story where good luck is mandatory."[72] Coincidentally or not, the theme of Leda and the Swan—whose union led to the conception of the twins—was the subject of a marvelous poem by Yeats, and Partch may well have seen during his long hours in the British Museum in 1934–35 the famous Greek bas-relief on the subject, in which the rape of Leda by the swan is depicted as a magnificent form of sexual assault. Partch's descriptions of his composition are close to the concerns of Yeats's poem, emphasizing the dual psychology of "the beautiful, mortal woman Leda and the rampantly fertilizing and immortal Zeus in the form of a swan."[73] While it is primarily the mood of exuberance and optimism that infects the music—he described *Castor and Pollux* at the time of its composition, sardonically but accurately, as an "atonal-dynamic dythiramb"[74]—the work embodies a number of dualisms on a structural level. It is in two equal parts, "Castor" and "Pollux." Both consist of three dances for two instruments: "Leda and the Swan" (originally subtitled "Insemination" but later toned down to "Seduction"), "Conception," and "Incubation," which are then played simultaneously as a fourth dance for six players, "Chorus of Delivery." The music is built almost entirely from short repeating phrases of irregular lengths. "In order to effect the kind of unity of the parts that I envisioned, it was necessary to repeat phrases frequently. Yet this helps in gaining familiarity with the themes, and on second hearing, with melodic and harmonic elaboration and contrapuntal accumulation (in the Choruses of Delivery), the juxtapositions cause each individual repetition to be heard under entirely different musical conditions."[75] This is the first clear manifestation of Partch's willingness to sacrifice subtlety of formal design in the interest of making a musical process blatant enough to be perceptible at first listening: compositional craft is directed toward immediacy of impression, not toward hidden structural depth.

Ring Around the Moon is, by any standards, one of the oddest compositions in Partch's output. Loosely slung together in four "phases" lasting a total of nine minutes, the music seems willing to gamble any claim to coherence on the chance of unleashing, before an unsuspecting audience, an outrageous "satire on singers and singing, on concerts and concert audiences, on music in forty-three tones to the octave, on grand flourishes that lead to nothing."[76] Indeed, it is hard not to laugh out loud at the singer's farcically irrelevant contribution to the proceedings: at sporadic intervals he injects a succession of nonsense phrases, all to be delivered with precise timing and delicate expressive control. Musically speaking, while hardly one of Partch's more important works, there is a refreshingly alert feel to *Ring Around the Moon:* a willingness to take risks, to explore new ensemble sonorities without worrying about their ultimate persuasiveness. The music is laced with Partch's idiosyncratic humor, from the amusingly meandering, densely microtonal chord sequence at the beginning (salvaged from his 1943 or 1944 exercise in tonality flux for the Chromelodeon) to the wonderfully melodramatic ending when the voice, accompanied only by glissandi on Adapted Guitar II, declares (and for no apparent reason): "Look out! He's got a gun!"

The conception of *Even Wild Horses* treats the poet Arthur Rimbaud's exile in Africa, forging a striking link between fragments from *A Season in Hell* and the rhythms of Afro-American and Latin American popular music. While bemoaning the fact that "the African sense of rhythmic subtlety has degenerated, in the course of its evolution from tribal ceremony to Cuban ritual to Hollywood nightclub,"[77] Partch recognized that, paradoxically, it was in these supposedly bastardized forms that the rhythmic motivations for the piece had presented themselves to him. In essence, his use of these vernacular musics is little different from that of Stravinsky or Milhaud thirty years before. In his treatment, "the samba, the ñañiga, the conga, are metamorphosed, developed into something different from their starting moods . . . and all become infused with an altered character as they move toward the child-like and explosive words of Rimbaud."[78]

Even Wild Horses is divided into three acts, with eight scenes in all, lasting a total of twenty-five minutes. The three mildly humorous scenes of Act 1 are purely instrumental. The five remaining scenes, more sober in tone, each conclude with a setting of a passage from Rimbaud, creating an effective structural "rhyming" of movements thanks to the voice entry near to their close. The "dark and humorous" program of the work concerns the individual's journey, which begins with "his coming into the world as a decent and honorable mistake, and long before his life has run its course he begins to be aware of the endless reaches of his innocence."[79] This is conveyed as a purely instrumental drama, in which the instruments personify ideas or forces relevant to the concept. For example, in the first scene, "A Decent and Honorable Mistake—Samba," the "insinuating" samba rhythm is maintained by high Bass Marimba, which "delicately teases the murmuring and melodious [Harmonic] Canon."[80] After a brief abandonment for a few measures of 13/16 time the Harmonic Canon explodes as though in protest—the "Mistake"—and the scene abruptly ends. In Scene 2, "Rhythm of the Womb—Melody of the Grave," an odd dual heartbeat rhythm—two players on Bass Marimba, playing two triplet eighth notes apart—is set against a melody on Adapted Guitar III, Chromelodeon, and Adapted Viola, "a melody that is sure of nothing—not even where it is going. The immanence of death in the fact of life!"[81] Scene 3, "Happy Birthday to You," "begins with an African-sounding marimba and somehow gets involved with a Chinese-sounding guitar in a pentatonic melody, and so I call it an Afro-Chinese minuet."[82] In each of the five scenes of Acts 2 and 3 the mood is firmly established before the voice enters, but each has an air of expectancy, as though waiting for the refocusing of perspective that the vocal part brings about. These scenes offer the exact opposite of Partch's intoning voice principle: here the vocal lines grow out of the instrumental music, not the other way around. There are many beautiful moments, particularly in the first scene of Act 2, "Nor These Lips upon Your Eyes—Rumba," which is sadly sensuous; and a skillfully achieved hysteria breaks out in the final scene, "Let Us Contemplate Undazed the Extent of My Innocence," a "Tahitian Dance" in which "slowly accruing and stormy tonal masses" rise and fall through the ensemble.[83]

Even Wild Horses as a whole seems to amount to less than the sum of its parts, and following its initial performances and recording it was not revived again in Partch's lifetime. Yet it is perhaps the most fascinating of his "forgotten" works, and shows him (as do the *Plectra and Percussion Dances* as a whole) in the midst of a period of creative growth, where emotional urgency goes a long way toward compensating for the occasional shortcomings of compositional technique.

In August Partch received a "very congenial" visit from Martha Graham, who was passing through northern California. They had met almost nine years before, in New York, and with her interest in his work rekindled by Wilford Leach they now talked seriously about a collaboration. Partch played her the recording of the *Intrusions* and mentioned the dance music he was then writing. Graham was, however, less interested in choreographing an existing work than in creating a new one. She proposed that he write a new thirty-minute dance work for performance in New York in January, to a scenario she would send him. Partch was a little alarmed by the proximity of the proposed performance, and outlined for her the amount of time it would take him to write and copy the music, to learn all the parts himself so he could teach and rehearse an ensemble, to pack and transport the instruments to New York and to set them up there. Had he known then the eventual fate of the proposed collaboration he would doubtless have impressed upon her more strongly that these were not minor considerations: the ultimate success of any such venture depended upon including these logistical considerations in the overall equation. As it was she failed, not unreasonably, to register their full importance. Partch declared that he must have a definite commitment to the idea by September 1, when his Guggenheim funds would finally run out. She agreed, promising him, if the decision were favorable, a check and a scenario at the same time.

His reservations notwithstanding, Partch was thrilled at the prospect of the collaboration, both artistically and simply as a way out of his present stalemate. He admired the originality of Graham's dancing and liked her strength of character: the prospect of a well-publicized New York event, moreover, offered an appealing solution to the continued indifference he felt from artistic institutions in California. It is all the more unfortunate, then, that her visit marked the beginning of an uncomfortable five-month episode of confusions and misunderstandings, typical of the difficulties that would cling to the majority of the large-scale collaborations Partch would undertake over the next twenty years.

Once fired by an idea, his basic attitude toward collaboration was that, as the project had become the primary focus of his own emotional energies, it had to be treated with the same intensity and urgency by the other party. He could not understand—or would claim not to understand—how his collaborator could have anything more urgent on his or her mind than clearing the ground so the working process could begin. This he demanded from someone as eminent as Graham as much as from the many other less famous figures with whom he worked. Moreover, as a freelance composer he was dependent to a considerable extent on financial support from the proposed collaborator. Very few of those with whom he worked understood the precariousness of his finances, not least because Partch would of course not dwell on money matters at the outset of a creative undertaking, nor the extent to which his life could be, and would be, taken over by the collaboration.

September 1 came and went with no further communication. Arch Lauterer, who had been in New York, returned to Oakland with the news that Graham was busy trying to raise money for the project. However, Partch was now in an awkward position. His Guggenheim funds were gone, so he had no steady income; worse, he had received an order from Mills College to move his instruments. Still confident that something would come of the plan he began the elaborate job of disassembling and packing the instruments, together with his tools and repair equipment, in preparation for the move east. By way of distraction he wrote an article entitled "The Rhythmic Motivations of *Castor and Pollux* and *Even Wild Horses*" and descriptive essays on both works, and began circulating them. The days passed, and by September 20 he was already writing to a friend in unreasonable irritation about the three-week delay without communication from Graham. "All my—and Arch's—letters remain unanswered. They've all dropped dead, I guess."[84]

No sooner was this missive in the mail than he received a special delivery letter from Martha Graham in Santa Barbara. Her tone was gentle and apologetic, explaining the reasons for her slowness in communication and outlining ideas for a choreography of the *Two Studies on Ancient Greek Scales,* which she suggested using as interludes in the new work. But her mention of funding for the project sounded an alarm bell in Partch: her offer was a sum total of $500 to cover commission fee and to bring him and the instruments to New York. She was shocked to read in his reply that a realistic fee for the transportation of his instruments alone would be in the order of $350, and told him that he would have to wait a week until she returned to New York to see if more money could be found. Although the amount was not nearly sufficient, as Graham herself acknowledged, he was willing to gamble on her interest in his work, hoping that further funds could be found in the weeks ahead.

A further delay, in many ways, was the worst of all possible outcomes, and this time also it was longer than promised. Graham, of course, had many things to attend to on her return to New York besides the thorny problem of drumming up further funding for a project involving a little-known composer. Thanks to Arch Lauterer's intervention Mills College agreed to store the instruments temporarily, but in a room that could not be locked and which had a leaky roof. Partch himself felt unable to carry on, as he had been for some weeks, living off "a few small loans": to make matters worse, he was evicted from his lodgings on MacArthur Boulevard in Oakland because he was no longer able to pay his rent. Early in October his attorney friend James Fletcher in San Rafael came to his rescue by finding him a temporary job helping with the voters' lists in the Marin County Courthouse, and by offering to let him stay for a while at his home in Mill Valley.

In the midst of all the uncertainty, the direct practical assistance offered by Fletcher seems to have given Partch the mental peace to settle to a task that had been on his mind since the spring. He had planned to issue the recording of one of the performances of *King Oedipus,* and had applied for the necessary permission to the Yeats Estate. What he had assumed to be a routine matter met with a determined refusal from an agent. Permission was denied in accordance with Yeats's overall policy on musical settings, notwithstanding Yeats's own sympathetic letter to Partch of January 6, 1934, granting him "permission with pleasure" to proceed with the projected setting "subject, in case of performance or publication, to the usual business arrangements." This refusal was a considerable disappointment, and Partch realized that now a recording could only be contemplated if he rewrote the text himself and mounted a new production of the work. He put together a version using only public domain sources, putting into his own words "a composite of the versions of Jebb, Gilbert Murray, Plumptre, and Sir George Young, and Yeats to a very minor extent."[85] He had thought originally to retitle the work *Sins of the Fathers,* but changed his mind thanks to forceful objections from Wilford Leach. The new text necessitated a rewrite of the score, and he exchanged some correspondence with Douglas Moore at Columbia University about the possibility of mounting a new production of the work in New York, using players he would have trained for the Martha Graham collaboration.

The next communication from Graham herself came in the middle of October. She reported that she had been in touch with both Moore and Otto Luening about further events that might offset the costs of the projected New York performance, but that nothing definite had been established. Meanwhile, Partch's daily existence was becoming ever more difficult. His county clerk job had ended—"perhaps because I smoked a pipe, wore a checkered shirt, or put [an Adlai] Stevenson sticker on my car. . . . So far [October 28] I've been unable to find anything else, and I've very nearly reached the end of my borrowing talents . . . even a definite negative answer would have advantages. The few people I know here ask me what my plans are, and I have to tell them that I have none, and cannot have any, and so they forego moves they might make if they were sure that I would be around."[86] At the beginning of November he stayed briefly with friends in Oakland while helping to move his instruments into storage in yet another room at Mills College.

He had decided to head for Santa Rosa, where rents were cheaper, and to wait for some kind of final resolution on the New York venture. There he stayed with his old friend Martha Zoller, who was still managing the same apartments on Second Street more than twenty years after he had first lived there. He settled down to rewriting the choruses of *Oedipus* to conform to his new text, completing the rough copy of the score on December 3. Significantly, he found that he could work with his own words "with maximal creativity" and "could change them whenever it suited my harmonic, rhythmic, or dramatic purpose."[87] It proved to be a decisive experience, and thereafter Partch remained his own librettist for all his large-scale dramatic projects.

With the draft score completed he moved back to Mill Valley, this time staying with John Ludlow and his family on Cascade Way. From here on December 7 he wrote to Lauriston Marshall about the miseries of his suspended existence: "I impose on people whenever they offer me a bed and a meal. So far the only job I've been offered was as a janitor in a bar from 2 A.M. to 10 A.M. 'It is the business of the gods to take the high and make them low'—so says Tiresias. Well, I was never so high, although, for the first time in my life, last spring, I had the mistaken feeling that something was at last going to open up for me." On December 18 he received another letter from Martha Graham, who promised to send him a check if he would confirm his interest in a collaboration. Partch replied immediately, trying to suppress his exasperation, but a further two weeks passed before their next contact, this time by phone, when she told him to send the instruments collect and she would send a check and scenario by the end of the week. "She mentioned a performance at the end of April," Partch wrote to Douglas Moore, "and even though I felt that I was making an almost insane commitment I still wanted to believe, I was still eager, and I agreed."[88] On the strength of her assurances he had a mover pick up the instruments from their room at Mills and crate them in preparation for shipment, and was presented with a bill for $106.81, full payment of which was demanded before the instruments would be dispatched collect.

The weekend came and went, *without a check from Martha Graham,* and without which I could not pay the charges which would send the instruments off to New York. In view of my experiences during the four months previous, I began to have a sickening certainty that Martha would fail me again.

Through all these months I have lived by hook, trick, and crook—to await the decision that never came—borrowing where I could, selling personal possessions where I could, working at odd jobs where I could, and imposing on a small group of friends where I couldn't do anything else. And these friends have watched my waiting—reading the pertinent letters and telegrams—with growing concern and disbelief.

I do not have $106.81, and at the time I had no idea how I might extricate myself from the trap, with accruing storage charges while trying to find a solution . . . when—on Tuesday, Jan 13th—Martha wired me that there would be another delay, I decided that the time of decision had come, that it was—and would be—too late, even though the delay of "a few days" that she mentioned *really turned out to be a few days.*[89]

In his disillusionment he sent her an angry telegram, making it clear that he was not prepared to wait any longer. He wrote more calmly to Douglas Moore that he was not abandoning all hopes for a future collaboration with her, nor the idea of a production of *Oedipus* in New York, "even though it will take quite another kind of experience to restore my faith in her awareness of the passage of time." He added a few days later that he blamed the failure on his own ignorance and naiveté.

On January 26, 1953, Graham wrote him a final communication, enclosing a small check to cover some of his present expenses. "My great mistake," she wrote, "was that I did not communicate with you as each thing arose."

I was endeavoring to find a way to meet the costs. This I hope you will believe. The matter of the long periods when I did not write are sins and I will have to deal with those as one always does with one's own. I regret that I could do no better. I think it is always difficult for each of us to realize the involvement of another's life and its great drives and needs. I did get snowed under this year. . . . I was always certain about you and definite in my belief in you and my eagerness to work with you never lagged. There was too much for me to encompass and when I did not write I know I did you a great injustice and made your year one of waiting and that is never good to do to another. I hope you will in time forgive me even though the involvement has been great for you. . . . I still hope we may be able to work together someday and I think you will then find that I can be a responsible person in ways that may seem hard to believe at this time.

A fortnight later Partch replied: "I am terribly sorry if I have hurt you. I have perhaps more than the average dislike of being hurt myself, and I believe that this makes me intensely reluctant to become the agent for hurting others. But there have been times—in the continuing struggle to exist as a composer— when harassments have come in such a rain that I felt I had to make the situation known as plainly as possible. If this has been one of those times I hope *you* will forgive *me*."90 It is tantalizing to imagine the work that might have resulted from their collaboration, the work lost in Partch's fuming dismissal of the project at the very moment it seemed set, finally, to come together.

Sausalito and Urbana

Partch regarded his compositional activity as having roots in two archetypal forms of music-making: the expressive power of human speech, and what he liked to call "the ancient rhythmic magic." His output begins with works for the medium of intoning voice, and he reaped a rich creative harvest, in fits and starts, until 1951, by which time his energies for this vein of composition seem rather depleted. From 1952 onward he began to work up toward a personal, genuinely *instrumental* manner, percussive in its derivation. The major works at the thin ends of the two wedges—*King Oedipus* and *Plectra and Percussion Dances*—are transitional works, signaling the change to the fully fledged percussion-based idiom of the "dance satire" *The Bewitched*.

These two archetypes succeed one another as themes in his writings as well. In *Genesis of a Music* Partch had expressed his belief in speech intonation as the wellspring of music, rejecting the "ecstatic, percussive, dance-inspired" hypothesis about music's origins. By the early 1950s he had come to feel the act of cleaving an instrument from a piece of wood as a tie to an ancient form of musical magic. In 1955 he wrote: "The forms that imagination may devise transform the primitive sound-generation ideas into vehicles for new and exciting adventures, and the act of transforming, in itself, like a fire by a stream, is an antidote to this age, a transcendence of its materials. And it is a small reaching back, through many thousands of years, to the first men who wished to find meaning for their lives through art."[1] The transition from the intoned speech manner to a percussive dance idiom follows his realization that the theater could be a suitable medium for both. The successful collaboration with Arch Lauterer on the *King Oedipus* production fostered in him the unshakable belief that the theater was the screen on which he should project all his future work. It spoke to the tendency of the "lonely child" in him to build "worlds of his own, both with objects and in fantasy,"[2] for which purpose the theater offered a more magically enclosed world than did the more rigid strictures of the concert hall. Moreover, Lauterer's acceptance of his instruments as dramatically compelling presences on stage both vindicated and transformed Partch's attitude to his instrument-building activity, and confirmed his belief in the sculptural and kinesthetic appeal of instruments as visual forms.

Although he had decided to stay in California following the collapse of the Martha Graham project in January 1953, Partch faced the prospect with his typical ambivalence. Back in September he had told Douglas Moore that he had "reached the limit of [his] endurance in California," his restlessness made worse by Mills College's refusal to offer any further support for his work despite the success of the *King Oedipus* production. Yet at the same time he told Peter Yates of a strong counterimpulse "to help in the fight to make [California] a center culturally independent."[3] By the end of January two separate events had conspired to strengthen his resolve to make the San Francisco Bay Area the base for his activities in the years ahead: the offer of an almost ideal new studio, and a sudden and unexpected upturn in his finances.

The new studio came about through the intervention of a new friend, the painter Gordon Onslow Ford. A modest, soft-spoken Englishman who had studied in Paris amid the later flowerings of Cubist and Surrealist art, Onslow Ford was a prodigious craftsman whose work grew from a calligraphy of circles, lines, and dots. To the untrained observer his work often looked, as Partch's sounded, Oriental: its apparent simplicity came from an aim he felt he had in common with Partch, that of "making a beginning."[4] The two men met at the home of their mutual friends the Dimitroffs, where Onslow Ford and his wife, Jacqueline, had been invited for a musical evening. Gordon, who was not especially interested in music, had gone under mild protest. "There was a man sitting in the corner," he recalls, "with a rather sallow complexion, very down in the dumps; and I said to myself, there's someone I don't want to get mixed up with tonight."[5] Once this man began to talk about his instruments and Lucienne Dimitroff began to play the tapes of *King Oedipus,* Onslow Ford recalls, "my heart melted." When he discovered that Partch was homeless and had been sleeping in his old Studebaker, he invited him to come and stay in their large, ramshackle home on Magee Avenue in Mill Valley—one of the oldest houses in the area, perched on the slope of a hill with redwoods on three sides.

The Onslow Fords became immediately devoted to their new guest, who was not in a good state either physically or psychologically. Jacqueline took it upon herself to nurse him back to health and listen to his outpourings of woe. Rather soon they discovered he could be difficult and charming by turns; but, as Gordon remarked stoically, "it was very good for us to have a little disruption."[6] They introduced Partch around their circle of artist friends in Mill Valley and adjoining Sausalito. Gordon's most impressive act of help came following a chance meeting with someone he knew who owned some property in the abandoned shipyards in Sausalito, across the Golden Gate Bridge from San Francisco. Over a cup of coffee Onslow Ford persuaded the owner, Jim Wilson, that he ought to do something to patronize the arts, eliciting a vague promise from him that if Partch thought the property contained the makings of a suitable studio he would let him use it for a modest rent. The next day Partch telephoned and, without further discussion, Wilson told him to move in as soon as he liked. In the end Partch paid rent of only $40 per month.

The Sausalito shipyards had been built feverishly during the war. After 1945 many of the buildings had been abandoned and others had gone into private hands. A number of people, mostly young artists, took over converted ferries, barges, and houses on stilts in the area. Partch found an attractive 200-foot-long shed in a property known as the Waldo Building at 3030 Bridgeway. Years later he explained: "The shipyard had five gates, and the sign: GATE 5, was still to be seen when Harry Partch moved his instruments into a building previously used by the Army at the entrance to it."[7] The area became known locally as Gate 5. Elsewhere in the confines of the Waldo Building was the M. W. Park Company, merchants of cotton and cotton linen; Al's Used Furniture, owned by Al Tatum; and in the autumn of 1954 these enterprises were joined by Lunquist and Kuhlman, importers of plastic eyeglass frames. Onslow Ford recalls that Partch's corner of the building was distinguished by the scent of spices and coffee, which was almost constantly brewing in a corner of his studio.

His financial situation had improved thanks to Martha Graham's check for $100, as compensation for the difficulties she had caused him, and an unexpected letter in January from Douglas Moore, who had secured him an award of $500 from the National Institute of Arts and Letters. With these remedies to his finances, plus two gifts from Bay Area friends, he was able to move into the studio at Gate 5 early in February 1953.

Sausalito, at the southern foot of Mount Tamalpais, was described by one of its more famous inhabitants, the philosopher Alan Watts, as "a steep slope of wooded and begardened villas going straight down to a colourful mess of shops and harbors . . . the nearest thing in the United States to a fishing village on the Italian Riviera."[8] By the beginning of the fifties it was already the scene of a bohemian artists' community, mostly based around the houseboats, of which Onslow Ford owned one of the earliest. Partch's Sausalito neighbors would include, at various times, the artist Jean Varda, whom he had known at Big Sur; the poet Maya Angelou; and Alan Watts himself. Watts, with his wide erudition in world religions and comparative mythology and his involvement in the American Academy of Asian Studies, was already a well-known figure. Although he was a good friend of the Onslow Fords—through him Gordon developed a consuming interest in Chinese calligraphy and a knowledge of its use in Taoism and Zen—Watts and Partch remained only casual acquaintances. On matters of religion their views could scarcely be farther apart. Confronted with religious practitioners Partch would often slip into the role of the diehard atheist, his father's role: in calmer moods he would present himself as a rational agnostic. He reputedly remarked on one occasion, when Watts was talking about religious ritual, that ritual was fine with him as long as it didn't have religion attached to it.[9] And yet this antipathy toward Watts's multifarious and disinterested attachment to Eastern cultures stands as an early sign of the distance Partch was to keep from the intellectual milieu of the San Francisco area.

The improvement in his financial situation enabled him to turn his attention to a performance and recording of the *Plectra and Percussion Dances.* Many of his new Sausalito and Mill Valley friends, together with some from Gualala days, were signatories to a circular issued by James Fletcher on February 7, 1953, soliciting subscriptions to a Harry Partch Trust Fund that would allow him to make a recording of the *Dances.* This new venture had been proposed by Fletcher as a solution to Partch's economic survival. The intention was to make records of his music which he could sell, and the profits from which would give him a modest income. The fund had hoped to raise "at least $1,500" for the *Dances* project: in fact it raised quite a bit more in the months ahead. Records were priced rather expensively at $7.50 each, and were promised by early July. The final impetus to embark on the project had been Partch's realization that the Gate 5 studio was easily large enough to hold rehearsals and even concerts, and the fact that the necessary musicians were already coming forward.

With the recording of the *Dances* in mind and with the help of money from the trust fund, the Gate 5 Ensemble, as Partch called it, was formed. Most of the players commuted from San Francisco for rehearsals, for expenses only; Partch quipped that "the Trust Fund . . . [was] sometimes hard pressed in the matter of paying bridge tolls." Most of them were young and from diverse musical backgrounds. What they had in common was that they "did not feel really at home in either . . . the serious or the not-so-serious . . . musical world": "In my studio they generally played music I had written, although now and then they had jam sessions, one of which started at 9 P.M. and ended only at 4 A.M.; but they occasionally achieved a kind of magic perception through their music."[10] Partch came to regard the players collectively as "lost musicians," and they continued to drift in and out of his studio throughout his stay in Sausalito. By designating them in such quasi-religious terms he was casting himself in the role of teacher, as someone who could impart a sense of musical direction, even—though he would hesitate to use the word—vision. It marked a new role for him, or perhaps the resumption of a role he had first played in "Cloud-Chamber Music," one linked to the fact of getting older: a willing acceptance of artistic responsibility, and an involvement with the concerns and aspirations of a younger generation.

The money in the trust fund placed him under considerable pressure to direct his energies toward preparations for the recording, as failure to deliver the promised product, or even a delay, would be a considerable embarrassment. On April 12 he wrote to Lauriston Marshall, who had offered to help gather together recording equipment for the sessions: "I am terribly pressed. In order to do this job on the money budgeted it must be done within five months from Feb. first. . . . I must learn every part on every instrument." Together with the usual work on instrument maintenance he was building a new instrument, the Surrogate Kithara, the first of the new creations in the Gate 5 studio. It was a small instrument with two horizontal canons with eight strings on each, similar to the earlier Double Canon he had built in Madison and left there. The instrument was intended to help with the very difficult Kithara part in *Castor and Pollux,* and allowed him to divide the part between two players.

Meanwhile, his name was becoming better known in the San Francisco area. In March the radio station KPFA in Berkeley broadcast a series of nine radio talks he had written and recorded for them with the general title "Toward a Creative Music." At that time KPFA was one of the main sources in the United States of enlightened broadcasting. Alan Watts featured regularly on the station, as did the poet Kenneth Rexroth; and KPFA had broadcast the series of recordings of Partch's old Big Sur friend Jaime de Angulo reading his *Indian Tales*. The talks fleshed out subject matter familiar from the first two chapters of *Genesis of a Music* on the misguided economics of the concert world and the recording industry. He also discussed the shortcomings of conventional music education, and his own work, illustrated by recordings.

Other public engagements were of a more transient nature. In April, at the suggestion of his friend Jordan Churchill, he presented two lectures at San Francisco State College: "The Human Ear: Its Ignored Capacities" and "The American Culture: Its New Music Potentialities." The lectures were well received and were even covered by the student newspaper *The Golden Gater*. A rather more bizarre official recognition of his standing as a composer followed in July, in the form of a letter from the institutional parole officer at San Quentin Prison, asking him to join the panel of judges for a composition competition at the Seekers Music Festival the following month.

The recording for *Plectra and Percussion Dances* was completed by the end of June. The Onslow Fords hosted a gathering and invited the ensemble players to come and hear the finished master tape. Because the music had been recorded in short fragments, none of them had much sense of the overall conception of the pieces; hearing the final product, Onslow Ford recalls, they were "transfixed."[11] The mixing and mastering proceeded swiftly, and Partch had the records—an edition of five hundred copies—in his hands by September. In the end the whole project had cost around $2,500, including Partch's living expenses; about $400 of this was provided by outright gifts to the fund from friends, and the remainder came from individual subscriptions. Partch was pleased with the outcome, telling Douglas Moore: "The whole thing has been extremely heartening, because it was made possible by 144 subscribers . . . without a subsidy, without an advertising agency to promote it, and without any assistance whatever from any of the business houses based on music." In fact, issuing his own recordings led him on a wholly unfamiliar excursion into the business world. "Besides being instrument-builder, composer, organizer and director of the ensemble, I find that I am also the manufacturer of the record (I own the masters and must pay federal excise taxes), the retailer (the

State of California has my bond to guarantee that I'll charge state sales taxes), the packer and shipper. It is all very time-consuming . . . but right at the moment it seems the only possible path that also involves continuing with my music."[12]

Although a private release, the record of the *Dances* was reviewed widely. It received "long and favorable" notices in the *San Francisco Chronicle* and the *Oakland Tribune,* which Partch found "surprising enough, . . . but the response in orders and checks was slightly sensational."[13] Further, and not always favorable, reviews followed in such national magazines as *Good Listening, High Fidelity,* and even, the following summer, the journal *Etc: A Review of General Semantics.* Partch sent some review copies, with covering letters, to likely publications: a few of his targets, such as *Saturday Review,* responded with "complete silence. No acknowledgment, no review, no mention. It was as though [it] had been dropped into the deeps of Long Island Sound."

Within the circle of Bay Area friends he had now made, one category was significantly underrepresented: other composers. Whatever sporadic contact Partch had with composers was with men based on the East Coast, and these figures remained at a distance, and more than just geographically; they were professional contacts rather than close friends. A significant exception to the rule occurred one afternoon in October, when Partch was browsing in the San Francisco Public Library. A young man approached and introduced himself as the composer Lou Harrison. Harrison, then thirty-six, had returned to California after many years on the East Coast. Partch recalled the unfavorable review of his League of Composers concert that Harrison had written during a stint as a music critic in New York in 1944, but was prepared to ignore it in the light of the younger man's evidently genuine enthusiasm for the tapes he had heard of *King Oedipus.* The two quickly became good friends: indeed, Harrison was to be Partch's only close composer friend for the rest of his life.

Largely thanks to the release of the *Plectra and Percussion Dances* record, the autumn of 1953 marked a time of consolidation, even of optimism. Record sales were bringing in a trickle of money; in the years ahead a significant part of Partch's income would derive from sales of his records, "though few Americans would consider my income from records a 'living.'"[14] Further acknowledgment of his professional status as a composer came in November in the form of a letter from Carl Haverlin at BMI (Broadcast Music, Incorporated) in New York, who invited Partch to become one of their affiliates. As his situation as a composer was very different from that of most with respect to performance, publication, and royalties, he was at a loss to know how to respond to the letter. At first he was slightly confused about what Haverlin was proposing, even thinking that BMI was somehow interested in a "stake" in his work. Once Haverlin had set him straight on that count they began to work out an affiliation that paid Partch fees for "broadcast rights" to his work.

Despite his protestations of naivete in business matters, Partch had a shrewd sense of the implications of contractual agreements. Beginning the following spring he entered into what was initially a three-year contract with BMI, stipulating a $250 advance on royalty payments per annum, a kind of minimum guarantee. As with his income from record sales, the intermittent checks from BMI would ease his way financially, providing an occasional, always modest sum of money that could make or break a new project.

Meanwhile, he had secured an invitation from KPFA to mount a complete performance of the *Plectra and Percussion Dances* at the International House in Berkeley for broadcast by the station. The occasion, on November 19, 1953, was not only the work's première but was the first public performance of any of his music since the production of *King Oedipus* at Mills. Partch prefaced the performance with a witty and charismatic introductory talk, which contributed substantially to the success of the venture. This kind of public lecture-demonstration, with a script, was his great public relations strength; by contrast he was, by his own admission, "hopelessly bad" in interviews, especially broadcast ones, when his humor would generally desert him and his capacity to respond to questions was annulled by his insistence on getting across, whatever the occasion, a nutshell account of his work and his creative philosophy.[15]

The performance at International House marked the first public appearances of the Surrogate Kithara and of Harmonic Canon II, known as Castor and Pollux, a new instrument he had built during the year. Harmonic Canon II had two canons side by side, with forty-four strings on each. It was originally designed to replace his existing Harmonic Canon, and he used the redwood base of that instrument to make the two endpieces of the new canons; in the performance, however, he used both instruments. Following the success of the KPFA event, three further performances were given in Partch's Gate 5 studio in December.

Audience response to the *Plectra and Percussion Dances* was highly favorable, and Partch attempted to rationalize the reasons for their success. He felt among the audience what he called a "here-and-now excitement," which "manifested itself in more intense listening . . . [and] in a general feeling that doors were being opened."[16] He attributed this to the predominant role of percussion in the

Dances: partly to the attractive timbres of his particular instruments, and partly to the instinctive, physical appeal of percussion as a sound source. He concluded, modestly, that the success of the *Dances* in performance was an "unconscious response to a longed-for antidote, a small and sudden relief because—in the face of wizardous dials and juke-box comic books—there is still such a thing as ancient rhythmic magic."[17] And he was pleased to see that the audiences contained a sampling of San Francisco's Asian community. Teased by a correspondent that this showed a latent Orientalism in his work, he responded: "Philosophically, I would call my music Western, if I have to place it. The initial response of many people is that it is 'Oriental,' but there have been many Orientals in my audiences here in California, and none of them who has bothered to express himself considers it 'Oriental.' In fact, the bewilderment of many Orientals is easily equal to the bewilderment of many Caucasians."[18]

A more modest concert appearance followed on February 13, 1954, when he introduced a new composition, "O Frabjous Day!"—a setting of Lewis Carroll's poem "The Jabberwock" for voice, Harmonic Canon, and Bass Marimba—at a program of the Young People's Concert Series of the Mill Valley Outdoor Art Club. The performance, including a demonstration by Partch of his instruments, was recorded by KPFA and broadcast as a forty-minute program on March 28. Several months later he composed a companion piece, "The Mock Turtle Song," for voice with Surrogate Kithara (which was proving to be a much more versatile and useful instrument than its original role as partner to Kithara I had suggested) and Spoils of War; together with "O Frabjous Day!" it became his *Two Settings from Lewis Carroll.*

As 1953 drew to a close, a new production of *Oedipus* became a priority in Partch's mind. The ban on the use of the Yeats text meant that not only could the recording not be released, but attorney friends had even suggested to Partch that both he and Mills College "could become involved in serious legal difficulties if the tapes are widely copied and played."[19] Moreover, the gratifying experience with the *Dances* had made Partch dissatisfied both with the Mills performance and, especially in loud passages, with the recording quality of the tapes. On a more positive note, he now had a willing, trained ensemble to hand and, crucially, the promise of the availability of Allan Louw, his original Oedipus, for the principal role. The drawbacks were the enormous amount of time the project would inevitably consume, and the considerable effort and anxiety involved in organizing a second trust fund, without which a new recording could not be contemplated.

With some reluctance Partch drafted a prospectus for the new fund, and in February 1954 a brochure was distributed, more elaborate than the one a year earlier, soliciting subscriptions to a projected recording of the rewritten version of the work. This time Partch had the added assistance of Gerd Stern, an artist and poet who had become a staunch supporter, and whom he appointed ensemble manager. James Fletcher, Partch's attorney friend in San Rafael, remained a trustee, "the guy who writes the checks." As rehearsals for the work got under way many of the necessary additional players were recruited from San Francisco State College. During the rehearsal period Partch tinkered with minor changes to the score as a result of problems encountered during rehearsal; even his new text received some revision following criticisms from Jordan Churchill, his friend at San Francisco State, who was a Greek scholar.

The ongoing developments in his ensemble of instruments were reflected in the new *Oedipus* score. Most significantly, he worked at a reconceived version of the Marimba Eroica. The vertical playing area of the original, built at Mills College, had proved awkward, and in his new conception the instrument was to have four horizontal Sitka spruce blocks over huge resonators, designed by his friend Bill Loughborough and built with the help of Loughborough and Gerd Stern. In addition, he rewrote the Kithara part to conform to a new tuning he had devised for the instrument, with revised hexad voicings spread over a wider pitch range. This tuning was desirable theoretically but did not sound well on the instrument, so he built Kithara II, a new instrument with the improved bass resonance necessary for the new tuning; Kithara II thus was conceived for this new tuning while Kithara I reverted to its original alto register tuning. Like its predecessor, the new Kithara had seventy-two strings arranged in twelve six-string hexads, over Sitka spruce resonators in a mostly redwood structure nearly seven feet high. The player was to stand on a riser, making the instrument— like the Marimba Eroica and Cloud-Chamber Bowls—visually and sculpturally imposing on stage. Partch also worked at rebuilding and retuning Chromelodeon II, though with less satisfactory results.

Subscriptions for the *Oedipus* recording were coming in more slowly than those for the *Dances* recording a year earlier, and although there was already enough money in the fund to record the work, there was not enough to pay for pressing the records and printing the jackets. In May James Fletcher issued a further circular to this effect, announcing in addition that subscribers and their friends would be invited to a studio performance of the work at Gate 5. This produced a worthwhile response, but in the end delays were avoided thanks to a timely royalty check from BMI rather than to further subscriptions. The performances in Partch's studio, which took place on June 2 and 3, served as a preview, and gave the musicians an opportunity to perform the work in its entirety before recording it. The principals were Allan Louw as Oedipus and Sue Bell Starck as Jocasta; the ensemble was conducted by Jack Hohensee. The musicians and singers worked essentially for free. When the singer playing Tiresias announced his unavailability for the recording sessions because of paid work elsewhere, Partch saved the day by taking the part himself.

The new recording was broadcast in its entirety by KPFA on July 16, and Partch prefaced it with an introductory talk expressing his wish for a shift away from specialization and purity toward an integration of the theater arts. "The theater has many separate and specialized forms in our contemporary world, but they were not always separate and specialized. The central idea of *Oedipus* is to bring together more of the elements that belong to theater with the purpose of increasing its power—its power of communication, its power to give meaning to our existence."[20] Yet even in so apparently clear-sighted a viewpoint lies an anomaly. Partch's willingness to issue the work as a sound recording, and to broadcast that recording on radio, can surely be seen in direct contradiction to his stated belief in a form of integrated theater in which stage action and music are inseparable. *Oedipus* does not truly depend upon its theater context any more than do the majority of operas.

A full production of the work followed on September 11 and 12, 1954, as part of the Sausalito Arts Fair. The performances, beginning at 4 P.M., took place outdoors on Shell Beach, the scorching sun and blue ocean conspiring to create a marvelously Greek ambience. The musicians, as well as the singers, were costumed, and were set against a simple but effective backdrop, largely the work of Gordon Onslow Ford.

The recording was released on two LP discs, and largely because of its price—$12.50—it never sold especially well. Reviews began to appear by the middle of October. The response was as varied as ever, but by now Partch was not afraid of incompetent or misguided reviewers and was even beginning to enjoy tackling them. He sent one such explosive response to a dismissive review that appeared in the *Los Angeles Times* on October 17: "Sir: How dare you waste my time with your 'reviews'? You . . . are a Euro-technique-inculcated hash-brain, who displaces a depth of water that a pollywog would die in. Go back to your histories, crawl between the pages, and get pressed for another century."[21]

The December issue of *Arts and Architecture,* on the other hand, carried a highly favorable review by Peter Yates. As one of a breed that Partch liked to consider his enemy—the academic musicologist—Yates had a continuing interest in and admiration for Partch's work, which provided considerable moral support, all the more so as his responses were not always favorable. A year earlier Yates had criticized the "arbitrary and rather abrupt intrusion of nonsense" in the liner notes for the *Plectra and Percussion Dances,* urging Partch to eliminate "the vestiges of your creative embarrassment" that he felt marred the composer's descriptions of his own work.[22] Yet at the same time Yates praised several aspects of the music, generally those that depended least upon Partch's verbal exegesis.

The *Oedipus* venture brought Partch a certain amount of local celebrity, though little in the way of financial reward. His modest lifestyle remained quite unchanged; Gordon Onslow Ford has described Partch's "sober, simple existence" at Gate 5 as being like that of a monk. Yet with a few exceptions he remained rather isolated from other Bay Area artists, refusing to integrate his work or his artistic concerns with theirs.

An instance of this is the brief but revealing exchange of letters with the San Francisco filmmaker Kenneth Anger which took place during April and May 1954, in the midst of the preparations for *Oedipus.* It concerned Anger's wish to use the recording of the *Plectra and Percussion Dances* in the soundtrack for his film *Inauguration of the Pleasure Dome.* Anger was one of the most radical of the young Bay Area filmmakers. His early films like *Fireworks* combined sadism and violence within an explicitly homoerotic context. Anaïs Nin, who appeared in *Inauguration of the Pleasure Dome,* described the film in her *Diary:* "[One] interpretation of Kenneth's film was that it was an extension of the masquerade. It was a portrayal of people's madness. The reality and the madness mingled and that made chaos and confusion. The links were missing, as in madness. There was a distortion. Love became hatred, ecstasy became a nightmare. Those who began with a sensual attraction ended by devouring each other. . . . The whole feeling was out of balance."[23] Partch denied Anger permission to use the *Dances* in the soundtrack, his refusal backed up by letters from representatives of the trust fund. On the one hand, this can be understood simply as the expression of a quite reasonable policy discouraging the use of his music in artistic contexts other than those he had intended. (It should be noted that some months earlier he had, albeit reluctantly, allowed fragments from the record to be used as theme music for the program *Discovery* on television station KPIX. This is not necessarily a contradiction: it might be simply that he was now wanting to clamp down on further use of the music in unintended contexts, which would progressively eradicate, even devalue, any sense of its own artistic purpose.) On the other, it seems more likely that the subject matter of Anger's film alarmed him, and Anger's reputation suggested a personality with which Partch did not want to have any association, artistic or otherwise. Such an overt treatment of homosexual subject matter as some of Anger's films contain made Partch uncomfortable; he remained discreet about his sexuality, not discussing the matter even with close friends like the Onslow Fords. His artistic isolation was such that he felt distant from even the radical elements of the San Francisco counterculture.

Feeling "both relieved and revivified" after the performances of *Oedipus* in September,[24] Partch began to plan a new dramatic work. This was the "dance satire" *The Bewitched,* the most substantial of the works from his years at Gate 5. Originally it was conceived for solo female voice (the Witch) and an ensemble of eleven instruments, and cast in ten scenes lasting some forty minutes. The score of this first version of the work was begun on December 17, 1954, and completed on January 19, 1955, the fifty-four manuscript pages evidently having taken him less than five weeks. He told Peter Yates that it was "the most 'unconscious' music I've ever written. One day later I had only a vague notion of what I'd written the day before."[25]

The theme of *The Bewitched* is the "unwitching" of human beings from their comfortable, mundane existences. The argument of the work is stated clearly by Partch himself: "We are all bewitched, and mostly by accident: the accident of form, color, and sex; of prejudices conditioned from the cradle on up. Those in a long-tenanted rut enjoy larger comforts of mind and body, and as compensation it is more frequently given to others who are not so easily domesticated to become mediums for the transmission of perception."[26] This unwitching is brought about by the central character of the work, the Witch, a demanding solo part for a female singer. Central to the concept is that the instrumentalists, the "Chorus of Lost Musicians," are co-conspirators with the Witch. As well as playing the Partch instruments they form a kind of "Greek Chorus, singing occasionally as well as playing, shouting, stamping [their] feet, even whistling,"[27] their presence on stage forming an indispensable part of the dramatic action.

From the outset, *The Bewitched* was conceived as a dance work with a story of Partch's own devising but no text: the Witch's part and the vocal interpolations by the musicians use meaningless syllables. The concept was closer in spirit to the *Dances* than to *King Oedipus,* closer to the conventions of Japanese Kabuki theater than to Greek drama. Whereas *Oedipus* had been his imaginative reconstruction of "an age . . . that has been discovered through digging and presuming and learning," *The Bewitched* was his search for "an ancient spirit of which I *know* nothing."[28]

The work is "a sequence . . . of ten psychological situations that call for some salutary witchery."[29] In each scene, thanks to the Witch's intervention, an unwitching takes place, "diametric changes . . . which bring a new perception."[30] The scenario is populated by more or less typical characters and scenes of 1950s America, with a discreetly Californian flavor, all of them rutted in "civilized" comforts of body and mind: undergrads, a pathological liar, a basketball team, a Sausalito love affair, police detectives, a courtroom, a lost political soul, and, to conclude, a room filled with "the Cognoscenti" drinking cocktails. In Partch's words: "These are stories of release—through salutary and whimsical witchery—from prejudice, from individual limitations, even from the accident of physical form—of sex, that creates mental obstacles to vision, and the release is the climax. In its characteristic way, each one is a theatrical unfolding of nakedness, a psychological strip-tease, or—a diametric reversal, with the effect of underlining the complementary character and the strange affinity of seeming opposites."[31] The concept involved three elements: the Witch, a singing part, but for a singer who was also a dancer or a mime; the "Witch's Chorus," the instrumentalists, who would be present on stage and who, besides playing their instruments, would respond vocally and by occasional body gestures to the action, but who would not be full-fledged dancers; and "the Bewitched," the characters in the ten scenes, played by the dancers. In a kind of "analogy with lyric tragedy," the Witch, the ancient, pre-Christian symbol, was "an omniscient soul, all-perceptive, with that wonderful power to make other people see"; the Chorus (the musicians) became "her instrument, always under the oracular power of suggestion"; and the dancers were the principals, who would "speak [only] with their bodies."[32]

Partch himself felt that *The Bewitched* had grown from three creative seeds. First was the "fascinatingly repulsive (or repulsively fascinating)" idea, suggested by a "man from a broadcasting organization" who had visited his studio at Mills College in the summer of 1952, that he write "a series of 'backgrounds' for television—for airplane crashes, drownings, and murders in the park, I suppose."[33] The suggestion of writing background music had a rather degrading ring to Partch, even though in his teens he had earned a partial living providing just that as a silent-movie pianist in Albuquerque. Now, given his renewed concentration on working in the theater, background music—the precipice over which all effective theater music threatens to fall—was exactly what he did *not* want to be writing, and he remained touchy about the subject for the rest of his life. Yet "some of this background music and the dramatic situations that I worked out [in the summer of 1952] are actually a part of *The Bewitched*."[34] Second was the idea of the "lost musicians," who are here banded together to become the agents of diametric change. And third was what Partch called "an old interest in the ancient idea of the *benevolent, all-knowing witch*"[35] which, as Ben Johnston has observed, is mischievously at odds with the monochromatic normality of the scenes of urban and suburban America that Partch presents in the work.[36]

In keeping with the idea of a possible tour, *The Bewitched* in its original form called for only nine musicians, and its forty-minute duration was tailored for a single LP record.[37] Partch hoped to have it ready for performance by about May 1955. He told Carl Haverlin of BMI in New York: "I'd like to present the thing at some hall in San Francisco, but if that is impossible we will certainly have some studio presentations [at Gate 5], without dancers of course." However, it seemed that getting an ensemble together, even so soon after the *Oedipus* performances, was not going to be as easy as he had hoped. "Young Americans are restless. I . . . find that in the projected music I can call on no more than three of my previous ensemble, which means a lot of training from scratch."[38]

In fact, his frustrations in maintaining a stable ensemble in Sausalito were to lead to significant changes in *The Bewitched* itself. During the spring of 1955 he pursued various paths to producing the work in California, but most of his contacts countered his rather ambitious proposals for a production and tour of the work by inviting him for a one-off lecture.[39] Partch found little appeal in most of these offers. He had by now given numerous presentations of his work in "schools, art festivals, clubs, [and] nightclubs" in California, but had grown discouraged with solo presentations, finding that "it is only when my ensemble presents *music* that I get a really spontaneous and significant response."[40] He tried to push a few places to "raise two hundred dollars more and have people to play the instruments I would bring" and told Peter Yates that an even better solution to the impermanence of his situation would be "a nominal—non-salaried—connection with an educational institution, such as I had at Mills College (where it was at least possible to have rehearsals every night). . . . My requirements are a room large enough for my instruments, some cooperation in the organization of an ensemble, and an understanding that I could make and sell records of the ensemble in order to exist. If, in addition, there were drama and dance departments that would like to use my music I'd be eager to cooperate." In the middle of April he wrote in exasperation to a friend: "I've tried for three months to form an ensemble to do an abbreviated version [of *The*

Bewitched], but it has never become complete, we've never even had a single full rehearsal, and I'm on the point of disbanding it."[41] He had been enthusiastic at the prospect of casting the poet Maya Angelou, a neighbor in Sausalito, as the Witch, but finally decided she lacked sufficient theatrical experience. Another candidate was the folk singer Odetta, who was an acquaintance, but she had too many other commitments.

Although the score had been finished in January, ideas for the work were still developing in Partch's mind. He prepared a detailed twenty-page scenario which he circulated among various contacts, with the ultimate hope that it might end up in the hands of a suitable choreographer. In writing it, he allowed his mind to "wander with little hindrance. My suggestions regarding stage-set, lights, costumes, and movements about the stage go into highly technical areas, and I would like to invoke experience and attitudes beyond my own. My statements are really questions: is this particular idea a good idea? in costume? in set? in lighting? in movement? is what I am asking, throughout. Even the music is subject to change—by lengthening, shortening, the changing of emphasis."[42] In particular he was concerned to clarify his ideas on the dramatic purpose of the musicians on stage, and in April he devised a new "prologue" to the existing scenario which made "the presence of the instruments on the stage a necessity, and provides a rationale for the power of the Chorus."[43] What he hoped to establish with the help of the scenario was "an agreed-on basis for performance, so that a true collaboration and integration results." One might however argue that, having prepared such an imaginative and detailed scenario, all he really needed was not a true collaborator but simply someone to translate his rather clear ideas into choreographic reality.

In the event, reactions to the "working script" he was circulating were mixed. One professor at San Francisco State College "almost became violent—said he got that kind of stuff every day from his students. . . . I'm inclined to think his reaction irrational, simply because if he had that reaction every day with his students he'd be catatonic by now."[44] He sent a copy rather apologetically to Peter Yates, mindful of Yates's criticisms of his liner notes for the record of the *Dances,* explaining: "The transmutation always comes in the music, and in its light the verbal element that precedes seems inadequate and even stupid. Yet, words are part of the process, because I can't for the life of me dissociate words and ideas, even musical ideas. I hear these ideas in music at the time the idea is formulating itself in words. I see the relationship, whether I communicate it or not."[45] Nonetheless, given the unusual and, for many readers, attractive nature of the scenario, Partch's verbal notes proved very worthwhile. A few years later he noted that during the period of composition "by far the major part of the extra financial help that I received was spontaneously given by people who found value in my satiric verbal notes."[46]

The 1955 scenario is an elaborate and highly colorful piece of writing. It provides a striking example of Partch's theatrical imagination at its most unfettered, and plunges headlong into areas that are usually the preserve of choreographers and stage designers, describing the stage set (a network of stairways), lighting, costume, and the integration of the musicians' movements with those of the dancers. The opening of his description of scene 8, "A Court In Its Own Contempt Rises To A Motherly Apotheosis," reads:

> The scene opens on a semi-dark stage, with a melody from the Indians of the Southern Californian desert—the Cahuillas, whose culture contains a race memory of centuries of hunger. The court stands rigid, as lights brighten, Your-Honor and Mrs. Witness on low pedestals, the two attorneys on the floor. All but Mrs. Witness wear frightening head-pieces and robes, violent in color and effect. As the [Harmonic] Canon enters, Your-Honor, whose pedestal adjoins the Spoils of War, swings a large Bass Marimba mallet, menacingly. Arguments and the questioning of Mrs. Witness begin, with sharp interruptions from the Canon (the law) and Your-Honor, who are virtually a single entity. After incredible wrangling, Mrs. Witness (with the Chromelodeon and rhythmic Kithara) finally gets a chance to use her graceful, feminine lilt, but she is ruthlessly interrupted by Your-Honor.

It is obvious that such a clearly imagined scenario presents an unusual challenge, even to the extent of robbing the choreographer of much of his or her traditional autonomy. In some passages Partch describes the dance movements in minute detail. The Witch's movements, for example, he characterizes as Kabuki-like, "slow, dignified movements with rigid trunk, and occasional quick, furious movements." His description of scene 9, "A Lost Political Soul Finds Himself Among The Voteless Women of Paradise," contains the following:

> *Dancers: Mr. Death, Miss Transfiguration, and any number of background houris.*
> The mood in paradise is static, suspended somewhere between ineffable joy and exquisite melancholy. Several beautiful women stand here and there on the stage, immobilized by Paradisian hypnosis as part of the set.
> Death and Transfiguration dance back to back throughout. When Death faces front, Transfiguration's movements are the exact reverse. With Transfiguration in front, Death's back is the mirror.
> The dancers enter simultaneously, he with a black frock coat with a white carna-

tion, and white leotards, she in a transparent Moorish veil and virtually naked beneath.

"Where am I?" says Mr. Death, obviously suffering from trauma. The Witch is abstruse. The antiphony of her Chorus and the melancholy of the echoing Harmonic Canon point up the poignance of a situation where there is no security to administer, where human charges and human defenses seem to have become organically fused into a timeless, sad ecstasy.

But the Harmonic Canon, through the Witch's power, begins to accelerate, and as it does so it engenders a high, witching, deathlike wail.

"Yah——Yoo——Yuh———!" (O Death, where is thy sting?)

Darkness descends. . . . The scene ends on a picture of Mr. Death agreeably at home with his counterpart, and among constituents who had no part in electing him.

Summing up his choreographic intent, Partch comments: "It is to be hoped that the lost musicians and the dancers, as opposing forces, will be mingled in the staging. That entrances and exits be made through the musicians or down the musicians' stairways occasionally. That close involvement of *a* dancer and *a* musician be planned occasionally, so that the work will come off as a bold and forthright venture into integrated art."

Abandoning his original plan of forming a small troupe of musicians and dancers to tour with the work, Partch spent the late summer rewriting *The Bewitched,* completing a second version in September. In its new form it lasted about seventy-five minutes. In addition to the new prologue, he appended an epilogue to the ten scenes, which now had reworded titles. Much of the new music drew on and developed the existing material, and the scenes underwent some internal expansion. He also rescored much of the music for a slightly larger ensemble. The conception of the players as a chorus of "lost musicians" and the integration of their dramatic function with the stage action became a significant part of his stage directions in the new score.

The rationale for making the work even larger—effectively, into an evening-long entertainment—was that it could now, realistically, only be staged using the resources of an institution, most likely a university or college. Rather than a touring version, with the organizational nightmare such a venture implied, mounting a production of the work now became a question of finding a single, suitable institution to take it on. During its brief existence, the Gate 5 Ensemble had freed Partch from the necessity of any such affiliation, allowing him to operate independently; but now he had no other recourse. He was heartened by the excitement shown toward the work by Arch Lauterer at Mills College, who was charmed by the scenario and was keen to direct it. The initial interest shown at San Francisco State College had evaporated, and both Partch and Lauterer felt that the other "schools in this area are too reactionary to waste time approaching."[47] Various other ideas were aired, including a film version, but as the autumn passed plans to mount the work seemed as far away as ever.

The impasse Partch had reached with *The Bewitched* fueled a growing sense of dissatisfaction with his life in the Bay Area, a feeling that had begun to take hold of him some months before. In February, suffering from stomach tension and "overwhelmed" by the difficulties of getting an ensemble together, he had cancelled a talk at San Francisco State and fled to southern California for a month. Just prior to his return to Sausalito in the middle of March he wrote to a friend that his instruments and music were "now positively repulsive" to him, and the thought of returning to Gate 5 was "anathema."[48]

Exactly why he was so reluctant to return seems, on the surface, not easy to explain. His first two years in Sausalito had been among the most settled and productive of his life. Gate 5 provided him with a comfortable and reasonably secure studio environment, a colorful and supportive circle of friends, and an existence that did not depend on a substantial income—by the spring of 1955 he was paying no rent for his studio because he was acting as a "pseudo (or crypto) night-watchman" for the Waldo Building.[49] We may ascribe his discontent simply to innate restlessness, or to fluctuating health. Or it may have more to do with the darker aspects of his outlook on life—his self-destructive impulse to crush anything or anyone that seemed to offer a lasting happiness. In fact, Sausalito was to be his home only for a further, uneasy few months; in the autumn of 1955, and almost without his knowing it, the milieu was to disappear as quickly as it had come into being.

The truth—uncomfortable for those who like to regard Partch as the embodiment of a Californian composer, whatever that might be—is simply that, even in this successful and productive period of his life, he felt isolated and out of place in the artistic climate of the San Francisco area. The city had become, by the mid-1950s, the scene of a great many exciting cultural currents, all conspiring to create what would become known a decade later as the San Francisco Renaissance, which Alan Watts characterized as "a huge tide of spiritual energy in the form of poetry, music, philosophy, painting, religion, communications techniques in radio, television and cinema, dancing, theater, and general life-style."[50] Already there was a burgeoning poetry renaissance, stimulated in great part by the presence in the city of the group of writers that would become known as the Beats—chiefly Allen Ginsberg, Kenneth Rexroth, Philip Lamantia, Robert Duncan, Gary Snyder, and Lawrence Ferlinghetti, who ran the City Lights Bookstore which served as their main locus. The novelist Jack Kerouac, soon to be the most famous of them all, paid intermittent visits to the area; the publication of his novel *On the Road* in 1957 stamped San Francisco as the Beat Generation's spiritual home.

Partch did not regard his own work as part of any of these currents. He was aware of the Beat poets and had seen some of their work, but although his name and theirs would later occasionally be linked (though chiefly by commentators outside the United States) he was never part of their world. His friend Gerd Stern, who was, has stated bluntly that "Harry had no use for the Beat Generation."[51] Although he was becoming ever more reliant on alcohol as a relief from tension, Partch felt no attraction to other recreational drugs and had no interest in smoking marijuana.[52] He was critical, too, of the emerging form of poetry recited to jazz which was becoming de rigueur at the clubs where the Beats first attracted attention. "Poetry-cum-jazz: I've heard a few very simple things I like," he told a correspondent a few years later, "but mostly, it seems to me, both poetry and jazz need a little more *cum*. They should be more *with it*. When poets are jazzmen, and jazzmen are poets we'll be closer to an art. I see little evidence that poets have studied the sounds of their own voices, and rhythms, to say nothing of the frequency sounds of their voices, and no evidence whatever that the jazzmen are doing anything different than they've always done."[53] And to another friend he complained: "It is undoubtedly my own fault, but I am soured on the S.F. Bay Area—almost to the point of psychosis. I asked James Broughton—experimental movie maker—why he left S.F., especially considering that he made his best films here. He replied that whenever he showed anything he always found the same small group in attendance. That is the way I feel—it sounds ungrateful but it really isn't. I feel that I am going around in a circle and meeting the same problems every five degrees."[54]

Partch spent most of 1955 trying to escape from the San Francisco area. His growing restlessness prompted him to disappear for another holiday toward the end of May with his painter friend from Madison days John McKinney and his wife, Rosalea. They "dropped in unexpectedly from Santa Fe" and invited him to go back with them: "Since there was nothing immediately pressing to hold me here I went."[55] Santa Fe had grown since his adolescent years in nearby Albuquerque, but its character had changed little. The elegant adobe architecture and the prevalence of a large Native American population and their handcrafts gave the place the charm of a small town, free from the encroachment of excessive commerce. The climate, too, was ideal for him, the clear, dry air smelling of piñon and sage. Although he was there on vacation he had, as ever, come prepared with samples of his work. On the evening of June 14, the McKinneys installed some good hi-fi equipment in one of the rooms of their restaurant-bar, The Pink Adobe, and Partch presented the records of *Oedipus* to a gathering of some two dozen of their friends. A brief report even made it into a local paper, the *New Mexican,* the following day, under the title "Partch Scale Introduced to Santa Fe."

Back in Sausalito in the middle of June he settled down, for a time, to a few weeks' work in composition. With *The Bewitched* still unperformed the way was blocked, mentally, for any new large-scale projects, but he worked at rewriting older pieces, producing new versions for his now much expanded instrumental resources. The previous November he had drafted a rescoring of *Barstow,* and now he tackled *U.S. Highball, By the Rivers of Babylon, The Potion Scene, San Francisco,* and *The Letter.* Although this spate of rewriting had a largely pragmatic aim, at least one task— *The Potion Scene*—involved a considerable amount of recomposition. These new versions took advantage of the current state of his ensemble of instruments, and conformed to Partch's wish to distance himself somewhat from the role of central performer in his own work. In *Barstow* and *U.S. Highball* the highly virtuosic Adapted Guitar parts, which he had originally played himself, were omitted entirely and the material rescored. Similar considerations, this time with respect to the Adapted Viola, governed the new versions of *By the Rivers of Babylon, The Potion Scene,* and *San Francisco,* in which the Adapted Viola parts were transferred to cello. The original Kithara parts were transferred to Kithara II, with its more extensive bass register. The other main transformation was the addition of percussion to most of the works—Diamond Marimba, Bass Marimba, Cloud-Chamber Bowls, Spoils of War, and later a new instrument he had "finished, in a rough way" by the end of September: the Boo. This was a bamboo marimba with originally fifty-five (later sixty-four) short sections of bamboo from the Philippines arranged in six rows of unequal length, with "the end sections of the lower two rows, being rather long . . . tilted upward, somewhat like the roofline of a Chinese temple."[56]

In July he produced a new composition, *Ulysses Departs from the Edge of the World.* In its first version the piece called for trumpet, string bass, and three sets of Boobams—(equal-tempered) bamboo drums built by his friend Bill Loughborough, which had inspired his own Boo. He described it as "a minor adventure in rhythm"; it is a genial piece, anticipating, in its modal tunefulness, parts of *Revelation in the Courthouse Park* and *Water! Water!* He wrote it for the jazz trumpeter Chet Baker, who was a friend of Loughborough's, and who had expressed an interest—which was not to materialize—in working with him. The piece was never played in its original version, but after completing his own Boo Partch made a second, slightly shorter version for B-flat clarinet, cello, Diamond Marimba, and Boo.[57] He had found, partly from his experience with the clarinetists in the *Oedipus* ensemble, that jazz players, being used to "bending" notes, could give him "almost any intonation" he wanted on their instruments, and the same applied to trumpet players.[58] In the rather optimistic remarks that preface the original score Partch explains his preferred tuning for the trumpet's modes, but both in this version and in the one for clarinet the intonational demands are considerable. A year later he included *Ulysses* and some of the new versions of older pieces he had produced in these months in a collection entitled *Summer 1955*.[59]

By the early autumn Partch was leading an uneasy existence at Gate 5, his affairs "way up in the air." The recompositional activity had left him high and dry, terribly unsure what to do next. He wrote to Peter Yates at the end of September that he needed to hear the works he had been writing or rewriting over the past year "in order to go on": "I'm no Charles Ives. . . . I've reached the point where any more composition is pointless."[60] Now, as with his other compositional hiatuses, ideas—chiefly dramatic ideas—continued to implant themselves while he focused his attention elsewhere, but few of these were ever to see the light of day. Perhaps most poignant are the verbal notes he made for a work conceived for record called *And I'll Tell You My Story*, a work that, rather in the manner of the voice and Adapted Viola works of 1930–33, was intended as "a communication from *one* individual to *one other* individual": "*And I'll Tell You My Story* is lonely music, with little or no conscious formality, confidential and conversational, fragmentary, episodic, unconnected. It is intended to have this quality: a lost soul in a rainstorm who has found someone who will listen to him briefly, while giving him shelter."[61] Although the work was destined to remain in his imagination, the autobiographical implications of the concept are clear: the "lost soul" looking for shelter seems to be none other than Partch himself.

Casting around desperately for a way out, a solution seemed to present itself, rather out of the blue, through Peter Yates, who had had the idea to organize a small-scale exhibition of Partch's instruments at a museum in Los Angeles. Partch was delighted with the suggestion, partly because it seemed to validate his growing awareness of the fine sculptural qualities of his instruments, and partly because it gave him the opportunity to put forward a proposal of his own for a much more ambitious undertaking: he would insist on a major retrospective in which all of his instruments would be on display, thereby involving himself in extensive preparation and regular maintenance. In his desperation he had grabbed onto Yates's original suggestion and had transformed it, in his own mind, to a much grander scheme implying the total relocation of himself and his instruments, providing both an escape hatch from the Bay Area and a way into a hopefully agreeable new milieu.

In haste he threw a few belongings into his car, and early on the morning of October 17 began driving south, intending to see Yates in Los Angeles and set the plan in motion. He stopped off en route to see various friends, and spent a few days with his friend James Sturgeon in Santa Barbara, where he did some further work on the still-unfinished Boo, which he had brought with him. From there he continued on to Los Angeles.

In the end he stopped only briefly in the city before continuing south. It transpired, much to his despair, that Yates had taken the idea of the exhibition no further, largely because Yates was concerned that the two would be unable to maintain reliable contact while Partch was on the road. Partch took this as a betrayal, a sign of Yates's insincerity. When a letter from Yates finally reached him a few weeks later in San Diego, Partch fired back a hasty reply, telling him there was no good reason why communication should have seemed a problem: he always left forwarding addresses, like "most responsible people." He concluded: "I am quite depressed, and mystified, wondering how serious you are in wishing (an assumption) to help me find a new milieu."[62]

It was a familiar pattern. Almost without realizing it, Partch was placing considerable, and unreasonable, pressure on a friend to help him escape from an intolerable situation. Yates was taken aback by the vehemence of Partch's reaction, and tried to explain that his suggestion of an instrument exhibition had been simply an idea, not a solid offer of any kind. On December 10 Partch wrote more calmly but no more amicably to Yates that the "detailing of difficulties and misunderstandings seems only to beget others—I want to end them."[63] The two eventually overcame the rupture, but only after several months of strained silence.

In the end his trip south proved thoroughly futile. It came as a "shock" that in all the weeks he spent in southern California no one offered any form of lecture or guest appearance for him. Worse still, while he was there he received notice that the Waldo Building in Sausalito, which he had occupied for three years, had been sold, and that his "effects—personal and instrumental—have already been put in temporary storage."[64] On December 10, staying with John Glasier in San Diego, he wrote in great depression to Yates: "I've not had anything that could be called a 'plan' since the date of my departure from Sausalito [in mid-October] . . . and I have none now, except that some time very soon I shall have to go north again to find a more permanent storage solution." The chapter of his life at Gate 5 had come to a sudden end.

By the close of the year a move was under way that would result, ultimately, in a solution to the impasse. Ben Johnston, who had not seen Partch since Mills College days but who had kept in touch with him, had proposed Partch's name to the committee responsible for giving commissions for the 1957 Festival of Contemporary Arts at the University of Illinois at Urbana-Champaign, where Johnston was then teaching. On December 28 Duane Brannigan, director of the university's School of Music, wrote to Partch, officially offering him a commission for a short work for the festival. The original suggestion was a modest one, and involved a work for "only one or two" of his instruments— and not the originals but duplicates, which they proposed to build at the university.[65]

In reply Partch wrote that because he was now homeless and all his belongings were in storage he could not accept the offer outright. Moreover, he had hit upon a solution for the immediate future, which would make any such new work impossible: he had been in contact with John McKinney in Santa Fe, and together they had conceived the idea of driving to Mexico—"to San Cristobal, very close to the Guatemala border, for three months"[66]—McKinney to paint, Partch to relax and temporarily to solve his problems of homelessness.

In the end they were gone for some two months, not three. Given the extent of the apparently intractable problems awaiting his return, Partch seems nonetheless to have found the peace of mind needed to enjoy their surroundings. He wrote, with obvious glee, that they lived "in a grass shack overlooking the Pacific, as far south as you can get in Mexico, and wore nothing but a loin cloth. It was exceedingly primitive."[67] In La Ventosa, Oaxaca, in February 1956, he began to copy the full score of *The Bewitched* and worked at it on and off for the duration of their stay. While a grass shack by the ocean seems an unlikely place to make a neat ink master copy of a score, he had worked before—and would work again—in less favorable conditions.

At some point during their stay in Mexico Partch paid a call on a man in Mexico City who had ordered his records: Conlon Nancarrow. Partch occasionally looked up subscribers to his records, especially those in out-of-the-way places, and it is not certain that he knew who Nancarrow was. Nancarrow had been living in Mexico since 1940, in virtual isolation from the musical life of the United States, and around 1947 had begun work on his series of *Studies for Player Piano,* compositions that explored a breathtaking range of new possibilities in the domains of polyrhythm, polymeter, and even polytempi. The only documentation of Nancarrow's meeting with Partch comes many years later from the young composer Peter Garland, to whom both men gave rather contradictory accounts. According to Partch (writes Garland), Nancarrow seemed a "strange guy. Real morose. Wouldn't play any of his music for me. We just sat there, had some drinks." Nancarrow, on the other hand, recalled (in Garland's words) that "the strange thing was that Partch never even seemed curious to hear my music. I took him around, showed him the studios and the [player] pianos . . . [he] didn't even ask to hear anything. We had a pleasant chat, about nothing in particular, and he left."[68] Nancarrow, whose work was quite unknown at the time in the United States, admitted that in retrospect it is quite likely Partch had no idea before the visit that he was a composer.

Partch returned with McKinney to Santa Fe on March 20. Waiting there was a letter from Ben Johnston, saying that the Festival of Contemporary Arts commission could only go ahead if Partch would write formally to accept the offer. The deadline was the very day of their return, but Partch, with remarkable sang-froid, wrote the following morning of his intention to accept, telling Johnston in a covering letter of their holiday which, he joked, was "exceedingly less grim than Gualala."[69] Their discussions now centered around an instrumental work involving no more than ten performers, and the idea of building duplicates of the instruments had been dropped. The university offered a mere fifty dollars to cover transportation of Partch's instruments from California. The situation must have reminded him not a little of his proposed collaboration with Martha Graham.

As had happened with Peter Yates's suggestion of an exhibition of his instruments some months before, Partch seized upon Johnston's offer and began to plan something more ambitious: he was determined to bend the festival committee's thinking round to the idea of *The Bewitched.* Told of the idea, Johnston pleaded that "because of the setup and small size of the dance department" at the University of Illinois the idea was a non-starter; but by the time of his next letter, on March 31, he had investigated further and now thought there would be some possibility both of finding extra money for transporting instruments and of involving dancers. The two or three dancers he had spoken to seemed interested, but although there was an open platform stage there was "no overhead from which to hang things, no proscenium arch, no way to erect flats except unattached to the floor." Johnston's cautious and noncommittal letter was as close as Partch felt he needed to a go-ahead on the idea.[70] He wasted no time completing copying the 183-page score of *The Bewitched*, which Johnston had requested, and dispatched it to him. Without waiting for a reply Partch decided to take matters into his own hands, and toward the end of April bought a ticket and got on a bus to Urbana. There he gave a "couple of talks to classes," and played some "very bad" demo tapes he had made at Gate 5 of short sections of *The Bewitched*. "After about a week, it was agreed that they would undertake it, provided the moving of my instruments and my living could be financed, but they had no suggestions on this score."[71] Encouraged, he made a "leisurely return," arriving back in Santa Fe on May 26.[72]

Now there was nothing to do but wait. He was living in a room at the back of the McKinneys' bar, The Pink Adobe, and had some serious discussion with them about moving permanently to Santa Fe if the Illinois project fell through. McKinney even offered to drive a truck to California, at his own expense, to move Partch and his instruments lock, stock, and barrel to New Mexico.[73] The instruments themselves remained in storage, some in San Diego and some in northern California. Anxious about their condition, Partch returned to Sausalito, in the hope that confirmation of the arrangements with the University of Illinois would follow, and he could busy himself preparing them for transportation.

It was to be a fruitless summer, with all his activities suspended and his future uncertain. Correspondence with Illinois was intermittent and developments regarding funding were painfully slow. He was living in "an unheated room in the Moldloft Building, inside Gate 5," his instruments stored on the same floor. It was only a stone's throw away from his former studio, but the situation felt appallingly temporary, and his keenness finally to leave the San Francisco Bay area had never been plainer.

The offer of money to transport the instruments came finally from Lauriston Marshall, who had undertaken to raise funds himself in the light of the inability of the University of Illinois to provide the realistic sum needed—$500. On September 11 the instruments were sent off, including a new addition—a koto, given to him by Gordon and Jacqueline Onslow Ford as a kind of farewell present, and which he immediately decided to incorporate into the scoring of *The Bewitched*. Partch himself finished packing up and followed some ten days later. On September 20, before departing, he wrote to Ben Johnston, who had been concerned about the anxious tone of Partch's recent letters, in mock-

Partch leaving Sausalito, 1956. Unsigned photograph, Harry Partch Estate Archive.

reassurance: "I do not feel that I am entering a trap, and, of course, the School of Music need not feel that it is stuck with me. If I cannot function, for whatever reason, I can remove my obnoxious person almost immediately, although it will require more time to arrange for the removal of my annoying equipment (if it hasn't already been destroyed on the road)—that would 'solve' everything."[74]

Urbana, Illinois, could scarcely have been a greater contrast to the San Francisco Bay Area. A small, quiet, midwestern university town beside the larger city of Champaign, Urbana gave Partch the definite sense of being in the middle of nowhere; he felt almost immediately that he was hemmed in within a rather self-contained academic community.

In general, the School of Music accorded him a warm welcome. He renewed his friendship with Ben Johnston and met several musicians on the faculty who would remain important to him, particularly John Garvey and Jack McKenzie; the students were enthusiastic too, especially the percussionists. Among those who gravitated to him early on was Danlee Mitchell, an eighteen-year-old freshman from Tacoma, Washington. And Partch was financially solvent. "About a month after my arrival in Illinois, a subscriber to my records sent me a check for a thousand dollars"; and Paul Fromm, patron and director of the Fromm Music Foundation who was giving the commissions for the 1957 festival, "upped my stipend from 400 to a thousand when he saw the magnitude of the project."[75] In the coming months this was supplemented by "gifts by friends of my work in California."[76]

The immediate problem, which he had not foreseen, was that of a suitable studio. On October 8 he complained to Lauriston and Lucie Marshall: "I've been given two places to work—both impossible—everything was moved into one, then nearly everything into the second." Even finding a satisfactory apartment proved not so simple. Kenneth Gaburo, himself just arrived at the university, recalls overhearing an early conversation between Partch, Garvey, and McKenzie about the problems of housing the instruments and finding a suitable home for Partch himself. Partch remarked: "My instruments need a home while I'm here. I can sleep on the ground. I'm used to that."[77] Gaburo remembers the first of the apartments he visited as "just a dingy room,"[78] and at the end of the winter Partch wrote to Marshall that "not the slightest effort was made by anyone—not even a single inquiry—to locate quarters for me before I arrived. I have been moving around from cockroach-infested basement to cockroach-infested basement (one night at three A.M. one ran over my face, and I finally crunched him to death in my ear) in the effort to get closer to my instruments so that I don't consume valuable time in transportation and parking."[79]

The instruments themselves were moved to three studios in quick succession, the first a top floor and the other two basements within a block of the music building.[80] Gaburo recalls Partch sleeping on the floor of the basement studios to check for any strange creaks from the instruments, indicating warping or cracking due to the heating system or dampness. The inadequacy of access caused him considerable trouble. "The catacombic hole I was forced into in Urbana required me to take instruments apart, in as many pieces as they would go without ungluing, and putting the pieces out windows, and up tiny tortuous stairways hardly intended for more than midgets."[81]

Partch made a modest formal debut on November 7, when the newly retitled *Ulysses Turns Homeward from the Edge of the World,* in the version for clarinet, cello, Diamond Marimba, and Boo, received its première at a faculty chamber music concert, sandwiched between works by Debussy and Beethoven. The four performers were all students, three of them from the ensemble for *The*

Bewitched, which had by then taken shape. *Ulysses* provided a useful, if not fully representative, introduction to his music, which puzzled some of the composers on the faculty even if they were sympathetic to it. Ben Johnston, still apparently untouched by his work with Partch, was then composing in an essentially neoclassical idiom owing something to Stravinsky and to his teacher at Mills College, Milhaud. Kenneth Gaburo recalls of his first impressions of Partch's music: "I could hear all this . . . complexity in some of his stuff, and in his head too, but I didn't really understand how he could, so easily, wipe out a very large amount of what I considered to be the operating basis for music."[82]

The faculty members were on cordial terms with him, but their circle was hardly one in which he felt comfortable, and for some months he made little headway finding friends. The occasional dinner parties he attended were sometimes colored by his scorn for some of his colleagues' wives, especially those who, as he thought, aspired to nothing more than the status of housewife, and he would vent his misgivings about their supposedly "tyrannical" dedication to matters of household economy.[83] Describing the situation a year later to friends he complained: "I was in Urbana three months and twenty-seven days before anyone even invited me to have a cup of coffee with him, and then the invitation came from a Texas piccolo player who also detested the place."[84]

These personal trials and tribulations, however, were as nothing compared to the hell that was to break loose over the production of *The Bewitched*. In an uncharacteristic delegation of responsibility, Partch had assigned Ben Johnston the task of choosing a choreographer for the work.[85] Johnston spoke to a number of choreographers before settling on Alwin Nikolais of the Henry Street Playhouse in New York. Almost from the outset of their correspondence, in October 1956, there was a distinct lack of common feeling on the part of Partch and Nikolais about the project.

Nikolais was some eleven years younger than Partch. His early experiences as an accompanist, puppeteer, and stage technician had all played a part in shaping his approach to dance, which concerned the integration of dance, music, and design. His work at the Henry Street Playhouse was regarded by many critics as controversial. *Masks, Props, and Mobiles* (1952), in which stretchable bags concealed and transformed the dancers' bodies, was the first fully achieved exploration of his concept of "the dancer in relation to external substances" and was branded in some quarters as dehumanizing. Nikolais himself was concerned to circumvent what he regarded as modern dance's preoccupation with the self, using props to extend the body, and looked to nonrepresentational art to nourish his interest in shape, color, and texture. A competent musician himself, his musical tastes were likewise adventurous; his newest production, *Prism,* used electronic music. Excluding "the drama of man," as critic Walter Sorell noted, Nikolais "permits the theater to function only on some magic level where the conflict lies in objects, not in man, and in a land where inanimate things are free from their subjection to animate beings."[86] In this sense Nikolais's work seemed to promise a refreshing perspective on *The Bewitched.*

For his part, Partch wanted a choreographer who could bring to life his vision of *corporeality,* of which *The Bewitched* was the first fully achieved manifestation. He had used the word in *Genesis of a Music* to mean "the essentially vocal and verbal music of the individual,"[87] but it was subtly changing its meaning to convey in addition the interaction between the musician and the instrument, and the self-projection of the performing musician on stage. By the time he began to devise the dramatic scenario for *The Bewitched* he had already had the experience of *Even Wild Horses,* which he had conceived as a kind of instrumental drama, the instruments personifying ideas, forces, and emotions relevant to the concept. In *The Bewitched* the role of the instrumentalists as the Witch's Chorus, the "lost musicians," is even more crucial to the dramatic action.

Nikolais's first letter to Partch, dated October 18, was cordial and enthusiastic but already drew attention to one aspect of Partch's scenario that "disturbed" him: Partch's insistence that the "lost musicians" be seen on stage and become a part of the dramatic focus. Nikolais's objection was a pragmatic one: "Although this is fine for the Urbana production," he wrote, "subsequent performances necessitating live [musicians] would immediately exclude the work from my repertory. This means that the labor and choreography (and expense) would be projected towards the single performance in Urbana. This I could not afford to do."[88] Adequate remuneration would come only if the work could be performed repeatedly, using a tape of the music, which Nikolais proposed to do in New York and Connecticut following the Urbana première. Although this struck at the heart of his concept, Partch initially suggested that "certain types of compromise" might be possible, even including Nikolais's suggestion "of the prologue occuring during a light play on stage."[89] For his part, Nikolais promised "to do anything that will allow us to continue to perform the work without undue loss of musical value and theatrical unity."[90]

There was relatively little direct correspondence between the two in the next few months, as Nikolais began to prepare the choreography on his own in New

York, without the benefit of discussions with Partch in person about the work. Nikolais was receiving letters from up to "six different sources" in Urbana concerned with other aspects of the production, and in his replies he would occasionally ask that messages be relayed to Partch, which usually happened either not at all or in garbled form. Partch, meanwhile, had plenty to do rehearsing the music. A rehearsal tape was eventually put together and sent to Nikolais in New York.

By early February Partch could no longer contain his impatience, and wrote bluntly asking Nikolais about his progress on the choreography. Nikolais's reply made it evident that he had no intention, and probably had never had, of following the dramatic outline of Partch's scenario. He protested that "the most I was able to do before the tapes arrived was to plan how I could manage to work within my own manner (which necessitates eliminating the characters and mimetics projected in the script) and yet state the fundamental idea of the total piece."[91] In addition, Nikolais was hesitant about printing Partch's satirical notes on each of the scenes in the program. While he liked their quasi-poetic vein, he was concerned about the "direct literal references which are not within my range of operation to bring about, and therefore the inclusion of such literal references when they will not actually occur will certainly be confusing to the audience."[92] In his defense, Nikolais pleaded:

In more than a couple of letters there has been indicated to me an assurance of freedom of treatment. The notes, however, throw me right back to literal situations of undergrads, chorus girls, basketball teams, boys chasing girls and situations in general which are not at all within the realm of my capabilities. My concern is with the semantically vertical statement, not the horizontal narrative line of the play-wright. It is more akin to music and poetry in this aspect. My task is the difficult one of making peace with the suggested literal concepts of the script. . . . The nature of my work is substantially known and . . . most definitely indicates a dance approach far and away from a Cocteau-esque mimetic substance.[93]

In the balance of the letter he went on to outline his proposed choreographic ideas at length.

Partch replied quite philosophically on February 18 that Nikolais's outline was "a wonderfully free creative effort. In these particular circumstances I am for it without reservation. At this late hour a strongly individualistic creative man has got to be free." He suggested that they make quite clear in the program booklet the extent of the overlap in their dramatic conceptions and the points at which they diverged, and he seemed prepared to leave most of the important theatrical decisions—including the placement of instruments on stage—in Nikolais's hands.

However, almost immediately Partch's mood seems to have changed, and he wrote again the following day, stating his attitude somewhat more pointedly and (reading between the lines) expressing regret that the collaboration had uncovered so little common ground. Partch defended his "starting point [in] the literal, the human, the dramatic, the narrative": "From this beginning I endeavor to create musical magic, and if I think I succeed I am not a bit ashamed of those beginnings. Quite the contrary. The literal motivation is as much a part of the work as one of the instrumental sounds, whether it occurs as words integrated with the music or not." He went on: "I am as incapable of functioning in your 'poetic' way as you are incapable of functioning in my 'narrative' way. I think that an example of what I can respond to in poetry is significant. I find that a Chinese poem giving names of characters, and exact place names, that describes some trivial incident in a narrative way, is more moving than a European poem portraying a grand and abstract state of mind and incapable of being located in *any* sense."[94] He ended the letter by adding: "I hope that this amplification does not discourage you. It is written only with the object of increasing the candlepower." Privately, though, he entertained more worries than he admitted to Nikolais. The day after the second letter he wrote to his choreographer friend Eleanor King in Arkansas:

> Do you hate satire? Do you hate humor? Do you reject—automatically—the idea of telling a story in dance? Do you oppose all situations that are recognizable as human in dance? Do you reject the idea of American situations, commonplace enough but unusual simply because they are not used, as dance themes? Well, Alwyn [*sic*] Nikolais does all these things. . . . He has thrown out all satire—rejected all human situations. His technical imagination seems tremendous, but his conceptual poverty is nothing less than appalling. To see my music reduced to the verbal and subject-matter level he suggests produces a pain in me almost too great to endure. . . . Nikolais does not propose to *extend* the [satiric] idea. He proposes to do a major job of plastic surgery on it.[95]

As the days passed Partch became increasingly distraught. His mood of stoic humor—which he was often capable of mustering in the face of oncoming disaster—gave way to an increasingly black interpretation of Nikolais's intentions. Gradually he was consumed by the feeling that an alarming sort of artistic violence was being done to his work. When the next letter arrived from Nikolais, attempting to placate Partch with the suggestion that a statement be included in the program to the effect that "Mr. Partch's narrative content has been treated generally rather than specifically," and that "direct delineation of character and incident, for the most part, have been translated into other abstract areas and metaphoric ideas,"[96] the tone of Partch's correspondence became immediately more self-assertive and hostile. In a letter of February 25, never mailed, he wrote: "The idea and the music of *The Bewitched* are my creation. As I have repeatedly stated, and as is obvious in the score, they are *one.* To assume that being 'free' means that you may use a composer's music and at the same time reject the dramatic motivation of that music, and without consulting him, is extraordinary indeed. It seems to me that the intolerableness of that kind of 'freedom' is beyond debate." The letter ended with the blunt suggestion that if Nikolais did not find it possible, "even at this late date, to follow my dramatic outline . . . I prefer to perform *The Bewitched* in semi-dramatic concert form." Before sending the letter he evidently reconsidered this final ultimatum, and the letter he *did* send, two days later, made no mention of it, merely outlining his objections and his original dramatic intentions in stronger and more concise terms.

There was still almost a month to go before the première, and Partch's ever-excitable nerves were under strain from the apparent antagonism he felt coming from the choreographer. He wrote to Lauriston Marshall, with one of the last traces of his vanishing humor: "I've fluctuated the past week between pro-longed release capsules and whisky—one prolonged release capsule, or one whisky, for each wrangle—or: one prolonged release capsule *and* one whisky for each wrangle."[97] Ben Johnston, too, came in for much of Partch's anger. Partch blamed Johnston for having put him together with the unsuitable Nikolais in the first place, and Johnston made matters worse by refusing simply to take Partch's side out of loyalty, arguing that *The Bewitched* was strong enough to withstand a choreographic interpretation as remote from the com-poser's conception as Nikolais's was proving to be.

Partch's letter of February 27 came as a slap in the face to Nikolais, who wrote back immediately that he was "much disturbed by its contents" and felt that "an atmosphere of apprehension has been created which will make the Illinois visit a very trying and negatively emotional one for all concerned. . . . I also feel that you have projected a negative anticipation of what I am doing and I'm inclined to feel that nothing I do will satisfy. At this point I feel far from being 'Unwitched.' "[98] He offered to withdraw from the Urbana performance, if that was Partch's wish, and agreed not to use the tape of the forthcoming perfor-mance of the music for future performances by his company. Partch decided that the performance should go ahead, comforting himself with the thought that he would be there in person to explain *his* conception of the work, and an introductory lecture was arranged for March 24, two days before the performance. In letters to Nikolais of March 2 and 3 he summed up his objections, even reinstating his permission, subject to certain conditions, for Nikolais to use a tape of the music in future performances. But by then it was much too late.

Nikolais and the dancers of the Henry Street Playhouse arrived in Urbana exactly three days before the production. If Partch, or Nikolais himself, had been waiting for a miracle, nothing of the sort transpired, and there was much tension and even antagonism between Partch and Nikolais during rehearsals, most of it smoldering quietly rather than bursting into flame. The two men were inclined to speak to one another mostly through the conductor, John Garvey. Partch's mind was already made up about the worthlessness of Nikolais's choreography, from his standpoint, before he had seen any of it, which totally precluded any genuine, honest response. A few months later he described it to Peter Yates as "shallow and tricky—plastic bags, many props, an immense plastic five-line staff pulled straight across the stage. This is not choreography, it is shallow spectacle."[99]

The program booklet distributed on the evening of the première printed both the "Argument" of the work, in Partch's words, and Nikolais's "Choreographer's Notes," in which he stated his intent. Nikolais wrote,

> The choreographer has translated the episodes of the "Bewitched" into a language of motion utilizing several semantic strata. He has interpreted the episodes generally, rather than specifically. Direct delineation of characters and situation have been defined in terms of scenes evolving in dance theater, each of which utilizes a different aspect of human entertainment as its framework. Within these scenes are contained the ideas of the "bewitched" and the "unwitching." . . . The titles are intended as catalysts, creating vantage points from which the details of the inner scene may be observed . . . While departing from the composer's specific narrative outline, the dances maintain the relative dramatic balance between the orchestra as chorus, and the witch, and follow the dynamic interplay of all involved.

The booklet also listed both Partch's scene titles and Nikolais's, which, far from clarifying the dramatic intent of the work, can only have clouded it in the minds of those in the audience who took the trouble to study the program booklet carefully.

The Bewitched, supported by funds from the Fromm Music Foundation and the University of Illinois School of Music, was premièred as part of the Festival of Contemporary Arts on March 26, 1957, with Freda Schell singing the part of

Table 3. Partch's and Nikolais's titles for the scenes of *The Bewitched,* from the program booklet distributed at the première, March 26, 1957.

Partch Titles		Nikolais Titles
Prologue—The Lost Musicians Mix Magic		Prologue
Three Undergrads Become Transfigured in a Hong Kong Music Hall	1	Dancer's Ritual
Exercises in Harmony and Counterpoint Are Tried in a Court of Ancient Ritual	2	Travelogue
The Romancing of a Pathological Liar Comes to an Inspired End	3	Dance Hall
A Soul Tormented by Contemporary Music Finds a Humanizing Alchemy	4	Art Show
Visions Fill the Eyes of a Defeated Basketball Team in the Shower Room	5	Puppet Show
Euphoria Descends a Sausalito Stairway	6	Flower Show
Two Detectives on the Tail of a Tricky Culprit Turn in Their Badges	7	Melodrama
A Court in Its Own Contempt Rises to a Motherly Apotheosis	8	Pageant
A Lost Political Soul Finds Himself Among the Voteless Women of Paradise	9	Mystery Play
The Cognoscenti Are Plunged Into a Demonic Descent While at Cocktails	10	Late Show
Epilogue		Epilogue

The Witch. Following the performance a moving van was placed at Partch's disposal for transportation of the instruments, without disassembling them, to St. Louis, where a performance was given the following evening at Washington University.[100] Back in Urbana, a studio recording was made using recording equipment loaned by Lauriston Marshall, with the assistance of recording engineer Lyle Dahms. On April 7 Partch held a gathering in his apartment for those involved in the production to hear the recording, even sending an invitation to Ben Johnston, to whom he had not been speaking for some weeks. Following the performances Partch and ensemble members Jack McKenzie, Danlee Mitchell, Thomas Gauger, Michael Donzella, and a small group of dancers went to Chicago with some instruments to record a program for WTTW-TV featuring short excerpts from *The Bewitched* and an interview with Partch.

Rubbing salt in the wound, there was almost universal critical acclaim for

Partch with an extract from the score of *The Bewitched*, WTTW-TV, Chicago, 1957. Photo by Robert Kostka.

Nikolais's choreography, and the production, Partch's antipathy notwithstanding, made a tremendous impact on many people. Only an occasional notice, such as one in the University of Illinois newspaper *The Daily Illini* on April 3, came down strongly on Partch's side "regarding the propriety of a choreographer changing totally the creator's concept." Most reviewers hailed the production as one of the crowning successes of the festival.[101]

The première of *The Bewitched* is a disconcerting chapter in Partch's career. His searing negativity toward the event is quite at odds with the critical acclaim for the production. His bitterness at Nikolais's "treachery" and his contempt for the resulting "disaster of choreographic integration" come across as a stubborn and blinkered refusal to acknowledge the obvious merits of Nikolais's work. Clearly, Partch was not prepared to strike a reasonable attitude; his position was and would remain that Nikolais had betrayed something he believed in. Sixteen years later he explained the matter thus:

> Nearly everyone in the art professions positively beams when I say that I believe in an integration of [music with] stage and film arts. Subsequent to this enthusiastic approval, however, I have seldom experienced anything but timidic back-pedaling, from either filmmakers or choreographers, because of an imagined threat to their

particular specialities . . . [what] choreographers really want is musical yardage goods, to constitute "background" for whatever spur-of-the-moment ideas they might concoct. To them it is literally inconceivable that a dramatic composer could fashion a purpose in drama that is equal to theirs. Collaboration is just a word.[102]

Against this, it may be argued that *The Bewitched* on paper was a finished concept that needed only execution, not the collaboration he claimed; and while the performance of the work indeed demanded talents beyond his own, these were of a technical rather than a creative nature.

There is no doubt that Partch felt a personal affront at Nikolais's disregard for the details of his carefully prepared scenario, a feeling exacerbated by his sense that artistic violence had been done to the work as a result. Not only had all the scenes been renamed, but his original idea for the set, a network of stairs to infinity, had been abandoned. Worst of all, Partch claimed, in Nikolais's production "the Witch was discarded totally as a dramatic element," because the singer had not been used on stage in the way he had envisioned.[103]

Added to this was the sense of exasperation he felt at seeing his original idea of a touring company of dancers and musicians come to nothing. *The Bewitched* was expensive to mount and, calling as it did for eleven of his own instruments, it was prohibitively expensive to take on tour beyond short forays to Chicago or St. Louis (as Nikolais had pointed out). In addition, because it could scarcely be expected to stand a chance in the commercial theater, the only likely venues for it were universities—in Wilfrid Mellers's words, precisely those "rich (usually industrially sponsored) academic institutions that were philosophically anathema to him."[104] On a deeper level, if one regards the work not merely as dance theater but, taking Partch's writings at face value, as offering an intimation of a form of music-making freed from the restraints of mechanized society, then the true "fulfilment of [the work's] ideals," Mellers continues, "would have implied the demise of the society from which he sought succour." It is possible, Mellers argues, to see some of the premises from which the work grew as inherently contradictory.

The final irony in Partch's attitude lies in the fact that the ever-larger projects he would undertake in the years ahead, with their demands for more performers and their more elaborate staging directives, make *The Bewitched* look modest in comparison. This gradual scaling-up, with all its attendant problems, has more than a hint of the self-destructive about it, as though he were determined to vindicate the kinds of demands he had made in *The Bewitched* in the very act of upstaging them. Indeed, only one major work in the years ahead—the score he wrote for Madeline Tourtelot's film *Windsong*—involves a significant reduction of forces.

Reflecting on the Urbana première some twenty-five years later, Ben Johnston wrote that the episode displays some of the less admirable aspects of Partch's artistic self.

> He was so possessive of his artistic creations that notwithstanding the manifest impossibility that any one person could be artistically skilled, let alone talented, let alone genius-endowed in all areas of a complex multimedia art work, Partch yet was unwilling, even unable, to collaborate. He either dictated to his collaborators in their own area or he fought with them all the way to an estrangement. Consequently almost all his productions were seriously flawed.
>
> This is the action of a man who was at least on that level (and there were others as well) self-defeating. In his attitude to society he demanded support for his own work as far as possible without any strings attached while he was capable even of violating a contract with another artist he had specifically directed to make decisions on his behalf and maintaining enmity for years because he was opposed. This goes far beyond artistic integrity; indeed the word integrity is an ironic one to use at all in this context. He orchestrated and all but guaranteed the oblivion his work so obviously courts.[105]

Yellow Springs, Chicago, Evanston, and Champaign

Partch regarded the première of *The Bewitched* quite un-equivocally as the greatest failure of his career. Once a semblance of calm was restored after the production he remained in a peevish, unforgiving mood, loudly announcing to his Urbana friends that he was proposing to leave, "in a manner that indicted the whole damned University."[1]

After the Urbana performance he had been approached by Keith McGary, who had reviewed *Genesis of a Music* favorably at the time of its publication in 1949, and who raised the idea of Partch coming to work at Antioch College in Yellow Springs, Ohio, where McGary was associate professor of philosophy. On the weekend of April 20–21, 1957, Partch paid a visit to the college, and on Sunday afternoon he gave a talk to students, playing excerpts from the recording of *The Bewitched*. The proposal he discussed with McGary and Walter Anderson, head of the music department, involved not only the use of a studio, but the possibility of doing a film of the new and still unperformed version of *U.S. Highball*.

Encouraged by the meeting, and rather in desperation, he made up his mind there and then to move to Yellow Springs.

Back in Urbana things seemed intolerable. And yet there were plenty of people who valued his work very highly. "I turned down an offer—a tentative offer—of a 12-year research appointment at Illinois," he told a friend, "and in doing so I became persona non grata immediately. From the standpoint of my personal security I was foolish, but from the standpoint of my music I couldn't have been more right. . . . [I] recall the atmosphere in Wisconsin where, in three years, I hardly wrote one page of music. I could see 12 years of sterility stretching ahead of me. I may not be around that long, but I'll be god-damned if what time I am around is going to be sterile."[2]

During May he busied himself with the recording of *The Bewitched,* with a sense of urgency that was financial rather than artistic. If he was going to move to Yellow Springs he would have to pay for it himself, and he was hoping that orders for records would cover the costs—about $100. Lauriston Marshall proved a continual support, helping him with things as mundane as packaging materials for the records. At the end of May Partch reported that orders had indeed come in, enough to tide him over. "I've told everyone I've seen that I'm going to Yellow Springs for the summer. For all I know it may only be for the summer."[3] On the evening of his departure many of the ensemble members in *The Bewitched* loyally assembled to help him pack the instruments, which had remained in a rehearsal studio following the production, and to load them into a U-Haul trailer. Warren Smith, who had played Bass Marimba, drove Partch and the instruments all the way to Yellow Springs. On July 5, some five weeks later, he wrote to the Marshalls: "I will never regret leaving that depressing Urbana, even if I had immediately run into poverty, destitution, treachery, mayhem, rape, perjury, subornation of whatever gets suborned, and anything else that the dictionary offers."

Partch arrived in Yellow Springs on June 1, 1957. The studio at Antioch College that Walter Anderson had arranged for him for the summer was a large class-room, "the most beautiful studio I've ever occupied—a new second-grade classroom, by a modern architect with imagination. A row of skylights—one solid glass wall, lawn and trees beyond."[4] He found lodgings at 130 Glen Street.

Yellow Springs, in southwestern Ohio, was then a small town of some four thousand inhabitants. Partch took an almost instant dislike to what he felt to be the "lethargy" of the place, finding it to be a town stifled by self-importance in the midst of "the stamping grounds of the abolitionists and Horace Mann." He wrote to the Marshalls that he was "convinced that everyone in town is living in a state of arrogance with the history of Yellow Springs as a kind of morphine— why the hell should *I* do anything—after all I've got Horace Mann in *my* history!"[5] In calmer moments he told correspondents that "Yellow Springs provided an immediate and feasible haven. I had hoped it would be more, but if it turns out to be nothing more than a momentary haven I shan't regret coming."[6] Yet he was clearly unhappy, resorting to tranquilizers to keep his nerves at bay. "For some reason I feel both depressed and abandoned. I've no business living anywhere east of the Rocky Mountains. Maybe it's the weather, which is depressing enough. No sun in days."[7]

Despite the pleasant environment of his new studio, virtually everything else he needed in order to function was lacking. The people he knew, including the two men who had expressed interest in filming *U.S. Highball,* "promptly abandoned" him, "as though to say—well, we've given you a studio, now go ahead, stimulate us!"[8] Worst of all, there were very few musicians around during the summer. The problem was the exact reverse of the one he had faced in Urbana. "So it goes—sewer pipes and flushing musicological toilets with every musical phrase *and* good musicians, or skylights and green lawns *and* no musicians."[9]

While in Urbana he had written to Christine Charnstrom, one of the musicians he worked with twelve years earlier in Madison, asking her to play the Chromelodeon part in the projected film of *U.S. Highball.* Now married with children and living in Binghamton, New York, she replied that it would be impossible for her to come to Yellow Springs. By the end of June there had been still no progress in forming an ensemble, and Partch wrote again with the "preposterous" suggestion that if she couldn't come to Yellow Springs to play the Chromelodeon, he and all the instruments could come to her in Binghamton. This letter was the last of five he wrote at the end of June to various contacts, proposing in each case to relocate himself: to Lima, Ohio, "where there is a small group interested in my work"; to Chicago, "where I have friends"; to the University of Arkansas, "which invited me . . . on the basis of a room to work in, and musicians" (with the idea of doing *The Bewitched* with Eleanor King); and to the McKinneys in Santa Fe.[10] Although sparked by the desperation he was feeling, these letters are quite controlled and rational proposals, showing that his old ability to take care of himself was still intact.

Throughout the lonely weeks he derived some comfort from the fact that Lauriston and Lucie Marshall were "only 135 miles away" in Indianapolis, and that they might come to visit him and—he hoped—help guide him out of the hole he had landed in. Longing above all for "a little human warmth," he found that his situation took an unexpected turn for the better in the middle of July when he met the sculptor Seth Velsey and his wife, Elinor. They showed an immediate interest in him and both "dedicated their lives" to his problems. "They've given so many parties for me, until 2 and 3 in the morning, that I can't remember the number, and Elinor has hung on the phone for hours in the effort to uncover musicians. They've also offered me a beautiful concrete block studio, back of their house, for my instruments, when I have to move out of the school on August 15."[11] The two-record set of *The Bewitched* had now been released, and the Velseys played it at the parties they gave for Partch, helping the steady trickle of sales and bringing him some money. The Velseys' companionship and their evident belief in his work changed his mood somewhat, and by the end of July he was announcing to friends that "I'll probably stay on, partly as the path of least resistance, because I do dread moving, and trying to establish myself in still another new location."[12]

Despite the frustrations, he was still intent on making a film. With the idea of trying actively to seek out other prospective filmmakers, he wrote a script for a projected film of *U.S. Highball* in July and sent it to several people. The script, broadly similar in intent to his scenario for *The Bewitched,* traces the history of the work and presents the "film idea," which was to operate on three levels:

> The seven instruments, their players, and the voice of the protagonist constitute the Initial or Objective Reality. Beyond this, and inherent in the idea, are two other levels of response which can also be exploited visually. The First Level of Subjective Reality contains recalled or imagined scenes: the highway, the steam engine, the freight train, the clouds, the mountains, the desert. The Second Level of Subjective Reality contains the emotions that this music, these recalled scenes, and this integrated concept arouse, and I believe that it can be represented both faithfully and tellingly by abstract animated art, in color.[13]

Translated into more mundane terms, his idea was to film a studio performance of *U.S. Highball,* with musicians and instruments to the fore, and to contrast these shots with footage of highways and trains, real-world images of travel and movement intended to bring to life the journey recreated in the work. At times, the realism of these scenes would give way to moments of "abstract animated art," nonrepresentational images intended to convey the emotional intensity of the work. His primary intention was to avoid turning the resulting film into a straightforward documentary or travelogue, on the grounds that the trip that had inspired the work, in 1941, was a personal ordeal and as such would mean little to anyone else; he wanted to render the "aloneness" of the protagonist by having the screen at times depopulated of human faces and by concentrating instead on locomotives, boxcars, clouds, desert, mountains, and highways.

Among the first to respond enthusiastically to the script was the Chicago filmmaker Madeline Tourtelot. On August 11 Partch flew to Chicago—the first commercial flight he had taken, although he had "been in the private air before"—to meet her.[14] Her name had been suggested by Robert Kostka, art director at WTTW-TV in Chicago, the station for which Partch had done the feature on *The Bewitched* some months before. Kostka recalls:

> I'd known her when we were both students at the Institute of Design in Chicago, an American recollection of the German Bauhaus. Madeline came from a wealthy family, and was married to an architect. She had a gallery, and then became interested in avant garde films, made many. We met at her studio, and I introduced Harry . . . another film maker was there, and a painter whose name I forget. They all talked, and Madeline offered to explore working with Harry and he immediately accepted. This surprised me as I had several others to have him meet. But I was naive. . . . Harry was dependent on wealthy patrons.[15]

Partch described Tourtelot to Lauriston Marshall as "very sensitive and imaginative,"[16] and found it "very refreshing" that a filmmaker saw some possibilities in his music "other than science fiction."[17]

Tourtelot was at that time only beginning to establish herself as an independent filmmaker. Her two completed films, *Reflections* and *One by One,* were both short nature films, the second of which she described as a "film poem on the theme of the passing of time" and for which she had written both the narration and the music. In showing Partch her work, Tourtelot screened the rushes for a film in progress, begun some weeks earlier at a summer school in Michigan. She and a sculptor friend had been amusing themselves filming each other in black-and-white on the sand dunes of the eastern shore of Lake Michigan, "more an afternoon's fun than any serious film," as Robert Kostka puts it. Kostka also suggests that the theme of the film these rushes eventually became—that of the Greek myth of Daphne and Apollo—was Partch's interpretation of the rushes, and not Tourtelot's original intention: "Partch saw it, and saw in it the myth of Daphne."[18] Greatly taken by her use of "nature symbols and the intense insight they bring into a dramatic incident," Partch proposed he write the music for the film.[19] The fact that the rushes were still in a raw state suggested to him that he might have some input into the editing process, promising the true integration of music and film art he had dreamed of. They agreed that he would work on the music for this project first and that they would turn their attention to the *U.S. Highball* film thereafter.

Partch returned to Yellow Springs the following day and began preparing for his move to the Velseys' at 1220 Xenia Avenue. All such moves were now "horribly difficult."[20] In Chicago he had discussed with Tourtelot and with Shirley Genther, a friend from Madison days with whom he had stayed, the idea of establishing a Gate 5 Record Company "as a quasi foundation." The Velseys too were keen to be involved, and with this in mind he began preparing second editions of the *Plectra and Percussion Dances* record and of *Oedipus*. When the test pressings of *Oedipus* came back he found the sound quality "pretty terrible," and decided with Lauriston Marshall's help to remaster excerpts from the work and issue it on one disc.

This project aside, he felt good having the new records of *The Bewitched* to distribute, fully three years after the last release. Clearly, Partch's faith in the work had not been shaken by the circumstances of the première. He sent a copy of the recording to Peter Yates as a gesture of friendship, together with a slightly defensive covering letter, in the concluding paragraph of which he wrote: "I am numb to tragedy, not because of any personal tragedy, of course, but a sensitive person does not need to be struck personally, in this overcast era of a threatened terminal tragedy and lightening communication of endless personal tragedies to others. *The Bewitched* is my individual and responsive laugh. A laugh may of course be anything from a percussive hollow blast to a profound Zen-Buddhist giggle. I am even somewhat numb about this—as to what category this work will be considered to fall into."[21]

Yates's response to the recording has not survived, but letters from other interested listeners came from time to time. One such was from a seventeen-year-old in New Hampshire, William Wilder, who, although he liked the music, criticized its lack of "advanced rhythm techniques" and the looseness of its form. Partch replied good-naturedly that a "Boston musicologist" had been quoted in the *Christian Science Monitor* to the same effect, but that coming from "a young partial believer" the criticism required some comment.

As for "advanced rhythm techniques," which you imply I do not use, I am quite at a loss to understand you. My rhythmic structure is very varied. . . . In *The Bewitched* I used, for example, alternating 25/16 and 5/4, 35/16 (in which accents created 5 against 7), and 15/16 (in which accents created 3 against 5), and basic 5, 7, 11 and 13 impulses and variations of them. . . . If by advanced rhythm techniques you mean large structural "rhythms," then you are getting into the area of "form," which in this case cannot be divorced from narrative. . . . The "form" of both *Oedipus* and *The Bewitched* was automatically determined by my interpretation of the narratives.[22]

In fact, Wilder's comments had touched upon the two technical aspects of Partch's music—rhythm and form—that are perhaps the most underdeveloped aspects of his musical language. To Peter Yates Partch had acknowledged: "Perhaps I *ought* to follow the pattern of other composers, and conceive in terms of "pure" form. . . . But I do not, and cannot." In his own defense Partch argued that this was to overlook the advances he had made in other ways:

> One becomes intimidated into believing something is "experimental" and "advanced" when allegedly respectable little people (such as musicologists) say it is. In this sad circumstance he often loses the ability to see, when demonstrable "advances" in another direction stare him in the face. . . . Composers with "advanced" techniques . . . enshrine the bodiless brain. The bodiless brain really needs no sounds at all, only theories. Based upon what I have seen, I would say that the deliberate beguiling of youth into the academic "modern idiom" is worse than an assault on the street. Both are malevolent, but the second is honest.[23]

Indeed, Partch's own musical tastes, on the rare occasions he mentioned them, were by now rather firmly oriented away from the "modern idiom" of the generation of composers who had come to prominence after World War II. To a correspondent he claimed that, "among others, I respond to Mussorgsky, Lou Harrison, and Gerry Mulligan. I emphasize *among others*."[24]

He spent most of September at the Velseys', rebuilding the Boo and preparing a sixteen-page booklet with photographs of his instruments to accompany the records of *The Bewitched*. This was partly in response to his awareness that *Genesis of a Music* now presented a rather outdated picture of his concerns and his achievements. He had heard from Jacques Barzun that the Carnegie Corporation had taken three hundred copies of the book for distribution abroad as part of their "American Shelf." He was of course delighted by this, and wrote to the University of Wisconsin Press suggesting that if the book had now sold out, or nearly so, they might contemplate a second edition with revisions to bring the story of his work up to date. Thompson Webb, director of the Press, replied that no such plans were being entertained, as they had not managed to break even on the first edition: "We undertook the publication of your book with the

Partch playing the Bass Marimba. Photo by Fred Lyon.

knowledge that we were going to lose money."[25] Partch toyed with the idea of writing "a short and simple exposition of my musical philosophy, something that would be more available because less expensive—comparatively free of 'scholarly' citations and mathematical tables, but with a few drawings or photographs of instruments, which I consider essential." (In the Gate 5 Records booklet he had described himself as "not an instrument-builder, but a philosophic music-man seduced into carpentry.") He hoped this kind of book "would not compete with [*Genesis*], but would actually promote it."[26] Although the press's response was encouraging, nothing came of the idea.

• If Partch had planned to stay in Yellow Springs to work on the music for Madeline Tourtelot's film on Daphne and Apollo, the disadvantages of the Velseys' studio, gradually becoming apparent to him, put an end to the idea. "This studio was fine in the warm weather," he wrote in the middle of October, "but now I've got to leave. Concrete block, concrete floor, no storm windows, no insulation on roof, gas heat, and water on the floor and drips in one end when it rains (a little bit of Gualala). It's quite impossible, and the sinus infection that was so bad in Wisconsin is plaguing me again (in Urbana's hot dry rooms I had no trouble)."[27] Moreover, although he had met a competent recording engineer there were still very few musicians in the town who would

Partch playing Chromelodeon I; the score
of *The Bewitched* is on the music rack.
Photo by Paul McAdams.

be likely prospects for an ensemble. His only hope was to move to Chicago to be
closer to Tourtelot, and rather despondently he began disassembling all the
instruments and packing them for shipment.

The last week of October 1957 found him unsettled, ready to move, and
entertaining contradictory thoughts. These find expression in two letters he
wrote on consecutive days, looking toward two very different futures. The first,
on October 24, was to BMI in New York, responding to their request for
materials for a brochure intended as publicity material on his work. The
second, the following day, was to Lauriston Marshall, proposing to draw up a
will leaving everything to Marshall in the event of his death. He apologized for
sounding "morbid," but the question of mortality was one that had been on his
mind. A couple of old friends had recently died, including Arch Lauterer, and
Partch himself was now of an age—fifty-six—when the subject could no longer
be avoided indefinitely. His only remaining family members were his two
nephews—Paul's sons—with whom he was on good terms, but who had never
been involved with his work. The request testifies to the closeness Partch still
felt to Marshall, personally and professionally.

Early in November he left for Chicago, leaving most of his belongings, including the instruments, in storage in Yellow Springs. As on his previous visit, he
stayed first with Charles and Shirley Genther, who had an apartment in Mies

van der Rohe's building at 860 North Lake Shore Drive. Charles was an architect and a partner of Mies, and at the parties he and Shirley hosted they introduced Partch to the artistic circles of Chicago. To keep himself busy, Partch worked off and on at compiling a document called "Gems from my Scrapbook 1930–1957," a collection of snippets from reviews of his work over the years, good, bad, and ugly.

The Genthers were happy to have him stay until he could establish himself, but much of the practical help came from Madeline Tourtelot. "She has driven me all over the old-city triangle looking for studios," Partch wrote to Lauriston Marshall on November 22, "and we've finally found one. She lectured the landlord on how he ought to do something for art, and he agreed to give it to me on a nine-month lease for $35 a month, plus utilities and heat . . . it begins to look as though I'll have more good musicians than I can possibly use. Since these records [the reissues] are draining my bank account to within about $30 of zero Madeline has offered to lend me all the money I need to establish myself here." A week later, staying with Tourtelot and her husband in their home at 2719 Sheridan Road, he seemed more hesitant about becoming indebted to her to such an extent: "I don't think I can accept the offer. My expected income from records would not enable me to repay the loan at any foreseeable time. And I think the best thing I can do is rent a housekeeping room, conduct my little record business, and wait for a break."[28]

Madeline Tourtelot seems, one way or another, to have changed his mind, and in the week beginning December 9 he moved into the studio they had found, at 1801 N. Orleans Street. The instruments were sent from Yellow Springs, and Partch was plunged into nearly a month of "debts, bills, and problems of organization" getting the place ready for work on the music for the Daphne and Apollo film, now called *Windsong*.[29] North Orleans Street was in the Old Town area of Chicago, which had been spared in the Great Fire of 1871. Robert Kostka recalls that "it had a good German beerhall . . . an old neighborhood. At first Harry loved it. . . . His studio was decorated with drawings from Gordon Onslow Ford and letters from the composer Lou Harrison, who wrote long letters that looked like medieval manuscripts in red and black."[30] The studio was a large room with a high ceiling, heated by a huge oil stove, and was rather cramped because of the instruments. It had a shabbily bohemian feel and only the bare essentials in terms of kitchenware: Kostka remembers that Partch used "the ceramic jars that a British marmalade used to come in as coffee cups." He slept on a makeshift bed beneath the Marimba Eroica, covered by Navaho blankets. Early in the new year he threw a housewarming party for his Chicago friends.

In January 1958 he began composing the music for *Windsong*, writing short passages timed to synchronize with the cuts between scenes; the resulting score became "a collage of sounds."[31] He notated the various sections at first in pencil in a small, eight-stave music notebook. The music was conceived so that he could play and record all the ten instruments himself by overdubbing: no more than four instruments are used simultaneously. He made demo recordings first on Tourtelot's two Pentron machines and, with the music nearly completed, began to record the final soundtrack early in February, with the help of a professional sound technician from Evanston, on a multichannel Berlant. He told Peter Yates proudly that he had been working "fourteen hours a day for three weeks on the sound track for an art film that will be entered in various European festivals. . . . Thirty hours of recording and sixty hours of editing."[32] Watching the process, Madeline Tourtelot had the idea to make a documentary on the making of the soundtrack, and toward the end of February she began shooting footage of Partch miming the instrumental parts. With the music recorded he made an ink copy of the score, adding the triumphant colophon: "Written, rehearsed, recorded, edited, and copied at 1801 North Orleans St., Chicago, January 16 to March 2, 1958." The completed eighteen-minute, black-and-white film was premièred on WTTW-TV in Chicago on March 19, preceded by an interview with Tourtelot and Partch.

Ten years later, in his preface to a "re-copying of the score" of *Windsong* (when he also changed its title to *Daphne of the Dunes*), Partch described the "subject of the film" thus:

> In the myth, or at least the Roman version of it, the god Apollo is enamored of Daphne, virgin daughter of a river god. Apollo pursues her. This is most natural—it is what he knows how to do. The story makes no sense whatever unless one remembers that almost any virgin, either male or female, automatically resists seduction, however beautiful and otherwise desirable the would-be lover. Apollo pursues, and Daphne calls on her father river-god for help. At the crucial moment—when she is only an inch away from becoming a non-virgin—her father changes her into a green laurel tree. Apollo, both appalled and frustrated—with arms clasping the rough bark of a tree—, nevertheless regains his sexual sobriety, and decrees that henceforth all victors in any area of competition are to be crowned with green laurel leaves.
>
> The story is at least some indication of the Greek sex ethic. But the film *Windsong* deals in fact with the Puritan American sex ethic, and Madeline Tourtelot, in a stroke

Partch with Madeline Tourtelot, Chicago, 1958. Unsigned photograph, Harry Partch Estate Archive.

nothing less than brilliant, turns the virgin American Daphne into a white, bare-limbed, dead tree at the top of a sand dune.

Perhaps the most beautiful sequences in the film are the nature shots, for which Partch believed Tourtelot had a gifted eye. Yet these images are charged with symbolic, often erotic, significance: "The eroding sand is female, the snakes wriggling up the sand male. The waving grasses female, the gulls flying overhead male." Interspersed among these sequences are shots of a man and a woman—a friend and Tourtelot herself—enacting parts of the Daphne and Apollo legend. The story is thus represented in three ways, more or less equal in importance: by the nature shots; by the man and the woman; and by the music.

In his score, Partch uses the percussive timbres of his ensemble to symbolize Apollo, and the strings, both plucked and bowed, to symbolize Daphne. (These two musics are kept quite distinct in the pages of the music notebook in which he sketched the work.) In addition, as Glenn Hackbarth has shown in his analysis of the work, both protagonists are assigned their characteristic pitch centers: 16/9 (F) becomes associated with Apollo, 3/2 (D) with Daphne.[33] The symbolism of this is quite clear. The two pitches are separated by the narrow and, in Partch's terms, dissonant "minor third" 32/27, and are not found together in any of Partch's consonant Otonalities or Utonalities: this implies that the two characters, like the two pitches, will never be able to achieve consonance or unity. The story is played out as a musical drama, moving unpretentiously through its several stages: the introduction of the characters, the pursuit, the encounter, the attempted seduction, and the transformation. Its overall conception provides a further instance of Partch creating, as he had expressed it to William Wilder, "a 'form' which . . . cannot be divorced from narrative."

The music for *Windsong* has often been regarded as one of Partch's most beautiful scores. Wilfrid Mellers has suggested that Partch was "at heart a composer of the desert," and that this music is "concerned with the desert, both within the mind and without."[34] While the "desert" in the film was achieved by cinematic sleight-of-hand on the sand dunes on the shore of Lake Michigan, something about the music suggests the vast emptiness of desert terrain: a feeling of great immobility, of a muted landscape of great richness with its isolated plants and living creatures, cottoning sound from the world outside. As Partch describes it: "The film technique of fairly fast cuts is . . . translated into musical terms. The sudden shifts represent nature symbols of the film, as used for a dramatic purpose: dead trees, driftwood, falling sand, blowing tumbleweed, flying gulls, wriggling snakes, waving grasses." For the most part the visual images and the musical material change synchronously one with the other. The music grows through discontinuity, by the juxtaposition of self-contained musical images: the rhythmic Boo, Diamond Marimba, and Bass Marimba passages associated with Apollo's pursuit; the languid Adapted Viola melody accompanied by Harmonic Canon and Kithara, which is first heard against shots of the poplar leaves associated with Daphne; or the haunting passage for Kithara with wailing Chromelodeon, first heard as she looks through the grass to the sky. Yet this discontinuity adds up to a satisfying and unified whole. Partch's recording has a dry quality, a lack of reverberation (the Kithara's Daphne motif, for example): the acoustic of his room on North Orleans Street, swallowing vibration, produced a result that is uncannily like the way the desert environment itself absorbs sound and dampens it.

No sooner was work on *Windsong* complete than he embarked on preparations for the *U.S. Highball* film. The prime mover behind this new project was a young master's student at Northwestern University, Elizabeth Gentry, who had been introduced to Partch's music by her teacher Leigh Gerdine as an undergraduate at Washington University. The housewarming party Partch had thrown at his North Orleans Street apartment had given Gentry a closer look at the man and his lifestyle, and she wrote a vivid article on him for the *St. Louis Post-Dispatch* and determined to help him in whatever way she could. She first persuaded the dean at Northwestern to allow the use of the condemned top floor of the old Victorian music school building, which was thought to be unsafe, as a studio for Partch's instruments, so that *U.S. Highball* could be rehearsed and filmed. In mid-March Partch moved his instruments there and simultaneously moved into the four-room student basement apartment in Evanston where Elizabeth lived with her then husband Thomas Coleman.

Partch remained in their apartment, sleeping on a pull-out bed in the living room, for "several weeks" before he moved to an apartment of his own on Lee Street. Elizabeth found him a "fascinating, if trying" guest. Each evening he would order a jug of cheap wine to be delivered from their local store and invite them to share it with him, settling into a conversational mode and content as ever to be around talented young people. Determined to impose his "anti-bourgeois ideals," she recalls, "he'd fuss about housekeeping notions, or any of my attempts at tidiness."[35] She was keen to learn the Chromelodeon, and persuaded her husband to undertake the role of *U.S. Highball*'s protagonist, Mac. "When Coleman, then a corporate executive, would leap off the last commuter train in his grey flannel suit for an evening rehearsal, Partch would laugh with cynical glee—'Imagine! A Yale Whiffenpoof has come to play the leading hobo role with Harry Partch! At last I have seduced the Ivy League.'"[36] Their attempts to recruit other musicians for the ensemble were not greatly successful, and they had enticed only one more—Melvin Wildberger, a graduate student friend of Elizabeth's at Northwestern—when a fortunate coincidence solved their problems.

Danlee Mitchell, one of the mainstays of Partch's ensemble in Urbana, was doing his student teaching practice in the Chicago area. He had heard that Partch was in town and, eager to renew their acquaintance, managed to track him down. Quite unexpectedly he appeared at Partch's door one day, and Partch, delighted to see him, explained about the *U.S. Highball* project and invited him to play in the ensemble. Mitchell agreed and suggested bringing other musicians from Urbana when the school year finished in June. This seemed the best way to proceed, and although it meant that Partch had to cool his heels for a few weeks, the Urbana players would already be familiar with the instruments and would not need to be trained from scratch.

Partch occupied himself in the meantime by building the Bloboy—more of an invention than a musical instrument. It was a bellows with a 1912 auto exhaust horn and three small organ pipes attached, intended for *U.S. Highball,* to render, in conjunction with Chromelodeon I, "a fairly realistic impression, even to the echo in the distant foothills, of a Southern Pacific freight train crawling through the steep pass sixty miles away, then racing down the near side."[37]

It was clear, once their friendship resumed, that Mitchell possessed a number of qualities that Partch valued highly. He was a first-rate percussionist, and found Partch's collection of instruments quite irresistible; he had a forthrightness coupled with a sense of patience that meant Partch would increasingly allow him to share the task of coaching an ensemble; he was quite willing to absorb from Partch some modest maintenance and repair skills and proved competent with common tools; and while no sophisticate, he was sufficiently wide-ranging and nondogmatic in his musical outlook to be aware of what Partch had achieved musically. Temperamentally, Mitchell could be strong-willed and seemed unlikely to soften into a servile nonentity: Partch described him to a friend as possessing "perception far beyond his years."[38] For his part, and despite the difference in their ages, Mitchell found the composer wonderful company. Partch's conversation was a heady mixture of discussion of the arts, culture, and society, and his often contentious views on everyday matters, including education. It was sprinkled with odd bits of hobo wisdom and, on occasion, with mystifying allusions. One evening in Evanston, Mitchell recalls, "Harry and I went out for a drink. We were sitting at the bar, and I was telling him about some minor problem I had: some small thing. Harry said what I should do when faced with a problem was to crouch down, make the sign of the goat, incant the problem or the name of the person causing the problem, and say three times, 'Get thee behind me,' to exorcise it."[39]

Madeline Tourtelot, meanwhile, was temporarily absent from Partch's life. At the beginning of May she took *Windsong* to Europe, where it and her earlier film *Reflections* were shown at the Brussels International Experimental Festival. Partch harbored some resentment that she had not invited him to accompany her, as the film was nothing if not a joint effort: but funding for his travel to Europe would have had to come from Tourtelot herself, which she declined to offer, perhaps worried that it might set an expensive precedent for future showings of the film. In the meantime, Partch entered into correspondence with Gordon Onslow Ford in California about visual ideas for the *U.S. Highball* film. Partch very much wanted to involve him, having in mind to ask Onslow Ford to provide the "abstract animated art" that he had proposed to use for some of the sequences in the film. Onslow Ford replied that although he "could not do animated abstractions at a distance," he would willingly discuss ideas for images, both Partch's proposed animated ones and shots from a train window.[40]

Following Tourtelot's return from Europe, the recording and filming of the ensemble's performance of *U.S. Highball* took place in the first half of June. Danlee Mitchell had recruited Jack McKenzie, who became the conductor, and four other musicians from Urbana. Partch had decided that, as a competent ensemble would be at his disposal, they should rehearse all the compositions in *The Wayward,* none of which had yet been tried out in the rewritten versions he had produced in Sausalito. Moreover, he wanted to come out of the project with a new record as well as the film, and as *U.S. Highball* was only twenty-five minutes long he needed additional pieces to fill the disc. Most of the rehearsal time was spent on *U.S. Highball,* however, rather to the detriment of the performances of the other works.

His rehearsal manner was as patient and exacting as ever. The instrumentalists in the work—"the bums" on the journey from San Francisco to Chicago—were obliged to become vocalists, "intoning or singing bits of conversations, signs, inscriptions."[41] Elizabeth Gentry remembers that "Harry usually sang [the lines] first with dramatic facial and hand gestures. . . . He conducted from a stool, wearing sandals or barefoot [and] an old plaid, open shirt."[42] The filming and recording proceeded without hitch, and Tourtelot and Partch worked also at the editing of the documentary on the making of the soundtrack of *Windsong,* now called *Music Studio.* Gentry was invited into Tourtelot's social circle, spending some time "at her home on the lake in Evanston and at her studio on the near north side." She observed that Tourtelot and Partch "seemed to have an 'on and off again' relationship which was not predictable."[43]

Throughout the recording sessions Partch was delighted with the assistance provided by Danlee Mitchell, and he was coming increasingly to value Mitchell's judgment on other matters. Mitchell stayed around to help with the tape editing after the other players had gone their separate ways, and when Mitchell himself departed in the middle of July Partch had a copy of the finished master tape made for him so that he could help judge which of the other recordings were good enough to release. Together they discussed Partch's next move. The idea of New York had been suggested, and Partch felt that, especially with the added benefit of Madeline Tourtelot's films, he had the incentive and the materials with which to try to create "some sort of congenial milieu" for himself in the city.[44] Talking to Mitchell about the pros and cons, Partch was gratified by the young man's encouragement and evident belief in him and relieved to have the human warmth of a real companion on whom he could unburden his worries.

Partch's feelings for Mitchell seem, at least outwardly, to have been warm and friendly, perhaps slightly paternal. The letters Partch wrote to him after his departure are adoring and express a degree of emotional attachment, but they are not flirtatious. In one letter Partch greets him as "Light-of-my-life Danlee" and signs off by saying "You have no idea how much I miss you."[45] But nowhere do these letters step outside the terms in which a doting father would write to his son.

Mitchell helped soothe Partch's anxieties in more practical ways as well. With the recording and filming finished, Partch felt "trapped" on the fifth floor of the Northwestern School of Music, which he had been told he had to vacate now that the *U.S. Highball* project was over. "Danlee rented a garage, paid for it himself, and virtually single-handed moved my instruments into it. He really saved my life."[46] This uncharacteristic helplessness in moving had to do with the fact that he had been feeling unwell throughout the whole process of putting out the *U.S. Highball* recording. With little in the way of capital, he had announced in July a third trust fund, and began again the extensive labor of mailing out leaflets to potential subscribers. This, the tape editing process (sometimes involving long stints of up to fifteen hours at a stretch), and the task of designing and, later, assembling the record jackets, had seemed unusually draining. With Mitchell gone he felt worse than ever. He joked that he had the energy of "a warm lettuce leaf." His room was an appalling mess, and he was "too damned weak" to sort it out. The conclusion of his dealings with the Northwestern School of Music, moreover, left him feeling cold: "I returned the key [to the rehearsal room]. . . . The ladies of the office were very kind, expressed great regret that I was gone, said—O but we were going to come up to see your instruments—and—You know, Northwestern University is proud that you were here, Mr. Partch. Well—I mumbled something that may have sounded congenial while staring off into space."[47]

The tiredness from which he had been suffering turned out to be the symptom of a serious problem. During the early part of July he had been suffering from cramps, so on the thirtieth, feeling weak, he saw a doctor "who promptly warned me that I ought to prepare myself for bad news, as though I ever expected to live forever."[48] Two days later he had X-rays taken—"about ten *U.S. Highball* subscriptions down the drain"—and on his return from a weekend in the country with the Tourtelots he had the verdict, which he reported to Mitchell in a letter of August 5. The cramps "were the onset of an ulcer, and it's been bleeding merrily away ever since. I have only about half the red blood I ought to have, which explains my constant weakness and dizziness." The doctor prescribed a new rigid diet of "seven small bland meals a day. No coffee, no liquor, no—or very little—smoking." By a morbid coincidence, he received on the same day the will that Lauriston Marshall had had drawn up for him. Thanking Marshall for his efforts Partch told him: "I'm on a very strict plan—the usual thing—Rest. Don't worry. Rest. Don't worry. Etc. Milk, Cream, Gelusil and constant sedation, with the threat of surgery if the bleeding doesn't stop." The letter goes on, poignantly: "I'm close to no-one, and the people that I might be close to are not here. . . . I'm trying to forget the instruments, and I truly do not care whether I ever write another note in my life. I've already written plenty, and I can't afford to bury myself, to set up my instruments, or even move them."[49]

Feeling lousy and generally depressed, he vented his frustration on his Chicago friends, complaining about the "flag-waving, church-lined streets of Evanston" (as Elizabeth Gentry put it) and berating them for the pervasive "apathy" shown by the "fashionable people" in the area toward his work. Although subscriptions to the *U.S. Highball* record were coming in at a pleasing rate, and over $450 had accumulated by the beginning of August, he had "yet to receive one wretched $4.50 subscription from either Evanston or the entire North Shore. . . . I want nothing so much as to separate myself from the scene of this degradation."[50]

By now he had resolved to head for New York in September—"if I have enough strength."[51] In mid-August he escaped for a week to nearby Paxton to visit his Urbana friends Lynn and Marilyn Ludlow. There, at a party given by a friend to hear the test pressings of *U.S. Highball,* he met John Garvey, who was "extremely cordial" and warmly encouraged him to return to Urbana, inviting him to visit on his way to New York. Partch returned to Evanston still in low spirits. He even complained in a letter to Mitchell that his instruments were still "rotting" in the "hot garage in Evanston" where Mitchell had put them. "I went in there one day, and it was truly suffocating—I expect every glue joint to be loose." With all his troubles he felt quite abandoned by the person who, he felt, had enticed him to the Chicago area in the first place—Madeline Tourtelot, who was off again "like a butterfly" to Europe, this time to the Edinburgh Festival.

U.S. Highball was released in September 1958 as a ten-inch record. The jacket offered an inelegant and rather makeshift cover design by Partch and Mitchell, with lines from the work's text scattered across it, rather too neatly to give the pseudo-graffiti impression they had intended. Of the other Evanston recordings Partch could countenance only the release of *Ulysses at the Edge* (as his 1955 composition was finally entitled) at some future time: the voice parts in *Barstow* were unsatisfactory, and *The Letter* seemed stilted. The *U.S. Highball* recording, as he was well aware, was far from perfect musically or technically; partly for that reason, and partly because of his poor health, he showed little interest in promoting the disc. Elizabeth Gentry, who was moving to St. Louis, offered to help launch it there with an autographing party, but, she recalls, "we never seemed to be able to get together at a convenient time . . . he became difficult and negative, as I was told was his pattern in the final implementation of his projects. He seemed to enjoy the outsider, underdog position. A successful sale would have undermined his posture."[52]

A week into September Danlee Mitchell stopped in Evanston, en route from his home in Tacoma, Washington, to Urbana for his senior year, to help him pack. Mitchell found him very depressed, and Partch made no attempt to hide his state from his young friend. "He told me he'd been contemplating suicide," Mitchell recalls, "that his career prospects were uncertain, that his health and his financial problems seemed insurmountable."[53]

The instruments remained in storage, as Partch's destination in New York was wholly unknown. En route he took up John Garvey's offer of visiting Urbana, and while he was there Garvey tried yet again to persuade him to return on a longer-term basis to the university. Reporting this a couple of weeks later to Lauriston Marshall, Partch added: "We'll see."[54]

Partch's arrival in New York had all the casualness of a student passing through at the end of a summer's traveling, not the anxiety of a distinguished man in his late fifties trying to establish a foothold for himself before it was too late. His bus pulled in at the Greyhound station at 4 A.M. on the morning of September 20, 1958, "in rain—a dismal horrible day." With remarkable sanguinity he spent "11 hours walking up one street and down another looking for a decent, cheap room" before he gave up and phoned the most promising of the New York phone numbers in his address book, that of Lyle and Barbara Dahms (Lyle had helped record *The Bewitched* in Urbana).[55] Barbara invited him to come and stay with them in their apartment on Seagirt Boulevard, Far Rockaway, a two-hour subway ride from the center of Manhattan; he ended up staying with them for a week.

At the outset he seems to have had few concrete plans or prospects on his mind, other than a vague resolution to promote interest in his music in the city "in the effort to change the drift of my fortunes."[56] After a day's rest at Far Rockaway he visited his contacts Oliver Daniel and Carl Haverlin at BMI, which seemed the best starting point. The affiliation he had rather grudgingly begun with BMI in the spring of 1954 had been to his benefit in numerous ways. Even though none of his compositions had been published and none were available commercially on record—the Gate 5 records were all private re-leases—the contract BMI devised for him had been renewed in April 1958, when his advance had been increased from $250 per annum to $400. Now, with Partch's help, BMI was preparing materials for a brochure on his work. "They had many suggestions," he reported to Danlee Mitchell, "including a *Bewitched* presentation at the Modern Museum this year, transporting [an] ensemble from Illinois."[57]

The idea of a new production of *The Bewitched,* and the chance of canceling out Alwin Nikolais's "treachery," evidently held a strong appeal, and from then on it became the focus of his efforts. His estimate of the amount of time needed to make the idea a reality, on the other hand, was quite unrealistic. Within a fortnight of the original proposal he had managed to discuss it with Henry Allen Moe of the Guggenheim Foundation and with Douglas Moore and Otto Luening at Columbia University, yet he grumbled to a correspondent that "if any wheels are moving their movement is so slow as to be imperceptible."[58] Moore suggested mounting the production at Columbia using, as far as possible, the players from the original Urbana production. By the middle of October Partch was sending a steady stream of letters to Mitchell and to John Garvey in Urbana asking impatiently about possibilities, and about Garvey's offer to try to secure him a grant from the University of Illinois Graduate School so that he could take up residence again to prepare the performance. Partch busied himself looking at theaters and meeting with prospective chore-ographers, for which purpose he had produced a lengthy revised version of the scenario for the work, entitled "Some New and Old Thoughts After and Before *The Bewitched.*"

His efforts to present his work to individuals in New York were aided considerably by the existence of Madeline Tourtelot's films. He had brought with him a copy of *Music Studio,* the twenty-minute documentary (still only provisionally finished) on the making of the soundtrack for *Windsong,* and on October 30 he gave an afternoon showing of it and of *Windsong* itself at Columbia University.[59] The same evening he gave a private showing to a group of about forty people at a studio in lower Manhattan, the audience consisting mostly of filmmakers, writers, and composers. Among them was Anaïs Nin. She had heard his Gate 5 recordings through Kenneth Anger in San Francisco and was instantly captivated. Nin wrote in her diary that in Partch's music "I recognized the sensation of fluidity . . . [this] was an entirely novel and modern expression, [with] the power to dissolve the senses, to multiply their receptivity, to expand the range of receptivity, to involve the senses completely. It was a delight, as if one had drunk the music instead of accepting it through the ears."[60] Partch himself she described as "an unusually handsome man, a man preoccupied with metaphysics, born in San Francisco and exposed to its Oriental influences. . . . He has extremely blue and candid eyes, a spiritual face." She gave him copies of her books, including the recently reprinted *House of Incest*. She was struck by the scenes in *Music Studio* of Partch packing and mailing his records, which paralleled her own activities of packing and mailing her books and, impressed by his "difficult, independent, individualistic life," she offered to lend him her tenth-floor penthouse on West Ninth Street in Greenwich Village while she was in California and her husband, Ian Hugo, was in Europe.

The use of Nin's apartment, as he told Henry Allen Moe, was "a real break," as it gave him the opportunity to finalize arrangements for *The Bewitched* while not worrying about rent. New York was proving even more expensive than he had imagined. During October he had been renting an apartment at 270 Riverside Drive but vacated it in great relief at the end of the month, partly to save money and partly because, as he told Mitchell, the house had been full of "mad people": "I get no sleep—vaudeville comedians, madams, Chinese scholars who love Puccini, marine cadets who drive MGs."[61] After a brief trip to Chicago in early November to check on his instruments and to fetch some winter clothes, he moved into Nin's apartment and began to bombard Danlee Mitchell and John Garvey with correspondence. On November 21 he complained to Lauriston Marshall: "I wrote three long letters to John Garvey, and I've had one phone call from him, that in early October. Since, there has only been silence. How does one collaborate with silence?"

Nonetheless, he had by now managed to find a suitable choreographer, Joyce Trisler, and, thanks in large part to Douglas Moore, Columbia University had agreed to fund a production of *The Bewitched* there. At the meeting of the university's Alice M. Ditson Fund Advisory Committee, held at the Guggenheim Foundation offices on December 20 with Moore, Otto Luening, and Henry Allen Moe among those present, the committee appropriated $10,000 from the fund, the largest amount yet raised for a production of Partch's work, for two performances the following April with Thomas DeGaetani of the

Juilliard School as producer and Joyce Trisler as choreographer, and with the Juilliard Dance Group.[62] With plans for *The Bewitched* consolidated, Partch faced the prospect of returning to Urbana to begin rehearsals as soon as students came back in the new year: the University of Illinois had also pledged an additional, smaller grant for the production.

A farewell gathering was held for him in New York on the evening of December 21 at the studio of Lenore Tawney, a tapestry-maker friend. Partch wrote to invite his old composer friend Quincy Porter and his wife, Lois, "to see a 20-minute color film on my instruments, and also some rhythmically swinging color (!), on three screens, by a man from Ann Arbor. Milton Cohen and his assistant *perform*—this is not a film—with various gadgets, and the result is a four-hand experience in rhythmically moving, dissolving, expanding color."[63] He reported the event to Bertha and Harold Driscoll, telling them of a distinguished guest who turned up at the gathering: the composer Edgard Varèse. Varèse "liked the film [*Music Studio*] so much he almost embraced me. This surprises me immensely, because his own music is so utterly different, even though I admire it and have frequently said so."[64] What had perhaps overwhelmed Varèse was his recognition that Partch had brought to life the very dream that had obsessed him for years: the building of new instruments free from the constraints of the tempered scale. Four years earlier, Varèse had emerged from some eighteen years of creative silence with his *Déserts* for orchestra and tape, finally having at his disposal the resources to produce electronic music and thus to expand the parameter of pitch: perhaps he felt a sense of kinship with that aspect of Partch's work. Partch told the Driscolls: "Altogether, I shall hate to leave New York, because in people it is the [liveliest] place I've been in a long long time." After he left her penthouse, Anaïs Nin wrote to thank him for renewing her husband's faith in human nature, and telling him that he was "the best and kindest guest" they had ever had.[65]

Partch returned to the campus of the University of Illinois at Urbana-Champaign in mid-January 1959. Danlee Mitchell drove the instruments in a truck to Urbana from the garage in Evanston, where they had remained throughout Partch's four months in New York. If he was unhappy to be back in "that depressing Urbana," as he had described it some eighteen months earlier, there is no sign of it in his correspondence. He took a small apartment at 300 S. Goodwin, in the married students' dormitory; unlike much of the other student housing it had no curfew, so he could come and go as he pleased. He was given a large studio in the university band building, even though he had no official appointment and only a nominal connection with the School of Music.

In February he received a check for $1,040 from Columbia University's Ditson Fund, "in partial payment for expenses and royalties" in connection with the production of *The Bewitched;* the balance of his honorarium, a further $150, was payable after the production. The part of the Witch was again taken by Freda Schell (now Freda Pierce), John Garvey again was the conductor, and several musicians from the 1957 production returned to the ensemble. The new choreographer, Joyce Trisler, proved more willing to take orders from Partch than Alwin Nikolais had been, and as a result the choreography was closer to his wishes. Partch described the staging, in a letter to Robert Kostka, as "sensationally good,"[66] and writing to Douglas Moore described himself as "fortunate" in the quality of his collaborators: "Altogether it was the kind of opportunity that one can expect only once, or very infrequently, in a lifetime."[67] He gave a very different assessment of the Trisler production in a "statement" on *The Bewitched* fourteen years later, stressing the two crucial aspects of his staging intentions that had been disregarded by the choreographer: "Not only was the Witch not allowed on stage but a white scrim was drawn before my instruments, along with the remark: 'Do you think we can compete with those instruments?'"[68]

The production opened at the Juilliard Concert Hall in New York on April 10, with a second performance the following evening. A further performance was given at the University of Illinois on April 24 as part of the 1959 Festival of Contemporary Arts; the now-completed film *Music Studio* was also shown as part of the festival. The performances were unquestionably successful, although opinion was divided, particularly in Urbana, about the relative artistic merits of the new production and the Nikolais one of two years earlier.

The New York reviews were mixed. Jay Harrison, in the *Herald Tribune*, commented: "The score itself is mainly incantational, an effect close to hypnosis seeming to be Mr. Partch's ultimate aim . . . [thanks to the Witch's vocal part] the flavor of the piece takes on a demonic voodoo air. Further, rhythmic counterpoint, especially as given out by bizarre or unfamiliar instruments, invariably takes on a quality of secret rites danced in dark places."[69] The *New York Times*, while very positive about the costumes and about Joyce Trisler's choreography, criticized both the "smarty-pants humor" of Partch's scenario ("without either theatrical content or continuity") and the idea of having the instruments on stage ("eminently visible even behind a scrim"). There was, however, "considerable musical variety in spite of the unavoidable monotony of the orchestra as a whole. . . . Mr. Partch, in effect, has reinvented the Indonesian gamelan for his own purposes."[70]

The *New York Times* remark about Partch's ensemble being a reinvention of the Indonesian gamelan typifies the incomprehension with which many in New York greeted his work. It was less a case of East Coast snobbery toward anything "west of the Hudson River," as Partch put it, than of genuine confusion about how to place his work in the broad panorama of contemporary music.

Comments about the supposed orientalism of his music would be made time and again throughout Partch's career. He seems not to have minded when they came from the pen of Anaïs Nin, who makes the point somewhat impressionistically in a passage from her diary to convey the aesthetic difference between Partch's work and the abstract symphonic music of Western tradition. Listening to his music, she wrote, she felt its "affinity with nature": "the sounds coming out of Sitka spruce, Philippine bamboo, Brazilian rosewood, redwood, Pernambuco, played with picks, fingers, mallets, and felted sticks. The affinity with Oriental music, which has a flowing, enveloping, oceanic rhythm. Rhythm was an essential part of Partch's music, a native, contemporary rhythm. The richness of it gave to contemporary compositions the depth and dimensions which so far existed only in the music of the East."[71] In contrast, comparisons of his music with specific non-Western traditions, such as the gamelan, irked him considerably. Most of the critics who made such comparisons, he felt, knew little or nothing about the non-Western musics they cited, and their comments betrayed an ignorance about how his own music was constructed.

In spirit and technique Partch's work is wholly Western: it is enriched more by his sensitivity to Eastern traditions than by his knowledge of them. He had a deep and abiding interest in non-Western instruments and theater traditions, but at no time in his life did he study or learn to play the music of a particular non-Western tradition, as some of his contemporaries had done—among them composers Colin McPhee, Henry Cowell, and Lou Harrison. While in New York for the performances of *The Bewitched* he talked to Alan Hovhaness, an American composer of Armenian descent whose music, like Harrison's, kept a weather eye open to Eastern traditions. Partch told Douglas Moore that Hovhaness "expects to spend a year in India under a Senior Fulbright. This is something I'd give a couple of eyeteeth to do, but I'd like to cover the whole of Southeast Asia also, and I think that my work has prepared me to profit from such an experience."[72] Partch's lack of direct practical familiarity with any form of non-Western music was therefore not from any conscious decision on his part, but simply from lack of opportunity—a lack, moreover, that he hoped to remedy.

The effect of such study on his music must remain a matter of conjecture. He held most of the emerging forms of musical orientalism in mild disdain, with Harrison's work as a notable exception. By the late 1950s Cowell had become a kind of American musical ambassador to the near and far East, and his music had begun to explore the meeting of non-Western instruments, scales, and forms with the Western concert tradition. The conductor Leopold Stokowski had recently directed the New York première of Cowell's *Persian Set,* for small orchestra and Persian *tar,* and was giving performances of music by Eastern composers alongside "exotic" music by Westerners.

Cowell's transplanting of Eastern instruments, scales, and forms into a Western context held no appeal for Partch. Neither did the very different interest in Eastern traditions shown by John Cage. Since the late forties, Cage had been obsessed with Zen Buddhism and with the Chinese *I Ching,* the Book of Changes. Beginning with his *Concerto for Prepared Piano and Chamber Orchestra* of 1950–51, his music had explored a variety of chance techniques, with or without recourse to the *I Ching,* but always mindful of the Zen attitude of non-intention, producing a music that, Cage argued, was free of the likes and dislikes of its creator. Partch viewed this whole enterprise with great suspicion; as Ben Johnston has put it, Partch "had no grasp" of this phase of Cage's work "and even less curiosity about it."[73] To surrender the responsibilities of making choices and to accept the outcomes of chance operations and indeterminacy was, in Partch's mind, to stop making art.

Partch saw no special affinity between his endeavors as a composer and those of fellow Californians like Cowell and Cage, their shared interest in the Pacific rim cultures notwithstanding. He continued to regard those East Coast figures who had been part of the musical scene he entered in the early thirties as his real colleagues. Some of the reviews of *The Bewitched* in New York surprised him by linking his name with composers of a younger generation, which fact he commented on in an unpublished introductory note to his article "The Ancient Magic":

> I find it strange indeed to see my name linked, as it is occasionally, with such composers as Gunther Schuller, Chou Wen-Chung, William Russo, and others equally young. Decades before they were even interpretable twinkles in the eyes of their parents I was deep in the composing and performing of music, just as deep—I might say—as Aaron Copland, Roger Sessions, Roy Harris, and George Antheil, to which generation I belong.

But I was in the Paris scene never, the New York scene seldom, and California was among the bushes. I am not complaining about the mentioned association of names; I am in fact honored. My emergence among composers roughly twenty-five years younger is simply a mad fact.

Partch's New York adventure in the autumn of 1958, and his return the following April for the performances of *The Bewitched,* had boosted his public profile considerably. His time in New York had given him a good deal of assurance and had planted some new ideas in his mind, including that of travel in Asia. By the late spring of 1959, however, his immediate future seemed relatively settled.

John Garvey wrote on May 14 with news that a grant had been awarded to Partch by the University of Illinois Graduate School for the forthcoming year, beginning June 1959, to enable him to prepare a new theater work for performance at the university. Keen to accept the offer, Partch moved his instruments in early June to a studio above the Co-Ed Theater at 614 East Green Street in downtown Champaign.[74] "The University has leased a studio of 1800 square feet for me," he told Thomas DeGaetani, who had produced *The Bewitched* in New York. "I use only about half the room for instruments, and one can walk freely around any one of them. All are floodlighted. The only disadvantage is that the room is a loft over a movie theater, and I cannot rehearse after 7 P.M."[75] At the same time he rented a five-room apartment at 507 South Sixth Street, convenient to the studio, and began work.

He was planning a dramatic work based on Euripides' *The Bacchae,* an idea that had been on his mind for several years. Back in the spring of 1955 he had written to Ben Johnston that Euripides' drama, concerning the revels of the ancient god Dionysus and his female devotees, the Bacchae, "certainly lends itself to dancing and percussion,"[76] perhaps conceiving the music as a further development of the percussive language of *The Bewitched.* From the outset he had in mind a very different treatment of the ancient drama than he had given to Sophocles' *King Oedipus* in 1951. He felt that "the drama of Oedipus, however compelling, was deposited by the mind in an ancient category called *classical*—that it was not brought home to the audience as a here-and-now work. Because of this insight, I first decided that I would bodily transfer Euripides' *The Bacchae* to an American setting."[77] In the earliest surviving sketches for the work, then called *Dion Isus,* the drama is transplanted to California: Cadmus, founder of Thebes, is a former state governor; and Tiresias, the blind prophet, is "an old general and retired justice of the California Supreme Court."[78] However, by the end of 1959, preparing an outline of the work for submission to the University of Illinois for consideration as part of the 1961 Festival of Contemporary Arts (the title now *Revel and Revelation*), he had decided that "the better solution seemed to be to alternate scenes between an American courthouse park and the area before the palace of ancient Thebes."[79]

In *Revelation in the Courthouse Park*, as the work would finally be called, two dramas are played out, rather than one. The three principal characters accordingly assume dual identities, one ancient Greek, the other contemporary American. The Greek characters are those of Euripides' play—Dionysus, god of the Bacchae; Pentheus, young king of ancient Thebes; and Agave, leader of the Bacchae and mother of Pentheus. Their American counterparts enact a contemporary parable, devised by Partch himself but modeled closely on *The Bacchae*, about a middle-aged woman (Mom) who falls under the spell of a Hollywood idol (Dion) to the mortification of her sensitive young adult son (Sonny). By alternating the action between a modern American courthouse park and the palace of ancient Thebes, the intention was to point up the "psychological parallel" between the erotico-religious frenzy of the Bacchae, the female followers of the god Dionysus, and the hedonism and submissiveness of American teenagers and those "not so young" (as the text puts it) to rock'n' roll idols, represented in *Revelation* by the sensuous Dion.

The work is thus more than simply a new version of an ancient drama, as *King Oedipus* had been. In *Revelation in the Courthouse Park* Euripides' drama alternates, scene by scene, with Partch's own contemporary recreation of it; and although the characters are somewhat different the stories are morphologically similar, allowing the audience to observe the parallel unfolding of the two dramas. Partch's reconception of Dionysus, from Euripides' play, as a contemporary movie star/rock'n' roll singer, allows him to show the common patterns in the idolatry that surrounds the ancient god and the behavior of the young female entourage following his own character Dion. The role of Dion was modeled on Elvis Presley, whose swift rise to fame Partch had observed with interest; in *Revelation* one of his starting points was the assumption that "the mobbing of young male singers by semihysterical women is recognizable as a sex ritual for a godhead." Partch regarded the idolatry for the young Presley, or at least its outward manifestation, as "delightfully innocent"; but he pointed out that just as "the frenzied women in the Euripides play threaten both degradation and annihilation for anyone unwilling to praise or at least respect their particular pattern of mediocrity and conformity," so too it was "apparent that similar pressures toward the same end are implicit in this country."[80] He adds that, with this in mind, he decided to treat the singing of hymns to

Dionysus in Euripides' play as American revival meetings, equating the "degradation and annihilation" brought about by the women with the pressures toward religious conversion.

If this equation seems to have a slightly autobiographical ring—recalling his lament in *Bitter Music* about the castrating effects of our "Christian abstract female age"—it is only one aspect of a more extensive, crucial theme in *Revelation:* the ambivalence of the relationship between mother and son, in which the son is destroyed by his unhealthy attachment to a domineering but wayward mother.[81] On a broader scale, Danlee Mitchell regards the whole conception of the work as a personal allegory, with Sonny and Mom as symbolic recreations of the tensions between Partch and his own mother. Jennie Partch's interest in Christian Science, Unity, and New Thought can be seen as analogous to Agave's obsession with the god Dionysus, an obsession that Partch, in *Revelation,* portrays as a form of madness. The adolescent Harry was too close to his domineering mother simply to make light of her interests in this area; the limited evidence we have suggests, rather, that he found this side of his mother exasperating and demoralizing. And although the intensity of their relationship did not destroy the young Partch's spirit, as Mom crushes Sonny in *Revelation,* the "succession of breakdowns" Partch experienced from the end of his teens made it painfully easy for him to empathize both with Sonny and with Euripides' Pentheus, killed in the frenzy of Bacchantic orgies by his mother, Agave.

Revelation is, therefore, a dramatic hybrid of an unusual kind, setting a "straight" version of an ancient Greek play alongside a contemporary drama that is closer to the territory of musical than opera. The score that Partch produced is likewise of a hybrid nature, amounting almost to a résumé of his compositional techniques to that time.

It was not until the beginning of February 1960 that Partch began serious work on the score for *Revelation.* In the middle of December he had written to Peter Yates that the work had been approved for the 1961 Festival of Contemporary Arts—"the idea that is (not a note of music as yet)."[82] He settled to work in his studio above the Co-Ed Theater and wrote at high speed; three weeks into the composition process he had almost finished Chorus One, the largest scene of the work, lasting twelve minutes. Danlee Mitchell recalls Partch not wanting people around during the period of composition and leading a fairly solitary existence tempered only by occasional meetings with friends in the evening.[83] The scoring of *Revelation* involves a large ensemble with almost all his instruments to that time plus cello, string bass, and prerecorded tape, with a band of entertainers on stage (piccolos, brass band, and drums, two guitarists, clog dancers, and tumblers). The cast comprises three principals, five smaller parts, a Chorus of Eight Women, and a Chorus of Four Men.

The challenge Partch had set himself in *Revelation* was a formidable one: that of integrating the many facets of the two dramas through music. Broadly speaking, his approach was to create two different musical idioms for the American and the Greek scenes, but not consistently; there are moments when the two worlds are quite close together musically. Much of the time, the Theban scenes are carried by intoned speech—setting his own, much abbreviated version of *The Bacchae*—in the midst of music recalling the dramatic serious-ness of *Oedipus*. The American scenes (which he calls Choruses) are musically more diverse, alternating between the stylistic eclecticism of the set pieces performed by Dion and his fans (Choruses One and Three), which draw on a variety of popular and folk idioms, and the haunting dream sequences for Sonny (Chorus Two) and Mom (Chorus Four). The beautiful fragmented vocal lines of Chorus Two, in which Sonny "sees himself in a dream vision, offered up as a sacrificial victim,"[84] use music elaborated from Partch's memo-ries of a passage in *Bitter Music*, setting Lao-tzu: "I am drifted about as on the sea. I am carried by the wind—As if I had nowhere to rest." (The use of this fragment gives further resonance to the autobiographical relationship between the character of Sonny and Partch himself.)

The stylistic eclecticism is nowhere more apparent than in the opening scene, set on a "late afternoon in the Courthouse Park," where Dion, the Hollywood idol, is visiting small-town America. The town band and a team of majorettes lead a welcome procession in his honor, following which he and his entourage, with Mom prominent among them, perform a sequence of "num-bers." In the space of ten minutes we hear marching band music, with brass and snare drum to the fore; then a slow, repetitive chant, "Forever Ummorra"; a clog dance; an up-tempo pop song with walking bass line, "Deep inside, way way down I am"; a "primitive percussion ritual," "Wunnantu Anda"; and finally a big "show" tune, to the words "Heavenly Daze and a Million Years." In the score Partch notes that the audience "will consider several of these 'numbers' as parodies of popular or religious singing styles and lyrics if it chooses to. But it must *never* be led to feel that the *actors* are thinking of them as parodies. They must be performed straight, with great will and enthusiasm." Against this, it may be objected that few of these numbers are sufficiently close to any recogniz-able popular idiom for their satiric intent to have much bite; and at least one of them, "Wunnantu Anda," seems like "straight" Partch, not so different in essence from parts of *The Bewitched.* The one idiom conspicuous by its absence is that of fifties rock'n' roll, which places a question mark over the contemporaneity of the drama. The scene as a whole makes a rather diffuse impression, and the characterization of Dion as a Hollywood idol requires a certain degree of imaginative effort from the audience.

The Greek scenes, on the whole, are without stylistic anomalies of this kind, although even here the pseudo-American religious revival idiom of the hymns to Dionysus sung by the Bacchae ("Holy Joy and Get Religion," "Glory to the Male Womb," and others) strike a somewhat odd note, although dramatically not an ineffective one. The most haunting music comes at the end of Scene One (the first Greek scene) when Tiresias warns Pentheus of the ominous implications of his name (*penthos,* sorrow), which is set to a simple but memorable instance of the narrow resolution Partch called tonal flux. The final scene, in which the Apollonian light of day brings Agave back to her senses, only to realize that she has murdered her son, is a hair-raising exercise in sustained dissonance, with the two Chromelodeons providing a harmonic minefield of false consonances and chords involving higher "identities" than 11 (33, for example), with only an occasional chord proving to be a "straight" Partchian hexad. The musical symbolism of this is clear: it is only with the last-minute appearance of Apollonian clarity in the drama that Partch gives us virtually the sole passage in the score that makes exploratory use of his extended harmonic resources.

Revelation is an adventurous work, but in no sense, either today or at the time it was written, can it be described as avant-garde. Indeed, perhaps partly in self-defense, Partch by this time reacted quite strongly against certain forms of avant-garde theater. One of the critics who reviewed the Joyce Trisler production of *The Bewitched* in New York referred to it as an "Artaudian concept"; Partch had not read Artaud but, his curiosity aroused by the reference, he read *The Theatre and Its Double* during the summer of 1959 while he was preparing the text of *Revelation.* He was not very impressed; although there were some areas of genuine overlap between Artaud's ideas and his own, he found he could "easily pull twenty more out of Artaud's verbal hysterias that to me are absurd, even insane."[85] By contrast, as Ben Johnston has remarked, "Partch aimed *Revelation in the Courthouse Park* at the most ordinary of audiences. It is aggressively devoid of any highbrow traits. Its satire is so broad as to be inescapable even to the most naive. Its imagery and symbolism are obvious and uncomplicated. But its message is profoundly unsettling."[86] It is as though, in a work commissioned for performance in the rather staid atmosphere of a midwestern university, Partch was aiming for an uneasy balance: a theater work of broad appeal that would at the same time not abandon the central themes of his art as a whole.

The composition of *Revelation*—text and music—occupied Partch from August 1959 to June 1960. He had hoped to spend most of the summer of 1960 in California, recharging his batteries before the long process of preparing the production, which had been scheduled for the spring of 1961. However, his plans were "knocked haywire" by the need to move his studio, which took "a solid month" out of his life.[87] He decided to postpone the long weeks of labor organizing the new studio until the beginning of the new academic year, and to revise his original intention and make a shorter trip to California—the first time he had returned in four years. He planned to travel by train via Santa Fe to San Diego, then to go north to Los Angeles and San Francisco. In southern California he saw some friends, "all the way from Northridge and Encino down to South Hope St."; among them were the young writer John Rechy ("with whom I've had a long correspondence") and his Madison friends James and Marion Jacobs. He visited Peter Yates in September, and they recorded a lengthy interview (broadcast by KPFK radio in Los Angeles the following January), one of the few such that Partch felt was a success.

Back in Champaign in the early autumn, Partch began rehearsals for *Revelation* in his new studio on Springfield Avenue, near the railway tracks. Individual rehearsals got under way in October and full rehearsals, held initially every Thursday evening, in the middle of November. For the first time in his professional life Partch had no time to work through and learn all the instrumental parts, "partly because of the short time between the completed composition and the rehearsals," and partly because of the sheer enormity of the task.[88] Danlee Mitchell and Jack McKenzie assisted him in the organization and running of rehearsals, while John Garvey once again conducted. The principals were Jeffrey Foote (Sonny/ Pentheus), Freda Pierce (Mom/ Agave), and John Bert (Dion/ Dionysus). During rehearsals, as Garvey puts it, Partch would "putter around," offering various kinds of practical assistance to the players.[89]

The problems that had beset the first staging of *The Bewitched* were nowhere in evidence in the preparations for *Revelation*. Both the producer, Barnard Hewitt, and the choreographer, Jean Cutler, proved willing in rehearsals to abide by Partch's wishes, and as a result the production came close to his intentions in most respects. The stage alternately represented the American and Theban locales, with silhouettes of trees to left and right, and a rocky crag doubling as a park bench to the right. A portico with two steps, doubling as entrance to the courthouse and to the Palace of Thebes, was far left. Upstage slightly to the right was a small Victorian fountain, in the shape of a young boy and girl holding an umbrella, which could be darkened and hidden by a scrim curtain during the Theban scenes. A stairway leading from the far left aisle to the stage was used by the band, the majorettes, and Dion and his revelers when they entered. Transitions to the Palace of Thebes were achieved by spotlighting the players' masks, which descended and were worn during those scenes. Hewitt remembers the masks as a wonderful idea that did not come off to best advantage in the performance: "If only we'd had enough rehearsal. . . . It only happened every once in a while that you got that kind of effect and chills up and down your spine . . . After the thing was all over [we talked about the possibility of] a workshop where you could work on some of [the things in *Revelation*] for months . . . get the coordination of the mask moving and the light. Get it just right."[90]

During rehearsals of the work early in 1961, Charles Pond, the gymnastics coach at the university, liking the "Tumble On" sequence in Chorus Three (which uses mat tumblers and a trampolinist), asked Partch if the scene could be performed "with added music" at the National Collegiate Gymnastics Championship meeting, which was to be held that year in Illinois. Partch "wrote the script and titled it *Rotate the Body in All Its Planes*."[91] Before composing the "added music" he visited the gymnasium to time the rhythms of the gymnasts on the trampolines with a stopwatch. He put the piece together in February and it was performed at the Huff Gymnasium on April 8. He gave it the subtitle "Ballad for Gymnasts," and wrote in the program for the performance that he had tried to forge a link with the meaning and place of gymnastics in ancient times. "The present idea tends to fill a mutual need: the need of music to rediscover a creative meaning in the daily activities and the common rituals of our lives; the need of gymnastics to rediscover a rightful place in music, dance, and drama—in shows and extravaganzas."

Although a *pièce d'occasion* that is feasible only with the personnel for *Revelation* (including brass players), *Rotate the Body* was preserved for posterity by Madeline Tourtelot, who made an elegant film of the exhibition. The result, which she showed at the 1961 Edinburgh Festival and in New York and Czechoslovakia the following year, was to be one of Partch's favorites of their collaborations.

Revelation in the Courthouse Park was performed twice on April 11, 1961, in the afternoon and evening. The dress rehearsal on the ninth was filmed by

Tourtelot but, partly because of the much more complex staging than that for *Rotate the Body*, Partch felt the film was inadequate as a representation of his work and would not countenance its commercial release.[92] Critical response to *Revelation* was generally favorable, and a few critics were overwhelmed—notably Peter Yates, who judged it "one of the most fully conceived, spiritually and technically independent dramas of the twentieth century . . . another in the succession of American musical shows which are neither light opera nor grand opera." He described the spectacle:

> Stacked up on platforms at each side of the stage, the great shapes of the Partch instruments towered like a cubist mountain, an abstract skyscraper. . . . The black-clad instrumentalists lighted their small lights or switched them off as they played or sat silent, as one sees the light and darkening of windows at a distance . . . [the music] preluded, accompanied, supplemented and complemented, set atmosphere, broke into interjections . . . the musical themes were commonplace . . . deliberately, as was the language, the lazy, insistent motion of the dancers, the terrifying grass-roots nostalgia which was becoming the real tragedy of the implicit drama.[93]

The stage set for *Revelation in the Courthouse Park,* University of Illinois, 1961. Unsigned photograph, Harry Partch Estate Archive.

A party for the cast was held on the night of the performances, and several dignitaries from the university attended. A few days later the dean of the College of Fine and Applied Arts wrote to Partch praising the production and saying he had been unable to congratulate him at the party because Partch had been continually swamped by admirers.[94] In May both *Revelation* and *Rotate the Body* were recorded, not entirely to Partch's satisfaction, with the intention of giving him a new record to sell. Perhaps the most gratifying outcome for Partch himself was that the success of *Revelation* prompted the Illini Student Union Board to commission from him a "new type of musical" for performance on campus the following year. He could now look forward to another year of financial support from the university, and had a commitment to a performance of the new work at the year's end.

By all accounts, Partch "cut quite a figure" around the campus of the University of Illinois.[95] He was in the enviable position of having official status as a research associate and yet having no teaching responsibilities whatsoever. This allowed him to play to great advantage the role of the footloose bohemian artist who is accorded only grudging recognition from the academic powers that be—although his salary, $5,500 per annum, lifted him comfortably out of the economic bracket of the student body.

With financial stability and the guarantee of performances of the works he was writing, his stay in 1959–62 was a good deal more settled this time than in 1956–57. He had loyal support from several of the faculty; and, perhaps more than ever before, his work was a source of great fascination for a number of students. Partch was naturally delighted by such expressions of interest, especially when they came from talented young musicians.

Among the first students to be drawn to him in Urbana was the young composer James Tenney, who played in the revival of *The Bewitched*. Tenney had come to the University of Illinois for graduate study and was then beginning work on his master's thesis on the subject of musical form.[96] He was sympathetic to Partch's music, but his primary concern lay in discussing theory, for which Partch had little inclination—theory, as he told a correspondent in 1961, no longer being "on the tip of my tongue."[97] Tenney's musical tastes lay squarely in the Modernist tradition, music that was central to his research into the "phenomenology of twentieth-century musical materials." Unfortunately, from Partch's point of view, he had little interest in hands-on instrument repair. Tenney writes of this time:

[Partch] wanted, needed—and surely deserved, if anyone ever did—an assistant who could be wholly devoted to his work, and I was not able or willing to do/be that. I was fascinated by the instruments, the tuning system, etc., but I was much too interested in other music as well, and must have been rather ingenuous about probing him and probably *arguing* with him when I didn't agree with one of his very strong—and mostly negative—opinions about other composers whose music I was also interested in (Webern, Cage, Xenakis, electronic music, etc.). . . . In any case, he eventually (after about six months as his assistant) dismissed me, complaining of my "arrogance."[98]

Another type of student attracted to Partch, generally with happier results, was the type who saw him as a kind, approachable older man who would always be willing to lend a dollar or to offer a student, penniless or simply homeless during the university vacation, a floor to sleep on. Such was the experience of Michael Ranta, a young percussion student who had played the Boo in *Revelation*. In August 1961, arriving back in Champaign from a conducting course in Maine, Ranta presented himself at the door of Partch's apartment and, being homeless until the beginning of the school year in September, asked if he could stay. Partch offered him the spare room, and over the next few weeks the two became good friends. Partch would play Ranta recordings of his music or show him scores; in the lazy summer days there was plenty of time to talk and to reminisce. Partch told him about his hobo travels, his friends in California (including Gordon Onslow Ford, one of whose paintings hung over his couch), and discussed his professional plans with his young friend, much as he had done with Danlee Mitchell in Evanston three years before.[99]

The student in the School of Music who was the most indispensable for Partch's purposes proved once again to be Mitchell himself, who combined the roles of student, assistant, and friend. As Partch grew older—the production of *Revelation* took place some two months before his sixtieth birthday—his need became ever greater for competent young assistants, assistants who could devote themselves to the countless practical tasks involved in maintaining his instruments. When Partch took up his research associateship at the university in the summer of 1959, he requested funds for a half-time graduate assistant, and Mitchell, who was just beginning three years of graduate study, began working with him on a regular basis that September. Very little serious maintenance work had been possible in the years since Partch left Gate 5, mostly because the instruments had been moved around so much or left for long periods in storage. In Illinois, as Partch later explained to the University Research Board, "the alternate expansion and contraction of woods, between the excessive humidity of summer months and the excessive dryness of winter," conspired to create "a serious repair and tuning problem."[100]

During his years at the University of Illinois, Partch's work on his instruments had the largely pragmatic aim of restoring them to good condition. He was less concerned with working on new instruments than in improving existing ones (he built only two during his time in Champaign, neither of them his own invention). He worked, with Mitchell's help, on various improvements to Kithara I (to accommodate a new tuning); Kithara II; Chromelodeon II, satisfactorily completing the adaptation and retuning begun in Sausalito in 1954; and the Spoils of War. In addition, Harmonic Canon I was radically reconceived and rebuilt with eighty-eight strings in two sets of forty-four; a clear Plexiglas base was substituted for the former redwood base, and changes were made in the soundbox and belly. He put the finishing touches to a new instrument, the Crychord, which had been built largely by John Thompson, a student in the industrial design curriculum of the university's art department, as part of a project in "creating imaginative musical instruments" prompted by the performances of *The Bewitched*.[101] Partch worked on the Marimba Eroica and on new resonators for the Bass Marimba, using wooden organ pipes he had salvaged from the Twin Cities Church of the Bible in Urbana, which was being demolished.

Partch occasionally held open house at his studio, both the one above the Co-Ed Theater on East Green Street and the subsequent one on Springfield Avenue. These informal gatherings let interested persons hear his music, either live or on recordings; they were in fact the only such forum, as no large-scale performances were mounted at the university in the two-year gap between the 1959 and the 1961 Festivals of Contemporary Arts. At one open house Allan Louw, who had been working in Chicago, performed a scene from *Oedipus;* and for another Partch and Mitchell worked up "O Frabjous Day!" and made a recording of it. These gatherings would sometimes feature, in addition to Partch's music, poetry readings or displays of paintings by various friends.

Prominent among these friends, by the spring of 1961, was Vincenzo Prockelo, a young painter, poet, and musician, who had come to Champaign from military service. Partch took him under his wing and introduced him to various members of the university community. He also tried to persuade Prockelo that he should leave the military and pursue his multifaceted artistic talents. Danlee Mitchell drove Prockelo up to Chicago on a couple of occasions, trying to help him sell paintings. Prockelo showed Partch the typescripts of his poems, and Partch made occasional corrections or suggestions in the margins. One of the poems, beginning "Thank me not, for Loving/ Love me not, for Thanks./ Love me, as I am/ As I love you," is dedicated to Partch.

Partch sketched a setting of Prockelo's "Bless This Home," an unpublished poem written for their friends Gary and Susie Everett, on April 19, 1961, in a characteristic moment of creative energy once the dust had settled after the production of *Revelation*. The three-page sketch is written, like a piano score, in treble and bass clefs, with only an occasional ratio indication suggesting any harmonic movement outside the resources of the chromatic scale. The music begins in a diatonic F major and wanders to G major for the second verse, then back to F for the final verse. It manages in this way to tread an unpredictable path between familiar, secure harmonic areas. This offers a parallel to the quite individual mixture of the comforting and the mystic in the poem:

Bless this home and all within—
The One within this home within the mother's womb within—
that those feet within darken not the Gateway
nor darken the Golden Path within

The final score was completed ten days later, using intoning voice and five instruments: Adapted Viola (intended for Partch himself), oboe (for Prockelo), Harmonic Canon II, Kithara I, and Mazda Marimba. The Mazda Marimba was another new instrument conceived by an industrial design student at the university and consisted of the glass shells of twenty-four light bulbs in four rows played with rubber-capped mallets (and sounding, Partch remarked, "like the percolations of a coffee pot").[102] The instrumentation—with its blend of oboe, plucked and bowed strings, and the gentlest of his percussion instruments—creates a beautifully incantatory mood. A recording of the song was made on May 14.

In May 1961 Partch began work on the scenario of the new theater work, *Water! Water!* which he subtitled "An Intermission with Prologues and Epilogues." The subtitle expressed his rather cynical belief that it was the intermission, when the audience rushed with "eager anticipation and outright relief" for a drink, that constituted the focal point of any concert or theatrical event: the actual contents of the two halves were only the "prologues and epilogues" to this central social ritual. (As though in revenge, all of his own full-length theater works except for this one play continuously, with no intermission.)

In *Water! Water!* the ninety minutes of music theater that he provided, with its farcical story and frequent excursions into silliness, can be seen as only a frame for the central non-event: the drinks at intermission. Hence, the first page of the score describes the setting: "Time: Now. Place: At the drinking fountains, University of Illinois Auditorium. Cast: The audience." The work would be another of his send-ups of formal concert occasions, in the same spirit as *Yankee Doodle Fantasy* or *Ring Around the Moon,* were it not for the conventional nature of the drama he actually presents in the "frame," which is as close as he ever came to writing a Broadway musical. Set in a mythical American city, Santa Mystiana, and the countryside nearby, the story alternates between two locales, as had been the case in *Revelation.* Here the opposition is not between the ancient and the modern, but between the world of progress and the world of regress, a characteristic Partchian theme. The two locales, moreover, are caricatured mercilessly for comic effect. The half of the stage to the audience's left

> represents a world in which there is only a casual interest in what is called progress. It is a world of intuition, spontaneity, of unspoken reconciliation with the powers of a mysterious nature. The half of the stage to the audience's right represents social order, duty, law, convention, and progress. It is a world which probes and analyzes and exploits nature to the point that it has virtually lost reverence for its mysteries. Foreground, right or left, should be variably mysterious—never brilliant. This foreground, like Christianity, must suggest promise only in the rosy distance.[103]

Santa Mystiana—symbolically peopled by Her Honor (a Lady Mayor), a disc jockey, and an alderman—is suffering from drought, despite the presence of a large dam. In desperation they call on Arthur, a jazz musician, who enlists the help of his Jazzmen and a coven of ancient water witches to invoke the rain gods. When the rain does eventually come it falls continuously for days, causing a flood. Arthur and Wanda (leader of the witches) are brought to trial, but proceedings are halted by power failure due to floods in the power plant. Throughout the Epilogues the ghosts of Native American runners, dancing and playing on empty liquor bottles, bring news of the progressive calamity and deluge on the white man's world.

The music of *Water! Water!*—with its popular feel and with "very few microtonal demands"—was a new departure for Partch, but here the parodistic mode seems more fluent and convincing than it does in *Revelation.* Ben Johnston has suggested that the style of the work as a whole may have something to do with his sponsors—the Illini Student Union—but that in aiming it at a general audience (as he had done with *Revelation*) he was expressing also his own dislike of elitism.[104] Partch outlined the less happy aspect to the work's popular idiom a few years later when, commenting that he had felt "discouraged" by the variable quality of the musicians in his ensembles, he observed that "in Illinois I found that I was writing progressively *easier* music because I lost confidence that difficult music would be played well."[105] The preface to the score contains some helpful comments on tuning, presented in a humorous, resigned manner, merely asking that clarinets and bowed strings listen closely to the Chromelodeon and match their intonation accordingly.

He completed the full score of *Water! Water!* in November 1961 and began to take steps toward the ambitious project of mounting the production in New York following the Urbana première. A few recent experiences, though relatively unimportant in themselves, had brought home to him the disadvantages of producing work solely for a captive audience at the University of Illinois. One such was a projected revival of *Oedipus,* which John Garvey had wanted to mount in New York (where he had spent his sabbatical in 1960), but which collapsed under the weight of organizational difficulties following Garvey's return to Illinois; another was a projected collaboration with the jazz musician Gil Evans, who had been impressed by the recording of *U.S. Highball* and wanted to perform and record the work for MGM's newly purchased Verve label. Evans had encouraged Partch to come to New York to set the project in motion, but by the autumn of 1961 Partch was much too busy with the preparations for *Water! Water!* to give it the attention it needed. At the beginning of December he wrote to Gordon Ray, general secretary of the Guggenheim Foundation: "Very frankly, I am sure that my situation here will continue to be year-to-year, controversial, precarious, and generally unsatisfactory, despite strong support from Barnard Hewitt and John Garvey, unless my work wins occasional approval outside Champaign-Urbana. And the fact that even Chicago reviewers cannot be enticed down here tends to strengthen my feeling that I am operating in a comparative vacuum."[106]

A distinct lack of enthusiasm for the possible New York production is clear from some of his correspondence with contacts in the city, among them BMI, Douglas Moore at Columbia, and a theatrical agent he had met in Chicago at a dinner party for the playwright Tennessee Williams following a production of *Night of the Iguana* (even though Partch admitted he had "no illusions about a Broadway production" of *Water! Water!*). Rehearsals began early in December, with the same team as for *Revelation:* John Garvey as conductor, Barnard Hewitt as director, and Jean Cutler as choreographer. Partch was working under some strain, as the performance was in three months' time. To make matters worse, early in the new year he received news that he would not be reappointed at Illinois after his contract expired in June. He told Ben Johnston a year later that in these months "my liquor bill must have been staggering. I felt like a man, last fall, beginning with casting frustrations and the emergence of intellectual jazz" (so-called "third-stream" music, to which he had been introduced by John Garvey), "on the end of a gangplank."[107]

As rehearsals continued Partch began to see, as he put it some years later, that *Water! Water!* "is not a finished work. The two or many more years really needed to ponder and develop such an idea were not available, nor was there time to evolve, through long rehearsals, the techniques of farce, which in some ways are infinitely more exacting than straight drama or tragedy."[108] Barnard Hewitt, the director, agrees that the problem was lack of time rather than anything else: "It would have taken six months to work it out, and we didn't have six months. . . . It was an idea that wasn't fulfilled."[109] There were some new departures in the work, including the use of a jazz band, which produced its own version of some of the songs in the show (these were arranged and directed by Jim Knapp, a jazz musician at the university). Partch's ever-evolving vision of the function of his instruments on stage received a comic twist in that six of them were placed on low platforms with casters so that they could move around on stage, "propelled by the player or by designated helpers." At one point in the Second Prologue they start to attack the producer, who tries to order them down to the pit ("where you belong!"); and in the Fifth Epilogue, when Arthur (leader of the jazz musicians) is on trial for causing a flood, Her Honor orders the Bailiff to arrest the noisy Bass Marimba for contempt of court.

Water! Water!—while perhaps the least characteristic of Partch's creations— is not at all the lemon he had thought it was. It can work—as, in the opinion of some people, Ben Johnston among them, it did work in Urbana—as an enjoyable, unashamedly amateur student production, where the gaucheries and silliness of the text and the music can be consciously exploited to good effect. It stands with such theater works as Benjamin Britten's *Paul Bunyan* or Aaron Copland's *The Second Hurricane* as a flawed but highly enjoyable curio item in its creator's output.

Water! Water! was performed on March 9 and 10, 1962, at the University of Illinois auditorium, with a good deal of advance publicity by the Student Union in its paper *The Daily Illini.* Although Partch's attempts to take the production to New York had come to nothing, it played on March 17 at the Studebaker Theater in Chicago, thanks largely to funding from Madeline Tourtelot. Yet Partch returned to Champaign disillusioned with the work, his low spirits made worse by the knowledge that Tourtelot had lost money on the Chicago performance. A recording session for *Water! Water!* took place a few

"Rain finally comes to Santa Mystiana": a scene from the production of *Water! Water!*, University of Illinois, 1962. Photo by Wallace Kirkland.

days later with many of the students absent and their roles taken by the principals; only parts of the work were recorded, and not all of them satisfactorily. In a letter two years later Partch complained: "My last ensemble, in the spring of '62, was a miserable lot—and I was never sure that they would even show up. I lost control, and even *wanted* to lose control."[110]

The production over, Partch's only thoughts were how best to leave Illinois. He entertained no hopes of a further appointment at the university, for, as John Garvey puts it, "we were running out of ad hoc ways to try to keep him here."[111] In artistic terms, the experience of *Water! Water!* had cooled Partch's enthusiasm for working with student performers, and he was no longer willing to endure the kinds of musical compromise he had felt compelled to make. The more troubling aspect of his general dissatisfaction was that he was now drinking too much in the effort to escape from his problems.

He settled to the major task of issuing a new, and the final, set of Gate 5 records, seven in all, which were paid for in part by a gift of $1,500 from Madeline Tourtelot; the remaining $4,000 Partch himself put up from savings from his salary at the university for the previous three years. In the midst of the preparations for *Revelation* his supply of records had finally run out, and he had been unable to fulfill orders that were a direct result of articles about him by Peter Yates and others throughout 1961 and the early part of 1962. As long as he remained on a salary this mattered only in the sense that it prevented the dissemination of his work; now that his salary had stopped, record sales would have to become, once again, his primary source of income. Issue A, *Thirty Years of Lyrical and Dramatic Music*, features six of the Li Po settings recorded in 1947, a shortened version of the soundtrack for *Windsong*, eight of the *Eleven Intrusions*, and recent recordings of *Bless This Home* and *By the Rivers of Babylon*. (He had wanted to include *Dark Brother* as well but changed his mind, perhaps feeling that neither of the two recordings was wholly satisfactory—as long ago as 1953 he had written to Lauriston Marshall that the Gualala recording was "unbearably bad.") Issue B, *The Wayward*, was a reissue of the 1958 recording of *U.S. Highball* with the 1950 recording of *The Letter* and the 1958 *Ulysses at the Edge*. Issue C was *Plectra and Percussion Dances*, with deletions of short sections from *Ring Around the Moon* and the deletion of all of act 1, scene 2, of *Even Wild Horses;* Issue D was excerpts from the 1954 *Oedipus;* Issue E, excerpts from *The Bewitched;* Issue F, excerpts from the recording of *Revelation in the Courthouse Park*, which he described to Peter Yates as "disappointing";[112] and Issue G, excerpts from *Water! Water!* and an abbreviated version of *Rotate the Body in All Its Planes*. He took great care over the technical aspects of the disc mastering and design of the jackets, which feature designs by Robert Kostka, Arch Lauterer, and Vincenzo Prockelo, photographs by Madeline Tourtelot and Robert Kostka, and two of Partch's own photographs taken early in 1940 during his soul-searching trip in the southwestern desert. He prepared a new, updated photo supplement on the instruments for inclusion with the records. Twice he determined to withdraw the recording of *Water! Water!* as a statement of his dissatisfaction with the work but, "being human and impressionable," changed his mind.[113] The record was finally withdrawn from sale later in the year, but he occasionally sent a copy, free of charge and with an apologetic covering letter, to buyers of his other records.

At the beginning of August he put many of his possessions into storage. He wrote to Peter Yates: "The spectacle of me and two tons of musical effects wandering around the country is becoming almost comical. I feel that the time is coming when I'll have to make an outright gift of the things to someone who wants them, or otherwise dispose of them. I can see my way through the move to California, but not much beyond that, if I do not continue to sell records."[114] In his last few days in Illinois he stayed with Ben and Betty Johnston.

Then, without any definite plans, he took to the road, "putting what I need in my car, and driving off." He headed west via northern Wisconsin, and ended up staying for three weeks into September at Madeline Tourtelot's summer house in Ephraim. He rejected over eight hundred Gate 5 records that RCA had manufactured for him because of poor sound quality, and straightening the matter out caused him considerable delay. He enjoyed the cool autumn weather in Ephraim, and found it "finally relaxing to do nothing. At first, I found it exasperating to do nothing."[115] Toward the middle of September he crossed the desert, heading for northern California.

Petaluma

Partch arrived in Marin County in the middle of September 1962 and immediately began looking for a studio. His return to California felt at first like a homecoming, and he wrote to Peter Yates that it was "very good to be back, and to see old friends."[1] However, the San Francisco Bay Area had changed in the six years he had been away; rents were higher, and there were waiting lists on those cheaper studios that might have been suitable for his instruments. On September 27 he traveled thirty-five miles north to explore the small town of Petaluma. There, thanks to the help of his former Gate 5 landlord Jim Wilson, he was shown a vacated chick hatchery, the Pioneer Hatchery, at 416 Sixth Street. With its 1,100 square feet of floor space in one room, it was easily large enough for his requirements. The building had been constructed in the nineteenth century, and had been vacant for some six years: "They found it less expensive to raise chickens in Mississippi and send them frozen to California."[2]

As Partch later recalled it, that very first visit gave rise to a musical concept, which would emerge many months later as *And on the Seventh Day Petals Fell in Petaluma*. "On the day I looked the place over, I walked down the lane that led to the hatchery, and the way was strewn with petals—roses, camellias, and many others. Since I had these studies [which would become *Petals*] in mind for some time, and considering my strange absence [from California], twice, for exactly six years, the title came to me almost immediately."[3] The work's less-than-metaphysical title was never intended to be mysterious: the "seventh day" was a reference to the new year dawning after his six-year absence. In a later "Statement" on the work he added rather cryptically: "However sentimental or Oriental [it] may sound, the fact remains: it was the time of falling petals, and this music followed."

He hesitated for some weeks before deciding on the new studio, considering Sacramento, Los Angeles, and San Diego. A "slightly nostalgic" commitment to Marin County notwithstanding, he had no significant ties to any particular corner of the San Francisco area; the choice of studio location was influenced now, as throughout his life, by the immediate demands of his creative work. His initial reaction to Petaluma in this regard is outlined in a letter to Peter Yates written on the day following his first visit.

> There are plenty of vacancies, and rents are normal. However, I don't know a soul in the town, and even though it is only 35 miles away [from San Francisco] it has a characteristic of being off the beaten track. I would like to be near a metropolitan area, if only because I would sell more records. Eventually, I would like to form an ensemble, and Petaluma would be hopeless in that regard. I could never attract people from San Francisco. Right now I want no ensemble. I want to work alone with instruments, without the pressure of production, such as existed at Illinois for the past three years.[4]

Finally, the consideration of adequate floor space and modest rent (only forty-five dollars a month) swayed his decision, and he moved in around the middle of October, even though the legality of his tenancy of the derelict hatchery according to city statutes was, and would remain, in some doubt. The place was essentially one big L-shaped room with large windows, "and three other rooms [divided by plywood separators], for workshops, bedroom, and guestroom. Also two restrooms—men and women, I guess. However, there is no shower or bath. And until Jim [Wilson] helped me get them installed, no cookstove, sink, hot water, or refrigerator."[5] Partch made arrangements for his possessions, in storage in Urbana and Evanston, to be forwarded; "after I pay the $900 they say I owe them you'll be able to drive a truck through the hole in my bank account."

The "pressure of production" associated with the largely negative experience of *Water! Water!* was something he wanted to avoid in the immediate future at any cost. Although there were happier aspects of the experience, the most lingering residue was that left by the sacrifices in control he had been obliged to make due to time constraints. The conditions of extreme haste under which the music was composed and rehearsed had resulted in an ensemble sound that, at its worst, was merely a "mass of instrumentation . . . [in which] the sounds of instruments have frequently been lost, wholly or partly. . . . Due to these experiences I determined, in the summer of '62, to concentrate on a series of duets, in which I would have complete control. . . . And I determined not to record until I had the *right* musicians."6 The instruments themselves had suffered under excess of use in the past year, and he intended to embark upon an extensive program of rebuilding, repairing, and tuning.

At first he found it hard to concentrate on anything. On November 2 he wrote to Ben and Betty Johnston: "I am doing nothing, in a state of nothingness. O yes, I wash socks, iron a shirt, pick roses, shell walnuts (there's a tree at one window), bake pears. . . . As I say, emptiness. Sometimes I don't like it, but I realise most of the time that it is exactly what I need. And—strangely—I feel little or no desire to drown myself in alcohol."

The first task he accomplished was the writing of a grant application for a year's study in Japan, "of Japanese theater, particularly Noh and Kabuki, and of Japanese instruments and music, as they relate to theater," which he submitted to the Graham Foundation in Chicago and to the Ford Foundation in New York.7 In the proposal he explained that he had been "drawn to the Oriental attitudes because, in the Orient, there has never been any great separation of the theater arts, therefore no need to conceive of integration. . . . As a result of this proposed study I would expect to produce at least one new major work, employing the ideas, techniques, and possibly instruments, which I would have known intimately. . . . I do not think or plan on the level of reproducing anything, but rather in terms of revitalization of the over-specialized Western theater, through transfusions of old and profound concepts."

What the Graham Foundation or the Ford Foundation thought of his proposal we do not know, though an ethnomusicologist might well have detected a degree of naivete in his comments about Japanese music. In due course he received rejection letters from both foundations. He was not particularly discouraged, attributing their decision to the general "timidity" of foundations with respect to unorthodox proposals in the creative arts, and to the fact that "I don't have friends among the 'right' people. Which doesn't really bother me."8

During the winter months in Petaluma he began some repair work on his instruments, but his efforts were hampered by a broken thumb and problems with muscular rheumatism. He had had rheumatic trouble in Champaign two winters in a row, but this time he was unable to shake it off, finding it difficult "to rise out of pill-induced daze" long enough to do much work.[9] By the middle of January 1963, however, he was able to write to Danlee Mitchell of his progress and to outline the extent of the task ahead: "I have managed to put five string instruments in good shape despite my disability: Koto, Surrogate Kithara, Kithara I, Castor and Pollux, and Harmonic Canon I. The big Kithara [II], which was the worst problem, with four absolutely warped tuning boards, peg boards, is not finished. I haven't touched any of the percussion. The Boo is in dreadful shape, and the whole top of the Bass Marimba needs to be planed off and the blocks retuned. . . . The Diamond Marimba, which was absolutely rigid when I finished it in 1946, now wobbles drunkenly, and needs a complete rebuilding of base. Well—you see. So much to do."[10]

Before he got any further, Madeline Tourtelot came to his aid by sending him $125 for a plane ticket to join her and her husband in Mexico City, and he made a reservation for January 19. This was partly a much-needed vacation, and partly an attempt to find a climate that would ease his rheumatic trouble. The original idea of staying in Mexico City itself was jettisoned because of its high altitude and pollution, and he and the Tourtelots headed south to Cuernavaca, where they remained for two weeks. "After five days in the warm dry air of Cuernavaca my rheumatism vanished."[11]

In Cuernavaca he began writing a document called *Manual on the Maintenance and Repair of—and the Musical and Attitudinal Techniques for—Some Putative Musical Instruments,* the first draft of which was completed back in Petaluma in March.[12] The *Manual* is energetic and detailed, a collection of the notes and instructions he was keeping during his mounting "fever" of activity on instrument repair. The text ranges across a broad spectrum of issues, from the aesthetic to the minutely practical. Examples of his fastidious attention to detail can be seen in passages such as this, on the Harmonic Canons:

A bad tone always results when the lip of the groove at one of the nuts is not decisive. The groove should climb at an angle to the lip, and there should be an acute drop *at* the lip.

If the lip groove is too wide, or if it is fuzzy, the string tends to vibrate *in* the groove, which causes the bad tone. Use a small triangular file and cut the groove (in the oak ends) *at an angle,* delicately.

If the lip is already too low a tiny piece of heavy, slick paper, such as that from a notebook or matchbook cover, glued under the string at the lip, sometimes helps. Remember that every time a bridge is moved the relation of string height to groove angle is changed.[13]

At the other extreme the *Manual* was intended to shake up the attitudes of prospective players, who "nearly always approach the playing of my instruments as a momentary adventure, like spending the night with a foreign whore. That is, one whose talents do not include spoken English." He suggested instead that "a true acquaintance with the whore" might lead to more gratifying results. This quip leads him, in the text, into a discussion of corporeality—a term which he now uses quite clearly to mean a particular performance aesthetic, a holistic mind-body interaction that is to be achieved by cultivating "attitudinal technique," the correct "attitude of the musician on stage":

> *At no time* are the players of my instruments to be unaware that they are on stage, *in the act.* There can be no humdrum playing of notes, in the bored belief that because they are "good" musicians their performance is ipso facto "masterly." When a player fails to take full advantage of his role in a visual or acting sense, he is muffing his part—in my terms—as thoroughly as if he bungled every note in the score. . . . There is surely some special hell reserved for the player of one of the more dramatic instruments who insists on deporting himself as though he were in tie-and-tails on a symphony orchestra's platform (such as experimental hanging by the gonads on a treble Kithara string until he relents).[14]

While the special form of oneness of musician and instrument that Partch describes in this passage is exciting and compelling, the precise nature of the musician's deportment on stage remains tantalizingly vague. The player, he writes, must "take full advantage of his role in a visual or acting sense"; but these two senses are not synonymous. Is it sufficient to look good (the "visual . . . sense"), besides playing well, or is the musician also intended to act? And if so, how? With what kind of movements? And how do these "acting" movements relate to the purely functional movements involved in playing the instrument? To these questions the *Manual* has no direct answers. Although Partch's vision of corporeality had evolved considerably since the time of *Genesis of a Music,* an unambiguous description of the idea in words proved as elusive as ever.

At the end of his holiday in Mexico Partch took the opportunity to visit friends in the Southwest and in southern California before returning to Petaluma. Although these were purely social visits, the question of his professional future was never far from his mind. He flew first to Dallas, where he saw Lauriston

Marshall, now provost of the Graduate Center for Advanced Studies in the Southwest, and discussed with him the possibility of finding some kind of affiliation with a college in the area. Marshall suggested New Mexico State, at Las Cruces, some forty miles north of El Paso, an area that Partch had known and liked from childhood. As the winter's experiences had shown, the matter of a favorable climate—"Texas or Rocky Mountains or the west"—was not entirely an aesthetic one: his rheumatism was now a significant consideration.[15]

From Dallas Partch traveled by Greyhound bus with a through ticket to Petaluma, making stopovers in San Diego, where he saw Bertha and Harold Driscoll, and Los Angeles, where Peter Yates introduced him to Sister Magdalen Mary, an unconventional Catholic nun who taught at Immaculate Heart College in Hollywood. A few days later Partch, still astonished by their meeting, reported to Lauriston Marshall: "She had bought all my records for the art dept., and had them in a jukebox, 25 cents to hear one side, 50 cents for a complete record. She has huge music boxes, mostly from saloons of the nineteenth century, and she said, 'If you get too excited I can lend you an opium pipe.' She did (I had to provide my own opium)."[16] Equally extraordinary, "phallic funerary idols from the Orient stood about. She didn't make any point about my seeing them, but how could anyone miss them? Bells are everywhere, and when she found one missing she said, 'I think the reverend mother has been poking around.'"[17] She offered to help find him a suitable studio in the Los Angeles area, should he ever wish to move there, and arranged a lecture for him at the college in April.

Partch returned to Petaluma on the morning of February 12, the northern Californian climate an unwelcome change after his weeks away. "Rain and fog greeted me, but through the mist and drops I saw acacia trees flaming into bloom, and camellias in nearly every yard."[18] Although he was not unhappy to be back, he was restless. For a few weeks he busied himself with more work on his instruments before leaving once more, this time for a month in southern California, where he presented a lecture at Immaculate Heart College on April 20. An apparently promising meeting took place a few days later with Charles Kaplan, "a dean at Valley State [California State University, Northridge] . . . [who] seemed very enthusiastic about my work. . . . I've found a possible studio about four or five miles from the campus, in a beautiful location in rocky semi-desert hills at the northwest edge of San Fernando Valley."[19] The studio proved to be bigger than he needed and too expensive, and the idea was dropped.

The trip south had the effect of making him feel somewhat more settled.

Back in Petaluma, as the days passed he realized, as he wrote to Danlee Mitchell on May 27: "I am very glad I came to California. I am now feeling more at ease, more poised, than I have in years." His records were not selling particularly well, "partly because I am in a backwash," but his personal expenses were somewhat lower than in Illinois, and he could scrape by.[20] Petaluma itself he found "very conventional," but it had one distinct advantage: "Nobody cares what you do here." He felt a maverick in little ways: in the spring "the whole of Sixth St. was lined with walnuts. I went down the sidewalk picking them up . . . those silly residents—they prefer to pay 49 cents a pound for them than demean themselves by stopping over their own sidewalks."[21]

The spring and early summer of 1963 in Petaluma, with the exception of his month-long trip to southern California in April–May, was devoted to mainte-nance work on his instruments. He spent some time tuning the Sitka spruce blocks of the Bass Marimba, using the facilities of the night workshop at Petaluma High School. He wanted to improve the coupling between the blocks and the new organ-pipe resonators, finally determining that the best coupling resulted from the irrational tuning of the block higher than the desired pitch and the resonator lower: the heard tone averaged out at the desired pitch. He also worked at the Boo, using some bamboo he had bought in New York three years earlier. In the interim, even though he had banded most of the bamboo at the time, "roughly half of it had to be thrown out, since it was split and warped too badly for any use except as kindling."[22] The remainder was used to improve the first row of the instrument; the new appearance of the Boo gave "the impression of a Chinese pagoda, high at the ends, lower in the middle." Also with visual aesthetics in mind he remade the cases of the two Chromelodeons using Philippine mahogany plywood, in the effort to make them less incon-gruous when placed among his other instruments. The vertical-grain white oak that originally cased Chromelodeon I was recycled for the fourteen blocks of the Zymo-Xyl, a new instrument that also incorporated the empty liquor bottles used in *Water! Water!* as well as two hubcaps and a kettle top. He also built his own version of the Mazda Marimba he had used in Illinois, with the shells of twenty-four light bulbs in four rows, preserving the tuning layout for *Bless This Home.* He attached two new long sections of bamboo to the Spoils of War, replacing the two pieces of giant bamboo that had been used on the instrument in *Revelation;* and, working again in the evenings at Petaluma High, he fashioned and tuned a large Sitka spruce block as a replacement for the original redwood no. 2 block of the Marimba Eroica. At the end of July he had completed ten months, on and off, of work on the instruments with nine days spent rebuilding the bellows of Chromelodeon I, and two weeks (ten hours per day) tuning both Chromelodeons. Following this, in great relief, he announced to Peter Yates on July 31: "Tomorrow I can finally get back to work, with instruments in *good* shape, for the first time in years." In August, with the repair work finished, he completed a revision of the *Manual* on the instruments.

Although Partch's plans for an immediate return to composition proved somewhat optimistic, the extent of his labors during these months itself bears witness to the resurgence of his creative impulse. Rather than attempt to wind down his activities now that he had passed sixty—even though advancing age and his rheumatic trouble made the strenuous physical work on his instruments increasingly difficult—his work in the Petaluma studio in 1963 shows him as youthful in spirit as ever, still trying out new ideas and making discoveries. A scrap of paper that has survived from these months records his exhilaration at this sort of endeavor. It reads: "EUREKA! Like, you know, man, I've found it."

In the midst of this activity Danlee Mitchell flew down from his home in Tacoma, Washington, to help Partch put together a concert he had been invited to give on June 20, 1963, for the Eighteenth National Convention of the American Symphony Orchestra League at the Sheraton Palace Hotel in San Francisco. The appearance had been arranged by Oliver Daniel at BMI and was intended as a lecture-demonstration, featuring short excerpts from several of Partch's works.[23]

A polite review of the program by Alfred Frankenstein—who had written some unfavorable reviews of Partch's Gate 5 records in the previous decade—was published in the *San Francisco Chronicle* on June 22, and a lukewarm one by Alexander Fried appeared in the *San Francisco Examiner* the same day.

However, the event—which Oliver Daniel had thought might provide a modest but worthwhile bit of publicity—backfired somewhat, when *Time* magazine, in the issue of July 5, published a sarcastic and potentially damaging article under the title "Harry Isn't Kidding." Ostensibly a review of the Sheraton Palace Hotel program, the article set out, quite maliciously, to undermine Partch's credibility as a creative artist and to ridicule Partch himself ("a hopeless, penniless outsider"), his instruments, and his music. The anonymous reviewer described the Surrogate Kithara as "a two-deck, 16-string zither that looks like a pair of overgrown abacuses without the beads," the Spoils of War as "a big and ugly one-man band strung up on a gallows," and the "clucks, gurgles, thumps and thunders" of the music Partch and Mitchell played were "reinforced by a recurrent and highly menacing *meeeEEEOOOW!* from his strings and an occasional unspecific crash that sounds like a Boo player collapsing." A *Time* reporter had visited Partch a few days before the performance, arriving in Petaluma at 11:15 A.M. and leaving at 10:15 P.M.. "I would guess that eight of those hours were spent explaining intonation and giving examples of intonation," Partch wrote to Oliver Daniel, who had written to express his horror at the article. "Not one word of this appeared in the *Time* story . . . the only fact gleaned from me during those eleven hours that was published was my father's atheism."24 Partch told another correspondent that the interview itself had been enjoyable enough, but that five hours into it "we both began to get a bit irritated, and I suggested a can of beer. By 10 P.M. beer cans were littered all over the studio."25

The article's "palpable impertinence" understandably annoyed Partch and enraged many of his friends and supporters.26 At first he was upset and concerned about the article's impact, but friends tried to reassure him: his doctor in San Francisco "just laughed, and said, *Time*'s readers . . . will never be interested in you." By the end of the month he had become highly philosophical about the whole thing, and wrote to Danlee Mitchell: "I might even feel honoured, since *Time* has reserved some of its best ridicule for me. I remember, but of course you don't, how Salvador Dali was ridiculed back in the 1920s. When you invite the public eye you have to take it, however depressing." He even began receiving religious literature in the mail, "anonymously, because—having had an atheist father—[some of *Time*'s readers] are deeply concerned about the salvation of my soul. I have a book entitled, 'The Romance of Redemption.'"27

The bad press and the correspondence that it entailed were time-consuming and exasperating disruptions to his calm existence—he had told Mitchell at the beginning of July that all he really wanted to do was "to sit under a tree"28—but the incident presented no serious blow to his professional activities. Composers Recordings, Incorporated, in New York was interested in releasing a record of his music, and occasional letters of admiration were reaching him from young musicians in California, including jazz players like Emil Richards and Gary Burton. It began to seem as though a new ensemble might be possible once he returned from the lengthy trip to the midwest he was now contemplating.

Partch's trip east in September–November was undertaken with the primary purpose of completing his film collaborations with Madeline Tourtelot. The *U.S. Highball* film begun in Evanston five years before was still unfinished, and Tourtelot was keen to complete it; she was also exerting some pressure on

Partch to help her salvage the film of *Revelation in the Courthouse Park* which he had not considered worthy of commercial release at the time it was made in Urbana.

Their three finished collaborations— *Windsong, Music Studio,* and *Rotate the Body*—had encouraged Partch to undertake small-scale lecture presentations on his work, something he had virtually abandoned since Sausalito days. He felt that the films were an acceptable substitute for a live demonstration of his instruments when he was there in person to insist on good sound quality. And their collaboration had obvious benefits for Tourtelot herself: *Music Studio* had the best rental record of any of her films to that time.

In resuming work on *U.S. Highball* Partch had hoped to retain, as far as possible, his original concept of juxtaposing the now five-year-old black-and-white shots of the ensemble performing the work with color sequences newly filmed along the route of the protagonist's journey from San Francisco to Chicago—footage of highways and trains, mountains and deserts. Even before he set out from California, Partch realized there would be problems in retaining this idea. In a letter in July Tourtelot had expressed her disappointment with the ensemble shots filmed in Evanston five years before: "This is not my type of work," she wrote, "and it is the reason I tried to back out of this part of the filming. I am a poet with the camera, not a reporter. I prefer to discover beauty, not to try to recreate it."[29] More alarmingly, she suggested that the overall length of the film should not exceed twelve to fifteen minutes: "To be so clever and artistic over so long a piece of music could visually tire the audience beyond their peak of enthusiasm. Listening to the music in its present length is a different thing." Partch, naturally, was opposed to cutting *U.S. Highball,* which lasted twenty-five minutes.

Partch seems to have approached their meeting in a combative mood. He still resented the amount of traveling she did with the films, especially to European film festivals and other prestigious venues to which he had never been directly invited. In August she had written: "As far as your coming away 'with nothing' from Festival showings, you are mistaken. Nothing tangible, perhaps, but don't think for a minute that your music doesn't get attention, and your name made known a little."[30] But he was not to be so easily appeased; and indeed, the whole period of work on the two films was fraught with difficulties. "It was all a farce," Partch later complained to Danlee Mitchell.

> She made the outdoor shots [for *U.S. Highball*] without reading my scripts. I had left three with her, all originals, and she lost all of them. She didn't invite me on the trip.

> She invited a guy who knew nothing about *U.S. Highball.* She lost the tape I left with
> her, and she threw away her own notes telling her *where* the various shots were taken.
> I was then obliged to try to decide whether a small butte on the trip was in western
> Nebraska or eastern Nevada. I'm not that good. She misplaced most of the shots of
> the ensemble, and insisted that what she had in Ephraim was all there was. I insisted
> it wasn't. So we made the 276-mile trip to Evanston to search. There—sure
> enough—were the good shots.[31]

Despite Partch's antipathy to the whole project, the film was completed in time
to be shown at the forthcoming Brussels International Experimental Festival;
he was not displeased with the finished product.

They also worked, no more happily, at resynching parts of the film of
Revelation with improved sound quality, for which Tourtelot paid some $1,500,
but which still failed to produce what Partch felt to be an acceptable film. Also,
"she made a film of a young man in black tights dancing in the autumn leaves.
As usual the photography was beautiful, but the idea escapes me. She wanted to
use *Castor and Pollux.* In my unutterable weariness I said go ahead. I hope I
never see it again." The film was later released under the title *The Renascent.*
The whole period of collaboration was painful and distressing for him, and he
wrote to a correspondent in November that "I'll never try again."[32]

Partch seems to have felt by this time that his artistic association with
Tourtelot had simply run its course. His initial attraction to her in the summer
of 1957 had come about partly because of her obvious qualities as a filmmaker,
and partly because of her potential as a patron of his work; in combination,
these had given him the sense of being able, at that time, to shape his life around
her. Six years on, this latter prospect no longer seemed so compelling. It may be
that he now felt that her presence in his life was simply a burden from more
desperate times; he now needed a new source of belief in his work, a source of
fresh promise and of hope for the future.

Partch and Tourtelot worked together only once more, in 1969, on a project
with which he was even less satisfied; and in an important sense he never truly
regained his artistic faith in her after their disagreements that autumn in
Evanston. The aspects of the *U.S. Highball* collaboration that had aroused his
wrath—her misplacing his scripts, her forgetting the extent of the footage they
had shot in Evanston five years before, and even her suggestion of cutting the
work to make a shorter, more marketable film (which suggestion she readily
withdrew under pressure from him)—he perceived as showing a lack of understanding of, and respect for, his work, and her general disorganization he
regarded as unprofessional. His evident feeling of maltreatment, and his bitter

complaints about Tourtelot herself, show the undiplomatic side of his nature, and—once again—how temperamentally ill-suited he was to collaborative ventures.

From Evanston he went on to New York where, on October 23, he met with Oliver Daniel to discuss BMI's suggestion that he do a tour of universities in the following season. He also had "a session with CBS, who might do a show. The tour would call for at least ten thousand. So, I spent two hours at lunch with one Rockefeller man, seven hours at a cocktail party with another Rockefeller man."[33] Neither meeting gave him much encouragement. "The first said, Why didn't I establish a school like Alwyn [*sic*] Nikolais? I said, Who is there who can go home and practise on his own Kithara? But I don't think he got the idea."[34] The experience left him weary, and "sick" of the general vagueness of the various possibilities. "I've no idea what may happen," he told a correspondent. "On the basis of past experience I would say: nothing."[35]

Partch returned to Petaluma, exhausted, on November 8, and found his studio in an appalling condition: "No heat, no gas, a huge leak in the roof, and dampness and even mold."[36] He and his landlord "dug a 50-ft. ditch for a new line, then fitted pipes, and after ten days of wrangling the city inspector finally put his okay on it."[37] But his troubles were only beginning. "The mayor decided my occupancy was questionable, so he would not allow gas to be connected until I put down $25 for a 'temporary use permit.'"[38] A public hearing of his case came up on December 3, to enable the local planning commission to decide whether or not he could stay. The hearing was covered by a reporter from the *Santa Rosa Press Democrat Empire News,* who published a story on him on December 8. "The city people were really very understanding," Partch told Danlee Mitchell. "They bent over backward to make it possible for me to stay. But I am in a firetrap—at least the instruments are—I can dive out the window. The electrical wiring is substandard."[39] The Petaluma authorities granted him a permit so that his gas could be reconnected but insisted he install new wiring to bring the place up to city codes.

The end of the year found him at something of a standstill, hampered by an accumulation of mostly practical difficulties. He wrote in disgust to Mitchell: "This has been an absurd fall, beginning [with] those wretched 'collaborations' with Madeline, and ending with more than a month [of] the present uncertainty in Petaluma. There has been no sense of security in the housing of the instruments in 17 years. They've become a Frankenstein, and I am sick of stop-gap measures." The seemingly endless problems with his studio made him uncertain about remaining there for much longer. On the other hand, as he

Partch in his studio in Petaluma, 1963. Photo by Chris Mannion.

well realized, "Petaluma is considerably warmer than San Francisco—we've had camellias since early December."[40] And he had by now grown fond of the place: "Even though I've been very lonely here . . . it represents the first peace I've had in seventeen years."[41] Finally, early in February, he spent $160 rewiring the studio, realizing that it was cheaper than moving again. No sooner was the rewiring complete, and Partch flat on his back with flu, than he was informed that the hatchery had been sold and was to be demolished to make way for a new apartment complex. "I may have another five or six months," he told Peter Yates, "and I'll take every month I can get."[42]

The eviction notice could scarcely have come at a worse time. Not only had he invested time and money in his studio to make it safe and habitable, but by the late autumn of 1963, to judge from his correspondence, ideas for a new composition were firmly on his mind—one whose conception may be regarded in part as a wish to savor the fruit of his labors with the instruments.

The first new work following Partch's return to California marks a radical departure from the works of the Champaign years. *And on the Seventh Day Petals Fell in Petaluma,* written in March–April 1964 and revised at various times and places until the completion of the final copy of the score in San Diego in October 1966, shows a renewed concentration on technical innovation and on fusing his activities as composer and instrument builder within the context of a single composition. Even given the somewhat unusual conception of the work as "studies in preparation" for the large dance-drama which followed, *Delusion of the Fury* (1965–66), *Petals* may be regarded both as a representative example of Partch's later work—if the term "representative" can be said to have any real meaning when applied to his sui generis output—and as a continuation of a line of development, leading from intoned speech works to a fully instrumental idiom, which had become rather fragmented after *Windsong*. Coming as it did after some two years of compositional inactivity, the music is both exploratory—the audible manifestation of a period of preparation during which new ideas were allowed to assemble themselves under the horizon—and reflective, in gathering those ideas, like falling petals, into an array.

The impetus to begin the composition of *Petals* was provided by Partch's confidence that the sine qua non of the undertaking, good musicians to perform what he wrote, would be available to him. When he returned from his holiday in Mexico in February 1963 he found letters waiting for him from Danlee Mitchell and from Michael Ranta, two of the most dedicated musicians in his ensemble at the University of Illinois, both expressing their willingness to come out to California to work with him. Characteristically, Partch never directly asked either of them to come: always wary of what Ranta describes as "half-assed help," he needed to be sure of intense commitment.[43] Given the remoteness of his location, and the fact that the undertaking would not bring any financial recompense—nor could it even be guaranteed to produce a finished result—the promise made by Mitchell and Ranta implied that kind of commitment. Perhaps equally important, Partch's faith in the abilities of Mitchell and Ranta not merely as virtuoso percussionists but also as musicians with the right kind of "attitudinal technique" gave him carte blanche to "exploit the instrumental resources to the full, exploring new techniques and . . . untried rhythms and polyrhythms."[44]

Thanks to the extensive cache of letters from Partch to the two young musicians in the months leading up to April 1964, and to the fact that Partch retained a folio of sketches, verbal and musical, for *Petals,* we can trace the history of the work itself. Writing to Ranta on November 20, 1963, he had complained that, with having to devote so much time and energy to maintaining instruments, to repairing his studio, and to coping with the exigencies of daily life, he had "written about seven lines in a year and a half." By the time of the next letter, January 17, 1964—with the threat of eviction from his studio hanging over his head—plans for the work had developed. "I've been trying to write 23 duets, exploiting instruments, for several months," Partch explained, "but I've gotten very little done. If I should be able to get to work on these, and finish them, and if I can find a dedicated recording engineer who has the time to record them—then—help [in performing them] would be a real help. I might also add—if I have a studio. A lot of ifs."

He was slow in getting down to work. With a "deluge of visits" from various friends and acquaintances throughout January (including a "most congenial" one from Karlheinz Stockhausen and David Tudor),[45] lectures at the University of Oregon (arranged by Jean Cutler) in mid-February, and illness and exhaustion upon his return, work on the duets did not begin in earnest until early March. He had fixed the visits of both Mitchell and Ranta for mid-April, hoping to have the music completed by then. Although he had heard by this point that the hatchery was to be demolished, the "only word" he could get from the new owner was that it would be "some time" yet before the demolition work would begin, so it seemed safe to proceed.[46] On March 11 he wrote to Mitchell: "Frankly, I dread moving so much, and I like the summers here, so I hope I can stay till September. . . . I've written very little more on the duets, but I truly think that I am now ready—I might have to put the duets on sprocketed tape, in order to be sure of synchronization in the quartets, sextets, and octet. I've written percussion parts that I can't possibly play well at the tempos indicated."

The original sequence of twenty-three duets—which he called "verses"—and the original grouping of the verses into five quartets, three sextets, and a concluding octet seems to have been established before composition proper was under way, and certainly before it was completed. On March 28 he sent Ranta a "tentative outline" of the duets, adding: "I've always hated composing under pressure, and here I am doing it again. But I have written eleven of the twenty-three duets. This much has taken me twenty-one days, and I have twelve to go. There are so many interruptions." The remainder of the verses followed at an even more rapid rate: the last page of the pencil sketch score of the work bears the colophon "Fine 5.35 p.m. April 15, 1964." Judging by the comparatively neat appearance of the sketch score, we may surmise that much of the music was worked out quite fully at the instruments before being committed to paper. The pages record several changes of mind and scribbled-in afterthoughts, but large stretches of the music remained unaltered from this first notation to the final score two and a half years later.

And on the Seventh Day Petals Fell in Petaluma is one of Partch's rare excursions into "absolute" music: a thirty-five-minute instrumental work, radical in form, apparently unrelated to text or program. Looking beneath the surface and delving into the imaginative world of Partch's sketches we find that, conceptually, *Petals* is not as "absolute" as it first appears; and in fact the music had not one but two essentially different layers of extramusical significance both during and after the period of its composition.

The first is Partch's insistence that the instrumental "verses" of *Petals* were studies for the music of the dance work he was already planning, *Delusion of the Fury;* during the composition of *Petals,* he wrote, "the placement of these musical ideas in the larger dramatic work . . . was constantly anticipated, although not indicated at the time."[47] The implication of this is that his intention was to use the verses quite freely in *Delusion* wherever their musical character suited the mood of the drama, even though the allocation of a particular verse to a particular point in the two-act story line was not on his mind as he composed *Petals.*

The second substratum of extramusical significance is of a more specific nature. Partch regarded the verses of *Petals* as musical portraits, in miniature, of various scenes and events of his daily life in Petaluma. In his sketches the verses were given titles, "verbal concepts" reflective of such everyday matters. In fact, the folio of sketches contains sheet after sheet of lists of these titles. No two such lists tally exactly, but a great many of the titles reappear from one page to the next. Although the titles were ultimately abandoned, Partch announced them in his introduction to the concert première of *Petals* at UCLA in May 1966. On that occasion he remarked:

> A small town, and Petaluma is a small town, tends to be introspective. It retains a kind of indigenous individuality—this despite TV waves from the nearest urban center. Little irritations become fantastically exaggerated, and it seems easier and more natural to observe small things, such as a fly getting dejuiced in a spiderweb in the corner. This is a commentary on my habits as a housekeeper, but it is also a commentary on the instability of life in traps—for men and nations. . . . I generally work with verbal concepts, and not unlike others at least as far back as Aristophanes my concepts are often whimsically satiric. One could at least call these working titles.

With allocations to the final sequence of twenty-three verses appended—these were not indicated by Partch in his typescript for the UCLA lecture—the titles he announced are as follows:

And on the Seventh Day Petals Fell in Petaluma—[1] They had been blooming for six days—[2] On the seventh they were tired of blooming. [3] They fall on historic ground—[4] An ant slept here, a spider died there. [5] Music for our times—[6] Pure music for pure people—[7] Nude at noon—[8] Transfigured on the postoffice steps. [9] Alleyoop in A Street (it is in A major)—[10] Bubbaloo in B Street. [11] Recognition Scene in the Pioneer Hatchery—[12] Pity! Pity! the white leghorn cockerel! [13] Good grief in G Street (it is in G major)—[14] Delight in fright at night. [15] Sad! Sad! [16] With crickets in the hedges—[17] And mating calls of attic ghosts. [18] Andante cantabile in F Street (it is in F minor)—[19] Death in Cobweb Corner—[20] And climax—in the public library. [21] The egg is wondrous! [22] It desires only to get fertilized—[23] Stay tuned for biology.

The autobiographical significance of most of these titles is clear enough; the more obscure ones (for example the insect allusions) are explained in the lecture. The first two have to do with the work's title, and the "historic ground" of the third perhaps refers to nothing more than his own personal history in northern California. The swipes at "Music for our times" and "Pure music" are familiar from his lectures and writings of the fifties. "Delight in fright at night," its word play aside, may refer to an attempted break-in to the hatchery in June 1963 which, as he wrote at the time to Danlee Mitchell, he had "been expecting," but which frightened him considerably. The F minor "Andante cantabile" sounds rather Chopinesque, whereas the reproductive theme of the last three titles seems to return to the world of *Castor and Pollux* as well as to the former activities of the Pioneer Hatchery. "Climax—in the public library" is anyone's guess, but may simply reflect Partch's lifelong tendency toward decisive encounters—of an intellectual kind—in public libraries, beginning at least as far back as his discovery of Helmholtz's *On the Sensations of Tone* in the Sacramento Public Library in 1923.

Its extramusical content aside, the overall form of *Petals*—a sequence of one-minute "verses"—is revealed in the folio of sketches as a return to the idea of musical "yardage goods" that had been so important to the conception of *The Bewitched*. This new "Musical Yardage in an Oriental Petal Pattern" could, he quipped, be sold by the beat, "2400 beats for $2.99, 4800 beats for $5.98." This goes some way toward explaining his determination to have each of the verses last exactly sixty seconds (although in practice this idea did not work out so precisely). Partch's approach was not to treat the one minute as a frame that cropped its materials arbitrarily, but to generate a metrical structure for each verse that yielded a precise number of bars (different for most of the verses) adding up, if played at the specified metronome mark, to sixty seconds. Clock time was thus less important than the radically new exploration of the relationship between meter and form suggested by the pieces of "musical yardage" of equal length.

In its final version, *Petals* is a sequence of thirty-four one-minute instrumental verses. Verses 1–23 are duets and trios: they are played through first singly, then pairs of verses (in sequence) are played simultaneously to form quartets or quintets, verses 24–33. After ten of these "double exposures," the final three verses of the original sequence of twenty-three are combined to form a concluding septet (verse 34). On the title page of the final score Partch described the work as "Studies in techniques, timbres, double rhythms, double tonalities." The rather complex nature of the instrumental textures thus created result, especially from verse 24 to the end, in his most virtuosic ensemble writing. This schema, familiar from *Castor and Pollux,* can be viewed as a way of building up toward new kinds of large ensemble texture to be explored further in *Delusion of the Fury.* Overall, the music is so obviously designed to make full use of all his instruments that it seems as though Partch were determined that this work should vindicate his continuing activity as an instrument builder. Six new instruments built since 1960 are used in the final version, which uses a total of twenty-two instruments (all of them his own, with no "extras"); the only major omission is the Adapted Viola, which was, however, used in the first version. Fully two-thirds of the instrumental timbres in *Petals,* in its final form, are percussive in nature.

In the decade before the composition of *Petals,* the increasing dominance of percussion in his ensemble had led to fundamental changes in Partch's musical language. The complex timbres of instruments like the Cloud-Chamber Bowls and the Boo (and later the Zymo-Xyl, the Mazda Marimba, and the Gourd Tree), together with their inability to produce sustained tones, obscured the prominence and the relevance of pitch as an organizational factor in the music written for them. His percussive idiom—of which *Petals* and *Delusion of the Fury* are the culmination—thus represents the furthest point on his musical spectrum from the voice and Adapted Viola works of the early 1930s, in which subtlety of intonation was paramount.

Partch's percussion instruments present a wide spectrum of relative difficulty to the ear's powers of pitch analysis, with respect to both assigning a definite pitch to single notes and hearing clearly their function in chords or aggregates. In the case of the Cloud-Chamber Bowls and the Boo, the complexity of timbre results in a relatively low level of pitch definition. Passages in which percussion is dominant are increasingly common in his music from *King Oedipus* onward.

In this music the possibilities of harmonic orientation, which depends on clarity of pitch definition, are greatly reduced; harmonic listening is therefore not always the primary intention. Instead, Partch is free to work with contrasts of timbre—often linked to dramatic characterization—and with rhythm. The resulting change in his musical language, beginning around 1951, was quite conscious and affected not simply the sound-materials of the music but its structure. In 1967 he commented: "In all my later work . . . my music is more bound up in the integrity, the daimon, of each instrument—separately and together, and although analyses can be made in [harmonic] terms, the results are so different, in respect of sound and pattern, in fact so wrong, that the originals become unrecognizable."[48]

Consideration of the character—the "integrity" or the "daimon"—of each of the instruments had become a central concern by the time of *Petals,* and a proper understanding of this music, or any of Partch's later work, is inconceivable without it. The "character" of an instrument depended on more than simply its timbre. The layout of blocks or strings or found objects gave Partch, in each case, a different palette of pitches; the visual pattern of pitches on an instrument influenced the sort of passagework he would write for it. These layouts may be complex, like the hexad tunings on the Kitharas, or simple, like the 43-tone scale sequence on the Chromelodeons, the Boo, and some of the Harmonic Canon settings.[49] The *gestural patterns* characteristic of especially the later, percussion-based works—which most often take the form of short, reiterated figures involving a particular mallet pattern (on the percussion) or arpeggiation pattern (on the strings) that stays constant as it is applied to different blocks or strings (i.e., different pitches)—result in figures that sometimes overlap with other structural configurations, such as Otonalities or Utonalities (as is often the case on the Diamond Marimba or the Kithara), scales (as on the Harmonic Canon or the Boo), tetrachords, harmonic formulae or suchlike, and at other times do not. These gestural patterns are often used together with more abstract musical materials as primary elements in the compositional process.

For all the work's harmonic adventurousness, the rhythmic language of *Petals* is still more exploratory. Verses 1–23 make use of seven metrical patterns. These range from regular ones notated in 3/4, 4/4, or 5/4, through the less common but still regular 20/16 (four quintuplets in the measure) or 18/16 (three sextuplets in the measure), to unusual repeating patterns of lengthening measures. (An earlier example of this latter kind of rhythmic expansion and contraction can be found in *Windsong.*) From verse 24 onward, when these verses are combined, a staggering array of polymetric combinations result (only two of the later verses—25 and 26—are not polymetric, but merely polyrhythmic). Some of these polymetric verses are relatively straightforward—verse 31, for example, has a proportional relationship of 3:5 within the measure—while others are highly complex. Verse 24 (a superimposition of verses 1 and 2) combines a lengthening-measure sequence in Zymo-Xyl and Crychord with a constant 20/16 rhythm in Surrogate Kithara and Bass Marimba, with only the very fast sixteenth-note pulse, constant in both layers, providing a useful common reference. The composer whose work most readily springs to mind in connection with these radical explorations in rhythm is Nancarrow; but as we have no evidence whatsoever that Partch knew any of Nancarrow's *Studies for Player Piano* by this time, the connection may be purely coincidental.[50]

It is striking that, in this first composition following his return to California, Partch should have reanimated the exploratory thrust of his earlier work. The opposite path, a much easier one, would have been to continue to produce ever more approachable, middlebrow theater works such as those of the Champaign years, and finally to enjoy the sedentary comforts of the aging pioneer. The image of the lane strewn with petals, which had stayed in his imagination since the day he had first set foot in Petaluma, is more apt than Partch himself perhaps realized. While on the one hand the array of fallen petals symbolizes the idea of a momentary pattern, and gives a sense of the arbitrariness of the attempt to grasp and fix those petals into an "ideal" configuration, there is also the sense that *Petals* was itself a pathway to something else; that even in the autumn of his compositional life the solitary path still held its old fascination.

On April 17, 1964, Michael Ranta arrived in Petaluma to find Partch's world "caving in."[51] Partch was now living from week to week under threat of eviction, and the two men spent some time driving in the countryside around Petaluma following up on offers of storage space for the instruments. But none proved to be even faintly hopeful; one was a dark, dirty barn with water dripping in from the roof, another a building on pilings over the water with sea salt spraying in. Partch was becoming increasingly depressed as the days went by, and in his drunken moods would threaten to put the instruments up for public auction or throw them on the city dump.

The problem of where he might go next had received what seemed like a promising solution in March, when Danlee Mitchell had written to say that he had been hired at San Diego State College to form a percussion section. Partch reported to Peter Yates that Mitchell would move there in August:

"He says that he will find a studio, rent a van, and move my instruments down there. Well—of course—the problem isn't that simple, but at least I do not feel so alone, now, with the problem."[52] A further complicating factor was that Mitchell was now married and had begun a family. This, as Partch knew only too well, would severely restrict Mitchell's involvement with his work. Nonetheless, he wrote encouragingly that San Diego was "certainly the best climate I've ever known—not as dry as Arizona, not as damp as San Francisco, neither as hot in the summer nor as cold in the winter as Southern Arizona, where I grew up. And it doesn't have the Los Angeles smog." The problem for Partch, however, was studio rent. "The going price would wreck me . . . within six months."[53]

Mitchell arrived in Petaluma toward the end of April, and he, Partch, and Ranta began to rehearse *Petals*. They also worked on instrument repair and "spent something like two weeks making tapes of metronomes in the required tempos" for *Petals*, which was to be recorded using the resulting tapes as click tracks.[54] On their occasional days off Partch took Mitchell and Ranta to some of his old haunts in the San Francisco area; he also introduced the young musicians to his friends, among whom were his dentist, Francis Crawford; Crawford's secretary, Mary Isaacs; and a young carpenter, Bill Symons. Artists, as ever, figured high on the list: in nearby Inverness were his old friends the Onslow Fords, and Jack Wright and his wife, Patty, whom Partch had known in Sausalito; and, in Petaluma itself, Robert and Mary McChesney.[55]

During the rehearsals for *Petals*, Partch would occasionally invite friends

Danlee Mitchell, Partch, and Michael Ranta, Petaluma, California, 1964. Unsigned photograph, Harry Partch Estate Archive.

around to listen to a play-through. He was interested in their opinion of his new music, although he took pains to explain that each individual verse was eventually to be combined with another verse on tape; Michael Ranta admits that he found the intended end product difficult to imagine.[56] The recording sessions began with Partch, Mitchell, and Ranta sealing all the studio windows with masking tape, trying to insulate against buzzes and rattles caused by the louder instruments, particularly the Marimba Eroica. Most of the duets were recorded satisfactorily, with the help of Mike Callahan, a recording engineer from San Francisco, and using a click track, but the cross-rhythms Partch had hoped to achieve in the quartets and sextets "were never fully realised, because of the absence of technical help and/or an adequate number of competent musicians."[57]

By the later stages of the recording sessions, the bulldozers had already arrived to demolish the Pioneer Hatchery. One morning Mitchell even had to ask the driver of one of them to stop for a while so the musicians could complete a take.[58] Partch reported to a correspondent two months later that the sessions were "prematurely ended by battering rams against nearby buildings, and a bulldozer supplied the climax on May 17. I think we actually have a take with the sounds of a collapsing wall. After that, all I could do was pack up and run."[59] Although nine of the twenty-three duets were "not acceptable, for various reasons and in varying degrees—bad performance, or bad recording, or both . . . [two of them] involved bad writing too," further recordings were impractical in the circumstances. Mitchell returned to his family in Washington State, while Ranta remained with Partch in Petaluma.

Early in April, when Partch was immersed in work on *Petals,* a letter had arrived from Martin Kamen, music adviser to the committee set up to establish a humanities division at the new University of California campus in San Diego. Partch had written to Kamen at Peter Yates's suggestion to inquire about the possibility of an affiliation, an attractive idea for a number of reasons, chiefly because it meant being near Mitchell in the new school year and because the climate was ideal both for Partch and for his instruments. Kamen's letter offered mild encouragement, saying that the university hoped to have a creative arts program running "in another year."[60] Kamen was familiar with Partch's work and showed his letter to Helen Raitt, wife of Russell Raitt in the Scripps Institute of Oceanography; she was, Kamen told him, "among the group desirous of seeing you here, and she is casting about now to see if a proper studio can be found for you." Once work on *Petals* had been halted, Ranta urged

Partch to follow up on the correspondence and offered to drive him down to San Diego to meet the people concerned.

Partch took this tentative gesture of encouragement from Kamen and Raitt to imply something much more substantial than either could have intended. By the middle of May he had made the decision to move south and informed them accordingly. Helen Raitt, delighted but somewhat taken aback, offered to let him stay in a small house she owned not far from the campus, on the assumption that he would soon have an appointment as composer-in-residence at the university.[61] On May 27, in the midst of the chaos of packing in Petaluma, Ranta drove Partch through the night to get him down to San Diego for a talk he had been invited to give the following afternoon on his work. The talk, illustrated with film and recordings, was given at the Scripps Institute of Oceanography, one of the most spectacular parts of the campus. Helen Raitt organized a cocktail party in Partch's honor so that he could meet some UCSD people, but Ranta recalls the evening as a harrowing experience: Partch got drunk before the party to try to relax, but went too far and made a bad impression on some of the university people.

Following the party Ranta again drove all night back to Petaluma, with Partch complaining about his never stopping for a rest. Hoping that something would emerge and that the move was the right one, and having in any case no choice, Partch set about closing up the studio and packing his things. Ranta saw how reluctant he was to leave the place, and he was still slowly sorting through his manuscripts when a bulldozer started to tear down the back wall of the hatchery. Partch reported a few weeks later, without any exaggeration: "I left Petaluma on June 4, permanently. The walls were collapsing around me."[62] Ranta rented a truck and drove Partch and the instruments south. Partch was despondent, burdened by uncertainties, with *Petals* still unfinished and his professional future a complete blank.

Del Mar, Van Nuys, Venice, and San Diego

Partch and Michael Ranta arrived in Del Mar, in San Diego's North County, on June 5, 1964, and moved into the house that Helen Raitt was loaning him at 12790 Via Esperia, about a mile from the Pacific Ocean. Almost from the moment of their arrival Partch began to unwind, feeling an overwhelming sense of relief that the move had been the right one. Ranta helped him get established and then, some two weeks later, departed for a summer job playing timpani with the Santa Fe Opera.

The house was much smaller than Partch's studio in Petaluma. The instruments were installed around the place so that they were minimally on display, making it extremely crowded. When a friend came to visit in July Partch "told him . . . that he would find instruments in every room, even the kitchen and bathroom. He thought I was kidding, but later—when he used the bathroom—he came out laughing."[1] In September he reported to Peter Yates: "There are four or five instruments in the living room, seven in a bedroom, one in my little office, several on the side screen porch, and three in the carport. At one time I had an instrument each in the kitchen and the bathroom, but this didn't work out."[2] At night he slept outside in the carport, which was "wonderful, because the climate is so good. No mosquitoes."[3]

The hot, peaceful weeks of summer made the tension and anxieties of the last months in Petaluma seem far away. "I am very grateful for this little place," he told Yates. "It has brought a peace of mind and a general good physical feeling that I haven't had in decades. I am quite happy in it when I am alone."[4] The summer months were quiet, but there was little to do but sit tight and wait for developments with UCSD. The cramped conditions precluded the organization of any serious rehearsals, although musicians frequently visited him— particularly Danlee Mitchell, who arrived in San Diego in August in preparation for his first semester's teaching at San Diego State College. Partch's hope of beginning work with the tape of *Petals,* synchronizing pairs of verses into the polyrhythmic quartets and quintets, was frustrated due to his inability to find a suitable studio in the San Diego area prepared to undertake the job.

Nonetheless, he began revisions to the score of *Petals* and spent much time thinking about the new theater work. On September 14 he wrote to Yates: "In a part of this projected work I want to use a variety of primitive instruments, the kind that it would be logical for people to play while moving about on stage, and which would not require disciplined musicianship, only a rhythmic sense and dramatic timing. I've been working on the idea this summer, acquiring instruments where possible, and making them when I could." By this time his collection included an Ugumbo, his version of a Zulu instrument with one string, "struck with a stick, extending over a curved branch of eucalyptus attached to a gourd resonator";[5] Philippine drone devils (jews' harps); Ceremonial bamboo poles (which he ultimately discarded); two Piris (Korean reed instruments), which had been given to him a few months earlier by Lou Harrison; and a variety of drums, gongs, calabashes, and rattles.

The most substantial instrument built during the summer was the Gourd Tree, a percussion instrument that is a beautiful piece of sculpture quite without regard to its sonic properties. The instrument is a tall eucalyptus bough from which are suspended twelve Chinese temple bells bolted to gourd resonators. The eucalyptus bough, as Partch told an interviewer years later, "I just observed in a trashpile . . . down the road to UCSD from where I lived in Del Mar. And so one day I went back to pick it up."[6] The bough gives the instrument its quasi-organic character, the smallest bells looking like "the smallest fruit" at the top of a papaya tree. He also began working "very tentatively" at the Eucal Blossom,[7] a new marimba consisting of thirty-three short sections of San Diego bamboo which, with its very thick walls, produced sounds even shorter than those of the Boo.

The prospect of establishing a new studio for his instruments remained, for the time being, an unlikely one. Although they had not quite ground to a halt, his discussions with UCSD were frustratingly inconclusive. He had occasional meetings with John Stewart, the new director of fine arts, and asked about the possibility of studio space, even though he had no appointment, but no definite answer was forthcoming. He even discussed with Helen Raitt, who was beginning to worry about the lack of progress, the possibility of forming a tax-exempt corporation to provide money for studio rental. He quipped to a friend that the university's "right hand has no idea what its left hand is doing," adding that "my life is half incertitude and half turmoil."[8] A letter dated October 5 arrived from John Stewart, explaining that UCSD was still trying to organize itself and was in the middle of the complex process of allocating space, assuring him: "This is not so discouraging as frustrating."

Yet discouragement was exactly Partch's response to the letter. By the middle of October, running out of patience, he had decided that San Diego was not a very promising milieu for his work and had resolved to move up to the Los Angeles area. Michael Ranta, who had returned in time to enroll for the beginning of the academic year at San Diego State in order to be close to Partch, had decided to leave the unexciting musical world of San Diego and to return to the University of Illinois to complete his B.A. and take part in the 1965 Festival of Contemporary Arts. Although aware that he was leaving Partch in a difficult situation, Ranta felt upstaged by a powerful new presence in Partch's life, one whose network of contacts in the Los Angeles musical world seemed to promise much: Emil Richards.

Richards had begun to deluge Partch with letters in Petaluma the previous summer, all of them, in Partch's words, "very wonderful and complimentary."[9] He was one of the most sought-after session players in southern California. Although essentially a jazz percussionist, Richards had a consuming interest in non-Western instruments, primarily percussion. Partch liked his warmth of character and was heartened by the evident belief he showed in his work, but he was slightly worried by the unrealistic suggestions Richards would occasionally put to him ("Are any of your instruments for sale or rent?" Richards had written in one letter). Partch entertained doubts about how well Richards understood his work, and felt vexed at how long it had taken to get across to Richards the fact that he had "abandoned 12-tone equal temperament more than 40 years ago," and thus could not "manufacture percussion or any other instruments in it."[10] Partch was also only moderately enthusiastic about Richards's involvement with non-Western instruments and about his plans for a percussion institute. But as he got to know Richards better, Partch grew to accept, even to like, his naive side, and Richards came to regard Partch quite unashamedly as his "musical guru," endeavoring to learn all he could from him.[11]

Partch had planned his move to the Los Angeles area to coincide with a lecture-demonstration he had been asked to give at the Pasadena Art Museum in late November. On October 12 he drove up to Pasadena to meet with those responsible for the museum's contemporary music activities, among them an influential patron of the arts, Betty Freeman. Partch's meeting with Freeman that October afternoon marked the beginning of a close ten-year relationship, during which time she would become not only an important promoter of his work but his chief patron and primary source of financial support. Thus he now had not one but two powerful new allies in the Los Angeles area.

In her early forties, married with four children, Betty Freeman had grown up in Brooklyn and New Rochelle, New York, and had moved to Los Angeles in 1950. There she began collecting art, notably works by American Abstract Expressionist painters. In 1964 she was just beginning active participation in the Encounters series of contemporary music concerts at the Pasadena Art Museum. She had graduated from Wellesley College with a minor in music and was a keen amateur pianist; like her tastes in the visual arts, her interest in music centered around the work of living composers. At their first meeting Partch and Freeman adjourned for lunch to the corner coffee shop. She found him "utterly charming"[12] and was captivated by his eccentricities—he was experimenting with smoking his pipe through a piece of gauze, which he had heard helped reduce the risk of cancer—and by his conversation about the arts and about his own extraordinary life.

Partch's charm was wholly without devious intent. Although Freeman was by then already known in southern California as a patron and promoter of the arts, he was largely unaware of this. When she and her husband invited him to stay with them that night in Beverly Hills so they could all attend a Schoenberg concert, he politely refused and set off back to Del Mar. However, it is clear that very soon Partch began to see in Betty Freeman someone who could take over the role in his life played until recently by Madeline Tourtelot. Freeman had an even more extensive and colorful circle of artist friends and acquaintances, and her generosity toward him and his work was already becoming apparent.

Partch came down with the flu a few days later, which brought rheumatic trouble in its wake, and he was obliged to rest—"I am resting my damnedest," he told Emil Richards on October 19. When he began feeling better he started dismantling the huge instruments crowded into the Del Mar house, which gave him an odd sense of relief—"I hadn't realized before that the towering shapes, in that small room, were psychologically crushing me"[13]—and began preparing to move.

In November he moved into a rented house in Van Nuys, in the San Fernando Valley. Partch subsequently calculated that this had been his fifteenth complete move in sixteen years, an astonishing record that led his friends to joke, with some reason, that the hobo in him was refusing to die. The house was found with help, both financial and practical, from Emil Richards, and, although pleasant, it was nearly as crowded as Helen Raitt's house in Del Mar had been. Danlee Mitchell recalls that "it had a beautiful backyard, and a big tree, and he used to sit under that tree in an overstuffed chair drinking mint juleps."[14] Soon after he had settled in, Betty Freeman visited and, seeing the cramped conditions, began talking immediately about trying to find him a proper studio.

A considerable boost to what Partch felt was a sagging public profile came in December, when Composers Recordings Incorporated in New York released *From the Music of Harry Partch*, the first commercially available recording of his work, which the company had compiled, with Partch's advice, from various of the Gate 5 releases. It contained *Castor and Pollux*, the Gualala recording of *The Letter*, *Windsong*, "Cloud-Chamber Music," and Scene 10 and the Epilogue from *The Bewitched*. The record was financed in part by the Alice M. Ditson Fund of Columbia University, which had so generously contributed money to the 1959 production of *The Bewitched*, and a photograph from the lecture-demonstration preceding the Columbia performance was used on the record jacket. Partch regarded the disc as marking a turnaround in the dissemination of his recordings. Even though he had originally planned to make *Petals* the next Gate 5 release, the CRI disc, with its generously designed insert of photos and descriptions of his instruments, seemed to signal the end of the need for private releases.

In every other sense, his professional stock had risen hardly at all in the more than two years since his return to California. His hopes for a senior appointment at the University of California, San Diego, had come to nothing. In a letter to Lauriston Marshall on January 12, 1965, he wrote: "I got so disgusted with the timidity of UCSD—this at the end of many months of silly lip service to the 'creative arts'—that I began to express myself, rather freely. If I am now persona non grata down there I really couldn't care less." Although his friend-ship with Betty Freeman helped him on occasion to brave the waters of contem-porary music concerts, he felt out of sympathy with most of the work of established composer colleagues, both those with and those without academic appointments. In January 1965 he asked Freeman to accompany him to a concert by John Cage at the Pasadena Art Museum.[15] He described the event to Lauriston Marshall: "[Cage] cut carrots with an amplified knife for ten min-utes, put them through an amplified juicer for another ten, then drank the juice through an amplified gullet for another ten (while smoking an unamplified cigaret). Knife, juicer, and gullet all came out the same—static. When he began to cut carrots again I left."[16] Partch's antipathy toward the experimentalism of the avant-garde, and in particular toward Cage's use of chance techniques to make music, only increased as the 1960s wore on. He felt betrayed by sup-porters like Peter Yates, who was becoming ever more enthusiastic about Cage and who was beginning to expend the same degree of proselytizing eloquence in writing about Cage's work as he had once done for Partch. In 1967 Cage asked Partch for a contribution to his book *Notations,* a volume of statements and manuscript extracts from a number of contemporary artists which Cage was editing, sometimes by subjecting the various texts to chance operations and presenting them in "composed" typesetting of the kind he was using for his own writings. Partch submitted a short statement taken from the liner notes he had offered CRI for *Petals,* which Cage edited to exactly forty-three words, corresponding to the number of tones in Partch's scale. Partch replied furiously: "I sent you a scrap of manuscript because I did not want to seem difficult. . . . But when you insist on a statement from me that is exactly 43 words you are being difficult. . . . You have done an unbelievably fine job of excerpting and editing. It is probably better than my original statement. However, if you dare to mention that number 43 you are deliberately misrepresenting me. It is the one-half truth of the one-fourth factor. And I shall *curse* you. You have been cursed before, but never by me, and if you are cursed by me there will be a difference."[17]

Once he had installed himself in Van Nuys Partch plunged into weeks of intense creative work. On December 30, 1964, he completed the first draft of the scenario for the new theater work, provisionally entitled *Cry from Another Darkness.* A host of afterthoughts and further details filled his mind in the following days, and he typed a second draft, twice the size of the first, dated January 17, with the new title *Delusion of the Fury.*[18]

Delusion of the Fury was conceived in two acts that would play without a break. They were to be mutually complementary, the first "intensely serious" and the second "highly farcical."[19] Act I is based on the Arthur Waley translation of the Japanese Noh drama *Atsumori*, the story line of which is retained and presented as a dance-drama. *Atsumori* tells the story of a princely warrior who has fallen in battle at the hands of a young rival. It begins with the slayer's remorseful pilgrimage to the scene of the murder, so he may repent at the shrine. The murdered warrior appears as a ghost. Then his son, born after his death, enters; he too is seeking the shrine in the belief that he may see a vision of his father's face. "Spurred to resentment by the presence of his son," Partch writes, "the ghost-father lives again through the ordeal of battle." Finally, realizing the error of his ways and the futility of his anger, he seeks "total reconciliation" with both his son and the slayer.

If act I is a "portrayal of release from the wheel of life and death," act II, in contrast, was to be "a reconciliation with life." It is based on an Ethiopian folk tale, "Justice," which Partch had come across in a book called *African Voices*. In it, a young vagabond is preparing to cook a meal over a fire of twigs when an old woman who tends a goat herd approaches, searching for a lost kid. She asks the vagabond if he has seen the kid. He, being deaf, does not understand what she is asking, and gestures impatiently for her to go away and leave him to enjoy his meal in peace. She misinterprets his gesture as an indication of where she might find her lost kid. She wanders off, finds it, and comes back to thank the vagabond for his help. Not understanding why he is being disturbed a second time, he becomes quarrelsome, and a dispute ensues. Villagers gather, and force the quarreling pair to appear before the Justice of the Peace, who is both deaf and myopic. He, in his turn, misunderstands the nature of the quarrel, thinking it is a marital dispute, and tells the vagabond to take his "beautiful young wife" and his "charming child" and "go home." Following the judge's pronouncement, the villagers exclaim in mock despair, "O how did we ever get by without justice?"

The two stories, for all their cultural diversity and differences of mood and characterization, are linked by their treatment of a common theme: the futility of human anger. In act I the dead warrior, in the presence of his son, reacts with fury at the sight of the slayer who took away his life. His anger is depicted as a loss of self-control, an emotion not worthy of the princely class to which he belongs; in the final scene his anger is sublimated in the act of seeking reconciliation with his murderer. In act II, the angry dispute between the vagabond and the old woman is the result of a farcical misunderstanding; the idea of communal justice is also parodied, the Judge's stern proclamation ridiculed as the nonsense it really is. *Delusion of the Fury* thus brings together in one work a tragedy and a farce, reminiscent of the ancient Greek custom of following a tragedy with a satyr play, rather as Partch himself had done by following the composition of *King Oedipus* with the *Plectra and Percussion Dances.*

As had been the case in *Revelation in the Courthouse Park,* the three principals in *Delusion* all play dual roles. The Slayer, the Son, and the Slain as a Ghost of act I become, respectively, the Young Vagabond, the Old Goat Woman, and the Justice of the Peace in act II. With this as a basis, some commentators have tried to find structural parallels between the two stories. Will Salmon, in an article on the work, points out that the tradition of dual roles is not uncommon in Noh itself; and, although acknowledging that the "guise changes in *Delusion* are more marked than is usual in Noh," he goes on to outline a set of correspondences: "The ghost is young and vigorous; the justice of the peace is myopic and deaf. The slayer is a noble and a priest; the hobo, an outcast. The son is in search of his father; the goat woman is in search of her goat. But each of these characters is similar to his counterpart in dramatic function."[20]

These parallels, however, do not stand up to close scrutiny. The Slayer in act I and the Vagabond in act II, Salmon suggests, have in common that they are both "wanderers who deny materialism"; but the pilgrim Slayer is motivated by remorse for past wrongs, the Vagabond only by an apparently carefree defiance of material values. The Vagabond inadvertently helps the Old Woman to find her lost kid, whereas the Slayer does nothing to affect a reconciliation between the Son and his father—rather it is the Son, whose very presence, provoking the father to unworthy anger, enables him to find reconciliation with his Slayer. The Son in act I and the Old Goat Woman in act II are both searching for a loved one; but there is no functional parallel between the dead warrior of act I and the Justice of the Peace of act II, the former being provoked to anger and then transcending his anger in a gesture of reconciliation, the latter passing a ludicrous judgment on the anger of others. *Delusion of the Fury* does not offer us two morphologically similar stories (as was true of *Revelation*); rather, the dual roles played by the three principals provides a more superficial sense of symmetry and aesthetic balance.

The theme that links the two acts is the delusory nature of human anger— justifiable anger, as in act I, or anger with no real justification, as in act II; anger sublimated by effort of will or anger simply forgotten about in the ongoing passage of time. We may well wonder about the personal significance of this theme for the composer. *Delusion* suggests the relativity of human ideas of right and wrong, and it both questions and mocks our recourse to anger as a response to perceived injustice. Can we view this as a gesture of self-admonishment, a way of confronting and transcending the recurrent bitterness and hostility that Partch himself felt at the multiple injustices dealt to him by the society in which he lived? An undated memo from these years, which he retained among his papers, seems to record his feelings of injustice at his mistreatment at the hands of uncaring fortune: "The evil things that I have done in my life may cause me to scream in my sleep, but it is the good and constructive things which have caused all my personal problems in my relationship to this society." In devoting his largest theater work to exposing the delusion that anger can heal the injustices of life, Partch, like the Ghost in act I, is making a gesture of acceptance. In this sense we may perhaps accept Danlee Mitchell's claim that *Delusion of the Fury* was "Harry's reconciliation with the world."[21]

Although the scenario for *Delusion* was complete by January 1965, it was almost a year before he began to compose the music. This was partly because at the beginning of 1965 he was not feeling well enough physically to undertake a lengthy spell of composition. His rheumatic pains in the autumn had passed, but he was now having problems with a swollen foot. On the recommendation of Anaïs Nin he began seeing a new doctor, Raymond Weston, in Beverly Hills.

Many years later Weston recalled his impressions of his new patient.[22] After examining him and listening to Partch recount his history of high blood pressure and hypertension, Weston quizzed him about his drinking. Partch remarked that a couple of drinks would be all he'd need to get drunk, a possible sign of alcoholic dependency, though after investigating further Weston came up with nothing substantial that led him to consider Partch's alcohol consumption to be seriously detrimental to his health. He was, however, concerned at the demands made by Partch's prolonged spells of intense creative work, especially as he would often work in states of considerable nervous excitement. (Weston's seriousness about this aspect of his "artistic" clients, who at various times included Anaïs Nin and Martha Graham, made him a valuable confidant, and Partch enjoyed talking to him.) Most important, Weston was worried about Partch's heart, warning him that he could be headed for a coronary thrombosis and recommending a change of diet. Partch dutifully obeyed, and he described the diet in a letter to Barnard Hewitt a few months later: "I can give lessons on how to make food palatable without one grain of salt or one drop of animal fat (yolks, cheese, cream, butter, all pork products). At first I didn't see how I could eat the white of an egg, but now I even like it. I simmer a few drops of olive oil with toasted garlic chips, lemon juice, curry [powder], and then beat up the white in this. I also make saltless bread from egg whites, dry skim milk, walnuts, raisins, coriander seed, soybean flour. It is by far the best thing on my menu."[23]

Part of the purpose of living in the Los Angeles area was to have access to good musicians willing to play in an ensemble, but his high hopes in this regard were dashed mostly on account of his generally poor health. The Encounters program at the Pasadena Art Museum had taken place on February 8; Partch showed some beautiful color slides that Danlee Mitchell had taken of his instruments, showed the films *Music Studio* and *Rotate the Body*, and, with the help of Emil Richards and Curry Tjader, played fragments from several works.[24] On March 20 a similar lecture-demonstration program followed at California State University, Northridge: this time the three musicians were joined by Danlee Mitchell and John McAllister. Partch could not, however, consider more ambitious undertakings. The musicians themselves were keen to do more, but Partch had very little energy and felt that the extensive cooperation he needed from his musicians was not forthcoming. At the end of March he wrote to Mitchell: "I am constantly weak, and much of the time I feel actually sick. I don't want to be so alone. Emil . . . is ruthlessly intolerant of illness. It is so strange I can't believe it, but he can't see why I don't build a new instrument at least once a month, write new music, and keep everything in beautiful tune and repair for him to play. I need peace, and rest."[25]

One day in the middle of March Partch had a minor accident backing his car out of his driveway. He had been feeling "increasingly nervous in traffic" for the past few years due to weakening eyesight, and the accident destroyed "what small self-confidence" he still possessed for driving.[26] Rather impulsively he gave the car to a friend. This contributed to his growing feeling that "this Los Angeles venture is a total failure," and he began once again to think about moving.

On April 20 he received news from Betty Freeman that was to shape the course of his life in the years ahead: the offer of permanent financial support in establishing and maintaining a new studio. Since their meeting in October she had occasionally been giving him presents, some of them merely thoughtful— a basket of pears at Christmas—others of more long-term use, such as sending an unsolicited check, or subsidizing anonymously a small grant from the Pasadena Art Museum. Now she was offering what amounted to a modest annual income, which—because he was used to living on very little and still

Partch with the Boo, 1966. Photo by Gil Cooper, *Los Angeles Times*.

had a small amount of money coming in from record sales, his annual check from BMI, and fees for occasional appearances—meant that he could afford to rent a studio and concentrate on creative work. He wrote to thank her, saying that the gesture "is momentous to me in a way that you probably cannot realize. It has been of tremendous moment to me that I find, somehow, a sense of continuity and permanence, and up to now this sense has eluded me. (I slept well Tuesday night for the first time in months!)" He explained that the

majority of the support he had received had been for "one-shot ideas, leading—
as far as I and my work were concerned—nowhere. For over twenty years I have
been the strangest kind of hobo—a hobo with over two tons of 'weird' instruments to take, wherever." The news gave him a "fantastic feeling of relief" in the
face of the continuing uncertainties of his professional life.[27]

During the spring and early summer of 1965 his energies received a perceptible boost thanks in no small part to Freeman's support. He concentrated on
instrument building, with the intention of completing the new instrumental
resources needed for *Delusion of the Fury.* He experimented with new blocks for
the Diamond Marimba using Osage orange, a highly resilient American wood,
large supplies of which he had been given by his friend Loran (Cloudy) French,
but without much success. This work on the Diamond Marimba, however,
may have prompted the building of a new marimba, the Quadrangularis
Reversum, conceived as a twin to the earlier instrument. Partch began work
early in April and continued "every day for over two months."[28] As with the
Gourd Tree, the structure of the instrument was based on eucalyptus boughs—
two of them, supporting a horizontal tori bar over eight feet long, "from which
the blocks—the instrument—seem to suspend."[29] At the sides are two alto
register flanks with ten blocks each, which were originally intended to have
resonators of square Japanese quadrangularis bamboo ("hence the name").
This proved much too expensive, so he decided "to retain the name while
staying with materials that I could afford."[30] The center section has thirty-six
blocks, originally of Guatemalan hormigo wood (which he replaced in 1971
with African padouk), with pitches arranged in a layout that is the exact mirror
reverse of the Diamond Marimba pattern. Partch arrived at the pattern of
pitches on the Quadrangularis Reversum intuitively, and the precise nature of
its relationship to the Diamond Marimba layout was only later pointed out to
him by his new friend Erv Wilson, himself a considerable authority on tuning,
who was beginning to design new marimba and keyboard layouts to accommodate microtonal scales.[31] Wilson also offered valuable practical help in building the instrument. The downward arpeggio patterns made possible by the
tiered rows of blocks on the Diamond Marimba were now complemented by
the upward arpeggios characteristic of the Quadrangularis Reversum. By the
beginning of July Partch had also made a number of small hand-held instruments, intended for those scenes in *Delusion* when the players of the large
instruments would move down to center stage and become a "moving, playing
chorus."[32] These included a gourd drum, a bamboo belly drum, a bamboo
hand drum, and several pairs of eucalyptus claves.

He had been invited to give a concert at the Deepest Valley Theater in the Alabama Hills near Lone Pine, California, at the end of August, with the possibility of repeat performances in San Diego and Los Angeles. Even though this would again be "a fragmented performance, fragments of instruments, fragments of compositions . . . nothing complete," he decided to take up the offer and to try to tie it to another move.[33] The Van Nuys house was too cramped for serious rehearsals, and he wanted to have all the instruments set up and accessible before plunging into the composition of *Delusion*. With no car he was now dependent on the good will of friends to drive him around to look at places, and with help from Emil Richards, Erv Wilson, and Betty Freeman, and after a good deal of fruitless freeway cruising, he had made a decision by the middle of August.

On August 15, 1965, Partch signed a lease on an abandoned laundromat at 1110 West Washington Boulevard, a noisy street in Venice, the bohemian coastal town on Santa Monica Bay. The place had been suggested by his sculptor friend Charles Mattox, who had a studio nearby. Partch then began what he later called "three months of turmoil" getting the place organized.[34] It was his "largest studio ever," with enough space to house all his instruments comfortably.[35] The rest of the furnishings were characteristically sparse; the living area had a bed, a low table, and a couch, with three Japanese parasols hanging upside-down from the ceiling above it.

Amid the turmoil, rehearsals began for the Lone Pine concert. Emil Richards recruited several new players, including Michael Craden, and Michael Ranta came back to California after another summer with the Santa Fe Opera for the performance. The concert took place on August 29, starting at twilight, in a spectacular setting—an open-air stage in the hills, lit by kerosene lanterns hoisted high on poles on all sides. It contained some of Partch's by now customary set pieces, such as excerpts from *U.S. Highball,* and a complete performance of *Castor and Pollux.* Two days later, the opening of his Venice studio was heralded by repeat performances there of some of the items from the Lone Pine concert.

Mounting these one-off concerts proved very exhausting, and only occasionally rewarding. The organizers of the Lone Pine concert had sent down an open flatbed truck for the instruments, which was hopelessly unsuitable, and Partch, in exasperation, decided on the spot to rent a closed van at his own expense. When he and the musicians arrived they found that the amplification system was poor. The players consequently could not hear each other clearly on stage;

Partch in his studio in Venice, California, 1966. Photo by
David Freund.

partly as a result of this, and partly because the musicians were in any case
largely new to one another, the performances were no better than adequate.
With the added complication of a scare with "chest pains, rapid pulse, and
tremors" in July, Partch began to be hesitant about accepting invitations.[36] He
began to turn down almost as many as he accepted, concentrating almost
exclusively on engagements in California. He told Peter Yates in connection
with one such unworkable offer, for a lecture on the East Coast: "If a proposal
were made involving a two to five-year project I would consider it very seriously,
because I need the facilities and the personnel of an institution, but one-shot
lectures and one-shot performances 3000 miles away are out of the question.
My decades of wandering about the country with five thousand pounds of
instruments have finally ended. . . . My first obligation is to my creative work,
and next to the people who made this [Venice] studio possible. It was their
understanding that I wanted to write music and build instruments, and money

was put up for that purpose. This, living quietly, I can do, and I can even put on performances when there is sufficient cooperation. In any other sense I have retired."[37]

During the autumn in Venice he fashioned two aluminum Cone Gongs, made from the nose cones of airplane gas tanks obtained from the salvage department of the Douglas Aircraft Company. "They are painted a greenish yellow," he wrote, "and the 'stems' that support them are green—a mounting that suggests a strange variety of giant mushroom."[38] They were intended, in an appropriately botanical coupling, to form one instrument with the Gourd Tree. He also built Harmonic Canon III, a new instrument, with two redwood canons along the same lines as Harmonic Canon II, necessitated by the new bridge settings and tunings for *Petals* and *Delusion*. He called it the Blue Rainbow because of the instrument's most beautiful new feature, the blue-painted plywood arch that supports the tray for the two canons. The top of the arch acts as a fulcrum and in vigorous playing the two canons "sway lightly up and down in rhythm with the action of the sticks, thus adding a visually dynamic element to the music."[39]

By the end of October Partch had received confirmation of an offer to mount a concert the following spring at UCLA. Partly in exasperation at the inconsequential nature of his recent performances, he determined to make this an important platform for his work, and in particular to feature the première of *Petals*. Several people at UCLA were also "taking a good look" at his scenario for *Delusion of the Fury*. Partch was determined to use the concert to demonstrate his powers, as a possible way in to a more extended affiliation with the university and, ideally, as a way of enticing them to undertake a production of *Delusion* (for which the music was still unwritten).

With this in mind he set about, for the first time since his last year at the University of Illinois, to form a full-fledged ensemble that would meet to rehearse on a regular basis, for a long-term period of rehearsals would be necessary if the players were to achieve the ensemble skills needed for the later verses of *Petals*. From the beginning, however, the sessions were beset by problems. First was Partch's own limited energy, and the tension caused in him by the weekly arrival of a group of musicians expecting to find the studio in readiness and all the instruments in good repair and in tune. There was also his unsuccessful attempt to delegate the direction of rehearsals to John Grayson, a young musician friend. By the middle of November he was writing to Danlee Mitchell—who, living two hours' drive away in San Diego, was not expected to attend weekly rehearsals at this stage—in some despair. "The Tuesday night 'rehearsals' have degenerated into a social evening where six or seven people come in to tell jokes and diddle on weird instruments for four hours. . . . [At the last rehearsal I] wore ear plugs, and read a book. Or tried to. John [Grayson] controlled nothing, taught no one anything. I guess he tried, but he has no experience with either the music or instruments."[40]

Even more pervasive problems were caused by the noisy and sometimes violent neighborhood he was now living in. The same letter to Mitchell continues:

> Life at 1110 is nothing but turmoil. Even when nothing happens in the small hours of the morning, I fully expect it to, and my sleep is far from satisfying. One night I was awakened by loud screaming and curses at my front door—a man and a woman (not Negroes). It went on for 20 minutes. This was 2:20. Later, someone banged furiously at the front door. This was 2:30. I put on a robe, turned up the lights. No one was to be seen, even on the street. Last night—this was 1:20, a car blocked my back door and a drunk fell over his car horn. It was deafening. I opened the door and screamed at him, and he fell off the horn, but I had little sleep last night. My ulcer is of course returning. (I wonder what kind of a frightening mistake I've made this time.)

His anxieties were such that he even returned the gift of an eye-catching purple shirt, from Emil Richards's wife, Betty, lest it make him too conspicuous on the street. As a consequence of the constant tensions of his daily existence he was drinking ever more heavily, ostensibly to help him unwind in the evenings, but perhaps also to help him vent some of the bitterness that was just below the surface. His Petaluma friends felt a change in him when he paid a brief visit in the autumn for free dental treatment from Francis Crawford. Robert and Mary McChesney threw a dinner party in his honor, inviting several friends, including the Onslow Fords. During the course of the evening, Partch—drunk and belligerent—latched onto a passing remark in the general conversation and loudly harangued all of the assembled guests, saying that they knew nothing about what it felt like to be a "starving artist," and that they shouldn't pretend to know. His vehemence shocked them, as did the extent of the character transformation his excessive alcohol consumption brought about.

It was in these frustrating conditions in Venice that, on November 1, 1965, he began the sketch score of *Delusion of the Fury*. The music called for all of his instruments with the single exception of the Adapted Viola, and is perhaps the most richly detailed and complex of all his scores. "As the composition of *Delusion of the Fury* progressed," he later wrote, "I found that I had used all but one of the duets and trios [of *Petals*], with elaboration and added instrumentation, and—in addition—two or three of the polyrhythmic ideas. . . . They became the structural sinews of the new work."[41] His use of the later, poly-rhythmic verses of *Petals* in the new score was more cautious than he had originally intended, possibly because, with rehearsals for the première of *Petals* proceeding around him during the period of composition of *Delusion,* he was realizing just how difficult some of the verses were. The process of fleshing out the duets into the larger ensemble of *Delusion* was sometimes one of developing further "multiple exposures," as he called them, sometimes one of superimposing similar types of material on instruments of the same family, and sometimes one of adding freely contrapuntal or accompanimental parts.

The score contained large stretches of new music as well, notably in the instrumental "Exordium" ("The Beginning of a Web") prefacing act I, and the "Sanctus" (its name suggested by the "Pray for me" sequence at the end of act I) that forms the entr'acte. There is considerable musical contrast between the two acts, the first dark and the second bright, but they form a coherent whole. A musical symbol of this fusion of apparent opposites—a characteristic theme of Partch's work as a whole—is the use of the Bolivian Double Flute, given to him in Venice by Erv Wilson. The instrument features prominently in the opening scenes of both acts, with not dissimilar material; given the dark and light contrasts of act I and act II, the flute aptly symbolizes the "complementary character and the strange affinity" of the tragic and comic modes.[42]

Partch liked to insist that, despite the Japanese and African starting points, the music of *Delusion* was "a development of my own style in dramatic music," a logical outgrowth of the language of *Oedipus* and *Revelation*.[43] Although a great many of its rhythmic techniques are foreshadowed by *The Bewitched* and *Windsong,* the work introduces a new—and indeed unique—ensemble sound, cleaner and clearer than the "mass of instrumentation" of parts of *Revelation* and *Water! Water!* It is a luminous and colorful score, "an adventurous work, but I cannot call it experimental. . . . I am sure—in this unreal world—that I knew what I was doing."[44]

The score of *Delusion of the Fury* was completed on March 17, 1966. The colophon on his pencil score adds: "After 3 years—Petaluma, Del Mar, Van Nuys, and now Venice, building the instruments and writing the music." His outward existence during the four and a half months of composition was as quiet as he could make it, his only distraction some instrument building. *Delusion* called for new tunings on many of his string instruments, and in the early months of 1966 he built two new canons for the Surrogate Kithara with this in mind.[45]

Fortunately, his hard work on the score was having no detrimental effect on his health. Shortly before Christmas 1965, with the Sanctus finished, he had seen Dr. Raymond Weston, who told him that his blood pressure was normal "for the first time since my once-a-month visits started. So maybe this pattern of ten hours work a day is exactly what I needed." He told Betty Freeman that "I simply could not have pursued [this pace of work] in the frustrations of the house in Van Nuys, and I am fantastically grateful for this opportunity."[46]

With *Delusion* now finished, Partch came increasingly to regard the concert at UCLA, set for May 8, 1966, as the most likely avenue of escape from the "terrible aloneness" he was feeling in Venice.[47] He was already thinking past the concert itself to the prospect of a performance of *Delusion* and even beyond, rather rhetorically, to the question of what would become of his instruments if and when this largest undertaking was brought to fruition. Especially in his periods of poor health—although most of this spring he had been feeling "pretty good"—he became "frightened" by the whole question of the future of his work. He told Betty Freeman on one occasion that he would "turn all the instruments over to the Pasadena Museum, sign them over, almost any time. They could at least put them in storage."

The UCLA concert itself was preceded by a good deal of modish publicity around the campus, of the kind that often prefigured appearances by intellectual gurus of the sixties like Marshall McLuhan. The campus newspaper *The Daily Bruin* printed a series of tiny ads for weeks before the performance, announcing "Partch is coming," and elaborating: "Partch is part of the dream"; "The inspiration is Partch"; "The others in captivity are not Partch." The concert, in Royce Hall, was rapturously received by the largely student audience. It opened with an extended lecture-demonstration, focusing on "the problem of finding a musically creative reason for being, in a promising and destructive, ordered and disordered, moral and anarchistic world."[48] The concert itself consisted of the *Two Studies on Ancient Greek Scales,* the première of *Petals* (with metronomic lights operated by John Grayson), and *Castor and Pollux,* choreographed by Virginia Storie. Peter Yates, who was present, wrote Partch an effusively enthusiastic letter the following day, praising *Petals* as an "exciting, challenging, and dizzying" breakthrough, and suggesting, to Partch's mystification, that its language was more demanding and ultimately more rewarding than that of European total serial works such as Pierre Boulez's *Structures.*[49]

However, the strain of mounting the concert had finally pushed Partch beyond his endurance, and a few days later he sent a depressing letter to all thirteen ensemble members. In it he complained about the shoddiness of some points in the performance ("There are moments that are great, and moments when things fall apart. At times, the notes are massacred with feeling. The massacres are executed with tremendous spirit") and about the lack of adequate tuning before the performance started: "Neither Harmonic Canon II (for *Castor and Pollux*) nor the Crychord was tuned. Both [were] badly off." He also noted their lack of cooperation in rehearsals: "Further rehearsals, unless I have conscientious and continued help in maintaining 25 instruments in playable condition and in tune, and help in cleaning up the hurricane of beer cans, pop bottles, coffee cups, half-eaten sandwichs, napkins, and overflowing ashtrays, after each rehearsal, are totally out of the question." The letter ends with the threat never to mount a concert again: "I've had it—permanently."[50]

Two gratifying developments followed from the UCLA concert. First, at the end of May he was awarded the Marjorie Peabody Waite Award of $1,500 from the National Institute of Arts and Letters, given every third year "to an established composer of distinction." Second, CRI in New York expressed willingness to release *Petals* on record. Emil Richards stepped in to finalize the business arrangements, and a further recording session was planned for the end of July to fill in those parts of the work not recorded, or not satisfactorily, on the Petaluma tape.

However, on the more important matter of UCLA's possible commitment to a long-term home for Partch's instruments and to a performance of *Delusion* there was little progress. Partch had discussions with Mantle Hood in the music department about a studio on the campus, but the exchange was shadowed by the suspiciousness that was a continuing impediment to his dealings with institutions. He reported to Betty Freeman that Hood seemed "very guarded. He seemed doubtful that he could find me studio space on the campus, and when I mentioned *storage*—the size of a two-car garage—he thought this might be possible. Regarding the gift of instruments, I'm afraid it is the old story. I can't quote him precisely, but he inferred that there was the very serious hazard that acceptance would mean UCLA was committed to my direction in the creative arts. . . . I do not see why acceptance of my instruments would imply anything except the accessibility of a philosophy which students may take, or reject, as they choose."[51] He left a copy of the score of *Delusion* with Hood, the question of both it and the instruments remaining open for further discussion.

In the middle of May, Partch fled temporarily to San Diego to avoid "the constant noise, the constant indecencies, and the abrasive hostility" of Venice.[52] He rented a small house at 4523 Kensington Drive which, he told Betty

Freeman, was "very cheap, very quiet—there are no traffic noises, all I hear are birds in the trees."[53] He began work copying the full score of *Delusion*. He needed tranquillity to produce the 250-page score more than he needed access to his instruments, and the little house proved to be "a wonderful place to copy music. Danlee isn't too far away." He was making the master copy largely "for UCLA's consideration."[54]

He finished the task on June 12 and made plans to go back to Venice. He was determined simply to close up the studio once the final recordings for *Petals* were finished, but even so he dreaded going back. John Grayson, who was staying in the house to guard the instruments while Partch was away, tried not to worry him with some of the incidents that were taking place in his absence, but news filtered through. On one particularly wild Saturday night, Partch later reported, a group of teenagers "began throwing rocks at my plate glass windows. I have a circle of shattered glass 14 inches in diameter as a result—no hole, but it could be pushed in very easily. They also shoved lighted firecrackers through my mail chute." In July, after he returned, "there was a two-car crash right in my parking lot. . . . I feel terrible that so much money was spent on this place, to make it pleasant and livable. The bad things happen only at night, when I am, or would be, quite alone. I can't seem to decide when to give notice. My dread of another move is at least equal to my fear of Venice, and I am consumed with a great weariness."[55]

In Venice on the weekend of July 30–31 two recording sessions were held to complete the work on *Petals*. Some of the verses recorded by Danlee Mitchell, Michael Ranta, and Partch himself in Petaluma two years earlier could be used, but the work had undergone several changes since the spring of 1964, partly as a result of Partch's decision to eliminate the Adapted Viola from the scoring. Partch, Mitchell, Emil Richards, Wallace Snow, and Stephen Tosh played in the newly recorded verses.[56] Cecil Charles Spiller, the recording engineer who had taken charge of the amplification for the UCLA concert, recorded the new verses and later, working with Partch's assistance mostly in his garage studio at home in Santa Monica, he tried with considerable difficulty to synchronize the duets and trios into quartets, quintets, and a concluding septet. The resulting recording was still problematic, though Partch decided it was adequate within the limits of the technical sophistication of the time, and the tape was dispatched to CRI at the end of August. At the same time *Source,* a new magazine devoted to contemporary music and edited by the young composer Larry Austin, had agreed to publish the score, making it the first of Partch's pieces to appear in print.

Two pages from the score of *And on the Seventh Day Petals Fell in Petaluma*. Harry Partch Estate Archive.

The level of street violence in Venice, particularly at night, was increasing all the time, so out of fear for his own safety Partch gave notice and started getting the instruments ready for storage. He was concerned how Betty Freeman would react to his wish to leave Venice, as it was her money that had made the studio possible in the first place, and was relieved when she wrote in the middle of August, on holiday in France, to reassure him that there was no problem. On August 18, "sunk in exhaustion," he explained to Lou Harrison that "I have to give up the studio not because I do not have the money but because I no longer have the strength to maintain the place and maintain the instruments in playable condition and in tune." As there seemed to be "no miracle on the horizon," he felt "doubtful that the instruments will come out of storage while I am alive."

He had decided to move to San Diego, a gesture that he felt at the time was almost equivalent to retirement. At the beginning of September he wrote: "Slowly, inexorably, I am getting ready for a new life, and already my health is better. I am throwing things away, giving them, destroying with glee articles that I have carried about for twenty years. Since it is my fate to be homeless it is my goal, within one year from today, to be able to walk away from my 'home' carrying everything I need for daily living in two arms."[57]

On September 15 his lease expired and he fled from Venice. John Grayson drove him down to San Diego. "I uttered hardly a single word on the entire trip," he told Betty Freeman. "I had the feeling that I was flying for my life, and wondered if I would make it."[58] He rented a small house at 4645 Wilson Avenue in "a very green, non-slum" part of the North Park area of San Diego. "I water the grass and flowers for about two hours every evening. What a wonderful change!"[59] Gradually he began to unwind after the tensions of his year in Venice, and he told Peter Yates a month later: "I am slowly regaining some serenity."[60]

The instruments were put in storage in several places, most of them in a garage in Santa Monica which he had rented simply because it was convenient to Venice. Despite his protestations of tiredness he was deeply concerned about them and about the prospects for future performances of his work, especially *Delusion*. It therefore caused a considerable stir when, at the beginning of October, an unsolicited letter arrived from Will Ogdon, chairman of the music department at the University of California, San Diego, saying he had learned of Partch's interest in obtaining a "permanent and useful home" for his instruments and suggesting that one of the Quonset huts on the campus in La Jolla might be suitable.[61] In reply Partch explained how weary he was of the constant effort to maintain his instruments, stating flatly that if any such deal were to be struck he would need Danlee Mitchell or another assistant somehow to be involved as well; but that, these reservations aside, he would be willing to discuss the idea further.

Partch's primary concern, if the instruments were given to an institution, was that they be kept in playable condition so they could be a "living, continuing influence." Implicit in this was the fact that "physical possession of scores and instruments is meaningless unless the knowledge, the usages, the traditions, the ethos, the daimon, that underlie and permeate them are somehow present. I speak to the intuitive and understanding human element. . . . If my music is considered important by some future generation these realities are basic. If it is not, my instruments become a pile of sculptural junk, and the scores fragments in a whirlwind."[62] The only person he felt able to assume these responsibilities was Danlee Mitchell. In fact, any performance of *Delusion of the Fury* was inconceivable to him without Mitchell's involvement. The problem was, as

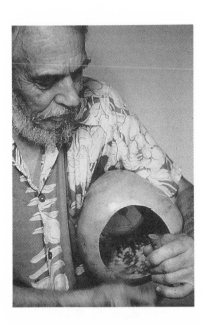

Partch hollowing a gourd, c. 1967. Unsigned
photograph, Harry Partch Estate Archive.

Partch explained to a correspondent, that "along with a deep interest in my
music [Mitchell] had a compulsive urge toward reproduction and now has a
wife and four small children. Consequently, he would need to be remunerated
better than I ever would."[63]

The question of what to do with his instruments remained tied in Partch's
own mind to the prospect of a performance of *Delusion*. He had received a letter
from the Koussevitzky Foundation offering a $2,500 award for "a dramatic
work of at least fifteen minutes in length": as a new work was "totally out of the
question" he offered them *Delusion,* but received no word of a decision.[64] He
worked at building or customizing the remaining small hand instruments for
use in the work. With wood from a "50-year old clump of bamboo in the
backyard next to me" he produced two Ektaras, Indian-inspired instruments
with one string attached to a gourd resonator by two long bamboo flanks which
met at the top. "Both are decorated in colored lacquer," he told Emil Richards,
"as though by an insane Navaho."[65] Yet the idea of a performance still seemed
rather hypothetical, and not a little worrying: "The thought of getting deep
into responsibilities again frightens me."[66]

In the middle of November, like a bolt out of the blue, he heard from Jan
Popper, director of the Opera Workshop at UCLA, that the music faculty had
committed themselves to a performance of *Delusion* "two years hence."[67]

Partch's reaction to the news was restrained, and he refused to regard it as a sign of the university's belief in his work. In a letter some years later he expressed the matter in even blacker terms, explaining that it had been Betty Freeman, "all by herself," who had backed UCLA "into the kind of corner where they could not refuse to do *Delusion*."[68] Freeman had agreed to UCLA's demand that she underwrite the production and cover any deficit incurred; with this financial safety net the university felt confident that matters could proceed.[69] Freeman remained his chief liaison, and thanks to her negotiations the performance dates were eventually finalized for January 1969. The two-year wait seemed "like an eternity, but I would probably have thought them an eternity at age 25 also."[70]

The most gratifying professional activity this winter was not a directly musical one. On November 28 Partch presented a lecture at the San Francisco Art Institute, in connection with an exhibition at the San Francisco Art Museum in which his Gourd Tree and Cone Gongs and Quadrangularis Reversum were on display as pieces of sculpture. In December the institute presented him with the 1966 Nealie Sullivan Award of $1,000, and he spent "a 22-hour day (4:30 A.M. to 2:30 A.M. next day)" in San Francisco to receive it. He described the event to David Hall at CRI as "a beautiful experience, meeting old old friends, a full house, a fine greeting."[71] The museum also mounted a photographic retrospective on Partch and his instruments.

Back in San Diego, December passed quietly. The news about *Delusion* had brought him a feeling of contentment, though one punctuated by moments of anguish. Telling the news to Peter Yates, he apologized if at times he sounded "lugubrious," adding that he was nonetheless "very content, more so than at any time since those quiet days in Petaluma."[72] He was living close to Danlee Mitchell, and not far from his old composer friend John Glasier and his son Jonathan, all of whom "have cars and see me frequently. So I'm not alone."[73]

In the early months of 1967 he was suffering from an adrenal depression, "a kind of anemia," which hit him suddenly, just like the attack he had had in Gualala in 1950. "The doctor gave me a shot of cortisone," he told Betty Freeman, "and within minutes re-designed my life. My blood pressure went from far above normal to far below normal. . . . So now I have switched from a pill *twice* a day to *decrease* blood pressure to another pill *three* times a day to *increase* blood pressure. I have the strange feeling that for seventeen years I've been kept alive by a chemistry teetering on the edge of uncertainty, that—in my case—in every eleventh hour, has somehow guessed right."[74] One consequence of this was a further change of diet. He had been observing his former no-salt and little-meat regime with remarkable determination, but now he was permitted salt again. He had reluctantly given up seeing Dr. Raymond Weston, being now too far away, especially without a car of his own, to maintain contact. The previous October he had told Freeman: "My physical weakness seems to be progressive and Ray has no explanation. Or hasn't, in the past."[75]

The recovery process was slow. He was "determined, if humanly possible, not to lapse into chronic invalidism," telling a correspondent: "I have too much to do, and I see no immediate prospect of anyone with the time and dedication to take my place right now."[76] His immediate plans included a new venture, the teaching of a course on his own music at UCSD at La Jolla in the autumn. The idea was attractive for several reasons, primarily because—and Partch was quite frank with the university about this—he could not bear the thought of his instruments simply remaining in storage for nearly two years before rehearsals for *Delusion* would begin at UCLA. He discussed the idea with Will Ogdon in the music department, showing his customary impatience in dealing with institutions—though in this case not unreasonably, as negotiations of one kind or another with UCSD had now been proceeding, on and off, for three years with no tangible result. By early March he had had enough, and Danlee Mitchell was landed with the job of issuing those communications that Partch himself could not face.

The first obstacle came when Ogdon told Mitchell that Partch's assistant—if and when there were to be such an appointment—must be a UCSD graduate student. Partch protested that "this is straight nonsense. I require of an assistant a large degree of willingness, aptitude, and dedication, and these qualities are not automatically implicit in a college degree. I need someone who will drive me around the country and city looking for the right piece of wood, the right eucalyptus branch, the right latex product, the right hardware, and literally a hundred other items, who will do tedious sanding of hundreds of strings, blocks, reeds. For the past six weeks Jonathan Glasier has been helping me in this way. . . . He's been a great comfort, and I am very grateful. He is the first genuine assistant I've had in five years. He has no degree, and wants none, for very much the same reasons I wanted none, a long time ago."[77] Partch went on: "After all, I was myself a school drop-out, back in 1919, because I felt convinced, even then, that the curriculum which faced me at the age of 18 had no solid basis in either acoustics or philosophy. I have seen, since then, decade after decade, a straight abdication by most music educators of their obligation to each new generation to examine the long-engraved milleniums-old truths, and if I were 18 in this year of 1967 I am fairly certain that I would again drop out." Yet for all his reservations he agreed, in a letter of March 30, to teach the course and accepted the university's offer of space for his instruments in one of the Quonset huts on campus.[78] Most of the other details concerning his complex requirements remained to be sorted out.

He made another, and quite uncharacteristic, foray into the world of musical academia during the early spring. He had been exchanging correspondence with Ben Johnston, still teaching at the University of Illinois, who had offered him a lecture spot at the April meeting of the American Society of University Composers in the context of a panel on microtonal music in the United States. Partch declined to attend, largely because of his unstable health, but thanks to Johnston's persistence agreed to complete the project for an alternative venue. He prepared a lecture on tape called "A Quarter Saw Section of Motivations and Intonation," in which—for the first time since he completed *Genesis of a Music*—he focused in detail on his use of just intonation. Musical examples were recorded on the Chromelodeons, which were brought to Partch's house on Wilson Avenue for the purpose at the end of May, and other examples were taken from recordings of his music. Johnston presented the tape, with slides, at that year's summer school at Tanglewood in Massachusetts.

Partch spent the spring and summer copying scores.[79] He worked first at *Petals,* which he sent to *Source* magazine in April; he also had an extensive correspondence with CRI over the release of the now-finished recording. Then he made some corrections and changes in the score of *Delusion,* working out possible distributions of the various instrumental parts so that ensemble players could double on the array of small hand instruments he had by now finished building. During July and August he worked on a new copy of the score of *Oedipus,* incorporating "many changes made during the six months of rehearsals the early part of 1954 in Sausalito."[80] Although there were no immediate plans for a production, suggestions of reviving the work had surfaced from time to time—most recently from a choreographer in Athens, who wanted to perform it in Greece—and, because of the comparatively modest resources called for, it was the least daunting of his stage works to produce. He also finished building the Eucal Blossom, the bamboo marimba he had begun three years before in Del Mar, so named because the "blossom" of tuned bamboo sections, arranged in three columns, appears to grow from a eucalyptus stem.

In August he received his copy of the second issue of *Source* magazine, with the full score of *Petals,* the first publication of any of his scores, together with an article on his music by Arthur Woodbury. After months of polite correspondence with individuals at CRI, who had run into delays over the release of the recording, his temper snapped, and he sent a furious telegram to David Hall: "The score of *Petals* has already appeared in *Source*. They have kept their word but you have not kept yours. It has been fourteen months since this record was authorized. If you did not like this work why did you not say so a long time ago? You seem to think that if you send love from Bernice [Hall's wife] everything is right. She, a human being, never writes to me. What the hell can I care about Bernice's regards, is this record to appear only in the lives of my heirs?"[81] More calmly he protested to one of the directors of the company that "in my Gate 5 experience there was never more than a six-week period intervening between an acceptable recording session and the advent of the manufactured record. In the instance of *Petals* the intervening period *has extended nine-fold!* . . . These endless delays—with never an explanation—constitute straight cruelty."[82]

Early in September he moved to a small wooden-frame house at 228 North Helix in Solana Beach, two blocks from the ocean and about eight miles north of UCSD at La Jolla. With the honorary title of Regents Professor, he taught a series of seminars ("the first in my life")[83] on his own music in the fall quarter, concentrating on intonation and instrumental practice. The classes lasted three hours and met weekly in one of the Quonset huts on the Camp Matthews section of the campus, starting at 8 A.M. He also felt obliged to spend about six hours a week "in office," "which means, in essence, giving individual instruction."[84] Twelve students took the class for credit, and a few others sat in.

In the seminars Partch presented the students with a heady mixture of the enthralling and the exasperating. His plan was to "analyze scores in terms of the musical theories expressed in my book,"[85] and some of the time he did just that, talking also about the philosophy of music education both as practiced in American universities and as might be practiced in an ideal world ("educo—lead out, open doors").[86] But although the lectures were always thoroughly prepared, he was easily sidetracked and would launch into various tangential subjects, his discourse laced with all manner of personal grievances. John Chalmers, a graduate student in biology with a passionate interest in tuning who was sitting in on the class, recalls one memorable session which, more than any other, impressed itself on the minds of students and faculty, and created an indelible image of Partch himself around the campus.

> The best classroom presentation we had unfortunately no-one took any notes, because we were all terrified. Harry came in drunk and absolutely furious, and denounced the Music Department . . . and the whole state of American music, for about forty-five minutes, and [let fly with] invective, just pouring forth. And then

sort of politely burped and excused himself and walked out the door. And we were just dumbfounded. Everyone was afraid he was going to have a coronary. . . . The next class [he was] fine. Never another word about it.[87]

Jack Logan, another student in the class, adds: "We became symbolic examples of the frustrations he must have felt continually in the larger world, where his music was so often misunderstood."[88]

Partch's attitude toward the students could at times be combative. "You can consider me a television set," he told them one week, "you can either turn it off or pick up a gun and shoot it. And I shall be totally indifferent."[89] Some of his quips, although funny, could be rather exasperating for those students who were genuinely struggling to follow his explanations of tuning. "One of the persons in this class once complained that the floor here was dirty. May I observe, with great conviction, that the sweeping of this floor would probably supercede nearly everything in his musical education in creative meaningfulness."[90] He made no bones about his anti-institutional stance ("Credits, degrees, honors—I am against all of them in the creative arts"), but was perhaps slightly less clear about exactly what function his teaching *was* intended to fulfill. Concerning its overall didactic value he concluded rather sadly: "The disorientation of my students during the first few weeks was . . . simply sad. . . . The bewilderment was so great at first that deeply serious requests were out of the question. I gave only reading assignments. Later, I asked for progressions or resolutions in ratios, and—at the end—a final paper. In a sense the class was a total failure. . . . It is not the teacher's fault that his class failed. Due to the general apathy of the students discussion of the ideas advanced never took place."[91]

His teaching responsibilities, and the "nervous tension" they caused, sapped his energies considerably.[92] "I retire from the world about five P.M.," he told a correspondent. "Sometimes I have a few drinks—sometimes I don't."[93] On December 17 he typed up a report on the quarter's activities, "My Seminar in Retrospect," and at Christmas he admitted to a friend that he was still in a state of "deep exhaustion" following the conclusion of his "seminar experience."

Partch did no more official teaching at UCSD, though he retained a nominal connection with the university and continued for a time to house his instruments in a Quonset hut on campus. In the spring of 1968 he was appointed as a (non-salaried) "professor of music in residence" for a year, and the appointment was later renewed for a second year. On May 11 and 12 two concerts of his music were mounted at the UCSD Art Gallery, featuring excerpts from *Petals* and a tryout of "Time of Fun Together" from act II of *Delusion*. Also on the program, with choreography by Susan Long, was *Daphne of the Dunes*, a "re-copying" and slight rescoring of the music for *Windsong*, which he had undertaken in the hope that it would make "an acceptable dance-drama."[94] The concerts and the excitement they generated, however gratifying, were very tiring for him. He told Peter Yates: "When I am able to live a hermit-like existence (almost never), seeing almost no one, going out in the evening never, I can maintain a degree of serenity, and perhaps a surprising level of energy. But when I am faced with rehearsals, public appearances, interviews, social obligations, well—I am torn apart; I anticipate this sort of thing with growing dread. What a strange reason for trying to prolong one's existence! It is too late."[95] During the summer in Solana Beach he continued the work of recopying scores, with forthcoming performances in mind. In June he finished a new copy of *Barstow*, making "a more readable presentation" of the revised version from Sausalito in 1954 and including changes made during rehearsals in Evanston in 1958; and in early July he copied *Castor and Pollux*, incorporating a new Cloud-Chamber Bowls part written three years previously and making clear the division of the Kithara part between Kithara II and Surrogate Kithara.

In the middle of July 1968 Partch moved up to the Los Angeles area to be near UCLA for the forthcoming production of *Delusion of the Fury*. He and Mitchell shared an apartment on Weyburn Avenue in Westwood. Partch described his situation to Betty Freeman: "Danlee and I have a large roomy flat right on the edge of campus, very pleasant. His family remains in San Diego. It is still a 35-minute walk up the hill to the studio, so I don't go too often. Westwood, after the quiet little town of Solana Beach, is a shock—frenetic and exhausting."[96] Besides Mitchell, another assistant was very much in evidence: Bill Symons, Partch's carpenter friend from Petaluma, came down to Los Angeles to help with maintenance work on the instruments. Describing him to Freeman, Partch declared that "[i]n my entire life no one has come close in approaching the talents of Bill—that is, in one who is deeply interested in my work. He has *common sense*, with tools, with construction."[97] Symons helped significantly in putting the instruments in shape, and Mitchell began teaching him, virtually from scratch, to play the Marimba Eroica part in *Delusion*.

When rehearsals got under way they were initially for a quite different venture. Thanks to the fund-raising efforts of Oliver Daniel of BMI, Partch and his ensemble had been invited to present two concerts in September at the Whitney Museum in New York. Because few UCLA students were around

during the summer, and because an eyebrow had been raised by Walter Rubsamen in the music department about UCLA students being involved in Partch's
activities outside the university, the ensemble consisted largely of Los Angeles-
based musicians who had worked with him before. The money for all the many
preparations for the New York concerts came initially out of Partch's own
pocket, to the sum of $3,000. "It wasn't just Bill [Symons], it was also the
immediate necessity to have good musicians, and I took care of fares to L.A. and
even rent occasionally. Also, materials expenses [for the instruments] were very
large." Partch even paid Michael Ranta's flight from West Germany, where he
had been living, so he could play in the ensemble. All of the expenses were
reimbursed in due course by Betty Freeman.

The Whitney Museum concerts took place on September 8 and 10, in
connection with the International Music Congress and with funds from the
Rockefeller Foundation. They drew capacity audiences—"standing-room-
only lines that twisted outside the Museum, down Madison Avenue, and
around the block," as one reviewer put it[98]—and were the occasion for unprecedented public exposure and acclaim, with reviews appearing in the *New York
Times*, the *Village Voice*, the *New Yorker*, and *Newsweek*. Although genuinely
enthusiastic, all the reviews shared a sensationalist tone, deflecting attention
from the critical examination of Partch's work to a largely uncritical adulation
of it. The *Village Voice* described the event in pseudo-Hollywood terms: "This
week New York City, the famous rich but parsimonious whore, rolled out one
of her red carpets. Not the better rug reserved for monosyllabic movie stars and
tricky politicians, but the tattered, modest one marked 'maybe an artistic
genius.'"[99] *Newsweek* described Partch as an "American visionary and stubborn
individualist" who had built "his own musical world out of microtones, hobo
speech, elastic octaves and percussion instruments made from hubcaps
and nuclear cloud chambers," calling his music "a richly erotic, primitive, fresh
and stirring drama of sound."[100] Following the final concert, *Barstow, Castor
and Pollux*, and *Daphne of the Dunes* were recorded by Columbia Records, with
John McClure producing, in a session held in the Whitney Museum beginning
around 10 P.M. and continuing until 8 A.M. the next morning.

While he was in New York Partch met briefly with Ben Johnston, who
attended the second of the Whitney Museum concerts, and visited La Monte
Young, a composer with a considerable though largely underground reputation
as the earliest exponent of minimalism in music. Young let Partch hear a just-
tuned electronic drone that he had set up in his studio. Partch was horrified, and
writing to Young a couple of months later—declining his request for a grant

recommendation—he confessed: "I realize that I was not pleasant when I met you in your studio. I don't think that I could have taken that New York ordeal much better twenty years ago. And I also doubt that if I awoke fresh as the rosy dawn I could stand an electronic drone very long without suffering."[101]

However gratifying, the whole New York venture had been highly taxing, and Partch was drinking heavily. An unfortunate conclusion came when he accidentally knocked over and smashed a valuable lamp in Oliver Daniel's apartment, where he had been staying. Saying goodbye to Michael Ranta he was resentful that Ranta should be intent on returning to Germany rather than staying on to play in the performances of *Delusion,* telling various of the ensemble members: "I'm going back to California to grow okra. Danlee's coming with me. And Mike, he's going back to Germany to play Stockhausen."[102] The difficult mixture of professional triumph and his own general weariness left him with the feeling that all the adulation was coming too late.

Back in California he moved into a new apartment in Culver City, and following the return of the instruments from New York Betty Freeman rented a studio for them nearby.[103] At the beginning of the new academic year the team for *Delusion of the Fury* quickly came together. Partch placed all the responsibility for rehearsing the work in the hands of Danlee Mitchell, who was on sabbatical leave from San Diego State College. The ensemble contained a mixture of old and new players, several of them recruited by Emil Richards; Richards and Linda Schell, who had joined the ensemble for the New York concerts, were the mainstays. The choreographer was Virginia Storie, who had choreographed *Castor and Pollux* at the UCLA performance in May 1966; and the sets were to be designed by her husband, John Crawford, whose work had impressed Partch at UCLA more than two years earlier.

The underlying aesthetic of *Delusion of the Fury* is revealed in the subtitle Partch gave the work, "A Ritual of Dream and Delusion." Before the production and subsequently he repeatedly stressed, in statements and interviews, that what he wanted to achieve in this work was a form of ritual theater, with a full integration of the musicians, dancers, and mimes into a kind of tribal vision, moving one step beyond the point he had reached in *The Bewitched.* Although *Delusion* is of course not truly a ritual, any more than is any work of dance theater, it is perhaps the most self-contained of all his achievements, allowing us to experience a heady sense of disorientation—a state of change, of a kind parallel to that undergone in ritual experience. In a statement of this aesthetic, he wrote:

I believe in many things: in an intonation as *just* as I am capable of making it, in musical instruments *on stage,* dynamic in form, visually exciting. I believe in dramatic lighting, replete with gels, to enhance them. I believe in musicians who are *total* constituents of the moment, irreplaceable, who may sing, shout, whistle, stamp their feet. I believe in players in costume, or perhaps half-naked, and I do not care which half. . . . I believe in a total integration of factors, not as separate and sealed specialities in the artificially divorced departments of universities, but of sound and sight, the visually dynamic and dramatic, all channeled into a single, wholly fused, and purposeful direction. *All.*[104]

In rehearsals at UCLA the problem arose as to what exactly the musicians ought to be *doing* on stage when they weren't playing their instruments. In Partch's conception, the musicians would be fully integrated with the stage action: they ought, he wrote, to become "actors and dancers, moving from instrument to acting areas as the impetus of the drama requires."[105] To a certain extent he had worked out the instrumental parts so that the musicians could at times move down to center stage and join in the dramatic action—the small hand instruments were intended to be brought down and played at such moments—but he became aware of logistical problems after completing the score. "My original concept involved a natural, musical, and motivated use of the hands in the act of playing small hand instruments—drums, claves, etc., which would contribute to the total dramatic effect, rather than hands hanging uselessly and awkwardly at the sides, which would contribute nothing. Now, after finishing the score, I realize that the music for the small instruments is rhythmically too difficult for a simultaneous singing-playing performance."[106] The problem, as he saw it, was the old one of specialization: the fact that a musician is usually trained only as a musician, and becomes awkward and self-conscious when asked to act or even to move on stage. The principals faced a similar problem. "Ideally, the singers would be skilled also in the arts of dancing, acting, miming, as they are in Noh and Kabuki. But in our specialist culture, singers are generally only singers, actors only actors, and dancers only dancers." The solution adopted in the production was to "put the singers in the pit, while the actor-dancers on stage mouth the words, the gibberish, or whatever."[107]

The only way around this impasse would have been to conceive of the whole rehearsal process as a form of prolonged interdisciplinary re-education, in which the musicians could attempt to acquire other skills. Faced with the practicalities of limited rehearsal time, and the lack of a multitalented individual to guide the process, any such optimistic schemes were out of the question. As the rehearsals entered the final stage, it became clear to Partch that the production would not live up to his hopes. In rehearsal he and Mitchell devoted most of their attention to "getting a good performance of the music."[108] "I never had time to do anything," he later protested, "except sit for hours and hours, teaching people to play well."[109] Moreover, "I did not know, being very very preoccupied with the music, what was being contemplated in the costuming and choreographical departments . . . until the last few days before performance—about three days in each case, when it was far too late to make substantial changes."[110] Three years later he declared himself unhappy with the costuming of the Chorus of Shadows at the beginning of act I, and with the Son, whose costume, "exactly calculated to emphasize bulging breasts and hips," made the performer—a woman—look exactly like a woman, not a boy. "On stage, I suffered through the scene entitled *A Son in Search of His Father's Face*"—in which the son looked like a daughter—knowing that "in Japanese mythology a daughter would never do this." As bad in his terms as the costumer's "treachery" was the choreography, which "was worse than I expected"; the scene of the Lost Kid in act II was "too stupidly gauche to comment on," and the "miming, all through Act II, is dreadfully over-acted, amateurish. No subtlety whatever—so that it is not only not amusing—it is

The Justice of the Peace delivers his verdict in the case of the Young Vagabond and the Old Goat Woman in act II of *Delusion of the Fury*, UCLA, 1969. Photo by Malcolm Lubliner.

pathetic. The Court Scene is at least better. And the judge reveals a mordant and ironic dignity."

Delusion of the Fury was premièred at the UCLA Playhouse on January 9, 1969, and repeated on January 10, 11, and 12. The work was recorded for Columbia Records and filmed, on a last-minute impulse, by Madeline Tourtelot. Many of Partch's old friends were in the audience, including Lou Harrison, Gordon and Jacqueline Onslow Ford, and James and Marion Jacobs. The performances were sold out long in advance, and the critical reception was uniformly rapturous.

The production over, the task of packing the instruments and of clearing up the "incredible chaos" in the studio left Partch feeling very depressed. Even worse was a distressing theft that took place in an unguarded moment, which he reported in a letter to John McClure of Columbia Records: "I suppose you already know about the loaded truck stolen just as Danlee was ready to take off permanently for San Diego. I've been troubled, sad, gloomy . . . [this] was no act of God. Danlee was only a few yards away. Danlee lost a great deal, Linda [Schell, who had many of her belongings in the truck] was practically wiped out. I lost only one master tape, from 1953 (second side of P[lectra] and P[ercussion] Dances), to the best of my knowledge."[111] Later he discovered that a collection of rosewood, which he had been storing up for replacement blocks for the Diamond Marimba, was also missing; and that during the eight months of his residency at UCLA "scores, tools, materials have simply disappeared."[112] "Was absolutely no one in charge of that studio from July through January?"[113] Then there was "the question of money. I personally put out nearly $600 for materials for repair, the past eight months (for new [Cloud-Chamber] Bowls—for example—senselessly destroyed by bad packing and untrained players), and I've put out about $1600 paying for various services. UCLA paid me nothing—I've spent about $9000 during these months; only six and a half [thousand] came back to me in fees and grants—I am out about two and a half." He told John McClure, "I won't do this again."[114]

After the production Partch spent several weeks in Culver City working with Madeline Tourtelot on her film, "editing, re-shooting, and post-synching."[115] Some post-production shooting of scenes with the principal mimes was done by Tourtelot, to Partch's dismay, in the Botanical Garden at UCLA: these shots were intended for insertion into the film to cover up scenes where the camera-work was inadequate. By the middle of March they had finished, and, with Mitchell's help, Partch had found a new home north of San Diego, in the coastal town of Encinitas.

Encinitas and San Diego

His new home was at 224 Sunset Drive in Encinitas, some eight miles north of his former home in Solana Beach. It was east of the main Amtrak railway line from San Diego to Los Angeles, and north of Moonlight Beach, a large sandy expanse, the proximity of which had attracted him. The papers were co-signed by Partch and Betty Freeman—after the bank had refused to give him a mortgage due to his lack of tangible assets—and Partch made the monthly payments. The house stood on a hill, with the Pacific Ocean visible from the living-room windows. A few days after he moved in, on the early morning of April 1, 1969, he had a strange, dream-like vision which he recounted to a friend three years later. As dawn came over the ocean, he imagined he saw in the sky a rainbow containing no color other than blue. At first he thought he was dreaming, but the image persisted. Although probably attributable to worsening eyesight or to a trick of the light, he took it as a good omen: that an image from one of his own instruments, the blue arch structure that supported Harmonic Canon III, was appearing over the ocean as a benediction on his new home.[1]

In Encinitas at first, as he reported to Betty Freeman, "the walking necessary to existing, the hill climbing, was pretty strenuous." After about six weeks he noted: "My legs are stronger, and I feel much better physically. I have the first small garden since I was 11–12. I've planted blue morning glories and white moon glories and lemon cucumbers along the south side of the patio, and zinnias and petunias in the yard. Also cucumbers and okra down below."[2] Later he would describe the place as the first real home since his childhood.[3]

Partch's move south implied a final abandonment of hope that UCLA would provide a permanent home for his instruments, and indeed any such agreement seemed as far away as ever following the production of *Delusion*. Instead, he renewed his discussions with the University of California, San Diego, and in April met with the now provost, John Stewart, and others to thrash out the issues involved in establishing a stable studio for the instruments on campus. The discussions were as trouble-ridden as ever. Betty Freeman had warned Will Ogdon, in the music department, that Partch was no longer able to maintain the instruments on his own and needed an assistant. On March 24 Partch wrote to Ogdon, protesting: "I am thoroughly capable of maintaining instruments for my own use, as a composer. I even have plans to build a new one, and I've been saving and looking for materials for it the past nine years. Where I stop short is under a weekly attack of some twenty musicians expecting every instrument to be in beautiful playing condition."[4] He had a "nervous session" in April with the provost and later reflected—with a touch of paranoia: "Everything that has happened in the five years of my slight association with UCSD has been consistent. Stewart is dedicated to electronics-indeterminacy, and he appointed [people] to implement his beliefs. . . . There are five disciples of the Cage-Tudor-Stockhausen beliefs. And not a single person on the campus who can teach my instruments, tune them, or repair them. . . . What a strange place as a repository of fifty years of my work!"[5]

The sense of being out of place in any of the main streams of contemporary music, and of being increasingly dependent on Danlee Mitchell to keep his music alive, shadowed the majority of Partch's exchanges with UCSD. He wrote to Ogdon on June 2: "Betty Freeman . . . was and is concerned that Danlee could not carry on my work, in the present situation, and of course she is right. But what are my alternatives? Long ago I reconciled myself to the very probable fact that there would be no extension beyond my death. In view of this old old feeling, I am not going to grasp at straws to try to make it possible . . . Danlee is irreplaceable."

During the late spring and early summer, various ideas were suggested to try to satisfy the interests both of the university and of Partch himself. Freeman wrote to the university that Partch was prepared to donate his instruments on condition that UCSD would hire Mitchell and Bill Symons, and she even offered financial help to make this happen. Madeline Tourtelot, meanwhile, met with John Stewart to attempt to move things along in a slightly different direction: their talk centered on UCSD's plans for a building to be devoted to experimental work in the creative arts which, Tourtelot proposed, should house Partch's instruments. Yet the extent of Partch's needs, the general vagueness about what exactly the proposed affiliation would amount to, and the added complication of mild but perceptible differences between Freeman and Tourtelot, combined to dissipate the small steps toward progress almost as soon as they had been taken.[6] Partch himself remained difficult and uncooperative. John Stewart protested to Tourtelot at the end of June that any kind of joint effort at a solution "is precisely what we are unable to bring about, not in the least because of Harry's own misgivings about people who bear him nothing but goodwill, which is in some danger of running out."[7]

The theme of what would happen to his work after his death found expression in a different form concurrently with his discussions with UCSD. In February the previous year, in Solana Beach, Partch had received a letter from Alan Marks of Da Capo Press in New York inquiring about reprinting *Genesis of a Music,* which had gone out of print at the beginning of 1964. Partch agreed unreservedly and proposed that he update some parts of the book for the new edition. The press offered him $750 as an advance against royalties. He had promised to begin work on the new material immediately after the performances of *Delusion.*[8]

At the beginning of May 1969 he began writing and collating the new material. The chapters on his instruments and notation clearly needed to be updated, but upon reflection he decided to let the historical and theoretical parts of the book stand. Although he would have liked to make "a few changes," these were more a matter of detail than of substance, so he elected to settle for an exact reprint in the hope that "the fire of youth" would be preserved.[9]

The most significant addition was a new preface. In the numerous typescript drafts of the text, which still survive, he gathered together his thoughts under three main headings. First was the autobiographical, in which he recorded memories of his childhood and his early musical experiences and provided a brief chronology of *Genesis* itself. Second was the shortcomings of academic musical education, with the subsidiary theme of the corruption of youth by fashions, musical and political, of the moment. Third was the spirit and motivation of his own creative work:

> The more I see of fashions the more I discern, with infinite clarity, another path— that of Man, the bright adventurer, the magic-maker. When I feel optimistic, it holds brilliant promise, like an Arizona morning before dawn, with its cardboard stage set and dark eastern silhouette in honor of the sun's holy rising. . . . The truly path-breaking step can never be predicted, and certainly not by the person who makes it at the time he makes it. He clears as he goes, evolves his own techniques, devises his own tools, ignores where he must. And his path cannot be retraced, because each of us is an original being.[10]

Of these three themes, the second, on the inadequacies of musical academia, was discussed only in passing in the finished text. Perhaps he felt it sounded too negative in the context of what was, after all, a document of creative fulfillment; but he was also worried that he was "setting up a straw man—the musical establishment—then taking a sadistic delight in beating it to death."[11]

The passage in the new preface recalling his youth in Arizona and New Mexico was the only piece of true autobiography Partch offered for publication in his lifetime (with the exception of *Bitter Music*). Written ostensibly as a way of answering the question, "repeated literally hundreds of times, . . . how did you ever get started?"[12] these paragraphs give a very clear impression of going on record, of setting down all that is worth knowing about these years. In the long span of time between the writing of the new material and the eventual republication of the book, Partch offered this preface to interviewers to read, partly to supplement the sparse and error-ridden biographical material available, but also, perhaps, to forestall further investigation and probing in what was, for him, a painful area. He had discussed with Lou Harrison the idea of writing his memoirs but had decided against it, not because of lack of time— there was plenty of free time now in his "retirement" years—but because his later childhood and teens had been so unhappy.[13] "The past comes screaming back at me," he told Betty Freeman, "and I just want to go away and hide."[14]

The six months from May to November 1969 were spent working on the new material. On July 11 he signed an agreement for publication, under the terms of which Da Capo Press agreed to publish the book within one year of receipt of the new material in satisfactory form. Accordingly, in August the contract with

University Microfilms, which had been the sole source of photocopies of the book since it went out of print, was terminated, as the book was officially once more in press. Partch submitted the final batch of new material on November 10. He also sent a set of Gate 5 records—"I wanted my editor to be aware of my music"[15]—and his only perfect copy of the first edition of the book.

His other professional activities centered around recordings. The Columbia disc with the Whitney Museum recordings of *Barstow, Castor and Pollux* and *Daphne of the Dunes* had appeared by the beginning of May 1969, under the title *The World of Harry Partch*. Partch considered it "a good record" though, as he told John McClure, "the Gate 5 record of *Castor & Pollux* was not perfect, but over the years I got used to its imperfections. Now, I've got to get used to a whole new set of imperfections."[16] He entered into extensive correspondence with McClure about the editing and balancing of the master tape of *Delusion of the Fury*, and about the liner notes, for which purpose Partch suggested using a long and beautiful letter he had received in response to the work from Jacqueline Onslow Ford. "She is a poet," he told McClure, "but with no wide recognition—she is a name in neither literary or musical circles. But she and her husband, Gordon, helped me financially, occasionally, during those rough days in Sausalito in the early 'fifties, and—more important—they were sources of constant strength in the matter of morale."[17] Partch was particularly drawn to passages from the letter like this one, which he even considered including in the new preface to *Genesis of a Music:*

> Such an experience [as *Delusion*] is not easily approached in words, it has its protection—, some beautiful element of silence keeps it whole in feeling, in contemplation, it has the attraction of its dark orb turning within thought . . . composition and spectacle are one to include the whole scale of our humanity, and beyond our ordinary limits to the great Thunder, it stretches us to the great celebration, ritual to reveal what we live that we cannot know . . . in the austere, bold, luminous progressions and harmonies I recognize everywhere your clarity and what I can only call the timbre of heroic life.[18]

McClure, however, felt that somewhat less poetic liner notes would be in order, and Partch agreed without complaint. Madeline Tourtelot's film of *Delusion,* on the other hand, was a different matter: "Frankly, I do not see how editing can save Madeline's film," he told McClure. "How do I tell her?" He found little to recommend the film, and as time passed became almost wholly damning of her inadequate record of the production's "academically static modern dance" and the "nadir" it had reached "in costume treachery."[19]

A new film project was in the air by the end of the year. Partch's choreographer friend Jean Cutler, now teaching at the University of Oregon, had had the idea to do a film portrait of him with the provisional title *"The End of Life is Perception"—Harry Partch.* Cutler visited Encinitas to record some conversations with Partch, and in December wrote to say that he was in the process of putting together a script and trying to find funding. The first filming sessions were scheduled for March 1970. By the time the letter reached him, however, Partch was "virtually bedridden by some kind of arthritis," which had hit him in November and persisted through the winter.[20] He was hospitalized briefly over Christmas in Scripps Hospital in La Jolla, and when he came out he was obliged to walk with a crutch. Even though Cutler eventually shot a considerable amount of interview material, the project stalled and never came to fruition.

Some welcome news arrived at the beginning of January 1970 in the form of an award of $2,000 from the Cassandra Foundation in Chicago "in recognition of past achievements in the field of art." On January 6 Partch wrote a grateful letter of acceptance: "Since I feel little affinity for the House of Atreus, and having already faced The Furies, I feel free to accept your generous grant—without shudders, without apprehension, and without any overwhelming consciousness of guilt. I hope that I do not sound flippant, because I want to write with dignity, a deeply serious note of appreciation. For obvious reasons, of course, but also because Cassandra is, to me, Aeschylus' most unforgettable character."[21]

With the materials for the new edition of *Genesis of a Music* dispatched to the publishers, and notwithstanding his problems with arthritis, Partch was thinking again about trying to establish a new studio for his instruments. He had virtually given up on the prospect of officials at UCSD proposing a viable solution and was beginning to distance himself from them. When the university informed him that his affiliation was to be changed from professor in residence to adjunct professor, he scribbled a reply to the effect that he would prefer to be called a "Disjunct Professor."

In January 1970 he and Betty Freeman visited a prospective new studio at 143 South Cedros Avenue in Solana Beach. Partch described his requirements in some detail to the landlord, and specifically asked "whether I might bother anyone nearby or whether anyone nearby might bother me."[22] What the landlord neglected to mention was that behind the flimsy south wall of the studio there was a surfboard shop. Once the lease had been signed and Partch had moved in, "something akin to hell developed beyond that south wall."[23] Fumes from the resin used in the manufacture of surfboards during the day became overpowering, dust from sanding filtered through the holes in the south wall and into Partch's studio, and the noise of power tools, when they were at full blast, was deafening. Partch's temper snapped, and he demanded that both Chromelodeons—the most vulnerable of his instruments—be returned to his home in Encinitas, and that all the instruments with tuning gears be covered with polyethylene.

His outbursts of bad temper were aimed at, or reenacted for the benefit of, a new development in his life: a Harry Partch Foundation, created mainly, though not exclusively, by Betty Freeman. In February 1970 Freeman loaned $10,000 for the purpose and enlisted the help of Karl ZoBell, a young lawyer friend of Partch's in La Jolla, to set up the foundation and to make it legally viable.[24] In order to obtain an IRS number for the foundation, Partch agreed to assign all his copyrights and royalties to it. As of June 30 the foundation was approved by the IRS as a charitable and educational nonprofit organization, and hence all contributions were tax-deductible: in consequence, Freeman turned her initial loan into a gift. Besides Freeman herself, the leading figure in the foundation was her friend and Gurdjieff teacher, Omar Zenman, who became the business manager. Freeman and Patty Wright, Partch's friend from Sausalito days, contributed further monies to the foundation, part of which was put toward the rent of a studio, the equipping of a workshop, and the full-time services of Bill Symons to assist Partch with the instruments.

The first meeting of the board of directors of the Harry Partch Foundation was held at the office of the accountant Gilbert Drummond in San Pedro on July 11, 1970; Drummond's son Dean had played in Partch's ensemble since the time of the UCLA concert in 1966. The nine board members were Betty Freeman (president and treasurer), Patty Wright (vice president and secretary), Gilbert Drummond (accountant), Emil Richards, Harold Driscoll, Danlee Mitchell, James Jacobs, Madeline Tourtelot, and John McClure (the last two were absent from the meeting). Peter Yates had been considered for the board, but Partch's disillusion with Yates was by now considerable: "I felt a man so passionately dedicated to chance, indeterminacy and silence would be an inappropriate representative of my thinking. In recent years he has become such a dogmatic spokesman for ideas that are even repugnant to me that there has been no communication at all."[25] Although much good feeling was generated at the meeting, concrete prospects seemed as vague and trouble-ridden as ever. The minutes of the meeting record the foundation's aims:

Long term goals were discussed and the directors decided these should include the expansion of Harry Partch's music through teaching and performances. This would include a scholarship center for training and furthering of interest in Partch's music along with the preservation and reproduction of the instruments. Danlee Mitchell would be hired as music director and to teach and Bill Symons to duplicate the instruments and instruct in instrument building. Also, plans would include liaison with any interested universities. Short term goals were to rent a studio to house the instruments and prepare productions and a workshop to maintain the instruments.[26]

The first substantial setback to these plans came when the National Foundation of the Arts and Humanities turned down the foundation's application for a grant to finance duplication of the instruments. Danlee Mitchell wrote to Freeman that "we were depending on this too much. Without it I see only long range plans, not immediate projects."[27] Even immediate projects buckled under the sums of money needed. The Smithsonian Institution in Washington, D.C., had offered to make an advance for a projected tour in the spring of 1971, but Mitchell calculated that the realistic costs of such an undertaking would be in the order of $250,000, which left a considerable shortfall. Partch explained to a San Francisco journalist the following year that the Smithsonian had been "trying to sponsor two tours, then only one, but both fell through. The H. P. Foundation had the idea . . . of finding money to build two sets [of his instruments], but the money for even one collapsed. And it hoped that Smithsonian would help discover sponsors. Maybe they tried, but they didn't succeed in getting one dollar."[28]

The renting of a new studio, another of the foundation's aims, was clearly a matter of some urgency. Thanks to the activities of the surfboard shop, conditions in the studio on South Cedros in Solana Beach remained intolerable. Partch was all for breaking the lease because of the irresponsibility of his landlord, but he was overruled by Omar Zenman, who had been making trips down to Solana Beach, without Partch's knowledge, to pressure Bill Symons "into building and organising a big [wood]shop."[29] On June 1, in exasperation, Partch took matters into his own hands and rented "a place where we could at least tune instruments," on the other side of Highway 101 in Solana Beach.[30] But this, too, was only a temporary measure.

Why Zenman was so keen to ensure the provision of a fully equipped power-tool shop became clear to Partch only sometime later. Under the pretext of providing a working environment for Partch, Zenman had intended to use the studio to manufacture frames for waterbeds. He wanted Bill Symons to work on the frames at those times when Partch was not using the studio—the majority of the time, the facilities of a fully equipped woodshop being already at their disposal. When he learned of this Partch was utterly mortified. By August his resentment of Zenman had reached its height, and he declared in no uncertain terms to both Patty Wright and Betty Freeman that the "tenure of Omar Zenman as the dominating advisor to the Harry Partch Foundation must end. If he does not bow out . . . there is only one alternative—dissolve the foundation."[31]

The temporary studio on Highway 101 proved essential for one project during the summer. At the end of June Partch began to record the narration for a bonus record which Columbia Records proposed to include with the forth-coming release of *Delusion of the Fury.* Brief demonstration passages on all his instruments were recorded, mostly by Danlee Mitchell, Linda Schell, and John McAllister, in the new studio at night, when there was virtually no traffic on the road outside. Mitchell recalls that one of the musicians would stand outside the studio windows along the highway to watch for approaching headlights, and when no cars were coming would tap on the window as a signal to start recording.[32] The sessions continued in this way into August, although Partch's commentary was not completed until October, when the producer Eugene Paul asked him for a new and more arresting opening, a "rouser," that would command instant attention. Partch wrote to Lou Harrison that "there is only a fine line between bitterness, which must be avoided, and strength";[33] and again a week later that he had "lost all confidence that I can give them what they want—be the person they expect me to be."[34]

Partch's differences with Omar Zenman were only the beginning of a num-ber of changes that took place in the foundation during its first year. James Jacobs and Harold Driscoll dropped out, and Partch admitted in retrospect that it was misguided of him to have offered their names. "They told me at the time of my invitation that they could not offer money, nor sustain any efforts to raise funds," Partch told Freeman; and fund-raising was a pressing concern. "San Diego has a lot of wealth, and here I am! If I were as active now as I was in Sausalito in 1953 I might attract some, but I truly can make no effort."[35] More significantly, at a meeting on September 19, Freeman resigned as president, on the grounds that, whatever her title might imply, it was Danlee Mitchell who had the real power in the foundation: every decision depended on his concur-rence, and nothing could be tried or done without it. Mitchell was elected by general consent as the new president. In situations that provoked a conflict of loyalties between Freeman and Mitchell, Partch stressed his dependence on

Mitchell, as only he seemed capable of ensuring the continued performance of Partch's music. This loyalty was reflected in his new will, dated October 8, 1970, in which he appointed Mitchell his sole heir, and willed to him all his instruments, manuscripts, miscellaneous papers, recordings, and personal effects. This decision was very much against the advice of Freeman, who urged him to leave his estate to an institution that could provide the sense of continuity that an individual could not.

Added to the frustrations in the spring with studio conditions and the aggravation with the Harry Partch Foundation in the summer was a new crisis over the republication of *Genesis of a Music*. Under the terms of the agreement signed in July 1969, Da Capo Press had undertaken to publish the book within one year after receiving the new material in satisfactory form; their original promise had been "to publish the work in midsummer" 1970.[36] Delays had occurred by April, and the publication date was amended to "early in the fall."[37] Plenum Publishing, Da Capo Press's parent company, were going through extensive personnel changes, but Partch was not kept up to date on the situation and complained that the press left him "in total ignorance."[38] The first proofs for the book promised by his editor had still not arrived by August, when Partch wrote to inquire about the reason for the delay.

This exchange marked the beginning of a long series of silences and broken promises from Da Capo which continued throughout the following years. In October, Partch enlisted the help of Karl ZoBell, the lawyer who had helped set up the Harry Partch Foundation, who wrote to Alan Marks at Da Capo "asking his intentions in regard to publication, inasmuch as all promises had been broken."[39] In reply, Marks sent a telegram announcing that he would come to Encinitas the following month to see Partch. He arrived on November 7, and over the next two days he, Partch, and Mitchell had satisfactory discussions. Marks admitted that the book should have been in print by this time and that the failure was entirely his own fault: he promised to have the proofs ready for Partch "around christmastime."[40] Heartened by the meeting Partch settled down to some final corrections, and on December 2 came up with the book's new subtitle, "An Account of a Creative Work, its Roots and its Fulfillments." When Christmas passed with no sign of any proofs, Partch wrote to Marks, "wishing him a Happy New Year and begging an end to his silences."[41] After more weeks passed with still no reply, Partch sent Marks a furious telegram, demanding an explanation. Immediately he regretted the act and wrote the following day to apologize. On February 2 a telegram from Marks arrived, saying he had been in touch with Columbia Records, which was scheduling the release of *Delusion of the Fury* for April 1971, and that he was "making every effort to get out your book at the same time."[42]

By late 1970, his health relatively stable, Partch's thoughts had turned once again to instrument building, an activity that had scarcely seemed possible since his work on the last of the small hand instruments for *Delusion of the Fury* some three years earlier. Things were now different thanks to the presence in his Encinitas home of a lodger, Jim Aitkenhead, who had just finished three years of military service, one of them in Vietnam. In early November Aitkenhead moved into the basement of Partch's house, where he lived rent-free in exchange for helping with everyday tasks. As Bill Symons was by this time no longer in the Partch Foundation's employ, Aitkenhead became the composer's main assistant in building and repairing instruments.

By the end of the year he and Partch were at work on a new Boo, using giant mottled Japanese Mozo bamboo open at both ends, producing a different tone quality than that of the original instrument. "I think it is going to be beautiful," Partch told Emil Richards, "and that it will STAY IN TUNE!"[43] As the layout and notation were the same as that for Boo I, the instruments were designed to be interchangeable, though "at least to the ear," Partch wrote, "Boo II is a different instrument."[44] Danlee Mitchell was less impressed by the result, regarding the instrument as "the activity of an old man just keeping his hand in."[45] The successful completion of the project briefly encouraged Partch to think about composition again, and he told Betty Freeman that he had promised "to write a score for a film about Antoni Gaudí, the celebrated Catalonian architect."[46] This "promise," made to his San Francisco friend Thad Kusmierski—who had filmed a lot of Gaudí's work in Barcelona—was sadly not kept.

Partch and Aitkenhead worked at other tasks in the following months. The blocks on the Quadrangularis Reversum were replaced with padouk, giving a much increased ring time, and the blocks on the Bass Marimba were replaced with new vertical grain Sitka spruce, which restored the pulverized blocks to their "earlier pristine resonance."[47] Aitkenhead recalls that work usually started by 7 A.M., even if Partch had been drinking heavily the previous evening, and although Partch's energies were slight they managed to accomplish much by sheer perseverance.[48]

Aitkenhead's presence also helped combat the loneliness Partch was feeling, which his general weariness made harder to bear. He wrote to former ensemble member Dean Drummond that "when people are with me that exhaustion point is seemingly unpredictable—it could be twenty minutes, two hours. The ironic part is that I am lonely, like most elderly persons, that I do like people, but don't quite know how to cope with them, under conditions of dissipating energy."[49] The amount of alcohol he was now consuming made his social behavior rather unpredictable. "Harry was at his best between his first and his third drink," Drummond recalls. "After three drinks it could be touch and go."[50]

During the spring Partch began planning a trip to Hawaii, partly as a revitalizing break ("only my third vacation in about 40 years," he told Lou Harrison)[51] and partly because, at the end of his happy stay there with his sister in the early months of 1922, he had thrown his gardenia lei into the harbor, "meaning that I would come back." He was counting on the assistance of Aitkenhead, who, in addition to his competence with practical tasks, was "a fabulous surfer," and who was thrilled at the prospect. Thanks to Harrison's help, a lecture was arranged for Partch at the University of Hawaii for July 9, largely to "help the financial situation."

In the end the trip was disastrous for him, demanding more energy than he had. "I blame only my bad judgment," he wrote to a friend on his return. "I assumed too much, that I had the energy, that people in Honolulu would guide me to acceptable accommodations."[52] The first night they stayed in "one of those high-rise Waikiki monstrosities,"[53] and although they moved to better accommodation the next night, he had become irascible and his spirits were low. He had "two good moments, seeing the Pali again, and seeing Kaneohe Bay," although he found Waikiki a "horror." The day after his lecture at the university he was taken to the airplane in a wheelchair and he flew back to San Diego.

During the months that followed he had little energy for anything. *Ulysses at the Edge* was recorded in San Diego under the direction of Mitchell, in a version for trumpet (played by Jack Logan), baritone saxophone, Diamond Marimba, Boo, Bass Marimba, Cloud-Chamber Bowls, and speaking voice, and was released the following year on Logan's record *New Music for Trumpet* on the Orion label. The Columbia Records release of *Delusion of the Fury*, long delayed, finally appeared in September as a two-LP set plus a bonus record featuring a demonstration of his instruments. Partch was delighted with the result, and his only reservations concerned details of the liner notes: no listing was given of the individual members of the ensemble (again, as with *Petals*, for "contractual reasons"), and there was no mention at all of Emil Richards who, Partch protested, was "crucial" to the work, as was Linda Schell.[54] Mention was made also of the interest shown in his instruments by the Smithsonian Institution, from whom he had not heard in over a year; and Da Capo Press was mentioned as the publisher of *Genesis of a Music,* the production of which remained in limbo. "This credit I regret more than anything."

This last matter was the only professional activity that aroused the passion of old, but to a largely negative end. Even the involvement of Karl ZoBell during the spring and summer of 1971 had proved ineffective, and through the year more promises had been broken despite Alan Marks's insistence that he was working on the project. During August two letters from ZoBell to Marks produced no response, and on September 1 Partch sent another furious telegram: "Your disrespect for me is beyond my understanding. Send everything back to me. Do I have to get a court order? I want to be able to sleep at night." Marks telephoned ZoBell and gave an "absolute guarantee" that proofs would be sent to Partch by the middle of the month; but this deadline, too, passed without result. Partch's volleys of temper had less to do with Marks's competence ("you are a good editor," he told him on one occasion, "you force one to think, to try to make better use of words")[55] than with his unreliability and his tendency to make unrealistic promises; their effect was to increase the sense of bitterness Partch sometimes felt about his whole career.

Partch's professional disillusionment is evident in his exchange of letters with the young Californian composer Peter Garland, who had founded a new magazine entitled *Soundings,* conceived as a forum for the work of younger composers and that of older, neglected figures that Garland perceived as constituting an indigenously American tradition, including Partch himself, Dane Rudhyar, Cage, Varèse, Nancarrow, Harrison, and others. The first issue of *Soundings,* in January 1972, contained a reprinting of Partch's old Madison article "Show Horses in the Concert Ring," and the second issue, in April, boasted the first publication of the 1968 score of *Barstow* and the 1960 article "A Somewhat Spoof." However sincere Garland's admiration for him, Partch was concerned about the inclusion of his work in a magazine such as *Soundings,* which presented a broad spectrum of American new music, much of it seeming to smack of what he considered Cagean gimmickry. He told Garland that the people who ran the magazine *Source,* which had published the score of *Petals* in 1967, "are very charming, but after about the fourth issue I had to conclude that it was becoming its own kind of monolith, and I lost interest. Focusing upon the drafting board, which may or may not have much relation to anything heard, and upon chance . . . these activities indicate abdication on the part of both composers, so called, and their publisher."[56] Clearly Partch felt some personal hurt in the fact that Cage's work was so overwhelmingly influential, especially in California, while his own, although respected, was very much more difficult to assimilate. He told Garland that when one of the composers featured in *Soundings* "speaks of Cagean innovations,"

> I laugh and say, come again?
>
> What?—tickling a big brass gong with a toothpick? Drinking carrot juice with an amplified gullet? Prepared piano? . . . Zen Buddhism? (A gimmick that has contributed substantially to a couple of careers.) Showmanship? Fine. Innovation? Not for me.
>
> At a private affair someone asked, "What do you think about Zen Buddhism?" I replied, "I don't give a fuck about Zen Buddhism," and someone at the back of the room muttered, "There is a true Zen Buddhist!"[57]

He told Garland that in the midst of this "absence of idea," "perhaps I do not belong in any case, but if so I would not like to feel that I was invited to a party, then abandoned. Please—please—abandon me *before* publication—not *in* publication."

This rebuke, and Partch's other complaints about slips in the proofreading of his articles, wounded Garland deeply, all the more so because Garland felt he had done Partch, whom he revered, a disservice. Writing to apologize, Partch remarked that "I have no right to take out my hurts on you";[58] and two months later, after another such reprimand: "I hate myself for causing you further emotional turmoil . . . I know you tried hard. Why didn't I keep my silly mouth shut!!!! Please forgive . . . I know what emotional pain is, because I am emotional too."[59]

Partch's irascibility was by now never far below the surface. Some of it was vented on Jim Aitkenhead, whose mild-mannered demeanor was rarely ruffled by his aggressive behavior, and for a time on Aitkenhead's girlfriend Nancy, who moved into the Encinitas basement late in 1971. Once while Jim was surfing, during their early-morning visits to Moonlight Beach, Nancy managed to get Partch into conversation. Later that day he left Jim a note saying he had wanted to stuff her mouth with seaweed to shut her up. Perhaps ashamed at his own misogyny he relented, and as a gesture of acceptance of Nancy picked them a bunch of flowers, attaching a note which he signed "from an old bastard to a pair of young lovers." He even attended their subsequent wedding, grumbling that the last wedding he had been to was his sister's, and that he didn't plan to attend any more.[60]

By now Partch struck several people who came into contact with him as a schizoid mixture of an old-style gentleman, rugged and proud but also charming, and a cantankerous old drunk. Danlee Mitchell, who admits he often could not predict or understand Partch's lightning mood swings, has commented:

> Harry was a very responsible person. He could scream at people toward the end of his life for doing dumb, immature things. He would fly off the handle—but not for too long or too deeply—when people wouldn't carry out a job in the most efficient amount of time. He was a completely unrepressed individual, never holding back any reaction to his environment, never suppressing anything. And yet you always knew where you stood with Harry. His tantrums would end, and later he would apologize to you with an equal amount of concern and care. Harry would never use something like guilt as a weapon of power. In fact, he hated all games of that sort. He was probably the most sane person you'd ever run across, and his fierce dedication never worked to the detriment of someone else.[61]

Kenneth Gaburo, who was teaching at UCSD, occasionally visited Partch in Encinitas, but found the experience dispiriting: "It was always very strained. It was like visiting somebody on his deathbed. I just could not face all of that and the immensity of his legacy that I could see was being corrupted already. I mean, he was corrupting it. One of his smaller marimbas was being used as an end table. It was sticky with wine that had been spilled and cigarettes were put out on it. . . . I couldn't take it."[62]

It was against this backdrop of petty but exasperating professional frustrations, declining health, and a volatile temper fueled by increasing alcohol consumption, that the final emotional drama of Partch's life was played out. At the beginning of November 1971 he flew to San Francisco for a performance of Lou Harrison's *Young Caesar*. Upon his return, enthusing about the work, Partch met Betty Freeman for lunch. During this meeting she put to him an idea that had been on her mind: to produce a documentary film on him, and to commission a new work from him for the purpose. Overwhelmed by the idea, he wrote a few days later that her gesture was "almost too much, far too generous."[63] Her intention to commission a new work was also a pretext for giving him money, which he needed badly but refused to accept as charity.

Moreover, Freeman had found a prospective director for the film: Stephen Pouliot, a master's student at the film school of the University of Southern California. One afternoon in November, Pouliot drove down from his home in Santa Monica to Encinitas and parked in Partch's driveway on Sunset Drive. When there was no reply at the front door he began wandering around. Standing on Partch's "patio roof, below which was his garage/workshop,"

Pouliot "looked over the railing and Harry walked out of the garage. He shielded his eyes from the sun, and said—'Well . . . it's the Strangford Apollo!'" Pouliot's profile brought to Partch's mind the Greek statue of a young man, from about 490 B.C., that he had fallen in love with at the British Museum nearly forty years earlier.[64] The member and both arms had been broken off the statue, and even though Pouliot "was still blessed with [those] three important limbs," the identification was important to Partch's perception of his young friend. He told Betty Freeman that he liked Pouliot "a lot. His presence is comforting, reassuring. Because he is gentle, and his reactions are always considerately human."[65] What he didn't at first tell her, but what was painfully clear to Partch himself from the very start, was that he had fallen in love.

Stephen Pouliot was twenty-five years old, tall, bearded, handsome, a sensitive conversationalist. He, for his part, was charmed by Partch, though his feelings had none of the desperate intensity that marked Partch's for him. The considerable gap in their ages—some forty-five years—was central to Pouliot's view of their friendship. Shortly after their meeting Pouliot wrote: "You've become a special person in my life. You are the warm wisdom I long for in my restlessness. . . . I would hate to think we could share nothing but respect. Let me be your friend."[66] And a month later: "In this year of 1971 I count you as a gift—priceless and patient, a wise river which has held back the flood of time

Partch in his garden at Encinitas, California, with Stephen Pouliot, 1972. Unsigned photograph, Harry Partch Estate Archive.

with humor, and a get-along grace. You are a thing of the spirit, and you shall be with me."[67]

In Stephen Pouliot, Partch saw, as he later put it, "a universal guy and a symbol—of timeless youth and timeless beauty, in body and spirit."[68] His lifelong attraction to male beauty, which Pouliot now personified, was one of the most poignant expressions of his belief in the human race. Personally, Partch was swept away by Pouliot's "loving and gentle nature," his "unfailing encouragement and dedication."[69] At the same time, especially given that the two were to work together on the film project in the months ahead, he felt torn about making an open declaration of his love. The tone of Pouliot's early letters to Partch is warm and caring, but not flirtatious: he was in any case involved with someone else at the time, and although aware of Partch's interest in him, felt there was no question of entering into a sexual relationship.

Pouliot came to Encinitas again for the weekend of January 15–16, 1972, to discuss some preliminary ideas for the film. Among the current projects Partch showed him was a New Harmonic Canon I, an instrument with alternating redwood and Sitka spruce soundboards and a blue-tinted Plexiglas base, designed to be set for the tunings for *Petals* and *Delusion*. With Jim Aitkenhead's help he was beginning work on a New Kithara I and starting to rebuild the two Chromelodeons. Pouliot immediately thought to film Partch in his workshop. Although Partch's movements were now slow, and he needed Aitkenhead's help in lifting even moderately sized pieces of wood, his old skill with tools was still there, as was the aggressively physical way he caressed each piece while working with it.

By the early spring planning was well under way for the film. Pouliot had written on February 21 proposing to start shooting, but Partch claimed to be camera shy and needed some more coaxing. Pouliot drove down occasionally to see him, and spent time "visiting his favorite beaches, listening to his stories, meeting his friends."[70] Many years later Pouliot recalled how they would sit out "in his yard, late at night, the two of us nursing cups of iced milk laced with Eagle Rock brandy, Harry's favorite panacea. He'd tell stories about his hobo days, of Spartan soldiers and their loyalty to one another, and a favorite tale, about the rebel Timotheos, a young Greek musician [banished] because he strung his lyre with too many strings . . . you could hear waves breaking far below on Swami beach. Midnight trains would whistle by, and the jasmine Harry had planted on the porch trellis filled our breath with cool perfumed air."[71] During a visit one weekend in mid-March they drove to the mountain town of Julian, about an hour outside San Diego. It was the beginning of apple

Partch in his workshop, Encinitas, 1972. Photo by Betty Freeman.

blossom season, and Partch amazed Pouliot by pointing out and naming a wide array of wildflowers, explaining their medicinal uses. Back home in Santa Monica Pouliot wrote that the weekend was "a memorable one for me. Many ups and downs to be sure, but I think we came closer to knowing each other than ever before. Thank you for being patient, and thank you for sharing your home and love with me. Apple blossoms and wild spring lilacs—the closest I will come to an eastern spring."[72]

Pouliot brought the cameraman John Monsour to Encinitas to explore the possibilities of filming in Partch's instrument-cluttered home. Since Partch gave up the studio in Solana Beach the instruments had dispersed, some to San Diego State University, where Danlee Mitchell was still teaching, and quite a few others to Partch's home. Partch offered to tidy up his studio for the filming, but Betty Freeman assured him that "both Steve and I do not want to pretty up the workshop—it must stay exactly as it is when you use it. You are not a neat housekeeper and it would be false to have an immaculate workshop as if you were Mondrian. You are you and that is what we want in the film, not a Beverly Hills housekeeper like me. So please, leave it exactly like it is, it's fine."[73]

Partch had wanted to celebrate Pouliot's birthday with him, on April 1, but Pouliot had business in Dallas at the beginning of the month. He wrote to reassure Partch that he would visit him at the end of the week: "Will be down

Friday afternoon [April 7] to light garage. Will have a quiet talk. Save the cake and candles till then." And with reference to a remark in Partch's most recent letter, he added: "Will be anxious to see what's hanging in the window."[74]

Hanging in the window, when Pouliot arrived in Encinitas, was a five-part sculpture that Partch had made as a "gentle gesture" for his birthday, which he called "The Garden of Eden." Top to bottom it consisted of a "serpent" (a large, S-shaped gourd); a sky-blue Plexiglas disc, representing the heavens; an "apple" (a large, round gourd almost a foot in diameter); eleven tuned pieces of bamboo; and a transparent surfboard dangle (a multicolored piece of resin, the collected drippings from the surfboard manufacturing shop in Solana Beach). The various pieces were linked together by heavy strands of blue yarn that matched the intensity of "the heavens." The symbolism of the sculpture was clarified in an accompanying letter, in which Partch made some of its imagery graphically clear. The bamboo pieces were "eleven stiff pricks of varying sizes" and the surfboard dangle represented "22 balls, of course." He went on to explain how the tuned bamboo pieces coupled with their resonators in the most sexually explicit of all his corporeal metaphors:

> The optimum resonance of a stiff prick occurs when the *blow* tone is virtually identical with the *tongue* tone.
>
> To ascertain the blow tone blow on the head of the prick. Keep this in your mind, and the best way to do this is to sing it.
>
> To ascertain the tongue tone, grab the prick and use it to strike something firm but soft, like the edge of your hand.
>
> . . . the blow tone and the tongue tone must couple. And I am speaking scientifically and acoustically. This is not an invention, an obscene farrago.[75]

The sculpture, with its symbolic recreation of the Biblical tale of a garden of beauty and contentment invaded by sexual temptation, made abundantly clear Partch's true longings for Pouliot. During the visit Partch told him quite directly: "You are the last of my loves." Pouliot wrote to him from Santa Monica on the Tuesday following: "I shall always remember that, Harry. That is what the Garden of Eden really says. That's what we're all about."[76]

Filming began in April, Pouliot and Monsour adapting to Partch's unusual schedule. He was often awake by 5 A.M., went bodysurfing at Swami's Beach around 6, worked until 10, and observed a mandatory rest period from 11 A.M. to 2 P.M. They shot sequences of Partch talking in his garden, and Pouliot recorded interviews with him which eventually became voiceovers in the film. They filmed Partch in his workshop, assisted by Mitchell and Aitkenhead, building two new instruments: New Kithara I, which was designed largely as a replacement for the original Kithara and which, Partch felt, was "an infinitely improved instrument, with much greater resonance"; and the Mbira Bass Dyad, "an extension, in the direction of much lower tones, of the tongue-with-resonator idea implicit in the Boos."[77] The instrument used two Osage orange blocks over large resonators, but although used in the film it remained "an experiment that is far from complete." On May 7 he wrote to Betty Freeman: "We saw the footage in workshop Saturday night. I think that it is great, but it also frightens me. With so much money and talent and love expended on it I realize the weight of my obligations even more. To perform, perform—always fresh and rested. My confidence is like the waves of the ocean—uncertain, up and down, full and receding."

By now he had been thinking for some months about the music he was to write for the film. On May 27 he completed a "very tentative" draft of the text for the piece, which was to be called *The Dreamer That Remains—A Study in Loving*. The title came from a poem by Roy Campbell, which Partch found at the beginning of Laurens van der Post's book *The Lost World of the Kalahari*.

This first draft of the text was intended to shock. The opening is harmless enough, focusing on Partch himself as the subject of the film, the "dreamer" of the title. The second part begins with his recollections of his childhood in Arizona, making the point that the increased pace of modern life does not allow us time to "loiter together" and to get to "know each another." The narration then drifts into a pointed discussion of a "booklet found inside a Victorian harmonium, entitled—How to Take Good Care of Your Organ," and from there to a discussion of "How to put on your panty hose" ("Never—a quick jerk!," the Male Chorus interjects). This second part was intended to feature a new percussion instrument to be called the Rhythmic Pudenda, and to climax on a chorus to the single word "Bullshit." Uncharacteristically, Partch had envisaged some scenes of female nudity in the film, presumably those involving the pantyhose.[78]

He sent the text to both Freeman and Pouliot. Freeman recalls that she found it "so horrible, with its references to organs and panty hose and jerks that I had to . . . telephone Partch immediately to revise it. Without argument he agreed. . . . I think that when he wrote this first version there was something very wrong, a perversity, in his mind."[79] Pouliot shared her reservations about the crude symbolism of the projected second part for "both personal and commercial" reasons, but reacted more mildly, feeling that the text was simply an unsuccessful attempt at risqué humor. A few days after receiving it he wrote:

"The narration of the 2nd movement is ironic, hip, contemporary, pertinent, and slightly pornographic. It is also confusing. The panty hose, pea, the organ, and the pope—can these be rewritten? I find the basic premise—'Do Not Loiter'—a universal concept. Our love song should be loiter together to know one another. That is so beautiful Harry. Ten years from now that thought will be valid. In the same 10 years the . . . panty hose may well be [a] social artifact."[80]

Partch duly revised the text, removing its offensive content, and work resumed. In June they filmed him picking apricots and yellow limes from the trees in his garden, and recorded more interviews, completing the documentary material for the film. Freeman drove down to see him on June 18 and she and Partch signed a contract for the film, under the terms of which Partch received a fee of $3,000 plus 10 percent of the profits.[81]

With the first stage of the film finished, Partch and Pouliot departed for a long-planned trip to San Francisco, ostensibly so that Partch could show him his old haunts. It was quite clear to Pouliot that Partch had hoped the trip would be an opportunity "to take our friendship in a direction that I didn't want it to go."[82] Danlee Mitchell drove Partch up to Pouliot's home in Santa Monica on July 5.

Partch and Betty Freeman, Encinitas, 1972. Photo by Danlee Mitchell.

Pouliot was out when they arrived, and he returned home to find Partch upset that he had not been there to greet him on arrival. Partch had also been drinking, and Pouliot knew him well enough to sense that trouble was in store. Pouliot had planned to take him out to dinner with a couple of friends, but after Partch's making a scene about having forgotten his tobacco he sensitively suggested that he and Partch go to dinner alone. They drove to Sinbad's restaurant on the Santa Monica pier, where Partch complained most of the evening about the widening beach, the high-rises, and the waitress. "The sunset is beautiful. I enjoy it," Pouliot recounted in his diary, "but am mad at Partch's obstinacy."[83] Back at Pouliot's home Partch sat "out on the balcony on a beach chair" while Pouliot finished packing. "Few words are exchanged. I play [the record of] Lou Harrison's *Pacifika Rondo* to help soothe nerves."[84]

When they arrived in San Francisco they hired a car, packed "a suitcase with booze" in the trunk, and took to the road. Partch was amazed at the high-rise look of the city, and at how much it had changed since his Petaluma days. They headed first for Sausalito, where Partch showed him the Gate 5 building—"a two story tan building," Pouliot noted, "not very impressive but lots of space." They also looked at the houseboats and searched in vain for one of Partch's favorite restaurants, which no longer existed. From Sausalito they traveled north to Inverness and called on the "warm and gracious" Jack and Patty Wright. They stayed one night, at the gentle insistence of Patty, who was delighted to see Partch again. Partch's fondness for them was apparent: on one occasion, in response to Pouliot's remark "When you go, Harry, it'll be the last of the eccentrics," Partch replied "No, there'll always be Jack." The Wrights, with Danlee Mitchell and Betty Freeman, he described to Pouliot as his "family."[85]

The following morning they visited Jack's studio, where they drank apple wine and talked. Pouliot noted in his diary: "Harry learns of [Jean] Varda's death and is disturbed. Many recaps of Varda's potent sex life between paintings." In the evening they went with the Wrights to a local inn, where conversation turned to the arts. Partch recalled "being insulted by Henry Miller and W. H. Auden. Miller listened to Partch's *U.S. Highball* and told him he better stick to music, not to words. Auden, who Partch describes as a megalomaniac, complained that Partch would never replace Mozart. Partch had a caustic comeback. Auden said Nonsense. Partch said Poop. Auden said Pure nonsense. Partch said Pure poop. It ended with Auden calling Partch a despicable, mean man and walking out."

The following afternoon they saw the Onslow Fords. Pouliot thought Gordon "shy, proper," and Jacqueline "a will-o'-the-wisp, elegant . . . the perfect hostess." From Inverness they drove to Petaluma, where they bought a bottle of brandy and had lunch on the corner opposite the apartment complex on the site where the Pioneer Hatchery had been.

Before leaving northern California they paid a visit to Lou Harrison and Bill Colvig in Aptos. Over the previous decade Partch's admiration for Harrison's music had increased steadily. The majority of Harrison's compositions by now used just intonation, and the chromaticism of some of his earlier work— inspired by his studies with Schoenberg, who regarded him among the most talented of his American students—had largely given way to a modal language in which subtleties of intonation could be heard more clearly. Harrison occasionally visited Partch in southern California, where Partch would take him proudly on a tour of his garden, picking lemons and avocados from his trees, or drink with him and discuss tuning.[86]

The visit in Aptos, however, made Pouliot feel "uncomfortable."[87] The tense atmosphere was not helped by an awkward conversation about where Partch and he would sleep; in the end the two hosts pitched a tent in their garden, Partch slept in their room, and Pouliot slept on the living-room couch. Exactly why the atmosphere was so strained around an old friend like Harrison was unclear to Pouliot. Most likely, Partch had hoped to be able to introduce Pouliot as his lover; seeing Harrison in a stable relationship, Partch felt the weight of his own loneliness more intensely than ever.

The San Francisco trip brought to the surface tensions that were developing between the composer and his young friend. Back home in the small hours of July 15 Pouliot poured out his confused feelings in a letter. "I feel cold to myself," he wrote.

> I know my work affects me deeply. The more responsibility I have the more distant I become. And I suppose I have reflected no warmth, or fostered little friendship over the past weeks . . . God forbid—maybe I have vicariously enjoyed torturing you. . . . Perhaps I have taken out my frustrations and loss of hope on you, whom I cherish. . . . I plan to pour myself into my work. . . . I must complete the film for you—my mentor, my wise and gentle friend. I have so often heard you say, "I am repulsive—don't touch me." I consider you beautiful and full of light. But . . . I love from afar much more than I love physically. I am starved for spiritual love. . . . There are many kinds of love, Harry. The Greeks had several names for it, didn't they? I don't know what class ours falls into, but let it be known that it is a love I have for you. It is not a passionate love, but a constant, growing affection. . . . You have talked about your shoulders, your ass, your hair. I give not a fuck about these. I do not put

them up for critique. You are whole, I am whole—and we both function with some help from science. This is all I ask. It is late now, and I must close. I want you to rest in the safety of our home on Sunset Drive. Yes, if I was there I would tuck you in and kiss you goodnight.

The score of *The Dreamer That Remains,* with a revised text, was begun back in Encinitas on July 15 and completed on October 6, despite a bronchial and lung infection which Partch contracted at the end of August and an ulcer which developed in September. The completed work is in two parts: the first was intended for the opening of the film, and the second, "entirely narrative and satirical, contrasting memories of my childhood (1905–1910) with the present," for the end. The day after completing the score he wrote a dedicatory page to Stephen Pouliot, acknowledging him frankly as the inspiration for the music, which he planned to subtitle "My Love Song for Stephen": "This score and the pencil notes that preceded it are Stephen's if he wants them. Stephen lurks behind every thought, every idea, every musical note in the work, in a won-derous way. It would be hypocritical of me to deny his presence, despite the inevitable personal hurts in the process of knowing him." The work was "very simply—an act of adoration for Stephen personally." He showed the dedica-tory page to Pouliot, who wrote on October 11: "In your dedication you mentioned the personal hurt. And I opened the familiar wound again. There is no part of you I hate. My affection is deep and constant. My passion is being faithful to you, and in some way to myself—However faulted accept me as I am." Partch copied the score in October, "Anno Domini 1972 and Anno Plymouth Rock 352." In his urge to testify to his feelings for Pouliot, Partch had forgotten about Betty Freeman, who had, after all, commissioned the music, and on November 1 he wrote a new inscription on her copy of the score: "For my Beloved Producer Betty—that unfailing source of Strength, Belief, Regen-eration—and with the hope that the work is worthy." It is clear that both dedications had validity in his own mind.

The rehearsals and filming for the musical portions of *The Dreamer That Remains* were arranged to take place at San Diego State University, and Partch took the opportunity to end once and for all his uneasy affiliation with UCSD. Back in December 1970 he had protested to Will Ogdon that his reappoint-ment as adjunct professor made no sense: "I am a partial invalid, I've not even been on campus in over a year and a half, I never go out at night, I am in touch with no one on the campus, in or out of the music school."[88] The following March he had written to the chancellor requesting that his name be deleted from all publicity material that implied he was part of the department. And at the end of October 1972, just before filming at San Diego State got under way, he declined a request to write in support of promotion for one of the composers on the faculty at UCSD: "It would be absurd of me to offer comments about 'the needs of our department.' I could have offered precise comments in 1964–65, but I was not permitted. For example, about the slavish insistence on following the newest fashions à la Princeton and Columbia—the fashions of gadgets, computers, with no real corpus of use, experience, maturity, philosophy, to back them up. I know nothing—totally nothing—about your 'needs' now. I do not even want to know."[89]

He was not especially concerned about San Diego State's "needs" either, but they were at least providing Mitchell with a room for his instruments. The performance segments for *The Dreamer That Remains* were shot at the university during Thanksgiving weekend, with an ensemble formed by Mitchell and consisting mostly of students and a few old friends, among them Emil Richards and Jonathan Glasier. New members included the young composer David Dunn, who played the Adapted Viola—"Harry said it sounded like him 40 years ago," Mitchell noted—and "Jack Logan saved the day by conducting."[90] Many of the new players remained friends, as did the sound engineer Mark Hoffman (whom Partch described as "the most dedicated recording engineer I've known since 1954").[91] David Dunn, although still in his teens, had by this time become a valued assistant and "factotum"; "experiencing Partch's dynamic personality and imagination at an early age," he recalls, made a profound impact. "I not only saw the beauty of that, but also the pain and suffering that can come with that type of gift."[92]

The scenario of Part Two of *The Dreamer That Remains* was the closest Partch would ever come to a public statement on the theme of homosexuality. The ostensible subject is simply the increased tempo of modern life, symbolized by the "Do Not Loiter" signs that adorn modern post offices, public buildings, and parks. These are contrasted with the slower pace of life the Narrator recalls from his boyhood in Arizona, the punchline being that today only by becoming one of the "congregated corpses in the funeral parlor" is one finally "permitted to loiter." Betty Freeman raised an objection to the line, "Even in public parks, where a couple of people want to improve the darkness with a little loving," which Pouliot had staged with two young men sitting together on a park bench.[93] Lou Harrison, on seeing the completed film, considered this sequence fairly "out of the closet," feeling that "the clear implication of the work is that [Partch] was objecting to modern barriers against casual male-male sexual encounters."[94] Partch defended the sequence, telling Freeman that it was "light-handed satire," "not *seriously* homosexual . . . we must be allowed our wry humor!"[95]

As a whole, *The Dreamer That Remains* offers a very mild treatment of its homosexual subtheme. Partch's comment that the film indulges in a moment or two of gay "humor"—admittedly, the remark was made to Betty Freeman rather than to one of his gay friends, to whom he might have expressed the matter differently—is a more modest claim than Lou Harrison's statement that the film is "a fairly public and if-you-will political 'coming out.'"[96] We may wonder, though, if the gay content would not have been greater had Partch been given a free hand in the film's production.

Partch had kept an eye on the growing movement for gay rights in the United States since its ostensible beginnings in the Stonewall riots in New York in the summer of 1969. On the one hand, as many friends have testified, Partch approved of the act of personal liberation implicit in the practice of homosexuality, with its radical contestation of the roles and sexual identities that modern society imposes on its members. Harder for him to accept was the gay movement's principal tactic, that of "coming out": the public declaration of one's homosexuality.

Part of his reservation about coming out may be ascribed simply to age. Partch belonged to a generation that did not consider public manifestation of homosexuality at all proper. But it was not simply that as a member of an older generation he felt shy about declaring allegiance with a cause espoused by the young: he felt also that coming out assumed that one had a fixed sexual identity that could confidently be declared in public. In *Bitter Music* he had responded to his hobo friend Pablo's declaration of having once kissed a man by saying that "Any real love is a beautiful experience . . . and real love is apt to fluctuate over the whole idea of sex, and beyond, too"; and his basic attitude—"Who cares who loves who?"—shows little sign of having changed in later years.[97] The act of coming out seemed to him less an avowal of personal liberty than a gesture of political alignment, and thus was of secondary interest to him. Stephen Pouliot recalls that he and Partch never discussed the matter.[98]

By the time of the November filming Partch's attachment to Pouliot had become obsessive and increasingly destructive. The tension between the two during the filming was felt by everyone. They stayed together at the Hitching Post, a hotel on El Cajon Boulevard, not far from San Diego State, where several others involved in the film were staying. One evening Partch fell in his room and injured his right arm. "He called it his 'symbolic death,'" Pouliot recalls. The symbolism was all the more nightmarish because of an incident that had happened the night before. After an exhausting day's filming, Pouliot was awoken in the small hours by the sound of arguing in Partch's room, adjacent to his.

> I heard two people arguing in the other room. And I sort of went back to sleep because people went in and out of this place all day long. But then I woke up and I sat up and . . . listened to the argument—there was a very ferocious argument going on; and one person was Harry, saying . . . I listened because the argument was about me, my name was being mentioned, and . . . Harry's voice was saying how much he liked me, and this other voice was saying that I must be destroyed and blotted out. And suddenly I realized that it was the same person. And I was scared to death. . . . I finally fell asleep towards morning. When I got up Harry was not there and I went to Danlee and I told him this; and when I came back there was an ice-pick [Partch's metal pipe cleaner] on my pillow. And then I moved out of the room.[99]

When Pouliot recounted this story to various of Partch's friends after his death it met with diverse reactions. Some took it as an instance of the destructive side of Partch's passionate nature, others as an almost childish cry for attention (among them Lou Harrison, who added that "children are terribly violent").[100] Still others regarded it as a sign of mental instability, as though the tensions in Partch's personality—exacerbated by his frustrated longings for Pouliot—had finally pushed him beyond the edge of his reason.

The practice of speaking in two voices was noted thirty years before by Partch's Big Sur friend Preston Tuttle, who remembers Partch "talking to himself" and "trying to resolve a problem by taking different sides"; Tuttle even recalls "Harry encouraging me to use such a technique in settling some personal problem I was wrestling with." He does not believe, however, that an incident such as the one described by Pouliot indicates that Partch, at the end of his life, "had become psychotic in his uses of these techniques. He remained the same 'paranoid' Harry, I should imagine."[101] For Pouliot himself the incident underlined his feeling that "there was always something unreal to me about Harry . . . an otherworldliness." Acknowledging many years later that what he heard "that night at the Hitching Post *did* terrify me . . . I can still recall being paralyzed with fear, thinking that Harry had actually conjured up demonic spirits or the devil himself," he stresses: "I can't imagine Harry ever hurting me. He used that ice-pick to clean out or unclog his pipe. Maybe that was the symbolism—cleaning me out of his life."[102]

The filming was completed under some difficulty and both men went their separate ways. Partch's warm feelings for Pouliot were still with him, and on December 4 he recopied the dedicatory page to *The Dreamer That Remains*. As his right arm was still painful he was obliged to use his left hand, noting that "true love is ambidextrous."[103]

By the end of 1972 the whole film was "in the can," but problems arose during the editing process. Partch was sometimes surprisingly uncooperative, and Freeman, in particular, felt things would be easier without him around. The tensions came to a head on December 26. "Betty told me, in effect, that I could get lost," Partch wrote to Pouliot. "I walked away in pain and depression. It was a traumatic shock."[104] The problem, ostensibly, hinged around the wish—on the part of almost everyone involved with the film other than Partch himself— to allow short fragments of his music to be used as background music to passages of him talking. "I am talking about 'background music,'" he complained to Pouliot.

> When I talk, theoretically, about integration, you and Betty are with me, but when you—by every virtue of reason, are asked to integrate—you exclude the composer. And this with a film about his work, his life, his integrity. . . . I will not be what Tantalus [the company that acted as co-producer in marketing the film] wants to make me. The fact is that I am far more interesting with my integrity intact.[105]

January 1973 passed in a furious silence. Freeman strongly advised Pouliot to leave Partch alone to cool off, thinking that no further contact at this point would be best. Meanwhile, Partch took his enforced inactivity as an opportunity to rethink his situation. For more than a year he had been considering moving down to San Diego to be closer to Mitchell, on whom he was increasingly dependent, and to San Diego State, where his instruments were now to remain. At the end of November 1971 Freeman had given him her share of the house in Encinitas, which they had owned in joint tenancy. It was, of course, a very considerable gift, but she approached it matter-of-factly, telling him: "I'm very happy that I can make this gift as I know you can put the money to good use. My thanks are in the joy your recording of 'Delusion' is giving me—how can I measure this against an abstraction of green printed paper?"[106] He sold the house to a musician friend from UCSD, and in January 1973 moved into a house that Mitchell had found for him at 4851 Felton Street in the Normal Heights area of San Diego. But the place was a considerable let-down. "The house I found is turning out to be a real lemon," Mitchell admitted to friends; "even I am disgusted with the place and should have had my head examined for buying it at the height of filming."[107] Partch himself, with problems with the film hanging in the air, was "very disagreeable and abrasive," Mitchell commented, "and I don't blame him."

For some six weeks there was no communication between Partch and Pouliot, "except haphazardly through Danlee and Mark [Hoffman] as go-betweens."[108] The complete cut-off was hard for both men. At the end of January Pouliot had written a long letter to Partch which Freeman urged him not to send. Finally, on February 4 Partch sent letters to the two of them, accusing them of having misled him into a production that, with its short sequences and background music, was too reminiscent of a commercial television documentary. He was also outraged by the fact that the second part of his score had been cut in the middle and a segment of further narration interpolated. He insisted on his right to veto decisions made by them or by Tantalus Films, and ended by suggesting that they would "live to regret your ill-considered dismissal of me—giving me the guillotine."[109] His explosion of anger had the effect of reopening communication, and letters arrived from Freeman and Pouliot in reply.

The next few weeks were very tense for all concerned. Pouliot wrote on February 21: "I am in such a dejected state that every new bit of correspondence just adds to the confusion. I can only wonder what will be in tomorrow's mail? A new threat? A more powerful bolt of criticism? My hope is that the mails will be empty so I can rest." The exchange had the gradual effect of putting the matter into better perspective for Partch, though with considerable hurt to Pouliot in the process. "The great joy of creation has been taken from me," he wrote. "I feel disgraced as a director when I need encouragement and faith in my career. . . . I will always respect you for your work and for the endurance of your vision. I thank you for all the good times we have shared during the past eight months. Perhaps in time it is only those moments I shall remember."[110]

Partch was finally shaken out of his anger by Pouliot's moving and dignified letter. On February 26 he wrote to Freeman, in great confusion: "I would never condemn the film. Too much devotion and dedication went into it, from several quarters. Anyhow, I couldn't condemn something that I have never experienced. I have said this to Stephen, as plainly as I know how. I want him to have exactly what he chooses to have. The turmoil must end. I would like to see it, and I am sure I will approve. I've always been sure of this, but I had no opportunity. Please forget about me."[111] *The Dreamer That Remains* was given a preview showing on March 25, 1973, at the Unicorn Cinema in La Jolla. Three days later Partch wrote to a friend that "I cannot talk about the value of the content, but I think that it is beautiful film art."[112]

Partch on the set for *The Dreamer That Remains,* San Diego, 1972. The instruments, in a spiral from bottom left, are Chromelodeon II (with Adapted Guitar II on top); Cloud-Chamber Bowls; New Kithara I; Quadrangularis Reversum; Ektaras; Eucal Blossom; Gourd Tree; Mbira Bass Dyad; Harmonic Canon I and New Harmonic Canon I; and in the center, behind Partch, Harmonic Canon III. Photo by Betty Freeman.

The Dreamer That Remains is a deeply moving and dignified film portrait, part documentary and part performance, which captures a sense of Partch's passionate intensity and something of his mordant vein of humor. The music he wrote for the film seems more like a postscript to his life's work than any new beginning. Throughout, the instruments of the ensemble—which number fifteen, omitting the usual staples of his percussion (Diamond Marimba, Bass Marimba, and Marimba Eroica), but including the New Kithara I, New Harmonic Canon I, Boo II, the Mbira Bass Dyad, and the Ektaras used in *Delusion*—have the dignity of funeral stelae given them by the composer's death so soon thereafter.

The film is very intense throughout, and the close-up impact of Partch's rage and zest as he recounts childhood memories and hobo lore, together with the imposing images of the dark wood, bright orange, green, tarnished plum red, and violet of the instruments, set against a pallid white backdrop, makes for a powerfully emotive experience. Despite the film's occasional gaucheries, Pouliot managed to capture in *The Dreamer That Remains* a real if fleeting sense of the beauty of Partch's instruments in performance, and succeeded in conveying a true image of the man himself—embarrassing, inspiring, exasperating, larger than life.

Toward the end of the film Pouliot included a sequence of Partch talking in his garden in Encinitas about the future of his work. He expresses the wish that the work be remembered for its own virtues, quite independently of the struggles and frustrations of its creator. "I would choose to be anonymous. Of course! I'm thinking of those fantastic cave drawings in southern France and in northern Spain, at Altamira I think it is. And there's no author there! And what a treasure they are! And who cares who did them, how many thousands of years ago. Of course, I'm not saying that anything I do is going to last that long. But who cares what the name was!"[113]

The reactions to this apparently self-effacing remark were various, even among those who had played in the film. Jon Szanto has argued that Partch's wish for anonymity was a strong affirmation of belief in what he had achieved, and that his was a private struggle which could now be laid to rest. "The music is so unique, so expensive to perform—since it can be performed only on the fragile instruments he made, which cost a bundle just to move—that maybe the music should be like Harry. Let it rest. It's done its thing. He did it, and it was great. End of movie. Credits. Like the cave painters, this was Harry's moment, and now it's gone."[114] David Dunn, to the contrary, feels that Partch's statement was a dramatic flourish intended as a deliberate promotion of his work, which should thus be promoted vehemently as a result. "You must remember the context in which Partch made the statement. He put it *on the record*, in a film about his work. . . . The time has come to get beyond glorification and deification of the man, which do him an extreme injustice, and begin to take his work seriously, looking at both its strengths and weaknesses . . . we should get beyond all the rhetoric and try to see what is actually there in Partch's work."[115] The debate embodies, in microcosm, the issues that have surrounded the legacy even to the present day.

By the spring of 1973 Partch's energies were so slight that any further professional activities were beyond him. Before he left Encinitas he had received a visit from the distinguished Hungarian composer György Ligeti, who found his work "very exciting" and proposed a performance of his music in Europe—among other places, at the Holland Festival. Partch wrote to the festival organizers to pursue the matter, but given the state of his health any such idea was wishful thinking. Diminishing energy also prevented his accepting an invitation to visit Amherst College in Massachusetts in June, to receive the degree of Doctor of Music *honoris causa*.

And yet he had not lost sight of his lifelong vision. Responding to a discouraged letter from Peter Garland, he wrote to "comment gently" on Garland's creative frustrations, "hoping that I may help a little":

> I must part with you when you say—" . . . there's virtually nothing left, nothing retrievable from the European past, no signs along the way, and nothing to lean on." I've said it many times, but I'll say it again. In three thousand years the West has abandoned values, beautiful and significant things, that in toto are at least as important as what we have preserved. But it is tough—no instruments, the culture, the milieu are absent. But they can be re-created or imagined. With Oriental music you don't have to re-create or imagine. In either case what you come up with is something new.[116]

In April Jonathan Cott, one of the best-known young American music journalists, came to San Diego to interview him. "The first thing that distinguishes Partch's home from any other on the block," Cott noted, "is a strange sign hanging on the door: 'Occupant is a Heathen Chinee./ Missionaries at this door will/ face the Dowager Empress/ and another Boxer Rebellion/ Please do not disturb/ 11 A.M.–2 P.M./ MISSIONARIES NEVER.'" "His living room looks a bit untogether," Cott went on, "but comfortably so: a Chinese coolie hat and a Balinese shadow puppet [a present from Betty Freeman] on the wall and a table filled with sharpened colored pencils, black pepper containers, post cards, jumbo Gem clips . . . and several books (including *Japan's Imperial Conspiracy* and *Maximum Security: Letters from Prison,* edited by Eve Pell—both of which Partch has been reading avidly)."[117] Despite Partch's protestations that he was "sick to death" of his career, Cott conducted an interview with him which appeared in *Rolling Stone* a year later.

Early in August 1973 Partch moved a couple of blocks, to 4809 Felton Street. He wrote to James Jacobs, his old friend from Madison days, that it was "the best living abode I've had in many years. A small lot, but landscaped to death, and I can't keep it up. It is only one long block to a fair shopping center."[118] A postcard dated September 8 arrived at his new home from Stephen Pouliot, in part as an acknowledgment of their reconciliation: "Just thinking of you," Pouliot wrote, "and hoping you are well, settled, and turning toward enclosures." This last reference was to a new piece of music that was on Partch's mind, a work that he intended to be his last. "He said," Pouliot recalls, "that like Anaïs Nin, he'd looked upon his work as a letter to the world; and the last thing he'd like to do was an enclosure. And he would have called this *The Enclosures*."[119] The idea remained with Partch for many months. Phil Keeney, a young musician friend who arrived in San Diego in February 1974 and who lived with him for a time, helping take care of him, recalls that Partch wanted to build another instrument for the piece and to retune another organ to a Pythagorean enharmonic scale.[120]

Throughout the year he grew progressively weaker. On January 4, 1974, he wrote to Betty Freeman: "I have two new doctors, an internist and a neurologist. They are trying to get to the bottom of my growing weakness and six years of stumbling and falling. I've had about six weeks of the fanciest tests of my life. I have an a-rhythmic heart, an arhythmic and a-symmetrical brain, and almost anytime I expect to hear that I am really a-musical as all hell." And a month later he told Samuel Mitnick, his new editor at Da Capo Press, which had resumed work on the republication of *Genesis of a Music:* "My health continues to deteriorate—a straight statement of fact. A series of minor strokes has left me much weakened, but I will offer you no sentimental garbage."[121]

It began to seem, in the new year, as though the world was finally catching up with him. He had received a visit from Herman Pedtke, inventor of the Scalatron, an electronic keyboard designed to accommodate microtonal tunings— the very instrument he had dreamed of as long ago as 1945 in Madison. Partch was fascinated by the instrument, but noted to a friend that his work had gone in a very different direction in the years since, and now involved "far more than a microtonal scale."[122] To another friend he added mournfully that the Scalatron was "just what I needed. Thirty years too late."[123] Toward the end of March he was visited by Ben Johnston, who was passing through San Diego on tour. They spent a whole day together, talking of many things, including an integrated notation system that Johnston had developed for microtonal just intonation, the very project that Partch himself had left unresolved after his experiments of 1928–33. Partch seemed "sympathetic and interested," Johnston recalls.[124] There was an equally valedictory air about the visit the same month from the musicologist Vivian Perlis, who interviewed Partch for the Oral History Project on American Music at Yale University. And in May the composer Roger Reynolds visited, inviting him to take part in an experimental workshop at UCSD beginning in October. Partch agreed, but made no secret of his poor health. Some weeks later the prospectus arrived, and he felt "despair" at being "plunged again into the vortex of tuning, repair, rehearsals," and could not face it.[125]

In the spring of 1974 rehearsals for a revival of *The Bewitched* got under way at San Diego State University, directed by Danlee Mitchell.[126] Most of the members of the ensemble for *The Dreamer That Remains* played in the work and several came to pay regular visits. To the young musicians Partch was a delight—unpredictable, outrageous, and generous. Randy Hoffman and Jon Szanto recall Partch preparing mint juleps for himself and the two of them one morning before 11 A.M.—"a tall glass full of bourbon, an ice cube, and a leaf of crushed mint," as Szanto describes it—and neither of them could drink it all. That night Partch phoned Mark Hoffman to complain that Randy and Jon were nothing more than "Plymouth Rock puritans."[127]

In the middle of June, a week before Partch's birthday, Stephen Pouliot saw him for what proved to be the last time. Partch was trying, with help from Phil Keeney, to transcribe rhythms from a recording of Balinese music, but the task proved beyond his limited energies. Pouliot remembers that "he was so weak, it just killed me to look at him."[128] Partch "sat on the handcrafted couch he had built of driftwood and rope. Propped up with cushions, and smoking his ever-present pipe, he . . . read chapters of *The Family,* the pop biography of mass killer Charlie Manson and the gang. Occasionally, when something in the book hit his sense of irony and wit, he'd read lines or paragraphs out loud to me. I recall that he got a kick out of the use of the word 'gobble,' the family's euphemism for sex. Contrast this with his weekly commitment to 'The Waltons,' a television series Harry found enjoyable because the lead character, John Boy, reminded him of his youth, and the security of a close family life that apparently he never experienced."[129] Pouliot had maintained a regular, warm, loving correspondence with Partch ever since *The Dreamer That Remains* had been completed, but the fire had gone out of Partch's replies: the passions were dimming.

In June Da Capo Press sent him a check for $375, which represented the second half of his advance on *Genesis of a Music,* due upon publication. A month later the book finally appeared, four years later than originally promised, and Partch joyfully and often light-heartedly inscribed copies for those close to him. Perhaps most touching of all was Danlee Mitchell's copy, which he inscribed simply "To Danlee—the *sine qua non.*"

Those close to him worried that his constitution would not stand up much longer given the amount of alcohol he was consuming. Betty Freeman told him so quite sternly on several occasions, and on August 13 Partch replied:

> I am quite a different person from you, Betty. You seem to revel in people and sometimes in large numbers.
>
> With me they create terrible tensions, and especially when I am already somewhat the center of attention. You are never around during the long weeks and months when I am alone. I drink, then, to relieve the pain.
>
> Doctors have *never* found anything wrong with my liver. If I drank as much as you seem to think I'd have been dead of cirrhosis years ago.
>
> . . . According to my present doctor, as with those in January, my trouble spins from a long history of heart trouble and hypertension. Liquor during times of intolerable tension has probably prolonged my life. My excessive weakness and my tendency to stumble and fall—no, the initial reason is not liquor—result in hardening of the arteries in my brain—visions swim before my eyes—when I am totally sober.

He died three weeks later, on the morning of Tuesday, September 3, 1974, alone in his home on Felton Street. The immediate cause of death was listed on the death certificate as acute cardiac failure. His body was found on his bedroom floor that afternoon by Phil Keeney.

Three years earlier, Partch had written to his friend Michael Craden, quoting lines that Craden had written to him. "Dearest Mike: 'Listen to the sound as it disappears, it is going home to rest, to sleep in silence.' I do not want a stone at my head in the ground, I want to be at the bottom of the Pacific, sometime. But if some misguided soul insists on one your words would be all I would want."[130] In accordance with his wishes, Danlee Mitchell had Partch's body cremated and his ashes scattered over the Pacific.

Epilogue

On September 22, 1974, less than three weeks after the composer's death, a Harry Partch Film Festival was organized at the San Francisco Museum of Art. Three films were screened: *The Dreamer That Remains, Music Studio,* and *Rotate the Body in All Its Planes.* Following the event, a memorial meeting was held for Partch at the home of Lou Harrison's mother in Redwood City. Some fourteen people were present, including Betty Freeman, Danlee Mitchell, Stephen Pouliot, Lou Harrison, Bill Colvig, Phil Keeney, Jack and Patty Wright, and Francis Crawford. The intention was simply to burn some incense in the composer's honor and to exchange stories and reminiscences over a glass of wine. The tape recording of the meeting, which still survives, is evidence of the warmth of affection in which he was held by all those present.

In the months following Partch's death several obituaries and tributes appeared in print. Perhaps the most prophetic, from our vantage point today, was a talk given at the University of California, San Diego, in January 1975 by Ben Johnston. Johnston's talk, subsequently published as "The Corporealism of Harry Partch," was intended in

Harry Partch, Encinitas, 1971. Unsigned
photograph, Harry Partch Estate Archive.

part to sound an alarm bell. Johnston declared that Partch's legacy would not
simply take care of itself: an immense and concerted effort needed to be made
by all those concerned to ensure "the rescue of his life-work, which could easily
slide into oblivion":

> More than is usually the case there is after Harry Partch's death little certainty that
> any continuity will result from his life's efforts. . . . A very great and original artist
> has died leaving a rich but fragile heritage. There is a Harry Partch Foundation, but
> as yet that guarantees perilously little. Try to imagine the expert man-hours and
> diverse materials it would take to duplicate his many and complex instruments, even
> to get one extra set. Then, maintenance problems would supervene, including
> housing, storage, and rehearsal space, available over a long enough time to get
> beyond first performances and premiere productions. The problem staggers concep-
> tion.[1]

The whole subject of the custody and maintenance of Partch's legacy—his
instruments, manuscripts, recordings and writings—has been a matter of in-

tense concern to the members of Partch's extended "family," and others, ever since his death. The uniqueness of that legacy, its many and complex demands, and above all its fragility and mortality, have given the matter an urgency that has inflamed passions and given rise to controversy. In an important sense, Partch himself had placed the matter squarely in the hands of Danlee Mitchell. In the terms of his will, his estate was now the personal property of Mitchell, and even though Betty Freeman had several times tried to change his mind, Partch's decision stands as a testament to the devotion Mitchell had shown to his music, through thick and thin, since 1956.

Partch's decision also makes a significant statement about the relative importance he attached to the several facets of his legacy. The primary sense in which Mitchell had been indispensable to him was in the performance of his music, in the training of musicians, and in the maintenance of instruments. Other concerns—the publication of scores, for example, which Ben Johnston, Peter Yates and Peter Garland, in their different ways, were keen to oversee—could well have been left in the hands of others. Yet rather than fragment his legacy, Partch left everything to Mitchell, knowing full well that no one individual could attend with equal competence to the many aspects of his life's work.

The subject of what exactly Mitchell's responsibilities as Partch's heir amount to has been rife with misunderstanding. The widespread expectation seems to have been that Mitchell should be to Partch what Robert Craft was to Stravinsky: not simply a close friend, a daily companion, and professional assistant, nor simply someone who would take over the responsibilities of rehearsing and conducting performances, all of which roles Mitchell had fulfilled admirably; but also someone who would document Partch's life and work, and see his manuscripts both musical and literary through publication. In addition to all this, it was somehow assumed—and here the expectations became vague and quite unrealistic—that Mitchell would help bring into being a permanent studio and workshop space where Partch's instruments could be housed and maintained indefinitely, the very ideal that had eluded the composer himself.

It is clear that it would take a prodigiously talented individual to fulfill all of these roles adequately; an individual, moreover, who would be prepared to forsake any creative projects of his or her own in order to devote the necessary time to the promotion of Partch's work. The new production of *The Bewitched* performed in California shortly after the composer's death seemed a hopeful portent. But very soon, even the activity of playing Partch's music received a considerable setback due to the first of the two main schisms that would tear apart Partch's extended "family" during the 1970s: that between Mitchell and Betty Freeman.

Mitchell and Freeman were at odds in their attitudes to the Partch legacy both before and after 1974. Their differences had been clear ever since the early days of the Partch Foundation, and Freeman was still vocal in her belief that Partch's instruments and papers should be placed in the hands of an institution. Perhaps in self-defense, fearing the instruments would somehow be taken away from him, Mitchell became, in Freeman's words, "guarded" and "protective" about the legacy.[2] The consequence was that she declined to offer any further financial support to Mitchell for performances.

The San Diego ensemble that Mitchell had formed for *The Dreamer That Remains* continued to exist, in ever-metamorphosing form, for virtually fifteen years, until 1987. The primary handicap it faced was financial, which meant that its performances and the related organizational and promotional activities were never very extensive. The most notable, perhaps, was another revival of *The Bewitched,* which played at the Berlin Festival and in Cologne in 1980, the first European performance of any of Partch's work. In his running of the ensemble Mitchell received both praise and criticism: praise for the high musical standards he set and for his refusal to use the legacy in a self-serving capacity; and criticism, first for replaying the same small repertoire of pieces (*Castor and Pollux, Daphne of the Dunes, Barstow*), with only occasional excursions into other terrain, and second, for not making it somehow possible for musicians outside San Diego to get their hands on Partch's instruments. (Not once did any of Mitchell's critics suggest how this latter idea could be put into practice.)

Further storm clouds gathered after Partch's death over the publication of his scores. The year before he died Partch had agreed to the publication of *The Bewitched* in Peter Garland's magazine *Soundings.* The project—a facsimile edition of Partch's 183-page score—would have been an enormous financial risk for Garland, but the work had been a crucial part of his own musical development, and he was committed to seeing it into print. Partch had asked him to wait until he could make a few corrections to the score, which he never found time to do. After Partch's death Mitchell did not respond to Garland's repeated requests for a copy of the unedited score. "After Partch died," Mitchell recalls, "my efforts went into productions of *The Bewitched* and *U.S. Highball,* and Peter was left on the back burner. He blasted me in his journal, and I can understand his anger. He was well intentioned, but I don't think it would have worked out, because neither Peter nor I were set up to distribute the material properly after the printing."[3] More than twenty years later *The Bewitched* still awaits publication, together with the vast majority of Partch's other works.

Publication of his scores had never been an especially high priority for Partch himself. He always claimed that their interest was largely academic without his instruments: because of his tablature notation, it is impossible to "read" them as one reads a more conventional score. The most impressive challenge to this rather defeatist attitude came toward the end of the 1970s from Ben Johnston. Yet his proposed solution was to lead to the second major schism between Partch's most loyal supporters, this time not over the instruments or the performance of his music but over the question of Partch scholarship and the publication of his manuscripts.

Johnston had been using extended just intonation in his own music since 1960 and had evolved a complex but fully consistent notation system that allowed for the unambiguous representation of just intervals, one that was as little different as possible from conventional notation. This was achieved by redefining the symbols of ordinary staff notation in terms of just intonation, and adding new accidentals when they were needed.[4] His system provides the resources to notate all of the pitch relationships of Partch's music with total accuracy: it is, in fact, the kind of integrated system Partch himself had striven for unsuccessfully in his experiments in notation in the 1920s and 1930s. With the willing assistance of several of his graduate students at the University of Illinois, Johnston initiated a project to transcribe Partch's scores into his own notation system. In 1978 he submitted a grant proposal to the National Endowment for the Humanities for funds to publish the results.

However, a problem arose with the publisher Johnston had named in the grant proposal as the intended distributor of the edition: Kenneth Gaburo's Lingua Press. Gaburo had founded Lingua Press in 1975 as a vehicle for his own work and for experimental compositions and writings by others. In 1978, the same year that Johnston compiled his grant proposal, Gaburo announced a Harry Partch Publishing Project, intended as a three- or four-volume series of materials by and about Partch. The basis of this was to be the materials in Partch's large filing cabinet, which Danlee Mitchell had loaned Gaburo so that he might undertake selective publication of its contents. The filing cabinet contained a random assortment of carbon copies of letters, typescripts, photographs, scrapbooks with clippings of reviews, and other items left in great disarray at the time of Partch's death and later catalogued by David Dunn. Gaburo staunchly maintained an "anti-censorship" policy and an anti-editorial stance toward all those materials that Lingua Press issued. The "essential condition" for the projected Partch series he expressed as follows: "Let Harry speak for himself; Let those who are willing to speak about him speak for themselves." Gaburo and Johnston had discussed the problems of publishing Partch's scores without, evidently, having reached any mutual understanding. When Gaburo was asked, in May 1979, to write to the National Endowment for the Humanities in support of Johnston's proposal, he made clear in his response that Lingua Press's editorial policies—which amounted, essentially, to a strong commitment to *Urtext* editions—meant he could not countenance the publication of Johnston's transcriptions. The letter planted doubts in the minds of the NEH, and Johnston's grant application was turned down. The incident had the effect of severing the friendship between Johnston and Gaburo, and of creating opposing camps in the world of Partch scholarship.[5]

By this time, Johnston had established a Harry Partch Archive at the University of Illinois. In 1976 Partch's friend Lauriston Marshall had donated to the university's Music Library the collection of letters, papers, microfilms, and recordings he had assembled during his long association with Partch. With these materials as a basis, Johnston and the musicologist Thomas McGeary set out to collect other documents, including collections of Partch letters in private hands or from other university archives in the United States and copies of scores and other papers in Danlee Mitchell's possession in San Diego, eventually assembling a very extensive archive. After a few years McGeary took the first step in disseminating these materials by beginning to compile a collection of Partch's writings. He therefore requested permission to go through the filing cabinet of papers still in the possession of Lingua Press, which by then had moved from California to Iowa City. Gaburo, feeling that his own Harry Partch Publishing Project would be compromised if some of its items appeared first in McGeary's proposed anthology, categorically refused him access to the Lingua Press holdings. McGeary's anthology, published in 1991 as *Bitter Music: Collected Journals, Essays, Introductions, and Librettos,* was thus assembled without the benefit of access to an important part of Partch's literary output.

When I began the research for this book in 1987, I rather quickly encountered the schisms I have described. While the motivations and the viewpoints of the individuals concerned are clear and worthy of respect, the net effect has been a suppression of Partch's work and a general and widespread dearth of materials which has been detrimental to his whole artistic standing. It has seemed that, through neglect, he is being written out of music history. Most of the blame for this dismal situation has been laid, indiscriminately and unfairly, on Danlee Mitchell.

In the 1990s there have been some hopeful signs. Acknowledging that the maintenance of the instruments and the mounting of performances demanded the energies of a younger man, Mitchell in 1989 loaned the instruments to Dean Drummond and his ensemble Newband in New York. This coincided with the award of a grant from the Andrew Mellon Foundation to Newband for the purpose of building copies of nine of the instruments. After Newband's performance of *The Wayward* at the Bang on a Can Festival in New York in 1991, Mitchell made the "loan" of the instruments permanent.[6] The result of this has been an increase in the number of live performances, with the promise of yet more performances and recordings in the future. And following Kenneth Gaburo's death in 1993, his assistant Philip Blackburn has begun the publication of materials from the Partch archives. In an important sense the collation of documents, the researching of Partch's life, and the analysis of his music have only begun.

In one of the typescript drafts of the preface to the second edition of *Genesis of a Music,* one of the last texts he composed, Partch wrote a moving passage on the future of his legacy. Although not included in the final text, it is a serious statement about the limits of his achievement, a final coming to terms with his own mortality. The fact that the statement came in the context of a discussion of his artistic beginnings seems to imply that he felt his life was coming full circle. "Just as one instinctively clings to life, he clings to a possible extension of his life through those who follow. But in candor I must face the probable fact that in my case there will be no extension whatever. I have only the hope of a continuing spirit—going where or how I do not know, and it is unimportant." This book has been my contribution to the search for that "continuing spirit."

Chronology of Compositions

The earliest of his compositions that Partch remembered was "Death on the Desert," composed in Albuquerque in the spring of 1916, a story with piano accompaniment. Further such "whimsical, melancholy" stories followed. Other early compositions included songs and piano pieces. Dating probably from his early years in California and prompted by his desire to learn "the disciplines of concert music" was an unfinished piano concerto ("the first two movements," on which he spent "four years"). In 1924–25, probably in San Francisco, he wrote a symphonic poem for orchestra and submitted it for a competition sponsored by the Los Angeles Philharmonic. "About 1925" he composed a string quartet in just intonation, for violin, two violas, and cello. During the later 1920s he wrote more music for "unfretted string instruments" in just intonation. In 1929 he had a brief spell writing popular songs for voice and piano—"one a day, words and music," for "a period of about two weeks." One of them, "My Heart Keeps Beating Time," was published (and later quoted in *Bitter Music*). All of these compositions, Partch affirmed, he burned in an iron stove in New Orleans in 1930 in a gesture he called "a kind of adolescent auto-da-fé." "But it is a curious fact that I destroyed nothing truly valuable to me. As late as 1960 I was still pulling out bits of ideas from that pot-bellied stove, ideas stored away in memory—that mysterious structure of cells and spirit." None of the manuscripts of these compositions are extant.

CHRONOLOGY OF MATURE COMPOSITIONS

The author of the text of a composition is given in parentheses after the work's title, followed by the place of composition. Unless otherwise stated, manuscripts of all these works and their various revisions are extant.

1930   December: Composes "The Long-Departed Lover" (Li Po), New Orleans

1931   January: Composes "With a Man of Leisure" (Li Po), New Orleans; "On Seeing Off Meng Hao-jan" (Li Po), New Orleans
April: Composes "On the Ship of Spice-wood" (Li Po), New Orleans
August: Composes "On the City Street" (Li Po), Santa Rosa, California; "An Encounter in the Field" (Li Po), Santa Rosa; "The Intruder" (Li Po), Santa Rosa; "By the Rivers of Babylon" (Psalm 137), Santa Rosa (later considered the second of the *Two Psalms* for Adapted Viola and intoning voice)
October 15: Composes "On Ascending the Sin-ping Tower" (Li Po), San Francisco
December 9: Composes "In the Spring-time on the South Side of the Yangtze Kiang" (Li Po), San Francisco
December 17: Composes "The Night of Sorrow" (Li Po), San Francisco
December 29: Composes "The Potion Scene" (from Shakespeare's *Romeo and Juliet*), San Francisco
c. December: Composes "Dialogue" (from Shakespeare's *The Merchant of Venice*), San Francisco (withdrawn, no longer extant)

1932   January 5: Composes "The Lord Is My Shepherd" (Psalm 23), San Francisco (later considered the first of the *Two Psalms* for Adapted Viola and intoning voice)
February 17: Composes "On Hearing the Flute in the Yellow Crane House" (Li Po), San Francisco; "On Hearing the Flute at Lo-cheng One Spring Night" (Li Po), San Francisco

February 29: Composes "A Dream" (Li Po), San Francisco

October: Revises the ending of "The Potion Scene," Pasadena, California

November 14: Revises "On Seeing Off Meng Hao-jan," Pasadena

1933   January 15: Revises "On the Ship of Spice-wood," Pasadena

January 16: Revises "With a Man of Leisure," Pasadena

January 17: Composes "A Midnight Farewell" (Li Po), Pasadena

August 7: Composes "Before the Cask of Wine" (Li Po), Gloucester, Massachusetts

August 8: Composes "By the Great Wall" (Li Po), Gloucester

August 10: Composes "I Am a Peach Tree" (Li Po), Gloucester; in August all the Li Po settings listed above are gathered together as *Seventeen Lyrics by Li Po* for intoning voice and Adapted Viola

1936   January: Notates the music for his journal *Bitter Music* (June 1935–February 1936), for voices and piano, Glendale, La Crescenta, and Covina, California (originally entitled *Cause All Our Sins Are Taken Away*) (withdrawn: microfilm copy only extant)

1941   April 14: Begins *Barstow: Eight Hitchhikers' Inscriptions* (anon., collated Partch), for Adapted Guitar and baritone, La Mesa, California

May 18: Completes *Barstow,* Anderson Creek, California

December: transcribes "The Lord Is My Shepherd" for voice and Chromelodeon, Chicago

1942   January 1: Adds a Chromelodeon part to "By the Rivers of Babylon," Chicago

January: Completes the "second draft" of *Barstow,* for voice, Adapted Guitar and Chromelodeon, Chicago

September: Begins *Dark Brother* (Thomas Wolfe), for voice, Adapted Viola, Chromelodeon, and Kithara, Chappaqua, New York

December: Composes *December, 1942,* for voice and adapted Guitar, New York: (1) "Come Away, Death" (from Shakespeare's *Twelfth Night*); (2) "The Heron" (Tsurayuki, trans. Waley); (3) "The Rose" (Ella Young) (withdrawn: microfilm copy only extant)

1943   February 14–March 24: Composes *U.S. Highball* (anon., collated Partch), for voice and Adapted Guitar, Ithaca, New York

May 1: Begins "second draft" of *U.S. Highball: A Musical Account of Slim's Transcontinental Hobo Trip,* for voices, Adapted Guitar, Chromelodeon and Kithara, Ithaca

June 21: Completes *Dark Brother,* Ithaca

June 27–28: Adds Kithara parts to his 1941 transcription of "The Lord Is My Shepherd"; to the 1942 version of "By the Rivers of Babylon"; and to the 1942 version of *Barstow,* Ithaca

June 29–July 1: Composes *San Francisco: A Setting of the Cries of Two Newsboys on a Street Corner,* for voice, Adapted Viola, Chromelodeon, and Kithara, Ithaca

July 2–4: Composes *Letter from Hobo Pablo* ("Excerpt from *Bitter Music*"), for voice, Adapted Guitar, and Kithara, Ithaca

October 1: Completes "second draft" of *U.S. Highball,* Ithaca

1944   March 25–30: Composes *Y.D. Fantasy* ("On the Words of an Early American Tune") for soprano, two tin flutes, tin oboe, Chromelodeon, and Flex-a-tone, New York

May 2–11: Composes *Two Settings from Joyce's Finnegans Wake,* for soprano, double flageolet (or two flutes), and Kithara, New York: (1) "Isobel"; (2) "Annah the Allmaziful"

1945   c. April: Composes *"I'm very happy to be able to tell you about this . . . "* ("a setting of a broadcast transcription by glider pilot Warren Ward"), for soprano, baritone, Kithara, and Indian drum, Madison, Wisconsin (no longer extant)

1946   c. March: Composes four *Studies* for Harmonic Canon, Madison: (1) Terpander's hexatonic; (2) Archytas's Enharmonic; (3) Olympos's pentatonic; (4) ancient Mixolydian (this version no longer extant)

1949   August: Composes *Three Intrusions* for voice, Adapted Guitar II, and Diamond Marimba, Gualala, California: (1) "The Rose" (Ella Young); (2) "The Crane" (Tsurayuki, trans. Waley); (3) "The Waterfall" (Ella Young) (later considered the third, fourth, and fifth, respectively, of the *Eleven Intrusions*)

1950   [no date]: Completes *Sonata Dementia* for speaking voice, Adapted Guitar II, Kithara, Harmonic Canon, Diamond Marimba, Cloud-Chamber Bowls, Hypo-bass, Chromelodeon I, Chromelodeon Sub-bass, and Bass Marimba, Gualala: (1) Abstraction and Delusion; (2) Scherzo Schizophrenia; (3) Allegro Paranoia (withdrawn, microfilm copy only extant: later transformed into *Ring Around the Moon*)

[no date]: Rewrites two of the *Studies* for Harmonic Canon as *Two Intrusions* (later retitled *Two Studies on Ancient Greek Scales*) for Harmonic Canon and Bass Marimba, Gualala: (1) "Study on Olympos's

Pentatonic"; (2) "Study on Archytas's Enharmonic" (later considered the first two of the *Eleven Intrusions*)

March: Composes *Three Intrusions,* Gualala: (1) "The Wind" (Ella Young, Lao-tzu), for voice, Harmonic Canon, and Bass Marimba; (2) "The Street" (Willard Motley), for voice, Harmonic Canon, and Bass Marimba; (3) a rewriting of *Letter from Hobo Pablo* as *The Letter,* for voice, Adapted Guitar I, Kithara, Diamond Marimba, and Bass Marimba (the first two later considered the sixth and seventh of the *Eleven Intrusions;* the third later not considered part of the *Eleven Intrusions*)

September: Composes "Lover" (George Leite), for soprano, speaking voice, Adapted Guitar II, Cloud-Chamber Bowls, and Bass Marimba, Gualala (later considered the eighth of the *Eleven Intrusions*)

November: Composes, in collaboration with Ben Johnston, incidental music for Wilford Leach's play *The Wooden Bird,* Gualala (withdrawn: recording only extant)

November: Composes "Soldiers—War—Another War" (Ungaretti, trans. Weaver), for voice, Harmonic Canon, Diamond Marimba, Cloud-Chamber Bowls, Adapted Guitar II, and Bass Marimba (later considered the ninth of the *Eleven Intrusions*)

December 19: Composes "Vanity" (Ungaretti, trans. Weaver), for voice and Adapted Guitars I, II, and III, Gualala (later considered the tenth of the *Eleven Intrusions*)

December 30: Completes "Cloud-Chamber Music," for voice, Adapted Viola, Adapted Guitar III, Kithara, Indian Deer Hooves Rattle, Diamond Marimba, Cloud-Chamber Bowls, and Bass Marimba, Gualala (later considered the eleventh of the *Eleven Intrusions*)

1951   [early]: Adds Bass Marimba part to *Dark Brother,* Gualala

March 10: Begins *King Oedipus: Music-Dance Drama* (W. B. Yeats), for four intoners-actors, actors, singing voices, dancers and eleven musicians, San Diego

July 31: Completes *King Oedipus,* Oakland

1952   July 1: Completes *Castor and Pollux* ("A Dance for the Twin Rhythms of Gemini") for six instruments, Oakland (later considered the first of the *Plectra and Percussion Dances*)

August 31: Completes *Even Wild Horses* ("Dance Music for an Absent Drama") (Rimbaud), for baritone and eleven instruments, Oakland (later considered the third of the *Plectra and Percussion Dances*)

[no date]: Composes *Ring Around the Moon* ("A Dance Fantasm for Here and Now") (Partch), for speaking voice and eight instruments, Oakland (a reworking of *Sonata Dementia;* the second of the *Plectra and Percussion Dances*)

December 3: Completes *Oedipus: A Dance-Drama* (Partch), for six principals, chorus and ensemble, Santa Rosa (a rewritten version of *King Oedipus*)

1954   January 29: Completes "O Frabjous Day!" (Lewis Carroll), for intoning voice, Harmonic Canon, and Bass Marimba, Sausalito, California (later considered the second of *Two Settings from Lewis Carroll,* the third part of *Summer 1955*)

October 30: Completes "The Mock Turtle Song" (Lewis Carroll), for voice, Surrogate Kithara, and Spoils of War, Sausalito (later considered the first of *Two Settings from Lewis Carroll,* the third part of *Summer 1955*)

November: Rewrites *Barstow: Eight Hitchhikers' Inscriptions from a Highway Railing at Barstow, California,* for voice, Surrogate Kithara, Adapted Guitars II and III, Chromelodeon, and Diamond Marimba, Sausalito

December 17: Begins (first version of) *The Bewitched: a Ballet Satire,* for female voice and ensemble, Sausalito

1955   January 19: Completes (first version of) *The Bewitched,* Sausalito

June 30: Completes rewrite of *U.S. Highball: A Musical Account of a Transcontinental Hobo Trip,* for Subjective Voice (baritone), Objective Voice (spoken), and eight instruments, Sausalito (later considered the fourth part of *The Wayward*)

July: rewrites "By the Rivers of Babylon" for voice, cello, Kithara II, and Chromelodeon, Sausalito (the first part of *Summer 1955,* "A Collection of Small Compositions Written or Rewritten in Summer 1955")

July 10: Completes rewrite of "The Potion Scene" for low female voice, two high sopranos, cello, Kithara II, Chromelodeon, Bass Marimba, and Marimba Eroica, Sausalito (second part of *Summer 1955*)

July 12: Completes rewrite of *San Francisco: A Setting of the Cries of Two Newsboys on a Foggy Night in the Twenties* for voice, cello, Kithara II, and Chromelodeon, Sausalito (later considered the second part of *The Wayward*)

July 13: Completes rewrite of *The Letter: A Depression Message from a*

Hobo Friend, for voice, Kithara II, Harmonic Canon II, Surrogate Kithara, Diamond Marimba, and Bass Marimba, Sausalito (later considered the third part of *The Wayward*)

July 20: Completes first version of *Ulysses Departs from the Edge of the World,* for trumpet, string bass, and three sets of Bill Loughborough's boobams, Sausalito (later considered the final part of *Summer 1955*)

September: Completes the second version of *The Bewitched: A Dance Satire,* Sausalito

December: Completes second version of *Ulysses Departs from the Edge of the World,* for B-flat clarinet, cello, Diamond Marimba, and Boo, San Diego (later considered the final part of *Summer 1955:* premièred under the title *Ulysses Turns Homeward from the Edge of the World,* Urbana, Illinois, 1956)

1956   February: Begins ink copy of full score of *The Bewitched,* La Ventosa, Oaxaca, Mexico

April: Completes ink copy of full score of *The Bewitched,* Santa Fe

1958   January 16–March 2: Composes the music for Madeline Tourtelot's film *Windsong,* for ten instruments, Chicago

June–July: Records slightly different versions of *Barstow* (for two voices, Surrogate Kithara, Chromelodeon, Diamond Marimba, and Boo) and *Ulysses at the Edge* (for alto saxophone, baritone saxophone, Diamond Marimba, Boo, Cloud-Chamber Bowls, and speaking voice), Evanston, Illinois (these versions of the pieces are considered the first and fifth parts, respectively, of *The Wayward*)

1959   August: Begins text for *Revelation in the Courthouse Park,* music-theater work based on Euripides's *The Bacchae,* Champaign, Illinois

1960   February 1–June 16: Composes *Revelation in the Courthouse Park* (Partch), for seven principals, Chorus of Eight Women, Chorus of Four Men, Entertainers (twelve musicians and twelve dancers), ensemble, and prerecorded tape, Champaign

1961   February: Composes *Rotate the Body in All Its Planes: Ballad for Gymnasts* (Partch), for solo soprano, chorus, and ensemble, Champaign (partly derived from Chorus Three of *Revelation in the Courthouse Park*)

April 19–29: Composes *Bless This Home* (Vincenzo Prockelo), for intoning voice, oboe, Adapted Viola, Harmonic Canon II, Kithara I, and Mazda Marimba, Champaign

May–November: Composes *Water! Water!: An Intermission with Prologues and Epilogues* (Partch), music-theater work for eleven principals, five chorus groups, jazz band, and ensemble, Champaign

1964   March–April: Composes (first version of) *And on the Seventh Day Petals Fell in Petaluma* ("23 One-Minute Duets, Which Later Become 5 Quartets, 3 Sextets, and 1 Octet") for twenty-one instruments, Petaluma, California

1965   January: Completes scenario for *Delusion of the Fury,* dance-drama, Van Nuys, California

November 1: Begins *Delusion of the Fury: A Ritual of Dream and Delusion,* dance-drama for large ensemble (instrumentalists/vocalists), Venice, California

1966   March 17: Completes *Delusion of the Fury,* Venice

June 12: Finishes copying score of *Delusion of the Fury,* San Diego

October: Completes the revision of *And on the Seventh Day Petals Fell in Petaluma* ("Twenty-three one-minute duets and trios which later become ten quartets and quintets and one septet: Studies in techniques, timbres, double rhythms, double tonalities")

1967   July–August: A "rescoring" of *Oedipus* (incorporating changes made during rehearsals in Sausalito, 1954), San Diego

1968   January: A "recopying" and slight revision of *Windsong* under the new title *Daphne of the Dunes,* for twelve instruments and prerecorded tape, Solana Beach, California

June 12: Completes a new copy of *Barstow* (a "more readable presentation" of the 1954 score and incorporating changes made during rehearsals in Evanston, 1958), Solana Beach

July: Makes a new copy of *Castor and Pollux* (including a new Cloud-Chamber Bowls part and a revision of the Kithara part), Solana Beach

1972   May: Rewrites *The Letter* for intoning voice, New Kithara I, Harmonic Canon III, Surrogate Kithara, Omicron Belly Drum, and prerecorded tape (of the six short instrumental interludes from the 1950 recording of the work), Encinitas, California

May: Begins the "concept and tentative text" of *The Dreamer that Remains,* Encinitas

July 15: Begins *The Dreamer that Remains: A Study in Loving* (Partch), for narrating voice, chorus voices, and fifteen instruments, Encinitas

October 6: Completes *The Dreamer that Remains,* Encinitas

October 9–22: Makes ink copy of *The Dreamer that Remains,* Encinitas

OCCASIONAL COMPOSITIONS

Partch did not include these four extant compositions in his list of works, presumably because of their insubstantiality.

1929: *While My Heart Keeps Beating Time* (Larry Yoell), for voice and piano, San Francisco

July 1945: *Polyphonic Recidivism on a Japanese Theme* (Tsurayuki, trans. Waley), for soprano, alto, tenor, and bass, Madison

November 1963: *Jine the Cavalry,* an arrangement of the traditional song as adapted by Carl Haverlin, for voice, Chromelodeon II, Diamond Marimba, and Bass Marimba, Petaluma

[no date: late 1963 or early 1964]: *Study* for Harmonic Canon I and Kithara I, Petaluma (perhaps originally intended for *And on the Seventh Day Petals Fell in Petaluma*)

PROJECTED WORKS

These projected works were mentioned by Partch in correspondence or in conversation. Most of these works were probably never begun. In a few (stated) cases, sketch materials (generally verbal) exist for a particular project. No finished manuscripts for any of these works are extant.

1933: Music for three string instruments, New York

1935: "Four chapters from the *Song of Solomon*" for voice with Ptolemy and guitar accompaniment, Malta. (A setting of a passage from the *Song of Solomon* is given in *Bitter Music,* entry for July 25, 1935.)

1935: "Sapphic trilogy" for voice with Ptolemy and guitar accompaniment, Malta

1942: "Mad Scene" (also known as "Storm Scene") from Shakespeare's *King Lear* for baritone, Chromelodeon and Kithara, Chicago

1942: *God, She,* a "musical satirization of women as the arbiters of the nature and color of American expression," Chappaqua (draft text only extant)

1943: *Letters from Sergeant Allen,* "a Setting of Excerpts from the Letters of a Man Now Serving in the United States Army," Ithaca

c. 1948: *Mendota Night* ("the dramatization of an instant of solitude"), California (one page of verbal notes extant)

1949: *Tonality Flux* for ensemble, California: transformed into *Sonata Dementia*

1953: *The Incident at Drake's Bay,* music-drama, Sausalito (verbal notes extant)

c. 1955: *Dion Isus,* music-theater work on Euripides' *The Bacchae,* Sausalito: transformed into *Revelation in the Courthouse Park* (verbal notes extant)

c. 1955: *Quick Transit,* dance drama, Sausalito (verbal notes extant)

c. 1955: *And I'll Tell You My Story,* for one male voice [and small ensemble?] ("lonely music, with little or no conscious formality, confidential and conversational, fragmentary, episodic, unconnected"), Sausalito (verbal notes extant)

1973: *The Enclosures,* for [voices and?] ensemble, San Diego

Chronology of Writings

PUBLISHED SOURCES

The two main published sources to date of Partch's writings are his book *Genesis of a Music* (two editions) and the posthumous collection of writings entitled *Bitter Music:*

Partch, Harry. *Genesis of a Music.* First edition, Madison: University of Wisconsin Press, 1949.

Partch, Harry. *Genesis of a Music: An Account of a Creative Work, Its Roots and Its Fulfillments.* Second edition, enlarged, New York: Da Capo Press, 1974.

Partch, Harry. *Bitter Music: Collected Journals, Essays, Introductions, and Librettos.* Edited with an introduction by Thomas McGeary. Urbana and Chicago: University of Illinois Press, 1991.

There is also a useful documentary source on Partch's music manuscripts, which includes a detailed bibliography of writings on Partch's work published in his lifetime and a discography:

McGeary, Thomas. *The Music of Harry Partch: A Descriptive Catalog.* ISAM Monographs, no. 31. Brooklyn, N.Y.: Institute for Studies in American Music, 1991.

WRITINGS

This section lists all of Partch's major writings: his extant literary manuscripts, whether they survive as typescript original, carbon copy, microfilm copy, or photocopy, and those writings published in his lifetime for which (in some cases) no manuscript has survived. I have divided the list into six categories, none of which is completely self-contained: theoretical writings; aesthetic writings (serious or satirical); essays on his compositions; autobiographical writings; lecture texts; and miscellaneous writings. Titles of lengthy manuscripts are given in italics. All of the writings published during Partch's lifetime (with the exception of *Genesis of a Music*) and several others are reprinted in the anthology *Bitter Music* (see above): the writings included in that volume are indicated here by the abbreviation BM in parentheses. Other manuscripts are in the Harry Partch Estate Archive, San Diego; photocopies of all the manuscripts here are in the possession of the author.

THEORETICAL WRITINGS

Exposition of Monophony, 1933. The fifth draft of Partch's early theoretical treatise, which would eventually be transformed into *Genesis of a Music.* This early text is an important document in its own right, and is much more than simply a draft of his book.

"A Quarter-Saw Section of Motivations and Intonation," 1967 (extract in BM). A lecture on theory, Partch's only extended written treatment of this subject after the publication of *Genesis of a Music* in 1949 (extract in BM).

AESTHETIC WRITINGS

"A Modern Parable I," 1934.

"A Modern Parable II," 1938.

"Show Horses in the Concert Ring," 1946 (BM: manuscript not extant).

"On G-string Formality," 1946.

"Musicians as 'Artists,'" 1947.

"No Barriers," 1952 (BM: manuscript not extant).

"The Umbilical Cord Still Vibrates," c. 1952.

"Life in the Houses of Technitution," 1953.

"Tentative WTTW script ideas," for WTTW-TV feature on *The Bewitched,* 1957.

"The Ancient Magic," 1959 (BM, without prefatory "Note" in the manuscript).

"Statement of May 22, 1960," 1960.

"A Somewhat Spoof," 1960 (BM).

"Statement for 'Arts in Society,'" 1963 (BM).

ESSAYS ON COMPOSITIONS

"*Barstow*," 1941. Written for and published in the *Carmel Pine Cone* (BM: manuscript not extant).

"*Barstow*," 1942. Notes for acetate recording made in Chicago, 1942.

"*U.S. Highball*," 1943 (BM).

"Composer's Statement of Intention" on *King Oedipus*, 1952 (BM: manuscript not extant).

"*Castor and Pollux*," 1952.

"*Even Wild Horses*," 1952.

"The Rhythmic Motivations of *Castor and Pollux* and *Even Wild Horses*," 1952 (BM).

"*The Bewitched*," scenario, 1955.

"*U.S. Highball*," film script, 1957 (extract in BM).

"*Windsong:* Script for Suggested Transformation Sequence," 1958.

"Some New and Old Thoughts After and Before *The Bewitched*," revised scenario, 1958 (extract in BM).

"Statement on *The Bewitched* Program Notes," 1959.

Folio of draft scenarios and sketch materials for *Revelation in the Courthouse Park*, c. 1955–60.

"Composer's Statement" on *Revelation in the Courthouse Park*, c.1960.

"Observations" on *Water! Water!* 1962 (BM: manuscript not extant).

"Statement" on *And on the Seventh Day Petals Fell in Petaluma*, 1966.

"*Delusion of the Fury*," scenario, 1965 (BM).

"*The Dreamer That Remains: A Study in Loving*," draft scenario and text, 1972.

"Statement" on *The Bewitched*, 1973: written for the CRI reissue of the 1957 recording.

AUTOBIOGRAPHICAL WRITINGS (INCLUDING JOURNALS)

Bitter Music, 1935–36, revised 1940 (BM: text and music examples only; manuscript not extant).

"Biography [sic] of Harry Partch," 1945: prepared at the request of the University of Wisconsin, Madison.

End Littoral: The Journal of a Hiking Trip, 1947 (BM: text only; manuscript not extant).

LECTURE TEXTS

KPFA radio talks, 1953: "Creativity in Music"; "Education and New Instruments"; "Education and the Record Repertory"; "Education and Acoustics"; "The Writers on Music"; "Musical Perspectives"; "My Instruments"; "*Castor and Pollux*"; "The *Oedipus* Dance Music".

Lecture preceding the KPFA broadcast of *Plectra and Percussion Dances,* 1953 (extract in BM: recording only extant).

Talk preceding the KPFA broadcast of *Oedipus,* 1954 (BM: recording only extant).

"A Soul Tormented by Contemporary Music Looks for a Humanizing Alchemy," 1957: lecture-demonstration given at the University of Illinois at Urbana-Champaign, two days before the première of *The Bewitched* (extract in BM: recording only extant).

Lecture at Columbia University before the performance of *The Bewitched,* April 9, 1959.

Lecture in St. Louis, April 1962.

Lecture for the American Symphony Orchestra League Convention, San Francisco, June 1963.

Lecture ("Monday morning") at the University of Oregon, February 1964.

Lecture ("Monday evening") at the University of Oregon, February 1964.

Lecture at Valley State College, Northridge, California, March 1965.

Lecture at UCLA, May 1966 (extract in BM).

Lectures at University of California at San Diego, autumn 1967.

Lecture at University of Hawaii, July 1971.

MISCELLANEOUS WRITINGS

"Six Months' Report on Projects to be Executed Under Carnegie Grant for the Year 1934–35," 1935. Submitted to the Institute for International Education, New York.

"A New Instrument," 1935. On the Ptolemy (manuscript not extant).

Author's Preface to *Patterns of Music,* 1940. The preface only to this version of Partch's book is extant (BM).

"Bach and Temperament," 1941. Written for and published in the *Carmel Pine Cone* (BM: manuscript not extant).

"The Kithara," 1941. Written for and published in the *Carmel Pine Cone* (BM: manuscript not extant).

"W. B. Yeats," 1941. Written for and published in the *Carmel Pine Cone* (BM: manuscript not extant).

Notebook, 1941: carried by Partch on his cross-country trek to Chicago in autumn 1941, this notebook contains the draft text of *U.S. Highball*, the draft text of *God, She* (see Chronology of Compositions, section on projected works) and other jottings.

"Report to the University of Wisconsin Research Committee on My Work Under Grant for 1945–46," 1946.

"Gems from My Scrapbook 1930 to 1957," 1957. A collage of quotes from reviews of his work.

"Expenses of a Research and Experimental Musical Instrument Project Dating from 1925 to the Present," c. 1963.

Manual: On the Maintenance and Repair of—and the Musical and Attitudinal Techniques for—Some Putative Musical Instruments, 1963. This manuscript was used by Partch in preparing the new chapters on instruments (chapters 12 and 13) in the revised second edition of *Genesis of a Music*, but is an important document in its own right and contains important material not found in his book.

"My Seminar in Retrospect," 1967. A review of his teaching at UCSD, Fall Semester 1967.

"Fragments from Partch," 1968. A collage of quotes from his writings and lectures compiled at the request of BMI, New York, for a publicity brochure.

Folio of drafts and memoranda for the Preface to the second edition of *Genesis of a Music,* 1969.

"Introduction to Bonus Record," 1970. Draft text of the narration for the bonus record issued with the Columbia Records release of *Delusion of the Fury.*

Notes

The majority of Partch's manuscripts are the property of Danlee Mitchell, heir to the Harry Partch Estate in San Diego, California. The materials of the Partch Estate, during the period of my research for this book (1987–92), included—besides Partch's instruments—his music manuscripts, literary writings, correspondence, scrapbooks, photographs, recordings, and miscellaneous papers. I have made extensive use of these primary sources in this book. The papers of the Partch Estate were organized and catalogued first by David Dunn and later by Thomas McGeary, and the work of these two scholars helped my own efforts considerably. During the years I was researching this book, and since, the holdings of the Partch Estate have been undergoing re-organization, and not all the manuscripts belonging to the Estate are actually housed in San Diego. Between 1978 and 1993 many of them were located in the offices of the publishers Lingua Press, where I studied them in January–February 1990.

Two important literary manuscripts, *Bitter Music* and *End Littoral,* exist (on microfilm only) in the other main archival collection on Partch: that of the Harry Partch Archive in the Music Library of the University of Illinois at Urbana-Champaign. This archive also contains copies of virtually all of Partch's music manuscripts, either as photostat, microfilm, or photocopy; collections of letters (including many originals), photographs, program booklets; a few original literary manuscripts plus photocopies or microfilms of many others; and the large collection of audio cassettes that forms the oral history project on Partch conducted by Ben Johnston and Thomas McGeary in 1978–79, with occasional additions thereafter. In addition, some miscellaneous papers formerly with Lingua Press, and some from San Diego, have recently been moved to the Urbana archive, and more shall undoubtedly follow.

Other sources used in my biography derive from the several archives in the United States, either in universities or other institutions, which contain Partch materials of one kind or another, particularly the University of Wisconsin; the University of California, San Diego; the University of Southern California; and Columbia University. Several collections of letters in private hands were made available to me by the recipients. In addition, a large amount of information derives from my own interviews and/or correspondence with many of those individuals who had been closely involved with Partch during his lifetime.

All quotations in this book from Partch's writings are taken from the typescript originals, or from carbon copies or photocopies of the originals.

The Harry Partch Estate Archive, San Diego, contains carbon copies of letters from Partch to: Steven Bookman, David Bowen, William Meiron Bowen, John Cage, the Cassandra Foundation, Oliver Daniel, Sally Fairweather, Albert Goldberg, Ronald Goldberg, Martha Graham, Lou Harrison, Carl Haverlin, Monika Jensen, Eleanor King, Rallou Manoy, Alan J. Marks, John McClure, James McEnery, Danlee Mitchell, Samuel Mitnick, Alwin Nikolais, Will Ogdon, the Harry Partch Foundation, Eugene Paul, Sybil Pincus, Peter Reed, the Rockefeller Foundation, Linda Schell, Ken Spiker, Madeline Tourtelot, Frederick Wall, William Wilder, Arthur Woodbury, Patty Wright, La Monte Young, and Karl ZoBell.

The Harry Partch Archive at the University of Illinois contains Partch's letters to: John Beckwith, Bertha Knisely Driscoll, Dean Drummond, Betty Freeman, Loran French, Barnard Hewitt, James and Marion Jacobs, Ben Johnston, Lauriston and Lucie Marshall, Quincy and Lois Porter, and Ross Santee.

Partch's letters to Peter Yates are in the Peter Yates Archive, Mandeville Department of Special Collections, University of California, San Diego; his letters to Livia Appel, Thompson Webb (of the University of Wisconsin Press), and M. E. McCaffrey are in the archives of the University of Wisconsin, Madison; those to David Hall and Carter Harman are in the files of Composers Recordings Incorporated, New York; his letters to Douglas Moore and Thomas DeGaetani are in the archives of Columbia University; his letters to Virgil Thomson are in the archives of Yale University; his letters to Henry Allen Moe and Gordon Ray are in the files of the John Simon Guggenheim Foundation, New York. The Elizabeth Sprague Coolidge Collection, Library of Congress, has letters from Partch to Elizabeth Sprague Coolidge; the Hans Moldenhauer Archive, Harvard University, has letters from Partch to Moldenhauer and to Adolph Weiss; the Otto Luening Collection, New York Public Library, has his letters to Otto Luening; and the Institute of International Education, New York, has letters written by Partch during his studies in Europe in 1934–35. His letters to Bill Biglow, Mike Craden, Peter Garland, Marshall Glasier, Lee Hoiby, Christine Charnstrom Lindsay, Stephen Pouliot, Michael Ranta, Emil Richards, and Elizabeth Gentry Sayad, are in private hands.

The Harry Partch Estate Archive has letters to Partch from: Larry Austin, John Read Brooks, George Cronyn, Edmund Dulac, Betty Freeman, John Garvey, Martha Graham, Carl Haverlin, Ben Johnston, Martin Kamen, Bertha Knisely, Don McGrath, Alan J. Marks,

Danlee Mitchell, Alwin Nikolais, Anaïs Nin, Will Ogdon, Gordon Onslow Ford, Jacqueline Onslow Ford, Adeline Partch, Jennie Partch, Paul Partch, Wilfrid Perrett, Stephen Pouliot, Kathleen Schlesinger, Madeline Tourtelot, Peter Yates, W. B. Yeats, and Nicholas Zoller. The archives of the University of Wisconsin, Madison, have copies of letters to Partch from Jacques Barzun and M. E. McCaffrey.

The following abbreviations are used throughout the notes.

HPEA/SD   Harry Partch Estate Archive, San Diego

HPA/UI   Harry Partch Archive, Music Library, University of Illinois at Urbana-Champaign

HPOHP   Harry Partch Oral History Project, Music Library, University of Illinois at Urbana-Champaign

Genesis   Harry Partch, *Genesis of a Music: An Account of a Creative Work, Its Roots and Its Fulfillments.* Second edition, enlarged, New York: Da Capo Press, 1974.

PREFACE

1. *Genesis*, xi.
2. Richard Ellmann, *a long the riverrun: Selected Essays* (London: Penguin Books, 1989), 114.
3. HP to Lauriston Marshall, Jan. 14, 1950.
4. Kenneth Gaburo, ed., *Allos: "Other" Language* (La Jolla, Calif.: Lingua Press, 1980) n.p.
5. Harry Partch, *Bitter Music: Collected Journals, Essays, Introductions, and Librettos*, edited with an introduction by Thomas McGeary (Urbana and Chicago: University of Illinois Press, 1991), xxiv.

PROLOGUE

1. *Genesis*, 296.
2. HP to Stephen Pouliot, Apr. 1, 1972.
3. *Genesis*, 294.
4. HP on the soundtrack of *The Dreamer that Remains*, 1972: cassette and transcript, HPA/UI.
5. HP, "A Quarter-Saw Section of Motivations and Intonation." Following the ellipsis, HP to David Hall, May 25, 1967.
6. "Sad compromise": *Genesis*, v; "genuine integrity" and "seen and heard performance": "Statement" preceding the manuscript score of *Delusion of the Fury*, 1966.
7. Kenneth Gaburo, "In Search of Partch's Bewitched: Part One: Concerning Physicality," *Percussive Notes Research Edition* (March 1985), 54–84.
8. HP, "A Quarter-Saw Section of Motivations and Intonation."
9. HP to Peter Yates, Sept. 25, 1952.
10. Anaïs Nin, *The Diary of Anaïs Nin, Volume Five: 1947–55*, edited and with a preface by Gunther Stuhlmann (New York: Harvest/HBJ, 1974), 240–41.
11. *Genesis*, xv–xvi.
12. Ben Johnston, liner notes to *Harry Partch/John Cage*, New World Records NW 214. Kyle Gann, "The Pierless Partch," *Village Voice*, Feb. 18, 1992, 90.

13. Henry Cowell, "American Composers," *Proceedings of the Ohio State Educational Conference, Eleventh Annual Session,* ed. Josephine H. MacLatchy, issued as *Ohio State University Bulletin* 36:3 (Sept. 15, 1931), 379; quoted in Rossiter, *Charles Ives and His America* (London: Gollancz, 1976), 222.

14. Jacqueline Onslow Ford to HP, July 18, 1958.

15. Ben Johnston to the author, Oct. 20, 1987.

CHAPTER 1. OAKLAND AND THE OLD WEST

1. *Genesis,* ix.

2. *Genesis,* x.

3. Paul Partch to HP, July 30, 1951.

4. According to the family stud book Virgil's father was also employed at the college for a time during his son's studies, although he is not listed among the faculty. The records of the university (which in 1913 became Highland Community College) note a payment to H. W. Partch of $374.55 in December 1880. Later, Homer's younger children went to the university, too. Grace, the youngest-but-one, is listed as an English teacher at the university in 1895–96.

5. George Enos Partch and Mary Dunlava Tellefson, *Quinton Patch and His Descendants,* unpublished monograph, 2.

6. HP to Alan J. Marks of Da Capo Press, New York, Dec. 13, 1971.

7. HP, manuscript drafts of the preface to the second edition of *Genesis of a Music,* 1969.

8. HP interviewed by Vivian Perlis, March 1974. Unpublished transcript: Oral History Project, Yale University School of Music. Hereinafter referred to as "Perlis interview."

9. Virgil Partch to the Commissioner-General of Immigration, Washington, D.C., Aug. 22, 1918.

10. HP to David Bowen, Oct. 3, 1960.

11. Virgil Partch to the Commissioner-General of Immigration, Washington, D.C., Aug. 22, 1918.

12. HP to Carl N. Ryer, Carrie Fisher, and Sue Ralston, June 26, 1963.

13. Recounted by Danlee Mitchell, interviewed by the author, Jan. 1989.

14. HP to David Bowen, Oct. 3, 1960.

15. *Genesis,* ix. Citation from the *Citizen* reprinted in Joseph Miller, *Arizona: The Last Frontier* (New York: Hastings House, 1956).

16. HP to Bill Biglow, Mar. 28, 1973.

17. *Arizona State Guide* (New York: Hastings House, 1940), 382–83.

18. Remark made during the filming of *The Dreamer That Remains,* 1972.

19. HP to Lauriston Marshall, Feb. 27, 1950.

20. HP to David Bowen, Oct. 3, 1960.

21. *Genesis,* viii.

22. HP to David Bowen, Oct. 3, 1960.

23. *Genesis,* ix.

24. HP to Eugene Paul, Mar. 2, 1971.

25. *Genesis,* ix.

26. *Genesis,* ix.
27. *Genesis,* xi.
28. HP to David Bowen, Oct. 3, 1960.
29. HP, film script for *U.S. Highball,* 1957.
30. Remark made during the filming of *The Dreamer That Remains,* 1972.
31. *Genesis,* ix.
32. *Genesis,* xiii.
33. HP, manuscript drafts of the preface to the second edition of *Genesis of a Music,* 1969.
34. *Genesis,* x.
35. HP to Alan J. Marks, Dec. 5, 1971.
36. Francis Crawford, speaking at the Harry Partch memorial meeting, Redwood City, California, Sept. 22, 1974: cassette copy courtesy of David Dunn.
37. Danlee Mitchell interviewed by the author, March 1991.
38. The story is given here as it was recounted by Danlee Mitchell in an interview with the author, January 1989, but it accords in every detail with the versions given to the author by other friends of the composer.
39. Lou Harrison to the author, Sept. 16, 1990.
40. Ken Cornish, "Petaluma's Experimental Composer Invents Instruments, Creative Music," *The Press Democrat Empire News,* Santa Rosa, California, Dec. 8, 1963, p. C-1.
41. *Genesis,* ix.
42. Paul D. Zimmerman, "A Prophet Honored," *Newsweek,* Sept. 23, 1968, 109.
43. HP to Betty Freeman, May 2, 1969.
44. Paul Horgan, *A Writer's Eye* (New York: Abrams, 1988), 25.
45. Perlis interview.
46. HP to David Bowen, Oct. 3, 1960.
47. HP to Peter Reed, Dec. 8, 1954. In *Bitter Music* he writes: "Until I trained myself to sing in many tones to the octave, which was far past my twenty-first birthday, I couldn't carry a tune either."
48. Anna Partch Couch to the author, Mar. 30, 1991. Their first son, Virgil Franklin Partch II, was born in St. Paul Island, Alaska, in 1916, and was to become well known as the cartoonist Vip.
49. Perlis interview.
50. HP to David Bowen, Oct. 3, 1960.
51. Remark made during the filming of *The Dreamer That Remains,* 1972.
52. *Genesis,* x.
53. HP, undated memo [c. 1969]: HPEA/SD.
54. HP to Alan J. Marks, Dec. 5, 1971, Perlis interview.
55. *Genesis,* viii.
56. HP to Oliver Daniel, July 15, 1963.
57. Perlis interview.
58. Perlis interview.
59. Remark made during the filming of *The Dreamer That Remains,* 1972.
60. *Genesis,* viii.
61. Perlis interview.

62. Perlis interview.

63. *Bitter Music,* entry for Aug. 15, 1935.

64. *Bitter Music,* entry for Aug. 14, 1935.

65. HP, journal [c. Oct. 1971—summer 1972], property of the author.

66. *Bitter Music,* entry for July 4, 1935.

67. Lou Harrison to the author, Sept. 16, 1990.

68. *Genesis,* x.

69. Remark made during the filming of *The Dreamer That Remains,* 1972.

70. Recounted by Michael Ranta in an interview with the author, July 1989.

CHAPTER 2. LOS ANGELES AND SAN FRANCISCO

1. HP, "No Barriers."

2. Perlis interview.

3. Catherine Parsons Smith and Cynthia S. Richardson, *Mary Carr Moore, American Composer* (Ann Arbor: University of Michigan Press, 1987), 106–7.

4. Perlis interview.

5. Perlis interview.

6. Rita Mead, *Henry Cowell's New Music, 1925–1936* (Ann Arbor, Mich.: UMI Research Press, 1981), 34.

7. The two quotes come from "A Somewhat Spoof" and his lecture at UCLA in 1966, respectively.

8. Remark made in 1972 during the filming of *The Dreamer That Remains.*

9. HP, lecture at UCSD, fall semester 1967.

10. Perlis interview.

11. Ben Johnston, "Beyond Harry Partch," *Perspectives of New Music* 22, nos. 1–2 (1984), 227.

12. HP, undated memo: HPEA/SD.

13. Stephen Pouliot, speaking at the Harry Partch memorial meeting, Sept. 22, 1974.

14. Perlis interview.

15. HP, "Biography [*sic*] of Harry Partch." Unpublished typescript, 4 pp., 1945; in Harry Partch File, University Archives, University of Wisconsin, Madison.

16. *Genesis,* vii.

17. In October 1932 and again in October 1933 Partch submitted grant applications to the John Simon Guggenheim Memorial Foundation in New York. His applications were unsuccessful, but the forms have survived, here referred to as "Guggenheim application, October 1932" and "Guggenheim application, October 1933"; Harry Partch File, John Simon Guggenheim Memorial Foundation, New York.

18. Due to water damage from a leaky roof around 1937, almost all the old records of the conservatory were destroyed, and the present-day conservatory (now part of the University of Missouri, Kansas City) has no record of him. LeRoy Pogemiller, associate dean for graduate studies, Conservatory of Music, University of Missouri, Kansas City, to the author, Mar. 11, 1991.

19. Although he says in the 1932 application that these studies continued "until 1921," this has become "until 1923" in the application submitted the following year; these dates can

be taken with some degree of latitude. No papers relating to his studies at the University of Southern California were among Partch's effects when he died.

20. Smith and Richardson, *Mary Carr Moore*, 113–16.

21. HP, tape-recorded conversations with Danlee and Georgie Mitchell, 1966: tape courtesy of David Dunn. Partch does not specify which of Field's piano concerti he is referring to. He mentions Field also in the preface to *Patterns of Music*, 1940.

22. Henry Brant interviewed by Danlee Mitchell, 1980: cassette courtesy of Professor Mitchell.

23. HP, "Show Horses in the Concert Ring."

24. *Genesis*, 4.

25. "Partch Devises 43-Tone Scale and Unique Instruments to Match," *Wisconsin State Journal* (Madison) [c. 1945–46].

26. Perlis interview.

27. HP to Lauriston Marshall, Jan. 14, 1950.

28. HP, "Show Horses in the Concert Ring."

29. HP to David Bowen, Oct. 3, 1960.

30. Perlis interview.

31. HP, unpublished typescript notes for a projected work to be called *And I'll Tell You My Story*: HPEA/SD.

32. HP, monologue on tape, recorded in the mid-1960s at the suggestion of the musicologist Peter Yates: tape in the Music Library, Central Library, University of California, San Diego.

33. HP to David Bowen, Oct. 3, 1960.

34. HP, "Show Horses in the Concert Ring."

35. HP to Elizabeth Sprague Coolidge, Jan. 13, 1932.

36. By his own account Partch began working as a copyholder in the proofroom of the *Los Angeles Times* in 1920: this would mean that he held the job concurrently with his studies. The *Times* has no record of Partch's having worked for the paper, though the sparseness of their records for this period doesn't preclude the possibility. A copyholder was part of a two-man proofreading team. One held the copy (as typed by the reporter or editor) and the other read the proof. Craig St. Clair, Historian, *Los Angeles Times*, to the author, Nov. 28, 1989.

37. Perlis interview.

38. Danlee Mitchell interviewed by the author, Apr. 1988.

39. HP to Lou Harrison, Apr. 19, 1971.

40. HP quoted in Jonathan Cott, "The Forgotten Visionary," *Rolling Stone* 158 (Apr. 11, 1974), 32–34, 36, 38.

41. HP to Lou Harrison, Apr. 19, 1971.

42. *Genesis*, 53.

43. Helmholtz, *On the Sensations of Tone as a Physiological Basis for the Theory of Music.* Second English Edition, translated by Alexander J. Ellis (London: Longmans, Green, 1885). In his Guggenheim application of October 1932 Partch mentions having previously encountered "a summary of the theories of Helmholtz" that would seem to have put him on the track of the book.

44. HP quoted in Jules Joseph, "Harry Partch Uses 43 Tone Scale to Preserve Natural Word Rhythm," *Daily Cardinal* (University of Wisconsin, Madison), Jan. 30, 1945.

45. Helmholtz, *Sensations of Tone*, 1.

46. Helmholtz, *Sensations of Tone*, 1.

47. *Genesis*, vii.

48. In the lengthy Appendix 20, "Additions by the Translator" (Ellis), Partch would have read—along with much else—of the calculation of cents values, of the incidence of ratio intervals in non-Western cultures as well as in ancient Greek theory, and of experimental instruments for demonstrating just intonation (particularly the harmonium), all of which concerns became central to his own work at different times.

49. HP, "Biography of Harry Partch."

50. HP, Guggenheim applications of October 1932 and (following the ellipses) October 1933.

51. HP to David Bowen, Oct. 3, 1960.

52. Franklin S. Clark, "'Seats Down Front!'" *Sunset* 54 (1925), 33.

53. Ronald Riddle, *Flying Dragons, Flowing Streams: Music in the Life of San Francisco's Chinese* (Westport, Conn.: Greenwood Press, 1983), 146.

54. *Genesis*, 13.

55. References to Oriental dance occur in "Some New and Old Thoughts After and Before *The Bewitched*," although the relevant section is not included in the excerpt published in Partch, ed. McGeary, *Bitter Music*.

56. HP, "Biography of Harry Partch."

57. HP, Guggenheim application, Oct. 1933.

58. *Bitter Music*, entry for June 13, 1935.

59. Perlis interview.

60. HP, Guggenheim application, Oct. 1933.

61. *Exposition of Monophony* (1933 draft, unpublished), 50.

62. A suggestion to the contrary is given in Rodney Oakes, "A Musician Seduced Into Carpentry: Harry Partch, 1901–74" in *The Composer* (Hamilton, Ontario) 16 (1976), 26–28. Oakes's obituary recalls a visit to Partch in Solana Beach in January 1968, during which Partch mentioned his early quartet. Oakes writes: "A performance of this work had been rather unsuccessful in San Francisco, but Howard Hanson heard it, liked it, and gave Partch encouragement." This is quite at odds with the impression Partch gives in his interview with Vivian Perlis in March 1974, and it may be that Oakes's memory, after an interval of eight years, was playing him false.

63. *Genesis*, vii.

64. HP, Guggenheim application, Oct. 1932.

65. Pitts Sanborn, [review]: *Modern Music*, May–June 1926, 3–9.

66. Mead, *Henry Cowell's New Music*.

67. *Genesis*, vii: HP, Guggenheim applications.

68. Perlis interview.

69. Leslie Dustin died in January 1927: *Quinton Patch and His Descendants*, 44. In the deeds Irene's address is given as Inglewood, California.

70. "New Instrument Invented to Demonstrate Musical Theory," *San Francisco News*, Feb. 9, 1931.

71. Perlis interview.

72. *Bitter Music,* entry for July 25, 1935. Partch's association with the UC Symphony Orchestra is frustratingly difficult to verify. His name is not listed among the orchestra personnel in the one surviving program from this season (its fifth), from January 1928. Steve Repasky, music reference librarian, University of California, Berkeley, to the author, June 19, 1990.

73. *Genesis,* x.

74. HP, Guggenheim applications, Oct. 1932 and Oct. 1933.

75. Nicholas Zoller, letters to the author, Aug. 13 and Sept. 13, 1990.

76. Josef Walter to the author, Oct. 8, 1990.

77. HP to David Bowen, Oct. 3, 1960.

78. HP to David Bowen, Oct. 3, 1960. It is possible that Partch's memory was deceiving him, and that the year in question is really 1929. The same letter continues: "I followed the harvest most of the rest of that season, then shipped out on an oil tanker"—this latter event, as we shall see, was at the end of 1929, not 1928.

79. HP in one of the manuscript drafts of the preface to the second edition of *Genesis of a Music,* 1969: HPEA/SD.

80. HP to David Bowen, Oct. 3, 1960.

81. HP, *Exposition of Monophony,* 1933 draft, 50.

82. Helmholtz, *Sensations of Tone,* 15.

83. HP, *Exposition of Monophony* (1933 draft), 50.

84. Some of the music of Ben Johnston from the 1970s onward introduces a modification to this idea by using incomplete systems; for example, by using ratios of 2, 3, and 11 but omitting ratios of 5 and 7. The result is still an 11-limit system, but an incomplete one.

85. This and other aspects of Partch's early work are explored in detail in my doctoral thesis "Harry Partch: The Early Vocal Works, 1930–33" (Queen's University, Belfast, 1992).

86. A good example of this can be found in the early works for voice and Adapted Viola: see the analyses in my paper "On Harry Partch's *Seventeen Lyrics by Li Po,*" *Perspectives of New Music* 30:2 (1992): 22–58.

87. If a cycle of twelve true perfect fifths—the ratio $3/2$—is tuned above any given starting tone, the tone that will be reached at the end of the cycle is seven octaves plus a small interval (about a quarter of a semitone) above the starting tone. (The mathematical proof is that $3/2$ to the power of 12, 129.74634, is greater than $2/1$ to the power of 7, which is 128.) In equal temperament one-twelfth of this small interval is "chopped off" each perfect fifth so that the cycle will fit exactly into seven octaves, causing a small but perceptible narrowing of the perfect fifth.

88. HP, author's preface to *Patterns of Music,* 1940.

89. "The One-Footed Bride": *Genesis,* 155.

90. Selby Noel Mayfield, "Student Devises 29-Degree Octave Theory of Music," *New Orleans Times-Picayune,* Nov. 16, 1930.

91. "Apparently dropped": we cannot be sure because Partch tells us that the 1933 *Exposition* was principally a "condensation" of the longer previous draft, completed the previous year and like its predecessors no longer extant. It is therefore impossible to know what exactly this 1932 draft contained.

92. Henry Cowell, *New Musical Resources* (New York: Knopf, 1930; 2d ed., New York: Something Else Press, 1969); 21–24.

93. HP, "A Quarter Saw Section of Motivations and Intonation."

94. HP to Peter Yates, Sept. 25, 1952.

95. Erv Wilson interviewed by Ben Johnston, Los Angeles, Jan. 1979: HPOHP.

96. Partch retained this certificate to the end of his life: it is now in the Harry Partch Estate Archive, San Diego.

97. Perlis interview.

98. Hulda Gieschen to the author, Nov. 30, 1989.

CHAPTER 3. NEW ORLEANS AND CALIFORNIA

1. HP to Michael Ranta, Feb. 27, 1964.

2. Edmund Wilson, *The Twenties,* edited with an introduction by Leon Edel (London: Macmillan, 1975), 184–87.

3. Perlis interview.

4. HP, "No Barriers."

5. HP, *Exposition of Monophony,* 1933 draft, 37. Contrary to expectation, the 29 pitches indicated on the Adapted Viola fingerboard do not correspond exactly to the 29 primary ratios within the 11-limit; sadly, we do not have Partch's rationale for the choice. One obvious consideration is that it is clearly undesirable (for practical reasons) to mark on the fingerboard two pitches very close to each other. We do not find, for example, both 10/9 and 9/8, both "essential" tones but only 21.5 cents (a fifth of a semitone) apart— only 10/9 is marked. It seems therefore that the "1928 theory of the more essential tones"—the 29-degree scale—did not include all the primary ratios within the 11-limit.

6. *Genesis,* x.

7. Perlis interview.

8. *Genesis,* x.

9. HP, "Biography of Harry Partch." In all his descriptions of the "auto-da-fé," Partch was adamant that he burned absolutely all of his music to that time. If so, this implies two things: first, that he kept all his manuscripts—even the earliest juvenilia from Albuquerque—together in one relatively tidy pile (which is somewhat at odds with his later habits, as Partch could be careless about the filing of his papers and lost or misplaced things fairly often, even scores or parts); and second, that all his manuscripts either accompanied him to New Orleans or were forwarded shortly after his arrival (he is unlikely to have brought them on board the oil tanker he worked on just prior to this, so one must assume that a trunk load of papers and books that had remained intact during his wanderings in the 1920s was forwarded to him). While none of this is impossible, we cannot rule out the tantalizing possibility that some manuscripts, or copies, or scraps, escaped the auto-da-fé simply because they were not part of the bundle of papers he had in New Orleans. The existence or the present location of such manuscript materials, if indeed there are any, is unknown.

10. Erv Wilson interviewed by Ben Johnston, Jan. 1979: HPOHP.

11. Perlis interview.

12. *Genesis*, 5–6.

13. HP, notes for an acetate recording, made in Chicago in 1942, of six of the Li Po settings. A copy of these liner notes is in the Harry Partch File, John Simon Guggenheim Memorial Foundation, New York.

14. The book is now in the possession of Ben and Betty Johnston.

15. Garland, *Americas: Essays on American Music and Culture, 1973–80* (Santa Fe: Soundings Press, 1982), 63.

16. *The Works of Li Po, the Chinese Poet*, trans. Shigeyoshi Obata (New York: E. P. Dutton, 1928).

17. It is interesting to speculate what Partch might have done with other translations of the verse—for example, with Ezra Pound's very different renderings of Li Po in his collection *Cathay* (1915); compare the lines set by Partch in "On the Ship of Spice-Wood" with Pound's "The River Song."

18. He quotes this passage in a letter to Henry Allen Moe, Jan. 29, 1934. The Yeats source is an appendix to the *Dramatical Poems* (London: Macmillan, 1907).

19. Perlis interview.

20. Cf. his description of the transcription process for Psalm 23 in the notes to the acetate recording of the setting made in Chicago in 1942.

21. This type of chord movement is a corroboration of, and an outgrowth from, the third of the "laws" of chord resolution in the *Exposition of Monophony* which states, in its later, clearer rewording in chapter 11 of *Genesis* (p. 182: the second and third "laws" of chord resolution of 1933 became respectively the third and second "observations" in this chapter) that the intensity of the urge for resolution in a satellite tone is in direct proportion to the proximity of that satellite to the magnet (or identity of a tonality).

22. The Dorian form of the Ptolemaic Sequence in the Utonality on 5/3: see *Genesis*, 166. The "alien mode" that occurs later in the setting is in the Utonality on 7/4.

23. For example, Dr. Ernest Schuyten, director of the New Orleans Conservatory of Music, who read the second draft of the *Exposition of Monophony* and who acted as a referee for Partch's first Guggenheim application some two years later.

24. HP to Ronald Goldberg, Tulane University, Oct. 11, 1961.

25. HP quoted in Ken Cornish, "Petaluma's Experimental Composer Invents Instruments, Creative Music," *Press Democrat Empire News*, Santa Rosa, California, Dec. 8, 1963, p. C-1.

26. Perlis interview.

27. Perlis interview.

28. Partch was making reference to Schoenberg's work in his Los Angeles solo performance in May 1932: see "Spoken Word Basis For New Musical Notation," *Los Angeles Times*, May 1932.

29. *Genesis*, 255–56.

30. Manuscripts of seven Li Po settings exist in this form, as do copies of both of the *Two Psalms* and *The Potion Scene*.

31. "Speech New Route To Music," *Oakland Tribune*, Nov. 12, 1931.

32. Redfern Mason, "Music Gamut of Speech is Noted Down," *San Francisco Examiner*, Nov. 29, 1931.

33. HP, film script for *U.S. Highball,* 1957.

34. HP to Betty Freeman, June 14, 1969.

35. HP to David Bowen, Oct. 3, 1960.

36. "Declamation Music Given By Originator," *San Francisco Chronicle,* Feb. 10, 1932, 9.

37. "Monophony and Monophone—Illustrated by Harry Partch," *San Francisco News,* Feb. 10, 1932, 9.

38. Paul S. Nathan, "Music Inventor in Oakland Concert," *Oakland Post-Enquirer,* Mar. 1, 1932, 10.

39. R.D.S. [R. D. Scofield], "Music Played in New Scale at Exhibition: Oakland Program Presented to Demonstrate 55 Gradations of Fractional Tone," *Oakland Tribune,* Mar. 1, 1932, 12.

40. Noel Heath Taylor, "Artist in the Wilderness," *California Arts and Architecture* 56:1 (July 1939), 8, 36.

41. As a token of the ill luck that seems to cling to Partch even in death, it is worth noting that the standard source book on Cowell's New Music Society, by the American musicologist Rita Mead, makes—inexplicably—not a single mention of Partch nor of the February 1932 concert. Mead, *Henry Cowell's New Music.*

42. *Bitter Music,* entry for July 20, 1935.

43. The work was for two pianos tuned a quarter tone apart, and was performed by the composer and Malcolm Thurburn for the New Music Society on May 15, 1932; the performance was upstaged somewhat by the second half of the evening's program, which featured a demonstration by Cowell of his new instrument, the Rhythmicon. Mead, *Henry Cowell's New Music,* 190–91.

44. The following year the *Pasadena Star-News* noted that Buhlig "was responsible for introducing Mr. Partch to Southern California." "Expounds New Music Theory," Feb. 16, 1933, 10.

45. Her first husband died in 1930. Bertha McCord Knisely Driscoll interviewed by Ben Johnston, La Mesa, California, Jan. 11, 1979: HPOHP.

46. Bruno David Ussher, ed., *Who's Who in Music and Dance in Southern California* (Hollywood: Bureau of Musical Research, 1933), 211.

47. Those whom Partch met in Bertha Knisely's company included the conductor Rodzinsky and the pianist Josef Hoffman.

48. Eleanor Barnes, "Musician Divides Notes: Shaves Sound Tones: Partch Has Novel Idea," *Illustrated Daily News* (Los Angeles), June 7, 1932, 16.

49. *Bitter Music,* entry for June 24, 1935.

50. Eleanor Barnes, "Musician Divides Notes."

51. *Bitter Music,* entry for June 12, 1935.

52. Earle Voorhies to the author, June 7, 1991.

53. The eight referees he listed in the application submitted in 1932 were Olga Steeb, George Davis, Mildred Couper, Roy Harris, Lester Donahue, Ernest Schuyten (of the New Orleans Conservatory of Music), Charles Seeger (in New York), and Richard Buhlig (who had read the 1932 draft of the *Exposition*).

54. The closest we have to an authoritative source on Partch's early notation systems is chapter 13 of the first edition of *Genesis of a Music,* a chapter that was discarded in the

revised edition of the book published in 1974, by which time it was badly out of date. The chapter was reprinted as "Experiments in Notation" in the anthology *Contemporary Composers on Contemporary Music,* ed. Elliott Schwartz and Barney Childs (New York: Holt, Rinehart, and Winston, 1967), 209–20.

55. See Bertha Knisely, "Music," *Saturday Night,* Nov. 12, 1932.

56. HP, *Exposition of Monophony* (1933 draft), 37.

57. Bertha Knisely, "Music," *Saturday Night,* Feb. 25, 1933.

58. Isabel Jones, [untitled], *Los Angeles Times,* Feb. 12, 1933.

59. HP to Lauriston Marshall, Oct. 20, 1949.

60. The March 1934 issue of the museum's magazine the *Masterkey* noted that a small sum was "raised by Mrs. Hodge [wife of the Museum's director, Frederick W. Hodge] to meet a part of Mr. Partch's expense" during his work on the transcriptions.

61. HP to Henry Allen Moe, Jan. 27, 1934.

62. HP, introductory comments to transcriptions of Indian songs from the Charles F. Lummis Cylinder Collection. Unpublished manuscript, property of the Southwest Museum, Los Angeles, Braun Research Library, Partch Collection, MS 1.

63. Perlis interview. See also Richard Kassel, "Harry Partch in the Field: Native American influence on his music," *Musicworks: The Canadian Journal of Sound Exploration* 51 (Autumn 1991), 6–15.

64. Perlis interview.

65. *Bitter Music,* entry for Aug. 5, 1935.

66. HP, *Exposition of Monophony* (1933 draft), 50.

67. Contributors included Richard Buhlig, Calista Rogers, Artie Carter (founder of the Hollywood Bowl), Helen Yankwich, and Louis Curtis. In his journal *Bitter Music* (entry for June 24, 1935) Partch notes that the fund provided "thirty-five dollars a month for eight months."

CHAPTER 4. NEW YORK AND EUROPE

1. *Bitter Music,* entry for July 25, 1935.

2. The letter was sent to Partch care of F. G. Goucher, Short Hills, New Jersey, and is now in the possession of the Harry Partch Estate. The idea to contact Schirmer may have come from Calista Rogers.

3. HP, Guggenheim application, Oct. 1933.

4. *Genesis,* 333.

5. The Abbey Theatre Players, from Dublin, had performed the play in New York in January 1933, but it seems impossible that Partch could have been at the performance.

6. HP, Guggenheim application, Oct. 1932.

7. Bertha Knisely, "Music," *Saturday Night,* Dec. 30, 1933.

8. HP to Adolph Weiss, Sept. 20, 1933.

9. For information on Clara Shanafelt I am grateful to Peter Flanders.

10. HP, "Experiments in Notation." The scale given in the "Key" to the notation in Partch's manuscripts has forty-three tones: the thirty-seven-tone scale that he describes in the *Exposition* augmented by six additional tones. These six are in fact suggested by Partch in the text of the treatise (p. 21) as ways of dividing the wide gaps in the scale.

11. HP to Otto Luening, Oct. 6, 1933.

12. HP to Otto Luening, Oct. 21, 1933.

13. HP to Otto Luening, Nov. 1, 1933. In addition to these were the "most ardent and loyal" of his supporters in California, among them Richard Buhlig, Bertha Knisely, Louis Curtis, Redfern Mason, and Artie Carter.

14. Partch quotes the letter in *Bitter Music,* entry for June 24, 1935: the original letter is in the Harry Partch Estate Archive, San Diego.

15. HP probably to Harold Driscoll ("P"), quoted in *Bitter Music,* entry for Nov. 6, 1935.

16. Wallace Stevens, "The Snow Man," from *Harmonium,* reprinted in *The Collected Poems of Wallace Stevens* (London: Faber and Faber, 1945).

17. HP to Henry Allen Moe, Dec. 13, 1933.

18. HP to Henry Allen Moe, Jan. 27, 1934. The first half of the program featured the poet Gilbert Maxwell, reading from his work "Look to the Lightning": Partch's presentation formed the second half. HP, scrapbooks, HPEA/SD.

19. Peter Flanders to the author, Feb. 11, 1990.

20. Reported by HP to Henry Allen Moe, June 22, 1934.

21. Bertha Knisely to HP, June 8, 1934.

22. *Genesis,* 203. Much later he fitted "high, stainless-steel frets into slots in a brass plate, which was then screwed onto the neck"; both *Barstow* and *U.S. Highball* were written for the guitar in this form and he used it in recording those pieces in the 1940s. In 1952 he removed the frets and played it with a weighted plastic rod: the instrument thereafter became known as Adapted Guitar I.

23. The letter is quoted in *Bitter Music,* entry for June 24, 1935. The original is in the HPEA/SD.

24. Two photographs which Partch retained from this time, later pasted into his scrapbooks, show the Pasadena model perched precariously on a balcony wall, with the (later) inscription "Pasadena Keyboard Model—abandoned to an unknown fate March, 1934."

25. *Bitter Music,* entry for June 24, 1935.

26. *Bitter Music,* entry for June 24, 1935.

27. HP to the Institute of International Education (IIE), New York, Oct. 18, 1934.

28. Partch discusses Perrett and his work in *Genesis,* 443.

29. HP to the IIE, Nov. 9, 1934. He arrived in Dublin on the morning of Wednesday, Nov. 14.

30. Partch describes his meeting with Yeats in *Bitter Music,* entry for June 24, 1935, from which the quotations in this paragraph are taken. He gives a further account in the article "W. B. Yeats," written for the *Carmel Pine Cone* six years later.

31. *Genesis,* 332.

32. HP to Henry Allen Moe, Dec. 24, 1934.

33. HP, "W. B. Yeats."

34. HP to Henry Allen Moe, Dec. 24, 1934; and, following the ellipses, *Bitter Music,* entry for June 24, 1935.

35. In *Ideas of Good and Evil* (Dublin: Maunsel, 1905), 16–28.

36. HP to Henry Allen Moe, Dec. 24, 1934.

37. W. B. Yeats to Margot Ruddock, postmarked Nov. 17, 1935. In *Ah Sweet Dancer: W. B.*

Yeats, *Margot Ruddock: A Correspondence,* ed. Roger McHugh (London: Macmillan, 1970), 27–28.

38. Edmund Dulac to HP, Nov. 22, 1934.

39. HP, "Six Months' Report" to the IIE, New York, Feb. 5, 1935.

40. *Bitter Music,* entry for June 24, 1935.

41. Arnold Dolmetsch to W. B. Yeats, Dec. 17, 1934: in *Letters to W. B. Yeats,* ed. Richard J. Finneran, 2 vols. (London: Macmillan, 1977), 2: 568–69.

42. *Bitter Music,* entry for June 24, 1935.

43. *Bitter Music,* entry for June 24, 1935.

44. This and the following quote are from HP to Betty Freeman, Jan. 4, 1974.

45. W. B. Yeats, "Rapallo," from *A Packet for Ezra Pound,* in *A Vision* (London: Macmillan, 1937).

46. *Bitter Music,* entry for June 24, 1935.

47. Yeats, cited in *Ezra Pound: The Critical Heritage,* edited by Eric Homberger (Routledge and Kegan Paul, 1972), 39.

48. *Pound/Joyce: The Letters of Ezra Pound to James Joyce,* edited with commentary by Forrest Read (London: Faber and Faber, 1969), 173.

49. HP to Betty Freeman, July 25, 1968. Another possible source of introduction to Pound would have been the composer George Antheil, whom Partch had evidently met in New York in the autumn of 1933.

50. HP to Henry Allen Moe, Dec. 24, 1935.

51. Willard Connely, director of the American University Union in London, to the IIE in New York, Dec. 20, 1934.

52. *Bitter Music,* entry for June 24, 1935.

53. *Bitter Music,* entry for June 24, 1935.

54. HP to Adolph Weiss, Oct. 13, 1933.

55. Remark recorded during the making of *The Dreamer That Remains,* 1972.

56. *Bitter Music,* entry for June 24, 1935. Partch included a diagram of one octave of the Ptolemy keyboard, showing the forty-three tones of his scale, on p. 206 of the first edition of *Genesis of a Music.*

57. Edmund Dulac to HP, Mar. 15, 1935.

58. W. B. Yeats to HP, undated (probably late Feb. or Mar. 1935).

59. HP, "The Kithara." Schlesinger mentions their earlier meeting in a letter to Partch dated Feb. 15, 1935.

60. Kathleen Schlesinger to HP, Apr. 2, 1935.

61. *Bitter Music,* entry for June 24, 1935.

62. HP, "W. B. Yeats."

63. *Bitter Music,* entry for June 24, 1935.

CHAPTER 5. WESTERN STATES

1. *Genesis,* 323.

2. HP to Meiron Bowen, Oct. 11, 1967.

3. Perlis interview.

4. *Genesis,* 322.

5. HP to the IIE, Nov. 28, 1935, in response to a letter from the director Stephen Duggan, Oct. 22, 1935.

6. Robert M. Lester, secretary of the Carnegie Corporation, to Edward Murrow of the IIE, Apr. 9, 1935.

7. *Bitter Music,* entry for June 24, 1935.

8. Nicholas Zoller to HP, postmarked Dec. 15, 1935.

9. Perlis interview.

10. HP to Henry Allen Moe, Dec. 18, 1936.

11. *Bitter Music,* preface (written in 1940).

12. *Genesis,* 322–23.

13. *Bitter Music,* preface.

14. The microfilm copy made by Lauriston Marshall is now in the Marshall Collection, HPA/UI. The edition of the journal by Thomas McGeary, which includes all of Partch's text and musical notations but excludes his drawings, was prepared from this microfilm.

15. *Genesis,* 323.

16. *Bitter Music,* entry for July 16, 1935.

17. *Bitter Music,* entry for Dec. 1935.

18. *Bitter Music,* entry for Nov. 16, 1935.

19. *Bitter Music,* entry for June 16, 1935.

20. Lou Harrison to the author, Sept. 16, 1990.

21. *Bitter Music,* entry for June 16, 1935.

22. The letter is addressed to James McEnery, Harrington Ranch, Oakley, California; a pencil copy in Partch's hand is in the Harry Partch Estate Archive, San Diego.

23. *Bitter Music,* entry for Oct. 16, 1935.

24. *Bitter Music,* entry for Oct. 29, 1935.

25. *Bitter Music,* entry for July 20, 1935.

26. HP to Ross Santee, Aug. 11, 1936.

27. HP to Ross Santee, Aug. 11, 1936.

28. HP to Henry Allen Moe, Dec. 18, 1936.

29. HP to Lauriston Marshall, Jan. 10, 1950.

30. W. B. Yeats to HP, Aug. 7 [1936].

31. George Cronyn to HP, May 27, 1937.

32. George Cronyn to HP, June 8, 1937.

33. *Bitter Music,* entry for Oct. 31, 1935.

34. On this subject we have the testimonies of Lauriston Marshall, interviewed by Ben Johnston, 1978; and Danlee Mitchell, personal communication, Feb. 1988.

35. *Bitter Music,* entry for Dec. 1935.

36. John Read Brooks to HP, Aug. 22, 1939.

37. Perlis interview.

38. Perlis interview. Discussing his jail history Partch added: "They would have no record of my being there, because I was released first thing in the morning."

39. Perlis interview.

40. HP to David Bowen, Oct. 3, 1960.

41. The only documentation of this comes from two postcards sent to him there by Jack Brooks.

42. Apr. 16, 1938.

43. HP to Peter Yates, Feb. 6, 1961.

44. Noel Heath Taylor, "Artist in the Wilderness," *California Arts and Architecture* 56:1 (July 1939), 8, 36.

45. Partch's own copy of the book, with his inscription "August 14, 1939," is now in the possession of Danlee Mitchell, who kindly showed it to me in San Diego in March 1991. Partch's salary, upon beginning employment with the WPA on July 14, 1939, was $94.40 per month.

46. HP quoted in Bruce Parsons, "Former Madisonian Harry Partch Does Strange Things with Music," *Daily Cardinal* (University of Wisconsin, Madison), Dec. 8, 1972, 3, 13.

47. HP, "Some New and Old Thoughts After and Before *The Bewitched.*"

48. *Genesis,* xiii.

49. HP, "Barstow" (article), 1941.

50. *Bitter Music,* preface.

51. Lillian Bos Ross, "He Would Upset the Whole Musical Applecart," *Monterey Herald,* Apr. 7, 1952.

52. *Bitter Music,* preface.

53. *Genesis,* 323.

54. Jaime de Angulo, "La Costa del Sur," in *A Jaime de Angulo Reader,* edited with an introduction by Bob Callahan (Berkeley: Turtle Island, 1979), 55–56.

55. Alan Watts, *In My Own Way: An Autobiography* (New York: Vintage Books, 1973), 326–27.

56. HP quoted in Cott, "The Forgotten Visionary."

57. HP to Larry and Lucie Marshall, July 5, 1957.

58. Preston Tuttle to Ben Johnston, Apr. 12, 1979: HPA/UI.

59. Henry Miller, *Letters to Anaïs Nin* (New York: Paragon House, 1988).

60. HP to Bertha Knisely Driscoll, Apr. 8, 1941 (the return address is care of Hamilton, 1516 N. Van Ness, Hollywood). Her letter appears not to have survived.

61. HP to the Rockefeller Foundation, July 21, 1973.

62. HP, liner notes to the acetate recording of Barstow made in Chicago, 1942.

CHAPTER 6. CHICAGO, ITHACA, AND NEW YORK

1. *Genesis,* 323–24.

2. HP, *U.S. Highball* film script, 1957.

3. HP, *U.S. Highball* (article), 1943.

4. HP, *U.S. Highball* (article), 1943.

5. HP, *U.S. Highball* film script, 1957.

6. HP, *U.S. Highball* film script, 1957.

7. HP to Ben Johnston, Aug. 2, 1952.

8. "Fingersnaps and Footstomps," *Time,* July 29, 1940.

9. HP to Ben Johnston, Aug. 2, 1952.

10. John Cage, "South Winds in Chicago," *Modern Music* 19:4, May–June 1942, 263.

11. *Genesis of a Music,* first edition, 199.

12. HP, "Harry Partch," mimeographed booklet, May 1942.

13. Partch's letters of February 1942 give his address care of Bishop at 823 East 46th Street.

14. HP to Henry Allen Moe, May 6, 1942. Recording equipment for these sessions was loaned by Philip Manuel and Gavin Williamson.

15. HP to Henry Allen Moe, Feb. 19, 1942.

16. HP to Otto Luening, May 6, 1942.

17. Otto Luening, *The Odyssey of an American Composer* (New York: Charles Scribner's Sons, 1980), 442.

18. HP to Otto Luening, Apr. 24, 1942.

19. The booklet he compiled on his work in May 1942 listed a new Shakespeare setting, the "Mad Scene" from *King Lear,* for baritone, Chromolodian, and Kithara, and several other projected works, still locked in his imagination: *San Francisco, U.S. Highball,* and *King Oedipus.* (The scoring of each of these works as given in the booklet is different than when the works were finally written: *San Francisco* is listed as two voices, Chromolodian, and Adapted Viola, *U.S. Highball* as voice, Chromolodian, and Kithara, and *King Oedipus* as voices, "the Monophonic Instruments," double bass, and timpani.) We do not know if the "Mad Scene" was ever completed; in September of the same year there is another reference to it in a Guggenheim application, in the list of his completed works, this time under the title the "Storm Scene."

20. HP to Henry Allen Moe, June 19, 1942.

21. This certificate, dated June 3, 1942, is now in the Harry Partch Estate Archive. His address is given as 1035 N. Dearborn Street, Chicago.

22. Peter Flanders to the author, Feb. 11, 1990.

23. HP, Guggenheim application, Sept. 1942.

24. Otto Luening to Virgil Thomson, Oct. 12, 1942.

25. Recalled by Michael Ranta, interviewed by the author, July 1989.

26. HP to Otto Luening, Oct. 12, 1942.

27. HP to Otto Luening, Oct. 30 and Nov. 17, 1942.

28. HP to Otto Luening, Mar. 27, 1943.

29. HP to Henry Allen Moe, Apr. 1, 1943.

30. HP to Henry Allen Moe, Oct. 20, 1943.

31. HP to Virgil Thomson, Oct. 21, 1943.

32. Luening, *The Odyssey of an American Composer,* 442.

33. HP to Otto Luening, Nov. 7, 1943.

34. HP to Otto Luening, Nov. 15, 1943. Among other meetings on this trip to New York was one with the maverick theorist Joseph Yasser, proponent of nineteen-tone equal temperament.

35. Henry Brant interviewed by Betty Freeman, Dec. 1985: HPOHP.

36. HP to Henry Allen Moe, Dec. 5, 1943.

37. HP to Henry Allen Moe, Dec. 21, 1943.

38. HP to Henry Allen Moe, Apr. 25, 1944.

39. Henry Brant interviewed by the author, Santa Barbara, Apr. 13, 1988.

40. Henry Brant interviewed by Danlee Mitchell, 1980.

41. Henry Brant has commented that the 1945 Madison recordings of the Joyce songs were much brighter than the intimate 1944 performances, especially thanks to the use of the tin flutes instead of the quiet double flageolet he had played. Henry Brant interviewed by the author, Santa Barbara, Apr. 13, 1988.

42. "Kitharist," *New Yorker,* May 27, 1944, 21–22.

43. *U.S. Highball* (article), 1943.

44. *Genesis,* 322–23.

45. HP, title page to *The Wayward,* 1956.

CHAPTER 7. MADISON

1. *Genesis,* v.

2. HP to Virgil Thomson, Mar. 28, 1943.

3. HP to Virgil Thomson, Mar. 28, 1943.

4. HP to Virgil Thomson, Oct. 21, 1943.

5. Johansen, interviewed in 1978 by Ben Johnston, was unsure which of the two concerts he had attended: HPOHP. The information given here is from Johansen, "Introduction to Harry Partch Records for FM Concert," WHA radio tape, Jan. 20, 1959, Wisconsin Music Archives, Mills Music Library, University of Wisconsin, Madison. Cited in Ronald V. Wiecki, "Relieving '12-Tone Paralysis': Harry Partch in Madison, Wisconsin, 1944–1947," *American Music* 9:1 (Spring 1991), 43–66.

6. HP to Lauriston Marshall, Jan. 10, 1950.

7. Perlis interview.

8. HP to Lauriston Marshall, Jan. 14, 1950.

9. Gunnar and Lorraine Johansen interviewed by Ronald V. Wiecki, Feb. 11, 1987, Blue Mounds, Wisconsin, quoted in Wiecki, "Relieving '12-Tone Paralysis'."

10. Warren Gilson interviewed by Thomas McGeary, Mar. 31, 1979: HPOHP.

11. HP to Harold and Bertha Driscoll, Dec. 24, 1944.

12. Johansen interviewed by Ronald V. Wiecki, in Wiecki, "Relieving '12-Tone Paralysis'," cf. footnote 18.

13. For information on Marshall Glasier and access to Partch's letters to Glasier I am indebted to Kenneth C. Lindsay and Christine Charnstrom Lindsay.

14. Perlis interview.

15. Christine Charnstrom Lindsay to the author, Nov. 26, 1989.

16. Lee Hoiby to the author, Mar. 25, 1990.

17. Christine Charnstrom Lindsay, quoted in Wiecki, "Relieving '12-Tone Paralysis.'"

18. "Harry Partch Has New Views on Native Music," *Milwaukee Journal,* Feb. 11, 1945.

19. HP to Otto Luening, Mar. 12, 1945.

20. HP to Peter Yates, Oct. 20, 1964.

21. Scudder Mekeel to David H. Stevens, Rockefeller Foundation, Mar. 6, 1945: copy in Harry Partch file, University Archives, University of Wisconsin, Madison.

22. HP to Henry Allen Moe, Mar. 11, 1945.

23. Lee Hoiby interviewed by Kenneth Lindsay, 1989: cassette in the possession of the author.

24. Lee Hoiby to the author, Mar. 25, 1990.

25. HP, "Statement for the Research Committee," April 1945: unpublished manuscript, 3 pp., Harry Partch file, University Archives, University of Wisconsin, Madison.

26. HP to Livia Appel, May 9, 1945.

27. HP to Livia Appel, May 9, 1945.

28. HP, undated memorandum to the University of Wisconsin Press, probably spring 1945.

29. Jacques Barzun to HP, May 18, 1945.

30. HP to Peter Yates, Oct. 20, 1964.

31. Leon L. Iltis to Professor E. B. Hart, chairman of the Research Committee, May 22, 1945: Harry Partch file, University Archives, University of Wisconsin, Madison.

32. E. B. Hart to President E. B. Fred, June 18, 1945: Harry Partch file, University Archives, University of Wisconsin, Madison.

33. M. E. McCaffrey, secretary of the Regents of the University of Wisconsin to HP, July 3, 1945.

34. HP to M. E. McCaffrey, July 12, 1945.

35. HP, "Statement for the Research Committee," April 1945.

36. Scudder Mekeel to the Rockefeller Foundation, Mar. 6, 1945: Harry Partch file, University Archives, University of Wisconsin, Madison.

37. Christine Charnstrom Lindsay to the author, Nov. 26, 1989.

38. *Genesis of a Music,* first edition, 197.

39. *Genesis,* second edition, 216.

40. *Genesis of a Music,* first edition, 211.

41. Warren Gilson interviewed by Thomas McGeary, Mar. 31, 1979: cassette in the Harry Partch Archive, University of Illinois.

42. "Extensively": HP to Otto Luening, Dec. 7, 1945.

43. *Genesis,* v.

44. Merrill Jenson to Ira L. Baldwin, dean of the graduate school, University of Wisconsin, July 11, 1945, cited in Wiecki, "Relieving '12-Tone Paralysis.'"

45. Howard Hanson to the University of Wisconsin Press, Mar. 12, 1946: cited in Wiecki, "Relieving '12-Tone Paralysis.'"

46. The only surviving typescript from the Madison years is of what is effectively the penultimate version, dated July 1946, though this is probably a starting date rather than a finishing date. This typescript is now in the Music Division of the New York Public Library, to which it was donated in 1977 by Warren Gilson.

47. HP to Peter Yates, Oct. 20, 1964.

48. HP to Peter Yates, Oct. 20, 1964.

49. HP, "Report to the University of Wisconsin Research Committee on my Work Under Grant for 1945–46": unpublished manuscript, June 26, 1946, University of Wisconsin Archives.

50. Christine Charnstrom, cited in Wiecki, "Relieving '12-Tone Paralysis'."

51. HP to Otto Luening, July 28, 1946.

52. HP, "On G-string Formality." Unpublished typescript, 1946, HPEA/SD.

53. HP to Peter Yates, Oct. 20, 1964.

54. HP to Henry Allen Moe, Apr. 9, 1950.

55. Hulda Gieschen to the author, Nov. 30, 1989.

56. James Jacobs interviewed by Ben Johnston, 1979: HPOHP.

57. Lee Hoiby to the author, Mar. 25, 1990.

58. Lee Hoiby interviewed by Kenneth Lindsay, 1989.

59. HP to Peter Yates, Oct. 20, 1964.

60. HP to Lucie and Larry Marshall, Oct. 20, 1949.

61. Quoted in Karen Monson, "Harry Partch: California's Musical Maverick," *Coast FM & Fine Arts,* Aug. 1969, 24–29.

62. *Genesis,* 8.

63. Jacques Barzun to HP, cited in Wiecki, "Relieving '12-Tone Paralysis'."

64. *Genesis,* 71.

65. *Genesis,* 60.

66. Schoenberg, *Theory of Harmony,* trans. Roy E. Carter (London: Faber and Faber, 1978), 21.

67. Schoenberg, *Style and Idea* (New York: St. Martin's Press, 1975), 216.

68. The earliest appearance of the Diamond shape itself is as the auxiliary diamond keyboard on the Ptolemy, built in the winter of 1934–35. Partch wrote that the "diamond keys" on the Ptolemy "are a substantiation of mathematics as the basis of musical materials. . . . they show that undertones, as the explanation of minor tonality, are intrinsically present in a logical system such as Monophony" ("A New Instrument," *Musical Opinion* [London], June 1935). There is no corresponding image in the Ptolemy's precursor, the Ratio Keyboard designs he drew up in Visalia in September 1932, suggesting that the image came to him sometime between then and his research in Europe.

69. As a reminder, an Otonality is that set of pitches generated by the numerical factors (which Partch calls *identities*) 1, 3, 5, 7, 9, and 11 in the numerator over a numerical constant (which he calls the *numerary nexus*) in the denominator. Conversely, a Utonality is the inversion of an Otonality, a set of pitches with a numerical constant in the numerator over the numerical factors 1, 3, 5, 7, 9, and 11 in the denominator.

70. The concept of the co-existence of major and minor was, of course, not original to Partch, and was noted by Zarlino as early as the sixteenth century. In the 1933 *Exposition of Monophony* Partch credits the discovery to Zarlino: in the published version of his book he is less direct, placing the acknowledgment not in the context of the discussion of the Diamond but mentioning it almost in passing in the final part, on the history of intonation. This may not be subterfuge: it is more likely that he was unwilling to distract from the theoretical discussion by introducing a snippet of history.

71. In the Diamond Marimba the arrangement of identities in each hexad is different from that in the Tonality Diamond: compare *Genesis,* 159 and 261.

72. Christine Charnstrom Lindsay to the author, Nov. 26, 1989.

CHAPTER 8. GUALALA AND OAKLAND

1. HP to Marshall Glasier, undated (probably late June 1947).

2. HP to Livia Appel, Aug. 29, 1947.

3. HP to Livia Appel, Aug. 29, 1947.

4. HP, *End Littoral*, entry for Sept. 17, 1947.

5. HP to Livia Appel, undated (probably early Nov. 1947).

6. HP to Livia Appel, undated (probably mid-Aug. 1948).

7. HP to Marshall Glasier, Mar. 10, 1948.

8. HP to Marshall Glasier, Mar. 10, 1948.

9. HP to Marshall Glasier, undated (c. May 1948).

10. HP to Marshall Glasier, undated (c. May 1948).

11. HP to Marshall Glasier, Aug. 15, 1948.

12. HP to Marshall Glasier, undated (c. June 1948).

13. HP to Marshall Glasier, Aug. 15, 1948.

14. HP to Livia Appel, June 19, 1948.

15. According to Lorraine Johansen (personal communication) the state of the smithy when Partch began work at it was such that "it required repairing and renovating but not reconstructing. The floor, walls, roofs, doors and (some) windows were already there."

16. HP to Marshall Glasier, undated (Sept. or Oct. 1948).

17. HP to Marshall Glasier, Oct. 9, 1948.

18. HP to Thompson Webb of the University of Wisconsin Press, Jan. 25, 1949.

19. HP to Thompson Webb, Jan. 25, 1949.

20. HP to Lauriston Marshall, Dec. 31, 1949.

21. HP to Lauriston Marshall, July 11, 1949.

22. HP to Lauriston Marshall, Aug. 27, 1949.

23. HP to Lauriston Marshall, no date (probably Oct. 1949).

24. HP to Lauriston Marshall, undated (probably late 1949).

25. Lorraine Johansen (personal communication) has suggested that this growing disillusionment, of which neither she nor her husband were aware, may have been due "to what Harry saw as too much preoccupation by Gunnar with his own projects and not enough with Harry's."

26. HP to Lauriston Marshall, Jan. 14, 1950.

27. The name "Azalean" that appears in the colophon on the manuscript was the name Johansen had given to the ranch, because of its large numbers of wild azaleas. Lucie Marshall to the author, May 28, 1990.

28. HP to Lucie and Larry Marshall, Dec. 31, 1949.

29. Partch described *Sonata Dementia* rather dismissively in a letter to Lauriston Marshall, Feb. 27, 1950: "Three of the six [ultimately eight] instruments involved I have never used in compositions before, and to get any facility in writing for them I must know what they sound like together. I just threw a lot of ideas into the thing, without trying to integrate them. It is an exercise."

30. HP to Lauriston Marshall, Feb. 27, 1950.

31. HP to Lauriston Marshall, June 10, 1950.

32. HP to Peter Yates, June 19, 1955.

33. HP to Lauriston Marshall, June 10, 1950.

34. HP to Henry Allen Moe, July 7, 1950.

35. HP to Lauriston Marshall, Oct. 20, 1950.

36. Ben Johnston interviewed by the author, Rocky Mount, N.C., Jan. 1990.

37. Lorraine Johansen (personal communication) has claimed that Partch's statements about gardening in the nude in various of his letters of this time are exaggerated, and that if it happened at all it was confined to the privacy of his immediate surroundings.

38. Ben Johnston interviewed by Thomas McGeary, Urbana, July 1983: HPOHP.

39. Ben Johnston interviewed by the author, Rocky Mount, Jan. 1990.

40. The privy was made from the box that Gunnar Johansen's Steinway piano was delivered in. Gunnar Johansen interviewed by Ben Johnston, 1978: HPOHP.

41. Ben Johnston, "Beyond Harry Partch," 226.

42. Ben Johnston interviewed by the author, Rocky Mount, Jan. 1990.

43. Ben Johnston, "Harry Partch's 'Cloud-Chamber Music,'" unpublished manuscript, courtesy of Ben Johnston.

44. HP to Larry and Lucie Marshall, Feb. 22, 1951.

45. HP to Larry and Lucie Marshall, Feb. 22, 1951.

46. HP to Lauriston Marshall, Mar. 21, 1951.

47. John Krich, *Bump City: Winners and Losers in Oakland,* 1979.

48. HP to Ben Johnston, Aug. 2, 1952.

49. Agnes Albert, thanks to Gunnar Johansen's intercession, provided Partch with a regular stipend during these months.

50. This and the following quotation are from *Genesis,* 334.

51. HP, "W. B. Yeats."

52. HP to Larry and Lucie Marshall, May 26, 1951.

53. HP, "Composer's Statement of Intention," in the program booklet for the production of *King Oedipus* at Mills College, March 1952.

54. HP, unpublished typescript of lecture at the University of Oregon, Feb. 17, 1964.

55. HP to Harold and Bertha Driscoll, Jan. 2, 1952.

56. Adeline Partch to HP, undated (early 1952).

57. HP, unpublished typescript draft of the preface to the second edition of *Genesis of a Music,* 1969: HPEA/SD.

58. HP, unpublished typescript of lecture at the University of Oregon, Feb. 17, 1964.

59. Arch Lauterer, "Comments on Stage Direction and Design," in the program booklet for the production of *King Oedipus* at Mills College, March 1952.

60. HP to Douglas Moore, Dec. 4, 1952.

61. *Genesis,* 332.

62. "Goblin Music?" *Time,* Mar. 24, 1952, p. 44.

63. Wood Soanes, "Mills Group Stages Ancient Greek Tragedy," *Oakland Tribune,* Mar. 15, 1952, p. D-11.

64. Alfred Frankenstein, "New Version of Oedipus at Mills," *San Francisco Chronicle,* Mar. 16, 1952, p. 13.

65. Wilford Leach, "Music for Words Perhaps," *Theatre Arts,* Jan. 1953, 65–68.

66. HP to Peter Yates, June 17, 1952.

67. HP to Lucie Marshall, May 24, 1952.

68. HP to Lucie Marshall, May 24, 1952.

69. A recording of *Castor and Pollux* was made at the end of July 1952, with two of the

musicians from the *King Oedipus* ensemble—Darlene Mahnke and Barbara Browning—overdubbing the instrumental parts.

70. In a letter to Peter Yates on Sept. 25 Partch provides a "Compositions Chronology" which makes no mention of *Ring Around the Moon,* but does list *Sonata Dementia,* dated 1950.

71. HP, spoken introduction to the performance of the *Plectra and Percussion Dances* for KPFA radio in Berkeley, Nov. 1953.

72. HP, spoken introduction to the performance of the *Plectra and Percussion Dances,* Nov. 1953.

73. HP, spoken introduction to the performance of the *Plectra and Percussion Dances,* Nov. 1953.

74. HP, "Castor and Pollux," unpublished typescript notes, 1952: HPEA/SD.

75. *Genesis,* 326.

76. HP, liner notes to "Plectra Percussion Dances," Gate 5 Records Issue C.

77. HP, "The Rhythmic Motivations of *Castor and Pollux* and *Even Wild Horses,*" 1952.

78. *Genesis,* 328.

79. HP, spoken introduction to the performance of the *Plectra and Percussion Dances* for KPFA in Berkeley, Nov. 1953.

80. HP, essay on "Even Wild Horses," 1952.

81. HP, essay on "Even Wild Horses," 1952.

82. HP, spoken introduction to the performance of the *Plectra and Percussion Dances* for KPFA in Berkeley, Nov. 1953.

83. HP, essay on "Even Wild Horses," 1952.

84. HP to Marshall Glasier, Sept. 20, 1952.

85. HP to Douglas Moore, Jan. 23, 1953.

86. HP to Douglas Moore, Oct. 28, 1952.

87. HP to Douglas Moore, Dec. 4, 1952.

88. HP to Douglas Moore, Jan. 17, 1953.

89. HP to Douglas Moore, Jan. 17, 1953.

90. HP to Martha Graham, Feb. 11, 1953.

CHAPTER 9. SAUSALITO AND URBANA

1. HP, "Some New and Old Thoughts After and Before *The Bewitched.*"

2. *Genesis,* ix.

3. HP to Peter Yates, Sept. 25, 1952.

4. Gordon Onslow Ford to the author, Jan. 10, 1990.

5. Gordon Onslow Ford interviewed by Betty Freeman, Jan. 1977: HPOHP.

6. Gordon Onslow Ford interviewed by Betty Freeman, 1977.

7. HP, in the photo supplement prepared in 1957 to accompany records on his Gate 5 label: quoted in *Genesis,* 485.

8. Watts, *In My Own Way,* 295.

9. Anecdote recalled by Betty Freeman at the Harry Partch memorial meeting, Sept. 22, 1974.

10. HP, "A Soul Tormented by Contemporary Music Looks for a Humanizing Alchemy": lecture-demonstration given on Mar. 24, 1957, at the University of Illinois at Urbana-Champaign, two days before the premiere of *The Bewitched*: cassette copy courtesy of Danlee Mitchell. Part of this lecture is published in Partch, ed. McGeary, *Bitter Music*, 239–43.
11. Gordon Onslow Ford interviewed by Betty Freeman, 1977.
12. HP to Douglas Moore, Oct. 19, 1953.
13. HP to Douglas Moore, Oct. 19, 1953.
14. HP to Peter Yates, Mar. 27, 1955.
15. HP to Herbert Feldman, Plenum Publishing Company, New York, Aug. 23, 1973.
16. HP, "Some New and Old Thoughts After and Before *The Bewitched*."
17. HP, "Some New and Old Thoughts After and Before *The Bewitched*."
18. HP to Peter Reed, Dec. 8, 1954.
19. HP to Douglas Moore, Oct. 21, 1953.
20. HP, spoken introduction to the KPFA broadcast of *Oedipus*, July 16, 1954.
21. HP to Albert Goldberg, Oct. 21, 1954.
22. Peter Yates to HP, Nov. 29, 1953.
23. Nin, *The Diary of Anaïs Nin: Volume Five: 1947–1955*, 140.
24. HP to Marshall Glasier, Feb. 23, 1955.
25. HP to Peter Yates, Apr. 15, 1955.
26. *Genesis*, 335.
27. HP to Peter Yates, Mar. 27, 1955.
28. HP, "The Ancient Magic," reprinted in Partch, ed. McGeary, *Bitter Music*, 184–87.
29. HP to Carl Haverlin, Feb. 4, 1955.
30. HP to Peter Yates, Mar. 27, 1955.
31. HP, *The Bewitched*, unpublished typescript draft scenario, 1955. An excerpt from the scenario is published in Partch, ed. McGeary, *Bitter Music*, 231–38.
32. HP, *The Bewitched* draft scenario, 1955.
33. *Genesis*, 334.
34. HP, "A Soul Tormented." In the original version of the score the music was described sardonically as "backgrounds" for the various dance episodes.
35. *Genesis*, 334.
36. Ben Johnston, "The Corporealism of Harry Partch," *Perspectives of New Music* 13:2 (1975), 85–97.
37. The original instrumentation involved clarinet, Adapted Viola, Adapted Guitar III, Kithara II, Harmonic Canon II, Surrogate Kithara, Chromelodeon I, Spoils of War, Diamond Marimba, Bass Marimba, and Marimba Eroica. In the final version of the score Partch replaced Adapted Viola with a cello, removed Adapted Guitar III, and added piccolo, bass clarinet, Koto, Cloud-Chamber Bowls, and Boo.
38. HP to Carl Haverlin, Feb. 4, 1955.
39. During the spring of 1955 the Museum of Man in San Diego and Orange Coast College near Newport Beach both invited him for one-off lectures; Professor Leigh Gerdine of Washington University in St. Louis was trying to raise funding to bring the ensemble to a large convention in the Midwest the following year; Oliver Daniel of Associated Music

Publishers had tried without success to interest the Columbia Concerts agency in subsidizing a tour of colleges in and around New York; and Peter Yates was suggesting several possible venues in California.

40. These and the two quotations following are from HP to Peter Yates, Mar. 27, 1955.

41. HP to Ben Johnston, Apr. 23, 1955.

42. HP, *The Bewitched,* unpublished typescript draft scenario, originally 20 pp., with a later insert of 3 pp. on the prologue. The original version must have been the one he sent to Peter Yates on April 15, 1955, and the insert pages are those he refers to in a letter to Yates in which he enclosed them, dated April 22. The address on the typescript, Box 387, Marin City, Calif., was the return address on his correspondence from the time he was composing *The Bewitched* until his departure from California in September 1956.

43. HP to Peter Yates, Apr. 22, 1955.

44. HP to Ben Johnston, Apr. 23, 1955.

45. HP to Peter Yates, Apr. 22, 1955.

46. HP, "Statement on *The Bewitched* Program Notes," unpublished typescript, c. 1959.

47. HP to Peter Yates, Sept. 27, 1955.

48. HP to Marshall Glasier, Feb. 23, 1955.

49. HP to Peter Yates, Mar. 27, 1955.

50. Watts, *In My Own Way,* 284.

51. Gerd Stern interviewed by Thomas McGeary, 1984: HPOHP.

52. Lou Harrison, personal communication, June 1985.

53. HP to David Bowen, Oct. 3, 1960.

54. HP to Ben Johnston and Wilford Leach, May 6, 1955.

55. HP to Peter Yates, June 19, 1955.

56. *Genesis,* 285–86. The bamboo had been brought to him by a friend, David Wheat, "who worked with the orchestra on one of the President liners and brought the bamboo back under his bunk."

57. A few weeks after completion of the work in December 1955, Carl Haverlin of BMI tried to interest Benny Goodman in playing this second version of *Ulysses.* Goodman, who had performed jazz-inspired pieces by Copland, Bernstein, and others, agreed to have a look at the score but declined to play it. Carl Haverlin to HP, Feb. 7, 1956.

58. *Genesis,* 315.

59. *Summer 1955* consists of the rewritten versions of *By the Rivers of Babylon* and *The Potion Scene;* the *Two Settings from Lewis Carroll* written the previous year; and the two versions of *Ulysses Departs from the Edge of the World.* This collection, quite unlike many of his other similar sets, seems a rather meaningless grouping, and *Summer 1955* has never been performed as a cycle—and perhaps was not intended to be. The only convincing reason why Partch should have put it together at all is for copyright purposes: this collection and the other fruits of his rewriting labors, *Barstow, U.S. Highball, San Francisco,* and *The Letter,* which he collectively entitled *The Wayward,* were both copyrighted on the same day, Sept. 26, 1956.

60. HP to Peter Yates, Sept. 27, 1955.

61. HP, unpublished typescript notes for *And I'll Tell You My Story,* no date (c. 1955): HPEA/SD.

62. HP to Peter Yates, Nov. 22, 1955.

63. HP to Peter Yates, Dec. 10, 1955.

64. HP to Peter Yates, Dec. 10, 1955.

65. HP to Peter Yates, Oct. 26, 1957.

66. HP to Ben Johnston, Jan. 12, 1956. Partch noted that the trip was made possible by "a gift of $200 from a new friend in California."

67. HP to Ben Johnston, Mar. 21, 1956.

68. Garland, who spoke with Partch about Nancarrow during a visit in February 1974, recounts the story in "Conlon Nancarrow: Chronicle of a Friendship," in Garland, *Americas: Essays on American Music and Culture, 1973–80* (Santa Fe: Soundings Press, 1982), 157–85.

69. HP to Ben Johnston, Mar. 21, 1956.

70. In the early planning stages Johnston in fact spoke both to Martha Graham and to Doris Humphrey about choreographing *The Bewitched*. Ben Johnston interviewed by the author, Oct. 1987.

71. HP to Peter Yates, Oct. 26, 1957.

72. HP to Lou Harrison, May 28, 1956.

73. During his stay at The Pink Adobe, Partch found some pleasant distraction helping McKinney's wife, Rosalea, with the final stages of a cookbook she had been writing, *Cooking with a Silver Spoon*. Rosalea's foreword, dated April 1956, records her "thanks to Harry Partch, our pioneer composer friend; with his help COOKING WITH A SILVER SPOON was finally edited and organized." A copy of the cookbook is still in the possession of Ben and Betty Johnston, who kindly showed it to me in March 1991.

74. HP to Ben Johnston, Sept. 20, 1956.

75. HP to Peter Yates, Oct. 26, 1957.

76. HP to Peter Yates, May 9, 1961.

77. Kenneth Gaburo, "In Search of Partch's *Bewitched*, Part One: Concerning Physicality," 71.

78. Kenneth Gaburo, personal communication, Feb. 1990.

79. HP to Lauriston Marshall, Mar. 5, 1957.

80. Danlee Mitchell, personal communication, Jan. 1989.

81. HP to Christine Charnstrom Lindsay and Kenneth Lindsay, June 30, 1957.

82. Kenneth Gaburo interviewed by Daniel Atesh Sonneborn, Apr. 4, 1984: in Sonneborn, "Corporeality in the Music-Theatre of Harry Partch," M.A. thesis, University of California, San Diego, 1984.

83. HP to Peter Yates, Oct. 30, 1957.

84. HP to Christine Charnstrom Lindsay and Kenneth Lindsay, June 30, 1957.

85. This decision was perhaps influenced by the fact that when Johnston joined the University of Illinois faculty in 1951 his employment was half-time in music and half-time in the dance department; he had in this way come in contact with a number of choreographers and had a good understanding of their work.

86. Walter Sorell, *The Dance Through the Ages* (London: Thames and Hudson, 1967), 252. See also Susan Au, *Ballet and Modern Dance* (London: Thames and Hudson, 1988), 158–60, and Joseph H. Mazo, *Prime Movers: The Makers of Modern Dance in America* (London: Adam and Charles Black, 1977), 231–43.

87. *Genesis*, 8. Arguably, Partch's concept of corporeality can be said to apply—even though it was not yet consciously articulated—to his very earliest work. What seems to be his first expression of the idea comes in his description of a projected composition from around 1948, *Mendota Night*, "the dramatization of an instant of solitude." The visual aspect of this never-to-be-written work was "subdivided into three parts: (a) movements of the dancers; (b) movements of the musicians in playing their instruments; (c) staging and lights." HP, unpublished typescript notes for *Mendota Night*, c. 1948.

88. Alwin Nikolais to HP, Oct. 18, 1956.

89. Alwin Nikolais to HP, Oct. 27, 1956.

90. Alwin Nikolais to HP, Oct. 18, 1956.

91. Alwin Nikolais to HP, undated [early Feb. 1957].

92. Alwin Nikolais to HP, undated [early Feb. 1957].

93. Alwin Nikolais to HP, undated [early Feb. 1957].

94. HP to Alwin Nikolais, Feb. 19, 1957.

95. HP to Eleanor King, Feb. 20, 1957.

96. Alwin Nikolais to HP, no date [Feb. 1957].

97. HP to Lauriston Marshall, Feb. 27, 1957.

98. Alwin Nikolais to HP, Feb. 28, 1957.

99. HP to Peter Yates, Oct. 26, 1957.

100. This second performance was recorded, but the result was unsatisfactory and not helped by the noise of "dancers' feet stomping on the stage." HP to Peter Yates, July 31, 1963.

101. The previews and reviews of the premiere of *The Bewitched* are listed in Thomas McGeary, *The Music of Harry Partch: A Descriptive Catalog* (New York: Institute for Studies in American Music, 1991), 136–40.

102. HP, statement for the Composers Recordings Incorporated (CRI) release of *The Bewitched*, originally written as a letter to Carter Harman of CRI, New York, June 6, 1973.

103. Ibid. Murray Louis, who danced in the première of *The Bewitched*, has pointed out (personal communication) that Partch was inaccurate in claiming that "the Witch was discarded totally as a dramatic element." The playbill for Nikolais's performances of the work in New York in October 1957 clearly lists the Witch among the dramatis personae in the prologue, played by the dancer Arlene Laub. Photographs of the later Nikolais performances are included in my article "'A Soul Tormented': Alwin Nikolais and Harry Partch's *The Bewitched*," *The Musical Quarterly* 79:1 (Spring 1995), 80–107.

104. Wilfrid Mellers, "An Authentic American Composer," *Times Literary Supplement*, May 31, 1991, 16. All the performances of *The Bewitched* during Partch's lifetime were given at academic institutions. Nikolais and the Playhouse Dance Company performed *The Bewitched* at the Henry Street Playhouse in New York, with a tape of the music, on Oct. 11–13, 1957.

105. Ben Johnston to Kipps Horn, undated [Feb. 1983]: copy courtesy of the author.

CHAPTER 10. YELLOW SPRINGS, CHICAGO, EVANSTON, AND CHAMPAIGN

1. HP to Lauriston Marshall, May 25, 1957.

2. HP to Christine Charnstrom Lindsay, June 30, 1957.

3. HP to Lauriston Marshall, May 25, 1957.

4. HP to Christine Charnstrom Lindsay, June 30, 1957.

5. HP to Lauriston Marshall, July 5, 1957.

6. HP to Christine Charnstrom Lindsay, June 30, 1957.

7. HP to Lauriston Marshall, June 11, 1957.

8. HP to Lauriston Marshall, July 5, 1957.

9. HP to Christine Charnstrom Lindsay, June 30, 1957.

10. HP to Christine Charnstrom Lindsay, June 30, 1957.

11. HP to Christine Charnstrom Lindsay, July 28, 1957.

12. HP to Christine Charnstrom Lindsay, July 28, 1957.

13. HP, film script for *U.S. Highball,* 1957.

14. HP to Lauriston Marshall, Aug. 14, 1957.

15. Robert Kostka to the author, Feb. 20, 1991.

16. HP to Lauriston Marshall, Aug. 14, 1957.

17. HP and Madeline Tourtelot interviewed by Charles Sharp, on the occasion of the premiere of *Windsong* on WTTW-TV, Chicago, Mar. 19, 1958.

18. Robert Kostka to the author, Feb. 20, 1991. In a letter to Partch of July 10, 1963, Tourtelot wrote that "I feel that 'Windsong' could never have come into being without you and that it is largely you and I shall be eternally grateful, believe me."

19. HP and Madeline Tourtelot interviewed by Charles Sharp, WTTW-TV, Chicago, 1958.

20. The three quotations in this paragraph are from HP to Lauriston Marshall, Aug. 14, 1957.

21. HP to Peter Yates, July 17, 1957.

22. HP to William Wilder, Sept. 3, 1957.

23. HP to William Wilder, Sept. 3, 1957.

24. HP to an unidentified correspondent, Aug. 31, 1957.

25. Thompson Webb to HP, Oct. 30, 1957. Sales of the book had been slow but steady. By April 1952 some 300 copies had been sold; by October 1957 about 720, including Carnegie's 300; and by Dec. 1962 about 850. Partch in consequence received almost nothing by way of royalties for *Genesis.*

26. HP to Thompson Webb, Jan. 13, 1958.

27. HP to Lauriston Marshall, Oct. 23, 1957.

28. HP to Lauriston Marshall, Nov. 28, 1957.

29. HP to Lauriston Marshall, Jan. 7, 1958.

30. Robert Kostka to the author, Feb. 20, 1991.

31. HP, liner notes for *Thirty Years of Lyrical and Dramatic Music,* Gate 5 Records Issue A, 1962.

32. HP to Peter Yates, postmarked Feb. 27, 1958.

33. Glenn Allen Hackbarth, "Tonality in *Daphne of the Dunes," Percussive Notes Research Edition* 21:6 (Sept. 1983), 57–71. The music and the film are discussed in even more detail in Hackbarth's "An Analysis of Harry Partch's *Daphne of the Dunes,*" D.M.A. thesis, University of Illinois at Urbana-Champaign, 1979.

34. Wilfrid Mellers, *Music in a New Found Land* (New York: Knopf, 1965), 176.

35. Elizabeth Gentry Sayad to the author, Dec. 8, 1989.

36. Elizabeth Gentry Sayad, "Partch's *U.S. Highball,*" written in 1958 and included in her

collection *A Scarlet Thread: Collected Writings on Culture and the Arts* (St. Louis: The Patrice Press, 1991), 128–30.

37. *Genesis,* 251.

38. HP to Lee Hoiby, July 23, 1958.

39. Danlee Mitchell interviewed by the author, Jan. 1989.

40. Gordon Onslow Ford to HP, Apr. 17, 1958.

41. HP, liner notes for *U.S. Highball,* Gate 5 Records Issue no. 6, 1958.

42. Elizabeth Gentry Sayad to the author, Dec. 8, 1989.

43. Elizabeth Gentry Sayad to the author, Dec. 8, 1989.

44. HP to Lee Hoiby, July 23, 1958.

45. HP to Danlee Mitchell, July 21, 1958.

46. HP to Lauriston Marshall, Aug. 5, 1958.

47. HP to Danlee Mitchell, July 21, 1958.

48. HP to Danlee Mitchell, Aug. 5, 1958.

49. HP to Lauriston Marshall, Aug. 5, 1958.

50. HP to Sally Fairweather, Aug. 8, 1958.

51. The quotations in this paragraph are from HP to Danlee Mitchell, Aug. 26, 1958.

52. Elizabeth Gentry Sayad to the author, Dec. 8, 1989.

53. Danlee Mitchell interviewed by the author, Jan. 1989.

54. HP to Lauriston Marshall, Oct. 5, 1958.

55. HP to Danlee Mitchell, Tuesday [Sept. 23, 1958].

56. HP to John Beckwith, Oct. 4, 1958.

57. HP to Danlee Mitchell, Tuesday [Sept. 23, 1958].

58. HP to John Beckwith, Oct. 4, 1958.

59. The editing of *Music Studio* was completed in January 1959 in Urbana with the help of technician Bill Godsey: Partch wrote on Jan. 19 to Tourtelot to tell her that they had cut some unnecessary shots and were recording a slightly altered narration.

60. Nin, *The Diary of Anaïs Nin, Volume Five: 1947–55,* 240–42. The date given by the editor for this entry, "Summer, 1955," for all its Partchian connotations, is clearly inaccurate by more than three years.

61. HP to Danlee Mitchell, Oct. 18, 1958.

62. Minutes of the Alice M. Ditson Advisory Committee Meeting at the Guggenheim offices on Dec. 20, 1958, courtesy of Central Files, Columbia University, New York.

63. HP to Quincy and Lois Porter, Dec. 14, 1958.

64. HP to Bertha and Harold Driscoll, Dec. 24, 1958.

65. Anaïs Nin to HP, undated (c. Dec. 1958).

66. HP to Robert Kostka, Apr. 30, 1959.

67. HP to Douglas Moore, undated (probably early May 1959).

68. HP, statement for the CRI release of *The Bewitched,* originally written as a letter to Carter Harman of CRI, June 6, 1973.

69. Jay S. Harrison, "The Bewitched," *New York Herald Tribune,* Apr. 11, 1959, p. 6.

70. John Martin, "A 'Dance-Satire' Is Offered Here: Columbia and University of Illinois Stage 'Bewitched' at Juilliard Concert Hall," *New York Times,* Apr. 11, 1959, p. 14.

71. Nin, *The Diary of Anaïs Nin, Volume Five: 1947–55,* 242.

72. HP to Douglas Moore, May 28, 1959.
73. Ben Johnston, liner notes to *Harry Partch/John Cage,* New World Records NW214, 1978.
74. His appointment was as "research associate in music" in the Graduate School, initially for one year beginning June 16, 1959. His salary was $5,500 per annum, considerably more than he was used to.
75. HP to Thomas DeGaetani, Oct. 11, 1959.
76. HP to Ben Johnston, May 6, 1955.
77. *Genesis,* 343.
78. HP, unpublished typescript notes for *Dion Isus,* no date: HPEA/SD.
79. *Genesis,* 343.
80. *Genesis,* 343.
81. Partch's friend Lynn Ludlow, reviewing the performance of the completed work in April 1961, suggested that this particular theme "probably was born during Mothers' Day Weekend at the University [in 1959]. The slogan was 'Mom's the Word' that year, and it intrigued Partch a great deal." Lynn Ludlow, "Partch 'Heresy' Began with Battered Viola," *Champaign-Urbana Spectator,* Apr. 17, 1961, 3.
82. HP to Peter Yates, Dec. 11, 1959.
83. Danlee Mitchell interviewed by the author, Jan. 1989.
84. *Genesis,* 347.
85. HP to Monika Jensen, Oct. 18, 1968.
86. Ben Johnston, "Ritual and Prophecy," unpublished manuscript written on request as liner notes for a projected release of the 1961 recording of *Revelation in the Courthouse Park* by Lingua Press, c. 1981.
87. The quotations in this paragraph are from HP to Peter Yates, July 17, 1960.
88. *Genesis,* 348.
89. John Garvey interviewed by Daniel Atesh Sonneborn, Mar. 1984, in Sonneborn, "Corporeality in the Music-Theatre of Harry Partch" (M.A. thesis, University of California, San Diego, 1984), 172.
90. Barnard Hewitt interviewed by Daniel Atesh Sonneborn, Mar. 1984, in Sonneborn, "Corporeality in the Music-Theatre of Harry Partch," 165.
91. *Genesis,* 344.
92. In his "Report by Harry Partch for 1960–61" to the University Research Board, dated May 12, 1961, Partch noted that thanks to "a gift of some $2200 from Madeline Tourtelot, a video tape of a complete performance of *Revelation* was made" by WILL-TV, University of Illinois, which broadcast it on April 25.
93. Peter Yates, "Music: Revelation in Illinois," *Arts & Architecture,* Aug. 1961, 4–6, 28–29.
94. Allen S. Weller, Dean of the College of Fine and Applied Arts, University of Illinois, to HP, Apr. 27, 1961.
95. Danlee Mitchell interviewed by the author, Apr. 1988.
96. This emerged in June 1961 as *META + HODOS: A Phenomenology of Twentieth-Century Musical Materials and an Approach to the Study of Form.* It was republished in book form a quarter-century later (Oakland, Calif.: Frog Peak Music, 1986; second edition, 1988).
97. HP to Peter Yates, Feb. 6, 1961.
98. James Tenney to the author, Aug. 22, 1990. As had happened in the case of Ben

Johnston—who did not begin to work with extended just intonation in his own music until around 1960—it was some time before an interest in tuning, and in particular the relationship between tuning and harmony, manifested itself in Tenney's work. "My early contact with [Partch]—and, more especially, his book—planted a seed that would only begin to sprout over a decade later (in 1972, with *Quintext*), and has continued to grow."

99. Michael Ranta interviewed by the author, Cologne, July 1989.

100. HP, "Report by Harry Partch for 1960–61" to the University Research Board, May 12, 1961.

101. HP to Peter Yates, Nov. 14, 1959.

102. HP, narration (recorded in 1970) for the bonus record for the Columbia Records release of *Delusion of the Fury.*

103. HP, preface to the score of *Water! Water!* The themes of progress and regress had featured in a short satirical essay called "A Somewhat Spoof," which he had written a few months earlier, in September 1960, at the request of Oliver Daniel. In this essay, the narrator introduces himself as a "humbled traditionalist from ancient ages," whom the gods have ejected from paradise back into the human world because, having (in his former life) stood for progress, he has learned "that man must also understand regress." The two main strands of this "progress" that the narrator lampoons are, first, purity—in music, dance, film, painting, and sex—and, second, the vogue for Eastern wisdom—"What was that again? All wise farts come out of the East?" The narrator has concluded that he should "let not one year pass when I do not step one significant century backward." By this freewheeling logic, he looks forward to the time when, having "regressed as far as I can possibly go, I shall have actually arrived at a point some years in the wild future, and maybe it won't be so godawful pure."

104. Ben Johnston in conversation with the author, Jan. 1990.

105. HP to David Hall, July 16, 1964.

106. This and the following quotation are from HP to Gordon Ray, General Secretary of the Guggenheim Foundation, Dec. 6, 1961.

107. HP to Ben Johnston, Nov. 2, 1962.

108. *Genesis*, 473.

109. Barnard Hewitt interviewed by Daniel Atesh Sonneborn, Mar. 1984, in Sonneborn, "Corporeality in the Music-Theatre of Harry Partch," 162–63.

110. HP to David Hall, July 16, 1964.

111. John Garvey interviewed by Daniel Atesh Sonneborn, Mar. 1984, in Sonneborn, "Corporeality in the Music-Theatre of Harry Partch," 179.

112. HP to Peter Yates, Aug. 19, 1961.

113. HP to Peter Yates, Aug. 4, 1962. Partch later excluded the previews and reviews of the performances of *Water! Water!* from the bibliography in the second edition of *Genesis of a Music.*

114. This and the following quotation are from HP to Peter Yates, Aug. 4, 1962.

115. HP to Peter Yates, Sept. 4, 1962. The photograph of Partch with his pipe that appears on the back of the Gate 5 Issue A record was taken by Madeline Tourtelot on her return from the Edinburgh Festival in September.

CHAPTER 11. PETALUMA

1. HP to Peter Yates, Sept. 28, 1962.
2. HP to Ben Johnston, Nov. 2, 1962.
3. *Genesis,* 348.
4. HP to Peter Yates, Sept. 28, 1962.
5. This and the following quote are from HP to Ben Johnston, Nov. 2, 1962.
6. HP to David Hall, July 16, 1964.
7. HP, "Proposal for Studies in the Creative Arts" (unpublished document, 8 pp., 1962), HPEA/SD.
8. HP to Danlee Mitchell, Feb. 14, 1963.
9. HP to Peter Yates, Jan. 15, 1963.
10. HP to Danlee Mitchell, Jan. 13, 1963.
11. HP to Michael Ranta, Feb. 23, 1963.
12. A copy of the first draft of the *Manual,* typed by Michael Ranta before the final draft was completed in August, was kindly put at my disposal by Mr. Ranta: quotations from the text in this chapter are, however, given with reference to Partch's own typescript.
13. *Manual,* 7–8.
14. *Manual,* 2. Partch's Mexican sojourn, during which the *Manual* began to take shape, prompted some of the allusions in the text. An example is his description of his failure to persuade Chromelodeon players to play tone clusters with an absolutely flat hand: "I say, 'Let me see you flatten your hand in the air. Perfect! Now do it on the keyboard.' But what I get is an eagle's claw, snatching the snake off the cactus in ancient Tenochtitlan, on an island in Lake Texcoco."
15. HP to Danlee Mitchell, Feb. 14, 1963.
16. HP to Lauriston Marshall, Feb. 15, 1963.
17. HP to Danlee Mitchell, Feb. 14, 1963.
18. HP to Lauriston Marshall, Feb. 15, 1963.
19. HP to Danlee Mitchell, Apr. 30, 1963.
20. HP to Michael Ranta, Feb. 23, 1963.
21. HP to James and Marion Jacobs, Mar. 2, 1972.
22. *Manual,* 23.
23. KPIX-TV in San Francisco made a video on the afternoon following the Sheraton Palace Hotel performance. Both Partch and the station were pleased with the result, which was shown on KPIX Channel 5 on Sept. 4 as a half-hour program entitled "The Music of Harry Partch."
24. HP to Oliver Daniel, July 15, 1963.
25. HP to Emil Richards, June 24, 1963.
26. HP to Oliver Daniel, July 15, 1963.
27. HP to Danlee Mitchell, July 10, 1963.
28. HP to Danlee Mitchell, July 2, 1963.
29. Madeline Tourtelot to HP, July 10, 1963.
30. Madeline Tourtelot to HP, Aug. 3, 1963.
31. This and the following quote are from HP to Danlee Mitchell, Nov. 22, 1963.

32. HP to Michael Ranta, Nov. 20, 1963.
33. HP to Michael Ranta, Nov. 20, 1963.
34. HP to Danlee Mitchell, Nov. 22, 1963.
35. HP to Michael Ranta, Nov. 20, 1963.
36. HP to Peter Yates, Nov. 27, 1963.
37. HP to Danlee Mitchell, Nov. 22, 1963.
38. HP to Peter Yates, Nov. 27, 1963.
39. This and the following quote are from HP to Danlee Mitchell, Dec. 13, 1963.
40. HP to Michael Ranta, Feb. 27, 1964.
41. HP to Danlee Mitchell, Mar. 11, 1964.
42. HP to Peter Yates, Mar. 12, 1964.
43. Michael Ranta interviewed by the author, July 1989.
44. *Genesis,* 348.
45. HP to Danlee Mitchell, Jan. 31, 1964.
46. HP to Michael Ranta, Mar. 7, 1964.
47. *Genesis,* 350.
48. HP, "A Quarter-Saw Section of Motivations and Intonation."
49. Harmonic Canon I is tuned this way in "The Wind" and "The Street" from the *Eleven Intrusions,* and in *Ring Around the Moon;* Harmonic Canon III (right canon) is tuned this way in *The Dreamer That Remains.*
50. The only two truly analytical articles on Partch's music published during his lifetime both concerned aspects of *Petals:* Elliott Friedman, "Tonality in the Music of Harry Partch: A Harmonic Analysis of Verse 3 of 'And On the Seventh Day Petals Fell in Petaluma,'" *The Composer* 2:1 (June 1970), 17–24; and Paul Earls, "Harry Partch: Verses in Preparation for 'Delusion of the Fury,'" *Inter-American Institute for Musical Research Yearbook* 3 (1967), 1–32.
51. Michael Ranta interviewed by the author, July 1989.
52. HP to Peter Yates, Mar. 12, 1964.
53. HP to Danlee Mitchell, Mar. 11, 1964.
54. HP to David Hall, July 16, 1964.
55. Mary McChesney, who under her maiden name Mary Fuller wrote articles mostly on Bay Area sculptors, published a piece on Partch in the December 1964 issue of *Art in America.*
56. Michael Ranta interviewed by the author, July 1989.
57. HP, introductory notes to the score of *Delusion of the Fury,* 1966.
58. Danlee Mitchell interviewed by the author, Jan. 1989.
59. HP to David Hall, July 16, 1964.
60. Martin Kamen to HP, Apr. 2, 1964.
61. HP to Peter Yates, Sept. 14, 1964.
62. HP to Emil Richards, July 24, 1964.

CHAPTER 12. DEL MAR, VAN NUYS, VENICE, AND SAN DIEGO

1. HP to Emil Richards, July 24, 1964.
2. HP to Peter Yates, Sept. 14, 1964.

3. HP to Danlee Mitchell, Aug. 5, 1964.

4. HP to Peter Yates, Sept. 14, 1964.

5. *Genesis,* 312.

6. Perlis interview. The Chinese temple bells were given to him by Emil Richards.

7. *Genesis,* 294.

8. HP to Emil Richards, Sept. 15, 1964.

9. HP to Oliver Daniel, July 15, 1963.

10. HP to Emil Richards, Feb. 24, 1964.

11. Emil Richards to the author, Feb. 5, 1992.

12. Betty Freeman interviewed by the author, Apr. 1988.

13. HP to Emil Richards, Oct. 23, 1964.

14. Danlee Mitchell interviewed by the author, Apr. 1988.

15. Betty Freeman, personal communication. Partch's own lecture-demonstration at the Pasadena Art Museum, originally arranged for Nov. 23, 1964, was postponed until the following February: the havoc of his move to Van Nuys prevented him from being able to prepare adequately.

16. HP to Lauriston Marshall, Jan. 12, 1965.

17. HP to John Cage, Oct. 14, 1967.

18. Partch had written to Peter Yates that ideas for the work had been on his mind from as far back as 1960, during the composition of *Revelation in the Courthouse Park;* letter of Sept. 14, 1964.

19. Quotations in this and the following paragraph are from HP, scenario for *Delusion of the Fury,* 1965. The sources are Arthur Waley, *The Noh Plays of Japan* (New York: Grove Press, 1957); and Peggy Rutherford, comp. and ed., *African Voices* (New York: Grosset and Dunlap, 1958).

20. Will Salmon, "The Influence of Noh on Harry Partch's *Delusion of the Fury,*" *Perspectives of New Music* 22 (1984), 233–45.

21. Danlee Mitchell, quoted in Salmon, "The Influence of Noh."

22. Raymond Weston interviewed by Ben Johnston, 1979: HPOHP.

23. HP to Barnard Hewitt, Apr. 30, 1965.

24. Around this time Mitchell wrote the most substantial article he published on Partch during the composer's lifetime, "Percussion in the Orchestra of Harry Partch," which appeared in *Percussionist* (Apr. 1966), 37–38.

25. HP to Danlee Mitchell, Mar. 30, 1965.

26. The quotations come from HP's letters to Danlee Mitchell of Apr. 4 and Mar. 30, 1965, respectively.

27. HP to Betty Freeman, Apr. 22, 1965.

28. HP to Betty Freeman, June 11, 1965.

29. HP, narration (recorded in 1970) for the instrument demonstration record included with the Columbia Records release of *Delusion of the Fury.*

30. *Genesis,* 270.

31. Erv Wilson, conversation with the author, Aug. 1993. The layouts of the two instruments are given in *Genesis,* 261 and 269. The Diamond Marimba and the Quadrangularis Reversum are played off to great effect in the Exordium from *Delusion of the Fury.*

32. HP, narration for the instrument demonstration record included with the Columbia Records release of *Delusion of the Fury.*

33. HP to Emil Richards, July 4, 1965.

34. HP to Peter Yates, Oct. 14, 1965.

35. HP to David Hall, Mar. 29, 1966.

36. HP to Danlee Mitchell, July 17, 1965.

37. HP to Peter Yates, Oct. 14, 1965.

38. *Genesis,* 298.

39. *Genesis,* 248.

40. HP to Danlee Mitchell, Nov. 11, 1965.

41. *Genesis,* 350.

42. The Bolivian Double Flute, although a gift rather than his own creation, was integrated quite naturally into the music of *Delusion;* this was somewhat different than the situation with Gordon and Jacqueline Onslow Ford's gift of a koto in Sausalito in 1956, a part for which he grafted onto the already completed score of *The Bewitched.* The flute has two bores going into a single mouthpiece: there are five pairs of holes on top, a pair of exit holes, and a pair of thumb holes. The instrument is notated in the score as Beta.

43. *Genesis,* 355.

44. *Genesis,* 357.

45. In Apr. 1966, with the score of *Delusion* complete, he received a psaltery as a gift from Lou Harrison for use in the projected performance of *Petals.* Partch regarded the instrument as a koto "because I had written for this instrument previously and I use the same number of strings as before—thirteen" (*Genesis,* 251). Because of its superior resonance he used it in *Delusion* to replace the koto given to him by the Onslow Fords ten years earlier.

46. HP to Betty Freeman, Dec. 22, 1965.

47. The quotations in this paragraph are from HP to Danlee Mitchell, Mar. 5, 1966.

48. HP, lecture at UCLA, May 8, 1966.

49. Peter Yates to HP, May 9, 1966.

50. HP to ensemble, May 14, 1966.

51. HP to Betty Freeman, July 28, 1966.

52. HP to David Hall, June 12, 1966.

53. HP to Betty Freeman, May 29, 1966.

54. HP to David Hall, June 12, 1966.

55. HP to Betty Freeman, July 28, 1966.

56. In a letter of June 6, 1967, to David Hall at CRI, Partch gave the breakdown of the 48 individual parts on the finished tape as follows: Partch 12, Mitchell 9, Ranta 9, Richards 8, Snow 5, Tosh 5. The names of the six players involved in the recording could not be listed on the LP sleeve "for contractual reasons."

57. HP to Arthur Woodbury, Sept. 5, 1966.

58. HP to Betty Freeman, Sept. 19, 1966.

59. HP to Lauriston Marshall, Sept. 24, 1966.

60. HP to Peter Yates, Oct. 18, 1966.

61. Will Ogdon to HP, Sept. 30, 1966.

62. HP, "Statement," Mar. 12, 1967: unpublished typescript, 3 pp., HPEA/SD.

63. HP to William M. Bowen, Oct. 11, 1967.

64. HP to David Hall, Sept. 19, 1966. The award finally arrived in 1974, only months before his death.

65. HP to Emil Richards, Jan. 3, 1967.

66. HP to Betty Freeman, Oct. 30, 1966.

67. HP to Peter Yates, Dec. 18, 1966.

68. HP to Patty Wright, Aug. 20, 1970.

69. In fact there was no deficit following the performances in Jan. 1969. Betty Freeman, personal communication.

70. HP to Peter Yates, Dec. 18, 1966.

71. HP to David Hall, Dec. 4, 1966.

72. HP to Peter Yates, Dec. 18, 1966.

73. HP to Betty Freeman, Jan. 13, 1967.

74. HP to Betty Freeman, Jan. 13, 1967.

75. HP to Betty Freeman, Oct. 30, 1966.

76. HP to Will Ogdon, Feb. 4, 1967.

77. HP to Betty Freeman, Mar. 4, 1967.

78. HP to Harry R. Wellman, Mar. 30, 1967.

79. Three performances of *Castor and Pollux* were given on May 12, 13, and 14, 1967, with a dance group in Los Angeles. For the first time Danlee Mitchell assumed all of the responsibilities for the preparations and the performances, including renting a room over an antique store in San Diego for rehearsals. Partch could not even bring himself to attend, unable to face another trip to the "screaming nothingness" of that city.

80. HP, introductory notes to the 1967 score of *Oedipus*. The score had new parts for Kithara II (conforming to the tuning adopted between completing the score and writing the part for the Sausalito performances), Chromelodeon II, bass clarinet, and Gourd Tree and Cone Gongs. The Gourd Tree was used to augment the part for Cloud-Chamber Bowls, as all the original Bowls had by this time been broken. The Bowls part itself he left blank; it was "to be filled in later if and when another performance is scheduled," the part to be recomposed in accordance with the pitches of the Bowls available. *Genesis,* 302.

81. HP to David Hall, Aug. 22, 1967.

82. HP to Avery Claflin, Aug. 23, 1967.

83. HP to Carter Harman, Oct. 14, 1967.

84. HP to Danlee Mitchell, Oct. 28, 1967.

85. HP to Emil Richards, Aug. 8, 1967.

86. HP, undated typescript for lecture at UCSD [autumn 1967].

87. John Chalmers interviewed by Thomas McGeary, 1984: HPOHP.

88. Jack Logan cited in Jeff Smith, "The Partch Reverberations: Notes on a Musical Rebel," *Soundings* 12 (Santa Fe, 1982), 46–59.

89. HP, undated typescript for lecture at UCSD [autumn 1967].

90. HP, undated typescript for lecture at UCSD [autumn 1967].

91. HP, "My Seminar in Retrospect," unpublished typescript, Dec. 17, 1967.

92. HP to Carter Harman, Oct. 6, 1967.

93. HP to Carter Harman, Oct. 14, 1967.

94. Following the performances, on May 17, 1968, KEBS-TV at San Diego State College filmed a performance of *Daphne of the Dunes* on the lawn in front of the UCSD Art Gallery. This, preceded by an interview with Partch by Will Ogdon, formed a 28-minute TV documentary called "The Music of Harry Partch," which was broadcast by KEBS Channel 15 in October, and shown again by several NET stations in the western states and Hawaii in July the following year.

95. HP to Peter Yates, May 25, 1968.

96. HP to Betty Freeman, July 25, 1968.

97. HP to Betty Freeman, July 2, 1969.

98. Peter G. Davis, "Composer Harry Partch—With Boo And Eucal Blossom," *High Fidelity,* Jan. 1, 1969, 30, 36.

99. Carman Moore, "Blo-boy to Chromelodeon: The Audience Catches Up," *Village Voice,* Sept. 12, 1968, 40, 42, 62.

100. Paul D. Zimmerman, "A Prophet Honored," *Newsweek,* Sept. 23, 1968, 109.

101. HP to La Monte Young, Dec. 4, 1968.

102. Michael Ranta interviewed by the author, July 1989.

103. Without the slightest solicitation on his part, Freeman sent him a letter enclosing a check for $3,000 for "help with some of the many extra expenses you must have now." Betty Freeman to HP, Sept. 26, 1968.

104. HP, "Statement," in the notes prepared for CRI Records on *And On the Seventh Day Petals Fell in Petaluma,* enclosed with a letter to David Hall, Dec. 7, 1966.

105. HP, introductory notes to the score of *Delusion of the Fury,* 1966.

106. HP, "Corrections and Additions to Data on Instruments," inserted in 1967 into the score of *Delusion of the Fury:* HPEA/SD.

107. *Genesis,* 351. The parts were taken by John Blount, Susan Marshall, and Glendon Hornbrook, respectively; the singers were John Stannard, Victoria Bond, and John Bergen.

108. HP to Madeline Tourtelot, Jan. 21, 1972.

109. HP to Danlee Mitchell, Feb. 14, 1969.

110. This and the following quotations in this paragraph are from HP to Madeline Tourtelot, Jan. 21, 1972.

111. HP to John McClure, Feb. 4, 1969.

112. HP to Will Ogdon, Mar. 24, 1969.

113. HP to Linda Schell, Feb. 17, 1969.

114. HP to John McClure, Mar. 12, 1969.

115. HP to Alan J. Marks, Apr. 15, 1969.

CHAPTER 13. ENCINITAS AND SAN DIEGO

1. Recounted by Stephen Pouliot, interviewed by the author, Santa Monica, Mar. 27, 1991.

2. HP to Betty Freeman, May 2, 1969.

3. Eugene Paul, liner notes to Columbia Records release of *Delusion of the Fury.*

4. HP to Will Ogdon, Mar. 24, 1969.

5. HP to Betty Freeman, May 2, 1969.

6. Freeman has stated that only after she realized that Tourtelot was not offering any financial assistance for these projects did she break off relations with her. Betty Freeman, personal communication.

7. John L. Stewart to Madeline Tourtelot, June 30, 1969.

8. Following this exchange he received a letter from the University of California Press with an identical enquiry.

9. *Genesis,* vii.

10. *Genesis,* xiii, xi.

11. HP to Betty Freeman, June 11, 1969.

12. *Genesis,* vii.

13. Lou Harrison interviewed by the author, June 1985.

14. HP to Betty Freeman, Dec. 4, 1966.

15. HP, "Resumé of Correspondence with Da Capo Press," Oct. 5, 1971: HPEA/SD.

16. HP to John McClure, May 12, 1969.

17. HP to John McClure, Oct. 27, 1969.

18. Jacqueline Onslow Ford to HP, Apr. 8, 1969.

19. HP to Madeline Tourtelot, Jan. 21, 1972.

20. HP to Alan Marks, Nov. 26, 1969.

21. HP to the Cassandra Foundation, Chicago, Jan. 6, 1970.

22. HP to the Harry Partch Foundation, May 21, 1970.

23. HP to the Harry Partch Foundation, May 21, 1970.

24. ZoBell's application for IRS clearance failed twice, after which he gave up. Freeman thereupon obtained the tax-deductible status by means of lengthy preparation and documentation, which convinced the clearance board. Betty Freeman, personal communication.

25. HP to Betty Freeman, Sept. 24, 1970.

26. Minutes of the first meeting of the board of directors of the Harry Partch Foundation, July 11, 1970: HPEA/SD.

27. Danlee Mitchell to Betty Freeman, Aug. 5, 1970.

28. HP to Ken Spiker, Apr. 22, 1971.

29. HP to Betty Freeman, Aug. 12, 1970.

30. HP to Patty Wright, Aug. 20, 1970.

31. HP to Patty Wright, Aug. 20, 1970. Freeman felt that combining the foundation workshop with a profit-making endeavor was not all bad, and would avoid the danger of her being the primary source of financial support. Betty Freeman, personal communication.

32. Danlee Mitchell interviewed by the author, Jan. 1989.

33. HP to Lou Harrison, Oct. 10, 1970.

34. HP to Lou Harrison, Oct. 18, 1970.

35. HP to Betty Freeman, May 23, 1972.

36. Alan Marks to HP, Feb. 9, 1970.

37. Alan Marks to HP, Apr. 29, 1970.

38. HP to Karl ZoBell, Apr. 6, 1971.

39. HP, "Resumé of Correspondence with Da Capo Press," Oct. 5, 1971.

40. HP to Karl ZoBell, Apr. 6, 1971.

41. HP to Karl ZoBell, Apr. 6, 1971.

42. Alan Marks to HP, Feb. 2, 1971.

43. HP to Emil Richards, Dec. 31, 1970.

44. *Genesis,* 289.

45. Danlee Mitchell interviewed by the author, Apr. 1988.

46. HP to Betty Freeman, May 4, 1971.

47. *Genesis,* 274.

48. Jim Aitkenhead interviewed by the author, San Diego, Jan. 1988.

49. HP to Dean Drummond, Apr. 7, 1971.

50. Dean Drummond interviewed by the author, Amsterdam, Nov. 1990.

51. The quotations in this paragraph are from HP to Lou Harrison, Apr. 19, 1971.

52. HP to Bill Biglow, Aug. 7, 1971.

53. HP to Bill Biglow, Aug. 7, 1971.

54. This and the following quote are from HP to Eugene Paul, Oct. 19, 1971.

55. HP to Alan Marks, Dec. 5, 1971.

56. HP to Peter Garland, Dec. 8, 1970.

57. HP to Peter Garland, Feb. 28, 1972.

58. HP to Peter Garland, Mar. 3, 1972.

59. HP to Peter Garland, May 19, 1972.

60. Jim and Nancy Aitkenhead interviewed by the author, Jan. 1988.

61. Danlee Mitchell, cited in Smith, "The Partch Reverberations," 46–59.

62. Gaburo interviewed by Daniel Atesh Sonneborn, Apr. 4, 1984, in Sonneborn, "Corporeality in the Music-Theatre of Harry Partch."

63. HP to Betty Freeman, Nov. 18, 1971.

64. Stephen Pouliot to the author, July 14, 1992.

65. HP to Betty Freeman, Nov. 10, 1971.

66. Stephen Pouliot to HP, Nov. 17, 1971.

67. Stephen Pouliot to HP, Dec. 11, 1971.

68. HP, "Dedicatory Page" to *The Dreamer That Remains,* Oct. 7, 1972: HPEA/SD.

69. HP, "Dedicatory Page" to *The Dreamer That Remains.*

70. Stephen Pouliot, "Filming the Work of Harry Partch or First Get to Know Your Genius," *American Cinematographer,* Mar. 1974, 322–25, 333.

71. Stephen Pouliot, "Remembering Harry," *1/1: The Journal of the Just Intonation Network* 8:4 (Nov. 1994), 23.

72. Stephen Pouliot to HP, Mar. 22, 1972.

73. Betty Freeman to HP, Mar. 29, 1972.

74. Stephen Pouliot to HP, Apr. 4, 1972.

75. HP to Stephen Pouliot, Apr. 1, 1972. I am grateful to Stephen Pouliot for further descriptions of the sculpture.

76. Stephen Pouliot to HP, postmarked Apr. 11, 1972.

77. *Genesis,* 226 and 290, respectively.

78. Stephen Pouliot to HP, June 3, 1972.

79. Betty Freeman, handwritten note (dated Nov. 23, 1985) on the typescript copy of Partch's first draft of the text for *The Dreamer That Remains:* HPA/UI.

80. Stephen Pouliot to HP, June 3, 1972.

81. The money came from Freeman herself. No money from the Harry Partch Foundation was used toward the film: its funds were, as ever, limited.

82. Stephen Pouliot interviewed by the author, Mar. 1991.

83. Stephen Pouliot, diary pages for July 5–8, 1972: photocopy, HPA/UI.

84. Stephen Pouliot, diary pages for July 5–8, 1972.

85. Stephen Pouliot, at the memorial meeting for Harry Partch, Sept. 22, 1974.

86. Lou Harrison to HP, Sept. 15, 1970.

87. Stephen Pouliot to HP, July 15, 1972.

88. HP to Will Ogdon, Dec. 12, 1970.

89. HP to Will Ogdon, Oct. 31, 1972.

90. Danlee Mitchell to Linda Schell Pluth and Allen Pluth, Feb. 13, 1973.

91. HP to Stephen Pouliot, Feb. 4, 1973.

92. Michael R. Lampert, "Environment, Consciousness, and Magic: An Interview with David Dunn," *Perspectives of New Music* 28:1 (Winter 1989), 94–105.

93. Freeman was hoping that a major distribution company would handle the completed film, and had even begun negotiations with one such firm. The company rejected the film because of the homosexual overtones of this scene. Betty Freeman, personal communication.

94. Lou Harrison to the author, Sept. 16, 1990.

95. HP to Betty Freeman, Nov. 18, 1972.

96. Lou Harrison to the author, Sept. 16, 1990.

97. *Bitter Music,* entry for June 16, 1935.

98. Stephen Pouliot interviewed by the author, Mar. 1991.

99. Stephen Pouliot, at the memorial meeting for Harry Partch, Sept. 22, 1974.

100. Lou Harrison, at the memorial meeting for Harry Partch, Sept. 22, 1974.

101. Preston Tuttle to Ben Johnston, Apr. 12, 1979: HPA/UI.

102. Stephen Pouliot to the author, personal communication.

103. HP, "Dedicatory Page" to *The Dreamer That Remains.*

104. HP to Stephen Pouliot, Feb. 4, 1973.

105. HP to Stephen Pouliot, Feb. 4, 1973.

106. Betty Freeman to HP, Nov. 26, 1971.

107. Danlee Mitchell to Linda Schell Pluth and Allen Pluth, Feb. 13, 1973.

108. HP to Stephen Pouliot, Feb. 4, 1973.

109. HP to Stephen Pouliot, Feb. 4, 1973.

110. Stephen Pouliot to HP, Feb. 21, 1973.

111. Freeman claims that the drama was resolved by a ten-page letter she wrote to Partch saying that she would "forget about using his music as background and instead would substitute something by Tchaikovsky. Needless to say, Partch relented and gave up his opposition." Betty Freeman, personal communication.

112. HP to Bill Biglow, Mar. 28, 1973.

113. HP, in the soundtrack of *The Dreamer That Remains: A Portrait of Harry Partch* (Los Angeles: Whitelight-Tantalus Productions, 1973).

114. Jon Szanto, cited in Smith, "The Partch Reverberations," 46–59.

115. David Dunn, cited in Jeff Smith, "The Partch Reverberations."

116. HP to Peter Garland, Apr. 14, 1973.

117. Jonathan Cott, "The Forgotten Visionary," *Rolling Stone,* Apr. 11, 1974, 32–34, 36, 38.

118. HP to James Jacobs, Sept. 6, 1973.

119. Stephen Pouliot, at the memorial meeting for Harry Partch, Sept. 22, 1974.

120. Phil Keeney, at the memorial meeting for Harry Partch, Sept. 22, 1974.

121. HP to Samuel Mitnick, Feb. 2, 1974.

122. HP to Steven Bookman, Nov. 10, 1973.

123. Remark made to Ben Johnston, 1974: Ben Johnston interviewed by the author, Jan. 1990.

124. Ben Johnston interviewed by the author, Jan. 1990. After the meeting Johnston told Mitchell how delighted he was to find Partch so lucid and in such good shape. Mitchell replied: "It's one of the better days."

125. HP to Betty Freeman, Aug. 13, 1974.

126. In 1973 CRI in New York had reissued the original 1957 recording of the work in full as a two-LP set. Partch prepared the liner notes for the sleeve and a new statement on his disappointments with the 1957 and 1959 productions.

127. Mark Hoffman interviewed by the author, San Diego, Nov. 1987. The story is recounted also in Smith, "The Partch Reverberations."

128. Stephen Pouliot, at the memorial meeting for Harry Partch, Sept. 22, 1974.

129. Pouliot, "Remembering Harry."

130. HP to Michael Craden, Nov. 10, 1971, quoted in Craden to Emil Richards, postmarked Sept. 11, 1974.

EPILOGUE

1. Ben Johnston, "The Corporealism of Harry Partch," 85–97.

2. Betty Freeman interviewed by the author, Apr. 1988.

3. Danlee Mitchell, cited in Smith, "The Partch Reverberations."

4. The "new" notational symbols include pluses and minuses, which symbolize respectively raising and lowering a pitch by a syntonic comma, the ratio 81/80. In his more recent music Johnston has expanded his notation system to make provision for intervals derived from the higher prime number relationships of the harmonic series—7, 11, 13, ad infinitum. He has needed to devise only one new symbol for each new prime number (from seven and upward Johnston calls these symbols chromas). These accidentals are used in combination for the more complex ratios: in his recent music it is not uncommon to find three such symbols applied to one note. This subject is discussed at length in my paper "Changing the Metaphor: Ratio Models of Musical Pitch in the Work of Harry Partch, Ben Johnston, and James Tenney," *Perspectives of New Music* 33 (Winter–Summer 1995), 458–503.

5. Copies of the relevant documents were kindly placed at my disposal by Kenneth Gaburo.

6. See Dean Drummond, "On Newband and the Partch Instruments," *1/1: The Journal of the Just Intonation Network* 8:4 (Nov. 1994), 14–15, 19.

Acknowledgments

The original suggestion that I should write a biography of Harry Partch came from Ben Johnston, on the occasion of our first meeting, in Paris, in June 1981.

Ben's suggestion was reiterated four years later by Professor Wilfrid Mellers, who encouraged me to expand an undergraduate paper I had written on Partch at the University of York into a book. For intellectual and moral support during my student days there I owe a lasting debt to Wilfrid, to Dr. Neil Sorrell, and to Professor John Paynter; also to Kipps Horn, whose own enthusiasm for Partch was an inspiration.

The book itself could not have been started without the Fulbright Scholarship which allowed me to spend the academic year 1987–88 in southern California. To the Fulbright Commission in London I extend my deepest gratitude for making it possible for me to carry out primary research.

In the writing of this book the most extensive debt I have incurred is to Professor Danlee Mitchell, president of the Harry Partch Foundation in San Diego, who gave me unlimited access to the instruments, manuscripts, papers, recordings, photographs, and other materials in his possession. Our many hours of conversation gave me considerable insight into Partch's personality. He has also been a valued friend. I can only hope that this book will go some small way toward repaying my debt to him.

I am also grateful to Dr. Thomas McGeary for access to and help with the Harry Partch Archive at the University of Illinois at Urbana-Champaign, and for many good times on my two visits there. Our correspondence and sharing of materials over the years since 1987, conducted in the best tradition of scholarly cooperation, has (I hope) been of benefit to us both. The Urbana collection for which he, following Ben Johnston's lead, is largely responsible, is an indispensable resource for materials on Partch; and even though I found it desirable to retrace many of the same paths, my research would have taken even longer without access to it. My grateful thanks also to William McClellan and Marlys Scarborough in the University of Illinois Music Library, and to Bill Brooks and Jacky Miles, for housing me during my two visits to Illinois.

Versions of parts of this book have been previously published. My thanks to Jerome Kohl, Ben Boretz, and an anonymous reader at *Perspectives of New Music* for their helpful comments in connection with two articles, expanding on parts of chapters 2 and 3 of this book, which appeared in that journal; and to Joe Fodor at *The Musical Quarterly* for his help with an article derived from chapter 9.

Grateful thanks are due to a number of individuals: to the late Kenneth Gaburo, for access to the Lingua Press Partch holdings and for hospitality in Iowa City in January–February 1990, and to Philip Blackburn for his encouragement and friendship on that visit and subsequently; to Mark Hoffman, who was a great friend during my year in San Diego and since, and who gave invaluable help with the recordings of the Partch Estate; to Richard Kassel, for the sharing of materials and exchange of ideas on Harry Partch over several years; to John Koegel, who rekindled my enthusiasm for archival research when it was in danger of going out, and for sharing his own research on Calista Rogers; to Ron Wiecki, for sharing his research on Partch's Madison years; to Mark Behm, for sending me his beautifully copied manuscript of Partch's *Seventeen Lyrics by Li Po* in the transcription into the notation system for just intonation devised by Ben Johnston; to Bertram Turetsky and John Silber, for encouragement during my studies at the University of California at San Diego; to Larry Polansky, for inspiration; and last but not least to my brother, Stephen Gilmore, for substantial help with the preparation of my manuscript.

I thank the many people I have interviewed about Partch, either in person or by correspondence: Andrew Partch, Anna Partch Couch, Maurine Partch

Ryan, Nicholas Zoller, Josef Walter, Earle Voorhies, Peter Flanders, Lee Hoiby, Christine Charnstrom Lindsay, Hulda Gieschen, Lucie Marshall, Lorraine Johansen, Gordon Onslow Ford, Murray Louis, Elizabeth Gentry Sayad, Rob Kostka, Kash Yamada, James Tenney, Jean Cutler, Emil Richards, Erv Wilson, Jonathan Glasier, John Chalmers, Dean Drummond, Jim and Nancy Aitkenhead, Randy Hoffman, Francis Thumm, Phil Keeney, Jon Szanto, Mary Hoffman. Michael Ranta provided hospitality and fascinating reminiscences when I visited him in Cologne. Betty Freeman met me in Los Angeles and discussed Partch with me. Stephen Pouliot met me in Santa Monica and shared his memories and encouraged me to present an honest account of his friendship with the composer. Henry Brant invited me to Santa Barbara and vividly recalled his concerts with Partch in New York in 1944. Lou Harrison talked with me in England and followed our early discussions with candid correspondence thereafter.

I should like also to thank the following individuals and institutions for answering my inquiries about materials relating to Partch: Thomas Tanselle, vice president of the John Simon Guggenheim Memorial Foundation, New York; Susan Hikida, University Archives, University of Southern California; Thelma Martin, National Personnel Records Center, St. Louis; Lynn Ochiltree, Simpson College, Iowa; Regine Morris, Albuquerque High School; Theresa Granza, Institute of International Education, New York; Bernard Schermetzler, archivist, University of Wisconsin, Madison; Kendall Crilly, Music Library, Yale University; James Cartwright, archivist, University of Hawaii, Manoa; Robin Wallace, publications and archives assistant, Los Angeles Philharmonic Association; Janet Michaelieu, Arizona Historical Society, Phoenix; Craig St. Clair, *Los Angeles Times;* Susan Coffman and Mary Borgerding, Pasadena Historical Society; Nina Myatt, Antioch College, Yellow Springs, Ohio; Marie Condon Thornton, University Archives, and Steve Repasky, Music Library, University of California, Berkeley; Carole Prietto, University Archives, UCLA; Bernard Crystal, assistant librarian for manuscripts, and Hollee Haswell, Central Files, Columbia University; Helene Whitson, Archives, San Francisco State University; LeRoy Pogemiller, Conservatory of Music, University of Missouri, Kansas City; Catherine Smith, University of Nevada, Reno.

My manuscript was read in its entirety by Ben Johnston, Danlee Mitchell, David Dunn, Frank Denyer, and by an anonymous reader for Yale University Press, and in part by Betty Freeman, Stephen Pouliot, Lucie Marshall, Lorraine Johansen, and Thomas McGeary: their comments have been most helpful. Maria Marquise took on the main editing of the complete manuscript and became my toughest critic, venturing into the murky waters of style and structure that others tactfully left undisturbed. Her sharp mind and even sharper tongue encouraged me to remove a great many infelicities of thought and expression, and helped me curb the excesses of my zeal for biographical detail.

At Yale University Press I thank Noreen O'Connor for her careful editing, Marnie Wiss for computer expertise, and Harry Haskell for his belief in and encouragement of my work.

Very special thanks are due to two individuals: to David Dunn, for friendship and guidance, for help with access to Partch materials, for accompanying me on a Partch trail through Santa Fe and Albuquerque, and for considerably enriching my understanding of Partch's work; and to Ben Johnston, who has been a central intellectual and musical influence over the past sixteen years, and to whom I am deeply grateful for hours of illuminating conversation and for sharing with me his own compositions and theoretical writings.

Over the inordinately long period of writing this book has begun to seem like a fond part of my misspent youth. I would like to acknowledge the love and support of my family, who sustained me through those many years. My son, Benjamin, had the good sense to be born on South Cedros Avenue in Solana Beach, California, a short walk away from the studio Partch occupied briefly in 1970.

Index

Abbey Theatre, 101, 106, 204, 423n5
Abstraction, 173–74, 178
Aitkenhead, Jim, 363, 364, 366, 369, 371
Albert, Agnes, 199, 433n49
Albuquerque High School, 26–28, 30–31, 33–34, 36
American Society of University Composers, 344
American University Union (London), 104, 109
Ames, Elizabeth, 139
ancient Greece: culture of, 29, 49, 75, 174, 175; musical thought in, 4, 7, 49–50, 62, 65, 69, 91, 105, 111, 175
Anderson, Walter, 253, 254
Angelou, Maya, 218
Anger, Kenneth, 226–27, 273; *Inauguration of the Pleasure Dome*, 226–27
Antheil, George, 100, 277, 425n49
Antioch College, Ohio, 253, 254

Appel, Livia, 163, 167–68, 170, 171, 180, 181, 182, 184
Artaud, Antonin, 282
Aswell, Edward, 142
Auden, W. H., 374

Bach, J. S., 135, 171
Baker, Chet, 236
Barzun, Jacques, 164, 174–75, 259
Beat Generation, 234
Benét, Stephen Vincent, 182
Bennington College, 123, 140, 144, 147, 198
Benton, Edwin, 72
Berlioz, Hector, 164, 174
Bert, John, 283
Bishop, George, 139
Blackburn, Philip, 394
Blake, William, 178
BMI. *See* Broadcast Music, Incorporated
Boulanger, Nadia, 55, 147
Boulez, Pierre, *Structures,* 336

Bowles, Paul, 150, 151
Boxer Rebellion, 14–15, 384
Brahms, Johannes, 43, 52
Brannigan, Duane, 238
Brant, Henry, 6–7, 43, 148, 149, 150, 151, 429n41; *Angels and Devils,* 148; *Music for a Five and Dime Store,* 148; *The Marx Brothers,* 148
Bricken, Carl, 158, 159, 164
British Museum, 90, 104, 105, 108, 109, 111, 206, 368
Britten, Benjamin, *Paul Bunyan,* 292
Broadcast Music, Inc. (BMI), 221–22, 224, 229, 261, 272, 291, 303, 307, 329, 347
Brooks, Jack, 126
Broughton, James, 234
Buddhism, 171. *See also* Zen Buddhism
Buhlig, Richard, 88, 201, 422n44
Busoni, Ferrucco, 159, 162

Cage, John, 6–7, 137–38, 277, 287, 324, 354, 365–66; *Concerto for Prepared Piano and Chamber Orchestra,* 277; *Notations,* 324
Cahuilla Indians, 93
California Institute of Technology (Pasadena), 90, 91
California State University, Northridge, 301, 328
Callahan, Mike, 317
Campbell, Roy, 372
Carmel Bach Festival, 135
Carnegie Corporation of New York, 103, 114, 115, 132, 141, 162, 259
Cassandra Foundation, Chicago, 358
Caxton Printers (Ohio), 131
Chalmers, John, 345–46
Chardon, Yves, 98–99
Charnstrom, Christine, 159, 161, 162, 165, 169, 172, 178, 255
Chase, Gilman, 139
Chavez, Carlos, 140
Childers, America, 12

Childers, John (grandfather), 12
Childs, Herbert, 134
Chopin, Frédéric, 43, 312
Chou Wen-Chung, 277
Churchill, Jordan, 220, 224
classification of intervals (in HP's theory), 66–67, 78, 94, 132
Clements, Ernest, 105
Cohen, Milton, 274
Coleman, Thomas, 266
Columbia Records, 140, 348, 352, 357, 361, 362, 364; *The Music of Harry Partch,* 348, 357; *Delusion of the Fury,* 352, 361, 364
Columbia University, 145, 151, 164, 205, 272, 275, 323
Colvig, Bill, 375, 388
Composers Recordings, Inc. (CRI), 304, 323, 324, 337, 338, 342, 344, 452n126; *From the Music of Harry Partch,* 323; *Petals,* 337, 345; *The Bewitched,* 452n126
consonance and dissonance, 4, 62–63, 66, 68, 176, 193, 203
Coolidge, Elizabeth Sprague, 86
Copland, Aaron, 55, 84, 100, 277, 292; *Music for the Theater,* 55; *The Second Hurricane,* 292
corporeality, 3–4, 30, 173–74, 244, 292, 300, 350, 438n87
Cott, Jonathan, 384
Couper, Mildred, 88, 114, 121
Cowell, Henry, 6–7, 56, 68, 83–84, 86, 100, 131, 138, 147, 148, 187, 276–77; character of, 83–84; relationship with HP, 84, 147; *New Musical Resources,* 56, 68, 84; *Persian Set,* 277
Craden, Michael, 331, 387
Craft, Robert, 390
Crawford, Francis, 23, 316, 334, 388
Crawford, John, 349
Crawford, Ruth, 6, 84
CRI. *See* Composers Recordings, Inc.
critics, reviews of HP's work by, 74–75,

85, 87, 89, 91, 204, 221, 225–26, 249–
50, 275–76, 277, 285, 303–04, 348
Cronyn, George W., 123–24, 128
Curtis, Louis, 122
Cutler, Jean, 283, 291, 310, 358

Da Capo Press, 355, 356, 362, 365, 385, 386
Dahms, Barbara, 271
Dahms, Lyle, 249, 271
Daniel, Oliver, 272, 303, 304, 307, 347, 349
de Angulo, Jaime, 132–33, 220
Debussy, Claude, 193–94, 242
DeGaetani, Thomas, 273, 278
Depression. *See* Great Depression
Dimitroff, Lucienne, 217
Dolmetsch, Arnold, 106, 107–8
Donzella, Michael, 249
Drake, Mary P., 135
Driscoll, Bertha Knisely, *see* Knisely,
  Bertha McCord
Driscoll, Harold, 110, 134, 161, 201, 274,
  301, 359, 361
Drummond, Dean, 359, 363–64, 394
Drummond, Gilbert, 359
Dulac, Edmund, 106, 107, 111
Dunn, David, xi, 377, 383, 392
Dustin, Leslie, 47, 57, 418n69
Dykstra, Clarence, 181, 182–83

Eastman School of Music, 144
Ellis, Alexander J., 48, 131
Ellmann, Richard, ix
equal temperament, 2, 42, 50, 53–54, 64,
  69, 131, 274, 419n87; defined, 64,
  419n87
Evans, Gil, 291
Everett, Gary and Suzie, 289

Fansler, Roberta, 103, 115
Federal Writers' Project, 122, 123, 128–29
Field, John, 43, 417n21
Fisher, Marjory M., 87
Flanders, Peter, 142
Flanders family, 103, 141–42

Fletcher, James, 211, 218, 224
Foote, Jeffrey, 283
Ford Foundation, New York, 298
forty-three tone scale, 64, 65, 142, 151,
  166, 176, 207, 324; on HP's instruments, 142, 166, 314, 444n49
Fox-Strangways, A. H., 103
Frankenstein, Alfred, 303
Freeman, Betty, 322, 323, 324, 328–30,
  331, 336, 337, 338, 339, 340, 342, 343,
  347, 348, 349, 353–63, 367, 368, 370,
  372, 373, 374, 376, 377, 378, 380, 381,
  384, 385, 387, 388, 390, 391, 449n6,
  449n24, 449n31, 451n93, 451n111;
  financial support to HP, 328–30;
  negotiations about *Delusion,* 342;
  Whitney Museum concerts, 348; helps
  HP buy Encinitas house, 353, 380; ne-
  gotiations with UCSD, 354–55; and
  Harry Partch Foundation, 359; *The
  Dreamer that Remains,* 367; and
  Danlee Mitchell, 391
French, Loran, 330
Fried, Alexander, 87, 303
Fromm, Paul, 242

Gaburo, Kenneth, xi, 4, 242, 243, 367,
  392–93, 394
Gann, Kyle, 6
Garland, Peter, 76–77, 239, 365–66, 384,
  390, 391
Garvey, John, 241, 242, 248, 270, 271,
  272, 273, 278, 283, 291, 292, 293
Gate 5 Ensemble: formation of, 219–20;
  performs *Oedipus,* 224–25; disbanding
  of, 229–30, 232
Gate 5 Records, 8, 130, 258, 260, 272,
  273, 293–94, 295, 323, 357; final "let-
  ter" series, 294
Gaudí, Antoni, 363
Gauger, Thomas, 249
Genesis of a Music (Partch). *See* Partch,
  Harry, *Genesis of a Music*
Genther, Charles, 262

Genther, Shirley, 258, 262
Gentry, Elizabeth, 266, 268, 270, 271
Gerdine, Leigh, 266
Gieschen, Hulda, 169, 172
Gilson, Warren, 166–67, 169, 170, 172, 430n46
Glasier, John, 183, 184, 185, 238, 342
Glasier, Jonathan, 342, 343, 377
Glasier, Marshall, 159, 171, 172, 181, 183, 184, 185, 192, 195
Gold, Julius, 58
Graham, Martha, 147, 205, 209–14, 216, 218, 239, 327, 437n70
Graham Foundation, Chicago, 298
Grant, Morton, 134
Grayson, John, 333–34, 336, 338, 340
Great Depression, 115, 116, 128, 136, 159
Grosz, George, 159
Guggenheim Foundation, 48, 90, 95, 98, 99, 100, 103, 132, 144, 146, 191, 272, 273; grants to HP, 146, 149, 191

Hackbarth, Glenn, 264
Hague, Eleanor, 93
Hall, David, 342, 345
Hanson, Howard, 56, 144, 148, 157, 158, 163, 168, 170
harmonic series, 50, 61–62, 63, 66, 67, 69, 91, 131, 176
Harms, Norman, 166
Harris, Roy, 55, 277
Harrison, Jay, 275
Harrison, Lou, 7, 24, 31, 118, 138, 151, 221, 259, 262, 276–77, 320, 339, 352, 356, 361, 364, 365, 375, 377, 378, 379, 388; *Young Caesar,* 367; *Pacifika Rondo,* 374
Harry Partch Foundation, 359–60, 361, 362, 389, 391
Haverlin, Carl, 221–22, 229, 272
H'Doubler, Margaret, 165
Helmholtz, Hermann, 48–51, 53, 60, 61–62, 65, 75, 132, 176, 193; *On the Sensations of Tone,* 48–51, 60, 75, 312, 418n48
Henry Street Playhouse, 243, 248

Hewitt, Barnard, 283, 284, 291, 292, 327
Hindemith, Paul, 144
hobos. *See* Partch, Harry, hobo experiences of
Hoffman, Mark, 377, 381, 386
Hoffman, Randy, 386
Hoiby, Lee, 159, 160, 162–63, 169, 172
Hollywood Bowl, 48
Hood, Mantle, 337
Horgan, Paul, 25
Hovhaness, Alan, 276
Hugo, Ian, 273
Hupa Indians, 93

Iltis, Leon, 164
Immaculate Heart College, 301
Institute of International Education (IIE), 103, 104, 109, 110, 114, 115, 120
Isaacs, Mary, 316
Isleta Indians, 93, 195
Ives, Charles, 6, 57, 83, 148, 150, 236

Jacobs, James, 159, 166, 169, 172, 283, 352, 359, 361, 384
Jeans, Sir James, *Science and Music,* 190
Jeffers, Robinson, 120
Johansen, Gunnar, 157, 158–59, 161, 162, 163, 164, 172, 180–81, 185, 187, 188
Johansen, Lorraine, 181
Johnston, Ben, 6, 8, 39, 69, 188, 192, 229, 241, 277, 278, 282, 290, 291, 292, 294, 298, 344, 348, 385, 388–93, 419n84, 452n4; "apprenticeship" with HP, 193–99; *The Bewitched* and, 238–40, 243, 247, 249, 252, 437n70, 437n85; *The Wooden Bird,* 194–95
Johnston, Betty, 193, 194, 294, 298
Joyce, James, 142, 151
Julliard Dance Group, 274
just intonation, 2, 54, 61–69, 75, 103, 105, 132, 176, 194, 392; definitions of, 49–50, 63, 64

Kain-tuck (HP's hobo pal), 119
Kamen, Martin, 317, 318

Kansas City Conservatory, 41, 416n18

Kaplan, Charles, 301

Keeney, Phil, 385, 386, 387, 388

Kerouac, Jack, 234; *On the Road,* 234

King, Eleanor, 246, 255

Knapp, James, 292

Knisely, Bertha McCord, 88, 91, 94–95, 97, 98, 99, 103, 110, 114, 134, 161, 201, 274, 301, 422n45, 422n47; relationship with HP, 88, 94, 110

Kostka, Robert, 257, 262–63, 275, 294

Koussevitsky Foundation, 341

KPFA (Berkeley), 220, 222, 223

KPFK (Los Angeles), 283

KPIX-TV (San Francisco), 226, 443n23

Kusmierski, Thad, 363

Lao-tzu, 76, 122, 191, 281

Lauterer, Arch, 144, 198, 200, 201–2, 205, 210, 211, 216, 232–33, 261, 294; collaboration with HP, 201–2

Leach, Wilford, 194, 195, 204, 205, 209, 211

League of Composers, 55, 147–48, 149–50, 221; HP's concert for, 149–51, 156

Leite, George, 194, 195

Lewis, Ted, 60

Ligeti, György, 384

"limit" (in HP's theory), 63, 419n84

Lindgren, Harry, 194, 198

Lindsay, Kenneth, 172

Lingua Press, 392–93

Li Po, 75, 76–77, 135, 195

Lloyd Campbell Publications (San Francisco), 60

Logan, Jack, 346, 364, 377

Long, Susan, 347

Los Angeles Philharmonic Orchestra, 38–39, 47, 48, 51–52

Loughborough, Bill, 224, 235

Louis, Murray, 438n103

Louw, Allan, 200, 223, 288

Ludlow, John, 212

Ludlow, Lynn, 270

Ludlow, Marilyn, 270

Luening, Ethel, 140, 142, 144, 147, 149, 150, 151

Luening, Otto, 99–100, 123, 139–47, 161, 163, 170, 172, 174, 205, 211, 272, 273

Macgowan, Kenneth, 182

MacNamee, Jamie, 185, 194

MacNamee, Ruth, 185, 194

MacNamee, Vernon, 190

Magdalen, Sister Mary, 301

"magnets and satellites" (in HP's theory), 67–68, 78, 81–82, 421n21

Mahler, Gustav, *Das Lied von der Erde,* 174

Malkin, Edwin, 108

Mandarin Theater, 52–53, 76

Manuel, Philip, 138, 428n14

Marks, Alan, 355, 362–63, 365

Marshall, Lauriston C. (Larry), 116–117, 186–200, 205, 212, 219, 240, 242, 247, 249, 254, 255, 257, 258, 261–62, 270, 271, 273, 294, 300–301, 323, 393; microfilm of *Bitter Music,* 116–17; befriends HP in Gualala, 186–200; Guggenheim award, 190, 191; *Partch Compositions,* 200; *The Bewitched,* 240; HP archive, 393

Marshall, Lucie, 186–87, 242, 255

Maruchess, Alix Young, 149, 150

Mason, Redfern, 85, 87

Mattox, Charles, 331

Mayfield, Selby Noel, 65, 74–75

McAllister, John, 328, 361

McChesney, Mary, 316, 334

McChesney, Robert, 316, 334

McClure, John, 348, 352, 357, 359

McGary, Keith, 253

McGeary, Thomas, xi, 393, 426n14

McKenzie, Jack, 241, 242, 249, 268, 283

McKinney, John, 166, 234–35, 238–39, 240

McKinney, Rosalea, 234, 437n73

Mead, Rita, 422n41

Mekeel, Scudder, 162, 163, 164

Mellers, Wilfrid, 251, 265

Mellon Foundation, 394

Mersenne, Marin, 63, 107

microtones: in common practice, 66; HP's use of, 2, 4, 7, 63, 65–66, 78, 79, 80, 81, 88, 93, 159

Milhaud, Darius, 199, 207, 243

Miller, Dayton C., 101

Miller, Henry, 134, 374

Mills College, California, 198, 204, 210, 212, 216, 222, 223, 224, 228, 229, 238, 243; HP's residency at, 199–12

Mitchell, Danlee, 43, 249, 283, 299, 302, 303, 304, 305, 307, 312, 320, 323, 327, 328, 333, 342, 343, 352, 354–55, 359–64, 370, 371, 373, 374, 377, 379, 380, 381, 386–94, 445n24, 447n79; as HP's heir, x, 362, 390–91; memories of HP, 21, 23, 47, 92, 267, 271, 280, 323, 367; first meets HP, 241–42; works with HP on *U.S. Highball* recording, 266–74; HP's assistant at University of Illinois, 287–88; work on *Petals,* 309, 310, 315–17, 338; work on *Delusion,* 340–41, 347, 349, 351; relationship with HP, 269, 287, 309, 354–55, 362, 390

Mitnick, Samuel, 385

Moe, Henry Allen, 100–101, 102, 103, 109, 123, 125, 132, 139–49, 158, 162, 167, 192, 272, 273

Monophony, 72, 100, 173–175

Monsour, John, 370, 371

Moore, Douglas, 145, 147–48, 151, 157, 158, 202, 211, 212, 213, 216, 218, 220, 272, 273, 275, 276, 291

Motley, Willard, *Knock on Any Door,* 191

Mueller, William Max, 191

Mulligan, Gerry, 259

Mussorgsky, Modest, 52, 174, 259

Nancarrow, Conlon, 6–7, 238–39, 315, 365

National Endowment for the Humanities, 392, 393

National Institute of Arts and Letters, 337

Native American music, 19–20, 93, 197

Newband, 394

Newell, Gordon, 128

New Music Society, 56, 85, 87, 88

Newsweek, 348

Nikolais, Alwin, 243–44, 244–52, 272, 275, 307, 438n103, 438n104; *Masks, Props, and Mobiles,* 243; *Prism,* 244; on *The Bewitched,* 243–52

Nin, Anaïs, 5, 8, 134, 226, 273, 274, 276, 327, 385; *Diary,* 5, 226, 273, 276; *House of Incest,* 273

Northwestern University, 266, 269

Novarro, Ramon, 47

Obata, Shigeyoshi, 77

Ogdon, Will, 340, 343, 354, 376

Oldham, F. G., 125

One Voice, HP's theory of, 100, 173

Onslow Ford, Gordon, 216–17, 218, 219, 225, 226, 227, 240, 262, 267–68, 287, 316, 334, 352, 357, 374–75

Onslow Ford, Jacqueline, 217, 240, 316, 334, 352, 357, 374–75

Otonalities and Utonalities, 68, 84, 91, 148, 170, 177, 196, 265, 431n69

overtones. *See* harmonic series

Pablo (HP's hobo pal), 118, 119, 378. See also *The Letter*

Paramount Studios, California, 194, 198, 205

Partch, Adeline (Doll), 201, 204

Partch, Anna, 27, 198, 201

PARTCH, HARRY: American Experimental Tradition and, 6–7, 55–56, 277–78, 365; ancient Greek culture and, 29, 60; autobiography and, xi, 10–11, 140, 173, 356, 372; and the army, 143–44; avant-garde and, 324, 365–66; background music and, 228–229, 380, 435n34; biography and, ix-xii, 9–11, 36, 124–25, 394; cars owned by, 129, 184, 185, 217, 328; childhood and adolescence of, 9–34, 356; circumcision of, 22–23, 24; collaboration with other artists, 194–95, 201–2, 209–10, 243–52, 275, 304–7, 439n18; compositional process in Li Po settings, 77–82, 86; compositional techniques in *Petals,* 312–15; compositional techniques in *U.S. Highball,* 152–54; death of, 387; destroys *Bitter Music,* 116–17; destroys early compositions ("auto-da-fé"), 73–74, 78, 420n9; drinking habits of, 144, 172, 234, 293, 298, 304, 327, 334, 345, 349, 363, 364, 367, 369, 374, 386, 387; early musical experiences, 19–20, 25, 26; education, 19, 24, 26–27, 33–34; electronic music and, 128, 287, 349, 377; European music and, 35–36, 38–39, 42–45, 55, 170–71, 178–79; father's death and, 34; grants awarded to, 103, 146, 149, 158, 164, 170, 191, 218, 242, 275, 278, 328, 337, 342, 358, 447n64; Guggenheim applications, 90, 98, 100–101, 141, 142–43, 190, 416n17; health problems of, 23–24, 44, 46–47, 125, 134, 140, 159, 160, 191, 191–92, 193, 197–98, 261, 269–70, 299, 301, 322–23, 327, 328, 332, 342–43, 358, 376, 385, 386–87; hiking trip in northern California, 181–82; hobo experiences of, 21, 31, 59–60, 113–14, 115–16, 117–22, 124–27, 136–37, 141, 151–52, 160; instrument building and, 1–5, 7, 20, 138, 165–66, 169–70, 260, 287–88, 299–300, 302–3, 330; instruments, fate of, 336, 337, 340, 383; irascibility of, 115, 172–73, 366–367; jail experiences of, 89, 127, 426n38; lecture-demonstrations of own work, 86–87, 91, 102, 139, 144–45, 161, 169, 171, 229, 248, 303, 328, 331, 336; loneliness and, 20, 133–34, 136, 186, 196, 308, 363, 375; mother's death and, 39–40, 41–42; musical academia and, 41–46, 102, 125–26, 164–65, 171, 251, 323–24, 343–44, 346, 356; musical studies (formal), 26, 35, 39–48, 73–74, 416n19;

musical studies (self-directed), 40–41, 47, 48–52, 53, 415n47; and Native American music, 93; new musical notations devised by, 5, 54, 79–80, 83, 85, 90–91, 99, 134, 392; as ordinary seaman, 69–70, 71, 141, 151; "Orientalism" of music of, 216, 223, 276–78; as "Paul Pirate," 60, 70; percussion instruments and, 169, 215–16, 222–23, 313–14; as photographer, 129, 130, 294; piano and, 25, 41, 42–44, 46, 48, 51, 53, 60; plans to study abroad, 90, 276, 298; posterity and, 8, 383, 389–94; as proofreader, 48, 52, 57, 75, 122, 151, 417n36; religion and, 28–29, 30, 117–18, 184, 218, 384; renovates Gunnar Johansen's smithy, 185–86, 432n15; romantic attachments, 47, 94, 110, 118, 121, 288–89, 369–76, 378–79; sexuality of, 24, 30–32, 72, 117–19, 149, 160, 193, 227, 377–78; as silent movie pianist, 27, 34, 46, 228; soul-searching trip in southwestern desert, 129, 294; speech-music, theories and descriptions of, 75–76, 77–78, 80, 92, 98, 104, 112, 119–20, 132, 135, 173–75, 203, 215–16; supposed sterility of, 24; as teacher, 51, 58, 122, 151, 157, 164, 219, 345–46; the theater and, 3, 4–5, 53, 201–203, 216, 225; theoretical work of, 4, 7, 49–51, 54, 58, 60–69, 78–79, 94, 105, 131–32, 175–78, 344; trust funds, 218–21, 223–24, 269–70; underachievement, periods of, x–xi, 188; violin/viola playing of, 53, 57; wills made by, 261–62, 362; women and, 27–28, 30–31, 88, 94, 103, 110, 243, 268, 280, 366; works for WPA, 123–24, 128–29, 427n45; as a writer, 111, 124, 168, 170–71, 212, 231–32

—*Works and Instruments:* Adapted Guitars, 103–4, 132, 134, 145, 146, 149, 150, 165–66, 194, 195, 196, 197, 207, 208, 235, 424n22; Adapted Viola, 72–73,

Partch, Harry (*continued*)

75, 76, 78, 80, 82, 85–94, 97, 106,
107, 108, 128, 169, 195, 197, 208, 235,
236, 265, 289, 313, 334, 338, 420n5;
"The Ancient Magic," 277–78; *And
I'll Tell You My Story*, 236; *And on the
Seventh Day Petals Fell in Petaluma*,
26, 154, 297, 308–15, 316–17, 318, 320,
323, 333, 334–35, 336, 338, 339, 344,
345, 347, 365, 369, 444n50; *Barstow*,
134–35, 137, 138, 139, 140, 142, 145, 146,
147, 150, 155, 162, 167, 235, 271, 347,
348, 357, 365, 391; "Barstow" (article),
135; Bass Marimba, 190, 191, 194, 195,
196, 201, 208, 231, 235, 265, 288, 299,
302, 315, 363, 364, 382; *The Bewitched*,
35, 93, 215, 227–33, 235, 238, 239–240,
243–252, 253, 254, 256, 257, 258, 259,
272, 273, 274, 275–76, 277, 278, 288,
294, 312, 323, 335, 349, 386, 390, 391,
392, 435n37, 436n42, 452n126; *Bitter
Music*, 29–30, 30–31, 113, 116–22, 123,
124, 125, 130, 131, 132, 135, 146, 153, 154,
281, 356, 378; *Bless This Home*, 289,
294, 302; Bloboy, 266–67; Bolivian
Double Flute, 335, 446n42; Boos
(Bamboo Marimbas), 235–36, 237,
242, 299, 302, 313, 314, 321, 363, 364,
372, 382; "By The Rivers of Babylon,"
see Partch, Harry, *Two Psalms; Castor
and Pollux*, 154, 205–7, 219, 306, 312,
313, 323, 331, 336, 347, 348, 349, 357,
391, 433n69, 447n79; Chromelodeons,
138–39, 140, 141, 142, 145, 146, 149,
150, 160, 165, 166, 169, 178, 187, 190,
191, 203, 207, 208, 224, 231, 255, 265,
267, 282, 288, 291, 302, 303, 314, 344,
359, 369; Cloud-Chamber Bowls, 190–
91, 194, 195, 197, 201, 313, 347, 352,
364; "Cloud-Chamber Music," 93,
195, 219, 323; Crychord, 288, 315;
Daphne of the Dunes, 154, 263–65, 347,
348, 357, 391, 448n94; *Dark Brother*,
142, 145, 162, 167, 196, 294; *Death on
the Desert*, 26; *December, 1942*, 145,
165, 189; *Delusion of the Fury*, 1, 3, 309,
311, 313, 320, 324–27, 330, 331, 333,
334–35, 337, 338, 340, 341–42, 344,
347, 349–52, 355, 357, 361, 363, 364,
369, 445n31; "Dialogue from *The Merchant of Venice*," 87; Diamond Marimba, 169–70, 177, 190, 195, 196, 235,
236, 242, 265, 299, 330, 352, 364, 382,
431n71, 445n31; Double Canon, 165,
219; *The Dreamer That Remains*, 93,
372–73, 376, 377–78, 379 (see also
Pouliot, Stephen, *The Dreamer That
Remains* (film)); Ektaras, 341, 382;
electronic organ (projected), 165, 166,
190, 191, 194, 385; *Eleven Intrusions*,
145, 188–89, 191, 194, 195, 196–97, 294;
The Enclosures, 385; *End Littoral*, 181–
82 Eucal Blossom, 2, 321, 344; *Even
Wild Horses*, 36, 205, 207–9, 244, 294;
Exposition of Monophony, 58, 60–68,
74, 84, 87, 89, 94, 97, 103, 109, 176,
419n91 (see also *Monophony is Expounded* and *Patterns of Music*); The
Garden of Eden, 371; "Gems from my
Scrapbook 1930–1957," 262; *Genesis of
a Music*, 1, 2, 23, 45, 61, 64, 66, 68, 75,
157, 163–64, 170, 173–79, 184, 187, 193,
201, 215, 220, 244, 259–60, 300, 344,
355–57, 358, 362, 365, 385, 386, 394,
430n46; *God, She*, 142; Gourd Tree
and Cone Gongs, 2, 313, 320, 330, 333,
342; Harmonic Canons, 166, 167, 169,
191, 196, 208, 231, 232, 265, 288, 289,
299, 314, 333, 354, 369, 382, 444n49;
*"I'm very happy to be able to tell you
about this . . . ,"* 161, 162; *King
Oedipus*, 29, 98, 99, 104, 106, 110, 112,
156, 168, 198, 199–205, 206, 211, 215,
216, 217, 221, 222, 227, 278, 313, 326,
335, 428n19; "The Kithara" (article),
135; Kitharas, 111–12, 128, 132, 136, 141,
142, 145, 146, 149, 151, 160, 162, 165,
169, 189, 195, 219, 222, 224, 231, 235,

265, 288, 289, 299, 314, 347, 369, 372, 382, Koto, 240, 299, 446n45; *The Letter*, 117, 146, 155, 189, 191, 235, 271, 294, 323; "The Lord is my Shepherd," *see* Partch, Harry, *Two Psalms; Manual on the Maintenance and Repair of— and the Musical and Attitudinal Techniques for—Some Putative Musical Instruments*, 299–300, 303, 443n14; Marimba Eroica, 200, 203, 224, 263, 288, 302, 317, 382; Mazda Marimba, 289, 302, 313; Mbira Bass Dyad, 372, 382; *Mendota Night*, 438n87; "A Modern Parable I," 102; "A Modern Parable II," 125–26; Monophone, *see* Adapted Viola, "Monophonic Cycle," 142–43, 146, 149, 157; *Monophony Is Expounded*, 110, 123; "Musicians as 'Artists,'" 171; "My Seminar in Retrospect," 346; "A New Instrument," 111; *Oedipus* (rewritten version of *King Oedipus*), 212, 213, 223–26, 235, 236, 258, 259, 281, 288, 291, 294, 344, 447n80; "On G-string Formality," 171; *Patterns of Music*, 131, 157; Piano Concerto, 45, 51, 73; *Plectra and Percussion Dances*, 205–209, 215, 218–21, 223, 226, 258, 294, 326, 352; *Polyphonic Recidivism on a Japanese Theme*, 165; "The Potion Scene from *Romeo and Juliet*," 86, 87, 90, 91, 97, 102, 162, 235, 421n30; Ptolemy, 65, 111, 114, 128, 132, 136, 138, 166, 425n56, 431n68; Quadrangularis Reversum, 330, 342, 363, 445n31; "A Quarter Saw Section of Motivations and Intonation," 344; Ratio Keyboard, 51, 89, 90, 91, 92, 94, 98, 104, 105, 107, 108; *Revelation in the Courthouse Park*, 29–30, 236, 278–86, 289, 290, 294, 302, 326, 335; *Ring Around the Moon*, 190, 205, 207, 290, 294, 434n70; "The Rhythmic Motivations of *Castor and Pollux* and *Even Wild Horses*," 210; *Rotate the Body in*

All Its Planes, 284, 286, 294; *San Francisco*, 142, 146, 151, 155, 162, 167, 235, 428n19; *Seventeen Lyrics by Li Po*, 75–82, 83, 84, 86, 90, 91, 92, 97, 99, 102, 132, 137, 139, 169, 170, 203, 294, 419n86, 421n13, 421n30; "Show Horses in the Concert Ring," 171, 178, 195, 365; "Some New and Old Thoughts After and Before *The Bewitched*," 272, 418n55; "A Somewhat Spoof," 128, 365, 442n103; *Sonata Dementia*, 189–90, 196, 205, 432n29; *Song of Solomon*, 110, 132; Spoils of War, 191, 223, 235, 288, 302, 303; *Summer 1955*, 236, 436n59; Surrogate Kithara, 165, 219, 222, 223, 299, 303, 315, 335, 347; string quartet, 51, 53–54, 56, 73, 418n62; symphonic poem, 51–52, 73; *Tonality Flux*, 189; *Two Psalms*, 86, 91, 106, 132, 138–39, 146, 162, 167, 235, 294, 421n30; *Two Settings from Joyce's Finnegans Wake*, 151, 162, 167, 429n41; *Two Settings from Lewis Carroll*, 223, 288; *Two Studies on Ancient Greek Scales*, 169, 189, 191, 196, 336; *U.S. Highball*, 20, 113, 137, 142, 145–46, 147, 149, 150, 151, 152–55, 162, 165, 167, 169, 235, 253, 255, 256–57, 265–67, 268, 270, 271, 291, 294, 331, 374, 391, 428n19; Ugumbo, 320; *Ulysses at the Edge*, 235–36, 242–43, 271, 294, 364 "W. B. Yeats" (article), 135; *Water! Water!* 236, 289–94, 298, 302, 335; *The Wayward*, 155, 268, 294, 394, 436n59 *(While) My Heart Keeps Beating Time*, 59–60; *Windsong*, 154, 252, 263–65, 294, 309, 314, 323, 335, 347; *The Wooden Bird*, 194–95; *Y. D. Fantasy*, 142, 149, 150, 151, 155, 162, 167, 290; Zymo-Xyl, 302, 313, 315
Partch, Homer Warren, 12, 414n4
Partch, Irene, 14, 19, 28, 32, 33, 36–37, 47–48, 57, 89, 364, 366
Partch, Jennie: character of, 13–14, 280; Christian Science beliefs of, 24, 28,

Partch, Jennie (*continued*)
280; death of, 39–40; education, 12–
13, 26–27; employment history, 13–14,
25, 40; music and, 13, 19; relationship
with HP, 17, 22–24, 29–30, 32, 36–37,
39–40, 280; women's rights and, 27, 28
Partch, Laura Ann, 12
Partch, Paul Chester, 11, 14, 19, 20, 27,
29, 34, 37, 57, 89, 122, 182, 187, 192,
198, 201, 261
Partch, Virgil Franklin (father): character of, 13, 28; Chinese culture and, 14–
15, 18–19, 21; crisis of faith of, 14–15,
28; death of, 34, 36, 40; education, 12;
employment history, 9–10, 14–17, 21,
25, 32–33; relationship with HP, 28,
36, 50–51, 152, 218
Partch, Virgil Franklin (nephew), 122,
261, 415n48
Pasadena Art Museum, 322, 324, 328, 336
Paul, Eugene, 361
Patch, Quinton, 11
Pedtke, Herman, 385
Perlis, Vivian, 385, 414n8
Perrett, Wilfrid, 105, 108, 131
Pippin, Donald, 195, 197
Piston, Walter, 55, 100
Pond, Charles, 284
Popper, Jan, 341
Porter, Lois, 274
Porter, Quincy, 147, 274
Pouliot, Stephen, 20, 22, 40, 367–76,
377, 378–79, 380, 381, 383, 384–85,
386, 388; and HP, 367–81; *The
Dreamer That Remains* (film), 8, 21,
22–23, 31, 77, 371–72, 373, 376, 380,
381, 382–83, 386, 388, 391
Pound, Ezra, 109, 421n17
Prockelo, Vincenzo, 288–89, 294
Ptolemy, 4, 91
Pythagoras, 4, 49, 62, 63, 64, 132

Radil, Rudolphine, 84–87, 90, 200
Raitt, Helen, 317, 318, 319, 321, 323

Raitt, Russell, 317
Ranta, Michael, 287, 309–10, 315–19,
321, 331, 338, 348, 349
ratios, as description of musical intervals,
50, 61–62, 63, 79–80, 175
Ray, Gordon, 291
Rechy, John, 283
resolution, HP's theory of, 66, 94,
421n21
Rexroth, Kenneth, 220, 234
Reynolds, Roger, 385
Richards, Betty, 334
Richards, Emil, 304, 321–22, 323, 328,
334, 337, 338, 341, 349, 359, 363, 364,
377, 445n6
Rimbaud, Arthur, 207; *A Season in Hell*,
205, 207, 208
Rinder, Cantor Reuben, 86
Rockefeller Foundation, 162, 164, 307, 348
Rogers, Calista, 89–92, 93, 101, 149,
423n2
Ross, Lillian Bos, 131
Rothwell, Walter Henry, 38
Rubsamen, Walter, 348
Ruddock, Margot, 106
Rudhyar, Dane, 6, 38, 52, 83, 365; *Soul of
Fire*, 38
Ruggles, Carl, 6, 55, 83; *Portals*, 55
Russell, George (pseud. A.E.), 112
Russo, William, 277

Salmon, Will, 326
Sanborn, Pitts, 55
San Diego State University, 315, 320, 321,
349, 370, 376, 377, 378, 380, 386
San Francisco Art Institute, 342
San Francisco Museum of Art, 342, 388
San Francisco State College, 220, 224,
230, 233
San Quentin prison, 147, 220
Santa Rosa Symphony Orchestra, 82
Santee, Ross, 122–24
Sappho, HP's projected settings of, 132, 135
Saunders, Frederick A., 101

Schell, Linda, 349, 352, 361, 364

Schell (Pierce), Freda, 248, 275, 283

Schlesinger, Kathleen, 105, 111–12, 128

Schoenberg, Arnold, 38, 69, 85, 131, 174, 176, 322, 375; *Pierrot Lunaire,* 85, 174; *Harmonielehre,* 176

School of Design, Chicago, 137, 257

Schuller, Gunther, 277

Scriabin, Alexander, 131

Sessions, Roger, 277

Shakespeare, 132, 135; *Romeo and Juliet,* 86; *The Merchant of Venice,* 87; *Twelfth Night,* 145; *King Lear,* 428n19

Shanafelt, Clara, 99, 103, 125, 141, 151

Sibelius, Jean, 52, 56

Simon, Henry, 151

Slonimsky, Nicolas, 147

Smith, Warren, 254

Smithsonian Institution, 360, 364–65

Snead, Bill, 194, 195

Snow, Wallace, 338

Snyder, Gary, 234

Sorell, Walter, 244

Southwest Museum, 93, 101, 195

Spengler, Oswald, *Decline of the West,* 171

Spiller, Cecil Charles, 338

Starck, Sue Bell, 225

Steeb, Olga, 41, 42–43

Stern, Gerd, 224, 234

Stevens, Wallace, 102

Stewart, John, 321, 354, 355

Stockhausen, Karlheinz, 310, 349, 354

Stokowski, Leopold, 277

Storie, Virginia, 336, 349

Stravinsky, Igor, 38, 55, 207, 390

Sturgeon, James, 237

Sweazey, Marjorie, 200

Symons, Bill, 316, 347, 348, 355, 359, 360, 363

Szanto, Jon, 383, 386

Tantalus Films, 380, 381

Tawney, Lenore, 274

Taylor, Noel Heath, 127–28, 192–93

Thompson, General Perronet, 105

Thompson, John, 288

Thomson, Virgil, 55, 143, 144, 146, 157

Tjader, Curry, 328

Tonality Diamond, 176–78, 431n68

tonality flux, 80–81, 142, 196, 203, 282

Tosh, Stephen, 338

Tourtelot, Madeline, 252, 257–58, 260, 262–64, 267, 268, 269, 270, 272, 284, 285, 292, 293, 294, 295, 299, 304–7, 322, 352, 355, 357, 359; *Reflections,* 257, 267; *One by One,* 257; *Windsong,* 257–58, 260, 262–64, 267, 272, 305, 439n18; *U.S. Highball,* 268, 304, 305–6; *Music Studio,* 263, 268, 272, 273, 274, 275, 305, 328, 388, 440n59; *Rotate the Body in All Its Planes,* 284, 305, 328, 388; *Revelation in the Courthouse Park,* 285, 305, 306, 441n92; *The Renascent,* 306; *Delusion of the Fury,* 352, 357

Trisler, Joyce, 273, 274, 275, 282

Tsurayuki, 145, 165

Tudor, David, 310, 354

Tuttle, Preston, 134, 379

Twaddell, Freeman, 162, 163

undertone series, 68, 84

Ungaretti, Giuseppe, 195

University Microfilms Incorporated (UMI), 357

University of California, Los Angeles, 41, 181, 182–83, 185, 311, 333, 336, 337, 338, 341–42, 343, 349, 352, 354

University of California, San Diego, 317–18, 320, 323, 340, 343, 347, 354–55, 358, 376–77, 386, 388; HP at, 345–46

University of California Symphony Orchestra (Berkeley), 53, 57, 419n72

University of Chicago Press, 139

University of Hawaii, 47, 364

University of Illinois, Urbana-Champaign, 238, 240, 248, 272, 274, 275, 278, 279, 286, 309, 321, 333, 344, 392; HP's residencies at, 241–54, 274–95

University of New Mexico, 26–27
University of Oregon, 310, 358
University of Southern California, 41–
46, 48, 204–5, 367
University of Wisconsin, Madison, 157–
73, 178, 182, 254; HP at, 158–73
University of Wisconsin Press, 157, 163–
64, 167, 187, 259
U.S. Immigration Service, 9, 17, 21
Utonalities, *see* Otonalities and Uto-
nalities

Varda, Jean, 133, 218, 374
Varèse, Edgard, 7, 49, 55, 274, 365;
Amériques, 7, 55; *Ionisation,* 7; *Déserts,*
274
Velsey, Elinor, 256
Velsey, Seth, 256, 258, 258, 260

Wagner, Richard, 174
Wahlin, H. B., 165
Waley, Arthur, 145, 165, 325
Walter, Josef, 58
Washington University, St. Louis, 249
Watts, Alan, 133, 218, 220, 233
Weaver, William Fense, 195
Webb, Thompson, 186, 259–60
Webern, Anton, 69, 163, 287
Weiss, Adolph, 83, 100
Wendlandt, William, 160, 169, 170
Weston, Raymond, 327, 336, 343
Whitney Museum, 347, 348, 357
Wildberger, Melvin, 266
Wilder, William, 258, 265
Williams, Tennessee, 291; *Night of the
Iguana,* 291

Williamson, Gavin, 138, 428n14
Wilson, Edmund, 71
Wilson, Erv, 69, 74, 330, 331, 335
Wilson, Jim, 217, 296, 297
Woodbury, Arthur, 344
Works Progress Administration (WPA),
122, 128–29, 159
Wright, Jack, 316, 374, 388
Wright, Patty, 316, 359, 361, 374, 388
WTTW-TV, Chicago, 249, 257, 263

Xenakis, Iannis, 287

Yaqui Indians, 19–20
Yasser, Joseph, 131, 428n34
Yates, Peter, 127, 172, 205, 216, 227, 229,
230, 248, 258, 259, 263, 280, 283, 294,
296, 297, 303, 315, 317, 319, 332, 340,
342, 347, 359, 390; reviews HP's work,
225–26, 230, 285, 294, 336; and exhi-
bition of HP's instruments, 236–38;
HP's disillusionment with, 324, 359
Yeats, W. B., 26, 29, 46, 60, 67, 77,
98, 108, 109, 111, 112, 124, 198, 199–
200, 204, 206, 223; letters to HP, 101,
104, 111, 123, 211; HP's meeting with,
105–7
Yoell, Larry, 60
Young, Ella, 133, 145, 189, 191
Young, La Monte, 348–49
Zarlino, Gioseffe, 431n70
Zen Buddhism, 218, 258, 277, 366
Zenman, Omar, 359, 360–61
ZoBell, Karl, 359, 362, 365
Zoller family, 58, 82, 102, 114–15, 212
Zoller, Nicholas, 58, 115